Roseboom, Eugene Holloway
A history of presidential
elections.

A HISTORY OF PRESIDENTIAL ELECTIONS

A HISTORY OF PRESIDENTIAL ELECTIONS

From George Washington to Richard M. Nixon

EUGENE H. ROSEBOOM

MACMILLAN PUBLISHING CO., INC.
NEW YORK
COLLIER MACMILLAN PUBLISHERS
LONDON

Macmillan Publishing Co., Inc.
866 Third Avenue, New York, N.Y. 10022
Collier-Macmillan Canada Ltd.

Library of Congress Catalog Card Number: 78-101726

THIRD EDITION
FOURTH PRINTING 1974

Printed in the United States of America

Preface

This is the third edition of a work designed to give a connected account of the history of national politics built around the quadrennial struggles for control of the office of President. It covers not only the elections themselves, but the developments in each administration that influenced the work of party conventions, and determined the character and outcome of campaigns. Otherwise the story would be fragmentary and incomplete. There are numerous biographies, autobiographies, and reminiscences of political figures, and many special studies of periods, elections, individual parties, and sectional and local politics, but there is no recent general work presenting the whole picture. A number of books in the field of political science discuss the party system; but their emphasis is on the present-day organizations, with no more than a brief historical background.

I attempt in the following pages to present the essential facts about conventions, campaigns, and elections, briefly to assess the effectiveness of Presidents and other important party figures as political leaders, to indicate the more significant Congressional struggles of a political character, and to explain the trends of politics in the social and economic settings of the different periods, with particular attention to periods of change.

The greatest problem has been selection. So much has been written on politics and politicians that the author of a book of this character cannot hope to escape criticism for omissions and emphasis. Yet the reader should remember that there have been forty-six Presidential elections, that thirty-six different men have served as President, that the also-rans outnumber the holders of the office, that an all-inclusive list of actual and potential candidates for nomination would run to an amazing length, that there are fifty states, each with its array of politicos—and that not everybody can get into the act.

This third edition adds two chapters to bring the story through 1968 and provides a classified and more selective bibliography.

I am indebted to my colleagues in the History Department at Ohio State University for encouragement and helpful suggestions, and to my wife, Thelma Matheny Roseboom, for many hours of typing and for assistance in revising the manuscript and making the index.

To the many graduate students whose theses and reports have assisted me at various points and in various ways, I can only express my deepest appreciation. To mention their individual contributions would be impossible.

For the errors that have eluded my best efforts, I assume sole responsibility. If my opinions offend, may the reader be charitable enough to remind himself that this is a book about politics.

EUGENE H. ROSEBOOM

Contents

	Preface	v
1	Politics Without Parties	1
2	The Rich and the Well Born Take Charge	15
3	Monocrats and Jacobins	29
4	Agrarian Liberalism in the Saddle	48
5	Mr. Madison's War and Mr. Monroe's Era of Good Feelings	62
6	The Politics of Sections in the 1820's	77
7	The Days of Andrew Jackson	92
8	Whigs and Democrats, 1833–1843	108
9	Expansion and Its Consequences	127
10	The Republican Party Is Born	149
11	The Failure of Parties	168
12	The Civil War Years	185
13	The Politics of Vengeance	203
14	The Grant Era	219
15	The Great Dispute and Its Aftermath	236
16	In the Doldrums—The Eighties	253
17	The Tariff Campaigns	275
18	The Great Agrarian Failure	293
19	The Golden Age of the Grand Old Party	321
20	The First Roosevelt	338
21	The Progressive Uprising	356
22	The Rule of Wilson	375
23	The Conservative Reaction	391

24 The Yankee Politician and the Great Engineer 406
25 The Second Roosevelt 430
26 The New Deal Landslide 446
27 "That Man" Again 460
28 And Again 477
29 The Great Surprise 492
30 I Like Ike 508
31 Ike Again 524
32 The Kennedys Take Over 543
33 L.B.J. All The Way 572
34 Nixon and Agnew 586
Selective Bibliography 614
Index 625

1

Politics Without Parties

On the last day of April of the year 1789—a watershed year in both Old and New World history—a great crowd converged on Wall, Nassau, and Broad streets in the city of New York to witness the inauguration of General George Washington as first President of the United States under the newly adopted Constitution. Around noon there appeared on the Broad Street balcony of the new Federal Hall a tall soldierly figure in a homespun suit of deep brown set off with eagle buttons, white stockings, and a bagwig, a dress sword hanging at his side. With him was Chancellor Livingston of the New York judiciary—the Supreme Court of the United States was not yet functioning—who formally administered the oath of office.

In the crowded Senate chamber, the first President then read his carefully prepared inaugural address; his voice was low and unsteady, and the pages shook in his nervous fingers, for he was never at ease before an audience. Well aware of the magnitude and difficulty of making the new Federal government a success, and too conscious of his own limitations, he was responding to the call of duty, assured that "no local prejudices or attachments, no separate views or party animosities" would misdirect the legislators assembled before him. This was his only reference to parties, and it was uncomplimentary. No army of eager job-seekers thronged the taverns and boarding houses of the little city and he gave no thought to politics.

A little more than seven years later Washington wrote a famed Farewell Address paying his respects to the dangers of political parties and the "baneful effects" of party spirit. This last will and testament of his public life warned his countrymen against party strife: "It serves always to distract the public councils and enfeeble the public administration. It agitates the community with ill-founded jealousies and false alarms; kindles the animosity of one part against another; foments occasionally riot and insurrection." It was a road to despotism, a spirit not to be encouraged. "A fire not to be quenched, it demands a uniform vigilance to prevent its bursting into flame, lest, instead of warming, it should consume." Having been scorched by the fire of partisan conflict, the first President saw in it little that was good. His high-minded selflessness could not understand, much less appreciate, the all-too-human proneness of less exalted Americans to divide into rival camps, to wage bitter war for ideals and offices, to call names and throw mud, and in the process to make government function as the majority willed, whether for good or for ill. For behind the party strife that bedeviled President Washington lay a long period of political apprenticeship.

Let us go back a little way over the road that our colonial ancestors traveled in acquiring their political education. Then we may understand why the warnings of the first President would not and could not be heeded.

Political parties were the fruit of a tree that had been long in growing. British Americans had been learning the art of self-government and the tricks of politics from the days when Virginia planters first elected a House of Burgesses, and when New Englanders began to hold annual "courts of election" and town meetings to provide governments tailored along Puritan lines. In time, each new colony acquired a representative assembly; and the transplanted tree of English liberty grew amazingly in a frontier environment of economic opportunity and social fluidity. By the middle of the eighteenth century, the growing independence of these elected assemblies was a thorn in the flesh of royal and proprietary officials, appointed from England. Controversies were frequent, and the political pot boiled vigorously in each of the provincial capitals strung along the seaboard.

Yet, while these years of America's youth produced politics, there were no permanent parties and no political professionals. Several reasons explain this strange and not unhappy situation. First of all, there was no central government with a hierarchy of offices to reward the victors in elections, and in the separate colonies the elected assemblies controlled the purse but not the patronage. Eleven of the thirteen colonies had governors commissioned from England for an indefinite term who handled appointments and dispensed favors with little regard for the ambitions and interests of local politicians, as the disgruntled fathers of James Otis and Sam Adams discovered. The sons repaid the rebuffs with interest, eventually; but, while Adamses and Otises might win control of the provincial assembly and sabotage the executive, their spoils cupboard contained few bones for their supporters. The material inducement for holding a party together was absent.

But there were other obstacles. Chief among them was the simple fact that the voters were not numerous enough to require formal party organization for guidance and discipline. There were no mass armies to be trained and deployed. The customary requirement for voting, that a man must own fifty acres of land (or its substantial equivalent), limited political power to a minority of the adult males; and these, it must be remembered, were divided into thirteen independent jurisdictions. Britain's colonies were like the spokes of a rimless wheel, held together only by the London hub. National parties were impossible, and local organizations largely unnecessary.

Physical and psychological obstacles also complicated the situation. Much of the population was scattered over vast areas with roads often impassable or, in the interior, non-existent. Outside populous New England, where town meetings performed electoral functions, the county seat was the usual polling place. This was a serious handicap for residents on the fringes of the county, twenty or more miles away. Add that the ballot was not secret, and that voice voting was practiced in the majority of colonies, and it is not surprising that timorous folk chose to abstain rather than to offend. The candidates for assembly seats were usually weighty local magnates, and the little man was sometimes in a tight spot when he walked up to the election judges and announced his preference. Another factor, which time has not remedied, was the sheer indifference of many voters, who did not trouble to use their privilege. The hard grinding labor of pioneering was not conducive to an active interest in government except when it directly touched some everyday problem.

In many colonies, infrequent elections also kept voter interest and political activity at a minimum. Where governors dissolved and renewed assemblies without restriction, a period of several years might elapse between elections—unbroken in the southern colonies even by local elections, as county officials were appointed by the governor.

By contrast, the annual elections of New England and Pennsylvania were forerunners of the democratic systems of the later American states.

But the ways and wiles of politics will be practiced wherever men are free to discuss and decide. George Washington as President inveighed against the spirit of party; but he may have forgotten that he himself in his younger days had not been above taking a hand in the political game. When he ran for the House of Burgesses in 1757, military duties kept him from electioneering at the polls; but he provided his friends with the following customary means for winning votes: 28 gallons of rum, 50 gallons of rum punch, 34 gallons of wine, 46 gallons of beer, and 2 gallons of cider royal. The voters, 391 in number, averaged a quart and a half per man. Washington wrote to his manager: "I hope no exceptions were taken to any that voted against me but that all were alike treated and all had enough." He was elected.

In Boston in the 1760's Sam Adams operated by somewhat different methods. The members of a long established Caucus Club, meeting secretly in a large garret, did their drinking as an accompaniment to the more serious business of drawing up a slate for town offices and assembly under Adams's direction. The Merchants' Club then was asked to approve the selections. Later these choices were duly nominated and elected at the town meeting of the voters, with Adams and his henchmen pulling the strings. Sometimes disputes were started and warm debates staged to entertain the assembled citizenry; but the machine was always in control when votes were counted. Harvard-educated Sam's range of friendship took in tavern politicians, preachers, lawyers, mechanics, and merchants—which explains his political prowess.

Pennsylvania, with a mixed population of English Quakers and Anglicans, Scotch-Irish Presbyterians, Germans, and other nationalities and religions, had its own brand of politics in mid-eighteenth century. The governor, representing the proprietary Penn family, was often at loggerheads with the Quaker Assembly; the frontier Scotch-Irish had grievances against both; and the Germans preferred to mind their own business. During tense election struggles for control of the Assembly stolid Germans were naturalized in droves, and the expenses handled by local politicians to get their votes. Bribery, repeater voting, and election affrays suggest the later Philadelphia of Quay and Penrose. Benjamin Franklin and his son were active leaders on the Assembly side.

In these same years New York, governed by Hudson valley landlords and city merchants, witnessed the battles of two rival houses, the De Lanceys and the Livingstons. They could march their tenants to the polls and watch how they voted; but they needed also to corral the votes of the rising middle class of small merchants, professional men, artisans, and independent farmers. New York City held a large proportion of these, and so the feudal magnates courted the popular leaders and sometimes used bruisers at elections to protect or intimidate, if need arose. Public meetings were held to nominate candidates and pass resolutions. Issues were played up in newspapers and broadsides. Neither faction was at all democratic, but the Livingstons catered more to the common man, later supported the Revolution, and established a family tradition of aristocratic liberalism that had a marked influence on New York state and even on national politics.

Propaganda, especially of press and pulpit, came increasingly into the political picture in late colonial politics. Some forty-two newspapers were being printed just before the Revolution, and their columns were open to all manner of space-filling contributions, because the printer-owners wrote no editorials and concentrated on setting type. Letters, usually long and signed by Cato, Publius, or some other distinguished Roman, discussed constitutional, economic, and political matters and played an important part in guiding public opinion. As the controversy between mother country and colonies approached its revolutionary climax, the friends of Britain were confronted with what was almost a one-party press. The local pressure of organized radical groups made subversives of the printers. Governor Thomas Hutchinson of Massachusetts, a victim of Sam Adams's diabolically clever propaganda, declared that seven-eighths of his people read only the Boston *Gazette*, "that infamous paper, and so are never undeceived." Ministers, usually New England Congregationalists or Scotch-Irish Presbyterians, frequently preached on political themes and were actively anti-British in the revolutionary controversy. Their own hostility to the Church of England, and the attitudes of their congregations, explain these political parsons of the northern colonies. In the southern colonies where the established church was the Anglican, the clergy steered clear of controversial questions.

While politics matured without benefit of permanent parties, there is much truth in the oft quoted statement of John Adams that a "court" and a "country" party had contended for power in every colony from the beginning. He was referring to the fundamental line of division that gave vitality to colonial politics, not to parties in the modern sense of the word. Two centers of power constantly worked at cross purposes. One was the appointed governor representing an authority beyond local control. Vested with broad executive powers and an absolute veto, and assisted by an appointed council, he was under instructions to promote England's interests and to safeguard royal or proprietary powers and privileges. At the opposite pole was the popularly elected assembly, concerned primarily with local matters and struggling to increase its power at the governor's expense. By various devices, but especially by omission of funds for gubernatorial salaries and other administrative expenses, it could pressure executive authority into submission; and in the decades before the Revolution it made itself a center of resistance against all forms of outside control.

Behind these contending authorities were ranged the various economic interests in colonial society. Supporting the governor was the "court party" of appointed officials and substantial citizens who profited from British measures or through privileges conferred by the crown or its agents. In the other camp were the "outs," who wanted more freedom and less discrimination from the top. This does not mean that the assemblies were centers of democracy. More often they were controlled by those merchants, lawyers, and landed aristocrats who were denied the blessings of special privilege. Yet the leaders voiced local sentiment, as the governors usually did not, and thus were closer to the views of the small farmers, shopkeepers, and laborers who formed the bulk of the population. In the arguments with governors and British ministers the assemblies spoke the language of democracy and encouraged the development of ideals that were far from being realized in practice. In these local forums before the Revolution appeared such influential figures as Patrick Henry, James Otis, Samuel Adams, and Thomas Jefferson.

Within most of the colonies a sharp social cleavage complicated the chronic controversies between governors and assemblies. The seaboard, dominated by merchants, planters, landlords, and land speculators, was usually at odds with the back country of farmers and frontiersmen over representation in assemblies, land policies, taxes, money and credit, the administration of justice, and defense. When assemblies proved too blind to reform demands the interior yeomanry even resorted to arms against their exploiters, who were eager enough in such emergencies for the military backing of crown and governor. Pennsylvania and the Carolinas are prime illustrations of this bifocal vision of the seaboard gentry, who could stand in the assemblies for their rights as Englishmen against arbitrary power but who turned their backs on the clamors of the back country for democracy and equality. In colony after colony a long pent-up flood of local discontents transformed the secession of 1776 from the British Empire into a genuine revolution. The local battles of colonial politics had set the stage for such upheavals.

In the years 1763-1776, the blunders of British ministers and the skillful leadership and propaganda of American Whigs created a national issue—the problem of Parliamentary supremacy versus local autonomy—and divided the colonists into two opposing camps without regard to colonial boundaries. British control was no longer a matter of a particular governor versus a particular assembly; it had become a momentous national problem. The spokes of the wheel at last had a rim. Two parties—in a loose sense—emerged, labeled with the familiar English terms of Whigs and Tories. In the former group were to be found those whose interests were injured or threatened by British policies or who might improve their lot by change; in the latter, the beneficiaries of the status quo. Between the opposing forces was a large body of indifferent or uncertain folk whose attitude was, "A plague o' both your houses." Fearful of the penalties that would be inflicted on the losers and hoping to be let alone, they followed a policy of nonparticipation.

The radical Whigs, like any revolutionary group, drew into their orbit the direct actionists, the more ambitious, the more discontented, the underprivileged. As in other revolutions these left wingers soon developed an organization, dynamic leadership, and a program; the conservatives were lacking in all three. Through a system of committees of correspondence, initiated at Boston by the first great American politician, Samuel Adams, the party of resistance developed an intercolonial organization that enabled it not merely to win elections and control assemblies (or the conventions which took their place when royal governors dissolved the legal bodies and fled) but, by propaganda, pressure, and finally force, to destroy the opposition and carry the Revolution along the path to independence. The Tories, isolated and unorganized, could offer only ineffective resistance to this Whig machine. One of its victims described it as "the barbarian rule of frantic folly, and lawless ambition—freedom of speech suppressed, liberty of press destroyed, voice of truth silenced, a lawless power depriving men of their natural rights, property taken without law—America arming east and west and pushing with madness in the high road of Sedition and Rebellion."

Yet the Whigs were more nearly representative of American desire for home rule than of American democracy. While they appealed to and made use of town workers and small farmers, they included too many conservative elements to accept a completely radical program. The Virginia planters, burdened with debts to British merchants, angry at restrictions on their land speculations, jealous of their control over the Old Dominion, and pushed toward revolt by the backfire of radicalism among the small farmers led by Patrick Henry, supported the war with as much zeal as the New England farmer-labor radicals under the banner of Samuel Adams. But they were not democrats. In the northern cities a considerable section of the merchants, under the pressure of British restriction on trade, joined the revolt, running the risks a propertied class takes when it plays with the fire of revolution. Planters and merchants began with the hope of forcing England to abandon its coercive policy through boycotts and then resistance; but the radical leaders were looking toward complete independence and popular rule.

The adoption of the Declaration of Independence by the Continental Congress was a victory for the radical Whigs of the Sam Adams and Richard Henry Lee type over the moderate group represented by John Dickinson, Edward Rutledge, and John Jay. The latter thought such a declaration premature and watched the rising revolutionary tide with forebodings. Rutledge, South Carolina Whig aristocrat, feared a confederation ruled by New England radicals. "I dread their low cunning," he wrote, "and those levelling principles which men without character and without fortune in general possess, which are so captivating to the lower class of mankind." Yet the radicals had their way as to independence, though the preliminary struggles in the different states were far closer than the vote of their representatives in Congress indicated. The pressure of the voteless lower classes, who now took part in the revolutionary movement, weighed heavily on the radical side.

Independence represented only the severing of the cord of empire. But who would now rule at home? On the whole, the radicals had their way in the writing of the Articles of Confederation. The powers of Congress were so limited that it could do little beyond managing the war and conducting foreign relations.

The states determined the internal course of the Revolution. Here conservatives battled radicals over new constitutions and for control of the new state governments to decide questions of suffrage, machinery of state government, apportionment of representation, relationship of church and state, preservation of landed estates, the fate of ungranted crown and proprietary lands, and confiscation of loyalist property. The radical gains were considerable, and the doors were opened to further changes by the large powers granted to the new state legislatures, no longer checked by royal governors or British imperial authority. With a general widening of the suffrage, even though it was still restricted to landowners or taxpayers, the agrarian democratic forces were in a stronger position than ever before. The results of the struggle varied from state to state; Pennsylvania and North Carolina, for example, swung sharply to the left, while Massachusetts and South Carolina steered a decidedly conservative course. Although those loyalists who gave open assistance to the King's forces went into exile and lost their property, that considerable body of the well-to-do who supported, or at least accepted, the Revolution suffered no inconveniences, and some even waxed fatter on war profits and speculations or through the virtual extinguishment of their debts to British merchants. The old seaboard ruling class was still a political force to be reckoned with, despite the exiling of its right wing. Fortunately, its democratic opponents respected private property and every man's right to get ahead in the world, and had no thought of liquidating patriotic aristocrats.

The period following the Revolution was one of economic depression and social unrest, caused by the disruptions and the devastations of the war. Confronted with an acute shortage of gold and silver, the state governments were under strong pressure to issue paper money, as in the Revolution, and to suspend the collection of debts. Debt-burdened farmers, suffering from low prices and unable to find cash for interest and taxes, demanded such relief. The commercial and creditor class, in the coastal cities and on tidewater, opposed measures that would delay the foreclosure of mortgages or force them to accept cheap paper as payment. Thus the old antagonisms flamed afresh, but this time the large propertied interests were decidedly on the defensive, without the backing of the British government to curb agrarian radicalism. Congress under the Articles of Confederation lacked both the power and the army to deal with crisis situations, and was almost bankrupt financially.

The conservatives, alarmed at the success of the paper money party in seven states and the outbreak of Shays's Rebellion in Massachusetts, where merchants, lawyers, and creditors still ruled, resorted to a double strategy. On the one hand, they fought a defensive battle to curb radicalism in the state legislatures; on the other, they skillfully inaugurated an offensive movement to set up a central government powerful enough to preserve order, protect property rights, place the public credit on a sound foundation, and facilitate the conduct of interstate and foreign commerce.

In this movement were merchants, shipowners, holders of government securities, money lenders, large planters, former officers of the Continental Army, lawyers and professional men generally, and a good many former Tories—the classes that had most to lose through social upheavals and civil strife. A few among them were whispering of monarchy; some were concerned chiefly over their speculations in depreciated government bonds; but more were level-headed men of means who wanted a reasonably strong government to provide security and stability against agrarian levelers and provincial-minded politicians. The masses had imbibed sufficiently of the heady wine of democracy; economic distress was not to be cured by paper money and weak government. If self-interest governed the framers of the Constitution, it was an enlightened self-interest, and they entrusted their handiwork to the verdict of the voters, not to the arbitrament of force.

The movement for a Constitutional Convention aroused surprisingly little opposition. The more radical elements, engrossed in state politics, paid slight attention to it. They assumed that such a convention would do no more than propose amendments to the existing Articles of Confederation, and that the state legislatures would pass on these. Consequently, conservatives in the legislatures chose men of their own kind to go to the Philadelphia convention. Since its proceedings were secret, the radicals were taken by surprise when the Constitution was submitted for ratification.

Not only was a complete instrument of government offered to the voters instead of a group of amendments to the Articles; but the state legislatures were by-passed, and the Constitution was submitted to popularly elected conventions for their approval. When nine states ratified, it was to go into effect for the nine. The others might come in later. The insuperable barrier to amendments to the Articles, acceptance by all thirteen legislatures, was thus hurdled in highly irregular fashion. Indeed, the whole procedure was unconstitutional—if one may use the term—for it discarded the old government by a revolutionary, though peaceful, process and substituted a new one in its place.

Though the issue of ratification, like the question of independence, was a national one, it had to be fought out in each state; and local considerations naturally influenced the outcome. The supporters of the Constitution, who called themselves Federalists, avoiding the more accurate but unpopular "nationalists," had certain distinct advantages over the opposition, whom they dubbed "Antifederalists." In leadership and political strategy the balance inclined decidedly toward the party that included Washington, Franklin, Madison, Hamilton, James Wilson, John Marshall, Rufus King, the Morrises, and the Pinckneys, to mention a few familiar names. In the other camp only Governor George Clinton of New York, Luther Martin of Maryland, and the Virginians, Patrick Henry, George Mason, and Richard Henry Lee, could rival the Federalist captains. At every juncture the Antifederalists were outmaneuvered. Where the Federalists were sure of their control, as in Pennsylvania and most of the small states, they called the elections to choose delegates to the ratifying conventions so soon that the opposition had no opportunity to organize effectively. Where the result was doubtful, they delayed action in the conventions and encouraged debate while they influenced wavering delegates to vote favorably. Pressure, flattery, all the arts of persuasion, even political deals, were resorted to with great skill. Thus in Massachusetts the two key popular leaders, office-loving John Hancock and liberty-loving Samuel Adams, were drawn into the Federalist net, the former by promises of support for the Massachusetts governorship and possibly high office under the new Constitution, the latter by the influence of the Boston workingmen, who had been induced to hold a meeting in favor of ratification.

Another type of Federalist strategy was the promise of future amendments to the Constitution. Several ratifying conventions took the Federalist bait and proposed amendments; but these were offered as recommendations, not requirements to be met before ratification became effective. Eventually, ten were passed by the first Congress and duly ratified, but they constituted a bill of rights to protect individual liberties and did not alter the machinery or powers of the new government.

Not the least factor in the Federalists' victory was the concentration of their strength in the populous coastal area. Here their wealth and power helped create a favorable public opinion and made the election of Federalist delegates comparatively easy. The unfair apportionment of colonial days, which overweighted the seaboard in the assemblies, had not been entirely removed; and this aided the friends of the Constitution, because the convention delegates were elected in the same manner as the representatives to the legislatures.

In the Antifederalist hinterland the opponents of the Constitution had their difficulties in getting the sometimes unruly rural democrats to come to the polls. Prosperity was returning, the paper money craze had subsided, and farmers generally were displaying an indifference toward politics and political issues. Franchise restrictions,[1] which in most states kept the propertyless from voting, have been regarded as a Federalist asset; but this may be questioned. Certainly, the mechanics, sailors, and fishermen of the seaports, voteless or not, resolved and paraded in support of the new ship of state, following the lead of their employers and customers.

Nevertheless, with all their advantages, the Federalists barely squeezed the Constitution past a reluctant electorate. Direct popular vote might have defeated it. Of the eleven state conventions that ratified in 1787-1788, four—Massachusetts, New Hampshire, Virginia, and New York—had hostile or doubting majorities when their sessions began; but persuasion and pressure and even sharp practices, such as holding up Antifederalist letters, tilted the balance, and ratification won out by the narrowest of margins. Democratic, individualistic North Carolina and farmer-ruled Rhode Island rejected the Constitution, and only later, when the new government was a going concern, did they yield. Rhode Island might have continued longer on her independent course but for proposals in Congress to slap a commercial boycott on her. Then her convention met and ratified.

With the Constitution in effect the way was paved for genuine national parties. Americans, after a long apprenticeship, had acquired as much experience in self-government as any people in the world. Now, with the political center of gravity shifted from states to federal government, and elections for national offices made necessary, some form of organization had to be devised for representative government to function on a nation-wide scale. The clashes of classes

[1] New York alone changed its voting requirements to permit all adult males to vote at the election of delegates.

and sections that had characterized colonial and state politics needed the tempering effect of national parties to keep them under control. Concessions and compromises were essential in this broader field. Contending propertied interests had composed their differences in the Constitutional Convention and presented a united front for ratification. That they would continue to cooperate in order to make the new system operate in their interests seemed reasonably certain. That the defeated agrarian democrats would rally their forces and presently continue the struggle on the new field seemed equally probable. Thus two national parties, built on the old foundations, would naturally come into being. Yet the founding fathers had made no provision for this vital institution of democracy. Realistic James Madison, chief architect of the Constitution, foresaw temporary combinations of special interest groups to put through particular programs, but not permanent parties.

Parties were needed for another reason. In the Philadelphia convention the members had been intent on building a structure of government that would insure the blessings of order and opportunity to men of property without being offensive to men of liberty. The result was a carefully balanced system with wide powers but divided authority. This would presumably prevent an excess of democracy and also make control by any special interest difficult. An aristocratic Senate, chosen by state legislatures for six-year terms, would balance a House of Representatives, elected every two years by those qualified to vote in each state, while an independent judiciary and an independent executive, neither subject to popular election, would checkmate Congress and each other. Such an arrangement, ideal in providing checks and balances, was also ideally unworkable. The executive in particular was set off against the legislative body in a manner almost designed to produce constant friction.

But the system worked in spite of itself. The President fortunately had complete executive powers, and a veto over the measures of Congress which could be overridden only by two-thirds of each House. And the original complicated method of election to the Presidency was soon found to be no barrier to popular choice. Thus a democratic tribune of the people evolved, responsible to the voters of the entire nation, as Congress was not, whose "administration" came to be judged not by how well he administered the laws but how successfully he administered the lawmakers. Two major parties appeared, with capture of the Presidency as a prime motivating force, for success at the polls carried with it the prestige, power, and patronage of the nation's highest office and usually control of Congress and of the majority of the states as well. Inevitably the independent, unbiased magistrate the framers of the Constitution had visualized faded into constitutional mythology, though each new incumbent at his inaugural continues to give the vision lip service. The successful Presidents have been those who accepted the responsibilities of party leadership and policy making and acted accordingly; the "Constitutional" Presidents—and they have not been nonpartisan—have generally won but a limited fame, if they have not actually been found wanting. The truth of this statement will be amply verified in the chapters following.

2

The Rich and the Well Born Take Charge

The First Presidential Election

In September, 1788, the last Congress under the expiring Articles of Confederation fixed the dates for the inauguration of the new system under the Constitution. The electors of President and Vice President, it decreed, should be chosen on the first Wednesday in January, 1789; they were to meet and vote on the first Wednesday in February; the new Congress was to assemble on the first Wednesday in March.

Election day, as later generations understood it, is that day when the people choose the Presidential electors. Yet the people had little to do with it in 1789. Each state could select its own method, and the variations were surprising. Five states had the legislatures name the electors, apparently because the necessary special sessions of the assemblies were called too late to provide for popular election. Pennsylvania, Virginia, and Maryland let the voters elect. In Massachusetts the legislature chose two electors at large by joint ballot and one for each Congressional district from the two highest elected by the voters of the district. New Hampshire had popular election of its five electors but required a majority to elect. In the absence of a majority, the legislature was to choose from the highest in the poll but was limited to twice the number of places to be filled. A strange multiplicity of candidates divided the vote and threw the entire election into the assembly. The two houses then wrangled over the question of joint ballot or separate voting, and it was nearly midnight of that first Wednesday in January before the lower house accepted the slate of the upper. The New York assembly displayed its party rancor by a deadlock between the Federalist Senate and the Antifederalist House and no electors were chosen. North Carolina and Rhode

Island took no part in the election as they had not accepted the Constitution.

The Antifederalists made a poor showing in both the Presidential and the Congressional elections. Their failure in the battle over the Constitution and improved economic conditions created an apathy among their farmer following that could not be overcome. Most Americans were willing to give the new plan a fair trial, and the prospective passage of amendments by the new Congress was a further reconciling influence. Only in New York and Virginia were die-hard Antifederalists still a potent factor in politics. In the Old Dominion unrelenting Patrick Henry, dominant in the legislature, saw to it that James Madison was turned down for the United States Senate. Antifederalists were chosen to both seats. To keep Madison from being elected to the House of Representatives, the Henry majority in the assembly put his home county in what was designed to be a hostile district—an early instance of the use of a gerrymander, though the term was unknown then. The Father of the Constitution took to the stump in the dead of winter and defeated his Antifederalist opponent, James Monroe, at the cost of a frozen nose. Seven of the ten Virginia Congressmen and nine of the twelve electors were Federalists. Henry retired, and Antifederalism dissolved. The New York deadlock ended in the spring state election of 1789 when the Federalists captured both houses of the legislature and elected the United States Senators. Antifederalist Governor George Clinton squeaked through to another term, but his power was slipping.

The electoral vote revealed the extent of the Federalist triumph. George Washington received one of the two votes of every elector, including the three Virginia Antifederalists, 69 in all. Their second votes were scattered among eleven persons, but John Adams led with 34 and became Vice President, the empty consolation prize provided by the Constitution for the second highest in the electoral total. He might have done far better but for Alexander Hamilton's maneuvering. Professing fears that Antifederalist opposition might reduce Washington's electoral vote below that of Adams and put the latter in the Presidency, he urged Federalist electors not to give equal support to both men. An emissary even appeared at Hartford to warn the Connecticut electors to divide their second votes. New Jersey was to do the same to insure Washington's success. Adams lost 7 votes in the two states and received only 5 south of Pennsylvania. Hamilton regarded the brusque New Englander, lately returned from foreign service, as a potential malcontent who had to be mollified by some high office—and the Vice Presidency would serve; but he did not intend to encourage the Adams ambitions for future preferment by a large electoral vote. And so the seeds of a mutual distrust were sown. Eleven years later came the harvest—the overthrow of Federalism.

Washington's unanimous election was a triumph of the popular will in spite of the complicated, undemocratic electoral system. It gave the nation a chief executive who had the complete confidence, even veneration, of Americans in every walk of life. "Integrity and firmness are all I can promise," he had written to a friend. He overlooked his fine sense of judgment in handling controversial issues, his strongest trait, which alone was enough to insure that the new Constitution would have every chance to prove its worth.

Washington, as has been indicated, had no liking for politics or parties. As he saw it, his administration was to be nonpartisan; and he struggled to keep it so. Yet, without realizing it, Washington was mildly and justifiedly partisan from the beginning of his term. He gave no offices to avowed Antifederalists, for they might try to scuttle the new craft. The crew must be composed of friends of the Constitution. But this was of little moment, for Antifederalism was rapidly expiring. Later, when Jeffersonian Republicanism arose from its ashes, Washington viewed it with distrust. As the critics of administration policies grew bolder he became more disturbed, and when he spoke of the spirit of party in his Farewell Address he was thinking of this group. He wrote in 1795 to Secretary of State Pickering: "I shall not, whilst I have the honor to administer the government, bring any man into any office of consequence knowingly whose political tenets are adverse to the measures which the general government are pursuing; for this, in my opinion, would be a sort of political suicide." It was not loyalty to a party organization but loyalty to his administration and its policies that he was demanding; but the effect was much the same. From the beginning the Presidency of the United States was bound to be a political office.

Washington picked his department heads with great care. He gave the State Department to Thomas Jefferson, then Minister to France. John Jay, who had handled foreign relations under the Confederation, preferred to become Chief Justice, and John Adams was Vice President, so that Jefferson was a proper selection. Alexander Hamilton, though only thirty-two, was made Secretary of the Treasury, a choice that suited financial magnates, including Robert Morris, and supporters of the Constitution generally. General Henry Knox, head of the army under the Confederation, took charge of the War Department, while Governor Edmund Randolph of Virginia served as Attorney-General. Randolph had failed to sign the Constitution at Philadelphia but had afterward favored ratification and was in the good graces of the Federalists. Congress was predominantly Federalist, and so was the Supreme Court. The Constitution was in the hands of its friends.

The Capitalists and the Agrarians

The proposals of Hamilton to Congress produced a financial system for the new government. He advocated the refunding of the old securities of the Continental Congress in bonds of the new government at par value, the assumption of the state Revolutionary War debts by the federal government, and the establishment of a United States Bank. Less fundamental were his recommendations for a protective tariff and an excise tax. The former was not realized, and the latter caused trouble out of all proportion to its revenue yield.

Hamilton's funding proposal to exchange the old depreciated Continental securities at par for those of the new government drew the fire of Madison, though earlier he had advocated such a measure. Stories, well substantiated, that speculators, including members of Congress, were engaged in buying up securities, troubled the Virginia leader, who now proposed that present holders, chiefly large-scale operators, receive only the highest market price, and that the original creditors, many of them veterans and small holders, be paid the rest. His motion failed in the House, 36 to 13, largely because it did not seem to be practicable, and the rift between Madison and Hamilton had started.

Assumption of state debts encountered stronger opposition. The agricultural South, excepting debt-ridden South Carolina, opposed the measure. The North, where state debts were larger and where speculator money had invested heavily in defaulted obligations, threw its weight largely behind it, and the House voted for it in committee of the whole, with a powerful lobby present including "officers of government, clergy, citizens, Cincinnati, and every person under the influence of the Treasury"—dour Senator Maclay's report. But the arrival of the North Carolina delegation reversed the earlier vote, and assumption was stalled. At this juncture Hamilton, greatly disturbed, conferred with Jefferson, newly arrived at the Capital to take over the State Department, and their famous deal was the result—the South to have the future national capital located on the Potomac, and Jefferson to provide two House votes for assumption. Madison was also involved, though he felt bound to cast a silent vote against assumption.

Speculator interest in the Hamilton debt plans was not confined to the lobby. The analysis of the historian Charles A. Beard shows that 21 of 32 members of the House and 11 of 14 Senators voting for assumption were investors in securities. Only a few of its opponents had such investments, in most cases for small amounts. William Duer, for six months Hamilton's assistant, was up to his neck in the business of buying for the expected rise and had associates in and out of the government. Here was a powerful array of "funding fathers" who would back the Constitution to a man.

The Hamilton proposal for a United States Bank brought the battle between capitalists and agrarians into the President's cabinet. The high-riding Hamiltonians put the measure easily through Congress, where Madison opposed it on constitutional grounds, but Washington was in doubt. He talked with the secretaries and with Madison, read the opposing statements of Jefferson and Hamilton, and finally signed the bill, giving the Treasury the benefit of the doubt. While the Bank bill for the first time drew the line sharply between broad and strict construction, both sides knew that basically the issue was economic with pronounced political overtones. Hamilton saw the financial utility of the Bank as an aid to business and as a further prop to the new government; Jefferson and Madison saw it as a moneyed monopoly which would add to the power of the financial oligarchy that seemed to be fastening itself on the federal government. Madison, the ardent nationalist, had not expected the Constitution to spawn anything like this; and so he turned to strict construction. Jefferson, ever mindful of liberty, saw monarchy in the offing with Hamilton its sponsor.

The alignments in the federal government soon spread outward. Hamilton's measures, however defensible financially, provided the fuel of political discord that ended the superficial harmony that followed acceptance of the Constitution. It was not that they created political parties *de novo;* it is even questioned that these early divisions were actual parties. But the old antagonisms of state politics were rekindled and the fires were now fed from the nation's Capital.

Yet there appeared after a time one significant change in the old alignment. The wealthy southern planters had been strong supporters of the Constitution and were prepared to continue their cooperation with the moneyed men of the North. Virginia and South Carolina were their special provinces. But the policies of Hamilton brought no benefits to landed aristocrats; they had no funds to invest in stocks, only taxes to pay. Soon the Virginia planters began to draw away from their old allies and enlist with the opposition. The planter-merchants of South Carolina, which shifted its heavy debt to federal shoulders by the assumption policy, were more sympathetic toward the Hamiltonian system and, for some years, constituted the chief center of Federalism in the South. But by 1800 their loyalty had become too perfunctory to withstand the popular Jeffersonian pull.

Hamilton's philosophy of statecraft in 1790 ran directly counter to the trend of American democracy. It involved the use of the power of the new central government to advance the interests of a special propertied class, which would form a bulwark to protect that government against the menace of the masses—to Hamilton, mob rule. "The people are turbulent and changing," he had said in the Constitutional Convention. "They seldom judge or determine right." Intent on erecting over the American people an economic superstructure of financial power similar to that in the British government, which he regarded as the best in the world, he seemed to forget, if he understood, the deep-seated American distrust of power, the heritage of conflicts with British officials in colonial days and with Parliament just preceding the Revolution. Americans looked upon the new government created by the Constitution as an experiment, yet Hamilton boldly offered proposals that seemed certain to arouse the suspicions and distrust of the classes that needed to be reconciled to it. However much he might argue that what was good for business was good for farmer and planter, the hard facts that the debt grew larger and taxes higher told heavily against him.

The slight, young-looking idol of the financial world created a party without becoming a good politician. Born in the West Indies of mixed Scotch and French Huguenot parentage,[1] he had come to New York at the age of fifteen, studied at King's College, served on Washington's staff during the Revolution, and married into the

[1] He was the illegitimate son of an impecunious Scotchman, James Hamilton, and Rachel Fawcett Levine, undivorced wife of a Danish-Jewish planter, herself of French Huguenot blood.

wealthy Schuyler family to become a kind of spoiled darling of the New York aristocracy. A brilliant lawyer, a gifted writer and speaker, and a keen student of politics and economics, he had matured early and acquired a self-confidence that amounted to arrogance in dealing with his inferiors and even antagonized his associates. He could be persuasive, clever, fascinating in the company of Rufus King, the Morrises, and their kind, and with women, but his contempt for the plain people unfitted him for political leadership. Despite his lowly origin—or perhaps because of it—he despised democracy. Ruthlessly efficient, he had writhed at the blundering ineptitude and weakness of government and politicians in the days of the Confederation. He would have welcomed a dictatorship and, given the chance, would have played the role himself, for his chief frustration was a never satisfied ambition to achieve military renown. Now that he was in a seat of power, he catered to the interests of the wealthy commercial and creditor class—the rich and the well born who would not be guilty of the follies of democracy.

But Hamilton ignored the first principle of practical politics, that political power is dependent on votes. Even in the 1790's the masses of small landowners, if not the city workers, possessed the suffrage. Prudence would have dictated the building of a strong party organization, the circulation of Federalist propaganda among the rural voters, the concealment of the party's aristocratic character behind catchy slogans and emotional appeals, and the abandonment by the leaders of their aloof, high-and-mighty attitude in favor of the arts of the politician. But, except for support of a few party newspapers, neither Hamilton nor his associates deigned to resort to such methods—demagogic, they called them. A political party that catered to the masses was something illegitimate. This contempt for practical politics opened the way for Thomas Jefferson, Albert Gallatin, Aaron Burr, and the rest of the Republican politicians to make the most of their opportunities.

The Federalists (the followers of Hamilton kept the old name) depended chiefly on personal contacts of leaders to maintain unity and to rally their supporters at elections. Hamilton, in touch with members of Congress and federal officeholders, had an informal organization at his disposal that the opposition could not at first match. The Treasury, much the largest of the departments, had some ninety employees at the Capital and several hundred in the field service in daily contact with the business world. More than that, in the larger cities the business and social connections of men of money, usually Federalist in sympathy, gave them means of cooperation the rural voters lacked. The coffeehouses, the dinners and other social gatherings of the élite, the chambers of commerce, the tax-supported New England Congregational churches, the chapters of the Society of the Cincinnati (an organization of Revolutionary War officers)—these were the local "cells" of Federalism. Influencing powerfully the attitudes of the newspapers, they gave the party a unity and a cohesion that were sufficient until the practical politicians appeared on the scene to organize the farmers and the town mechanics. Then Wall Street and its cohorts succumbed to the back-country democrats and the Sons of St. Tammany. In New England, where commerce, shipbuilding, and the fisheries owed much to the beneficent measures of the federal government, Federalism put forth deeper roots than elsewhere. Thrifty Yankee farmers, prospering along with seaport merchants, capitalists, mechanics, and fishermen, and influenced by the Congregational clergy who linked Jefferson with atheism, acquiesced in the rule of the rich and the well born—often phrased as "the wise and the good." Here and in a few other conservative coastal areas, notably the little state of Delaware,[2] the Federalists could withstand the adversity of national defeat. But generally speaking, when control of the federal government was lost in 1801, the imposing façade of Hamiltonian Federalism collapsed.

The Republican politico-economic philosophy, as expressed by Thomas Jefferson, was primarily agrarian. This middle-aged Virginia planter, himself a pioneer in scientific farming, saw the United States as still a nation of farmers and wished to keep it so. With land easily obtainable, every man could become a possessor, and political democracy would then be possible and safe. The new industrialism, with its concomitant evils of a congested urban population and a small ruling class, he would keep beyond the Atlantic. "The mobs of great cities add just so much to the support of pure government as sores do to the strength of the human body," he had written in "Notes on Virginia" (1781-1782). Even the shipping necessary to carry to other lands the surplus of farms and plantations and to bring back manufactured goods, he would let Europe provide. It would be less troublesome and less expensive, for the carrying trade required

[2] In Delaware the more isolated rural areas were Federalist; commercial Wilmington, Republican. This does not fit the orthodox pattern of early party division.

the protection of a navy. Jefferson, who was born and brought up near the Virginia frontier and later became the owner of a dozen farm properties of some ten thousand acres, remained fundamentally rooted to the soil despite his legal training, his familiarity with English and French political thought, his European experiences and contacts as Minister to France, his cultured cosmopolitan outlook, and the amazing versatility of his interests.

Disliking the capitalist-creditor class with its investments in paper securities and the merchants with their dependence on British business and credit, he patterned his political strategy on the natural class antagonism of the "honest farmers" for these "paper aristocrats." Because the latter profited from the policies of the federal government, he assailed any extension of its powers, particularly in the executive branch, as a threat to the liberties of the individual and the rights of the states. He saw the struggle as one between liberty and power. The Jefferson who was opposed by "the fashionable order" of the cities, "merchants trading on British capitals," and "paper men" (his own classification in 1793) has found a welcome in strange quarters in modern America. His belief in laissez-faire individualism and weak government has been torn from its agrarian setting and offered by conservatives as an argument against all forms of governmental control. They conveniently overlook the fact that Jefferson's narrow concept of the powers of government grew out of his belief in a farmer democracy, which needed little government. When the two conflicted, as in the Louisiana Purchase, he sacrificed his constitutional views.

But Jefferson, like Hamilton, was a practicing politician rather than a political theorist. He never produced a systematic treatise on government, though his ideas found expression in letters and state papers, and in his "Notes on Virginia." His writings reveal him as more of an idealist, even a visionary liberal, than his actions bear out. He could write in private: "A little rebellion now and then is a good thing, and as necessary in the political world as storms in the physical," and again: "The tree of liberty must be refreshed from time to time with the blood of patriots and tyrants. It is its natural manure." He once set up the proposition that "the earth always belongs to the living generation"; therefore, every nineteen years (a generation, by his figures) constitutions, laws, and public debts should terminate and a fresh start be taken. Small wonder his critics called him a speculative theorist.

But the pressure of political considerations and an innate aversion to controversy made him a practical reformer who knew when to compromise and propitiate. Persuasive, subtle, indirect in his methods, gifted as a conversationalist and a letter writer but not as an orator, shrewd in judgment, skillful in managing men, the tall, freckle-faced, ungraceful, carelessly dressed planter-philosopher set about convincing the voters that his Declaration of Independence and the Constitution were in danger of being subverted, that a ruling class was taking over the government with monarchy just over the horizon.

Each of the incipient parties posed as the true defender of the Constitution against its supposed enemies in the other camp. Since the Antifederalist leaders of 1787-1788, on the whole, were turning to Jefferson, it was easy for the Hamiltonians to call all their opponents Antifederalists—an unpopular term now that the Constitution had been successfully launched. The Jeffersonians refused to wear this label and insisted that they were the true "Republicans." They could accept "Democratic Republican" but were divided about the term "Democrat," loosely defined by their critics as an upholder of rule by the mob, and frowned upon in the South, where so many of the landed gentry followed Jefferson. Consequently the Hamiltonians—and their later historian apologists—used it in place of "Republican," along with "Antifederalist," which it outlasted. The French Revolution provided them with another favorite epithet: "Jacobin," the party of the bloody extremists. The Jeffersonians were content to damn the opposition with such general names as aristocrats, monarchists, speculators, Anglomen, and Tories, though the designation Monocrats had some vogue. In another generation the term Federalist, adopted proudly by the Hamiltonians, was to fall into disrepute and become an adjective of political disparagement, synonymous with aristocrat.

New York offered the best opportunity for Jeffersonian infiltration, for here the old Clinton Antifederalist machine was still functioning and the powerful Livingston family, once Federalist, was now alienated. Hamilton, ignoring the Livingston claims to preferment, had secured the election of his father-in-law, General Schuyler, and of Rufus King to the United States Senate. Robert R. Livingston had also been passed over for Chief Justice of the United States in favor of John Jay. A Clinton-Livingston alliance had the satisfaction of replacing Schuyler with Aaron Burr in 1791. Burr was a rising figure in New York politics and a dangerous ally, but the Clintonians needed his support. Here was a powerful anti-Hamilton movement, which might be drawn into an understanding with the Virginia Republicans.

In the spring of 1791 Jefferson and Madison made a leisurely trip into New York and western New England to see the country and relax from the cares of government. They observed rural life in the North, visited battlefields, examined plants and flowers, caught some fish, and called on Governor Clinton at Albany. They had already been received by Burr and Robert R. Livingston at New York. Hamiltonians wondered at this "botanical excursion," and historians have not penetrated the mystery since, if there was one. Neither Virginian wrote a line to indicate that politics was discussed. It has been inferred that the alliance of Virginia and New York had its inception in these casual meetings; the election of 1792 indicated its existence. But one cannot be sure. Jefferson's devious methods place him under suspicion; yet he was quite interested in botany.

On October 31, 1791, at Philadelphia, appeared the first issue of the *National Gazette*, edited by the poet Philip Freneau. Innocent enough at first, it soon gave evidence of pronounced Republican leanings. It was actually the subsidized organ of the anti-Hamilton leaders, for Jefferson, Madison, and Henry Lee had induced Freneau to come to Philadelphia, and Jefferson had given him a part-time clerkship for foreign languages in the State Department at $250 a year. They also aided him in securing subscriptions, and the *National Gazette* was soon a pronounced success.

The administration had stanch editorial support from the outset in the *Gazette of the United States*, edited by John Fenno, once a Boston schoolteacher. It speedily became Hamilton's particular organ and received substantial aid from Federalist sources through Hamilton and Rufus King, as well as public printing subsidies. To counteract its aristocratic and—to Jefferson—monarchical tendencies, Freneau had been brought to Philadelphia.

A series of articles by "Brutus" in Freneau's paper assailing the funding system, the Bank, and speculator influence brought Hamilton into the fray in the *Gazette of the United States* under the signature "T. L." He pointedly questioned whether Freneau was not paid his clerk's salary to vilify the administration, oppose its measures, "and by false insinuations to disturb the public peace." This jab at Jefferson did not bring the Secretary of State into the lists—he was too shrewd for that; but Freneau and several anonymous writers, James

Madison among them, replied, and soon a heated newspaper debate was under way. The discord between the two Secretaries had become an open scandal, and Washington was much disturbed at the growing bitterness.

Jefferson had indicated in February that he might soon resign, but the President would not hear of it. When matters grew worse in the summer of 1792, the distressed executive appealed by letter to the two rivals to compose their differences and work together for the public good. Each replied with a defense of his position, and both expressed a willingness to cooperate with their chief; but that was all. The ink was hardly dry on Hamilton's answer before he was penning further anonymous articles for Fenno to print, in an attempt to force Jefferson to resign. The latter was ready to retire, though not at Hamilton's urging; but Washington again refused to consider such a suggestion.

A Vice Presidential Election

Upon one point the rivals were in complete agreement. This was that Washington should accept a second term. Jefferson was insistent. "Your being at the helm will be more than an answer to every argument which can be used to alarm and lead the people in any quarter, into violence and secession. North and South will hang together if they have you to hang on." Washington, now sixty and afflicted with deafness and bad dentistry, as well as the cares of state, reluctantly accepted as a matter of duty, though he longed for the peace and freedom of neglected Mount Vernon.

But the Republicans regarded the second office in the government as fair prey, and they set to work to get rid of John Adams. The Vice President, with his peculiar propensity for getting into trouble, had written a series of essays, "Discourses on Davila," for the *Gazette of the United States* in 1791. They constituted a learned disquisition on governmental theory in which he elaborated his belief, long held, in a balanced government as a necessity for the preservation of liberty. Aristocracy and democracy must be kept in equilibrium by a careful division of powers among the three branches of government. There was no direct criticism of the American Constitution; but unfriendly critics detected a leaning toward monarchy, and unfortunate private utterances by Adams supplied additional fuel. Jefferson involved himself through a note indorsing an American edition of Tom

Paine's *Rights of Man* (recently published in France), not knowing that the printer would use it as a preface. It reflected on "political heresies which have sprung up among us," and was taken as a criticism of "Davila." "Publicola" (young John Quincy Adams, son of the Vice President) attempted to answer Paine and Jefferson, other "Romans" entered the fray, and an awkward situation developed between the two old friends.

The Federalists accepted Adams as their Vice Presidential choice without any formal action. Hamilton, at heart more of a monarchist than Adams, nevertheless thought the latter too indiscreet; but he made no attempt to offer another candidate. His efforts were centered on defeating the original opposition choice, New York's Governor George Clinton, an old enemy. The governor's chances were dimmed, however, by a bitter state election in the spring of 1792. Although Chief Justice Jay, the Federalist candidate for governor, actually had more votes, the state canvassing board threw out the returns from three counties on technical grounds and counted Clinton in. This aroused intense feeling in the state, and there was some doubt as to the wisdom of supporting the veteran governor for the Vice Presidency. In the fall an under-cover project to make Senator Aaron Burr the Republican choice was launched from New York. He was stronger than Clinton in New York City but less well known elsewhere. Jefferson attended a Philadelphia conference of middle-state politicians on October 16, which indorsed Clinton, and Burr gracefully acquiesced, perhaps with the hope of future support. He was only thirty-six and could wait. Hamilton, alarmed at the possible candidacy of Burr, an "embryo Caesar," now discovered virtues in Clinton, "a man of property, and in private life, as far as I know, of probity"; but his opinion had no influence on the Republican decision.

This campaign, though only the Vice Presidency was involved, at least proved the existence of two embryonic parties. Neither had a formal organization, but the degree of unity achieved by private correspondence and through the newspapers was surprising. The advantages were with the Federalists, but the Virginia-New-York alliance did yeoman work in creating a Republican opposition. In almost every state little groups of Jeffersonians were active in nominating Congressional candidates and laying the foundations for a powerful party. Adams, sulking in Massachusetts when Congress met in November, bore the brunt of their assaults. He was antirepublican, an aristocrat, a monarchist at heart, they charged, and the Federalists were corrupt speculators and a moneyed aristocracy. In retaliation the Adams men brought up Clinton's opposition to the Constitution and referred to their opponents as the "mobocracy."

Congress had changed the dates for elections to make the first Wednesday in December the day for the Presidential electors to cast their votes, and the second Wednesday in February for Congress to tabulate the result. The electors were to be chosen in each state any time within thirty-four days preceding the first Wednesday in December.[3] This spread the election period over the first two weeks of November. As in the first election there was no uniform method. Legislatures chose the electors in ten states; the voters, in three; and the Massachusetts and New Hampshire legislatures selected the electors only where candidates lacked a majority of the popular vote.

Most of the excitement over the election seems to have been confined to a few newspapers, for the popular vote was light. The choice of a Vice President was not a matter to arouse widespread interest. Nevertheless, the electoral vote reflected sharply the growing party solidarity. Adams had all of New England, New Jersey, Delaware, Maryland, 14 of Pennsylvania's 15, and 7 of South Carolina's 8—a total of 77 electoral votes. Clinton had 50, carrying New York, Virginia, North Carolina, and Georgia, and receiving 1 vote from Pennsylvania. Newly admitted Kentucky gave 4 to Jefferson, while a South Carolina elector cast a vote for Burr. Every elector gave Washington one of his votes, making a total of 132.

The Republicans might have elected Clinton but for Pennsylvania. Below the Potomac they had all the states except South Carolina; in the North, only New York. The victorious Federalists had good reason to be alarmed at the rapid growth of the opposition. Adams had won; but Jefferson believed that his personal worth and past services were responsible, not his political creed. The House, where the popular will was better expressed, seemed to be almost under Republican control. The "monocrats" had been checkmated there.

[3] This was changed in 1845 to the Tuesday after the first Monday in November. In 1887 the day for the electors to meet was changed to the second Monday in January. In 1934, as a result of the Twentieth Amendment, this was shifted to the Monday after the second Wednesday in December.

3

Monocrats and Jacobins

Anglo-Gallic Politics

The French Revolution was greeted at first with general approval in the United States. France seemed to be working toward a constitutional monarchy through orderly constitutional means. But the wheel of revolution presently whirled off on a radical course. In 1792-1793 Americans learned of the deposition and guillotining of Louis XVI, the establishment of a republic, the proscriptions of the nobility, the mass executions of the Terror, and the proclaiming of a holy war to free oppressed humanity in other lands. Conservative Americans saw in all this only bloodshed and anarchy, Paris ruled by a bestial mob, property and religion swept away, liberty, equality, fraternity a mockery; and they feared that even the broad Atlantic might not stop the spread of this contagion. Liberals insisted that the liberty of all humanity was at issue, and they became apologists for the Revolution and even the Terror. "Was ever such a prize won with so little innocent blood?" wrote Jefferson in 1793. He believed that the victory of republicanism in France would dishearten the monarchists in the American household. Enthusiastic American sympathizers with France formed Democratic societies modeled on the original Jacobin Club. Some of these began to take part in politics.

When France declared war against England early in 1793, divisions among Americans were immeasurably sharpened. An old enemy was fighting an old friend. The nation which had aided them in their time of trial, and with which they still had a treaty of alliance, needed their help in her struggle for liberty against the allied monarchs of Europe. When England, in the exercise of her usual wartime prerogative of defining neutral rights to suit her interests, began to seize American ships, the feeling against her reached a fever pitch. The West, already inflamed against Britain for her retention of several border posts in violation of the treaty of 1783, blamed her for the incitement of the Northwest Indians by Canadian officials and traders. Southerners also resented the efforts of British merchants to collect certain pre-Revolution debts and the failure of England to pay damages for hundreds of slaves carried away by departing troops. Out of this widespread antipathy toward the mother country the Republicans were in a position to make much political capital.

The Federalist leaders, however, refused to be swayed from their anti-French viewpoint. Their political principles were based upon the solid foundation of economic interest. Much of American foreign trade was with Britain, whose merchants sold to Americans on a credit basis. The United States needed their goods and could ill afford to lose British markets. The prospects of wartime profits made the commercial interests prefer neutrality, in spite of inconveniences and even losses from Britannia's rule of the waves, to any rupture of peaceful relations. Then, too, war with England would endanger the stability of the new fiscal system and disturb investments in public securities. The mobs might erect their liberty poles and cheer for Citizen Genêt, the new French Minister, but the hardheaded men in the chambers of commerce would go about their business unmoved by the clamor. Hamilton, their spokesman, would see that the administration held to a neutral course.

Business relations were strengthened by social ones, for leading Federalists such as Hamilton, Gouverneur Morris, and Senator William Bingham were connected by blood or marriage with English families, and the Pinckneys had been educated in England. Old Tory families in particular, now Federalist in politics, were likely to have kinsfolk across the water. Thus a community of feeling as well as interest drew the American aristocracy toward the British ruling classes.

That Americans remained neutral in act was due to the firmness and courage of Washington and Adams; neutrality in feeling proved to be impossible. But the fairly even balance of parties kept both sides within reasonable bounds. The tide of battle ebbed and flowed too uncertainly to give either a pronounced advantage. When it did seem to swing sharply toward the Federalists after the "X Y Z" Affair in 1798, their misuse of power brought about their downfall.

The neutrality proclamation, the Genêt affair, Jay's Treaty, and the Whiskey Insurrection furnished the issues to emphasize the divisions between the French and British parties in Washington's second term. Jefferson, though reluctantly giving his assent to Washington's neutrality proclamation of 1793, thought it should have been deferred, and Hamilton and Madison (as "Pacificus" and "Helvidius") crossed swords in a newspaper duel over the problem.

The natural enthusiasm of most Americans for the new French Republic was still working in the interest of the Republicans when Citizen Edmond Genêt, the new French Minister, made his triumphal journey from Charleston, South Carolina, to Philadelphia. That dangerous young diplomat, by his plan for a western invasion of Spanish Louisiana and his insolence toward the President, soon became a thorny problem for his Republican sympathizers. Jefferson hastened to dissociate himself from any responsibility for Genêt's misconduct and tried to get his friends to differentiate between the cause of the French Republic and the indiscretions of its representative. But the pendulum was definitely swinging toward the Federalists when Washington demanded the recall of Genêt.

The Anglomen were still rejoicing over this discomfiture of the Gallomen when England, by high-handed seizures of American merchantmen, stirred traditional dislike into demands for immediate retaliation. Only with great difficulty were Republican proposals for restrictions on British commerce defeated in Congress. Already President Washington was acting to check the drift toward war by sending Chief Justice John Jay to England to negotiate a peaceful settlement of all outstanding difficulties.

Jay, condemned in advance by Republicans as pro-British, brought back a treaty that was as roundly denounced as any ever made by an American diplomat. Hamilton, in close communion with George Hammond, British Minister at Philadelphia, had given secret assurances to His Majesty's government that knocked the bottom out of Jay's demands and threats. As a result, fearful that war might follow from his failure, he gave way on important points and yielded too much in return for too little. The treaty's limited trade concessions and its failure to settle the vexing issues of neutral rights angered even the commercial interests; but the Federalists had to support it, and the Senate ratified in secret session by a bare two-thirds.

All this had been done without making the treaty public. But Benjamin Franklin Bache, redoubtable Republican editor, obtained a copy from a Senator and published it in the Philadelphia *Aurora*. Anti-British feeling flared up in mob demonstrations: Jay was burned in effigy in the larger cities, and Hamilton, attempting to address a New York meeting, was struck in the face by a stone. The Federalist leaders, working through the chambers of commerce and merchants' clubs, brought the businessmen into line. Hamilton assisted powerfully with his "Camillus" articles in the newspapers. Washington hesitated for several weeks before signing the unpopular document; but, as usual when confronted with a hard choice, he took the Federalist road.

Relations with England improved after Jay's Treaty, and the war clouds lifted. But the effects on Federalism in the South were bad. Planter debtors were indignant over a treaty which placed upon the government of the United States the burden of paying the pre-Revolutionary debts to British merchant-creditors, and yet made no provision for compensating slave-owners for the hundreds of slaves carried away by British forces in the Revolution. Even in Federalist South Carolina there was little support for the treaty, and John Rutledge, Pierce Butler, and Charles Pinckney led a chorus of denunciation. Whatever benefits there were went north. The commercial clauses of the treaty and the surrender of the Canadian border posts by the British meant nothing to southern planters. Hamiltonian Federalism thereafter was in retreat south of the Potomac.

The Whiskey Insurrection of 1794, while Jay was in England, was a protest against the excise tax on distilled liquors in which the frontier Scotch-Irish of Pennsylvania let off steam against the British and the administration. Although its violent spirit did not meet the approval of Gallatin and other critics of the unpopular Hamiltonian tax, they thought the army of fifteen thousand that marched to Pittsburgh to suppress a non-existent insurrection, with Hamilton riding along to advise, an unnecessary display of military power. It did not help the cause of Federalism on the frontier. After the suppression of the outbreak Washington bitingly referred, in his address to Congress, to "certain self-created societies" as contributing to the opposition to the excise. This reference to the radical "Democratic Societies" was sharply debated in the House, where Republicans defended them and insisted upon the right of any group to express opinions on governmental policies. Nevertheless, the President's open condemnation was a deadly blow to the societies. Already hampered by a lack of central organization and the fall of their Jacobin model in France, they began to dissolve, and their political influence was soon gone. In 1794 they had contributed to Republican victories in the Congressional elections in New York City and Philadelphia and might have served in many places as the nuclei for local organizations.

Washington had become practically a Federalist by 1795. His cabinet was now entirely from that party. Jefferson had retired in December, 1793, and Randolph, the mild Republican who succeeded him in the State Department, was forced out in the summer of 1795, his reputation under a cloud. Timothy Pickering, a lean-faced, narrow-minded, self-righteous Massachusetts Puritan and persistent office seeker, took his place. Hamilton resigned early in 1795 to return to the practice of law and make some money for his family; but a satellite, affable, industrious Oliver Wolcott of Connecticut, took his cabinet seat. Pickering, Wolcott, and Irish-born Dr. James McHenry of Maryland, who became Secretary of War in 1796, all owed their places to the "Colossus" and looked to him for guidance. The Republican press was now assailing Washington himself, led by Bache of the *Aurora* who showed little restraint and much bad taste. Freneau had ceased to publish the *National Gazette*. John Fenno continued to support the Federalist cause in the *Gazette of the United States* until his death from yellow fever in 1798.

The election of 1796, with Washington eliminating himself,[1] soon became a struggle between Adams and Jefferson. Members of Congress of each party and some outsiders seem to have discussed the problem of candidates informally and to have reached an agreement as to their choices for first place. But there was no formal meeting of the "caucus," as in later elections, and there was nothing to bind the electors. Hamilton, doubtful about the wisdom of supporting Adams, had considered Patrick Henry; but that old Antifederalist, now a conservative, showed no interest. The need for a southern running mate for Adams pointed toward South Carolina, and Thomas Pinckney, negotiator of a popular treaty with Spain, was selected. Since there was no separate vote for Vice President, Pinckney's southern friends chose to regard him as a Presidential candidate. He was expected to take votes from Jefferson in the South and thus insure a Federalist victory for both offices. In this situation Hamilton took a hand. His plan was innocence itself. All he asked was that

[1] He did not consciously set a precedent against a third term. He would have retired after one term if circumstances had permitted it. Now, disgusted with party bitterness and eager to enjoy the peace of Mount Vernon, he refused to consider another term. At the time of the adoption of the Constitution he had written to Jefferson defending the reeligibility of the President and opposing any restriction on the number of terms.

the northern electors should be loyal to their party and give an equal support to both Federalist candidates, ostensibly to keep Jefferson from finishing first or second. Behind this plausible appeal was the possibility that Pinckney might do better than Adams in the the South. Thus the New Englander would end up in second place —an outcome which Hamilton admitted afterward "would not have been disagreeable to me." The Adams electors in New England, however, took care of the scheme, as the electoral vote reveals.

Burr's nomination for second place on the ticket with Jefferson seems to have been taken for granted, certainly in the North and West; but if the Virginia leaders favored him they failed to inform their electors. Perhaps the fact that the New York legislature, which would choose the state's electors, was Federalist made Burr's candidacy of little value to the Virginians, as he had proved unable to control his home state.

The campaign raged up to the day in December when the electors were to meet. Though elected on partisan tickets, there were no binding pledges to prevent the exercise of individual judgment by an elector. Consequently, the party newspapers continued the battle until the results were known. While Jefferson and Adams remained in bucolic retirement far from the seat of government, their ardent supporters used every weapon of propaganda, from poisoned arrows to mud. Adams was traduced as a monarchist, a lover of titles, an enemy of liberty; Jefferson, as an atheist, a coward in the Revolution, a tool of France, and an enemy of the Constitution. The French Minister, Adet, meddled in the campaign by supplying the Republican *Aurora* with copies of his notes to Secretary of State Pickering for immediate publication. His praise of Jefferson and his hostile tone toward the administration were obviously intended for public consumption. His actions proved more embarrassing than helpful to the Republicans.

With legislatures choosing electors in ten of the sixteen states, it is difficult to estimate the influence of campaign propaganda. Federalist electors were chosen from New England, New York, New Jersey, and Delaware, and the majority of Maryland's districts. One Maryland elector judiciously voted for both Adams and Jefferson. The Republicans carried Georgia, Tennessee, Kentucky, North Carolina, Virginia and Pennsylvania, though each of the last three had a solitary Adams elector. A second Pennsylvania elector, reputedly a Federalist, voted for Pinckney and Jefferson. The South Carolina electors also coupled these men as their choices. A bipartisan deal in the legislature was responsible for this all-southern ticket. This might have made Pinckney President had the Adams electors supported him equally with Adams elsewhere, as Hamilton had hoped; but 18 votes were thrown to other Federalists, and Pinckney lost even the Vice Presidency. Adams had 71 votes; Jefferson, 68; Pinckney, 59; and Burr, 30. Nine others received votes. Republican newspapers charged the Federalists with fraudulent voting in Pennsylvania, where the popular vote was very close, and in one Maryland district where four votes separated the two parties; but their protests were unheeded.

On the Republican side, Burr's poor showing was a surprise. The southern Republican electors from Virginia, North Carolina, and Georgia had given Jefferson 35 votes to Burr's 7. The alliance of the Old Dominion and New York had been dissolved without notice to the junior partner. Burr said nothing but was to be more canny when the Virginians looked northward for support in 1800.

Jefferson's defeat had its compensations. In the Vice Presidential chair he could see and hear much, keep in touch with his friends in Congress, and yet preserve a discreet silence in public. Votes and speeches are not required of Vice Presidents.

Adams and His Party

John Adams took the oath of office on March 4, 1797, before House and Senate members in a simple ceremony completely devoid of the pomp for which he had been reputed to have a true monarchist's love. The new President was off to an excellent start. This crusty New England lawyer, short, bald-headed, with a little too much belly—"His Rotundity," his critics called him—had as much learning stuffed in him as any man in America. He sometimes seemed overfond of displaying his knowledge of peoples and governments, ancient and modern, in a pedantic parade of illustrations; but his observations were often acute, and his conclusions were a challenge to the toughest intellects.

Though he had signed the Declaration of Independence, the wine of liberty and equality had not turned his head. He believed that men were governed by their interests and passions, and that neither the rich nor the masses could be trusted with unrestrained power. In this age-old class struggle, liberty could be preserved by a balanced government which represented both classes in its legislature, and included three departments, each a check on the others. He lacked Jefferson's faith in the people and Hamilton's belief in the rule of the few. Adams distrusted human nature. In his economics he was nearer to Jefferson. Brought up on a farm, he viewed property in terms of land; and in middle age he had become the proud possessor of a substantial New England farm. Without investments in trade or securities, he was not a sympathetic representative of the class interest of his party. Neither was he pro-British in feeling, for he resented the selfishness and the snobbishness of the British ruling class, which he had experienced at first hand when Minister to England; and he saw the dangers to the young nation in European involvements. Hamilton's distrust of him was well founded.

Adams was also unfitted by temperament for party leadership. He was proud, independent, suspicious, tactless, cursed with a sarcastic tongue and a quick temper. He even antagonized when he meant to conciliate. Franklin described him as "always an honest man, often a wise one, but sometimes wholly out of his senses." His wife, Abigail Smith, also of an old Puritan family, was his intellectual equal, cultured far above the feminine norm of the eighteenth century. Her published letters are a contribution to American literature. Yet this strong-willed first mistress of the White House—occupied in 1800—accepted and shared her husband's likes and dislikes, if she did not at times activate them. Her jealousy for his fame did not help to soften his asperities.

Adams retained Washington's cabinet—a serious mistake, as later events proved. The department heads were a mediocre group, and they were loyal to Hamilton, who expected to remain the power behind the throne. The new President, obsessed with his idea of a balanced government and coordinate departments, did not realize that his failure to provide leadership played into Hamilton's hands. The result was that Congress and cabinet looked to the ex-secretary, not to the chief executive, for guidance. To make matters worse Adams disliked Philadelphia, loved his country home at Quincy, Massachusetts, and was away from the seat of government 385 days in four years—in 1799 for a seven-month stretch. The result was a lack of supervision over administrative matters and a lack of consultation between President and secretaries on matters of policy.

Adams appeared in his inaugural address as the patriot statesman pledged to uphold free government at home and peace with all nations. With a bipartisan foreign policy in mind, he sounded out Jefferson on the possibility of his or Madison's serving on a commission to be sent to France to negotiate over matters then in controversy. Hamilton, not without guile, had the same idea. Jefferson wisely declined for himself and, a little later, for Madison. Meanwhile, Adams had been informed by his cabinet that party considerations made such an appointment inadvisable. He yielded, but later did put Elbridge Gerry, a political neutral and personal friend, on the commission with C. C. Pinckney and John Marshall, Federalists.

Otherwise, in matters of patronage the President followed the orthodox Federalist line. Two or three removals in the Treasury Department smacked strongly of partisanship. In one case the effect was reported as "good" upon some employees who had been "very Jacobinical." In making appointments, Adams took care that the recipients were steady supporters of the government, and his department heads were equally careful. The latter were inclined, also, to find jobs for impecunious or importunate relatives or for relatives of influential Federalists. Senators and Representatives were usually consulted about federal appointments in their localities, but in this respect the Adams administration merely continued a policy Washington had found advisable.

The troubles of the Adams administration with France are too familiar to require a retelling in a study of politics. They culminated in the "X Y Z Affair," an attempt by agents of the Directory, then the government of France, to secure a bribe from the three American negotiators. The wave of indignation that swept the country united the Federalists on a war policy and reacted against the pro-French Republicans. Congress made preparations for war and also passed a group of harsh repressive measures, the much criticized Alien and Sedition Acts, of which more later. The Congressional elections showed Federalist gains, though their House majority included a group of moderates, chiefly from the South, who would not accept the leadership of the New England extremists.

The creation by Congress of a standing army whetted Hamilton's appetite for martial glory. To command it became his consuming ambition, and not even the opposition of the President could thwart him. Washington was induced to accept nominal command but preferred an inactive role and named Hamilton to take the field for him. Adams felt that Knox and C. C. Pinckney, who outranked Hamilton in the old Continental Army, should have precedence; but he was forced to yield when Washington was adamant and the cabinet stood with him. Hamilton received the coveted command. At Washington's suggestion Adams nominated Colonel William S. Smith, his own son-in-law, to be adjutant general; but Secretary of State Pickering secretly influenced Federalist Senators to reject the nomination—another snub for the President. The army, officered chiefly by Federalists (for the loyalty of Republicans was suspect), never got beyond the training stage. Though Hamilton had a grandiose scheme to use it against Spanish America—with British aid—and the equally agreeable notion that eventually it might be turned against rebellious democrats at home, he never had the opportunity to test its mettle. Adams threw off the Hamiltonian octopus that was strangling his administration, broke with the warmongers in Congress, and overruled Pickering by sending a new special commission to France. Napoleon Bonaparte, now in control, agreed to a peaceful settlement. The army was disbanded in June, 1800, to the accompaniment of Republican celebrations.

A caucus of Federalist Senators and Representatives in May, 1800, nominated Adams and General C. C. Pinckney as the party candidates for the approaching election. Even the Hamiltonians agreed to the nominations, for it seemed possible that Pinckney might run ahead of Adams. In any case, with all their talented leaders, the Federalists had no other available candidates. If Adams had been put aside for a war candidate, he might have gone over to Jefferson to insure the defeat of his party enemies.

On the heels of the caucus action came a belated purging of the cabinet by the President. Inept, likable McHenry, a stooge of Hamilton, resigned from the War Department after a stormy scene with his irate chief. The malevolent, intriguing Timothy Pickering, "whose manners are forbidding, whose temper is sour and whose resentments are implacable" (Abigail Adams's description), clinging to office like a leech, had to be dismissed as Secretary of State. The smiling, slippery Wolcott, a better deceiver than his colleagues but at least an efficient Secretary, continued as head of the Treasury, though his private correspondence reveals the extent of his treachery. In John Marshall, Virginia member of Congress, as the new Secretary of State and Samuel Dexter as Secretary of War, Adams at last had capable men whom he could trust.

While the outraged but helpless Pickering continued to fulminate against the President, it remained for Hamilton to complete the discredit of the war faction. Traveling through New England in the summer of 1800, he conferred with various leaders and was especially well received in Massachusetts, where the "Essex Junto" was hostile to Adams. But George Cabot, Fisher Ames, and other influential men saw no way to repudiate the President without wrecking the party in the midst of the campaign. Adams was stronger with the rank and file than with the leaders. Nevertheless, Hamilton would not restrain his flowing pen. He wrote directly to Adams to inquire the truth of statements attributed to him that his enemies were a "British faction" led by Hamilton. Receiving no reply after a second letter, he prepared in October a pamphlet, "The Public Conduct and Character of John Adams," to be printed and privately circulated among Federalist leaders. Aaron Burr in some manner secured a copy as soon as it was printed and sent excerpts to Republican newspapers. Hamilton then had to make public the entire production.

It was a sorry performance. In the closing days of the campaign he had assailed with unsparing pen his party's Presidential candidate, not even overlooking his personal faults. Yet Hamilton concluded lamely that under the circumstances he would not advise withholding from Adams a single vote. Even his friends were dismayed at the publication. But the election was already decided. A Republican legislature had been elected in New York in the spring, and in South Carolina in the same month in which Hamilton was writing his pamphlet.

The Republican Triumph

In the dark days of the undeclared "French War" of 1798, Jefferson refused to despair. By merely observing his customary silence toward his critics he was a model of propriety as Vice President, though the Senate atmosphere was anything but friendly to him as presiding officer. But he was privately planning and conferring and writing, patiently intent on holding his lines until the Federalist fury wore itself out. Not once did he lose his head. The Republican opposition in Congress could do little to stem the tide of war; but when the anti-French, anti-Republican crusade produced the Alien and Sedition bills, the leaders put up a hard fight, though outvoted. The Alien Act[2] gave the President, for a two-year period, the power to deport without trial any aliens he thought dangerous to the peace of the country. A separate act increased the residence period for naturaliza-

[2] To be distinguished from the Alien Enemies Act, which applied only in case of war.

tion from five to fourteen years. The Sedition Act was even more partisan, forbidding "false, scandalous and malicious" criticisms of the government, Congress, or the President. All elements of the Federalist party supported this legislation, with John Marshall a solitary critic.

No alien was actually deported under the Alien Act, because most of the prospective victims left before it was passed or soon afterward; two or three were indicted under the Sedition Act. Federalist dislike of French "Jacobins," "United Irishmen," and refugee English liberals—Republicans, all—was well expressed by a writer in a New York paper: "Would to God the immigrants could be collected and retransported to the climes from whence they came." Adams, in rejecting a proposal to give passports to Du Pont de Nemours and a group of French scientists to come to the United States, wrote to Pickering: "We have had too many French philosophers already, and I really begin to think, or rather to suspect, that learned academies not under the immediate inspection and control of the government, have disorganized the world and are incompatible with social order."

The Sedition Act was aimed at Republican editors and writers primarily. It caught such experts in vituperation and vilification as John Daly Burk, Irish exile, who edited the New York *Time Piece*, William Duane of Irish ancestry and uncertain citizenship, who took over the deceased Bache's Philadelphia *Aurora* (Bache died of yellow fever while under indictment), Scotch-born James T. Callender, who wrote for Virginia newspapers, Matthew Lyon, belligerent Vermont member of Congress, and Dr. Thomas Cooper, English liberal, who wrote Republican pamphlets. There were ten convictions. Duane hid out to escape contempt proceedings by the Senate, was then indicted under the Sedition Act but never tried; Burk discontinued his paper and agreed to leave the country; and others were intimidated merely by indictment or frightened by these examples into suppressing their opinions. Even Vice President Jefferson felt the pressure. He wrote to a friend: "I know not which mortifies me most, that I should fear to write what I think, or my country bear such a state of things." The partisanship of federal judges, notably Supreme Justice Samuel Chase, on circuit duty, placed freedom of speech in grave danger. The courts were not to be depended upon to defend the civil liberties of Republicans. Federalist editors, such as venomous William Cobbett, an English subject, could castigate Republicans freely, since this was not sedition, and later could even assail Adams after his break with the war party, without fear of prosecution!

In Jefferson's opinion the Constitution had been clearly violated; and he conferred with his lieutenants on a plan for public protests. The outcome was the passage by the legislatures of Virginia and Kentucky of a group of resolutions declaring the Alien and Sedition Acts unconstitutional. Though it was not known at the time, Jefferson was the real author of the Kentucky Resolutions while Madison wrote the Virginia ones. The compact, or state sovereignty, theory of the nature of the Union set forth in them is more significant for constitutional history and need not be considered here. The political purpose of the resolutions came first in the minds of the authors. By calling attention to the extreme character of Federalist measures, they hoped to obtain responses from other states that would arouse public opinion against the laws. The replies were generally unfavorable in the states that noticed them, but the Republican cause was probably aided by the agitation and discussion that ensued.

As the war fever subsided and the Federalists fell to fighting among themselves, Republican hopes rose. Working quietly through conferences with small groups and through a wide range of correspondence, Jefferson, Madison, Gallatin, Burr, and other key leaders welded together a powerful party. Newspapers were financed, pamphlets were printed and circulated, Congressmen wrote letters to their constituents, and the propaganda mills ground steadily through the campaign. New York, Pennsylvania, and South Carolina were the key states that must be won, though the Jeffersonians refused to concede even New England to the enemy without a battle.

In New York the election of the legislature, which was to choose the Presidential electors, was held in the spring of 1800. Colonel Aaron Burr, whom Jefferson had been courting since 1797, became the Republican man of the hour. His task was to make Federalist New York City Republican and swing the balance of power in the legislature to the Jeffersonians. The arrest and harsh treatment of Jedediah Peck for circulating petitions for the repeal of the Sedition Act helped upstate; but in the city the clever tactics of Burr accounted for the result. The Society of St. Tammany proved to be a useful ally. Organized in 1789 by William Mooney on the foundations of earlier groups of the Revolutionary period, it was at first a fraternal order with a membership of mechanics, artisans, and laborers. Its democratic personnel caused it to evolve into a Republican club, which met in Martling's Tavern in a room the scoffing Federalists called the "Pig Pen." It was soon playing an important part in local elections, and Burr, though not a member, worked with it.

In order to draw the widest possible popular support, Burr drafted an assembly ticket of big-name Republicans including Clinton, General Gates, and a Livingston, and offered it to the voters in opposition to a group of Federalist mediocrities whom Hamilton had named to insure control of the city delegation. Burr also created some new voters by a clever legal device which made them landowners. The polls, open for four days, were scenes of great excitement as the two great rivals electioneered in person, though Burr depended more upon his disciplined organization to get results. The county voted Republican, and its assemblymen furnished the margin by which the new legislature chose Jeffersonian electors. An average majority of 490 votes was the balance of power in the county, and indirectly in state and nation.

One last card remained for the stunned Federalists to play. After conferring with friends, Hamilton proposed to Governor Jay that he call the old assembly into special session at once to enact a law providing for the choice of Presidential electors by popular vote under a district system. This would give the Federalists a second chance and would insure them at least a part of the New York electors. "It is easy to sacrifice the substantial interests of society by a strict adherence to ordinary rules," he wrote, urging the governor not to be "over-scrupulous." But austere John Jay had none of the arts of the political manipulator. He filed away the letter after inscribing on it, "Proposing a measure for party purposes which it would not become me to adopt."

The outcome of the spring election in New York made it certain that the Vice Presidential candidate would come from that state. But would it be Clinton or Burr? Gallatin asked his father-in-law, Commodore James Nicholson, to sound out the New York Republicans and let him know their preference for the benefit of the Republican Congressional caucus. The details of the negotiations were later a matter of controversy. At least Clinton seemed unenthusiastic toward the nomination while Burr's friends were quite insistent. Burr agreed to take the nomination provided assurances were given that the southern Republicans would act fairly toward him. He had not forgotten their treatment of his candidacy four years earlier. The party Congressional caucus met on May 11 and unanimously agreed to support Burr for Vice President.

In Pennsylvania the Senate, containing a number of holdover members, was Federalist, but the House of Representatives, elected in October, 1800, was strongly Republican. Had a state-wide popular vote been permitted for Presidential electors, as in past elections, all fifteen would have been Republican. But the Federalist Senate blocked all attempts in this direction, refused to vote by joint ballot, and forced a compromise which gave the Federalists seven electors, the Republicans eight. The outcome in no sense represented public opinion, for the state elected ten Republican Congressmen to three Federalists.

In South Carolina, which also elected through its legislature, the Republicans carried the assembly in October, though the city of Charleston, as usual, was Federalist. The energetic Charles Pinckney, breaking completely with his Federalist kinsmen,[3] had organized the Republican cause upcountry and stirred up planters and farmers against Federalist tax burdens on lands and slaves. He wrote to Jefferson that the "Federal interest" at Charleston voted "the lame, crippled, diseased and blind," whether taxpayers or not, and used colored ballots as a check on how their underlings voted.

While only four states permitted a popular vote, even the indirect choice through the legislatures reflected the swing toward Jefferson. The Republicans had found plenty of fuel for their propaganda in the record of the Adams administration. Militarism, high taxes, debt increases, and unconstitutional measures were played up along with the old refrains of aristocratic rule, the dangers of monarchy, and the power of the "monied interest." Republican journals joyfully quoted from Hamilton's pamphlet on the defects of John Adams.

The Federalists, thrown on the defensive by the effectiveness of the Republican appeal, resorted to a campaign of fear and smear in a vain attempt to save the day. Jefferson, they thundered, was an infidel, a fanatic, a believer in French revolutionary doctrines, who would destroy religion, set up agriculture over commerce, repudiate the public debt, and lead the country into bloodshed and anarchy. "Tremble then in case of Jefferson's election, all ye holders of public funds, for your ruin is at hand," wrote "Decius" in a Federalist newspaper. "Old men who have retired to spend the evening of life upon

[3] Charles Cotesworth Pinckney, Federalist Vice Presidential candidate, and Thomas Pinckney.

the fruits of the industry of their youth. Widows and orphans with their scanty pittances. Public banks, insurance companies, literary and charitable institutions . . . will be involved in one common, certain, and not very distant ruin." A pamphlet addressed to "Religious Republicans" charged that Jefferson, looking at a church building in a ruined condition, had said, "It is good enough for Him that was born in a manger." A Connecticut Federalist wrote in his diary: "I do not believe that the Most High will permit a howling atheist to sit at the head of this nation."

The electoral count gave Jefferson and Burr 73 votes each, Adams 65, Pinckney 64, and Jay one. At last party discipline had been made completely effective. Only one Rhode Island elector, fearful that Pinckney might lead Adams, refused to support both Federalist candidates. Adams had all the votes of New England, New Jersey, and Delaware, five of Maryland's ten, four of North Carolina's twelve, and seven of Pennsylvania's fifteen; Jefferson had all the rest.[4]

With Jefferson and Burr in a tie, the House of Representatives had to choose between them, though everyone understood that the latter was intended for second place. Burr, in a letter to General Samuel Smith before the final results were known, made it clear that he "would utterly disclaim all competition." A little later he was equally positive, in a letter to Jefferson, that his friends would not think of "diverting a single vote from you."

Nevertheless, Federalist leaders, bitterly disappointed over their defeat, turned hopeful eyes toward Burr. He might prove to be the lesser evil. He was a northerner, a lawyer and not a farmer, a practical politician rather than a Jacobin fanatic, and he was on friendly terms with many of his opponents. His election by the House would disorganize the Republicans and might destroy the leadership of the man the Federalists hated most, Thomas Jefferson. These opinions were well summed up by one Federalist: Burr's "ambition and interest will direct his conduct—and his own state is commercial and largely interested in the funded debt. If he will honorably support the government for which he has undoubted talents, he will have support of the federalists and some of the Jacobins whom he may detach—and his election will disorganize and embarrass the party who have given him their votes."

But Hamilton, in the unhappy role of choosing between two men

[4] Only Virginia, Rhode Island, Maryland, and North Carolina chose their electors by popular vote, the last two using a district system.

he thoroughly disliked, differed with his party colleagues. There was for him but one choice. Burr was the "Catiline of America," a man devoid of scruples and possessed of an inordinate ambition and the "boldness and daring necessary to give success to the Jacobin system." Jefferson at least had "pretensions to character," though he was unscrupulous, not very mindful of truth, and was a "contemptible hypocrite." "Nor is it true that Jefferson is zealot enough to do anything in pursuance of his principles which will contravene his popularity or his interest. He is as likely as any man I know to temporize—to calculate what will be likely to promote his own reputation and advantage; and the probable result of such a temper is the preservation of systems, though originally opposed, which, being once established, could not be overturned without danger to the person who did it." To Representative James A. Bayard of Delaware and others Hamilton wrote in the above strain. But his pleas fell on deaf ears. The Federalist members of the House held a caucus, and though some dissented, the majority voted to support Burr.

Voting as individuals the Federalists controlled the House, for this was a lame-duck Congress, elected when the war fever was mounting; but the Constitutional requirement that the members vote by states in choosing the President placed them at a disadvantage. Their strength was too heavily concentrated in New England, while the vote of the Republicans was better distributed and gave them control of more states. In addition, there were enough Federalist defections to deprive Burr of two states, New Jersey and Georgia, and to divide Maryland. Vermont was also evenly divided. Burr had four New England states, Delaware, and South Carolina; Jefferson was supported by New York, Pennsylvania, New Jersey, Virginia, North Carolina, Georgia, Tennessee, and Kentucky, eight in all. In the case of the last three, four members cast three votes for Jefferson, while twenty-five Federalists in New England could give Burr but four votes, voting by states. The vote by individuals gave Jefferson 55, Burr 49.

From the 11th through the 17th of February the House balloted with the result always the same: eight states for Jefferson, six for Burr, and two divided. The New Yorker needed three changes of votes—in New Jersey, Maryland, and Vermont—to get nine states. Maryland would have been his if Joseph Nicholson had let illness and a raging fever keep him away. Through a heavy snowstorn he came to the House to cast his vote for Jefferson from a bed fixed up in a committee room. This kept Maryland evenly divided. Gallatin, the cool-headed, was the floor leader of the Jeffersonians, carefully holding his lines intact while he waited for a break in the Federalist ranks.

The balloting started on Wednesday, but not until the week-end were there signs that the Federalists were weakening. Burr was apparently doing nothing to get the three Republican votes necessary to win, and some of his supporters were losing heart. Fears of what might happen if the 4th of March came with the deadlock unbroken had some effect on the sober-minded. The Republican governors of Pennsylvania and Virginia were reported as ready to call out their militia to prevent a Federalist usurpation of the Presidency. Bayard of Delaware, sole representative of that little state, was now prepared to shift it to Jefferson. Hamilton's importunities or Burr's failure to act or fears of a civil war or some other factors may have determined his course. In any case, he announced in the Federalist caucus that the deadlock must end. The die-hards from New England denounced him, but had to yield. On the thirty-sixth ballot a Vermont Federalist was purposely absent, Bayard and the Maryland and South Carolina Federalists voted blanks,[5] and Jefferson had ten of the sixteen states. Four New England states still voted for Burr on this final trial.

The whole plot—for it was hardly more than that—to elect Burr and frustrate the popular will had finally broken down. The good sense of the moderates had at least prevented the supreme blunder, a prolongation of the struggle until Adams's term expired. Without a constitutionally elected President or Vice President, the nation might have found itself plunged into civil strife. Before the next election the Twelfth Amendment was added to the Constitution. This provided that the electors should vote separately for President and Vice President. The original purpose of the electoral college had been altered by the development of parties.

Rumors of an understanding or even a bargain between the Federalists and Jefferson were circulated at the time of the election; but not until Bayard of Delaware lifted the curtain several years later was the nature of the negotiations revealed. Denials promptly followed from Jefferson and his henchmen, and a sharp controversy ensued. Bayard insisted that he had received assurances about Jefferson's poli-

[5] This gave Vermont and Maryland to Jefferson, since the Republicans now cast the votes of these states. South Carolina and Delaware had no Republicans and thus cast no votes on this ballot.

cies on such points as support of the public credit, maintenance of the navy, the protection and encouragement of commerce, and the retention of subordinate officials in office, including a particular Delaware officeholder. General Samuel Smith, who lodged at Conrad's boardinghouse with Jefferson and was in his confidence, had acted as a self-appointed intermediary to confer with Bayard and other Federalists. Smith's explanation, made years later, was that he had sounded out Jefferson on these points to quiet Federalist fears "without his having the remotest idea of my object." Then the busy go-between had let Bayard believe that he was authorized to speak for the Republican candidate. Jefferson's emphatic denial of any understanding or bargain still leaves unanswered the question whether he knew that he was being pumped when he expounded his views to General Smith.

Poor Burr was roundly denounced by the Federalists for his failure to give them pledges and to render aid in securing his election. "The means existed of electing Burr," wrote Bayard to Hamilton, "but this required his co-operation. By deceiving one man (a great blockhead) and tempting two (not incorruptible), he might have secured a majority of the States. He will never have another chance of being President of the United States; and the little use he has made of the one which has occurred gives me but an humble opinion of the talents of an unprincipled man." This remarkable left-handed compliment to Burr certainly exonerates him from any charge of activity in his own interest. The Machiavelli of the Republicans had behaved like an honorable man! The archintriguer had refused to use his base talents, and the Federalists were confounded in their efforts to help him. The humor of the situation was utterly lost upon them, for Thomas Jefferson had been elected President. The leaders of the party of "the wise and the good" had dug themselves a pit of their own misdeeds and follies and had fallen into it never to emerge.

4

Agrarian Liberalism in the Saddle

The Master Politician

When the tall, loose-jointed figure of Thomas Jefferson arose to take the oath of office from the new Chief Justice, tall, somber-faced John Marshall, in the unfinished Capitol at Washington on March 4, 1801, the office of President of the United States for the first time passed into the keeping of a man who had mastered the art of politics. Little did it matter that his inaugural was scarcely audible in the rear of the crowded Senate chamber, for Jefferson was not at his best in the forum. It was directed to a wider audience, the American people, who were waiting to learn how complete an overturn would be made of the Federalist system. The friends of democracy had a popular mandate for reform. Why not proclaim it from the housetops?

To the surprise of both friend and foe, the inaugural address was a document of conciliation and good will. Had embittered John Adams remained for the ceremony instead of slipping away from the Capital at dawn, he could hardly have withheld approval from such sentiments as equal and exact justice to all men; peace, commerce, and friendship with all nations, entangling alliances with none; a jealous care of the right of election and acquiescence in the will of the majority; economy and the honest payment of all debts; freedom of religion, the press, and the person; the encouragement of agriculture, and of commerce as its handmaid. To later generations they read like well worn platitudes; yet to Jefferson's listeners they were a proclamation of faith in the fundamental principles of the American system of government, and their utterance by the new President was a direct refutation of the oft repeated charge that he was a Parisian revolutionary ready to inaugurate a Red Terror in this land of liberty.

Even the skeptical Chief Justice called the speech "well judged and conciliatory." But it was more than a collection of aphorisms. Jefferson referred directly to the party struggle in a notable passage:

> During the throes and convulsions of the ancient world, during the agonizing spasms of infuriated man, seeking through blood and slaughter his long-lost liberty, it was not wonderful that the agitation of the billows would reach even this distant and peaceful shore; that this should be more felt and feared by some and less by others; that this should divide opinions as to measures of safety. But every difference of opinion is not a difference of principle. We have called by different names brethren of the same principle. We are all republicans—we are federalists.

These were the happiest expressions in all Jefferson's political writings. He was offering the olive branch to the opposition. The wish to conciliate reveals the wisdom of the statesman; but the ability to do so is the mark of the master politician. The new President was both. Thousands of voters, drawn to the Federalists by the troubles with France in 1798, had been sufficiently disillusioned to support Jefferson in 1800, while many others, alarmed and disgusted at the Federalist intrigue to elect Burr, were ready to follow a similar course. A temperate policy by the new administration would "give time for a perfect consolidation." The Federalist leaders, of course, were too unregenerate to ask forgiveness or to accept it. But they could be isolated and ignored.

Yet moderation must not mean an abandonment of principles. The ship of state must be put "on her republican tack." Rigid economy and simplicity in government, drastic reductions in the military establishment, repeal of the unpopular excise tax, gradual reduction of the national debt, and divorce of the government from the influence of "paper capitalists" constituted the Jeffersonian program. The Alien and Sedition Acts had expired and were not renewed; but Hamilton's financial system, except for the excise, was undisturbed. Bondholders and Bank stockholders had no cause for complaint. Business, despite the Federalist alarmists, went on as usual. The laissez-faire views of the Republicans left commerce free to develop, and, with growing foreign markets, the merchants and shipbuilders of the seaport towns enjoyed prosperity and profits and forgot their fears of Jefferson and revolution. There was as yet no manufacturing interest to clash with the planting interest over protective tariffs. Agriculture and commerce for a time proved to be harmonious partners.

Jefferson's policy of good will toward his enemies had limits, however, where jobs were concerned. Adams had hurriedly filled every possible vacancy after the result of the election was known, and Jefferson was under strong pressure from hungry Republicans to make wholesale removals. But this might wreck his conciliation policy. Luckily, Washington, with its muddy streets winding around the stumps of trees, its unfinished public buildings, and its limited and expensive accommodations for visitors, was too isolated and unattractive to draw the hordes of office seekers that came to later inaugurals. Jefferson himself spent much time at his beloved Monticello.[1] Applicants for office wrote letters and used Congressmen and other persons of influence to help their cause. This type of pressure was easier to withstand.

Jefferson's solution was to remove the Adams "midnight appointments" and any other Federalist officials who had been guilty of offensive partisanship, and to restore to office men removed by Adams for political reasons. In the great majority of cases he waited for vacancies to occur—a slow process. As he remarked ruefully: "Those by death are few; by resignation none." Misconduct in office provided some opportunities. He might have made further concessions to the spoilsmen but for the strong stand of that administrator *par excellence,* Secretary of the Treasury Albert Gallatin, who prized efficiency above party profit and made enemies of Editor Duane and others as a result. Jefferson aimed at party equality in federal offices but brought about a Republican preponderance gradually and with no loss of administrative efficiency.

One of the most emphasized of Jeffersonian axioms had been the exaltation of the legislative branch as against the executive, or "monarchical," element in the government. But Jefferson as a critic of the dominant group and Jefferson as the victorious leader of his party were in totally different positions. His theory of legislative control now rose to mock him. The success of his administration required the cooperation of President and Congress, particularly with a fighting minority of Federalists in the two Houses alert to capitalize on the mistakes of the majority. Leadership was necessary, and Jefferson was forced to supply it, as too many members of Congress had

[1] His wife had died in 1782, his two daughters were married, and the executive mansion (not yet called White House) had no official hostess.

little experience in public life. Yet it was not the fiery, challenging leadership of a Jackson or a Roosevelt, appealing for public support against a recalcitrant Congress and whipping a reluctant majority into line. It was subtle, concealed, skillful, and more efficient. Jefferson was at his best in informal touch with little groups of individuals, suggesting and directing and ironing out difficulties, not commanding obedience. These tactics, he applied to the members of Congress.

Here Gallatin proved to be an invaluable lieutenant. Diplomatic and cautious and wise in handling men, the European-born Secretary of the Treasury helped organize the Republicans in Congress into a compact, reasonably well disciplined body. Madison, the third member of the Jeffersonian triumvirate, gave advice and assistance but was better as Secretary of State than as a politician. A floor leader was necessary in the House, and William Branch Giles and John Randolph first acted in this capacity. Neither was a fortunate choice, and Randolph eventually became an insurgent. The party caucus proved to be most useful because it permitted policies and measures to be discussed, agreements reached, and discipline enforced. Under Jefferson the caucus operated as the White House willed; but he had created a machine which took over the management of the party when Madison was the executive and made him do its bidding in a time of crisis.

High Tide for the Jeffersonians

Jefferson's message to Congress in 1801 asked it to consider the judiciary system "and especially that portion of it recently enacted." This hint, which was not lost on the majority party, referred to the Judiciary Act of 1801 creating a new set of circuit judges with complementary officials and relieving the Supreme Justices of burdensome circuit duty. The merits of the act were lost when President Adams hastily filled the new positions with Federalists in the closing hours of his term. The Republicans could not remove the judges from office but could remove the offices from the judges. Congress in the session of 1801-1802 battled over a repeal bill, with the Federalists posing as defenders of the independence of the judiciary and the administration men criticizing the new court system as a waste of money and a Federalist refuge. In the end, Republican discipline overcame the Federalist eloquence of James A. Bayard and others, and repeal carried. "The fatal bill has passed; our Constitution is no more," groaned the Washington *Federalist*. Actually the bill simply restored the old situation and eliminated some Federalist officeholders.

Far more serious to the new administration was the problem of the older judgeships, where Federalist control might checkmate the will of the people as expressed by President and Congress. Judges could be removed by the impeachment process only if found guilty of "treason, bribery, or other high crimes and misdemeanors." This did not cover partisanship or unbecoming conduct unless "misdemeanor" received a liberal interpretation. Nevertheless, impeachment was attempted and was successful in the first case. Judge John Pickering of the federal district of New Hampshire was removed by a Senate vote of 19 to 7. He was a hopeless drunkard, mentally unbalanced; but the use of "misdemeanor" was open to question.

Justice Chase of the Supreme Court was the next target, and here the issue was clear. Not content with his past offenses against judicial decorum, he had let loose another blast at the Republicans to the grand jury at Baltimore, which Jefferson regarded as a "seditious and official attack on the principles of our Constitution." The House impeached Chase in March, 1804, but the Senate did not try him until February, 1805. In an atmosphere tense with excitement and partisan feelings, six Republican Senators—five from northern states—deserted their party on every vote, and the two-thirds vote necessary for conviction could not be obtained. Impeachment as a political weapon had failed the Republicans. Jefferson called it "a farce which will not be tried again." At least it curbed open partisanship, for Chase gave no more grounds for criticism.

Meanwhile, a far more dangerous enemy to Republicanism than Chase was beginning to read Federalist constitutional views into Supreme Court decisions. Strong-willed Chief Justice John Marshall, a near-midnight appointment of John Adams who concealed his partisanship under his judicial robes, wrote a decision first asserting the right of the Court to set aside an act of Congress. This was the famous Marbury versus Madison case of 1803. Jefferson, believing in the equality of the three branches of government, saw the danger but could not stop it. His efforts to bring the courts into line with the election returns of 1800 had failed with the Chase impeachment. In the long years ahead John Marshall preserved the best of Federalism—its broad conception of the Constitution—for future generations to use for ends that would have repelled the great jurist.

The purchase of Louisiana from France was the outstanding accomplishment of Jefferson's administration. His admirers could acclaim it as a great diplomatic victory, but circumstances beyond his control made it possible. Before the purchase the Federalists in Congress were pushing the resolutions of Senator James Ross of Pennsylvania demanding immediate seizure of the mouth of the Mississippi before the French could take possession. The West was eager for action, but the Republican majority defeated the resolutions in order to give diplomacy a chance. To the amazement of both parties Napoleon, for reasons of his own, decided to sell not merely the much desired mouth of the river but the entire western Mississippi valley to the Rockies.

The stunned Federalists now showed their real feelings toward the West by opposing ratification of the treaty in the Senate. They argued that the clause promising to incorporate the inhabitants of Louisiana in the Union and to admit them to citizenship violated the Constitution, which applied only to the original territorial domains of 1789. Louisiana must remain a colonial dependency until every state consented to the admission of new states from the area. Back of this constitutional camouflage were the real reasons. The Federalists did not want Louisiana because it would add to the wealth and power of the agricultural—and Republican—South and West and to the tax burdens of the commercial East. Senator William Plumer of New Hampshire recorded in his diary: "The United States are now doomed to pay a large sum for a vast wilderness world which will I fear prove worse than useless to us. . . . It will increase the patronage, etc., enrich the minions, of the Executive." Such shortsighted attitudes destroyed the last faint hopes of the Federalist party west of the Alleghenies.

Meanwhile, the Republicans were suffering from constitutional qualms also. Jefferson doubted that territory could be purchased without a constitutional amendment. Why he hadn't thought of this before he sent Monroe to Paris is not clear. Republican Congressional leaders soon convinced him that time was of the essence in dealing with a Napoleon, and that ratification could not wait on constitutional clearance. And so one of the greatest accomplishments of any administration was consummated because the President and his party put national security ahead of constitutional scruples. Liberal construction was now useful to the Republicans, as it had been to the Federalists when in power.

With Jefferson at the pinnacle of his popularity, the demoralized Federalist leaders saw their poorly organized forces facing annihilation. These Jeremiahs found consolation in writing long letters to one another bewailing the evil days that had come and predicting revolution and catastrophe as the ultimate fate of the American people. "Our disease is democracy," wrote Fisher Ames. "It is not the skin that festers—our very bones are carious and their marrow blackens with gangrene." Some held out the hope that the Jacobins would fall to fighting among themselves and give honest men a chance at their just dues. Their only remedy was to let the evils run their course. "The many do not think at all, and the few think only to despond. Indeed, most men are compelled to admit that our evils must be borne until their intolerability generate their cure," wrote George Cabot from his Boston listening post. Hamilton's proposal for a national Christian Constitutional Society with a branch in every town fell on deaf ears. Political organization on such a scale was deemed democratic folly.

But some active spirits, chiefly in Congress, saw a way to combat the Jeffersonian sweep: dismemberment of the Union. Pickering, now a Massachusetts Senator, Griswold of Connecticut, and a few others would save New England before it was too late by setting up a northern confederacy. The South and West could go their way under their idol, whose fanatical admirers, according to Pickering, were ready to choose him President for life. These New England extremists included New York in their calculations and looked hopefully toward British Canada. But to win New York required aid from a faction of the Republicans, and this brought Aaron Burr into the picture. Suspected of secretly conniving with the Federalists in the House election of 1801, Burr found himself overlooked in the distribution of federal patronage, while his enemies, the Clintonians, now led by the shrewd and ambitious DeWitt Clinton, enjoyed the loaves and fishes. Disgruntled, Burr attended a Federalist banquet on Washington's birthday in 1802 and offered a toast, "To the union of all honest men." After this indiscretion he took no further steps to break with his party and seemed to be on good terms with the administration. He dined and conversed with Federalists occasionally but was vague in his commitments. "Perhaps no man's language was ever so apparently explicit, & at the same time so covert & indefinite," commented the observant Plumer.

But it was clear before 1804 that Burr would not be named again for the Vice Presidency. He would have accepted in its place an appointive office, but Jefferson was politely noncommittal. This caused Burr to seek the governorship of New York at the spring election of 1804. The Clintonians, of course, had their own candidate, Judge Morgan Lewis; but Burr hoped that a combination of his own following with the Federalists would be sufficient to win. Although Pickering and Griswold were unable to commit him to their disunion project, the Federalists of New York inclined in policy to support Burr and did not name a candidate of their own.

Hamilton, busy with his law practice, was skeptical over any revival of Federalism and was pessimistic as to whether "the frail and worthless fabric"—the Constitution—could last. Nevertheless, he was not drawn into any New England intrigues to dismember the Union, and Burr's candidacy for governor aroused his old hatred. Whether Hamilton's opposition kept New York Federalists from supporting Burr cannot be determined; but at least it was a factor in his defeat. The Vice President's political prospects were blasted in his home state, and he was virtually ostracized by the national administration, so that he was in a mood to resent Hamilton's repeated strictures on his character. The challenge to a duel was the consequence, and the founder of Federalism was fatally wounded on the field at Weehawken. Burr's failure in New York and their inability to secure any widespread Federalist support for a northern confederacy led Pickering and his co-conspirators to postpone that project.

Burr, though under indictment for murder, returned to Washington to preside over the Senate during the Chase impeachment trial. His conduct was scrupulously fair and won encomiums from men of both parties. Indeed, the Jeffersonians were conciliatory toward the Vice President, apparently through fear that his rulings might hamper the prosecution. After the trial Burr retired from office and presently was embarked on his western schemes, the purposes of which have been matters of conjecture ever since. The ultimate collapse of his supposed conspiracy, ending in a trial for treason and his acquittal, closed the door of opportunity to a talented, if unscrupulous, political leader. More considerate treatment at the hands of the Jefferson administration might have saved him from the ignominy to which history has consigned him.

Jefferson was renominated at a formal caucus of Republican Senators and Representatives on February 25, 1804. George Clinton of New York received 67 of the 108 votes cast on the one ballot for

Vice President. An informal understanding among Federalist leaders made Charles Cotesworth Pinckney and Rufus King their choices.

Republican national victory was conceded, but New England Federalists fought desperately to save their states from democratic defilement. The Massachusetts legislature enacted a law for popular election of Presidential electors but required that all nineteen be chosen by a state-wide vote. The Republicans had demanded a return to the old district system, used before 1800, which would insure them a share of the electoral vote. To the chagrin of the Federalists, the state went Republican by over four thousand votes and Jefferson secured all nineteen electors. In Connecticut, Abraham Bishop led a Republican assault against the ruling Federalist-Congregational oligarchy. He denied the validity of the old royal charter, which had been used as a state constitution, and demanded a reform constitution with a simple taxpaying requirement for voters and an end of high property qualifications. Denunciations from press and pulpit and the power of the ruling hierarchy were too much for the reformers, and Connecticut voted Federalist as usual.

Where the Federalists campaigned at all, they were hard put to find issues. Peace, prosperity, the repeal of internal taxes, economy and the acquisition of Louisiana were too much for them. Old issues and old prejudices were dusted off but made little impression. The godless, pro-French President had disappointed his detractors. On the more solid grounds of his attack upon the judiciary, his reduction of the navy, and the expense of Louisiana, it was difficult to arouse the voters. Even the charge that Louisiana cost every person in Massachusetts four dollars fell flat. The benefits were too obvious.

Seven states chose electors through their legislatures; seven used state-wide popular vote; and three had a district system. Jefferson had 162 votes; Pinckney, 14. Connecticut, Delaware, and two of Maryland's nine went to the loser. Federalism was almost extinct.

The Scepter Passes

The political course of Jefferson's second term centered around two developments: a revolt within his party led by John Randolph, and a revival of Federalism occasioned by the problems of neutral rights. The first was annoying rather than serious; the second created a dangerous situation that threatened the security of the Union.

John Randolph of Roanoke, at first a Jeffersonian leader in the House of Representatives, was an impossible man in any political party. He was impulsive, passionate in speech, gifted with a caustic wit, and untroubled by consistent adherence to any very fixed set of principles. Usually he held to an extreme state-rights viewpoint—the doctrines of 1798. He became increasingly a defender of southern sectionalism and boasted that he was an aristocrat: "I love liberty, I hate equality." But these attitudes were complicated by personal feuds, possible sexual impotence, and, at times, sheer perversity. He developed into a perennial insurgent who seemed happiest when hunting alone. He broke with the Jefferson administration over two issues.

A friend of Speaker Nathaniel Macon, Randolph had been made chairman of the House Ways and Means Committee, a key financial post. In 1803 he opposed a bill to provide compensation for certain claimants to Yazoo lands on the lower Mississippi where the United States, the state of Georgia, and some land companies under grants from Georgia, later revoked, all were involved. A compromise settlement arranged by a commission of which Madison was a member had made a liberal provision for the claimant companies. Randolph, already suspicious of Madison, whom he regarded as a nationalist, now blamed him for the Yazoo "abomination." He succeeded in blocking the measure whenever it came up until his temporary retirement from Congress in 1814. In his feud with Madison, which became an assault upon the administration, Randolph acquired a small group of southern supporters, old-fashioned Republicans such as Speaker Macon of North Carolina, Joseph Hopper Nicholson of Maryland, and the Virginia agrarian philosopher John Taylor of Caroline. They were popularly termed "Quids."

Randolph warred with the administration over another issue in 1806 when a secret message from the President asked for an appropriation of $2,000,000 to buy West Florida, then in dispute with Spain. He expected to use the money to get French support. Randolph objected to such devious tactics, delayed the appropriation until the propitious moment for negotiation had passed, and was openly anti-administration thereafter. Perhaps twenty Republican Congressmen were more or less in sympathy with him by this time.

Without directly attacking Randolph, Jefferson skillfully reduced his power to make mischief within the party. In 1807 the administration forces effected the defeat of Macon as Speaker. This deprived Randolph of his committee chairmanship and much of his strength. Nicholson of Maryland, who had referred to Jefferson's unbounded popularity as "our present infatuation," was retired to a Maryland judgeship. He had once been under consideration for the Supreme Court and also for Attorney-General, but his chances had slipped away with his insurgency. Randolph, his influence impaired, nevertheless remained a threat to Madison's prospects in 1808. Monroe was his candidate.

But Jefferson had more serious problems than John Randolph. The great war in Europe had become a duel between England and Napoleon—the one supreme on the Atlantic, the other on the Continent. Unable to attack each other directly, both resorted to economic pressure; and a war of decrees and orders followed, in which neutral rights were almost entirely ignored. Hundreds of American ships were seized in the years 1805-1812. England also was impressing American sailors for service in her navy in greater numbers than ever before.

Matters were rendered suddenly acute in June, 1807, by the attack of the British ship *Leopard* on the American warship *Chesapeake* in an attempt to recover British deserters supposedly on the American vessel. Three men were killed and eighteen wounded; and four of the *Chesapeake*'s crew were carried off as British deserters, though three of them were Americans. This outrage might well have resulted in war, but Jefferson was not prepared for such an extreme step. Failing to secure an abandonment of impressments by the British government, he recommended "an inhibition of the departure of our vessels from the ports of the United States." This, he hoped, would put such economic pressure on the warring powers that they would abandon the violation of neutral rights.

The embargo speedily passed both Houses in December, 1807, with the Federalists and John Randolph in opposition. Its drastic economic effects were equaled by its political effects. Federalism, backed by the injured commercial interests, suddenly revived; New England turned against Jefferson, and nullification was openly advocated. Ships escaped in violation of the embargo, it brought no concessions from the belligerent powers, and finally Jefferson had to consent to its abandonment. In the meantime, the 1808 Presidential election had taken place.

James Madison had long been regarded as Jefferson's successor. Their harmony of views and Madison's services made him the logical choice. Accordingly, a caucus of Republican members of Congress in January, 1808, named him for the Presidency and renominated George Clinton for second place. The action was almost unanimous, for the friends of Randolph and some other dissenters were absent. A group of them denounced the caucus system of nominations as a violation of the Constitution. The arrogant, acid-tongued Randolph hoped to create a diversion for Monroe in the Old Dominion and destroy Madison's prestige at home. Curiously enough, although Clinton was the administration candidate for Vice President, he was also the Presidential candidate of certain northern Republicans who were opposed to the succession of another Virginian. His ambitious and aggressive nephew DeWitt Clinton was the real force behind the candidacy of the cheerful old gentleman of sixty-nine, who found even the duties of Vice President too arduous and was manifestly unfit for the office of chief executive. He told the diarist Plumer that "the sitting three hours in the Chair at a time was extremely fatiguing to him." His chances depended on the amount of insurgency in Pennsylvania and New York and the possible support of the Federalists.

Monroe, despite Jefferson's efforts to reconcile him to Madison, lent himself to Randolph's schemes. He had acted as a kind of diplomatic errand boy for the administration to the courts of France, Spain, and England with little to show for it. The Louisiana Purchase had been largely settled before he arrived in France, and his work elsewhere was unsatisfactory. He had faced difficult situations in both Spain and England, but the treaty he and William Pinkney had arranged with England went beyond his instructions and was not even sent to the Senate. As a result Monroe felt that Jefferson had repudiated him.

The Virginia legislature divided between the two native sons, 124 members holding a caucus in January to name Madison electors, while 57 indorsed Monroe. John Taylor of Caroline, an old-fashioned agrarian Republican, favored Monroe but tried to induce him to withdraw so as not to disrupt the party. The anti-administration men—the Quids—used the embargo as an argument against Madison and expressed fears that war would soon result. Monroe's candidacy probably was not helped by the indorsement of a group of Virginia

Federalists, while the possibility of victory for Clinton as a result of the Virginia split drew support to Madison. Before the election it was clear that Monroe had no chance.

Some twenty-five or thirty Federalist leaders from seven states north of the Potomac plus South Carolina, taking heart from the unpopularity of the embargo, held a secret conference at New York in August. The chief question at issue was whether the conference should support Clinton as the best means of defeating Madison. The majority accepted Rufus King's view and decided in favor of separate Federalist candidates. C. C. Pinckney and King were then named.

Fortunately for Madison, a bad factional fight in Pennsylvania—where Simon Snyder, Michael Leib, and William Duane, editor of the powerful *Aurora*, a radical trio, and Governor Thomas McKean, a conservative, had been at swords' points—was compromised sufficiently to unite Republican support for him. In New York DeWitt Clinton failed to control the legislature, and it chose six electors for his uncle to thirteen for Madison. Largely as a result of these developments in Virginia, Pennsylvania, and New York, the key states of the Republicans, Madison won with 122 electoral votes to 47 for Pinckney and 6 for George Clinton.[2] Clinton was reelected Vice President with 113 votes to 9 for John Langdon of New Hampshire and 3 each for Monroe and Madison.

Jefferson had passed his scepter to his closest friend, but his joy was far from complete. The embargo had failed and now had to be repealed. Federalism, apparently defunct in 1804, had revived and was in control of New England. Its powerful business leaders, quiescent in times of prosperity, were aroused against a President who, they believed, aimed at the destruction of commerce and the dominance of agriculture. They continued hostile to the Republicans for many years.

Yet Jefferson had laid the solid foundations on which American liberalism was to build. He had demonstrated the falsity of the Federalist dogma that the propertied few alone were fitted to govern and that democracy meant mob rule. He had shown the possibilities in wise, patient, skillful political leadership and—surprisingly, in view of his earlier predilections—had established the pattern of Presi-

[2] One Kentucky elector was absent. Pinckney added to all the New England electors except those from Vermont three each from Delaware and North Carolina, and two from Maryland.

dential direction of the party majority in Congress, which came to be the mark of reformer chief executives. He had secured an empire for his country that would give future generations of farmers the room they needed and would strengthen and prolong frontier democracy's influence. He was the master political architect of his day, and few have equaled him.

5

Mr. Madison's War and Mr. Monroe's Era of Good Feelings

Madison Fails to Take Charge

On March 4, 1809, an unimpressive, nervous little man who would soon be fifty-eight stood before John Marshall and took the oath that made him Jefferson's successor. Most of the great crowd in the newly completed hall of the House of Representatives had difficulty hearing his weak-voiced inaugural generalities. The more fortunate listeners near the front could observe his agitation and comment on the made-in-America woollen suit he was patriotically wearing for the occasion. If James Madison was no man of distinction in appearance, he certainly deserved that title in every other respect. A student of government from boyhood, a co-author of the famed Federalist papers of 1787-1788, wielder of a skillful pen in political controversies, and a writer of able state papers, he had become expert in statecraft through his work in state and national legislatures, in the Constitutional Convention, and at the head of the State Department. In the grasp of governmental problems he was not excelled by any of his contemporaries, even Jefferson. In fact, his level head more than once helped bring Jefferson back to earth from ideological flights into the stratosphere of political abstractionism. A final asset of the new master of the executive mansion was his wife Dolley, seventeen years his junior. Dolley Madison's beauty and charm as first lady were to make her a Washington legend.

In spite of his unusual qualifications for his great office, Madison proved to be one of the less capable Presidents. He lacked his predecessor's skill in political manipulation and ability to appraise and use men. He was guilty of bad appointments and proved inept as an administrator. He was irresolute and undecided when crisis statesmanship was needed. Possibly the great inconsistency of his life—his shift from nationalism to state sovereignty—made him unsure of himself and too fearful of the criticism that might come if he displayed vigorous executive leadership or advocated strong measures. In his defense it must be said that, whereas Jefferson had Madison and Gallatin to depend upon, Madison had only Gallatin; and Jefferson had not been any more successful in using peaceable coercion against tricky Napoleon and hard-boiled George Canning. The times were rough in international politics, and Madison was neither a lion nor a fox.

At the very outset President Madison showed reluctance to do battle with the opposition in the party. Gallatin, equally able in finance and in diplomacy, deserved the State Department. The new President wanted him for the place, but factious opposition reared its head. William Branch Giles of Virginia, ambitious for himself and jealous of Gallatin, threatened to make trouble if the appointment went to the Swiss-born Pennsylvanian. A vehement partisan and a rough-and-tumble debater in the halls of Congress, he had rendered valuable service to his party; but his failings were so clear that appointment to an administrative office seemed to be out of the question. The influential Senator from Maryland, Samuel Smith, whose brother Robert was the Secretary of the Navy, opposed the appointment of Gallatin. Allied with them were their brother-in-law Wilson Cary Nicholas of Virginia and Gallatin's Pennsylvania opponents, Senator Michael Leib and William Duane, editor of the *Aurora*. Madison yielded to the pressure. Fearful that this insurgency in his own party, aided by the Federalist group, might defeat confirmation of Gallatin as Secretary of State in the Senate, the President chose to retain him in the Treasury Department and to promote that cabinet mediocrity Robert Smith to the Department of State.

Madison might well have forced the issue and asserted his independence of the Senatorial clique at the outset. In the end, he incurred their hostility and gained nothing by the attempt to placate them. Robert Smith was so incompetent as Secretary of State that Madison had to perform the duties of the office himself. Finally, in 1811, he dispensed with his services in an unpleasant interview in which the irresolute Madison had to speak with unusual bluntness. He offered to make Smith Minister to Russia, where he could do no harm; but the displaced secretary insisted on England or a Supreme justiceship. Madison would not consider either demand, and so the Smiths became hostile.

Gallatin was largely responsible for forcing Madison's hand. The Secretary of the Treasury all along suffered from Congressional opposition. When he recommended a recharter of the United States Bank, the bill failed by a narrow margin in both Houses. Part of the opposition was based upon principle, for many old-fashioned Republicans could not bring themselves to support this Federalist institution. Yet, had someone else been at the head of the Treasury, the Bank bill would probably have passed. The balance of power held by Gallatin's personal enemies defeated it. Then he attempted to resign—a move which forced Madison to break with Smith, as indicated above. The President could not afford to lose the ablest member of his cabinet. But he had to replace Smith with an influential Republican to strengthen the administration, and James Monroe was his choice.

Monroe, while not openly hostile, had been sulking in his tent since his defeat and required careful handling. However, the offer of the State Department was an act of such magnanimity that he quickly forgot his resentment and accepted, particularly since no pledges were required as to policies. He knew that the position had its potentialities for a man with Presidential ambitions. John Randolph and the Quids could well be left in the lurch.

The President, involved in a maze of diplomatic dealings with England and France, had little time for politics. The "war of orders and decrees" kept up, neutral rights ceased to exist, and the danger of war was growing. Persuasion, threats, economic pressure, were alike ineffective. Only the end of the European struggle could bring relief. Before that fortunate time arrived, a party revolution occurred in the United States and a new leadership seized the reins from the fumbling hands of Madison and precipitated the country into war. The Congressional election of 1810 signalized the advent of the War Hawks.

The War Hawks Take Charge

The West played but a minor role in national politics before 1810. Ardently democratic and agrarian in viewpoint, back-country farmers and frontiersmen found the rule of Jefferson entirely to their liking. The Louisiana Purchase, Republican friendliness toward the admission of new states, and land cessions from Indian tribes confirmed them in the faith that had first shown itself in the days of their opposition to the whiskey tax. Consequently, Westerners had had no occasion to assert themselves nor to do more than serve as tail to the Republican kite.

Federalism, on its part, had neglected no opportunity to arouse distrust and suspicion in the Mississippi valley. From their efforts in 1796 to delay statehood for Tennessee to Josiah Quincy's extravagant statements in 1811 against the admission of Louisiana as a state, the party leaders had shown their active dislike of "the wild men of the back country." Without completely altering in fundamental character, aristocratic Federalism could draw no support from these democratic tillers of the soil.

New Englanders of conservative cast, moving to the frontier, became infected with democracy and equality. Western New York is an excellent example. Because of the heavy Yankee influx in the 1790's, this area became strongly Federalist and contributed to the hold of that party on the state. But in 1800 the Republican cause triumphed even in the western counties. The harsh application of the Sedition law to Jedediah Peck, a moderate Federalist member of the legislature who dared to circulate a petition for the repeal of the law, aroused hundreds of western New York Federalists against their party. This incident was typical of the lack of understanding and the arrogant disregard shown by the seaboard ruling class for the rights of the common man. New England settlers on the frontier sensed this feeling as they had not sensed it back home, and responded accordingly.

In the middle Atlantic states blocks of conservatives kept Federalism alive and won occasional local victories; but in the new states beyond the mountains the party never took root. Ohio, despite its considerable New England element, was conceded by the Federalists to the Republicans, except for a nominal offering of a Presidential electoral ticket every four years.

Yet western Republicanism tended to develop along lines of its own. It was more democratic, more aggressive, more nationalistic than the Virginia brand. Loyalty to the state and rigid construction of the Constitution had no traditional basis in newly settled areas whose population came from many states. Problems of lands, Indians, and markets were national, not local, and required national action. Nor was the western spirit willing to accept patiently a diplomatic policy of commercial coercion and fruitless negotiation with the European rivals when war, it seemed, could cut the Gordian Knot. The Congressional election of 1810 furnished the opportunity for western intervention in national affairs. It produced the "War Hawks."

The Congress that met in extra session on November 4, 1811, contained a remarkable group of Young Republicans. Henry Clay of Kentucky, John C. Calhoun, Langdon Cheves, and William Lowndes of South Carolina, and Felix Grundy of Tennessee appeared in the House for the first time. The oldest, Cheves, was thirty-five while Lowndes and Calhoun were only twenty-nine. Already members but entirely in sympathy with the newcomers were Peter B. Porter of western New York, Richard M. Johnson of Kentucky, and George M. Troup of Georgia. At no time has the Lower House been blessed with so much brash young talent. Not all were actually westerners; but all were from states that had frontier areas and were in contact with the Indian problem, either in its British or in its Spanish aspect. This, plus their lack of years, accounts for their aggressive nationalism.

The Indians were no longer a grave danger but rather a troublesome obstacle to frontier expansionists. Land hunger required the extinction of Indian titles everywhere east of the Mississippi. In the Northwest, Tecumseh was organizing an Indian confederacy, and though his plans were disrupted by Harrison's victory at Tippecanoe in 1811, the belief that he had British support created a demand for the seizure of Canada. To end the Indian menace and add a vast area for northward expansion was the program of those War Hawks who came from the northern and northwestern frontier districts.

The southern and southwestern expansionists looked toward the Spanish Floridas. These provinces had caused the Virginia Presidents much concern. Spain had refused to sell; and, with Napoleon controlling that unfortunate country, Jefferson and Madison had had some uneasy moments. At last, in 1810, an American-inspired uprising in the western province turned that region over to the United States at a time when Spain, in the throes of a rebellion against Napoleon, was helpless to act. East Florida was also much coveted in the southern states, for it was badly governed, was a refuge for hostile Indians, fugitive slaves, smugglers and pirates, and might be used as a base of operations by Great Britain in case of war. Since the Spanish uprising against Napoleon was receiving military aid from England, the expansionists in Congress were ready to seize East Florida along with Canada in 1812. The War Hawks found the existing grievances against England—impressments and the wanton violations of neutral rights—sufficient cause for war but their real purpose—and there was no concealment—was territorial expansion.

Their first move was to take control of the House of Representatives. Henry Clay, thirty-four years old and just beginning his years of service in the House, was chosen Speaker—a surprising overturn of the old order. Yet Clay was not unknown in Washington. He had represented Kentucky in the Senate for parts of two unexpired terms, the first in 1806-1807 when he was actually under the age requirement for membership. Plumer's ready pen furnishes this picture:

> Henry Clay, the senator from Kentucky, is a man of pleasure—very fond of amusements—gambles much. He told me that one evening he won at cards $1500—that at another evening he lost $600—He is a great favorite with the ladies—is in all parties of pleasure—out almost every night—gambles much here—reads but little. Indeed he said he meant this session should be a tour of pleasure.
>
> He has talents—is eloquent but not nice or accurate in his distinctions—He declaims more than he reasons. He is genteel polite and pleasant companion. A man of honor and integrity.

To the end of his days the ultrapuritanical regarded Henry Clay as a dissolute gambler even when they voted for him; but his warm, engaging personality won him hosts of friends, while his talents in politics placed him in the front rank of great American politicians. He was always "a man of honor and integrity."

The affable young Speaker filled the important committee posts with colleagues as young, energetic, and warlike as himself and made his office the directing force of the House. When John Randolph railed at this new crowd and attempted his usual obstructionist speeches, the Speaker promptly applied the House rules to squelch the fiery Virginian. But all was not easy sailing for the War Hawks. The older Republicans opposed their preparedness measures; the Federalists, numbering fewer than twoscore members in the House and half a dozen in the Senate, sowed dissension between the groups, while the President, hesitant and wavering, had to be prodded into action. The war party itself was divided along sectional lines, the northern group eager for Canada, the southerners looking toward

Florida. It was no small task to make all these horses pull in the same general direction.

Fortunately for the majority group, a Presidential election was at hand. Here was their opportunity, for the Congressional caucus was under their control. The power to nominate lay in their hands. There has been no proof that Madison bargained with the war party; but no bargain was necessary. He knew that only an aggressive attitude toward Great Britain would win him War Hawk support. In the spring of 1812 his actions foreshadowed a war message; in May the Congressional caucus renominated him; in June war was declared. The caucus met much later than had been the custom. Was the war party waiting to see what the President would do?

John Langdon, a New Hampshire Revolutionary War patriot and a successful businessman, who had served as United States Senator and as governor of his state, was named for the Vice Presidency. He declined, perhaps because he was past seventy, and a second meeting of the caucus named Elbridge Gerry, "Gentleman-Democrat," governor of Massachusetts and leader of his party in New England. Formerly an independent and a friend of Adams, he had been ostracised by the Federalists for his part in the X Y Z affair. While he was governor, his party had used redistricting to deprive the Federalists of control of the Massachusetts Senate. The device was not new, but it had lacked a name. The governor's enemies called it "gerrymandering," and the name has stuck.

The Virginia-New-York alliance, which had monopolized Republican nominations for national office since 1796, was now at an end, killed by George Clinton's death and DeWitt Clinton's insurgency. The younger Clinton's friends had not attended the caucus. With New York's backing he intended to try for the Presidency as an anti-administration Republican, appealing especially to northern jealousy of Virginia domination and New England antiwar bitterness. He was too shrewd to carry the peace banner, as this would hurt him where the war was popular. In his calculations the Federalists might be won without definite pledges because of their eagerness to divide the Republicans and defeat Madison.

The elder statesmen of Federalism, after consultation and correspondence, held a conference at New York in September to which the dwindling remnant of the party in South Carolina sent delegates; otherwise the region south of the Potomac was unrepresented. Rufus King proved to be the stumbling block in the way of outright indorsement of DeWitt Clinton. Accompanied by John Jay and Gouverneur Morris, he had conferred earlier with Clinton and found him ready to promise much in private but unwilling to make public commitments. Dissatisfied, King bluntly told the assembled Federalists that an alliance with the Clintonians might place a "Caesar Borgia" in the Presidency, and he favored a separate Federalist ticket. The majority, however, influenced by Harrison Gray Otis of Massachusetts, turned down this proposal; and, without formally indorsing Clinton, the conference adjourned, understanding that the shrewd New Yorker would get Federalist support in each state.

Publicity was avoided, and this suited Clinton well enough as he had no desire to appear openly as the Federalist-Peace candidate and thus offend his war following. The Federalist-Clinton understanding included support of Jared Ingersoll, a moderate Pennsylvania Federalist, for the Vice Presidency. Although the term "Federalist" was dropped in some places in favor of "Friends of Peace," Clinton was pictured as a war supporter wherever it meant votes.

Some dissatisfaction with Clinton developed in the Federalist ranks. A Virginia convention put forward King and William R. Davie of North Carolina, and Federalist members of the New York legislature refused to support the Clinton electors; but these defections were not serious. Far more important was Clinton's failure to draw Republican votes, notably in Pennsylvania. The factionalism characteristic of the Republicans of that state did not prevent united support for Madison, and this was fatal to the hopes of Clinton. He had 89 electoral votes to Madison's 128.[1] The West and the South alone could not have elected Madison, but Pennsylvania's 25 saved the day. To all New England except Vermont, Clinton added New York, New Jersey, Delaware, and 5 of Maryland's 11. His coalition had come very near to success.

The election was a weak vote of confidence in the administration. Madison had no better control over his party than before; New England was strongly Federalist, while many old-fashioned Republicans like John Taylor of Caroline had no confidence in the President and desired an early peace. War matters went from bad to worse. Gallatin was disgusted at the disregard by Congress of his recommendations and eagerly embraced the opportunity to go abroad as a member of the peace commission, leaving Monroe as the only first-rate man in the cabinet. Military reverses along the Canadian bor-

[1] For Vice President, Gerry had 131; Ingersoll, 86.

der in 1812 and 1813 and the failure of an American-engineered uprising in East Florida dampened the ardor of both wings of the War Hawks. The southern expansionists had little enthusiasm for the conquest of Canada in any case, and the cooperation that had forced a declaration of war was lacking in its conduct. After all, the management of the war rested with the executive department, and the War Hawks could hardly be blamed for its lapses. Under a parliamentary system, Clay, Calhoun, Lowndes, and their supporters would have administered as well as legislated. The American system of divided responsibility did not permit this.

With the defeat of Napoleon in 1813, the British government turned its attention to America. Veteran troops reenforced Canadian militia, the British navy was used to attack at strategic points, and the war became a life-and-death struggle for the American nation. At this juncture secession reared its ugly head in New England.

The New England Madmen

Federalism, threatened with overthrow in its New England strongholds, was becoming more extreme, more embittered, more state-rights in its outlook. Unable to endure defeat, its most aggressive leaders became potential secessionists who would withdraw their section from a Union they could not control. Such a step would be a denial of the fundamental principle of majority rule, but it would cut off the aggressive democratic elements of its section from the aid and comfort of the national government and the triumphant democrats of the other sections.

Yet it is easier to criticize than to understand the emotions of men who celebrated the overthrow of Napoleon, lauded Czar Alexander of Russia and the restored Bourbons in public resolutions, and ignored the American victories of Perry and McDonough. To them Federalism was more than a political party. It stood for the old New England way of life with its tax-supported Congregational churches and its public schools, its respect for magistrates and ministers, its belief in the rule of the well born and the well off, its social hierarchy with the "poorer sort" looking up to their betters for guidance and, if in want, for charity, and each man knowing his proper place, and its sincere conviction that wisdom and virtue were distilled in New England as nowhere else in the world. The

Jacobins who would seize control by demagogic appeals to the underdogs—debtor farmers, mechanics, fishermen, non-Congregationalists, immigrants—were hated and reviled with a bitterness that was not confined to politics. The few businessmen and lawyers of Republican persuasion became social outcasts. Young Joseph Story (later a Supreme Court justice) felt "the coldness and estrangement resulting from this known diversity of opinion, and was left somewhat solitary at the Bar." There were Federalists who even severed business relations with Republicans. Yale dropped a professor of mathematics, it was charged, because he was a Republican. In some places separate celebrations marred the Fourth of July. Dr. Nathaniel Ames refused to attend the funeral of his brother, Fisher Ames, Federalist Congressman, because it was a party affair of the Federalist Junto.

Both sides were equally guilty of vituperation and slander; but the arrogance and intolerance of the Federalist leadership, centering in the powerful Essex Junto of Massachusetts, hurt their cause with the moderates. John Adams never forgot the opposition of this "British Faction" to his administration, and his son John Quincy openly supported Jefferson's embargo at the cost of reelection to the Senate and the calumny that goes with apostasy. The genial, sociable New Hampshire diarist Senator William Plumer eventually joined the party of that President about whom he had once written, "I wish his French politics were as good as his French wines." Samuel Dexter, who had been in the cabinet of John Adams, supported the war and ran for governor of Massachusetts with Republican support in 1814. In Connecticut the "Standing Order," a politico-clerical oligarchy headed by Dr. Timothy Dwight, president of Yale and the "Pope" of Republican pamphleteers, held too tight a grip to be shaken until the war ended; but a "War Federalist," Oliver Wolcott, led the "Toleration" party to victory in 1817-1818.

The Republican minority in Federalist New England had one advantage, the support of the national administration. Around the federal patronage they built strong, surprisingly centralized organizations. In political technique and management they were more advanced than their aristocratic opponents, who criticized their methods and then copied them. Even the Tammany societies of Republicans in the middle states, Ohio, and Rhode Island had Federalist counterparts in the Washington Benevolent Societies of New England. These pseudo-charitable societies appeared about 1810 and lasted through the war years as political clubs to round up Federalist votes.

In the crisis of 1814 the Federalist extremists saw their opportunity. In the summer British warships blockaded New England ports, and enemy forces occupied part of the Maine coast. On the heels of news of the capture of Washington and the burning of public buildings came word that a veteran British army was advancing down Lake Champlain, and that the Gulf coast was in danger of invasion. The federal treasury was bankrupt; Madison was helpless; Monroe, now heading the War Department, was demanding conscription; and New England was withholding her militia from federal service to provide for her own protection. With Federalist newspapers talking openly of secession, a northern confederacy, and a separate peace with England unless the war was soon ended, Federalist leaders, through the Massachusetts legislature, called a convention to meet at Hartford and bring about common action in the crisis. Secret negotiations with the British commander at Halifax were opened by prospective collaborationists looking toward a separate peace and possible military aid.

The story of the Hartford Convention is an anticlimax. The "madmen"—the fanatics of the Pickering and John Lowell stripe known as the Essex Junto—did not appear at Hartford. The delegates, representing the Massachusetts, Rhode Island, and Connecticut legislatures and some local meetings in New Hampshire and Vermont, were guided by the moderate Harrison Gray Otis, and contented themselves with a report stating New England's grievances and offering some corrective amendments to the Constitution of the United States. These would require a two-thirds vote of Congress to declare war, lay embargoes, and admit new states, and would limit a President to one term with no two in succession from the same state. The three-fifths rule for counting slaves in apportioning representatives and direct taxes was also to be abolished. New England's dislike of Republican policies and Virginia Presidents found vent in these demands.

What the Federalists would have done if the war had continued may only be conjectured. The most reasonable conclusion is that the extremists would have failed in their secession scheme if they had dared to attempt it. The Republican minority in Massachusetts was so near a majority—45,953 votes to 56,374 in the spring election of 1814—that it could have prevented any extreme steps, aided as it would have been by many moderate Federalists. The other New England states, Connecticut excepted, were less Federalist. The unity necessary for a New England confederacy was lacking.

January, 1815, dispelled with surprising suddenness the twin dangers of disunion and British invasion. Andrew Jackson and his frontier militia won the most decisive victory of the war at New Orleans. While the national Capital was still rejoicing over this unexpected event, word came of the signing of the Treaty of Ghent—"a damned bad treaty," in Clay's words, but as good a treaty as such a war deserved. Without territorial gains or settlement of the questions of neutral rights, it left America free to pursue its own course, for Napoleon, save for the Hundred Days ending at Waterloo, was to plague Europe no more. Great Britain and the United States could well afford to wipe the slate clean.

For Federalism the peace was the end of everything. The dire predictions of the collapse of the government and the end of the Union suddenly seemed ridiculous. Fear and indignation, aroused by the Hartford Convention, turned into laughter at the three delegates Massachusetts sent to Washington to present her demands. Yet the Hartford gathering was not forgotten. The great majority of Americans made no distinction between the Hartford moderates and the Pickering extremists but damned all as Federalist plotters and disunionists. The once powerful party of Hamilton sank in a sea of popular opprobrium with the leaden load of Hartford around its neck.

The Indian Summer of the Virginia Dynasty

The final two years of Madison's presidency were peaceful and untroubled. Released from the dangers of war, invasion, and sectional strife, the country entered upon a period of nationalism and political peace. Patriotism, so lacking during the war, burst all bounds, and the young nation, exulting in its power and vigor, set about to remedy the national weaknesses revealed by the war. With the War Hawks, now called the Young Republicans, in charge, Congress passed measures for a larger peacetime army and navy, for the creation of a second United States Bank to remedy financial disorders, and for the continuance of high wartime tariff rates with some increases, now regarded as essential to protect American industries against English competition. The war had produced a powerful sentiment for economic self-sufficiency.

The votes in Congress on the Bank measure reveal one of the strange paradoxes of American politics. The party of Jefferson furnished the votes to pass it, and Jefferson's disciple and successor, James Madison, signed the bill while most of the Federalists were in opposition. Hamilton's nationalism had been taken over bodily by Clay, Calhoun, and their confreres, who, ignoring or openly flouting constitutional objections, rode roughshod over Federalists and old-fashioned Republicans who dared to object. John Randolph shrilled in vain against this abandonment of the agrarian doctrines of earlier years, but the control of the Republican party had passed to the younger men, who, in Calhoun's words, regarded a discussion of constitutional interpretation as a "useless consumption of time." Similarly, the Tariff of 1816 was the work of these nationalist Republicans, and the opposition consisted chiefly of commercial New England and the Randolph agrarians south of the Potomac. The financial interests of the middle states and the infant industries everywhere were drawn into the Republican ranks. In a series of great decisions John Marshall added the blessings of the Supreme Court to complete the posthumous victory of Hamilton. Madison, rationalizing a little, explained afterward that there had been a great change of circumstances which reconciled the Republican party to "certain measures and arrangements which may be as proper now as they were premature and suspicious when urged by the Champions of federalism."

Monroe received the Republican nomination for President in 1816 after a sharp contest. William H. Crawford of Georgia, who had worked with the Young Republicans in Congress, had fifty-four votes in the caucus to Monroe's sixty-five—a very narrow margin for the Virginian, who had been regarded generally as the heir apparent to Madison from the time of his acceptance of the primacy of the cabinet. Daniel D. Tompkins, the energetic governor of New York, favored at first to head the ticket by that state, was named for the Vice Presidency, thus restoring the old Virginia-New-York alliance of earlier years. No Federalist nominations were made, but the electors of Massachusetts, Connecticut, and Delaware, chosen by the legislatures, cast thirty-four votes for Rufus King.[2] Three Maryland Feder-

[2] For the Vice Presidency the Federalist votes were as follows: John E. Howard of Maryland, 22; James Ross of Pennsylvania, 5; John Marshall of Virginia, 4; Robert G. Harper of Maryland, 3. Three electors died before the meeting of the electoral college.

alists and one from Delaware did not vote. Monroe had one hundred and eighty-three. The only spark of interest in the campaign was provided by critics of the caucus system, and these accepted its choices.

The new President, well aware of northern discontent at the succession of another Virginia Secretary of State, went to New England for his foreign minister and named John Quincy Adams, experienced diplomat and former Federalist. This checkmated the ambitions of both Crawford, who remained as head of the Treasury, and Clay, who disdainfully rejected the War Department, preferring to return to the speakership of the House, where he became an occasional critic of the administration. Calhoun accepted the War Department, and William Wirt became Attorney General. On the whole, the cabinet was a strong one, and Monroe, in no sense a dynamic or inspiring leader, could afford to allow his strong-willed subordinates free rein in their departments while he ironed out their differences. It is to his credit that he kept three cabinet secretaries, all ambitious to succeed him in the Presidency, in office to the end of his second term in spite of a sometimes strained atmosphere and ill concealed envy and jealousies. Poise, patience, and a mellow dignity that approached statesmanship were the President's signal contributions. "He rather turns his eyes from misconduct," wrote his Secretary of State, "and betrays a sensation of pain when it is presented to him."

Fortunately the decline of Federalism and the sweep of nationalistic feeling eliminated party rancor and gave Monroe a political security that no other President except the "Father of His Country" has ever enjoyed. As a mark of his desire to appear as the head of a united nation, the new President set out on a triumphal tour of the North and West. The acclaim with which he was received caused his administration to be termed the "Era of Good Feelings"—a phrase first used by the Boston *Centinel* in describing his visit to that city. New England, which had never looked upon the faces of Presidents Jefferson and Madison, outdid itself to honor their successor.

When Monroe was reelected in 1820 without opposition, the venerable John Adams served as a Massachusetts elector, and only William Plumer of New Hampshire cast a dissenting vote.[3] Monroe had not been formally nominated. A poorly attended Congressional caucus decided against any action. That he survived the disastrous

[3] He voted for John Quincy Adams. Tompkins had 218 votes for Vice President; Richard Stockton (N.J.), 8; Daniel Rodney (Del.), 4; Robert G. Harper (Md.), 1; Richard Rush (Pa.), 1.

financial Panic of 1819 and a bitter sectional struggle over the admission of Missouri as a slave state without apparent loss of popularity is one of the anomalies of American political history. Yet Monroe himself was in part responsible for this. In his desire to blot out party differences he followed a course entirely compatible with his temperament, accepting Congressional solutions to perplexing problems.

This tendency had developed under Madison when the leaders of the caucus seized control, and Monroe was not the man to reverse the process. In a negative way he asserted himself against the Clay-Calhoun policy of liberal construction of the Constitution, particularly over internal improvements at the expense of the federal government. Like Madison, he urged the need for a constitutional amendment and vetoed the Cumberland Road bill, thus checking the movement for a national system of highways and canals. Yet there was little else upon which he left a strong imprint. Even the doctrine that bears his name was chiefly the work of his Secretary of State. Fortunately for the country, his immediate successors had more positive qualities, and the power of the President was not allowed to slip into the hands of Congressional politicians. Monroe had achieved the miracle of a partyless administration, but it was an abnormality. American political life was too vigorous to endure long an "Era of Good Feelings."

6

The Politics of Sections in the 1820's

The New Sectionalism

The nationalism of the Era of Good Feelings turned into bitter sectionalism in 1819-1820 when Northern opposition to the admission of Missouri as a slave state brought the question of slavery extension into the halls of Congress for the first time. If Missouri became a free state, control of the Senate would shift to the North, and legislation unfavorable to southern economic interests could not be checked. Slavery itself might be attacked as northern preponderance grew. But the crusading fervor of later abolitionism was absent, and this helps explain the willingness of both sides to accept a compromise.

An important force for sectional peace was the fear of Republican leaders that the old party would split into northern and southern wings with disturbing consequences for Presidential candidacies. They suspected that Rufus King, veteran New York Federalist and leader of the anti-Missouri forces in the Senate, was trying to revive Federalism under an antislavery cloak. In the end, large majorities in both Houses of Congress agreed to the admission of Missouri and Maine, one slave, the other free, and the prohibition of slavery in the Louisiana Purchase north of 36° 30′, and the embers of the bitter struggle cooled quickly. Its immediate political consequences were slight. In the election of 1824 John Quincy Adams, the one northern candidate, probably gained a few votes from the ardent antislavery men, but otherwise Missouri mattered little.

More directly important was a growing sectional pattern far more complex than the North-South division. New England, the middle states, the old South, and the Mississippi valley West were beginning to pull in different directions over protective tariff, internal improvements, and public lands. New England, in transition from foreign commerce to manufacturing, divided its votes in Congress on the tariff question, for the lords of loom were not yet dominant; but its influence was thrown against federal spending for internal improvements and against further reductions in the price of public lands, already low enough to lure too many ambitious young Yankees westward. The middle states, especially Pennsylvania, were developing industrially and favored tariff increases. They also supported federal subsidies for roads and canals to tap western markets and raw materials, although New York, once it completed the Erie Canal at its own expense, was less inclined toward federal aid for the projects of other states. Like New England, the middle Atlantic region viewed land policy in terms of revenue and objected to any liberalization of land laws that would draw population westward.

The South, more and more committed to a cotton-slavery economy, saw the trend toward rising tariff rates with grave misgivings. Higher duties placed barriers in the way of freedom of trade with England, its chief customer, and increased the cost of finished goods, whether domestic or imported. The older South also was suffering from the competition of cotton produced on the rich lands of the new Gulf states, but its statesmen attributed its woes to tariff burdens. As to internal improvements, the lower seaboard could expect few benefits and heavier tax burdens. It was too remote from important western centers, and its high mountains made canals impossible and roads expensive. Land policy aroused less concern than in the industrial Northeast except that lower land prices might create a need for greater tariff revenues.

The West, centered in the Ohio valley, was as strongly in favor of protective tariff and internal improvements as the South was opposed. Confronted with an unmarketable surplus, made worse by the collapsed farm prices after the Panic of 1819, Westerners saw in high tariff rates a partial solution. Protection would build up a home market for western raw materials and food supplies and create a better balance between manufacturing and agriculture. But transportation problems must also be solved, and Congress must come to the aid of the new states by constructing roads and canals and improving natural waterways, or at least by giving financial aid to state projects. Henry Clay made himself the spokesman of the West on these issues; his proposals, which he called "the American System," aimed to make the United States a great, self-sustaining economic empire. But, while the West looked eastward for support on these measures, it broke company with the East on land policies. In spite of the farm surplus, most westerners wanted land sold at lower prices and on easier terms, for the growth of the new states must not be restricted. The West would have its cake and eat it as well.

This new sectionalism ended the one-party system of Monroe's administration and created serious problems for ambitious political leaders. A candidate for President had to retain the loyalty of his own section while winning support elsewhere by catering to more distant provinces. The pattern of American politics was increasingly complex.

The Rivals of 1824

Big, good-humored William H. Crawford of Georgia, Secretary of the Treasury under Monroe, was at first well ahead of his rivals. An astute politician, he developed strong southern support both because of his Virginia birth and Georgia residence and because of the general impression that he accepted his section's viewpoint toward the tariff and constitutional construction. Yet Crawford was too shrewd to commit himself openly, as he needed votes in the North and the West. The dominant wing of the party in New York, headed by Martin Van Buren and the Albany Regency, was friendly. Old-line party leaders, such as Nathaniel Macon and Albert Gallatin, liked Crawford, as did many federal officeholders. Clearly he was a politician's, rather than a people's, favorite.

Henry Clay, jealous of Adams and Crawford, had carried on an intermittent warfare against the Monroe administration in the House, hoping to draw dissatisfied elements to his banner. Standing on the twin policies of internal improvements and protective tariff, he took an early lead in the Ohio valley. Although his platform had an economic appeal in the East, he had little strength among the politicos of Pennsylvania and New York; and John Quincy Adams seemed likely to carry New England. The anti-tariff South, of course, gave slight consideration to the Kentuckian, so that he had only his own section to show for his efforts. Even here, he was to encounter an unexpected obstacle.

John Quincy Adams had not been regarded as a Presidential possibility when he took over the State Department. This stocky, bald-domed, sharp-tongued, undiplomatic diplomat was an Adams, and therefore could never be "a popular man, being as little qualified by nature, education, or habit, for the arts of a courtier, as I am desirous of being courted by others." In intellectual stature, training, and experience in public life, he was eminently qualified for the position of chief executive; but his aloof, suspicious personality repelled people. His diary was his only intimate friend, and his sole recreations in the White House were to be swimming the chill Potomac before sunrise in summer and long walks at the same hour in the colder seasons. Yet this lonely Puritan became an increasingly formidable candidate, in part because the field was so divided and the party so badly split. Except for the Essex Junto Federalists, who could not forgive his apostasy, New England backed him, as did transplanted New Englanders in New York and the West. He was the only northern candidate, and voters who put antislavery principles first favored him. He was sympathetic toward the West on tariff and internal improvements, but gave no positive proof when the Clay men demanded it. He would not let his private letters on these matters be made public, as he was opposed to electioneering. This hurt him in Ohio, where he was charged with hostility to western interests, but it may have been good politics. In Virginia and even farther South state rights men seemed to favor him as a second choice to Crawford.

Calhoun's ambitions far exceeded his prospects. At first his home state, South Carolina, indorsed William Lowndes; but Lowndes's death in October, 1822, opened the way. Elsewhere in the South Calhoun's past support of tariff and internal improvements ruined his chances as against Crawford; and he was forced to look northward for votes. The Ohio valley was friendly, but Clay's copyright on the American System and Kentucky residence were too much for the South Carolinian. In Pennsylvania, which had no candidate of its own, Calhoun's friendship with party politicians and tariff record were in his favor; but the Scotch-Irish and Germans went "Jackson-mad," and a state convention early in 1824 ratified their position. The Vice Presidency was a consolation prize that the youngest of the candidates might claim, and so Calhoun retired from the race, and his following was soon allied with the Jacksonians.

Andrew Jackson was the great surprise of the campaign, at least to party wiseacres. The tall, gaunt, white-maned old soldier, whose high-handed measures in Spanish Florida in 1818 had stirred up a hornets' nest for President Monroe, seemed to be the antithesis of all that a President should be. Poorly educated, inexperienced in civil administration, high-tempered, military-minded, with a record including duels and acts of violence, he was a good hater; and Washington politicians did not take him seriously until the groundswell from the back country hit them. Then they realized that Jackson was developing tremendous popular strength. He was Scotch-Irish, anti-British, self-made, and was a fighter, a man of the people, who would, it was argued, drive the aristocrats and the corrupt politicians from the temple of government. His candidacy was launched in 1822 with an indorsement by the Tennessee legislature, but it made no great headway until the spring of 1824 when a Pennsylvania convention declared for him. Thereafter, many local politicians hurried to ship with Old Hickory.

The picture of Jackson as a backwoods democrat was fictitious. He was a frontier conservative with experience as a merchant, land speculator, judge, and cotton planter. His own original choice for President was John Quincy Adams. But a shrewd Nashville group led by Major W. B. Lewis, Senator John H. Eaton, and John Overton persuaded him to enter the race and played him up as the common people's candidate. The unprosperous and the discontented, numerous in the early twenties, were ready for a leader; and a mythical Old Hickory was created for them. The Nashville Junto secured his election as Senator from Tennessee against his wishes, and he appeared at Washington for the session of 1823-1824, in which he voted for a protective tariff and internal improvement bills but said little. The votes were proof of his fidelity to western interests but did not seem to hurt him in the South. All in all, Jackson and his managers played shrewd politics in 1824. They made it seem almost unpatriotic to criticize the Old Hero, who had saved his country at New Orleans. It was the man, not the issues, that mattered.

One other name rounds out a galaxy of candidates almost without parallel in Presidential elections before or since: DeWitt Clinton. As governor of New York and as canal commissioner, Clinton had rightly won the title "Father of the Erie Canal." In the West, where similar projects were planned, he was immensely popular, and several public meetings were held in his interest. Had he been able to control New York, he might well have won the Presidency in 1824. But the Albany Regency had the upper hand, and it seemed unlikely that he could get any electoral votes from his home state. His enemies brought about his removal as president of the canal board in 1824, and riding a wave of popular resentment against this petty political proscription, he was triumphantly returned to the governor's office.

But the hostile legislature chose the electors and passed over Clinton.

In 1822 Crawford had seemed to be far in the lead. But two factors combined to wreck his candidacy before the electors were chosen. The first was a stroke of paralysis, in September, 1823. Despite efforts to conceal his condition, it became evident that his health was seriously impaired. For months he could not attend cabinet meetings and was unable to sign official papers. When he reappeared at Washington he was but a shadow of his former self. "He walks slowly like a blind man," wrote an observer. "His feet were wrapped up with two or three thicknesses over his shoes and he told me that they were cold and numb. His recollection seems to be good, and he conversed freely. But it is the general impression that a slight return of his disorder would prove fatal to him." This was in April, 1824. He seemed to improve gradually, but Adams recorded in November that his articulation was still much affected and his eyesight impaired.

The second factor was not an unkind Providence but the blundering of Crawford's friends. In spite of every indication that the move would be unpopular, they called a Congressional caucus to make him the official nominee. Of the 216 Republican members, only sixty-six attended, two others voting by proxy. New York, Virginia, Georgia, and North Carolina sent forty-eight members. Crawford was formally nominated, receiving sixty-four votes, while Albert Gallatin, close to him for many years and coming from the important state of Pennsylvania, was named for the Vice Presidency. The holding of the caucus was a strategic mistake. The friends of the other candidates stayed away, making it appear as a rump affair with no authority to voice the will of the old Republican party. The chief effect was to direct against Crawford the guns of all his rivals, who eagerly presented the caucus as proof that he was an intriguer and a political manipulator who would achieve the Presidency through the machinations of Congressional politicians. Their charge was especially effective in the West, where the new democracy regarded party machinery as a means of perverting the popular will. Jackson probably was the chief gainer, as he appeared to be most removed from party politics, and the Tennessee legislature had been the first to oppose the holding of a caucus. Clay, Jackson, Adams, and Calhoun had been nominated by state legislatures, though popular conventions had been held in some instances, as in Pennsylvania and Ohio.

Foreseeing that the election would go to the House unless the field could be further reduced, friends of the rival candidates tried to use the Vice Presidency as a bait to eliminate an opponent. The Jackson and Calhoun men did arrange a joint ticket. Adams earlier had expressed approval of Jackson as his running mate, thinking that the second office would afford "an easy and dignified retirement to his old age."[1] The rapid growth of the Jackson movement ended such a scheme, and, with no other possibility for second place, the Adams electors generally voted for Calhoun, thus giving him an easy victory. The Crawford men, seeing that Gallatin's name brought no strength to their ticket, induced him to withdraw in favor of Clay and intimated to the Kentuckian that Crawford might not live out his term, if elected. Clay thought too much of his own chances in the probable event of a House election to listen. In the end, Clay and Crawford electors scattered their votes for the second office.

Eighteen of the twenty-four states chose electors by popular vote; but among the six using the legislative method was vitally important New York. A clean sweep here would give the successful candidate a block of thirty-six electoral votes, insure him at least second place in the national total, and add to his chances in the House of Representatives. The Albany Regency, refusing to permit a popular choice, expected to control the legislature for Crawford; but the popular uprising which elected Clinton governor weakened their hold and offered an opportunity for Clay and Adams. Thurlow Weed, a young Rochester newspaperman just winning his political spurs as an Adams strategist, outwitted the veteran politicians of the Regency and made a secret deal with some of the Clay men. When the vote was taken in the joint session of the two houses, in an atmosphere murky with duplicity and intrigue, Adams emerged with twenty-six electors; Crawford had five, Clay had four, while one preferred Jackson.

Weed had promised the Clay men enough electors to place their candidate among the three highest before the House but was unable to make good. Even so, Clay would have achieved that goal had he secured Louisiana. But a combination of Adams and Jackson men got control of the legislature of that state and divided the five electoral votes between them. The Kentuckian finished with only thirty-seven electoral votes in all, four below Crawford, and was eliminated from consideration by the House.

The New York result was almost equally fatal to Crawford. Had he received the entire vote of that state, as Van Buren and the Re-

[1] Adams was about four months younger than Jackson.

gency expected, he would have finished well ahead of Adams and in a strong position to bargain for the support in the House of Representatives necessary to elect him. With but forty-one electoral votes the odds were very much against him. Adams with eighty-four and Jackson with ninety-nine votes were the logical contenders for the House majority when the balloting began.[2]

The House Election

Henry Clay had the hard choice of throwing his influence to one or the other of the two rivals he most cordially disliked, Adams and Jackson (Crawford, because of the state of his health and his reputed hostility toward the economic policies favored by the West, was out of the question). He had to choose either the cold, suspicious New Englander, with whom he had crossed swords in negotiating the Treaty of Ghent, or the frontier military idol, who had wrecked the Speaker's chances in the West with his own ambitions. While he delayed any public pronouncement, Clay actually had little difficulty in making up his mind. There was in reality but one possibility. That was Adams.

Clay had long regarded Jackson as utterly unfit for the Presidency. How could a hot-tempered, dictatorial military chieftain with so little experience in civil office be seriously considered? He had seen Jackson's star rise with mingled anger and disgust, and, it is possible, with no small amount of jealousy. What did Jackson know or care about tariff and internal improvements and other western measures? Yet Clay's friends saw another problem in the elevation of Jackson: Would the country give the West a President soon again? He might have to wait many years for his turn.

Adams, the impulsive, warmhearted Kentuckian respected, even though the strait-laced, aloof Puritan was as unlike him as any man could be. "Clay is essentially a gamester," Adams had confided to his diary on one occasion; and again, "His morals public and private, are loose, but he has all the virtues indispensable to a popular man"; and more fairly, "Clay has large and liberal views of public affairs, and that sort of generosity which attaches individuals to his person."

[2] Edward Stanwood, *History of the Presidency*, gives the popular vote as follows: Jackson, 152,901; Adams, 114,023; Crawford, 46,979; Clay, 47,217. But six states elected through legislatures, and in most of the others a light vote was cast. Not much significance can be given to the popular vote.

The "large and liberal views of public affairs" proved to be the bridge between the former rivals. With the Latin-American question settled [3] and their old differences at Ghent forgotten, they found it easy to think alike on domestic questions.

Yet Clay was not willing to walk into the Adams camp without pledges. He must inform himself as to the good intentions of his former rival and have at least some assurances as to the recognition he might receive from the new President. Intermediaries—Washington was full of busybodies trotting from one candidate to another—helped to arrange the preliminaries. But, by chance, Clay and Adams were seated in adjacent chairs at the great Lafayette dinner given by the members of Congress on New Year's Day. When Adams showed unmistakable signs of thawing the friendly Clay suggested a confidential conference "upon public affairs." Adams readily agreed, and a few days later—on Sunday evening—the two conferred. Denying any personal interest, Clay declared that he wished to be satisfied with regard to "some principles of great public importance." Adams's diary is cannily silent as to his own side of the conversation, but Clay made it clear that he was ready to support him in the coming House election. The die was cast. Thenceforth the two men were friends.

Yet Adams had other obstacles to overcome. Not all his visitors were as discreet as Clay. Missouri's lone Congressman, with that state's vote in his hands, was concerned about his brother, an Arkansas territorial judge, who had killed a man in a duel. Adams avoided definite promises, but his general attitude assured the Missourian that the brother was safe from removal. Daniel Webster, worried lest Federalists be proscribed, conferred and was satisfied. This involved the vote of Maryland, where a Federalist held the balance of power. One is surprised at the dexterity of Adams in playing the game. Possibly his diplomatic training stood him in good stead, or perhaps his conscience was being subjected to a process of liberal construction. Through his own efforts as well as Clay's, he seemed to be reasonably sure of the votes of the six New England states and of Maryland, Ohio, Kentucky, Illinois, Missouri, and Louisiana. He needed one more to win. Virginia and Delaware were possibilities on later ballots if Crawford were abandoned, but New York seemed to offer better prospects.

[3] Clay had been an ardent advocate of the independence of the revolting Spanish-American colonies and had criticized Monroe and Adams for refusing immediate recognition; but this step was taken in 1822, and the issue disappeared.

Seventeen of the thirty-four House members from New York were ready to vote for Adams; but the wily Van Buren, straining every effort to hold the Crawford lines intact, seemed to have the rest under his control. What his game was, may only be conjectured. Did he plan to transfer his supporters to Adams on the second ballot and claim the honor of electing a President? Crawford's cause seemed hopeless, and Van Buren had as yet no liking for Jackson. His autobiography, written years later, is too disingenuous and is colored by his later relations with Jackson. Whatever his purpose, he seemed to be determined to prevent the election of Adams on the first ballot.

Van Buren's weak point in New York proved to be General Stephen Van Rensselaer, head of an aristocratic family. Elderly, religious, muddleheaded, and much disturbed at the crisis confronting him in the pressure of the Clintonians to support Jackson and of the Van Buren men to vote for Crawford, Van Rensselaer was taken into the Speaker's office by Clay and Webster on the morning of the election and told that the safety of the country depended on the choice of Adams on the first ballot. How an average human being, left alone with Henry Clay and Daniel Webster, could withstand their eloquent persuasiveness is past understanding; yet, according to Van Buren's account, written later, the general held out. Then Providence—or the Adams goddess of luck—intervened. As the vote was about to be taken, Van Rensselaer bowed his head in prayer, seeking divine guidance. It came at once. On the floor in front of him was a ticket someone had dropped with the name of John Quincy Adams written on it. His startled eyes rested on the bit of paper. A few moments later it was in the ballot box: New York had cast eighteen of its thirty-four votes for Adams, and the New Englander was elected President by thirteen of the twenty-four states.

Crawford had Delaware, Virginia, North Carolina, and Georgia; Jackson, the remaining seven—New Jersey, Pennsylvania, South Carolina, Alabama, Mississippi, Tennessee, and Indiana. In five of the twelve Adams states a change of one vote would have cost him their support. Perhaps a prolonged deadlock would have been disastrous. Yet it is equally possible that much of the Crawford vote would have swung his way. Election on the first ballot without Crawford aid left that group under no compulsion to support the new administration. Van Buren had lost, but he was free to choose his future allies. The prospects for a clever staff officer in the swelling Jackson army soon decided his course.

Bargain and Corruption

Before the House had voted, the Capital, though alive with rumors of bargains and intrigues, was genuinely startled when one was brought into the open. The *Columbian Observer* of Philadelphia printed an anonymous letter definitely charging that Clay had sold out to Adams to obtain the Secretaryship of State. Jackson, it was averred, could have had Clay's support at the same price. Clay, furious at the charge, published a card in the Washington *National Intelligencer* challenging his critic to a duel and demanding that he make public his name. The accuser ignored the challenge but revealed his identity. To Clay's surprise it was George Kremer, a slow-witted member of Congress from Pennsylvania who had done nothing heretofore to distinguish himself except wear a leopardskin overcoat unlike any other garment in Washington. Obviously he was the tool of shrewder men in the Jackson group who were working to destroy Clay's influence and prevent the election of Adams, or at least to place the Kentuckian in a difficult position if the State Department were offered to him. It would smear the Adams-Clay alliance with the calumny of a corrupt bargain to cheat the will of the people.

Clay demanded a House investigation and had his way. Kremer, refusing to appear, sent a long letter. The committee took no action as it was evident that proof was utterly lacking. Adams, after his election, cast caution to the winds and appointed Clay to the top cabinet post. Thus was the bargain consummated, at least in the minds of the angry Jacksonians. Clay had helped Adams; Adams appointed Clay. More recent generations have been inclined to wonder at the furore and to speculate on the number of Presidents who have gained office without pledges and bargains.

Two public addresses issued by Clay in 1825 and 1827 made it clear beyond any reasonable doubt that he had never considered Jackson for the Presidency, and that it required no bargain to induce him to support Adams. Furthermore, he could not have casually transferred his western colleagues of the Ohio and Kentucky delegations to Jackson. Most of them regarded Old Hickory as an unfit candidate and at the same time doubted his friendliness to tariff and internal improvements—vital factors in determining the vote of the Ohio valley. No defense, however, could undo the damage.

The Jacksonians not only played up the charge of a corrupt bargain but pointed out that Jackson was really the people's choice: he was first in electoral votes and led in the total popular vote, and therefore the House of Representatives was morally bound to elect him.

This argument rests on a questionable basis. Six states had elected through their legislatures, and the voters had had no direct means of expressing themselves. In several others one candidate had dominated, and the one-sided character of the contest had lessened popular interest. In only a few states were all four candidates offered to the voters. Throughout the nation the general expectation was that the election would go to the House. Jackson was merely first among four contenders in an election marked by a light vote. There was no method of determining either the second choices of the majority who had voted against Jackson or the first choices of the thousands who had not voted. The popular will had been so dimly revealed in 1824 that the House could not have subverted it.

Jackson himself believed that he had been victimized, because he had refused to bargain and his enemies had had no scruples. On February 14 he wrote to his trusted friend and political adviser Major W. B. Lewis that Clay would be Secretary of State: "So you see the Judas of the West has closed the contract and will receive the thirty pieces of silver. His end will be the same. Was there ever witnessed such a bare faced corruption in any country before?"

Jackson's mind was now made up. Vindication was not a personal matter; it was a solemn duty to the American people. When the Tennessee legislature named him as its choice for 1828, he resigned from the Senate and returned to the Hermitage to await his country's call. The Old Hero, now "the Cincinnatus of the West," was far better off away than in Washington where his votes and his every move would be subjected to hostile criticism. In Tennessee the voice of the people would sound more clearly than where the air was filled with the contentions and fulminations of politicians.

The Downfall of the Second Adams

For John Quincy Adams the Presidency brought only burdens and disappointments, bitterness and sleepless nights. His title tarnished by charges of corruption, he was acutely conscious of a lack of public confidence, which his morbid, suspicious, sensitive nature exaggerated because he had not been chosen by the electoral college. In any case, his own predilections would have led him to pay slight regard to political considerations; but the fires of criticism hardened this tendency into a determination to concede nothing to politics. His policies and appointments would be governed solely by the country's needs and his own sense of right and wrong. Such lofty idealism received its own reward, the crown of political martyrdom. The conscientious Adams fell a victim to his own uprightness.

Adams retained three of Monroe's department heads and would have included Crawford also, if he had been willing. One of the three was ambitious John McLean of Ohio, Postmaster General, who had been a Calhoun supporter, and who preserved such a political neutrality that administration men regarded him as disloyal and demanded his head. Adams kept him to the end, and Jackson rewarded him with a place on the Supreme Court in 1829. Adams reappointed the incumbents to lesser offices unless there were strong reasons to the contrary. All together, he made twelve removals during his term. Clay and other supporters protested that at least disloyalty should be punished, but to no avail. The President was adamant, though he believed four-fifths of the customs officers had been hostile to his election.

In enunciating policies he was equally inflexible. His first message declared that the object of government was to improve the condition of the governed, and offered a system of national planning with revenues from land sales to finance roads and canals, river and harbor improvements, a national university and a national astronomical observatory. Congress should legislate to promote not only all areas of economic life but literature and the arts and sciences. Such pronounced nationalism gave pause even to Clay and destroyed any hope of southern Crawford support. Western individualism and western desire for cheaper public lands were also antagonized by Adams's paternalistic doctrines.

The heterogeneous opposition was held together only by the prospect of victory with Jackson. There was no unity on tariff and internal improvements; the ruling class in the older planting states did not like rubbing party shoulders with frontier farmers and urban workers; Crawford hated Calhoun but could not swallow Adams's nationalism. In New York, Martin Van Buren and the Albany Regency led the Crawford following into the Jackson camp; but DeWitt Clinton had gotten there first. The factions battled at the polls as in the past, Clinton squeezing in as governor again and Van Buren returning to the Senate; but the embarrassing problem of Jacksonian leadership in the Empire State was solved by Clinton's death early in 1828.

In Congress every administration measure had to face a battery of political criticism. An Adams-Clay proposal to send delegates to a Panama Congress of American republics was finally approved, but only after misrepresentation by critics of its purposes, with charges that the slave trade and recognition of the Negro republic of Haiti would be discussed. With regard to internal improvements and the tariff, the Jacksonians, unable to offer a united front, voted the interests of their states and districts, and their candidate back in Tennessee was discreetly silent. In the case of the tariff, much maneuvering produced the political "Tariff of Abominations" of 1828, constructed by the Jacksonians to divide the Adams supporters sectionally. It was not intended to pass, but did by narrow margins. Its political effects were probably unimportant. The voters are not moved by economics when emotions are aroused.

As the election approached, personal abuse seemed to displace all other considerations. Adams men, angry at the vicious attacks upon the President for misuse of the patronage and the supposed bargain with Clay, retaliated by bringing up various acts of Jackson's career that showed a violent temper and a quarrelsome nature which unfitted him for the chief office. A Philadelphia editor, John Binns, printed the "Coffin Handbill"—a circular ornamented with coffins, which described purported acts of violence and brutality in Jackson's career. But the Cincinnati *Gazette* and *Truth's Advocate*, a campaign paper—both edited by Charles Hammond, brilliant journalist and friend of Clay—capped the climax by reviving an old story that Jackson's marriage to Mrs. Jackson had occurred before her divorce from her first husband. Legally, the charge was justified; but both parties had been innocent of intentional wrongdoing, and a second ceremony had satisfied both the law and public opinion. Other papers copied the story, and it appeared in pamphlet form. Jackson was aroused to a white heat against Adams and Clay: Why had they not used their influence to suppress the slander? Social relations with the two were thereafter impossible.

Had Jackson followed his natural impulses the printing of these stories might well have produced further acts of violence. Certainly his enemies hoped for some such result. But the Old Hero realized that he was no longer a private citizen, free to defend his own honor. A committee of friends at Nashville was set up to meet and refute all charges against him and to handle correspondence, while Duff Green, editor of the Washington *Telegraph*, Calhoun's organ, retaliated with counter slanders, even concocting a cruel canard that Adams, while Minister to Russia, had been involved in bringing about the seduction of an American girl by the Czar. A billiard table in the White House, privately purchased for the President's son, was said to have been paid for with public funds. Such a "gaming table," whether sinful or a mark of frivolity, was politically damaging.

The result of the election was foreordained. A new democracy, ignorant, impulsive, irrational, but rooted in the American soil, had its way in 1828. The protagonists of the old order fought not for John Quincy Adams, whom they could not love, but against the new monster, the common man, whom they feared. To a degree, the candidates were symbols of a renewal of the old conflict between popular rule and property rule. This intensified the bitterness and the mud slinging.

When the electoral votes were counted Andrew Jackson had 178; John Quincy Adams, 83. Adams had New England (except for one Maine elector), Delaware, New Jersey, sixteen of New York's thirty-six, and six of Maryland's eleven. All the rest went to Jackson.[4] Only Delaware and South Carolina chose their electors through the legislature, and so the result was a genuine popular verdict. The total vote for Jackson was 647,376; for Adams, 508,064. Nearly half of Adams's total came from New England and New York. Clay's support brought to the ticket not a single western electoral vote; and only in two states in the West and South, Ohio and Louisiana, was the result even close. Calhoun won the Vice Presidency over Richard Rush of Pennsylvania, but seven of Georgia's nine electors voted for William Smith of South Carolina, in a Crawford gesture of dislike for Calhoun.

[4] In this election Maine, New York, Maryland, and Tennessee used the district system; the other states (except South Carolina and Delaware) used a general ticket. Twenty-four states took part.

7

The Days of Andrew Jackson

The Reign Begins

John Quincy Adams—ignored by the President elect, who omitted the customary call of courtesy upon the outgoing chief—retired from the White House on the night of March 3 to a residence on the outskirts of Washington. Overwhelmed with bitterness, he regarded his public career as closed and resigned himself to the dismal prospect of an inactive life as ex-President. His library and his writing, he supposed, would occupy his mind, for old Federalist enemies had renewed their feud with the Adams family late in the campaign, and a book of exposure was to his liking.

Two years later, to his secret joy his home district in Massachusetts called him out of retirement by electing him to Congress. From that time to his death in 1848, he served in the Lower House—a remarkable figure, independent, courageous, barbed-tongued, irrepressible, an ex-President who refused to be shelved and, accepting public service in a humbler role, won new honors and a popularity that had been denied him in the highest office.

Andrew Jackson on the way to Washington in February, 1829, was greeted everywhere by enthusiastic crowds but his heart was full of grief and bitterness. A few weeks before, he had buried his beloved wife—"Aunt Rachel" to her friends. He believed that the slanders of the campaign had hastened her death. Small wonder that he refused to call on the man who, he felt, could have suppressed the scandalmongering. Unfortunately, Adams found it equally hard to forgive. Enemies they were, and enemies they remained.

On the 4th of March, Jackson was inaugurated before a crowd of ten to twenty thousand, with a simple ceremony in keeping with the accession of the people's choice. The address, inaudible to the majority of listeners, had been toned down by his advisers to include nothing to which any group could take exception. The reception at the White House, which made this inauguration memorable, turned into a mass onslaught upon the President and the refreshments by a rabble that far outnumbered the well groomed ladies and gentlemen in attendance. Eventually the crowd was diverted to the lawn by tubs of punch but not before enthusiastic democrats had broken dishes, wrecked furniture, and ruined carpets in their efforts to reach the Old Hero, guarded by a circle of friends, and to seize refreshments from the unprotected waiters.

The first problem was patronage. Cabinet appointments had been determined by factional and geographical considerations. Jackson, relying upon his Tennessee advisers but giving special consideration to Vice President Calhoun, chose a rather mediocre cabinet with Martin Van Buren of the Crawford faction, its only first-rate man, as Secretary of State. New England and Virginia were unrepresented. The break with the past was complete. For lesser positions the pressure was overwhelming. An avalanche of office seekers had descended upon Washington. Jackson's fumblings and the poor judgment of his advisers might have wrecked his administration at its outset had it not been for the opportune arrival of Van Buren near the end of March. Delayed at Albany by his work as governor, he came to Washington filled with forebodings because of Jackson's inexperience and the wails of disappointment from leading politicians whose wishes had been disregarded. Making friends with his new chief, whom he hardly knew, he became his trusted counselor and presently his companion on horseback rides, supplying sound advice and the tact and skill in management that Jackson lacked, and helping direct the native force and energy of "Old Hickory" into the right channels. The President was the popular hero of the masses, but the "Little Magician" from New York dealt the cards with the politicians and laid the groundwork for a great party.

The introduction of the spoils system is a familiar story that requires no retelling. Jackson can hardly be blamed for inaugurating a practice that the democratization of the party system made inevitable. To the masses of new voters, an aristocracy of permanent officeholders was intolerable. To the practical politicians, control of offices meant control of votes. To the new department heads, honesty, efficiency, and loyalty required new blood, and the corruption charges against the Adams administration in the campaign must be made to look good. Jackson defended the removals as "rotation in office," a democratic reform, while his editorial supporters preferred "turn the rascals out." Some petty rascality was uncovered here and there, and some elderly clerks with hands so crippled that they could hardly grasp a pen, who had been retained by kindly superiors, were justifiably replaced, as were some active workers for the Adams cause; but most of the removals were to make room for Jacksonians. Praise of the new President for his moderation in changing fewer than one-fifth of the federal officers overlooks two hard facts. Many officeholders, seeing the light, had voted for Jackson in 1828 to save their own heads. More important, it was not numbers that mattered but the institution of a new concept of service: the officeholder's first loyalty was now to his party. When it went out of power, he was expected to go out with it. The spoils system thus became an institution, and Jackson had set it up.

Van Buren, accustomed to the system in New York, gave it his expert attention. The President sometimes was not a good student. His emotions often got in the way of his judgment, especially if an old soldier was involved. An occasional rascal was rewarded. Samuel Swartwout, who wangled the collectorship of the port of New York over Van Buren's disapproval, defrauded the government of more than a million dollars. On the other hand, needy newspapermen often fattened at the federal crib, especially in the field service where a postmastership could provide the proper sustenance to enable an editor to follow the party line laid down by the Washington administration organ.

In handling the problems thrust upon him at the beginning of his term, Jackson turned for advice and ghost writing to a "Kitchen Cabinet" of trusted friends, most of them unknown in Washington. Usually included in this shifting inner circle were big, expansive, busy Major W. B. Lewis, an old Tennessee friend who took a Treasury office but who was also self-constituted head of the department of petty intrigues; sallow-faced, retiring Amos Kendall, also holder of a Treasury post, a Massachusetts-born Kentucky editor, whose chronic semi-invalidism did not prevent him from acquiring an undeserved reputation as the "moving spring" of the administration; Andrew Jackson Donelson—beloved nephew and efficient private secretary of the President—whose attractive young wife was mistress of the White House; Francis P. Blair, who came from Kentucky in 1830 to edit a new administration organ; and Van Buren and Eaton from the official cabinet. Others occasionally were called in for consultation. The Kitchen Cabinet lost much of its influence after the reorganization of the regular cabinet in 1831. Kendall later became Postmaster General.

Jackson had no program when he came into the Presidency. Only in upholding Georgia's determination to remove the Indians from her borders was his position clear. His first annual message in 1829 hedged on the tariff and internal improvements, offered a vague criticism of the United States Bank, and favored payment of the national debt. But before the session of Congress was ended he had taken a stand on federal aid for internal improvements. With Van Buren's collaboration, he wrote a strong veto message returning to Congress the Maysville road bill, which provided federal assistance for a road from Maysville to Lexington in Kentucky. The veto worried party leaders in Pennsylvania and the Ohio valley and probably cost the Jacksonians the state election in Ohio in 1830. But in the long run Jackson's arguments against extravagance and his constitutional objections to federal spending for local improvements added to his popularity. He actually signed many bills for internal improvements when convinced of their national character, but he had checked raids on the Treasury for all manner of projects and had put his economy preaching into practice. The veto was also a blow at an old Calhoun policy.

The Downfall of Calhoun

The growing coldness between President and Vice President, both men of the strictest morality, had its beginning in an affair involving a fascinating little brunette whose reputation became a political football. Jackson and Calhoun were on opposite sides. Margaret (Peggy) O'Neale, daughter of William O'Neale, a Washington innkeeper, had married at sixteen John Timberlake, a purser in the navy who was frequently absent on long voyages. The vivacious young wife was the life of her father's boardinghouse, where Jackson in his senatorial days and his wealthy Tennessee colleague John H. Eaton had lived. Eaton had helped O'Neale get onto his feet after business reverses, and also had come to Timberlake's rescue when his accounts as purser were found to be in bad shape. Scandalmongers said that Eaton had a selfish interest in keeping Timberlake at sea. Jackson found the young wife both charming and correct in deportment. In April, 1828, Timberlake died on shipboard in the Mediterranean; and gossip had it that, aware of rumors connecting his wife with Eaton and with others, he had committed suicide. Jackson, not blind to Eaton's infatuation, now ordered him to marry the lady, and he complied in January, 1829.

Unwisely, Jackson offered him the War Department and Eaton, prodded by his ambitious bride, accepted. The top-level wives and daughters proceeded to snub Mrs. Eaton, starting with the inaugural ball. To get at the truth of the stories in circulation, Jackson called a cabinet meeting on the subject of Mrs. Eaton's earlier conjugal fidelity. After reviewing the evidence, he pronounced a favorable verdict. This settled nothing, and the winter social season of 1829-1830 only made matters worse. When the President called in Secretaries Ingham, Branch, and Berrien and warned them that he disapproved of the treatment they and their families had accorded to a colleague's wife, they were properly surprised and minimized the affair. Presently his own household was disrupted when young Mrs. Donelson, the acting first lady, balked at his commands and departed for Tennessee.

The matter had already taken a political turn. Van Buren, a widower, and the soul of courtesy, had shown friendliness toward the Eatons; and he had induced the British and Russian ministers, both bachelors, to follow his lead. The other camp was led by Mrs. Calhoun and the pro-Calhoun cabinet wives, so that his motives are not above suspicion. The lonely President began to suspect that Calhoun was at the bottom of the affair and was aiming to discredit the administration and win the succession.

Other influences were operating to estrange the President and the Vice President. The animus of the old Crawford following was at work. To block Calhoun's path to the White House, Major Lewis let Jackson discover by way of a Crawford letter that Calhoun, as Secretary of War in Monroe's cabinet, had criticized his actions in the Seminole campaign and the 1818 invasion of Florida and had advocated punishing him for insubordination, while permitting the general to think of him as a friend. The revelation shocked Jackson and he demanded an explanation from the Vice President.

Calhoun replied in a long letter probably intended for eventual publication. Acknowledging that he had disapproved of Jackson's conduct in 1818 and had favored an investigation, he noted that in the end he had agreed with the other cabinet members on a different course. This was enough for the irate old President, perhaps overeager to expose a false friend. "I repeat," he wrote back, "I had a right to believe that you were my sincere friend, and, until now, never expected to have occasion to say to you, in the language of Caesar, *Et tu, Brute*." Calhoun had pointed to the political motives of the plotters and to Crawford's bitter hatred as sufficient explanation of their desire to discredit him, but the President was unmoved. Further letters in the summer of 1830 only widened the breach.

Conscious that the intriguers were close to the Secretary of State, Calhoun published the entire correspondence in Duff Green's *Telegraph* in February, 1831, when nearly everyone in Washington knew about it. His aim was to injure Van Buren, and he even hoped that Jackson would pay no further attention to the matter and would assume a neutral atttitude; but he was sadly mistaken. Already the administration leaders had prepared for the open break by setting up a new party organ, the Washington *Globe*, and importing Amos Kendall's Kentucky friend Francis P. Blair to edit it. A cadaver of a man in a seedy frock coat, carrying the poundage of a jockey on a fairly tall frame, he arrived in November, 1830—his chief assets a slashing pen and an unwavering loyalty to Jackson. Administration patronage soon made his paper prosperous while his own genius, supplemented by the assistance of an able partner, John C. Rives, made it the leading party organ in the country. Duff Green and his *Telegraph* were read out of the party along with Green's chief, Calhoun.

Even before the break, the President had warned the South Carolinians that he disagreed with the nullification ideas propounded by Senator Robert Y. Hayne in the famous debate with Daniel Webster. The occasion for Jackson's stand was a Jefferson birthday dinner staged by the nullification group. His famous toast, "Our Federal Union—It Must Be Preserved," shocked the extremists. Calhoun, divested of his once pronounced nationalism, would have been in a difficult position even if the break with the President had not occurred.

Meanwhile, Van Buren had carefully refrained from taking part in the controversy and had professed utter ignorance as to plotting by his friends. He refused even to read the Jackson-Calhoun correspondence: there was wisdom in ignorance, for he was walking over fires. Regarded in many quarters as a trickster and not yet well known in the West and South, he did not relish the role of arch intriguer against Calhoun in a rivalry over the succession. Carefully surveying the situation from every angle, he concluded that his resignation from the State Department was the solution. Only in this way could the cabinet be reorganized, the Calhoun men eliminated, and harmony restored. If Van Buren had cast an evil spell over the President, as his enemies charged, his departure at least would terminate it. Eaton, now a dead weight on the administration, might be induced to resign at the same time.

Jackson at first did not grasp all the implications when Van Buren made this suggestion. He took offense at the proposal as a desertion of his cause. But presently he saw the light; he and Van Buren met with Lewis, Postmaster General Barry, and Eaton, and the plan was discussed and accepted. Van Buren and Eaton resigned, the latter reluctantly, and Jackson then called for the resignations of the rest of the cabinet, excepting the innocuous and inefficient Barry. The reconstructed cabinet, headed by Edward Livingston of Louisiana, was an abler group than the old and had the President's confidence. No Calhoun men were included. The "Kitchen Cabinet" declined in importance, as the new cabinet was a Jackson group.

Jackson had hoped to take care of both Van Buren and Eaton but his plans miscarried. Eaton wanted to return to the Senate, and the President thought he was clearing the way when he obligingly offered the War Department to his old friend Hugh L. White, Senator from Tennessee. White refused the honor for family reasons but was apparently well aware of the game being played. A coldness developed between him and the President, and he later went over to the opposition. Eaton then sought the other senatorship, failed to get it, but was made governor of Florida Territory and later Minister to Spain. He repaid Jackson and Van Buren for exiling him by supporting the Whigs in 1840.

Jackson, now committed to running again, had appointed Van Buren Minister to England. Unexpectedly the Clay and Calhoun men produced a tie on the confirmation vote in the Senate, and the grim-faced Vice President cast the vote that brought his enemy home from London where he had already been received. "It will kill him, sir, kill him dead," Calhoun is reported to have commented on the vote.

The Democratic Republican (or Democratic) national convention, the first in the party's history and the third of its kind, met at Baltimore in May, 1832. Such a convention had been recommended by the Jackson members of the New Hampshire legislature at the suggestion of Major Lewis and Amos Kendall, and the Jackson press had heartily approved. The President had already been renominated by the Jacksonians in several state legislatures; consequently the delegates to the national convention merely declared their cordial concurrence in the "repeated nominations" he had received. Their chief purpose was to name a candidate for the Vice Presidency. Adopting a two-thirds requirement for a choice, they gave the absent Van Buren 208 votes out of 283 cast.[1] No platform or address to the people was prepared. Only Missouri was unrepresented when the roll of states was called.

Yet the opposition to Van Buren did not end with his nomination. A Pennsylvania convention had already pledged the electors of that state to a favorite son, William Wilkins, and he was not withdrawn. In the national convention Henry A. Wise of Virginia announced his intention of bolting Van Buren and supporting Philip P. Barbour of his home state. Jackson-Barbour tickets were projected in Virginia and North Carolina, and the South Carolina electors, chosen by the legislature, were of course hostile even to Jackson. But Barbour withdrew late in the campaign, and Van Buren could feel more secure. The President had had his way, and Calhoun, who in Jackson's mind was condemned to the lowest level in the political hell—below Henry Clay—had been made a political outcast. Van Buren was in line for the Presidency.

The Struggle with the Money Power

While Jackson was establishing his control over the Democratic Republican, or Democratic party,[2] the opposition, assuming the name National Republican, had its troubles. The Adams-Clay group had

[1] The convention adopted the unit rule—namely, that the majority of the delegation from each state should determine how the entire vote of the state should be cast—but did not enforce it strictly. Each state had the same number of votes that it had in the electoral college. Some states sent more delegates than they were entitled to; others, fewer. There were 334 in attendance. There was no uniform method of choosing delegates.

[2] In the campaign of 1828 the opposing groups had had no official names. Both were Republicans and were distinguished by such designations as "administration" and "opposition," or Adams men and Jackson men. About 1830 the term "National Republican" began to be used by the Clay following, thus combining the old party name with the adjective which seemed to suggest its policies. The Jacksonians clung to the name "Republican," but often prefixed the adjective "Democratic" in 1832, as had been done earlier in some states. The use of the latter term alone was a gradual development after 1832.

never been effectively organized into a party, and after the defeat in 1828 it lapsed into the status of a discredited minority with little solid strength outside New England. Only portions of the middle Altantic states and the Ohio valley could be regarded as fighting ground. With the federal and most state governments in hostile hands, there was little patronage on which to build a successful organization. Hopes rested chiefly on the expectation that the victorious but ill united Jacksonians would destroy themselves and bring about "a speedy restoration of the reign of reason and common sense."

National leadership was supplied from the Senate, where Clay joined Webster in December, 1831. The *National Intelligencer* at Washington, edited by Joseph Gales and William W. Seaton, served as central organ of the opposition. The policy of internal improvements had the hearty support of Clay, Webster, and their friends, and they seized upon the Maysville veto with glee. Soon afterward Clay's Presidential candidacy was under way. Public meetings and banquets were held to denounce the veto and praise "Prince Hal." In a series of speeches in the West he reiterated his devotion to the "American System" and criticized the administration. He seemed ready to go before the country with the same policies Adams had favored and the same economic appeal, trusting to his more spirited and inspiring leadership and the blunders of the Jacksonians to reverse the verdict of 1828.

State conventions in Delaware, Connecticut, and Kentucky nominated Clay in 1830, but a New York City committee suggested a national convention. The *National Intelligencer* approved, and a Maryland legislative caucus in February, 1831, named Baltimore as the place and the second Monday in December as the date. Other states accepted the proposal and began to choose delegates. There was no uniformity of method. Some states held state conventions; others, legislative caucuses; and still others, local conventions or meetings in the congressional districts.

Eighteen states and the District of Columbia were represented at the Baltimore convention by 168 delegates.[3] It lasted four days and nominated Clay without opposition although he seemed to be pessimistic about party success and urged the delegates to pass him

[3] Preceding the convention that nominated Jackson and Van Buren, this was the second national convention in American history. The first was an Antimasonic gathering.

by if they deemed another better fitted. A committee notified him at once, and his letter of acceptance was read to the convention next day. John Sergeant of Pennsylvania was the unanimous choice for the Vice Presidency. A system of committees was recommended for each state to provide an adequate organization, and an address to the people attacked the policies of Jackson. Another convention, to be composed of young men, was called to meet at Washington in May to indorse Clay and Sergeant.

The Washington convention is remembered chiefly for its series of resolutions that served as a platform. They committed the party to a protective tariff, federal support of internal improvements, and recognition of the final authority of the Supreme Court on constitutional questions;[4] stressed the importance of the Senate in preserving the balance of powers in the government; and attacked Jackson for his use of the spoils system and for his handling of relations with Great Britain with regard to the Maine boundary and the West India trade. The National Republicans thus took issue with the leading policies and acts of Jackson. But the campaign did not turn on these points. Two factors not suggested by this platform loomed large as the election approached: the Antimasonic movement and the United States Bank. Both require explanation.

The Antimasonic agitation began in 1826 with the abduction and disappearance of William Morgan of Batavia, New York, a Freemason, while he was preparing a book purporting to reveal the secrets of Masonry. The excitement that ensued was far greater than anything the book could have evoked. Investigations were held, and several persons were tried and convicted for the abduction; but Morgan never returned. Bitter opposition to Masonry developed in western New York, and entered into local politics. Antimasonic tickets were nominated, and in 1828 the movement affected the Presidential election in New York. Since Jackson was a Mason and Adams was not, the latter received the support of the Antimasons.

The defeat of the Adams party in New York discouraged some National Republican leaders, and Thurlow Weed and a coterie of active young politicians including William H. Seward and Francis Granger undertook to make the Antimasonic groups the basis for an

[4] Jackson had disregarded the decisions of the Supreme Court in cases involving the Georgia Indians. He believed in the equality of the three departments of the federal government and refused to let the opinions of the Court determine his interpretation of the Constitution.

anti-Jackson party. Weed, editor of the Albany *Evening Journal*, was the master mind in propaganda and in the subtle art of political manipulation. A state convention early in 1829 declared in favor of a separate political movement in New York, and also called a national convention to meet at Philadelphia in September, 1830. The politicians were planning to enter the national scene. Meanwhile New England, Pennsylvania, and the Western Reserve of Ohio were reverberating with the agitation. It had a certain democratic appeal, and many rural churchgoers were inclined to be sympathetic, regarding secret societies and secret oaths as subversive. Under its wings a new national opposition to Jackson might be formed, carrying none of the load of opprobrium that had borne Adams down. The 1830 convention drew ninety-six delegates from ten states—none from the states west of Ohio or south of Maryland. There was no difficulty in voting resolutions of hostility toward Masonry; but a sharp difference of opinion developed over nominating a Presidential candidate. The political element favored this step, and a committee, appointed to settle the issue, recommended a second convention to meet at Baltimore, September 26, 1831, and name candidates for President and Vice President.

The nomination of satisfactory candidates confronted the incipient party. It had developed its own crop of leaders with local reputations; but a national figure was needed to challenge Jackson and Clay. Some of the Antimasons hoped that Clay, though a Mason, might give satisfactory pledges and thus unite the opposition to Jackson. When he was unwilling to commit himself the Antimasons turned elsewhere. Justice John McLean of the Supreme Court, though a Jackson appointee, had grown cold toward the administration and was looking warily over the political field. He was sounded out, as were Richard Rush, former Secretary of the Treasury, and John Quincy Adams.

The Baltimore convention of the Antimasons was the first national nominating convention of elected delegates in American history. Groups of Federalists had met in 1808 and in 1812 to decide their party's preference for President; but were hardly more than an informal caucus of party leaders. The 116 delegates to the Antimasonic convention represented thirteen states—the six of New England, New York, New Jersey, Pennsylvania, Delaware, Maryland, Ohio, and Indiana. It was supposed that Justice McLean would be nominated; but on the eve of the convention word came that he would not accept. With Clay almost certain to be the National Republican candidate, McLean had no desire to sacrifice himself in a hopeless cause. Thaddeus Stevens of Pennsylvania wanted to name him in spite of his refusal; but the New York group led by Weed and Seward turned to William Wirt, Attorney General under Monroe, after finding that John Marshall was not interested. Wirt had been a Mason but gave satisfactory assurances as to his views, and he was nominated, receiving 108 of 111 votes cast. A rule requiring a three-fourths vote for the nomination had been adopted. Amos Ellmaker of Pennsylvania was named for Vice President. The convention adopted an address to the people and appointed a national corresponding committee. The precedent for national conventions was thus established. Yet the party that instituted the greatest of American political spectacles never held another convention.

Wirt's statement accepting the nomination virtually repudiated the party's principles: He did not believe that any proscriptive tendencies had existed in Masonry as he knew it, and he had withdrawn from it through lack of interest. He regarded the nomination as a personal honor but would gladly give it up if the convention disapproved of his sentiments. Wirt probably would have withdrawn had National Republicans and Antimasons been able to unite later on one man.

By far the most stirring and significant event of the campaign was Jackson's veto of a bill to recharter the United States Bank. He had never been friendly toward the Bank, and his attitude should not have surprised anyone. Coming from a section which had had unfortunate experiences with banks and paper money, he hated "ragg, tagg banks" and inclined toward a hard money currency. Ignorant of banking and often the victim of prejudices, he made little distinction between the "wild-cat" banks of the West and the well managed, highly centralized institution at Philadelphia under the efficient Nicholas Biddle. He disliked and feared the Bank, and it was easy for him to say, in bland disregard of John Marshall's decisions, that it was unconstitutional.

Jackson's first two annual messages raised the constitutional issue and questioned whether the Bank had established a uniform and sound currency. He suggested another type of institution "founded upon the credit of the Government and its revenues." Meanwhile, Biddle had established friendly relations with Major Lewis and other politicians, was lending money to Congressmen and editors—including $20,000 to Duff Green—and secured favorable reports from Congressional investigating committees. In the new cabinet Secretary of the Treasury Louis McLane was friendly and only Attorney General Roger B. Taney was openly hostile. The Bank's charter did not expire until 1836, and Biddle was not inclined to ask for a recharter before the election of 1832. Jackson's message of 1831 merely expressed a willingness to leave the matter to the investigation of an enlightened people and their representatives. Henry Clay was not so willing. At first in favor of postponing the recharter question, he felt the need of a popular issue after his nomination—particularly one that would divide the Jacksonians. Biddle was wary, but after sounding out nearly everybody in Washington through a special agent, he accepted Clay's view that the omens were favorable. Congress would pass the bill, and Jackson would hardly dare veto it with the election so near. If he did, he would lose Pennsylvania, home of the Bank, and other eastern states, and Clay would win.

A recharter bill, in charge of a Calhounite in the House and a Jacksonian in the Senate, passed by safe margins, 107 to 85 and 28 to 20. Jackson met this challenge with a ringing veto message that blasted the Bank as monopolistic and unconstitutional. His arguments—or those of Taney, Kendall, and Donelson, who wrote the message—ranged all the way from the clear logic of the strict constructionist to the blatant appeals of the demagogue. Biddle wrote to Clay that the veto had "all the fury of a chained panther, biting the bars of a cage. It is really a manifesto of anarchy." He even circulated it as a campaign document. With the business classes and two-thirds or more of the newspapers aroused against Jackson, the hopes of the Clay men ran high.

But the old Tennessean was wiser in the ways of the common man than Clay, Webster, Biddle, and the whole army of financiers and businessmen who thought the voters would listen to reason and logic. Jackson's instincts told him that, sound or unsound, the Bank was a "Money Monster" and must be crushed, or it would crush democracy. The masses could understand his appeal, and their confidence in his judgment was unshaken. Torchlight processions and hickory-pole raisings showed what they thought. The Bank spent heavily but could not stem the tide. Leading Bank Democrats, seeing the direction of the wind, hastened to make peace with Jackson. Pennsylvania, whose Democratic legislature had urged recharter, remembered only its old loyalty to Jackson. George M. Dallas, who had introduced the Bank bill in the Senate, declared for the Old Hero, "bank or no bank."

In the face of these portents of a Jackson victory, the opposition attempted to unite. Coalition electoral tickets were arranged in New York, Pennsylvania, and Ohio, with the understanding that the electors, if successful, should vote so as to bring about the defeat of Jackson. Whether this meant Clay or Wirt, no one could tell. Calhoun took no part in the election, but many of his southern friends supported Clay.

Yet the result was even more overwhelming than in 1828. Clay won his home state of Kentucky, Massachusetts, Rhode Island, Connecticut, Delaware, and 5 electors from Maryland, the only state to use the district system—a total of 49 electoral votes. Antimason Wirt had Vermont's 7. South Carolina, through her legislature, chose 11 electors who voted for John Floyd of Virginia. Jackson had 219; Van Buren, 189, as Pennsylvania's vote for Vice President went to William Wilkins.[5] The popular vote is difficult to estimate because of the fusion electoral tickets in some states, but Jackson's majority over both his opponents was at least 150,000 in a total vote well over 1,200,000.[6]

The New Machinery

The emergence of the national convention in 1832 was part and parcel of the democratizing of politics that had begun long before. Party nominations for local offices had produced the convention system in the early 1800's, when it began to supersede the more or less haphazard methods of self-nomination common in the South, and the mass meeting or nomination by the candidate's friends used in the North. The Federalists, generally disdaining party machinery and democratic innovations, left to their Republican opponents the establishing of extralegal methods of voicing the will of the voters.

In the middle states the county convention first came into general use. In New England the town (township) was the chief political unit, and the town meeting of the voters served for most purposes. But in the middle states, where county officials were elected by the voters and party unity was necessary for success at the polls, the delegate county convention was a logical outgrowth of the local mass meetings or primaries. In the early 1800's Delaware and New Jersey

[5] Two Maryland electors were ill and did not vote.

[6] The popular votes usually cited are: Jackson, 687,502; Clay and Wirt, 530,189.

Republicans also developed the state convention. Physical obstacles to state-wide meetings were not serious in these small states, and county conventions were already functioning. In Delaware Federalist use of this Republican device may help explain the persistence of Federalism after it ceased to function elsewhere. The use of a party caucus of members of the legislature retarded the development of the convention system for state nominations in other northern states, though occasionally the caucus was modified by the introduction of delegates from counties where the party was unrepresented in the general assembly, making it a "mixed caucus."

With improvements in transportation, and the growing distrust of the masses of new voters for the undemocratic caucus system, the state convention came into its own outside the South in the 1820's. The national convention, for the same reasons, made its appearance in the 1830's to fulfill a need that the old Congressional caucus and the state legislative or state convention nominations of Presidential candidates could not supply. It was representative in character; it divorced nominations from Congressional control and added to the independence of the executive; it permitted an authoritative formulation of a party program; and it concentrated the party's strength behind a single ticket, the product of a compromise of personal rivalries and group or sectional interests. Despite its defects, less evident then than later, it has remained fundamentally unchanged in general structure through well over a century of usage.

Yet, compared with the modern national convention, the early nominating body showed certain irregularities or imperfections. Delegates were chosen in a variety of ways—by state conventions, district conventions, local meetings, informal caucuses—dependent on the organization and strength of the party in each state. A national convention might even recognize as delegates visitors in attendance from a state which sent no delegates. Edward Rucker cast the entire vote of unrepresented Tennessee in the national Democratic gathering of May, 1835, because he happened to be in Baltimore and was a Van Buren man. At this gathering 181 sons of Maryland appeared as delegates from that state. In the Whig national convention of 1848, the Louisiana delegates cast both their own votes and those of Texas, because a Texas Whig convention had given them its proxies. Distance or lack of interest kept some states from sending delegates to the early Whig and Democratic conventions, while the gatherings of antislavery parties were sectional in character and attracted few southerners. From the beginning, however, the major parties limited the voting strength of a state in the national convention to its electoral vote, regardless of oversize delegations or other irregularities.

With the development of a system of committees to accompany this hierarchy of conventions, all unrecognized by the laws, the party organization began its rule of politics, and, indirectly, of government itself, ostensibly as the representative of the voting masses but actually developing into a powerful oligarchy of professionals intent on carrying elections and maintaining the party in power. As a necessary adjunct, the party press flourished as never before. In a state capital the faithful editor of the majority organ expected to receive the public printing of the state government, just as F. P. Blair at Washington benefited from the Jackson administration. In the county seats plums in federal or state civil service or nominations for local elective offices rewarded the editor-printer of the county partisan newspaper, whose struggle for subsistence usually kept him a bare jump ahead of his creditors. In time it came to be almost a tradition in many localities that he should operate the post office for the four years following a national victory.

The Whigs, like the old Federalists, somewhat standoffish toward the masses, soon copied Democratic practices, and the later antislavery Republicans took over and improved upon the methods of both. The President found himself the chief dispenser of favors for his party and its national leader, whether he relished the role or not. More than ever the Presidency became a political office, with its control the great aim of each party. Candidates were nominated by conventions of politicians who made availability their prime consideration. More often than not, the nominees were either secondary figures in public life or popular military men. Yet the results were surprisingly good, despite such dubious choices as Pierce, Buchanan, and Frémont.

8

Whigs and Democrats, 1833-1843

His Majesty's Opposition

The smoke of the campaign of 1832 had not cleared away before Jackson was confronted with South Carolina's attempt to nullify the tariff. A moderate lowering of duties in the summer of 1832 only convinced the nullifiers that protection was becoming a permanent burden; and with Calhoun's Presidential prospects blasted they decided the time had come for their state to assert its sovereignty and defy the will of the majority. The struggle that ensued cut across party lines. Jackson's strong stand for the Union divided the Democrats and drew praise from Webster, John Quincy Adams, and other National Republicans, though Clay, bitter in defeat, was silent. Many southern state-rights Democrats, while dismayed at South Carolina's extremist position, were aghast at Old Hickory's military preparations and his talk of hanging traitors. Among them were such Virginia leaders as Governor Floyd, John Tyler, and John Randolph, again an insurgent after enjoying a lucrative but brief service as Minister to Russia. Even Van Buren tried to restrain his fiery chief. A solution was found in the compromise tariff of 1833, offered by Henry Clay after he and Calhoun were brought together by John Tyler. Tariff rates were to be lowered gradually for ten years, and South Carolina rescinded her ordinance of nullification.

The political effects were significant. The controversy detached from the Democratic party a state-rights wing of southern conservatives who had never been too happy under the banner of the great western Democrat. It also restored in a measure Henry Clay's badly damaged prestige. The high priest of protection became the Great Compromiser, and for the first time southern planters began to look with favor upon the persuasive Kentucky Senator whose crisis statesmanship had averted civil war. But Jackson strengthened himself in the North by his stanch stand against the nullifiers. Harvard awarded him a doctor's degree, and New Englanders nearly killed their distinguished visitor with receptions, dinners and parades in his honor.

Renewal of the Bank war, however, soon cost the President the good will of northern conservatives. Clay, Calhoun, and Webster joined forces to put through the Senate a resolution of censure upon the President for forcing the removal of the government deposits from the Bank. The nomination of Roger B. Taney as Secretary of the Treasury was rejected because he had followed orders in the removal. The Senate rang with the angry, denunciatory voices of the Great Triumvirate. In the end Jackson had his way about everything. After three years of effort Benton of Missouri finally marshalled enough votes to expunge the censure resolution from the earlier Senate journal. Jackson rewarded the "expungers" with a White House feast. This same Senate ratified the nomination of Taney as Chief Justice to succeed John Marshall. Biddle's attempt to pressure a recharter by suddenly calling in the Bank's loans reacted against him, and the final victory rested with Jackson. After 1836 there was no United States Bank. Public money went into state banks.

Though land policy was a sectional rather than a party matter, Clay's idea of apportioning the proceeds of land sales among the states, first proposed in 1832, had the support of most of the anti-Jackson men. It appealed to the older states but not to the frontier, which wanted land prices lowered. A veto blocked Clay's bill, but the President reluctantly signed a Calhoun proposal to turn over to the states the mounting Treasury surplus—the national debt had been paid off. Such a government handout was too popular to turn down with the election of 1836 at hand.

The Congressional battles of 1833-1836 brought conservative Democrats, chiefly Bank men, over to the opposition. Executive usurpations by King Andrew the First were threatening the destruction of constitutional government. Congress and the courts, they feared, would soon feel the heel of the dictator. The Senate, quiescent under the Virginia Presidents, was discovering its powers for mischief. It was now the forum for the nation's greatest orators and parliamentary leaders, who were establishing the tradition that thwarting the White House was a major Senate function. But Jackson was hard to thwart.

The Whig party was emerging nationally in these Senate battles with the Jackson administration. Locally, groups of leaders, building chiefly upon existing foundations in North and West and upon secessions from the Jacksonians in the South, were developing the organizations essential to success. In most parts of the North Antimasons merged with National Republicans. The joint electoral tickets in New York and Ohio in 1832 had paved the way. In New England it proceeded more slowly; but it was substantially achieved by 1836, though many Antimasons had turned to the Democrats. Democratic divisions and local issues enabled Antimasonry, with National Republican support, to capture Pennsylvania in 1834. Thaddeus Stevens was an able, energetic leader, and the Whig party was actually functioning under the Antimasonic name. In all the free states small groups of Bank, or conservative, Democrats driven from the Jacksonians by the Bank struggle and the radical tendencies of their old party entered the ranks of the new opposition party. But the general tone of the Whig party in the North was that of the National Republican. Its leaders and its policies came from that element.

In the South the situation was reversed. Except for the border states of Delaware, Maryland, and Kentucky, and sugar-planting Louisiana, the National Republican element was a small minority. The more particularistic lower South had had little use for the economic doctrines of Henry Clay; but Jackson's measures and methods now appeared as the greater evil. State-rights men, friends of the Bank, the business and professional classes generally, and various insurgent groups slighted by the administration formed the southern wing of the Whig coalition. Its core was essentially conservative in the cotton South and centered in the areas of the large plantations and their urban hubs, where businessmen and planters cooperated in politics as they did in the business world.

Thus the Whig party was born, with its coat of many colors. It embraced protectionists and anti-protectionists, pro-Bank and anti-Bank men, state-rights zealots and ardent nationalists, planters and manufacturers, businessmen and farmers, in a strange combination. Yet it was the rallying place of the propertied interests, alarmed at the elements arrayed under the banner of the tribune of the people, who had even picked his own successor. Actually, Jackson's strict construction views, like Jefferson's, gave a wide latitude for state action. This forced conservatives to fight agrarian and urban radicals in each state over such issues as taxation, corporate monopolies, banking and currency, debt repudiation, and humanitarian reforms. Platforms had to be adapted to local situations. Sectionally, the Whig party was strong in conservative New England and where transplanted New Englanders lived, in the old Federalist seaboard area of the middle Atlantic states, in the wealthier, longer settled parts of the Ohio valley, and in the Black Belt of the South. Here and there the complex Whig pattern acquired a democratic pigmentation, for it included Tennessee and North Carolina mountaineers, many native-born (as opposed to Irish) workingmen of New England, and the small farmers of certain areas where transportation problems required federal aid. Middle-class Protestants, temperance advocates, and nativists found the Whig party a more suitable vehicle than the Democracy with its growing German and Irish segments.

The name "Whig" grew naturally out of the party's opposition to executive usurpation, the leaders likening themselves to the English Whigs who had resisted royal despotism. Given a good American usage at the time of the Revolution, it was now revived and applied to the opposition to King Andrew almost simultaneously in several places. The New York City election in April, 1834, was apparently the first appearance of the party name in a campaign.

The Whigs insisted that they were true Jeffersonians in constitutional theory. They emphasized the supremacy of the legislative branch, and criticized Jackson's free use of the veto power. In effect, they argued for an adulterated parliamentary system with a weak executive and the real power in the hands of Congressional leaders. But too much can be made of constitutional theories. The Whigs, like the wealthier classes on other occasions, raised a hue and cry about destruction of the Constitution by the President because his policies threatened their interests. Executive power was dangerous because Jackson was President.

The election of 1836 was a testing time for the Whigs. It was considered inexpedient to hold a national convention, and this left the leaders in each state free to offer local favorites. In New England Daniel Webster, representing the economic views of the National Republicans, and on friendly terms with the Antimasons, had strong claims. But, as a former Federalist and the paid attorney of the United States Bank, he was too vulnerable to Democratic shafts, and his hopes elsewhere were dashed by the failure of the Pennsylvania Antimasons to indorse him. Their state convention committed itself to General William Henry Harrison of Ohio, a hero of the War of 1812 and a man of considerable political experience, not hitherto regarded as of Presidential caliber. Because of financial reverses, he was then holding the position of clerk of the courts at Cincinnati. Availability was the keynote of his candidacy, for he was popular in the West, had been a Jeffersonian in other days, and had no damning record on national questions. John McLean, kept aloof from party controversies by his position on the Supreme Court, had the support of a number of Whig leaders in Ohio and Pennsylvania; and friends in the Ohio legislature nominated him in 1835 but the movement went no further. The western states were taking up the popular Harrison.

The Democratic legislature of Tennessee furnished a candidate for the Whigs in the South when it nominated Senator Hugh L. White, only recently estranged from Jackson. The Alabama legislature took similar action, and an independent Democratic movement for White was soon under way all through the South, as he was a moderate state-rights man. Van Buren, the "Little Magician," was not popular in this section, and all Jackson's efforts could not bring him a united Democratic support. Except in the border states, where Harrison was favored, the southern Whigs indorsed White electoral tickets.

Meanwhile a Democratic national convention at Baltimore, packed with federal officeholders, had nominated Van Buren in May, 1835. There was no opposition, but Jackson's choice for Vice President, Colonel Richard M. Johnson of Kentucky, barely received the two-thirds vote required. Johnson, a genial politician and war veteran, reputed slayer of Tecumseh, and long-time foe of imprisonment for debt, provided western balance for the ticket. But he had lived with a mulatto woman, now dead, and had two daughters, whom he educated and presented socially. Such disregard of southern social conventions made him of doubtful value to the head of the ticket, and the Virginia delegation greeted his nomination with hisses.

Whig strategy aimed to defeat Van Buren by running sectional "favorite sons" and throwing the election to the House, where Harrison or White might be chosen. As Biddle put it, "This disease is to be treated as a local disorder—apply local remedies." The scheme failed chiefly because the might of Jackson was behind Van Buren, who received 170 electoral votes to Harrison's 73 (Vermont, New Jersey, Delaware, Maryland, Kentucky, Ohio, Indiana), White's 26

(Tennessee, Georgia), Webster's 14 (Massachusetts).[1] The South Carolina legislature, hostile to White because he had voted for the Force Bill in the nullification crisis, chose eleven electors who voted for Willie P. Mangum of North Carolina. R. M. Johnson had 147 votes for Vice President, one under a majority; the northern Whig states cast 77 votes for Francis Granger of New York, Democratic Virginia gave her 23 votes to William Smith of Alabama, and South Carolina, Georgia, Tennessee, and Maryland cast 47 votes for Whig John Tyler of Virginia. The Senate, for the only time in American history, chose the Vice President, Johnson receiving 33 votes, Granger 16.

The Whigs had cause to feel encouraged. Unlike Clay in 1832, they had polled a large southern vote. They had carried two Jacksonian strongholds, Georgia and Tennessee, and three border slave states, and had given Van Buren a close race elsewhere. Furthermore, Harrison's good showing in the Ohio valley states and in Pennsylvania, which he lost by 4,300 votes, stamped him as a good prospect for 1840. The opposition groups were on the way to becoming a party.

Van Buren's Problems

On the 4th of March, 1837, Andrew Jackson, pale, feeble, disease-racked, rose from a sickbed to see his successor inducted into office. It was his, rather than Van Buren's, day of glory. Taking the oath of office was the man whom he had chosen for the place, though once rejected by the United States Senate as Minister to England. Administering the oath as Chief Justice was Roger B. Taney, whom the Senate had rejected for the Secretaryship of the Treasury. Yet these were mere outward symbols of the old man's power. His real greatness lay in a spirited leadership that drew its strength from an intuitive understanding of the hopes and beliefs of the common people. He had led a loose alliance of discordant factions into power; he retired as the head of a great, compact, well organized party whose principles were his own. He had destroyed the Bank of the United States, stood like a rock against nullification, refused to let the Supreme Court interpret the Constitution for him, and bequeathed to his party the role of defender of the humble

[1] The popular vote was: Van Buren, 762,978; Whig candidates, together, 736,250.

folk. Richly did he deserve the honors that were his on March 4, 1837.

Van Buren earnestly intended to walk in the Old Hero's footsteps, but unfortunately Jackson's boots were seven-leagued ones. This first New York President, the son of a tavern keeper, was a true democrat in principles; but his very appearance was against him. Short, plump, baldheaded, his good-humored face rimmed with side-whiskers that were once a brilliant burnished gold but now a decorous gray, he presented a strange contrast to the tall, lean, soldierly Jackson. His well groomed appearance provided scoffers with stories that he used Cologne water and laced himself in corsets—a pamphlet by Davy Crockett spread this libel in 1836—charges so damaging in a country where men "with the bark on" predominated that they amounted almost to a major issue in 1840. His unfailing courtesy and correct manners were liabilities with the voting masses. His cautious political generalship had created for him the reputation of an artful dodger—"noncommittalism" was the word commonly hurled at him—that weakened public faith in him. He had served Jackson better than he served himself. When his courage and tenacity of purpose revealed themselves in his Presidency, they won no popular acclaim. The dynamic personality of the Old Hero was missing from the picture.

Yet even Jackson's widespread popularity would have been placed under a tremendous strain in the White House during the late 1830's. Rapid business expansion, credit inflation from unregulated state banks, ballooning sales of public lands, and feverish speculation produced the inevitable consequences. Van Buren was scarcely inaugurated before the top-heavy structure of business and finance crashed to the ground. Bank suspensions, bankruptcies, deflated prices, and unemployment took their toll. A prostrate country turned to Washington for relief.

Van Buren had no solution. The government had not caused the panic, and things would have to right themselves through the good crops and good sense of the masses of farmers. People looked too much to the government for aid, he said—a shaft directed at the business classes. He did recommend an Independent Treasury system to protect the federal government from involvements with state banks. He also refused to revoke Jackson's Specie Circular of 1836 requiring hard money in payment for public lands. Angry businessmen argued that it had precipitated the crash.

A group of conservative Democrats—supporters of state banks and paper money—revolted and blocked the bill for an Independent Treasury. Nathaniel P. Tallmadge of New York and William C. Rives of Virginia led the insurgents and eventually joined the Whigs, as did other state-bank men.

As conservatives moved away on the right, radicals asserted themselves on the left, notably in Van Buren's home state. To understand the ferment of the 1830's, the organized activities of the workingmen must receive brief consideration. The beginnings of industrialism had depressed the wage-earning classes in the eastern cities and aroused a class consciousness which invited organization for economic and social betterment. Labor unions appeared, and in the years 1827-1834 labor became a definite force in politics. In Philadelphia, New York, and New England local workingmen's parties or independent workingmen's tickets contended for local offices and for seats in state legislatures. A few "workies" were elected, usually with the aid of one of the major parties, and though attempts were made to extend their activities into state politics the movements failed as third parties. Internal dissensions, lack of political experience, and the manipulations of local politicians tell the story of their failure. But they presently merged with the Democratic party, and Jackson recognized his working-class support through an executive order putting into effect a ten-hour day in the Philadelphia navy yard. The labor element, broadly reformist and humanitarian, contributed to the success of a number of reforms, notably free common schools, but its political influence was most effective in the Democratic party.

In 1836 Ely Moore, a Tammany-labor member of Congress, startled that body with what John Quincy Adams called "a thundering Jack Cade or Wat Tyler speech" in defense of labor's rights. Moore was affiliated with a Locofoco group, so called when, at a New York City Democratic convention, the radicals continued the meeting by lighting the new friction matches—popularly called "locofocos"—and candles after their opponents had turned out the gas lights. They organized a third party, supported by a part of the labor element, and launched a crusade for equal rights, calling themselves the Equal Rights party, but still were better known as Locofocos. They attacked all forms of monopoly and special privilege, but directed their guns particularly at banks and "paper capitalism"—"a nascent proletarian party," says one writer, "while the Democratic party of the time was essentially agrarian and the Whig commercial and capitalistic." William Leggett, associate editor of the New York *Evening Post* and later in charge of the *Plain Dealer*, a radical organ, was their intellectual leader, though he refused to leave the Democratic party.

The panic made the banking problem acute and placed Governor William Marcy and the state organization, controlled by the Albany Regency, in a difficult position. Senator Tallmadge and the conservatives were defending the credit system and the use of paper money, but the insurgent Locofocos and many radicals still in the Democratic party were demanding destruction of all specially incorporated banks and elimination of a paper currency. Van Buren, in close touch with the New York situation, courageously met the issue with his Independent Treasury plan, removing control of federal funds from state banks. This, with his expressed wish to limit the use of paper currency and encourage the circulation of gold and silver, converted the Locofocos into Democrats again. As Tallmadge and many conservatives departed, the Locofocos and their working-class allies came back. The national administration had been "locofocoized."

The Democrats of the West found Locofoco doctrines easy of acceptance if, indeed, they were not indigenous there. Jackson and his loyal western lieutenant, Benton, had come to distrust banks of issue and bank paper of all kinds before the Locofocos took their stand. Benton's home state, Missouri, was supplied with much Mexican silver from the Santa Fe trade. The crash of western banks in the panic and the sufferings of note holders encouraged the hard-money, antibank advocates to assert themselves. Equal rights and opposition to corporate monopolies of all kinds became cardinal principles of the agrarian Democrats of the West, though the local conservatives held out for regulated state banks. New constitutions in state after state reflected the reforming spirit in the next few years. The Locofocos, like the third parties of later periods, were the "incipient fermentation" which was "fast leavening the whole lump." Even southern Democrats slowly imbibed some of the faith of the radicals, especially in the new cotton states, Alabama and Mississippi. In general, the South was stony ground. Property in land and slaves did not encourage doctrines that might lead to social upheaval.

A further collapse of banks in 1839, including Nicholas Biddle's, persuaded Congress in 1840 to enact Van Buren's Independent Treasury proposal into law, with the provision that in 1843 all payments to or from the federal government should be in gold or silver. An order requiring a ten-hour day on all government works also pleased his labor following, and temporary preemption laws gave squatters on government lands the first right to purchase at the minimum price —a recognition of frontier democracy. Van Buren had been true to Jackson's principles. The Red Fox was displaying unexpected courage.

Oddly enough, the Independent Treasury bill brought recruits from a most unexpected source—Calhoun and his following. Professing fear that the Whigs would attempt to charter another United States Bank, the South Carolinian declared for the bill and drew away from his Whig allies. In December, 1839, in a formal reconciliation the old enemies broke bread together at the White House. Van Buren's narrow conception of the power of the federal government suited the state-rights position of Calhoun, who felt that the danger of executive usurpation had departed with Jackson. Nor was this all. The abolitionist movement was spreading in the North, and northern Democrats seemed safer guardians of the interests of slavery than the Whigs. Southern rights would not be infringed upon by a party with the negative viewpoint of Van Buren. With Clay in Calhoun's way in the Whig party, there were better prospects for the ambitious Southerner in the Democracy. Trooping back with Calhoun were his personal following in his home state and a few stanch state-rights men elsewhere.

The Little Magician secured a unanimous renomination from the Democratic national convention at Baltimore in May, 1840. Opposition to Vice President Johnson, however, was so great that the convention resolved that it was inexpedient to name anyone for the place. Affable "Tecumseh," according to reports from Kentucky, had been indulging in further experiments in race amalgamation. The platform declared for strict construction of the Constitution and opposed internal improvements, a protective tariff, and a United States Bank. It also disapproved of abolitionist agitation for Congressional interference with slavery. On the positive side it approved of the separation of government money from banking institutions and upheld the principles of the Declaration of Independence. Locofoco hard-money ideas were ignored. Had the campaign turned solely on platform issues, Van Buren might have won. Fate and the shrewdness of the Whig leaders willed otherwise.

Tippecanoe and Tyler Too

The business interests had turned against Van Buren in 1837. Disagreeing with his Treasury plan and his nonaction policy toward the panic, they were increasingly alarmed at the spread of Locofoco ideas. The Whigs, eager to take advantage of the fears of men of property, attempted to fasten on the whole Democratic party all the vagaries of extremists among the Locofocos; and their newspapers substituted "Locofoco" for "Democratic" as a designation for their opponents—a practice that lasted until the Whig party itself disappeared. "Locofoco" was defined in much the same loose terms as "radical" in more recent times: "in favor of an equal distribution of property, an uprooting of the institutions of the country, and the substitution of some monstrous and impracticable fancy of his own in their stead." The Democrats were charged with arousing poor against rich, with encouraging a class war.

While it was well to frighten men of property to the Whig camp, victory in an election required popular support. Thurlow Weed had opposed Clay's attempt in 1832 to use the Bank as an issue; and he was convinced in 1834 that the Whigs must find new weapons and new leaders. His fellow New Yorker, William H. Seward, deprecatingly wrote, "The rich we have always with us." The problem was to win the masses. The shrewdest Whig leaders saw the parallel with the old Federalists, who had doomed themselves because they were never able to forget that theirs was the party of the rich and the well born. Virginia Whigs might boast that Whigs knew each other by the instinct of gentlemen, but the votes of the common herd were needed on election day.

This desire to win explains the developing hostility toward Henry Clay and Daniel Webster as candidates in 1840. The "god-like Daniel," as in 1836, had a set of disabilities so generally recognized that his Massachusetts friends dropped him from consideration long before the convention met.

Clay, on the other hand, had distinct elements of availability: a devoted personal following, a captivating personality, and a wide support in the slave states that he had not had in 1832. This new-found southern enthusiasm for him had been aroused by his change of front on the tariff in 1833, which awakened the admiration of many southerners. The Union had been saved, they felt, by his broad patriotism in that crisis. Furthermore, he was not urging a national bank unless the people favored it, was no longer pressing the internal improvements issue, and was defending the cause of state banks in opposing the Independent Treasury. State-rights men were reconciled to him, conservatives trusted him, aristocrats thought of him as a southern gentleman in contrast to the tricky New York politician in the White House; and slave owners accepted him as one of their own kind. Leaders like John Tyler, Henry A. Wise, and Hugh L. White indorsed him, and most of the southern states, through conventions, chose Clay delegates.

Clay was not favored by the Whig leaders in New York, Pennsylvania, and Ohio, the key states to Whig victory. He had failed to carry them in 1832, and his long career constituted a record that made him vulnerable to Democratic attacks. The poor farmer and labor elements would not be drawn to Clay. A commoner was needed, preferably one without a long public career to defend. General William Henry Harrison seemed to be the man of destiny. The hero of the battle of Tippecanoe and the War of 1812 in the Northwest, a westerner of democratic background, he had no record on national questions to embarrass supporters beyond a brief service in the United States Senate. He had demonstrated his popularity in 1836 by carrying the Northwest and coming close to victory in the Democratic stronghold of Pennsylvania; and the Webster men in New England preferred him to Clay. His age—almost sixty-seven—was his only liability.

The national convention, called by a group of Whig members of Congress, assembled at Harrisburg, Pennsylvania, in December, 1839. Clay was the leading contender, but Weed and the New York leaders, privately friendly to Harrison, had encouraged a movement for General Winfield Scott, whose delegates from New York and New Jersey held the balance of power. It was charged later that the Scott delegates were really for Harrison, and that his candidacy was intended to head off Clay. The adoption of the unit rule by the Scott-Harrison majority makes this plausible, for it suppressed a Clay minority in several states. The first ballot under this rule gave Clay 103, Harrison 94, and Scott 57.[2] The southern states plus Connecticut, Rhode Island, and Illinois were for Clay; New York,

[2] Twenty-two states were represented by 254 delegates. Georgia, South Carolina, Tennessee, and Arkansas were not represented. The ballots were taken informally in the different state delegations and reported by committees.

New Jersey, Vermont, and Michigan were for Scott, and the rest were for Harrison. After a number of ballots, Harrison added most of the Scott support and had 148 votes to Clay's 90 and Scott's 16. The convention then formally declared Harrison the nominee.

The angry Clay men refused the offer to suggest a Vice Presidential candidate; two or three names were mentioned but withdrawn, and then John Tyler of Virginia, who had shed tears at Clay's defeat, was nominated. As a state-rights man, a Clay supporter, and a southerner, he balanced the ticket properly. No platform was made, as differences of opinion were all too evident on nearly every significant question.

The result at first did not seem to augur victory. Clay, disappointed as deeply as a man can be who sees the ambition of years thwarted at the moment of achievement, found liquor and profanity a temporary outlet but not a solace. "It is a diabolical intrigue, I know now, which has betrayed me. I am the most unfortunate man in the history of parties: always run by my friends when sure to be defeated, and now betrayed for a nomination when I, or any one, would be sure of an election." Whether the friend who reported these words quoted him correctly or not, they picture the state of mind of the man who had been most instrumental in creating the party that now rejected him. He had been shabbily treated, but he should not have been surprised. The northern politicians, and behind them the conservative business interests, wanted victory. They could win by an appeal to the democratic masses. Clay was not their man.

The key to victory was furnished by the Democrats. With incredible stupidity a Baltimore newspaper suggested, in disparagement of Harrison, that he be given "a barrel of hard cider and a pension of two thousand a year, and, our word for it, he will sit the remainder of his days in a log cabin by the side of a 'sea coal' fire and study moral philosophy." A Harrisburg Whig sensed the possibilities in the statement, and the sneer became the slogan. Harrison thenceforth was "the log cabin, hard cider" candidate, the simple man of the frontier pitted against the New York aristocrat living in splendor amid the luxuries of the White House. The arguments for Jackson in 1828 could now be used for Harrison, the frontier soldier. Glossed over were his aristocratic Virginia ancestry, his political activities in Ohio, his years of office holding and office seeking. He became the simple soldier-farmer of North Bend who would restore government to the people. His substantial country home was metamorphosed into a pioneer's log cabin.

Conventions and mass meetings, parades and processions with banners and floats, long speeches on the log-cabin theme, log-cabin songbooks and log-cabin newspapers, Harrison pictures, Tippecanoe handkerchiefs and badges, log-cabin headquarters at every crossroads, with the latchstring out and hard cider always on tap—all these devices and more were used to arouse enthusiasm that soon surpassed anything the nation had ever experienced. Crowds of unheard-of proportions turned out for Whig rallies. Ten acres of people (numbers would not suffice) were reported present at a Dayton, Ohio jamboree. The Democrats also held meetings and parades but, with an unaccountable display of moral rectitude, rejected hard cider and posed as the party of virtue. Democratic orators attempted to discuss the issues and—of all things—to belittle Harrison's war record when Van Buren had none. Old Andrew Jackson, on the stump in Tennessee, committed this *faux pas*.

Evading any expression of his bank views except to say that he favored paper money, Harrison talked in crowd-pleasing generalities at a soldiers' rally at Fort Meigs and made briefer speeches confined to Ohio. A Cincinnati committee handled all the correspondence. Whig orators assailed Van Buren's aristocracy with stories of gold spoons in the White House and a gilded coach and the trappings of British royalty. When issues were discussed, the hard times were played up, the Independent Treasury was attacked, and, to alarm state-rights men, a proposal of Secretary of War Poinsett to federalize the state militia was exposed as monarchical centralization and executive usurpation. But always the Whig orators returned to the log-cabin theme. Imposing Daniel Webster, without log-cabin nativity, claimed its virtues by association, through his older brother and sisters.

In the cotton South, Whig tactics were more moderate. Here businessmen and planters, indifferent to log cabins and much concerned about slavery, were assured that Harrison's membership in an antislavery society years before had been a youthful indiscretion, and the candidate himself declared against Congressional interference with their institution. He was pictured as an antique Jeffersonian Republican in contrast with the corruptionists who controlled the Democratic party. Clay recovered from his sulk and did yeoman service in selling Harrison's merits to the South. Even in Georgia, where a

State Rights party had operated independently, the Whig candidate was finally accepted.

In the northern cities businessmen used economic pressure for the "Hero of Tippecanoe." Workingmen were warned of the dangers of continued low wages and unemployment if Van Buren should win: prosperity would return if he were defeated. "The subscriber will pay five dollars a hundred for pork if Harrison is elected, and two and a half if Van Buren is." So ran an advertisement in a New York paper. But song and hard cider were better arguments than fear. One of the most popular ditties tells the story:

What has caused this great commotion, motion,
Our country through?
It is the ball a-rolling on,
For Tippecanoe and Tyler too, Tippecanoe and Tyler too.
And with them we'll beat the little Van, Van, Van;
Van is a used-up man.

More expressive was this:

Old Tip he wears a homespun suit,
He has no ruffled shirt-wirt-wirt;
But Mat he has the golden plate,
And he's a little squirt-wirt-wirt.

Tobacco chewers spit when they came to the "wirt."

And so Van Buren was sung and drunk out of the White House and back to Kinderhook. One of the most sincerely democratic of Presidents was overborne by a wave of popular enthusiasm for a log-cabin myth. Marching in the Whig ranks with simple artisans and rustic cultivators were bankers, merchants, landed gentry, mill owners, speculators—for the log-cabin cult, spreading through the land, had made strange bedfellows. The rich and the well born had at last learned that in politics the votes of the humble were not to be despised. "The Goths have taken Rome," wailed Thomas Ritchie, Virginia editor. But he did not add the bitter explanation that they had borrowed their weapons and their tactics from the Romans.

The electoral votes indicated a landslide. To Van Buren went only 60 votes (Virginia, South Carolina, Alabama, Missouri, Illinois, Arkansas, New Hampshire) out of 294. The popular vote was less conclusive: 1,275,016 for Harrison, 1,129,102 for Van Buren.[3] Both houses of Congress were won by the Whigs. Tyler had the same electoral vote as Harrison, but R. M. Johnson had twelve fewer than Van Buren. South Carolina cast eleven for L. W. Tazewell of Virginia, while one Virginia elector voted for James K. Polk of Tennessee.

Tyler Versus Clay

President Harrison in his long (an hour and forty minutes) and platitudinous inaugural decried the growth of executive power, pledged himself to a single term, and promised to use the veto only in extreme cases. He condemned the Independent Treasury but was vague on other matters. The cabinet, headed by Daniel Webster, included at least three Clay choices, but Harrison did not intend to let the Kentucky Senator direct his administration.

Clay, naturally assuming that the leadership in Congress and, with it, dominance in the administration would fall to him, was annoyed at the growing influence of Webster and the Weed group from New York, whose manipulations had defeated him at the Harrisburg convention. While engaged in a bitter but losing struggle over the collectorship of the port of New York, he went ahead with plans to direct legislation until he was stopped short by a note from the White House. Harrison frankly declared him too impetuous, said that others must be consulted, and intimated that written communications were preferable to personal conferences. The rebuke stung Clay to the quick. He saw the hand of his enemies in the move and wrote a sharp note in his own defense, assuring Harrison, however, of his continued friendship. He then left for home. The breach was never closed. The unfortunate Harrison, overwhelmed with "office-hunting locusts," as Horace Greeley termed them, and none too strong physically, broke under the strain, developed pneumonia, and died one month from the day of his inauguration. Upon the shoulders of that state-rights

[3] South Carolina voted through her legislature and continued to do so to the Civil War. Election statistics for this and later elections are only approximately correct. Votes cited are from Stanwood, checked by other sources. W. Dean Burnham, *Presidential Ballots, 1836–1892*, and E. E. Robinson, *The Presidential Vote, 1896–1932*, with supplements through 1944, are careful compilations by counties but group votes of minor parties under the heading "other." A more recent book, Svend Peterson, *A Statistical History of Presidential Elections* (New York, 1963) differs in detail from earlier compilations. See footnote 6, p. 319.

Republican John Tyler, reared in the Virginia strict construction school, fell the burdens of government and party management.

The special session of Congress, called by Harrison for May 31, repealed the Independent Treasury and adopted a series of resolutions favoring incorporation of a United States Bank, imposition of higher duties, and distribution of the proceeds of the land sales to the states. All this was the work of Clay, who took over the role of Senate majority leader and unofficial prime minister. He was back on old National Republican ground and ignored the state-rights element of Whigs. President Tyler had been indefinite in his message, especially on the Bank question, and Clay assumed he would cooperate with the majority. But when a bill to charter another United States Bank reached his desk he surprised and angered Whig Congressional leaders with a veto. Negotiations with cabinet representatives of the President produced a revised bill, but it suffered the same fate. Open war between White House and Capitol Hill followed, with mutual recriminations.

Tyler was angered by Clay's imperious assumption of leadership, but the clash was something more than one of personalities. Clay represented the ideas of the National Republicans, the majority element in the Whig alliance, and felt that an accidental President had no right to block the will of that majority. On the other hand, Tyler, as a state-rights southerner, had not favored a bank in the past, and, in the absence of a platform in 1840, could insist that his interpretation of the party's position was as valid as Clay's.

The verdict of the party was soon rendered. All members of the cabinet resigned except Webster, who remained in the State Department partly because he wanted to complete certain difficult negotiations with the British government, and partly because he had been playing second fiddle to Clay in party affairs long enough and a partnership with Tyler might advance his Presidential prospects. The Whig caucus denounced Tyler, and most of the party newspapers went along; but the program Clay had outlined was wrecked. Congress did pass a preemption-distribution bill, but distribution was not to take effect if the tariff was raised above 20 per cent, and the tariff of 1842 increased rates above that level. Tyler vetoed a separate distribution bill. Preemption, which Clay had not favored, remained in effect, thus giving squatters the right to buy land on which they had settled at the minimum price. This measure was more Democratic than Whig.

Before the tariff bill finally passed, Clay retired from the Senate, delivering his valedictory before crowded galleries, shaking hands with his rival Calhoun, and then leaving the scene of his many triumphs and disappointments—"something like the soul's quitting the body," wrote his devoted friend Crittenden. But his retirement was like Jackson's in 1825. As the "Sage of Ashland" he could rule his party no less effectively than at Washington, and without the embarrassments of Senate membership.

In the next two years Clay's sun was at the zenith. He had drawn away from the President all but a "corporal's guard" of state-rights Whigs. Webster saw the light and resigned from the cabinet after completing the negotiations with Lord Ashburton over the Maine boundary. There was no future for him with Tyler. Clay's strength was as great with the southern as with the northern Whigs, though the President was a southerner and a state-rights man. The explanation lies in the fact that most southern Whigs were not doctrinaire state-rights worshipers but practical bankers, businessmen, lawyers, and planters. Clay's program offered attractions after years of depression, deranged currencies, and low cotton prices, and there were industrial stirrings and railroad projects that Whig policies encouraged. As the party of conservatism it would checkmate radicalism, whether the radicals were abolitionists, Locofocos, poor southern whites, frontier squatters, or immigrant labor. Whiggery would insure stability to the Union and security to property; and Clay, not Tyler, was its true representative. His leadership was conservative and compromising—and he was a Kentucky gentleman and a slaveholder to boot.

Clay was too good a salesman to let matters drift. He attended dinners, conventions, and other gatherings, was acclaimed as the man of the hour by thousands of devoted followers, and was nominated for the Presidency by state after state long before the time for the national convention. He traveled to New Orleans in the winter of 1842-1843 and visited the chief cities of the older South a year later, refraining from direct electioneering, but drawing closer the loyalty of Whig voters.

The political skies had never appeared brighter to the gallant Kentucky statesman, gray-haired and elderly, but still the most eloquent and beloved of American political leaders. Andrew Jackson, feeble but able to hurl darts from the Hermitage at his pet enemies, watched helplessly while the friends of the "unprincipled demagogue" made Tennessee a Whig state.

But John Tyler was still to be reckoned with. Derided and ostracized by all good, orthodox Whigs, "His Accidency" had found a new weapon. When he hurled it in the spring of 1844, the effect was so devastating that the two most skillful party leaders of their generation, Clay and Van Buren, were overborne by it. The weapon was labeled "Texas."

9

Expansion and Its Consequences

The Texas Issue

Texas, after winning virtual independence from Mexico in 1836, had been disappointed in her hope of annexation to the United States. Jackson was sympathetic but contented himself with recognizing Texan independence as his term ended. President Van Buren let matters rest, for northern opposition to adding a huge slave area was evident, and sectional peace was preferable to more territory. President Tyler, an expansionist, became concerned at British interest in the Lone Star Republic, and Secretary of State Abel Upshur began negotiations for annexation that his successor, Calhoun, completed. The treaty was sent to the Senate April 22, 1844. Even earlier the secret had leaked out, and the Presidential candidates had to face the music.

Van Buren, with a majority of the delegates to the Democratic national convention already pledged to him, declared against annexation on April 20 in a long letter to W. H. Hammett of Mississippi. It had typical Van Buren loopholes, but the purport was all too clear—there was no immediate necessity for annexation. His stand, which had the approval of his closest friends, was the most damaging, and perhaps the most courageous, act of his long career. Possibly he knew that Clay, almost certain to be the Whig nominee, would take a similar stand, and the issue would be dropped; but he did not realize that it might cost him the nomination.

Almost at once his southern supporters began to drop away. The veteran editor Thomas Ritchie and the Richmond Junto, having eliminated Calhoun and tied the Virginia delegation to Van Buren, now found the wave of annexationist sentiment too strong to resist. They turned to Lewis Cass of Michigan, a pro-Texas man. Andrew

Jackson was distressed by Van Buren's letter. Already an old letter of his own favoring annexation had been exhumed and printed in Democratic newspapers. Privately he began to look around for another candidate, while expressing confidence in a public letter that his old lieutenant would soon see the light on Texas. His new choice was a Tennessee protégé, James K. Polk, then a strong contender for the second place on the ticket.

Meanwhile, Blair, Benton, and Silas Wright, loyal to the Squire of Kinderhook though divided over annexation, fought it out with the southern expansionists led by Senator Robert J. Walker of Mississippi, who was close to Tyler. Calhoun had been trying for three years to expand his following into the northern states and had even produced his own campaign biography; but he withdrew his name and entered Tyler's cabinet in March, 1844. His friends joined the clamor for annexation and against Van Buren.

The fourth Democratic national convention met at Baltimore, May 27, in an atmosphere of bitterness and suspicion. Only South Carolina sent no delegates. The two-thirds rule for nominations had been used in the first two Democratic conventions but not in the third. Now Walker secured its adoption by a vote of 148 to 118, with help from disloyal Van Buren delegates. On the first ballot Van Buren had 146 of the 266 votes cast, a clear majority; but his support faded away to 99 on the seventh ballot while Lewis Cass, his chief rival, rose from 83 to 123. "Tecumseh" Johnson and James Buchanan had the rest. The convention adjourned overnight in what seemed to be a hopeless deadlock. Polk's Tennessee friends, led by Congressman Cave Johnson, were now ready to offer his name, and George Bancroft, a Massachusetts Van Buren delegate, had been rounding up northern support in midnight conferences. When the eighth ballot was taken next day, Polk had 44 votes. On the ninth a stampede gave him the nomination by a unanimous vote. He was the first "dark horse" winner in convention history. Not yet forty-nine years old, he had been twice chosen Speaker of the House of Representatives and had served a term as governor of Tennessee, but this was followed by two defeats.

To conciliate the Van Buren following, the Vice Presidential nomination was given almost unanimously to popular Silas Wright, Senator from New York. The newly invented telegraph was used to notify him at Washington but he telegraphed his refusal at once, feeling that his views were like Van Buren's and that he should not profit at his friend's expense. After waiting for a messenger on horseback to verify the new gadget's message, the delegates named George M. Dallas of Pennsylvania.

The platform declared for "the re-occupation of Oregon and the re-annexation of Texas at the earliest practicable period," opposed distributing to the states the proceeds of land sales, and repeated the stand of the convention of 1840 on other subjects. The coupling of Texas with Oregon was a shrewd bid for expansionist support in both North and South, intended to controvert the charge that the convention was under southern control.

Although candidates and platform had Jackson's enthusiastic approval, the convention ended the domination of the Jacksonian old guard—Van Buren, Benton, and Blair. Walker of Mississippi and a southern contingent seemed to be using the Texas issue to bring about southern control of the party. Benton, angry at the defeat of Van Buren, continued to wage furious war upon the Calhounites, even though he supported Polk. He charged that an intrigue had nullified the choice of the people. Jackson believed that Benton's injuries in "the explosion of the big gun" on the man-of-war *Princeton,* which had killed Secretary of State Upshur, had affected his mind; but the southern wing made no such allowances and warned Polk not to be influenced by the old clique. It was only with difficulty that the candidate preserved harmony during the campaign.

The Senate, by rejecting Tyler's annexation treaty in June, left the issue to the voters. Tyler himself had not given up hope of another term. A mass convention of friends and officeholders had named him at Baltimore at the same time that the Democrats were in session. Angry at Blair's attacks in the *Globe,* he refused to withdraw until assurances were given that his friends would be received in full communion in the party. Polk did not like to give promises; but Jackson told Blair "to let Tiler alone," and, through Major Lewis, urged the President to withdraw, as his candidacy would help Clay—a potent argument. From other quarters pressure and flattery were used to good effect. Consequently, Tyler withdrew in August and announced his support of Polk.

Meanwhile, as expected, the Whigs had nominated Henry Clay. A convention at Baltimore on May 1, in which all the states were represented, disposed of all its business in one enthusiastic session. It was a love feast, to which Webster added the final touch in an eloquent eulogy of his old rival at a ratifying meeting after the nomination. Senator Theodore Frelinghuysen of New Jersey was named for Vice President on the fourth ballot. A brief series of resolutions, lauding the candidates and presenting Whig principles, constituted the party's first platform. These included "a well-regulated currency," "a tariff for revenue to defray the necessary expenses of the government, and discriminating with special reference to the protection of the domestic labor of the country," distribution of the proceeds of the land sales, one term for a President, a reform of executive usurpations, and an efficient and economical administration. There was no mention of a United States Bank or of Texas. On the old Jacksonian issues the Whigs had at last achieved unity, just when they had ceased to matter.

Three days before Van Buren's letter to Hammett, Clay sent to the *National Intelligencer* at Washington a letter from Raleigh, North Carolina. It contained a flat statement opposing the annexation of Texas as "involving us certainly in war with Mexico and probably with other foreign powers, dangerous to the integrity of the Union, inexpedient in the present financial condition of the country, and not called for by any general expression of public opinion." His letter was franker than Van Buren's, for his nomination was certain. The appearance of the two letters at almost the same time has led to conjectures as to whether the two men acted by prior agreement. On Van Buren's visit at Ashland nearly two years before, had the friendly enemies, enjoying their wine together, foreseen the Texas problem and reached an agreement to oppose annexation and keep it out of the campaign? There is no evidence that they did, but their views were strangely alike.

Unexpectedly Van Buren had lost the Democratic nomination, and Clay faced the expansionist Polk on a platform that threatened to make heavy inroads into his southern strength. In general, the Whigs of the South had rallied loyally to Clay, and in the Senate all but one had voted against Tyler's Texas treaty. The large planters and their business allies, except speculators in Texas land, had no stomach for war with Mexico and a stirring up of sectional hatred. "The Union without Texas rather than Texas without the Union," was their slogan. But the powerful appeal of Texas to the land-hungry small farmers and even to some planters, plus the argument of Calhoun that it was necessary to save the institution of slavery, played havoc with Clay's hopes. He began to soften the views of his Raleigh letter and in two letters to Alabama friends made it clear that he had no objection to annexation accomplished without dishonor, without war, with the common consent of the Union, and upon just and fair terms. He would be guided as President "by the state of facts, and the state of public opinion existing at the time I might be called upon to act." The letters encouraged his southern friends, but they damaged him in the North.

Here the Liberty party darkened the Whig sky. On November 13, 1839, eastern antislavery radicals led by Myron Holley, in convention at Warsaw, New York, had nominated James G. Birney for President. Birney, executive secretary of the American Anti-Slavery Society at New York, was formerly of Kentucky and Alabama and for a time had published the *Philanthropist*, an antislavery paper, at Cincinnati. He declined the nomination, feeling that the movement was premature; but when the Whigs and the Democrats, with Harrison and Van Buren as their nominees, showed no antislavery leanings a second convention at Albany in April, 1840, with six states represented renamed Birney, with Thomas Earle of Pennsylvania for Vice President. The convention was an eastern affair. Abolitionists were far from agreed as to the feasibility of a third party, and the national vote of 7,069 was discouragingly small.

Three years of agitation and organization followed, and new leaders appeared, notably in the Northwest: Salmon P. Chase and Samuel Lewis of Ohio, Owen Lovejoy of Illinois, and Birney, now of Michigan, were active, with at least half a dozen newspapers to advocate the cause. The national convention at Buffalo in August, 1843, with twelve states represented by 148 delegates, named Birney and Thomas Morris of Ohio as the party's candidates; its resolutions emphasized the need of separating the federal government from any connection with slavery but fell short of complete abolitionism. Texas had not yet become an issue. When it emerged in the spring of 1844 it placed the Liberty party leaders in a difficult position. The moral fervor of the antislavery movement appealed particularly to New Englanders and New England émigrés, who were usually Whig. A heavy Liberty vote would reduce the Whig vote in New York, Ohio, and other close states and might elect Polk, advocate of Texas, over Clay.

The Liberty party leaders, chiefly enthusiasts and fanatics, had little use for Clay under any circumstances; but their opposition would have mattered less had Clay not wavered on annexation. He attempted in September to return to his Raleigh letter position, undoing some of the damage. Whig hopes rose in October when the news spread that Birney had accepted a Democratic nomination for the Michigan legislature—seeming proof of a Liberty-Democratic bargain to defeat Clay. Birney attempted to explain it on the ground of purely local issues, but did openly admit his preference for Polk over Clay for the amazing reason that the latter, far more able, might lead his party to bring about annexation, while Polk was too incompetent to accomplish it. The effect was damaging to the Liberty party and was made more so by a forged letter, appearing in Whig newspapers a day or two before the election, in which Birney promised not to agitate the slavery question in the Michigan legislature. His refutation of it came too late. The Liberty party lost hundreds of votes. But its power in New York still proved decisive.

Yet expansion and slavery were not the sole issues on which the election turned. Oregon and Texas might be Democratic vote getters in South and West, but protectionist Pennsylvania, as important as New York in Democratic strategy, had to be propitiated in other ways. A letter from Polk to John K. Kane of Philadelphia made it clear that he favored a revenue tariff with only incidental protection, but his ardent supporters in the Keystone State used it to prove that he was as good a tariff man as Clay. "Polk, Dallas and the Tariff of '42" was their slogan. "Fifty-four Forty or Fight," long associated with this campaign, appeared after this election.

Organized Native Americanism also appeared locally in New York and Pennsylvania with both parties angling for its support without the curse of its blessing. The Whigs had the advantage here, for the foreign-born were generally Democrats. An antiforeign American Republican party, which had gained some local successes, indorsed Clay and Frelinghuysen. The latter had been active in Protestant evangelical movements, such as the American Bible Society and foreign missions, which weakened Whig appeal to Irish Catholics. The Democrats accused the Whigs of allying with the "church-burning" nativists, and countered by speeding up the naturalization of Irish and German newcomers in the East.

Both candidates were victims of slander and mud slinging. All Clay's chickens came home to roost. He was branded a gambler, a duelist, a profane swearer, a corrupt bargainer. Democratic newspapers printed an alleged letter of a Protestant minister who had traveled on a steamboat with him and bore witness to Clay's free use of strong language and his love of cards. Polk's character was quite exemplary, but Whig journals carried a story that a traveler had observed a gang of slaves being marched to a slave auction in Tennessee, each one branded with the letters "J. K. P." It purported to be an extract from a certain Roorbach's account of a tour of the South and West. Democratic defenders of Polk exposed the story as a Whig fabrication and the name "roorback" passed into the American political vocabulary for a preelection falsehood. One way of belittling the Democratic standard-bearer was to repeat the question many Americans asked just after his nomination: "Who is James K. Polk?" Tom Corwin, popular Whig stump speaker, added, "After that, who is safe?"

The election revealed that the relatively obscure Polk had defeated his more illustrious opponent, 170 electoral votes to 105.[1] Clay had carried only Ohio in the expansion-minded Northwest and only the upper tier of slave states in the South (North Carolina, Tennessee, Kentucky, Maryland, and Delaware). In the East, Massachusetts, Rhode Island, Connecticut, Vermont, and New Jersey gave him their votes. The South and West had voted for Texas and Oregon, but Polk also had Pennsylvania and New York by narrow margins. Clay needed New York's 36 electors to win. Birney had 15,812 popular votes in that crucial state. One-third of that number added to Clay's total would have meant victory. Had he not wavered on the Texas issue he might have gained these antislavery votes. But there is another side to the picture. His concessions to southern sentiments on Texas possibly tilted the balance to him in Tennessee. His margin there was only 113 votes. Defeat in Tennessee even with victory in New York would have lost him the election. Tyler in throwing Texas into the campaign had confronted Clay with a problem he could not solve, so long as the Liberty party warred on the Whig flanks. It was his misfortune that his Presidential candidacies ran counter to the two most powerful forces in the America of his generation: Jacksonian democracy and territorial expansion. One might add a third, just beginning to build up—European immigration. Millard Fillmore, himself the losing candidate for governor of New York, wrote that the abolitionists and the foreign Catholics had defeated Clay.

While the importance of Texas had tended to give Polk's victory the aspect of a southern triumph, the result in 1844 was more nearly an indorsement of a general expansionist program. The West,

[1] The popular vote was as follows: Polk, 1,337,243; Clay, 1,299,062; Birney, 62,300.

as ever, was land-hungry, and the Democrats had pointed the way by linking Oregon and Texas. Locofoco reformism had been diverted into a new channel that was to lead the Democratic party southward, as Benton and Van Buren sensed; but the South was not yet in the saddle. To the West, Polk was the heir of "Old Hickory" and even was sometimes called "Young Hickory." Jackson was his mentor, not Calhoun.

Polk's Presidency

Polk as President displayed marked executive ability and an unexpected determination to direct his own administration. Addicted to grinding labor (except on the Sabbath, which he carefully observed), methodical, careful of detail, patient with others, he gave himself unsparingly to his position. Yet he had serious defects as a party leader. He was drab, rather suspicious, self-contained, self-righteous, always on his guard, trusting no one overmuch and inviting no confidences. Most of the party bigwigs came to dislike him. They had catalogued him as a compliant mediocrity—he had the earmarks of one—only to discover that he had a mind of his own and would not take orders. Though he accomplished his major aims and led the nation through a great war with large accessions of territory, Polk was amazingly unpopular at the close of his term. His own party disliked him, though accepting his policies; the opposition Whigs and third-party men disliked both "Polk the mendacious" (Alexander Stephens's label) and his measures. Only now that the last slow embers of the great sectional struggle have turned to ashes, has this purposeful, capable, unloved man come into his own. Fortunately, the conscientious executive kept a careful diary, in which he plods his determined way into the history books.

Polk's difficulties in his party were primarily over patronage. The dark-horse President blundered in choosing his cabinet. James Buchanan of Pennsylvania, Secretary of State, Robert J. Walker of Mississippi, Secretary of the Treasury, and William L. Marcy, Secretary of War and former Governor of New York, were able men; but the appointments antagonized the still angry Van Buren supporters and, at the opposite pole, the Calhounites, who wanted their idol retained in office. The western states from Ohio to Missouri also were aggrieved at not being represented in the cabinet, when they had cast 56 electoral votes.

The Van Buren men were especially incensed at the appointment of Walker to the patronage-rich Treasury post, for he had spun the "vile intrigue" that defeated their favorite at the Baltimore convention.[2] The Jacksonians also resented Polk's treatment of Blair. He was forced to sell the *Globe*, which, renamed the Washington *Union*, became the voice of the administration. Major Lewis went back to Tennessee without a job, and Senator Benton was estranged for personal or family reasons by 1847. The old guard was on its way out.

Polk was equally unfortunate in passing out the lesser offices. He took personal charge of all manner of appointments, tried to treat all factions fairly, usually chose competent men, but often did not consult Senators and other party nabobs. He even retained some Whigs in office. The Mexican War increased both the number of jobs and the pressure on Polk. The sorely burdened President recorded in his diary his intention to write a book exposing politicians and their ways.

The New York situation grew steadily worse. There were two factions. The Barnburners led by Van Buren and Silas Wright, who was elected governor in 1844, had taken an anti-bank, hard-money position, had opposed canal extensions involving an increase in the state debt, and were generally reformist or liberal. They had a somewhat wider rural support than the Hunkers, who took the opposite stand on all these matters. But by the mid-forties leaders on both sides seemed more concerned with pelf than principles. The breach widened in 1846 when Silas Wright, who had run ahead of Polk in 1844, was defeated for reelection and friends charged that the Hunkers, aided by federal officeholders, had knifed him. When he died the next summer, his devoted following added his martyrdom to the list of Hunker iniquities. His death deprived the Barnburners of a possible Presidential candidate, for no man in their ranks was held in higher regard, even by Whig enemies, than this friendly homespun, unselfish, but too often inebriated Senator and governor.

No true admirer of the Jackson-Van Buren political principles could have found fault with Polk's policies; yet "the little mole," as Blair dubbed him, won few plaudits. The West disliked his veto of a rivers and harbors bill, and Pennsylvania and New England grumbled at Walker's tariff reductions. The Independent Treasury was restored,

[2] Strangely enough, the former Mississippi Senator during the Civil War was a loyal Union supporter and represented Lincoln's administration as a Treasury agent in Europe.

but the old trinity of tariff, banking, and internal improvements had been pushed aside by expansion and sectional conflict.

Tyler had secured the consent of Congress to the annexation of Texas, and his successor had only to complete the negotiations. But Oregon was acquired through Polk's own shrewd diplomacy, leading to an agreement with Great Britain to divide the region at the forty-ninth parallel. However, this aroused the Northwest, which believed literally in "54°40′ or Fight." Senator Hannegan of Indiana charged the South with "Punic faith" in thus yielding on Oregon after Texas was acquired, when the two had been "nursed and cradled in the same cradle." When the Senate ratified the Oregon treaty, William Allen of Ohio resigned as chairman of its Foreign Relations Committee.

Polk's attempts to settle the Texas boundary and to acquire California brought on the Mexican War. While there was slight opposition in Congress to the formal declaration, antiwar sentiment grew in the North. Antislavery men regarded the war as a proslavery affair; General Taylor's early victories seemed to be barren of results; Polk was not an inspiring leader; and the tariff and Treasury changes were at first unpopular. Consequently, a Whig Congress was elected in 1846.

The war also stirred up the smoldering dissensions in the President's own party. In August, 1846, David Wilmot, Pennsylvania Democrat, offered as an amendment to an appropriation bill the famous Proviso forbidding slavery in any territory obtained from Mexico. Jacob Brinkerhoff, an Ohio Congressman of Van Buren affiliations, may have originated it, but Wilmot, who was more friendly to the administration and had supported the annexation of Texas, sponsored it. Both Congressmen had patronage grievances. Northern Whigs and a group of northern Democrats forced it through the House but the session ended without a vote in the Senate. Preston King, a New York Barnburner, brought the Proviso up in the next session, and it continued to plague the White House Job to the end of his term, never passing the Senate but stirring up sectionalism and threatening to split both parties.

The New York Barnburners, at a seceding mass convention in October, 1847, accepted the principle of the Wilmot Proviso and appealed to antislavery men for support. The activities of "Prince John" Van Buren, the brilliant and ambitious son of the former President, and other aggrieved politicians make it clear that the antislavery ingredients were diluted with a certain amount of anti-administration animosity and with a larger amount of hatred toward their Hunker enemies in New York.

Northern Whigs supported the Proviso, while the southern wing opposed it; but both groups realized that the day of reckoning would come at their next national convention. A partial solution lay in the growing unpopularity of the war. Whigs of both sections used it to discredit the Polk administration in attacking the program of expansion through conquest. If nothing more was won than recognition by Mexico of the Rio Grande boundary, there would be no occasion to argue the slavery question. Eloquent Senator Tom Corwin of Ohio sounded off against the war in February, 1847, and expressed open sympathy with the Mexicans in one of the most extreme antiwar speeches ever delivered in Congress. But he was also moderately antislavery. More to the point were expressions of proslavery men like John M. Berrien and Alexander Stephens of Georgia and J. M. Clayton of Delaware, who attacked the dismemberment of Mexico as unjustified and productive of sectional discord in the United States. Clay in a speech at Lexington brought up resolutions against acquiring foreign territory "for the purpose of propagating slavery."

Successful termination of the war and ratification of the Treaty of Guadalupe Hidalgo left the Whig program of opposition high and dry. Congress was unable to agree upon any formula for organizing governments in newly acquired California and New Mexico, and left the riddle of sectional strife to the party conventions.

The Free Soilers Emerge

The Democrats at Baltimore on May 22, 1848, found the New York situation a harder problem than slavery. The Barnburners and the Hunkers sent separate sets of delegates. After long deliberation the convention voted by a bare majority of two to seat them both and thus divide equally the vote of the state. Both groups rejected this solution, and New York was unrepresented.

Senator Lewis Cass of Michigan was nominated for President on the fourth ballot over James Buchanan of Pennsylvania and Levi Woodbury of New Hampshire. General William O. Butler of Kentucky was named for Vice President. Cass, a New Englander by birth, had spent most of his adult life on the Ohio and Michigan frontiers in a variety of civil and military positions, including eighteen years as territorial governor of Michigan. Jackson had made him Secretary of War and Minister to France. A cautious elder statesman, who had opposed the Wilmot Proviso, he was one of the "doughfaces"—northern men with southern principles—and had declared in a letter to A. O. P. Nicholson for "squatter sovereignty," which Stephen A. Douglas later preferred to term "popular sovereignty." This would leave the decision of slavery in a territory to its voters.

The Democratic platform included resolutions defending the Mexican War, saluting the new French Republic, praising the acts of the Polk administration, and congratulating the President on "the brilliant success" of "his patriotic efforts." Yet not half a dozen delegates would have voted to renominate Polk. A resolution offered by William L. Yancey of Alabama upholding noninterference with property rights in states and territories was voted down.[3] Anxious to avoid the slavery pitfall, the convention did not even discuss the Wilmot Proviso. It had chosen a candidate popular in the Northwest and satisfactory to the South. Only the Barnburner defection marred its harmony; but this was serious.

The war failed the Whigs as an issue for 1848, but it furnished them with two potential candidates. Generals Winfield Scott and Zachary Taylor, sensing early in the war that the path of military glory might lead to the White House, had been as temperamental as prima donnas toward the harassed Polk and toward each other. Scott, an able soldier, was no novice in politics. Years of residence at Washington had given him a knowledge of politicians and their ways; and he had been considered for the Whig nomination in 1840. But he was vainglorious, at times asininely pompous, and lacked discretion and common sense in nonmilitary matters. Taylor, a less capable soldier, was brave, unsophisticated, poorly educated, roughhewn. Scott came to be known as "Old Fuss and Feathers"; Taylor, as "Old Rough and Ready" or "Old Zach." The Whigs naturally turned to Taylor. This unspoiled old soldier, mistreated—so they charged—by the Polk administration, was the candidate needed to cover up their lack of unity. Public meetings, some of them nonpolitical, offered him as a Presidential candidate long before the convention met. Now in his sixty-fourth year and without previous political affiliation, "Old

[3] It went much further than a resolution repeated from the platform of 1844, readopted by this convention, declaring Congress had no power to control the domestic institutions of any state and disapproving of all efforts to induce Congress to interfere with slavery.

Zach" had never voted. He regarded himself as a people's choice and announced that he would run, regardless of what the national convention did; but astute Whig leaders guided him into their camp. His "Allison Letter," composed by Congressman Logan Hunton, was produced to confirm his orthodoxy as a Whig.

Henry Clay, stirred by the unpopularity of the Polk administration and the war, began to look longingly again at the prize that had eluded him so long. Tremendous crowds when he traveled through the East misled him into allowing his name to be used once more; but the party politicians were not moved by popular acclaim—Clay had always drawn crowds. Even the faithful Crittenden was convinced that he could not win. The Whigs of the South, so long his loyal friends, were now ready to trust Taylor, a Louisiana slaveholder. When the national convention met at Philadelphia on June 7, Old Zach was well in the lead. The first ballot gave him 111 votes; Clay, 97; Scott, 43; Webster, 22; others, 6. On the fourth ballot Taylor was nominated, and Clay's vote fell to 32. Millard Fillmore of New York was named for second place on the ticket.

To avoid sectional discord, no platform was made. But all was not harmonious. The Whig party contained a strong antislavery element, particularly in New England, New York, and Ohio, and when a motion to indorse the Wilmot Proviso was tabled by a large majority there were threats of a bolt. Even outside the antislavery group, there was ill concealed dissatisfaction. Webster, who had spurned a suggestion that he run for Vice President, and had called Taylor "an illiterate frontier colonel," declared the nomination an unfit one. Only late in the campaign did he make speeches for the ticket. Clay never did. But their discontent was confined to private fumings and fulminations. The earnest antislavery men went ahead with plans to bolt.

The Liberty party held its convention in New York City in November, 1847, and nominated John P. Hale of New Hampshire and Leicester King of Ohio.[4] However, its abolitionist composition repelled Whigs and Democrats who regarded the anti-extension principle of the Wilmot Proviso as sufficiently radical. The situation seemed to call for a new third party, broad enough to include all the dissenters. The first step was taken in June, 1848, by a state mass convention at Columbus, Ohio, which called a national convention to

[4] A Liberty League and an Industrial Congress held national conventions and nominated Gerrit Smith of New York for President but made no campaign.

meet at Buffalo, August 9. The dissatisfied of other northern states began to elect delegates.

In Massachusetts divisions between "Cotton" and "Conscience" Whigs rent the party asunder. Robert Winthrop, Rufus Choate, Abbott Lawrence, and the "Olympian Daniel"—representing the lords of the loom—led the conservatives; Charles Sumner, Charles Francis Adams, Henry Wilson, and the younger men, moralists and keepers of the Puritan conscience, wended their way to Buffalo to join the heretics.

The Barnburners in convention at Utica, New York, nominated Van Buren for President on a Wilmot Proviso platform. The death of Silas Wright had deprived them of their strongest leader, and Van Buren reluctantly agreed to return to the political wars. John Van Buren, B. F. Butler, Preston King, John A. Dix, William Cullen Bryant, David Dudley Field, and other familiar figures in New York liberal Democratic politics, compounding Locofoco ideals with antislavery sympathies and revenge motives, prepared to take the Barnburners into the Buffalo movement. In the West men of the stamp of Salmon P. Chase and Joshua R. Giddings were organizing for the crusade.

At the enthusiastic Buffalo meeting in August eighteen states were represented, including three slave states. In a huge tent, the perspiring delegates, of Whig, Democratic and abolitionist persuasion, put aside their differences to organize the Free Soil party. Hale had already received the Liberty nomination; Van Buren, the Barnburner; and some antislavery Whigs had been sounding out Justice John McLean of the Supreme Court, who was too wary to commit himself. The Barnburners—by far the shrewdest politicians present—insisted on Van Buren, and their favorite was named over Hale by a vote of 244 to 181. The radical antislavery men, more concerned over principles, acquiesced in a candidate whose conduct they had deplored more than once in the past. Charles Francis Adams, Conscience Whig and son of John Quincy Adams, was named for second place.

The platform pledged the new Free Soil party against any extension of slavery; denied the power of Congress to establish slavery anywhere or, on the other hand, to interfere with the institution within a state; favored cheap postage, river and harbor improvements, free public lands to actual settlers, and a revenue tariff. Its motto was, "Free Soil, Free Speech, Free Labor, and Free Men." In advocating free homesteads for the public lands, the party appealed to eastern labor as well as to western farmers. For years labor groups had been advocating free land for the landless as a solution of the labor problem, giving every man a chance to become an independent farmer. Yet it was in line with the Jackson-Benton idea of cheap land and projected into the Free Soil movement a frontier ideal which alone would imperil any hope of southern control of the trans-Mississippi West. In its antislavery and its public-land policies it was a forerunner of the Republican party of Lincoln and Seward.

The Free Soilers waged a strenuous campaign to attract antislavery Whigs and Van Buren Democrats. With the former they were less successful. Though the Conscience Whigs in Massachusetts and Giddings and his following in Ohio lent aid, William H. Seward of New York and Tom Corwin of Ohio took the stump to allay antislavery dissatisfaction in Whig ranks. Van Buren's name had no attractions for northern Whigs, and many, doubting his sincerity, were persuaded that Taylor's opposition to the veto power would permit the Wilmot Proviso to become law if Congress passed it. The Free Soil movement played havoc with the New York Democracy but did only slight damage elsewhere. Wilmot, Brinkerhoff, and the Blair family joined the revolt; but Benton, embarrassed by a proslavery backfire at home, remained regular. Former Governor Marcus Morton of Massachusetts favored Van Buren but not the third party. Cass was popular in the Northwest, where he was not regarded as proslavery, and held most of the Democrats in line. He was the first Democratic Presidential candidate from that section, and it proved loyal to him.

Both the major parties fought sectional, rather than national, campaigns. The Whigs of the South argued that southern rights were secure only if a southerner sat in the White House. The Democrats defended Cass as "safe" on slavery and warned that Taylor might die in office, bringing Fillmore, possessor of an antislavery past, into the White House. In view of what actually happened, this has a curious significance. In the North, Democrats praised Cass as faithful to northern interests and asked how antislavery Whigs could stomach Taylor. The Whig answer was to call Cass a doughface and to argue that the North would control a Whig Congress.

The election, the first to be held on the same day everywhere, gave Taylor 163 electoral votes, Cass 127. Taylor carried Massachusetts, Vermont, Connecticut, Rhode Island, New York, Pennsylvania, and New Jersey in the North; the usual Whig states in the upper

South, Delaware, Maryland, Tennessee, Kentucky and North Carolina; and Georgia, Louisiana, and Florida in the lower South. Cass carried Maine, New Hampshire, all of the Northwest (Ohio, Indiana, Illinois, Michigan, Wisconsin, Iowa), and seven slave states (Missouri, Arkansas, Texas, Alabama, Mississippi, Virginia, and South Carolina). Taylor ran well in the usual Whig areas of the South and gained noticeably over Clay's vote of 1844 in the small farmer sections, where his personality seemed to be reminiscent of Andrew Jackson. Pennsylvania, disgruntled over Polk's revenue tariff, and New York, lost through the Barnburner bolt, bitterly disappointed the Democrats. In New York, Taylor received 218,603 votes; Cass, 114,318; Van Buren, 120,510. A united Democracy apparently could have defeated Taylor, though it must not be forgotten that a Liberty party vote was concealed in the Van Buren total and might, as in 1844, have held the balance. Taylor's pluralities were generally larger than those for Cass and his popular vote totaled 1,360,099 to his rival's 1,220,544 and Van Buren's 291,263.

The Free Soilers, though their vote fell below their early expectations, had the satisfaction of holding the balance of power in eleven states and in the national House of Representatives, where they won thirteen seats. The Ohio legislature, controlled by a coalition of Free Soilers and Democrats, sent Salmon P. Chase, Free Soiler, to the United States Senate.

The Politicians Make Peace

On March 5, 1849 (the 4th fell on Sunday), a strangely contrasted pair rode to the Capitol together: the stocky old soldier, roughhewn and unsophisticated, the most ignorant and inexperienced man yet chosen to the chief office, and the slight, studious-looking Polk, who had acquired a proud mastery of every detail of the Presidency. What consternation must have swept over the ardent expansionist to hear the general's casual remark that Oregon and California were too remote to become states, and that they would be better off independent! But he did not live to see the new President develop his policies. Exhaustion from hard work and chronic diarrhea ended Polk's worries forever three months later.

In the new House of Representatives the Free Soilers held the balance of power, and only after a bitter struggle was a speaker elected, by a plurality. Howell Cobb, Georgia Democrat, was the man. But sectional, rather than party, interests governed Congress, and slavery in the newly acquired Southwest was the burning issue. Taylor's first message offered a "nonaction" policy. He would have Congress merely recognize the *de facto* state government already set up in California, and act similarly on New Mexico, which was soon to hold a constitutional convention. This would remove the vexatious question of slavery in the territories from the halls of Congress; but it would mean two new free states, as slavery did not exist in the Mexican cession. The proposal was well received in the North; but the South, despite state-rights doctrines, would have none of it. Southern Whigs—notably Toombs and Stephens of Georgia—drew away from the slaveholding President, who seemed to be unduly influenced by antislavery Senator Seward of New York and his office broker, Thurlow Weed. Genial Seward was a welcome visitor at the White House, receiving federal patronage that the skillful Weed passed out, to the annoyance of Vice President Fillmore, his bitter enemy.

The ultimate solution was drawn up by Henry Clay—back in his old seat in the Senate, political ambitions ended—in a compromise to take care of all the sectional issues in the Congressional hopper, which was nearly full. He proposed to appease the North by admitting California as a free state and abolishing the slave trade (but not slavery) in the District of Columbia; to give the South a stricter fugitive slave law; to assign to New Mexico a border area disputed with Texas, which would receive a large money payment from the federal government; and to divide New Mexico into two territories, leaving the legality of slavery in them to the determination of the courts. Clay's skill in piecing together in one framework proposals already made by others, and his great prestige in both sections, sent the compromise on its way through the Senate with Webster, Cass, Douglas, and other moderates of both parties working with him. Douglas was particularly effective in parliamentary management, but Webster attracted the most attention with his famous Seventh-of-March speech, which drew public letters and addresses of thanks, and even gifts from substantial citizens, and vilification from antislavery radicals.

In the opposition were southern rights men, such as Calhoun and Jefferson Davis, and the northern sectionalists Seward and Chase. Calhoun, too ill to deliver his own speech, listened while Senator Mason read it on March 4. Before the month was out he was dead.

But the greatest obstacle to compromise was President Taylor. He held to nonaction on California and New Mexico and, with northern support, was prepared to defy the southern disunionists. The Great Compromise seemed to be stalled.

Then Fate intervened. Taylor unwisely exposed himself to the hot sun at a Fourth of July celebration, drank iced drinks, and was taken suddenly ill with cramps. The illness soon took a more serious turn—possibly it was typhoid fever—and in five days he was dead.

Millard Fillmore, handsome, middle-aged, statesmanlike in appearance, whose political fortunes seemed to have struck bottom with his enemies Seward and Weed in the ascendant both at Washington and at home, suddenly found himself in the driver's seat. Cautious, conservative, friendly to Clay, he dropped Taylor's policy and threw the weight of the administration behind the Compromise after putting Daniel Webster at the head of a new cabinet. Douglas of Illinois took over for feeble, weary Clay, and the various Compromise measures were put through by a bipartisan combination.

Antislavery radicals staged public meetings in the fall to protest against the new Fugitive Slave Law, but these were more than counter-balanced by great bipartisan Union gatherings in the larger northern cities. There was even talk of a Union party to support the Compromise. In the South, radical southern rights men, chiefly Democrats, agitated for disunion, believing that most of the benefits of the Compromise went to the North; but when a Unionist coalition captured control of a convention called in Georgia to consider secession they lost heart. The booming prosperity of the early fifties, an excellent sedative for sectionalist nerves, was a great factor against radicalism in both North and South.

The Compromise struggle split both parties, but the Whigs were the worse off. The elections of 1850-1851 showed general Democratic gains. Senator Seward and Governor William F. Johnston, controlling the Whig organizations in New York and Pennsylvania, were critical of the Compromise settlement, and so was Horace Greeley, editor of the increasingly influential *New York Tribune*. A House resolution in the Congress of 1851-1852 indorsing the finality of the Compromise had the support of only seven out of forty-two northern Whigs, though two-thirds of the northern Democrats voted for it. Southern Whigs, struggling to checkmate southern rights extremists in their own section, were dismayed at the anti-Compromise tendencies of the northern wing, and some turned toward the Democrats; most of them, reluctant to abandon the old ship, awaited the national convention.

The Whig national convention, held at Baltimore on June 16, made genuine concessions to southern members. The platform accepted the principle of state rights, "acquiesced in" the Compromise measures, and deprecated further agitation. Sixty-six northern delegates, favoring the nomination of General Scott, voted against the Compromise plank. Other northerners seemed to be willing to concede the platform to the South in order to get southern support for Scott. The balloting was long drawn out. Nearly all the northern delegates outside New England voted for Scott; the southerners voted for Fillmore, and most of New England for Webster. On the first ballot, Fillmore had 133 votes; Scott, 131; Webster, 29. With little change forty-nine ballots were taken. Then "Old Fuss and Feathers" began to gain, and he was nominated on the fifty-third with 159 votes, 12 more than a majority. Fillmore would have withdrawn in favor of Webster, but a little group of his supporters from the border states favored Scott as their second choice. Webster's friends were asked to raise their total to 41; Fillmore could then safely withdraw and transfer his bloc to the elder statesman. But Seward, directing the Scott forces, held them intact; Webster could not reach 41, and in the end went down to defeat, heartbroken. William A. Graham of North Carolina, Secretary of the Navy, received second place on the ticket.

The Democrats had already met at Baltimore on June 1, with unity largely restored. The Barnburners had come back; Benton and the Blairs were again loyal; and all shades of opinion were present, from southern rights men to former Free Soilers. But, even with a large field of candidates, finding a man to suit the wide diversity of views was not easy. Party veterans active since Jackson's day were in the lead. Cass, nearly seventy, sluggish and stout, bore no grudge for his defeat in 1848 and was not overeager to be named but had a large following of northern Compromise men. Buchanan, far more eager, had added to Pennsylvania a large southern rights support by his silence on the Compromise and his past record. Marcy of New York, astute and able, had Barnburner aid but was opposed by Senator Dickinson and some of the Hunkers. A brash newcomer, Senator Stephen A. Douglas of Illinois, threatened the prospects of these "Old Fogies" by collecting a motley crew of land and railroad speculators, lobbyists for government favors, and a "Young America" group favoring expansion and an aggressive, even interventionist, foreign policy to encourage democratic revolutions in the Old World. The "Little Giant"—he was five feet, four inches tall, squat, short-legged, and had a huge head—overplayed his hand and antagonized the older men. The two-thirds rule eventually killed off all the leading candidates and produced the darkest of all dark horses, Franklin Pierce of New Hampshire. His friend Edmund Burke had been carefully cultivating support in the South and keeping the good will of friends of all the candidates. On the forty-ninth ballot the weary delegates, most of whom had never heard of Pierce before the convention, stampeded to him. William R. King, Senator from Alabama, was named to run with him.

The platform, mostly a repetition of that of 1848, added a pledge to "abide by, and adhere to" the Compromise measures including the Fugitive Slave Law, and to resist all attempts to renew the slavery agitation. The convention had successfully surmounted all its difficulties, but the query "Who is Franklin Pierce?" was genuine, not a Whig sneer. The nominee had to be explained to the voters, though his availability could not have been higher. Forty-seven years old, handsome, friendly, once a victim of the liquor habit but now a good temperance man, he was a fluent speaker and had no enemies to conciliate and no record to explain away. He had served in both houses of Congress without particular distinction, retiring before sectional issues became acute. He had a Mexican War record as a brave but not brilliant officer. Every element in the party seemed to be pleased with its good-looking New Hampshire nonentity. The Van Burens and the Blairs rejoiced with the southern rights men over the defeat of the leading Compromise candidates, while Compromisers were happy that Pierce and the platform were right on the Compromise.

But the Whigs had no reason to rejoice. Southern party members were disappointed in Scott's letter of acceptance, which merely accepted the nomination "with the resolutions annexed," making no specific mention of the Compromise or the Fugitive Slave Law. To make matters worse, Seward's warm support convinced them of the candidate's unsoundness on slavery. Had not the wily New Yorker drawn poor General Taylor, himself a slaveholder, into his web? Stephens, Toombs, and a few other members of Congress formally repudiated Scott; others were silent, and nowhere in the lower South was there much enthusiasm. Some Georgia bolters, led by Stephens, ran a Webster electoral ticket; elsewhere the dissatisfied either voted Democratic or stayed away from the polls. In the North, Webster's friends were unreconciled to Scott, and those in Massachusetts would have supported a separate electoral ticket but for the great orator's death in October. His bitterness had caused him to hope for Pierce's election. The "higher law" Whigs, as they were dubbed after Seward's Senate speech against the Compromise, were enthusiastic for Scott but not the platform. As Greeley put it, accepting the nominee, they "spit upon the platform."

Yet the Free Soil men had no use for Scott or his platform. In Ohio the Ashtabula *Sentinel*, organ of the redoubtable Giddings, declared, "We do not desire to smuggle antislavery men or measures into the coming or any administration." The third party, under the name Free Democratic, held its national convention at Pittsburgh in August and nominated John P. Hale of New Hampshire for President and George W. Julian of Indiana for Vice President. The platform attacked slavery, condemned the Compromise and the Fugitive Slave Law, and indorsed a number of proposals including the homestead policy, cheap postage, river and harbor improvements, and international arbitration. The Barnburners had gone back to the Democrats, leaving behind hardly more than the old Liberty men and some unreconciled antislavery Whigs. Senator Chase of Ohio, after consorting with the Democrats for a year, returned to the fold. Charles Sumner, elected from Massachusetts to the Senate by a coalition of Democrats and Free Soilers in 1851, was the eastern leader.

The campaign was issueless, spiritless, and hopelessly dull. The Whigs made a strong bid for Irish Catholic support, as General Scott's daughters had attended church schools and one, now deceased, had become a nun. He declared in favor of citizenship for foreign-born soldiers after a year of wartime service. The Democrats retaliated with an unwise nativist letter he had written ten years before, and accused him of executing German and Irish soldiers in the Mexican War. The Whigs happily discovered a clause in the New Hampshire constitution disqualifying Catholics from officeholding and blamed Pierce for it. Quotations from English newspapers approving the Democratic low-tariff attitude were reprinted in Whig newspapers to arouse anti-British feeling in Irish breasts. Pamphlets in German were circulated by Whig postmasters. Politicians were aware of the swelling tide of immigration and its political import.

Efforts of both parties to revive the tariff question and to arouse interest in foreign policies accomplished little, and the campaign degenerated further into personalities. Pierce was charged with cowardice in the Mexican War and with habitual drunkenness. Scott, an imposing figure in military regalia, was ridiculed as a pompous ass, and he almost demonstrated this in an ill disguised electioneering tour of the North; his military career was belittled; and the dangers of electing a soldier despot were held before the voters. On this exalted plane ended one of the dullest campaigns in American history.

The Democrats triumphed by a landslide. Scott salvaged only Massachusetts and Vermont and the border Whig states of Kentucky and Tennessee—42 electoral votes. Pierce had all the rest—a total of 254. The popular vote was: Pierce, 1,601,274; Scott, 1,386,580; and Hale, 155,825.[5] The country was voting to uphold the Compromise. The Democratic stand was clearer, and the candidate safer, on this issue. The decline of the third-party vote is additional proof of the revulsion against agitation. More businessmen and more planters voted Democratic than in any previous election, while large numbers of conservatives gave only perfunctory support to Scott or had refused to vote. The Democratic party, divested of Jacksonian radicalism, was now safe for men of property.

The Whig party was demoralized. Had Webster or Fillmore been nominated the defeat would have been as bad. Thousands of northern Whigs would have repudiated the Compromise nominee, just as the southerners had rejected Scott. With its most available candidate, the party had suffered its worst defeat. Clay's Compromise had saved the Union but had wrecked the party whose foundations he had laid twenty years before. It might have passed away in any case. The growing moral sentiment against slavery, nurtured in Protestant churches, was stirring the middle classes, the backbone of Whiggery. The party was splitting apart in the North. In New England, there were Cotton and Conscience Whigs; in New York, Woolly Heads and Silver Grays; in other places, "higher law" and "lower law" Whigs. The conservatives who sought to repair the breach between the sections were pale reflections of Clay and Webster: Fillmore, Everett of Massachusetts, Bell of Tennessee, Crittenden of Kentucky, all were thin-blooded elder statesmen. The task required dynamic leadership, and this they lacked. Whiggery had gone to seed.

[5] Thirty-one states voted, California having been added in 1850. Webster had 7,425; Troup (Southern Rights), 3,300; Broom (Native American), 4,485.

10

The Republican Party Is Born

Pierce, Douglas, and Co.

The weather on March 4, 1853, was abominable—a gray March day with a raw wind whipping snow into the faces of the cheering thousands—but the handsome new President made a fine impression, speaking, not reading, his inaugural with a fluency and confidence acquired by years of courtroom practice and stump speaking before critical New England audiences. He unhesitatingly indorsed the Compromise measures, pleasing conservatives, and committed his administration in general to expansion and the ideal of America's "manifest destiny," pleasing the "Young America" zealots and southerners who looked toward Cuba. Even from antislavery sources there was little open criticism. Blessed with prosperity and sectional peace and backed by impressive majorities in Congress, Franklin Pierce began with prospects more favorable than had greeted any President since Monroe.

But President and Mrs. Pierce may have been the unhappiest pair in Washington. Their only son, thirteen years old, had been killed before their eyes in a tragic accident not two months before the inauguration. The White House was a mansion of sorrow, and its new tenant was in no fit frame of mind to cope with the heavy burdens of his position.

Despite an overwhelming triumph in 1852, the party of Jackson was in an unhealthy condition. The Cincinnati *Enquirer*, in contrasting the two parties, expressed happily the traditional viewpoint of the average faithful Democrat toward his party: "The one is full of Veneration and Fear. The other is strong with Courage and Hope. The one adores and consecrates Institutions. The other worships Ideas. The one temporizes with petty and patched up expedients. The other, with the determination and remorselessness of Fate, with the undeviating needle of Logic, explores the wide, illimitable theory of Truth." The writer of these lofty sentiments would have needed more than the lantern of Diogenes to discover Ideas and Truth in Washington in the weeks just before and after the inaugural. He would have found Courage and Hope only in the breasts of office seekers. In the mad scramble for spoils the victors seemed to be hardly more than a loose collection of splinter factions that had held together with difficulty until the election and now were battling one another for government jobs and handouts.

Pierce tried to be geographically correct and factionally wise in naming his cabinet. It was headed by the New York political veteran William L. Marcy as Secretary of State, but Jefferson Davis of Mississippi, Secretary of War, was more influential with the President. In the lesser positions, harmony was difficult to attain.

In New York the dominant Hunker faction had split into Softshells and Hard-shells over readmitting the bolting Barnburners of 1848 to party fellowship. Marcy leaned Softward, former Senator Daniel S. Dickinson headed the Hards. The Hards landed the prize plum, the collectorship of the port of New York, but the appointee proved to be so unrelenting toward the Softs that he was soon removed. The two factions then held separate state conventions and thereby handed victory in the fall elections to the Whigs. In Ohio bitterness within the party eliminated a prominent Democrat from consideration for the cabinet.

Soon after Congress met in December, 1853, Senator Douglas of Illinois, influential spokesman for western railroad interests, wrecked the President's hopes for party harmony and sectional peace. Douglas seems to have been interested primarily in a Pacific railroad when he brought up his Nebraska bill. He wanted the government to subsidize a northern road with Chicago as its eastern terminus. To accomplish this, the Indian country west of Missouri must be organized as a territory and opened to settlement. The Missouri Compromise of 1820 had forbidden slavery north of 36°30′, and southern members of Congress and Secretary of War Davis, more interested in the southern route for a railroad, were unenthusiastic over his bill. Douglas, intent on the immediate problem, then accepted a proposal of Senator Atchison of Missouri[1] to remove the restriction

[1] Senator Atchison was president pro tempore of the Senate, and—Vice President King having died—would have become President in the event of Pierce's death. He was involved in a bitter struggle in his home state with former Senator Benton.

on slavery and let the people of the territory settle the matter for themselves—popular sovereignty, he called it. Expecting a storm of opposition from antislavery men, he hastened to secure Presidential sanction. On a fateful Sunday in January, 1854, Pierce yielded to the persuasions of Douglas, Atchison, and others and agreed to the repeal of the Missouri Compromise, one of the costliest blunders in White House history. The bill was also changed to provide for two territories, Kansas and Nebraska.

Even the astute Little Giant underestimated the violence of the opposition. The Senate passed the bill easily enough but the storm raged in the House of Representatives until May. Party lines were shattered. Defying administration pressure, forty-three northern Democrats joined northern Whigs and Free Soilers against the bill. Southern Democrats and Whigs and the administration bloc from the North provided the votes that carried it. The sectional controversy had been reopened, and the Democratic party was threatened with demoralization. The man most responsible was neither an abolitionist nor a fire-eater, but an ardent believer in compromise, who insisted that he was merely extending the principles of the Compromise of 1850 to the Nebraska country. He was caught in a Congressional snake pit of sectional, factional, and personal rivalries, and tried to provide the leadership that should have come from the President.

Antislavery men seized upon the hated measure as manna from a proslavery heaven. Here was proof of the diabolical plottings of the never satisfied slavocrats who, with their Douglas allies, would ban freedom in the territories and endanger it in the whole North.

The tocsin was sounded on January 24 when the "Appeal of the Independent Democrats in Congress to the People of the United States" appeared. Giddings, a veteran antislavery Congressman, sketched the first draft; but Senator Chase was its chief author, assisted by Charles Sumner, Free Soil Senator from Massachusetts, and Gerrit Smith, Congressman from New York and avowed abolitionist. Two other Congressmen signed it. It denounced the Nebraska bill as "part and parcel of an atrocious plot" to exclude free labor from the new territory and convert it into "a dreary region of despotism inhabited by masters and slaves." More logically, it argued that the principles of the Compromise of 1850 had never been intended to apply to the Nebraska region or to disturb the Missouri Compromise. Here clearly was the weak point in Douglas's proposal

—the attempt to associate the measure with the Compromise of 1850; but the authors of the Appeal marred their logic with much inflammatory rhetoric. Published in northern newspapers, it accomplished all its authors could have hoped. Whig, Free Soil, and even many Democratic papers assailed Douglas and his bill; mass meetings were held in protest, and a political hurricane swept the North before the measure passed the Senate.

The Triumph of the Isms

In the Old Northwest came the first stirrings of a new party. This requires a brief explanation. Many northwestern Democrats had been out of harmony with the party's leadership since Polk's day. His failure to press the American claim to all of Oregon, his veto of a rivers and harbors bill especially popular in the lake area, Cass's defeat in 1848, attributed by northwesterners to lukewarm southern support, and a widespread feeling that the West had been neglected in patronage matters were old sores. Pierce also vetoed a rivers and harbors bill in 1854, and frowned on land grants for western railroads, while the strongly Democratic Senate killed a much desired homestead bill. Antislavery and pro-homestead Democrats, including many Germans, regarded the Nebraska bill as further evidence of proslavery—and administration—hostility toward the expansion of the free North. Simmering insurgency turned into open revolt, and thousands of Democrats looked to a new party to realize Jacksonian ideals.

In the Northwest the Whig party was disintegrating. It had carried but one state in three Presidential elections (Ohio, in 1844). Lacking the more solid social and economic basis of eastern Whiggery, it was ready to abandon its separate existence and make common cause with new allies on new issues. Experienced Whig politicians, Whig newspapers, Whig local machines, and Whig votes provided a ready-made framework for a new opposition party. The almost insuperable problem of a new party, creation of a grass-roots organization, offered no difficulties in the Northwest. The new Republican party was never a third party. Its transmutation from Whiggery was immediate. Whig policies, however, were soft-pedaled.

But the crusading zeal and humanitarian idealism of the new reform movement came chiefly from the Liberty and Free Soil men. Undismayed by the Barnburner defections after 1848, they continued an unrelenting battle against compromise with slavery and were ready, when the Nebraska crisis came, to join old enemies on the one principle of opposition to slavery in the territories. They put aside abolition for another day. As one editor wrote, "If men offer to join us in doing that which is good, without requiring us to join in anything wrong in return, shall we refuse because they do not offer to do all the good things we would like to accomplish?"

One other factor had been pulling the Northwest slowly and steadily away from its old partnership with the South. For some years a heavy migration from New England and New York had been flowing into the lake region, tying it commercially and culturally with the Northeast. The railroads of the 1850's were to strengthen these bonds. In the upper Northwest the anti-Nebraska cause received its warmest welcome. The Ohio valley still looked southward.

Numerous local meetings paved the way for fusion among antislavery men before the Kansas-Nebraska bill was passed. One at Ripon, Wisconsin, on March 1, 1854, led by Alvan E. Bovay, has been acclaimed as the first to propose independent political action; but others were taking similar steps almost simultaneously. A state-wide convention of several thousand voters, in an oak grove at Jackson, Michigan, on July 6, organized the first state party and named candidates for state offices. Wisconsin, Ohio, and Indiana followed with conventions on July 13—anniversary of the Ordinance of 1787, which forbade slavery in the Northwest. In Illinois there was no formal fusion of the opposition but a reasonably effective cooperation.

The Michigan convention adopted the name "Republican." A. E. Bovay had proposed it to Greeley, who suggested it in the New York *Tribune* on June 16; but other origins have been claimed for it. In any case, it simply revived the good old Jeffersonian name, which had been dropped by the Democrats in Jackson's day. Chase, who regarded himself as an "Independent Democrat," would have adopted the name "Democratic," a confusing choice, and would have called the old party the "Slave Democracy." However, the name "Republican" did not come into general use at once. "People's Movement," "Anti-Nebraska," "Reform," and other terms were applied to the fusionists. The Democrats at first preferred to call all the opposition "Know-Nothing," connecting it with antiforeignism, but presently began to use the term "Black Republican."

This anti-Nebraska movement, a crazy-quilt of parties and classes with a variety of reforms, discontents, and personal ambitions—Abolitionists, Clay Whigs, Jackson Democrats, disappointed politicians, Know-Nothings, Germans, temperance reformers, land reformers, and even businessmen dissatisfied with Democratic state administrations—swept to an amazing victory in the six northwestern states. Even the weather plagued the Democrats. A terrible drought in the summer and fall of 1854 made the farmers aggrieved at the world including the party in power. Douglas returned to Illinois and fought desperately to restore his party's shattered morale. At Chicago on a Saturday night a huge crowd heckled the undaunted orator and interrupted with angry yells and groans while he struggled to state his case. A story of uncertain authenticity has it that, after midnight, he defiantly ended: "Abolitionists of Chicago! It is now Sunday morning. I'll go to church, and you may go to hell." The defeat at the Illinois polls was bad enough: Five of the nine Congressmen elect, and the legislature which was to choose a Senator were anti-Nebraska. In the rest of the Northwest the rout was worse: the anti-Nebraska state tickets won everywhere, and the great majority of the Congressional candidates. Ohio's entire delegation was of the new faith.

In this major triumph an insidious silent partner was creeping in from the East. Know-Nothingism was making its bid for power. On the Atlantic seaboard the broth of nativism, which had long been simmering, boiled over with amazing suddenness. For years eastern cities had had occasional outbursts of antiforeignism—usually anti-Catholicism. Local parties had won temporary victories around 1843–1844 and had supported the Whig national ticket in 1844. A Pennsylvania Native American party, with slight strength outside Philadelphia, functioned for several years. A "national" convention of one hundred delegates from six eastern states and Ohio at Philadelphia in September, 1847, proposed Zachary Taylor for President, but was disrupted over a resolution that only native-born should be citizens. The party persisted in a few localities until July, 1852, when a handful of delegates from nine states at Trenton, New Jersey, named Daniel Webster for President. Webster's failure to decline was construed as an acceptance; but he died in October, and Jacob Broom was chosen by the national committee to run. His vote was insignificant.

But the situation was ripe for a new movement. Thousands of Whigs, discouraged at their defeat in 1852 and angry at the foreign-born for rebuffing their blandishments, were ready to embrace nativism. Lacking unity on the slavery issue, they sought to ignore sectionalism and raise questions that would divide and distract the Democrats. The Know-Nothing movement added to and profited from the political confusion of 1854. Many anti-Nebraska men in the East joined the nativists.

While Know-Nothingism sprouted out of party chaos, it was more than political opportunism. Many good Americans were alarmed at the tidal wave of immigration. Poverty-stricken Irish peasants settled in the slums of eastern cities, competed with native American labor, drank too much whiskey, added to the problems of pauperism and crime, mobbed anti-Catholic orators, and were herded to the polls by Democratic ward bosses, sometimes without the formality of naturalization papers. Although the Germans were less unpopular they were the despair of temperance reformers, and their beer gardens failed to observe the Puritan Sabbath. German radicals were classed as "Red Republicans" and atheists; and nearly all Germans were stubborn Democrats, though their party allegiance was not so fixed as that of the Irish.

Antiforeignism, however, played second fiddle to anti-Catholicism in the Know-Nothing movement. For many years professional Catholic-baiting editors, lecturers, writers, unfrocked priests, and "escaped" nuns had been appealing to prejudices and love of sensationalism with "exposures" of the evils and dangers of Popery, and the American Bible Society and other Protestant organizations had been propagandizing against the religion of Rome. Suggestions from Catholic sources that parochial schools receive part of the common-school funds, and protests against the reading of the Protestant Bible in the public schools, had fed the flames of anti-Catholicism. The hostility of Pope Pius IX toward liberalism and revolutionary movements in Europe stirred foreign-born liberals as well as anti-Catholic Americans, and when Archbishop Bedini, the papal nuncio, arrived in the United States in 1853, a trail of riots marked his tour. President Pierce's appointment of a Catholic as Postmaster General damned the administration in the eyes of Protestant bigots.

The secret Order of the Star-Spangled Banner supplanted earlier nativist organizations, and from it emerged the political party called "Know-Nothing" because members answered "I don't know" to queries of outsiders. With degrees, a ritual and a requirement of secrecy, the new order appealed mightily to the "joining" propensities of many Americans who might otherwise have been unaware of the "Jesuit peril." Within a few months in 1854 the new secret order became a power in politics, upsetting the calculations of the old-party leaders in the East and adding its volume to the anti-Nebraska wave that was just preceding it in the Northwest.

The Know-Nothing order spread southward in the spring and summer of 1854. The adoption by the national council of a Union oath as part of its ritual in November, 1854, at the instance of Kenneth Rayner, a North Carolina Whig, appealed to southern Whigs and helped the progress of the movement. It appeared as a Union-saving force which might draw together conservatives of both sections in a revived Whig party under the Know-Nothing name. But it also had a sectional appeal. While the border slave states and Louisiana had enough foreign-born to feel the nativist ferment, most of the South did not come into direct contact with immigrants. Rather, the slave section feared the alien influx because the foreign-born provided the North with a surplus population to fill up the vacant lands of the West. Southern Congressmen supported amendments to both the Nebraska and the homestead bills to exclude unnaturalized foreigners from their benefits. Northerners, by sending to Nebraska and Kansas the first half-dozen shiploads of immigrants arriving after the passage of the Nebraska bill, might give them an antislavery character for all time, argued a southern newspaper.

While there was much vague talk of "Americanism" as the fundamental principle of the new movement,[2] its concrete aims were to extend the naturalization period to twenty-one years, to place some restrictions on immigration, to exclude Catholics and foreign-born from office, and to support the use of the Protestant Bible in the public schools.

As if Know-Nothingism and Black Republicanism were not enough to muddy the political waters, the enemies of Demon Rum in several states decided that their hour had struck. Out of Maine in 1851 had come the Maine Law agitation to put a legal end to the liquor traffic by state action. Years of activity by various temperance societies preceded the plunge into politics. With state prohibition as its aim, the movement was essentially local; but it upset the calculations of party leaders. Independent candidates, Maine Law tickets, and anti-liquor pledges by party nominees were used to advance the cause. Free Soilers, enthusiastic for moral reforms, favored the movement;

[2] The Know-Nothings were popularly termed "Sams."

Whigs—in general, middle-class Protestant churchgoers—were usually friendly; Democrats, with some exceptions, hostile. Workingmen wanted their liquor; the Irish and Germans were insistent on this point, and the Democratic party refused to meddle. When the anti-Nebraska movement got under way, Maine Law men usually joined it or made fusion arrangements for state offices, as in New York, Maine, and Vermont.

The Know-Nothing, Maine Law, and anti-Nebraska uprisings played havoc with the old parties in the East. A Seward Whig, anti-Nebraska, temperance combination carried New York State against Democrats and Know-Nothings—the latter, mostly anti-Seward Whigs. In Pennsylvania an alliance of Whigs and Know-Nothings drew anti-Nebraska support and won. In Massachusetts the Know-Nothings ran roughshod over Whigs, Democrats, and a little Republican group. Fusion parties, in which temperance was a factor, carried Maine and Vermont. Connecticut and Rhode Island voted Whig in the spring, and New Hampshire elected an anti-Nebraska legislature. The trend was certainly anti-Democratic. But whose was the victory? Would these variegated fusions coalesce into one national party? If so, would it be Know-Nothing or Republican or Maine Law, or some strange hybrid of "isms"?

Know-Nothings Versus Republicans

The year 1855 proved to be critical for both the aspiring new organizations. At first sight the Know-Nothings seemed in the stronger position. Southern recruits poured into the lodges; eastern Whiggery, except Seward's New York following, had been swallowed; and the budding Republican party in the Northwest was honeycombed with nativists. It is true that the secret order's appeal was emotional and irrational; but its Republican rival was little better off. Popular sovereignty, as the excitement subsided, seemed likely to make Kansas and Nebraska free; Douglas would be vindicated, and the sectional Republican movement would lose its chief stock in trade. Know-Nothingism at least was not sectional. As the nativist craze subsided, there was a chance that a solid basis of economic interest, of northern and southern conservatism, might replace it, and a new and more virile Whig party might emerge. But Fate was unkind to the Know-Nothings and more than generous to the Republicans.

Misfortunes beset the secret order in 1855. After a bitter fight, Virginia went Democratic in the spring election. Know-Nothing blundering and Henry A. Wise's fiery leadership of the Democrats gave him the governorship and damaged the prestige of the nativist party in the slave states.

At Philadelphia in June the national council of the Know-Nothings wrangled over the slavery issue. The result was a secession of antislavery delegates, led by the Ohio and Massachusetts groups when they were outvoted on restoration of the Missouri Compromise. This division brought up the problem the Know-Nothings would face in the next national campaign.[3] Their chief successes in the North had come by coupling nativism with anti-Nebraska sentiment. Such a platform was impossible for the South.

On the other hand, three significant developments in 1855—in Ohio, New York, and Kansas—favored the Republican party. At a state convention in Ohio that adopted the name "Republican," the old Free Soil men, by threats of a bolt, forced the Know-Nothings in the anti-Nebraska movement to accept the nomination of Chase for governor. The rest of the state ticket was composed of Know-Nothings, but the antislavery men saw to it that nativism was kept out of the platform. A small minority of dyed-in-the-wool Know-Nothings and old Whigs rejected Chase and named their own candidate. Chase's election over Democratic and Know-Nothing opponents greatly heartened the Republicans in a year of failures by giving them control of the most populous state in the Northwest. Most of the Ohio Know-Nothings were then absorbed into the Republican party. A few months earlier the reverse process had seemed probable.

The second development was Seward's transfer of his New York State Whig following, the Woolly-Heads, to the Republicans. Reelected to the Senate by an anti-Nebraska legislature, he was now ready to join the new antislavery party. This gave it a powerful local organization under such able leaders as Seward, Weed, Greeley, and

[3] With the appearance in 1855 of the "Know Somethings" and the "Sag Nichts," secret societies seem to have become epidemic. The former organization admitted Protestant naturalized citizens and was aggressively antislavery and Republican. It appealed to Germans especially and, as one member wrote, was designed to "keep K. N'ism from doing mischief until the fever for secret societies is past." The more obscure "Sag Nichts" were hardly more than groups of Democrats organized to defend the foreign-born and religious liberty. They appealed to liberal Germans for support.

Henry J. Raymond. Seward, a friend of the Catholic archbishop, had no truck with the Know-Nothings.

But happenings in Kansas were even more important. After fraud and violence at the first election, attributed to Missouri "Border Ruffians," produced a pro-southern territorial legislature, the free-state men set up their own government at Topeka under an unauthorized state constitution. When President Pierce upheld the legal but unrepresentative territorial legislature, the Republicans charged him with favoring slavery in Kansas. In the following months violence on both sides, greatly exaggerated by the press, completed the discrediting of popular sovereignty. "Bleeding Kansas" became the favorite Republican theme in 1856, though the bleeding was far more in Congress, in the newspapers, and on the hustings than from bullets and knives.

The Know-Nothings, now formally christened the "American" party, had to face the slavery issue in 1856 and could find no formula to preserve unity. Their national council met at Philadelphia in February, just before the nominating convention, to make a platform. There was no difficulty over the nativist planks, which included demands for limitation of officeholding to native-born, requirement of twenty-one years' residence for naturalization, exclusion of paupers and criminals from entry into the United States, and denial of political station to anyone recognizing allegiance to a "foreign prince, potentate or power." But, though critical of the Pierce administration for reopening the sectional agitation, the platform lamely indorsed popular sovereignty for the territories. True-blue antislavery men could not accept this, and when the nominating convention assembled a northern delegate presented a resolution denying the right of the council to make a platform and demanding the nomination of candidates who favored restoring the Missouri Compromise line. The rejection of this resolution by a vote of 141 to 59 caused antislavery men—nearly all the New England and Ohio delegates and a few from some other northern states—to withdraw. The American party thus lost the backbone of its northern support outside New York; there the old Silver Gray, or conservative, faction of the Whigs still supported the nativists.

In the balloting New York had two candidates for President, Millard Fillmore and George Law. Several other names were considered, including Justice McLean, Commodore Robert Stockton of

New Jersey, Sam Houston of Texas, and Garret Davis of Kentucky; but each was found lacking in some respect, and it was felt desirable to take the candidate from New York, whose delegates had not bolted. Fillmore was then nominated with Andrew Jackson Donelson named to complete the ticket. Fillmore's popularity with southern Whigs and his compromising record as President explain his selection. The American party was now scarcely more than an original core of nativist fanatics and the conservative wing of the old Whigs. Only in the border states did it seem likely to secure electoral votes.

The seceding Americans (Know-Nothings), usually termed "North Americans," though not all the northerners seceded, held a convention in June just before the Republicans. John C. Frémont would probably have been named for President but for the fears of his friends that it might hurt his chances with the Republicans. A way out was found in nominating N. P. Banks, Speaker of the House, who was committed to Frémont and would withdraw in his favor.[4] Former Governor William F. Johnston of Pennsylvania completed the ticket.

The Republicans had already held an organizing convention at Pittsburgh on February 22 with delegates present from twenty-three states. In the chair was Francis P. Blair, Sr., veteran Jacksonian editor, who felt that his old party had turned to false gods. The principal business of the meeting was to call a national nominating convention and set up a national comittee.

On June 17 the first Republican national convention assembled at Philadelphia with all the free states, four border slave states, the District of Columbia, and three territories represented in some fashion. The six hundred or more delegates, plus alternates and visitors, crowded the hall and made the gathering almost a mass convention, disorderly but tremendously enthusiastic. Past greats and future greats guided affairs. David Wilmot, Francis P. Blair, Sr., Preston King, Joshua R. Giddings, Thurlow Weed, Horace Greeley, Thaddeus Stevens, Charles Francis Adams, John M. Palmer, Henry S. Lane, Henry Wilson, and many others of every shade of antislavery feeling and political affiliation were there. Robert Emmet of New York, an Irish Democrat, was temporary chairman, Henry S. Lane of Indiana permanent chairman.

The platform, as reported by Wilmot, indorsed the principles of the Declaration of Independence and the Constitution, denied the

[4] Commodore Stockton was named by the New Jersey delegates, who seceded from the "North American" convention; but he withdrew in favor of Fillmore.

legal existence of slavery in a territory, and upheld the right and duty of Congress to prohibit in the territories "those twin relics of barbarism, polygamy and slavery." [5] A long resolution dealt with the disorders and frauds in Kansas and laid the responsibility at the door of the President and his supporters. Other planks demanded the admission of Kansas as a free state; denounced the Ostend Manifesto as "the highwaymen's plea that might makes right";[6] declared for a Pacific railroad "by the most central and practicable route" with federal aid; favored rivers and harbors improvements of a national character; and opposed legislation impairing liberty of conscience and equality of rights of citizens. Except that the last resolution could be construed as a slap at the Know-Nothings, there was nothing in the platform to arouse opposition from any element in the new party. The planks for a Pacific railroad and for rivers and harbors were bids for the votes of California and the Old Northwest, although they might seem to have a Whiggish slant. But there was no mention of the tariff and no plank for free homesteads. The party was frankly sectional and had nothing to offer the South.

The candidate, John C. Frémont, had been selected before the convention met by certain astute eastern chieftains. They passed over Senator Seward, because his radical reputation and his hostility to the Know-Nothings would win no votes in the doubtful states, Illinois, Indiana, and Pennsylvania. Seward unhappily concurred in this action. Chase had cooperated with the Know-Nothings in Ohio but was too close to the abolitionists and was unpopular among Whigs. Only Justice John McLean remained a dangerous possibility in the way of Frémont. He had availability of a high order. He was a conservative antislavery man, believing in the power of Congress to prohibit territorial slavery, but had upheld the Fugitive Slave Law. He had regarded the Know-Nothing order at its inception with "unmeasured satisfaction" and had been considered for its nomination. He had friends in the South. Most important of all, the Pennsylvania conservatives regarded him as the one Republican who might carry that all-important state. With promises of support from Ohio, Indiana,

[5] Polygamy, practiced in Utah Territory by some of the Mormons, was attracting attention. Under popular sovereignty, the territory could decide such matters for itself.

[6] The Ostend Manifesto was the statement of the American ministers to England, France, and Spain that, if Spain refused to sell Cuba, the United States would be justified in seizing it. The Pierce administration did not indorse this proposal.

and Illinois he seemed to be nearer the goal of a lifetime than ever before. The chief obstacles were hostility of radical antislavery men, who looked upon him as an "iceberg," and the feeling of Greeley and other easterners that this "marrowless old lawyer" would not do—that the new party needed a fresh young leader, with no political past.

Their choice was John C. Frémont, aged forty-three, former army officer and explorer, participant in the California uprising against Mexico at the outbreak of the Mexican War, hero of a romantic elopement with Senator Benton's sparkling daughter Jessie, and recipient of the not wholly deserved title of "Pathfinder" for his explorations. In his brief service as Senator from California he had given little evidence of pronounced antislavery feelings; but this was handled discreetly in his campaign before the convention. In a letter he attributed his defeat for reelection to the Senate to proslavery opposition and expressed sympathy for a free Kansas. Frémont had been a Democrat but had turned against the Pierce administration. He was actively supported by F. P. Blair, Sr., the Massachusetts leaders N. P. Banks and Henry Wilson, and John Bigelow of the *New York Evening Post*. The Germans admired him, Greeley was friendly, Seward and Weed were not averse to his nomination, and he had a glamorous name familiar to all.

Judge Rufus P. Spalding of Ohio, manager for McLean, gave up the fight and withdrew his candidate before the voting; but the Pennsylvania delegates, led by Thaddeus Stevens, objected so strenuously that he rescinded the withdrawal. The damage could not be repaired. An informal ballot gave Frémont 359, McLean 204, Banks 1, Sumner 2, Seward 1. In the formal ballot that followed, McLean received 37 votes and Frémont 520. The nomination was then made unanimous. Frémont would probably have been named in any case; but McLean never forgave Spalding for his bungling.

For the second place the disgruntled Pennsylvanians were allowed to choose; but they could not decide between former Governor Johnston and David Wilmot. The convention then named William L. Dayton, former Whig Senator from New Jersey, over Abraham Lincoln of Illinois. To a committee was left the task of arranging for cooperation with the "North Americans," who had supposed that their choice for Vice President, Johnston, would be named.

The North American convention reassembled, Banks was withdrawn, and Frémont was named, but with Johnston as his running mate. The problem of two Vice Presidential candidates troubled the party committees all summer, and much negotiating failed to solve it. Finally Johnston withdrew, understanding from Frémont that his friends would not be overlooked in the event of victory, and Dayton had a clear field. But Pennsylvania leaders, deprived of both McLean and Johnston, were not enthusiastic. Besides, a popular son of the Keystone State was heading the Democratic ticket.

"Bleeding Kansas" and the Election of 1856

The Democratic convention met at Cincinnati. Factional strife, even violence, marked its opening session on June 2. An insurgent Benton delegation from Missouri, when admission was refused, crashed the door. Later the committee on credentials denied them seats, and it solved the perennial New York contest by dividing the vote equally between "Hards" and "Softs." The platform, according to custom, repeated the planks of earlier platforms on traditional policies; in addition it denounced Know-Nothingism, indorsed the Kansas-Nebraska Act, and favored a vigorous foreign policy in line with "manifest destiny" ideas. A resolution for a Pacific railroad was tabled, but was brought up again after the nomination of Buchanan and carried.

Buchanan was well in the lead long before the convention. As Minister to England, he had escaped involvement in the Nebraska struggle; he had a long record of inoffensive conservatism; he came from Pennsylvania, an important state in all Democratic calculations; and he had never given offense to the South. Pierce wanted the nomination, and he had much southern support and some strength in New England; but his availability had been destroyed by the Kansas situation and his lack of the forceful qualities Americans expect in a President. Douglas had northwestern support but, like Pierce, was damned with Nebraskaism and was opposed by the shrewder northern politicians. With the two-thirds rule in effect, a long deadlock seemed to be in prospect.

The first ballot gave Buchanan 135-1/2, Pierce 122-1/2, Douglas 33, Cass 5. Buchanan and Douglas both picked up support until the fourteenth ballot; then the former had 152-1/2, the latter 63, and Pierce 75. Overnight the Pierce men decided to withdraw their candidate; and Douglas went up to 122 on the sixteenth ballot. But Buchanan now had a majority, and rather than deadlock the convention further, Douglas's friends abandoned the fight. "Old Buck" received a unanimous nomination on the seventeenth ballot. John C. Breckinridge of Kentucky, a friend of Douglas, was nominated with him. The party was thus harmonized behind a colorless conservative candidate. Even Benton accepted the nominee, though his son-in-law was leading the Republicans.

A radical antislavery convention at Syracuse, New York, named Gerrit Smith of New York for President on an abolitionist platform. The nomination benefited the Republicans by lessening a little the force of the oft-repeated charge that they were abolitionists: the radicals had disowned them.

Groups of Whigs also followed an independent course. A convention at Louisville on July 4 made no nominations but recommended support for the candidates in nearest conformity to Whig views. A second convention at Baltimore in September with delegates from twenty-one states indorsed Fillmore and Donelson but not the American party platform. Preservation of the Union was all that mattered to the old guard of Whigs.

The course of the campaign was largely determined by the long session of Congress, from December to August, which was marked at every step by sectional and partisan bitterness. It required nine weeks to elect a Speaker, because Republicans, "North" and "South" Americans, Democrats, and Republican-Americans could find no common ground. At last Nathaniel P. Banks of Massachusetts, an American-Republican, was chosen by a plurality. Much time was consumed by the Kansas question. Long debates between "shriekers for freedom" and "subduers of freedom" produced no solution. Democratic Senate and anti-Nebraska House could not agree. Accompanying the excitement in Congress a series of events in Kansas culminated in the "sacking" of Lawrence by a marshal's posse of which former Senator Atchison was a member—really a proslavery mob. This produced other acts of violence, all luridly misrepresented by reporters for eastern newspapers.

On May 19, while the drunken mob was in possession of Lawrence, Senator Charles Sumner of Massachusetts, eloquent, vain, stuffed with classical learning and master of the dictionary, delivered his carefully prepared and rehearsed masterpiece, "The Crime Against Kansas." Not content with arguments and near-obscene metaphors, he indulged in offensive personalities against Douglas and, for no apparent reason, singled out for special chastisement the elderly South Carolina Senator, Andrew Pickens Butler, who was not present to defend himself. Douglas struck back with caustic comments, but Butler was avenged by his nephew, Congressman Preston Brooks. Two days after the speech, Brooks approached Sumner at his desk in the Senate after adjournment and attacked him with a gutta-percha cane, finally breaking it over his head. Opinion differed then and afterward over the severity of the wounds; but Sumner did not reappear in the Senate for two years, going abroad in search of health. Massachusetts reelected him as a mark of her esteem.

The assault on Sumner was, next to "Bleeding Kansas," the best argument the Repulicans had in 1856. A southern bully, fit product of the slavocracy, had brutally assaulted a northern Senator for words used in the supposedly free forum of the Senate. When his district reelected Brooks after he had resigned as a result of a vote of censure, here was further proof of southern depravity. A leading Democrat predicted that the affair would cost his party 200,000 votes.

The campaign rivaled that of 1840 in excitement and far excelled it in importance. A major party was contesting a national election on frankly sectional grounds. An old Whig, Robert C. Winthrop of Massachusetts, now a Buchanan supporter, caustically described the Republican appeal as one-third Missouri Compromise repeal, for which northerners were largely responsible, one-third Kansas outrages, with no regard for northern provocation, and one-third "disjointed facts and misapplied figures . . . to prove that the South is, upon the whole, the very poorest, meanest, least productive, and most miserable part of creation and therefore ought to be continually teased and taunted and reviled, by everybody who feels himself better off." This anti-southern crusade with its strong moral appeal aroused the Protestant pulpit and gave a religious fervor to the Republican cause. Songs, so effective as campaign weapons in 1840, reappeared as Republican writers exhausted the possibilities of "Freedom, Freemen, and Frémont." And it must not be forgotten that northerners had been exposed to *Uncle Tom's Cabin* in print and on the stage for four years.

The Democrats, with no young hero to exploit and no crusade to conduct, appealed to the fears of conservatives and Union lovers: The elderly, colorless Buchanan typified experienced statesmanship and security for the old American order; Frémont, disunion and possibly civil war. Toombs and Howell Cobb, the Union savers of 1850, publicly announced that the South would not submit to Republican victory. Because Fillmore could not win, Clay Whigs were urged to support Buchanan and northern business did not need to be reminded of southern markets and investments at stake. Democratic leaders in the North forgot their earlier diatribes against the nativists and appealed to Fillmore men to make common cause with them against the specter of sectionalism. In the South, where Fillmore and Buchanan were the only contenders, the battle was sharply fought, with the "Americans" insisting that their candidate was national and at the same time sound on southern rights.

Fillmore's supporters in the North were under the disadvantage of appealing to the same general constituency as the Democrats. Had another Democrat than Buchanan been named, their chances might have been better. Even so, they charged the Democrats with southern leanings, the Republicans with northern fanaticism, and described their own party as the truly national one. To stir up the dying embers of nativism, they concocted a story that Frémont was a Roman Catholic.[7] This invention, taken up by the Democrats, caused the Republicans much embarrassment because they were wooing the German Catholic vote and a public statement by Frémont would be unwise. Friends attempted to refute the charge, but it persisted through the campaign and may have cost some Know-Nothing support.

Republican success depended on victories in Illinois, Indiana and Pennsylvania. In these border free states the antislavery crusade backfired. Too many voters were frightened at Republican radicalism. Attempts to arrange fusion tickets with the Fillmore men were ineffective. In spite of the combined efforts of three of the nation's shrewdest and most unscrupulous political manipulators—local managers Simon Cameron and Thad Stevens helped by Thurlow Weed of New York—the Republicans failed to carry Pennsylvania. After all, it was Buchanan's home state, and it had never had a President. Weed later believed that $50,000 was the margin of Democratic victory.

The electoral college gave Buchanan 174 votes (Pennsylvania, New Jersey, Indiana, Illinois, California, and all the slave states except Maryland); Frémont 114 (the remaining free states); Fillmore 8

[7] Frémont, an Episcopalian, had been married by a Catholic priest, and an adopted daughter had attended a Catholic school. His enemies went on to insist that he had been reared as a Catholic, still attended mass, and had shown his Catholicism on various occasions. Witnesses were produced to vouch for the statements.

(Maryland). Buchanan had 1,838,169 popular votes; Frémont, 1,341,264; Fillmore, 874,534. The "Americans" were now a conservative third party, their antislavery strength having gone to the Republicans. Nativism had failed utterly as a national issue, but "Bleeding Kansas" had carried the Republicans through their critical period.

11

The Failure of Parties

Buchanan Blunders

"Old Buck" came to the Presidency through a combination of astute politics and sheer availability. This cautious, elderly bachelor, a diner-out of repute in London and Washington, was looked upon as the man of the hour, the experienced political physician whose skill would heal the nation's wounds. Whigs like Edward Everett, who had supported Fillmore, regarded the "Squire of Lancaster" as the right man in the right place. Unfortunately, Buchanan had never been a leader.

Buchanan's inaugural address hinted at what the South had long awaited: settlement of the issue of slavery in the territories by a court decision. He had been in correspondence with two of the justices and knew what was impending. Two days later the United States Supreme Court handed down the fateful Dred Scott decision. Traveling different roads to their conclusions, the majority upheld the southern view that the Missouri Compromise, repealed in 1854, had been unconstitutional, and that Congress had no power to prohibit slavery in a territory. The venerable court[1] had at last involved itself in the sectional controversy. That the dissenting justices, Curtis and McLean, were responsible for forcing the court to decide the case rather than to refuse jurisdiction seems reasonably clear; but the attempt of the majority to pass on a sectional and political issue shows a strange lack of wisdom. The fact that five justices were southerners was not overlooked by critics.

For the Republicans the decision was a blessing in disguise. Their

[1] With four justices past seventy and three beyond sixty the average age of the Supreme Court was greater than at any time until the administration of Franklin D. Roosevelt.

platform plank for Congressional exclusion of slavery from the territories was declared unconstitutional; but that they would abandon their one fundamental principle at the behest of the Supreme Court was too much to expect. Instead, the leaders fell upon the court and treated it with even more disrespect than Jefferson and Jackson had shown. Seward openly threatened reorganization or packing, and other Republicans echoed his sentiments. The Ohio state convention called the Dred Scott decision "anti-constitutional, anti-republican, anti-democratic, incompatible with State rights and destructive of personal security." J. S. Pike, Washington correspondent of the *New York Tribune,* sneered at the conclusions of "five slave-holders and two dough-faces upon a question where their opinion was not asked"; the court had "draggled and polluted its garments in the filth of pro-slavery politics."

The decision produced a sharp swing to a state-rights position by many Republicans. Northern states must defend freedom by limiting the power of the federal government to extend slavery. A leading Republican newspaper advocated requirement of a two-thirds vote by the Supreme Court to set aside state laws. In this connection the Fugitive Slave Law came under fire. Northern states in several instances had passed personal liberty laws to nullify the hated act. State courts were clashing with the federal judiciary in fugitive cases. The Wisconsin supreme court actually declared the federal statute unconstitutional—a plain case of nullification—but was overruled by the United States Supreme Court. In 1859 the highest Ohio court escaped a similar defiance by the margin of three votes to two. The state Republican convention promptly refused renomination to the judge whose deciding vote had upheld the law.

The Democrats now attempted to defend the Supreme Court and proclaimed, with little regard for the traditions of Andrew Jackson, that all good citizens must accept the Dred Scott decision in good faith. But there was a fly in the ointment. If Congress lacked power to prohibit slavery in a territory, could a territorial legislature, created by Congress, do so? If not, what became of the Douglas doctrine of popular sovereignty? This was the dilemma that confronted the Illinois Senator in his campaign of 1858. But Kansas provided a more immediate problem.

Pledged to a fair trial of popular sovereignty in Kansas, Buchanan was off to a good start in appointing as territorial governor Robert J. Walker of Mississippi, former Secretary of the Treasury. Walker accepted the thankless task of preserving order and guiding the territory to statehood. He was assured of the President's support in insisting on a fair submission of a state constitution to the voters. But when the free-state men refused to vote the proslavery forces captured control of the constitutional convention. That body, meeting at Lecompton, drew up a constitution, which it refused to submit to popular vote. Instead, the voters were permitted to vote for or against slavery in Kansas, not on the whole constitution. Even rejection of slavery would not affect slave property already in the territory.

Governor Walker denounced the scheme but found the President unwilling to support him. Alarmed at southern criticisms of Walker and influenced by southern cabinet members, Buchanan refused to demand submission of the Lecompton Constitution to the voters, and referred in his message to Congress to the approaching Kansas vote on slavery as an adequate compliance with popular sovereignty. Walker resigned in disgust.

Douglas entered the picture even before Congress convened. In a stormy interview with the President, he refused to support the Lecompton travesty and defied the administration, backed as it was by southern Democrats.

While Congress debated the question, Kansas voted on the Lecompton Constitution with or without slavery; and slavery won, as the free-state men refused to participate. The President accepted the vote as conclusive and recommended that Congress admit Kansas as a slave state. He had his way in the Senate, where only three Democrats joined Douglas and the Republicans in opposition; but in the House the anti-Lecompton Democrats were stronger, and the statehood bill failed. Then Democratic compromisers set to work and, over the objections of Douglas, produced the English bill. This provided for a Kansas referendum on the proslavery Lecompton Constitution and offered a land grant to the new state if the vote was favorable. The bill carried, but Kansas voted down the "bribe" and continued as a territory until 1861.

The controversy drove a wedge between northern and southern Democrats. While only a minority of the party in Congress voted with Douglas, public meetings and Democratic newspapers support made it clear that the Little Giant was on the popular side in the North. In the South, on the other hand, he was charged with party treason and was even stigmatized as a "Black Republican." Governor Henry A. Wise of Virginia was among the few who saw the folly of

Buchanan's course in wrecking the party in the North. The prospects of harmony in 1860 grew dim.

Meanwhile the Illinois Senator had been making strange political friendships. The Republicans, disbelieving in popular sovereignty, nevertheless were compelled to support his war on the administration. Schuyler Colfax of Indiana, Galusha Grow of Pennsylvania, and other Republican Congressmen conferred with him, ostensibly over the Lecompton matter, but actually to sound out his future course. Shrewd Senator Henry Wilson of Massachusetts commended him, and Horace Greeley made it a point to call at his Washington home. The *Tribune* and other Republican organs teemed with praise of his courage. Presently Greeley, voicing eastern opinion, suggested that the Illinois Republicans should not oppose reelection of Douglas to the Senate. This hinted at an alliance of Republicans and Douglas men in 1860.

Western Republicans blocked the move. Governor Chase of Ohio, distrustful of Douglas, opposed any trimming of sails, and was concerned lest the availability argument be used to keep genuine antislavery men out of the Republican picture in 1860. Even more potent was the hostility of the Illinois Republicans toward Douglas. "I think I see his tracks all over our state," wrote the editor of the *Chicago Tribune*. "They point only in one direction; not a single toe is turned toward the Republican camp. Watch him, use him, but do not trust him, not an inch."

The Republican state convention had a candidate for Douglas's seat in the Senate who had been patiently biding his time since 1855, when he was put aside for Lyman J. Trumbull. This was an extremely tall, angular Springfield lawyer, self-educated but highly respected by the Illinois bar, who had served one undistinguished term in Congress—moderate Whig in principles, antislavery enough for the Illinois atmosphere without being abolitionist, neither remarkably eloquent nor particularly inspiring but endowed with an unusual talent for clear, cogent expression and a deep vein of humor, which revealed itself in droll anecdotes and homely illustrations that caught the fancy of the crowd. A melancholy strain marked him off as a man apart, though he was jovial enough in a group of friends. Too conscious of his ungainly appearance, homely face, and lack of polish, he longed to distinguish himself. An ambitious, at times nagging, wife was a further incentive. Adept at local politics, he could be noncommittal and devious; but he was no unprincipled trickster. He had the wise opportunism of a great political leader who kept his ear to the ground. Aware of the mixed composition of his party, he carefully kept to a middle course. Kindly disposed toward everyone, he cherished no hatreds, burned with no grievances. He was a dangerous opponent because he did not permit personal animosity or the acclaim of the crowd to warp his judgment. Douglas recognized Abraham Lincoln as the best man the Illinois Republicans could have named.

Yet it was not merely Lincoln versus Douglas. The Buchanan administration, when the Little Giant fought the Lecompton measure, had inaugurated a drastic purge of Douglas postmasters, revenue collectors, marshals, and other federal officers. Anti-Lecompton Congressmen found the White House doors closed to them. After the passage of the English compromise there was a brief lessening of pressure; but Douglas's campaign for reelection reopened the war. Illinois federal officeholders held a bolting state convention and named an administration ticket to oppose the Douglas nominees. They also ran candidates for the legislature in as many counties as possible to defeat the regular Democratic candidates. This backfire threatened to unseat Douglas despite his hold on the masses of Democrats.

The story of the famous Lincoln-Douglas debates does not require repetition here. Politically they added to the laurels of both men. Yet Douglas at Freeport was forced into a position—his "Freeport Heresy"—of virtual repudiation of the Dred Scott decision; for he insisted that local police regulations by a territorial legislature could control slavery no matter what the Supreme Court might decide on the abstract question of legal right. He had said the same thing earlier but had attracted little comment. Now the southern leaders and an unfriendly administration scanned his every word for evidence of heresy. He won in Illinois by a narrow margin and retained the leadership of the northern Democracy; but the South was further alienated and prepared a bitter cup for him to drink in 1860.

The state and Congressional elections of 1858 were highly satisfactory to the Republicans. The Lecompton issue proved to be of great value both for propaganda purposes and in dividing the Democrats. The severe Panic of 1857 also was helpful. Northern business lay prostrate, and unemployment mounted. A revulsion against the administration was natural. The depressed industrial interests now brought up the tariff issue to plague the Democrats. A lower tariff, unsatisfactory to Pennsylvania in particular, had been enacted in the closing months of the Pierce administration. That state, suffering from the collapse of the iron industry in the depression, now demanded higher rates. With the tariff argument as a unifying force, Republicans, Americans (Know-Nothings), and anti-Lecompton Democrats united to create an opposition party which elected all but three of the twenty-five members of Congress. In the new House of Representatives the administration was in a minority. Dred Scott, Lecompton, and economic distress had undone the victory of 1856.

The Conventions Meet

The new Congress did not meet until December, 1859. By that time John Brown had made his fateful raid on Harper's Ferry to provoke a slave uprising, and had suffered the supreme penalty. Southern fears, inflamed by his insane act, turned Washington into a sectional battlefield. The House took weeks to elect a Speaker. John Sherman of Ohio, Republican choice, had indorsed Hinton R. Helper's book *The Impending Crisis of the South*, an attack on slavery from the standpoint of a non-slaveholding southern white, regarded with more alarm by southerners than *Uncle Tom's Cabin*. "American" party Congressmen held the balance of power and would not support Sherman. At last William Pennington, a New Jersey conservative Republican, was elected by a majority of one vote.

In the Senate, Douglas and Jefferson Davis crossed swords. Davis insisted that Congress could pass protective legislation for slavery in a territory; Douglas held out for local control, as in his Freeport utterance. Davis had a series of resolutions upholding his position adopted by a caucus of Senate Democrats. This was the southern ultimatum to the Little Giant.

The convention of the Democratic party met on April 23 at Charleston, South Carolina, under conditions of intense excitement, with the galleries packed with southern partisans, and elected Caleb Cushing of Massachusetts permanent chairman. The anti-Douglas men captured the resolutions committee of one from each state, the California and Oregon representatives voting with the South. This majority reported a platform with a plank declaring it the duty of the federal government to protect slavery in the territories. A dissenting minority report approved the Cincinnati platform of 1856 with an additional pledge to abide by the decisions of the Supreme Court on rights of property in states or territories. A bitter debate followed in which the Alabama fire-eater William L. Yancey led the advocates of the majority report, and Henry B. Payne and George E. Pugh of Ohio spoke for the minority. Recommittal of the platform to the committee only produced two similar dissenting reports. After a further long drawn-out debate the minority, or Douglas, platform carried, 165 to 138. The southern extremists—including most of the delegates from Alabama, Mississippi, Florida, Texas, South Carolina, Louisiana, and Georgia, and some from Arkansas, Delaware, and North Carolina—then seceded from the convention.

The convention then balloted for President. The two-thirds rule was held to apply to the total vote of the convention, not two-thirds of those present. The New York delegation voted with the anti-Douglas men to sustain this ruling of the chairman, which made the nomination of Douglas almost impossible. The first ballot gave him 145-1/2, R. M. T. Hunter of Virginia 42, James Guthrie of Kentucky 35, and Andrew Johnson of Tennessee 12 votes. For fifty-seven ballots the deadlock continued. Douglas reached 152-1/2 at one point, but was unable to gain further. At last the convention voted to adjourn to Baltimore, after recommending that the party in the different states fill any vacancies in the delegations. It had been a memorable two weeks of bitter strife, and the situation seemed hopeless.

Meanwhile the southern seceders had organized their own convention and adopted the platform rejected by the regular convention. They did not nominate, but adjourned to meet at Richmond on June 11. Only a handful came, and an adjournment was taken to the 21st to await the outcome of the Baltimore adjourned session. There was much confusion in southern Democratic ranks over the question of sending delegates to Baltimore. Douglas men and other conservatives organized and chose new delegates in some cases; but many of the bolters seemed ready to return, and conventions in several states accredited them to both Baltimore and Richmond. The problem of regularity was a puzzling one.

When the convention reassembled at Baltimore on June 18 the Charleston seceders, led by Yancey, demanded readmission. After much wrangling the committee on credentials agreed to admit them where there were no contests. But where new delegates had been chosen, as in the cases of Alabama and Louisiana, these were received. The decision only produced further secessions, including the returned seceders, a block of delegates from the upper South, and the

Buchanan men from Massachusetts, California, and Oregon. The convention, consisting now chiefly of northern and border-state men and the replacements from the lower South, then balloted. Douglas received all but 17 of the 190-1/2 votes cast. Another ballot gave him 181-1/2 out of 194-1/2. The convention then declared him the nominee by a unanimous vote. Senator Benjamin Fitzpatrick of Alabama was named to run with him but later declined. The Democratic national committee substituted Herschel V. Johnson, former governor of Georgia.

With Caleb Cushing in the chair the seceders, new and old, assembled in another hall. Vice President John C. Breckinridge of Kentucky, a moderate by reputation, was named for President with Senator Joseph Lane of Oregon, an administration supporter, as his running mate. The rump Richmond group, chiefly South Carolinians, then reassembled and repeated these nominations. Congressional protection of slavery, rejected by the majority at Charleston, was adopted by the seceders.

The blunders of Buchanan and the extremism of southern leaders had broken the party, but the immediate issue was a legal abstraction. Slavery could not exist in the remaining territories, and no court decision or Congressional code could give it life; but the South had evolved its formula, and compromise was impossible. Yancey of Alabama, Rhett of South Carolina, and other extremists, aiming at a southern confederacy, had whipped up southern opinion to such a pitch that the moderates had to fall in line. Both groups insisted on defining Democratic orthodoxy in terms that were impossible of acceptance in the North. They argued, plausibly enough, that the slave states had provided the majority of Democratic electoral votes in 1856 and should determine party policies. They forgot that three close northern states had provided nearly as many electors for Buchanan as the entire cotton South; that elsewhere in the North were large Democratic minorities that might, by careful strategy, become majorities again as in the recent past; that free-state Democrats outnumbered slave-state Democrats in total count by a goodly margin. And they ignored a fundamental axiom of American politics—that national elections are won by tailoring the party's program to fit doubtful areas and wavering groups. The "Dixiecrats" of 1860 would have fastened on their party a principle that, as Douglas knew only too well, would cost it every northern state; but he could not argue with blind emotionalism.

The other parties held their conventions between the Charleston and Baltimore Democratic assemblages. A Constitutional Union convention (called "National Union" in the invitation issued by a group of southern "American" Congressmen) met at Baltimore on May 9. Its personnel reflected the Fillmore Whig and American movement of 1856. Since the Lecompton struggle, border-state conservatives such as Senator Crittenden of Kentucky had been looking with interest at the growing conservatism of the Republican party. Kansas was out of the way, protective tariff was coming into favor, and conservative Republican papers like the *New York Times* and the Cincinnati *Gazette* were eager to desectionalize their party. The Richmond *Whig* reciprocated this feeling when it declared that it would "support Seward a thousand times sooner than any Democrat, Northern or Southern, in the land." The obstacles to fusion would have been difficult to overcome, but John Brown's raid ended any possibility of cooperation. The conservatives of the upper South then turned their attention to an independent Union-saving movement, and the result was the Baltimore Constitutional Union convention.

This convention was a gathering of graybeards, men of the faith of Clay and Webster, assembled to attempt the impossible task of pouring oil on the fiercely troubled waters. There was no dearth of candidates; but Sam Houston of Texas, favorite of the "Americans," and John Bell of Tennessee, one of the best known of the old Whigs and an opponent of both the Nebraska and Lecompton bills, were in the lead. On the second ballot Bell was nominated. Edward Everett of Massachusetts, a New England patrician famed as an orator and scholar, was named as his running mate and reluctantly accepted. The resolutions committee offered as a platform a simple pledge to support the Constitution and the Union against all enemies at home and abroad, and this was accepted. The Constitutional Union movement was the last effort of old-fashioned conservatives to resist the sectionalism that was engulfing the two great parties. Its chances were not hopeless, for the Democratic party had just been wrecked at Charleston and the Republicans might nominate Seward.

The Republicans chose Chicago for their national convention, and May 16 was the date. The accessibility of this young city by lake steamboat and the new railroads attracted visitors from all parts of the North. A carnival spirit replaced the crusading fervor of 1856, and whiskey-drinking politicians far outnumbered abolition zealots. A specially constructed "Wigwam" held ten thousand spectators, and convention orators entertained thousands of others who milled around outside. Delegates and spectators were rude and disorderly. Delegations representing somewhat shadowy Republican organizations in five border slave states were seated. Six delegates purportedly came from Texas and were accepted, though four were said to be Seward recruits from Michigan. David Wilmot of Pennsylvania was temporary chairman, and George Ashmun of Massachusetts permanent chairman.

The platform was shrewdly constructed to catch votes where votes were needed. A denunciation of the Dred Scott decision as "a dangerous political heresy," a strong statement in favor of Congressional action to preserve freedom in the territories, their "normal condition," and a demand for statehood for Kansas pleased antislavery men. Yet abolitionism was disavowed in a plank upholding the right of a state to determine its own domestic institutions and denouncing lawless invasion of any state (John Brown's raid) as "among the gravest of crimes." Doubtful Pennsylvania was wooed with a vaguely worded tariff resolution which could be construed to mean protection for the industrial interests. When it was read the Pennsylvania delegates rose and cheered vociferously.

The Germans, represented by Carl Schurz and Friedrich Hassaurek, were well pleased with two "Dutch" planks, one of which opposed any change in the naturalization laws and any state legislation abridging rights of citizens. Massachusetts Republicans, chiefly of old New England stock and hostile to Irish newcomers, had recently secured the adoption of an amendment to the state constitution under which foreigners would not receive the vote until two years after naturalization. Northwestern Republicans were alarmed: the German vote might be lost to the party in 1860. Lincoln had condemned the "Two-Year Amendment," and the practical politicians at Chicago now soothed the naturalized with the plank described. A significant factor was a meeting of delegates of German Republican clubs in Chicago the first two days of convention week. The second "Dutch" plank demanded passage by Congress of a homestead law granting public lands to actual settlers. This appealed not only to immigrants but to eastern labor and western pioneer farmers who had long been agitating for such a law. "Vote yourself a farm" was a slogan that drew in support where antislavery propaganda failed.

Platform demands for river and harbor improvements, federal aid for a Pacific railroad, and a daily overland mail—measures defeated or sabotaged by southern opposition—were aimed at the Old Northwest and the Pacific Coast. These and the tariff plank smacked of old Whiggery and helped convince conservatives that the Black Republicans were no longer men of one idea. Henry Clay would have approved such a program.

The old guard of antislavery men sensed these trends with growing alarm. After the platform was read tall, whiteheaded Joshua R. Giddings of Ohio, one of the abolition prophets, rose to propose an amendment. The "inalienable rights" statement of the Declaration of Independence, included in the 1856 platform, had been omitted. It ought to be inserted. After considerable turmoil he was defeated by a voice vote and walked out of the convention; but George William Curtis of New York appealed to the delegates not to go on record as rejecting the humanitarian ideals of the forefathers, and they reconsidered and accepted the amendment. This appeased the old Liberty men. Yet, taken as a whole, the platform was practical, rather than humanitarian. It was not primarily antislavery, but northern-sectional. Industrialists, railroad interests, labor, farmers, immigrants, moral reformers, all could find planks to stand on.

The selection of a candidate was handled in an equally practical way. This required blocking leaders with radical reputations. Chase, in this category, had attempted to save himself by recanting his free-trade views; but conservatives had other counts against him, and he had enemies in his own Ohio delegation. Seward, popularly regarded as radical, no longer talked about "a higher law" and "an irrepressible conflict." He had the best organization and the most money. New York City street-railway interests, recipients of legislative favors at Albany, were reported as ready to help Thurlow Weed finance Seward's campaign, if he were named. A large delegation of New York boosters headed by a well known bruiser, Tom Hyer, and accompanied by a brass band, paraded the Chicago streets and yelled for Seward at every opportunity in the convention. Free champagne and cigars were available for delegates. New York, perhaps half of New England, and the upper Northwest—a near majority—favored the New York Senator; but he encountered obstacles of no small moment. Horace Greeley, estranged for personal reasons and holding a proxy for Oregon, used every influence at his command to undermine Seward. More important was the opposition of Pennsylvania, New Jersey, Indiana, and Illinois—the border North, Democratic in 1856 and to be won only by a conservative platform and candidate.

They had the one; they now pleaded for the other. Two Republican candidates for governor, Henry S. Lane of Indiana and Andrew G. Curtin of Pennsylvania, spearheaded a "Stop-Seward" movement.

More available than Seward were Edward Bates, Justice John McLean, Abraham Lincoln, and Senator Ben Wade of Ohio (held in reserve as a dark horse). Simon Cameron, a favorite son, had Pennsylvania's nominal support but was ready to sell to the highest bidder. The elderly, bewhiskered Bates seemed to be the most likely choice. As an old Whig from slave Missouri, strongly backed by the Blair family and liked by Greeley, he would temper the sectional character of the party. Yet the Germans, represented by their convention of Republican clubs, were unfriendly because he had cooperated with the Know-Nothings, and the radicals had misgivings. McLean's age—in the seventies—virtually eliminated him. Lincoln was well regarded in the Northwest; but elsewhere he was thought hardly strong enough: the Vice Presidency seemed to be more suited to his talents. However, on the night before the balloting Lincoln's boom grew amazingly. The anti-Seward group, almost despairing of success, turned to him as the least objectionable of the lesser candidates and the holder of a large bloc of western votes. David Davis, his manager, misused his authority and gave pledges in return for votes. Cabinet seats were promised to Cameron of Pennsylvania and Caleb Smith of Indiana. Delegates from these states pleaded with wavering delegates from other states that nomination of the New Yorker might defeat their state tickets as well as lose the Presidency.

When the convention assembled to ballot, Lincoln enthusiasts, supplied with freshly printed tickets, hurried to fill the best seats and outroared the Seward men when the candidates' names were presented, fortunately without speeches. It was Lincoln's good fortune to have the convention meet in a city that knew him so well. The first ballot gave Seward 173-1/2, Lincoln 102, Cameron 50-1/2, Chase 49, Bates 48, and scattering 42. On the second, Pennsylvania, Vermont, some of Ohio's waverers, and a few others shifted to Lincoln, giving him 181 to Seward's 184-1/2, with 99-1/2 for the remaining candidates. Seward had been stopped. The stampede for Lincoln started. He had 231-1/2 before the third ballot was announced; but Ohio, seeing that he was within 1-1/2 votes of a majority, shifted 4 votes to him, and other states changed in quick succession. Availability had triumphed over experienced statesmanship. The battle-scarred Weed, outmaneuvered by prairie politicos, wept at his favorite's defeat; the loaded cannon on the lawn of Seward's Auburn home was never fired; but the joy in the Old Northwest was unbounded. Its favorite, a frontier rail splitter, had taken the prize. Pennsylvania, Indiana, and Illinois had had their way. The party had gone conservative. The convention completed the ticket by naming Senator Hannibal Hamlin of Maine—a Democrat before the Nebraska bill—for Vice President.

To believers in the hand of Providence in American history, the Chicago nomination must afford an amazing example of its mysterious ways. Midnight conferences of liquor-stimulated politicians, deals for jobs, local leaders pulling wires to save their state tickets, petty malice, and personal jealousies—a strange compound, and the man of destiny emerges.

The Struggle of 1860

Nominally four candidates contested for the chief office in 1860. Yet in most states—excluding two or three border slave states and the Pacific coast—it was a two-party fight: Lincoln against Douglas in the North, Bell against Breckinridge in the South. Valiant little minorities of Douglas men put electoral tickets into the field in most of the cotton states, but the great majority of southern Democrats voted for Breckinridge. The Bell-Everett ticket drew the old Whig, "American," and Unionist vote. Both Breckinridge and Bell groups professed loyalty to the South; but the "submissionists" were to be found in the Constitutional Union movement, the "secessionists" in the Democratic camp.

In the North the Bell movement attracted only remnants of "Americans" and old Whigs. The failure of Fillmore in 1856 and the newfound conservatism of the Republicans caused many former Whigs like Thomas Ewing of Ohio and Edward Bates of Missouri to support "Lincoln, the Whig," and the Whig policies in the Republican platform. The Breckinridge following in the North was little more than a corporal's guard of Buchanan officeholders seeking to destroy Douglas, even though it meant Republican success.

The real battle was between Douglas and Lincoln with the cards stacked in favor of the "Rail Splitter." His party was united and seemed to be reasonably sure of New England, New York, Ohio, and the upper Northwest—all carried in 1856. It needed Illinois, Indiana, and Pennsylvania to win. Lincoln's Illinois residence strengthened the Republican cause in his home state and neighboring Indiana. His Whig background attracted conservatives in the Ohio valley, and the homestead plank helped with the foreign-born. Buchanan vetoed a modified homestead bill in the summer; southern members of Congress had voted almost solidly against it, while both Democratic platforms had ignored it. Using a pamphlet, "Vote Yourself a Farm," and speeches in German by Carl Schurz, Gustav Körner, and other popular German orators under the special direction of a "foreign department" of the national committee, the Republicans made heavy inroads into the German vote in Cincinnati, Chicago, and St. Louis. These were centers of the newer German immigration, more radical and less fixed in party affiliation than the older groups, who still clung to the Democratic party.

In Pennsylvania and southern Ohio the tariff issue was used to win the coal and iron interests and their workingmen. The success of the fusionist "People's" party in Pennsylvania in 1858 prepared the way for 1860 and a similar victory. There was plenty of money, and Simon Cameron, Andrew G. Curtin, Thad Stevens, and other experienced leaders directed the strategy.

There was not the excitement in the North that had prevailed in 1856. The Republican party was neither so novel nor so radical, and its appeal was less emotional. Kansas had long since ceased to bleed; the territories were in little danger of ever becoming slave states; and —a strange vindication for Douglas—some Republicans even accepted popular sovereignty as a safe solution. "The operation of the natural forces of free labor and free emigration is worth a thousand Wilmot Provisos in building up free states," declared the Cincinnati *Commercial*, a powerful western Republican organ. However, most Republican speakers and newspapers were more orthodox in favoring Congressional action against slavery. The southern "intervention" idea—a Congressional slave code for territories—was subjected to bitter attacks; and the South was charged with schemes to reopen the African slave trade. A well organized campaign with numerous speakers and the usual parades and processions aroused moderate enthusiasm but no great excitement. The Wide-Awakes, drilled like military companies, marched in Lincoln-Hamlin parades. Seward overcame his bitter disappointment at his defeat and made what historian James Ford Rhodes has called "the most remarkable stump-speeches ever delivered in this country." He, rather than Lincoln, seemed to be leading the party. The candidate received callers daily at an office in Springfield, was in close touch with campaign strategy, but kept a muzzle on himself.

The opposition parties thundered at the sectionalism of the Republicans and repeated the danger-of-disunion argument of 1856. This was singularly ineffective in the North. "For ten, aye, for twenty, years," taunted Seward, "these threats have been renewed, in the same language and in the same form, about the first day of November every four years . . ." He was certain the Union was in no danger. Republican newspapers were equally sure.

But Douglas, facing certain defeat, was alarmed about the South. Unlike the other candidates, he had made speech after speech, all over the North—a new departure for Presidential candidates and a shattering of old traditions. In August he turned his attention to the South, not to gain votes, for his cause was hopeless there, but to arouse national feelings and bring that section to accept Lincoln's election quietly. There is nothing finer in Douglas's career than his sturdy Union speeches in Virginia and North Carolina, where he declared that no grievance could justify secession, and that he would support the President in enforcing the laws. He returned North to campaign from New York west to Missouri, but after the unfavorable state elections in October he said to his secretary, "We must try to save the Union. I will go South." Taking a steamboat down the Mississippi, he spoke at Memphis, crossed Tennessee to Chattanooga, invaded Georgia, and was in Alabama when the election took place. Threats were made against him, and a few eggs were hurled in Montgomery; but his crusade against secession went on. After the news of Lincoln's election he made his trip up the Mississippi from New Orleans a good-will tour in an attempt to reconcile the South to a Republican administration.

Desperate efforts to unite the anti-Lincoln forces upon fusion electoral tickets characterized the closing days of the campaign in the North. Complete or partial fusion was effected in Pennsylvania, New York, New Jersey, Connecticut, and Rhode Island. The candidates for electors were apportioned among the Bell, Breckinridge, and Douglas groups with the understanding that, if elected, they would cast their votes so as to bring about Lincoln's defeat in the electoral vote. This would throw the election to the House, where no party had a majority, but where one of the anti-Lincoln candidates might win.[2] A House deadlock beyond March 4 might even make Joseph Lane President, as the Senate was Buchanan-controlled and Breckinridge's running mate, elected Vice President by that body in the event no one had a majority, would assume the Presidency. The Republicans made much of this in criticizing fusion, but the danger was slight. Jefferson Davis wanted all three anti-Republican candidates to withdraw and unite upon Horatio Seymour of New York; but Douglas refused, believing that thousands of his supporters would turn to Lincoln if he abandoned the race. In the South the Bell and Douglas men cooperated in assailing the Breckinridge "disunionists," but only in Texas was there fusion.

The South was the more troubled section in 1860, divided, distracted, fearful—the very antithesis of the antislavery picture of a section held in the grip of a malevolent, aggressive slavocracy. Conservative southern newspapers charged that Breckinridge party leaders such as Yancey and Jefferson Davis were plotting to destroy the Union, and that their demand for Congressional protection of slavery was a subterfuge to divide the national Democratic party. The Breckinridge following held forth on the dangers of disunity in the South and played up stories of abolitionist-slave plots, burning of houses, and poisoning of masters with distant and thinly settled Texas as the favorite locale. This fear campaign may have added votes to the southern rights Democracy, but the large vote polled by Bell in the lower South, especially among the large slaveholders, is proof that the section was far from solid.

The election of Republican governors in doubtful Pennsylvania and Indiana in October indicated the outcome in November; but a vigorous, last-minute fight for the fusion ticket in New York held out faint hopes. Worried about disunion, the city's financial interests poured money into the campaign, but to no avail. Lincoln carried all the free states, except three of New Jersey's seven electors; Bell had Kentucky, Virginia, and Tennessee; Douglas had only Missouri and three electors from New Jersey;[3] Breckinridge won the remaining states, all slave and all from the lower South except Maryland and

[2] Actually Lincoln's chances in the House were excellent. The Republicans had fifteen of the thirty-three states and needed but two more, with Illinois and Oregon offering good prospects, especially if Douglas were eliminated.

[3] In New Jersey a fusion opposition had a small popular majority; but only three of the seven candidates received united support. Four Lincoln electors won.

Delaware. The electoral total gave Lincoln 180, Breckinridge 72, Bell 39, Douglas 12. The popular votes were 1,866,452 for Lincoln, 849,781 for Breckinridge, 588,879 for Bell, and 1,376,957 for Douglas. But in the Senate and the House the Republicans would be in a minority—a strong argument against immediate secession. The "Black Republican" President would have his hands tied.

Sectionalism triumphed in both North and South in 1860. The two moderate candidates, Bell and Douglas, were in a minority. Equally striking was the fact that conservative southerners preferred Bell, a southerner, over Douglas, a northerner, while in the free states the reverse was true. Even conservatives voted for a man from their own section. National parties, so long a unifying force, broke down. The sectionalists had their way.

12

The Civil War Years

Lincoln Takes Charge

In the critical months between Lincoln's election and the firing on Fort Sumter the Union was ruptured and politics received a new orientation. The role of party leaders in the crisis was to discover, as in the past, a formula for compromise. But southern disunionists playing upon southern fears of evils to come, and exaggerating grievances, brought about secession in state after state almost before the compromisers had a chance. Committees of the lame-duck Senate and House wrestled with the problem, but found no solution that offered any hope of acceptance. Crittenden of Kentucky and Douglas worked unceasingly for compromise, but in vain. Crittenden's proposal of a free and slave West divided at 36°30′ had wide popular support but was rejected in the Senate.

The Republican attitude, as the secession crisis developed, was one of uncertainty and confusion. Peaceable secession, compromise, and coercion each had its advocates, and some inconsistently changed camps. Greeley in the *New York Tribune* was not the only editor who would have let the erring sisters depart in peace. Such a view was widely expressed before the seriousness of the situation dawned on the North. Let the cotton states secede, and they would soon come to their senses. When the awful reality of the crisis dawned on them, many of the pacifists dropped this pose, and strangely enough, joined the non-compromisers.

An important group of Republicans, led by Thurlow Weed, favored compromise. Eastern business, alarmed at the prospect of losing loans and markets in the South, supported them. Senators James Dixon of Connecticut and Simon Cameron of Pennsylvania, and Representatives John Sherman and Thomas Corwin of Ohio and David Kilgore of Indiana represented a moderate viewpoint. Seward, strangely silent, was supposed to sympathize with them, though he voted against the Crittenden proposal, which Weed publicly indorsed. Opposed to them were radicals like Wade, Sumner, Stevens, and Giddings, representing small-town and rural Republicans, who upheld the Chicago platform without perhaps realizing the imminence of civil war.

The position of Lincoln was crucial, yet he continued his campaign policy of silence. Emissaries to Springfield found him evasive and unwilling to commit himself on the various compromise schemes. On one point—and it was fundamental—he did prove adamant. There must be no abandonment of the party's position against slavery in the territories. As long as he held to this course no Republican Senator could yield either to Crittenden's 36° 30′ line or to Douglas's proposal of popular sovereignty by a constitutional amendment. Efforts to get the President elect to commit himself to a plan for a national convention to consider constitutional amendments, or to approve the submission of a compromise plan to a popular vote brought no responses. He felt that his past statements had made clear his conservative viewpoint, and that anything he might say would be twisted and misinterpreted. Some felt that he was a weakling, but Douglas was reported as of a different opinion. "He does not know that he is President-elect of the United States. He does not see that the shadow he casts is any bigger now than it was last year. It will not take him long to find it out when he has got established in the White House." The Springfield politician was just emerging from his cocoon.

Lincoln's inaugural address was conciliatory but suggested no basis for compromise. He would not interfere with slavery in the states and would enforce the Fugitive Slave Law; but he declared secession a revolutionary measure. He announced that government places and property in the South would be retained but no offensive measures would be undertaken. The door was still open to conciliation.

Lincoln's cabinet selections were the products of past commitments, geographical and factional considerations, and a fierce under-cover struggle between a Seward-Weed (mostly Whig) group and an anti-Seward (more non-Whig) element composed of Chase, Greeley, and other active battlers. The result was a cabinet which included the party's outstanding men, four of them Lincoln's chief rivals at the Chicago convention. It was also outstandingly inharmonious and difficult to handle.

Seward, as Secretary of State, was a logical choice. Slight of stature, careless of dress, the loquacious New Yorker, waving his inevitable cigar, displayed admirably the two faces of Republicanism, humanitarian idealism and the sordid Weed system of practical politics. Salmon P. Chase of Ohio, for whom the path of duty always led to public office, accepted the Treasury headship. A man of imposing appearance, deep piety, and high reputation in antislavery circles, he was encased in an armor of self-righteousness, and his voluminous correspondence pictured himself as the conscience of the cabinet and its strong man. Edward Bates of Missouri as Attorney General fitly represented old Whiggery in age, appearance and viewpoint. Gideon Welles, a Connecticut Yankee and one-time Jacksonian who looked like a Hebrew prophet, brought efficiency to the Navy, and scored heavily, historically, against cabinet rivals and administration critics in a remarkable diary. Montgomery Blair of Maryland, son of Francis P. Blair, Sr., and brother of the Missouri Congressman Francis P. Blair, Jr., became Postmaster General. He was a border-state conservative and a loyal Lincolnian. Simon Cameron, Pennsylvania machine politician, and Caleb Smith of Indiana received the War and Interior departments, as promised at the Chicago convention; but Cameron proved to be so unfit that he was packed off to Russia as American Minister in less than a year. Edwin M. Stanton of Pennsylvania, War Democrat, who took his place, was distrusted in some quarters as a wily double-dealer. He was an able administrator, often ruthless and high-handed, and antagonistic toward his chief.

In the weeks that followed the inauguration, the very time when the new President had to deal with the problem of the two remaining federal forts in the South, he was overwhelmed by the patronage-hungry. Yet Lincoln did not object to spoils politics; and eventually he removed 1,195 of the 1,520 Presidential officeholders and distributed jobs to build up support for his policies.

The uncertainties of the situation, with civil war hanging in the balance, led the self-assured Seward to propose to the President that the Secretary of State become a kind of chief minister responsible for devising a policy. His "policy" was to inaugurate a foreign war and thus unite the country by ignoring domestic issues! Lincoln tactfully but firmly rejected the proposal and let Seward know who was to be the master of the administration. Cautiously he was developing his own policy, and early in April he determined to provision the garrison of Fort Sumter at Charleston, South Carolina. This provoked an attack by the Confederates, but it made them appear as aggressors. A distracted, wavering North united behind the President, and civil war began with the outburst of national spirit so necessary when the war drums beat. The South, too, had its hysteria of flag waving and martial ardor. It overflowed into the hesitating upper South, and Virginia, North Carolina, Arkansas, and Tennessee joined the Confederacy. Kentucky, Maryland, and Missouri had their troubles but remained loyal to the Union.

To the united front of the North, Douglas contributed his powerful influence. He had hoped against hope for a peaceful solution of the crisis, but after Sumter he assured Lincoln of his loyal support and set out for home, speaking to enthusiastic throngs from Wheeling to Springfield. At Chicago ten thousand people heard his last speech. "There can be no neutrals in this war; only patriots—or traitors." Broken in health, he became seriously ill and on June 3 breathed his last. His loss was indeed, as Greeley said, "a national calamity." He was but forty-eight years old and might have rivaled Lincoln in stature, had he lived.

New Alignments

In the summer and fall of 1861 a new fusion party took form. A large body of Douglas Democrats, small numbers of Bell and Breckinridge men, and all the Republicans acted together in state elections. The Republican majority, out of deference to the Democrats, accepted the name "Union Party" for the alliance. Republican policies were to be dropped, and a simple program of supporting the war was adopted. Slavery was not to be an issue. All differences were to be submerged in the common cause.

Yet the Chicago Republican platform of 1860 was not forgotten. The lame-duck Congress of 1861, after the withdrawal of members from seceding states, admitted Kansas as a free state and enacted a protective tariff. Higher rates came later. Free homesteads and the Pacific railroad were voted in 1862. Northern sectionalism was triumphant, with the South no longer a barrier in Congress. Republican threats to reorganize the Supreme Court were not carried out. Deaths and resignations helped solve the problem, though one justice was added to the Court in 1863. The President found it necessary to disregard a writ of habeas corpus issued by Chief Justice Taney in 1861, while military commanders and tribunals often infringed on the functions of civil courts. Congress answered the Dred Scott decision by voting in 1862 to exclude slavery from the territories. It is hard to see that in policies the Union party, in the end, was anything more than the Republican party of prewar days. Even the subordination of slavery to the problem of the war was but a postponement; but it served its purpose. Into the Union party came many Democrats like Daniel S. Dickinson of New York, Edwin M. Stanton of Pennsylvania, David Tod of Ohio, and Andrew Johnson of Tennessee. Among these, Ben Butler of Massachusetts and John A. Logan of Illinois followed the road of military glory to political eminence, becoming as ultraradical as any Republican toward the southern states.

The majority of northern Democrats held aloof from the fusion movement. Not prepared to oppose the war and reluctant even to criticize the administration in the face of the war fury that spread over the North in 1861, they quietly held their organizations intact and offered candidates in the few state elections of that year without any clear formulation of policies. The Union party triumphed; but the trend of events was developing a strong opposition party. Several factors gave it vitality in 1862. First and most important was failure on the field of battle. The disasters of that year shattered hopes of a speedy victory and created a war-weariness upon which the Democratic opposition fed. The Lincoln administration, it was argued, was unfit to conduct the war and must be repudiated. Mismanagement and corruption must be rooted out. Another potent force was the discontent aroused by the suppression of civil liberty. In the border states and occasionally in the free North, arbitrary arrests of outspoken critics of the war raised the issue in its most troublesome form. Were the constitutional guarantees meaningless in war time?

The administration attitude toward slavery also came into the picture. In Congress radical opponents of slavery, encouraged by the surge of war passions throughout the North, pressed for drastic measures. Lincoln, concerned over the border states, moved slowly. Emancipation with compensation to loyal owners was his policy for these states; but they were cold toward it, and the radicals were scornful. Emancipation in the District of Columbia and prohibition of slavery in the territories were voted, as well as confiscation of the slaves of disloyal masters. Any general emancipation in the slave states, Lincoln believed, would have to be by the President under his war powers as a measure to weaken the rebellion. By midsummer of 1862 he was ready to act but awaited an opportune time. At last, in September, after the northern victory at Antietam, he surprised the radicals with a proclamation freeing all slaves in states still in rebellion on January 1, 1863. Montgomery Blair had opposed it in the cabinet on the ground that it would cost the party the fall elections and prove especially injurious in the border states.

The Democrats seized upon the Emancipation Proclamation as proof of Lincoln's hypocrisy:

> Honest old Abe, when the war first began,
> Denied abolition was part of his plan;
> Honest old Abe has since made a decree,
> The war must go on till the slaves are all free.
> As both can't be honest, will some one tell how,
> If honest Abe then, he is honest Abe now?

Many War Democrats left the Union party, feeling that the President had yielded to Sumner, Greeley, and the radicals. The Democrats carried New York, Pennsylvania, Ohio, Indiana, and Illinois in the fall elections of 1862. Luckily for the Union party, only one of these states was electing a governor: New York chose Horatio Seymour, Democrat but not an avowed peace advocate. Oddly enough, the new Lower House had a Union party majority of about twenty in spite of the heavy losses mentioned. The upper Northwest and New England were pleased with the Emancipation Proclamation while the border slave states, contrary to Blair's prediction, elected almost solid delegations of Unionists. The secret here was the presence of federal troops and the more or less enforced absence from the polls of Confederate sympathizers. The majority of free-state voters actually repudiated the administration. But were they voting against the Emancipation Proclamation, against the war, or against the unsuccessful methods of conducting it? Many of the new Democratic Congressmen denied that they were antiwar.

The divisions in the regular Democratic party during the war were not sharply defined, as they were differences of degree. There were two groups: the radical Peace Democrats, or Copperheads, and the Regular Democrats, who at times showed peace propensities, at other times were merely critical of the administration and its management of the war. They acted together at the polls but could not offer a consistent policy or a satisfactory alternative to the Lincoln program. They thrived on military defeats and northern discouragement and lost ground when the skies brightened. They gambled in 1864 on the continued failure of the war but lost the election and discredited the party for years to come. All Democrats came to be called "Copperheads"[1] by their enemies; yet the distinction should not be lost between the open advocates of peace and the more moderate elements.

The Peace Democrats had their center and their leader in the Northwest. The East had its representatives, particularly in New York City, where the draft law aroused bitter opposition, and where Benjamin Wood, member of Congress and publisher of the New York *News*, did his part in fomenting antiwar feeling. But eastern Democrats were not so easily swayed by peace arguments: war orders and high tariffs brought a return of prosperity to manufacturers, financial interests were lending to the government, and business was reconciled to the war. The West, however, suffered severely for a time: the Mississippi River was closed until 1863; southern business was gone; and, while the railroads carried grain and animals East, this was only a partial compensation for the loss of the southern outlet, especially in the Ohio valley. In this area lived thousands of small farmers, many of southern origin, whose viewpoint was but little different from that of the non-slaveholding southern whites. Disliking the Negro, they were susceptible to propaganda that emancipation would release thousands of blacks to flood the border areas and create problems.

But the traditionally accepted explanations of Copperheadism—trade with the South and southern blood ties—tell only part of the story. There were equally ardent Unionists of southern stock in the Ohio valley, and there was much antiwar sentiment in areas remote from the Ohio River and among people of middle-state or other non-southern ancestry, particularly in Ohio. These Peace Democrats were provincial-minded conservatives who disliked the war, the draft, high taxes, violations of civil liberties, abolitionists, Negroes, profiteers, eastern capitalists, high railroad rates, and everything connected with the bloody struggle that threatened their established way of life. Not only physical but intellectual and cultural isolation contributed to Copperheadism. Older German communities, urban Irish, extreme religious conservatives, hard-shell Democrats of the hills and backwoods, doctrinaire Calhounites, all were represented in the peace agitation. Their slogan, "The Constitution as it is, the Union as it was, and the Negroes where they are," was the epitome of their political philosophy. Like the isolationists of a later day, they failed to grasp

[1] The term "Copperhead" came into general use in the latter part of 1862 but it was applied to Confederate sympathizers in Maryland and Ohio as early as the summer of 1861

the broader implications of the struggle of democracy for survival. They have been pictured as the agrarian forerunners of the reforming Populists of the nineties. It is more accurate to describe them as retarded Jacksonians whose idea of reform was to turn back the clock.

The aim of the peace group was to overthrow the despots at Washington, bring the war to an end at once, and call a convention to restore the old Union on a compromise basis, with the Northwest in the role of mediator. The Peace Democrats were not pacifists, for they did not disbelieve in the use of force. Many of them joined secret, oath-bound societies and collected arms. They denied that they were Confederate sympathizers, as they wanted the Union restored; but, to the embittered Unionist, the only distinction between a rebel and a Copperhead was that one fought in the open, the other stabbed in the back.

The leader of the Peace Democrats was Clement L. Vallandigham, member of Congress until 1863 from a doubtful southwestern Ohio district. Vallandigham was an able lawyer, possessed a persuasive eloquence, and was cursed with a Scotch tenacity of purpose and a one-track mind. Even before the war he had envisioned the nation as an alliance of four sections, East, West, South, and Pacific Coast, each of which, he believed, should have a veto power. As a northwestern sectionalist who ignored the effects of east-west rail lines and saw only the physical unity of the Mississippi valley, he set about to end this fratricidal strife. Defeated for reelection to Congress in 1862, he made antiwar speeches in Ohio until arrested by General Burnside in May, 1863. He was tried by a military court and sentenced to prison, but President Lincoln exiled him to the Confederacy. Leaving on a blockade runner, Vallandigham eventually reached Canada. He had already been nominated for governor by the outraged Ohio Democracy, who regarded him as a martyr to the cause of civil liberties. After a bitter campaign, he was defeated overwhelmingly by a War Democrat. Gettysburg and Vicksburg, in July, 1863, had made his defeat a certainty. Indiana and Illinois, where the peace movement was stronger, had passed under Democratic legislative control in 1862; but Republican governors, elected in 1860, had four-year terms. The Ohio setback hurt the Copperheads, and the moderates in the Democratic party were in a generally stronger position in 1864.

Lincoln's Triumph

Within the Union party, preservation of harmony constituted a major problem. As Lincoln caught up with the radicals on the slavery question, they advanced on other grounds. Many had felt all along that he was a misfit in the Presidency. As Senator Fessenden put it, "We went in for a rail-splitter, and we have got one." Yet radical critics assigned part of the blame for the administration's deficiencies to the cabinet conservatives, particularly Seward and Montgomery Blair. The genial Secretary of State, who appreciated Lincoln's earthy humor, was his frequent companion and presumably a bad influence.

In the dark days of late 1862, Senate radicals led by Sumner, Wade, Grimes, and Trumbull put through a caucus resolution for a change in the cabinet. Seward, knowing that it was aimed at him, promptly offered his resignation. Lincoln brought together the cabinet and a caucus committee, with Seward absent, and matters were threshed out. Secretary of the Treasury Chase, who had privately criticized Seward and was working with the radicals, found himself in such an awkward position that he, too, offered to resign. The President ended the crisis by tactfully refusing both resignations, outmaneuvering his critics and saving Presidential authority from a dangerous Congressional encroachment. But the Committee on the Conduct of the War under Wade's chairmanship continued to investigate and pillory able generals, push its favorites—stanch radicals—and hamper Lincoln's management of military affairs.

The Blairs now drew the fire of the radicals by two indiscreet speeches: Montgomery Blair, the Postmaster General, at Rockville, Maryland, in October, 1863, and Francis P. Blair, Jr., of Missouri in the House in February, 1864. Both assailed the purposes and program of the radicals; but the Congressman attacked Secretary Chase in savage fashion for his management of the Treasury. "When the Blairs go in for a fight," said Montgomery, "they go in for a funeral." Personally hostile to Chase and Frémont, Lincoln's prospective rivals for 1864, they brought down upon themselves the full weight of radical animus toward the administration. Removal of Montgomery Blair from the cabinet came to be a leading purpose of the anti-Lincoln group, for he was using the patronage of the Post Office Department for the renomination of his chief.

A movement to nominate Chase for President got under way in the winter of 1863-1864. The ambitious and long frustrated Ohio statesman, working through the large amount of patronage at his disposal and backed by Jay Cooke, Philadelphia banker and fiscal agent of the Treasury in selling government bonds, seemed to be in a strong position to challenge Lincoln. He saw no disloyalty in remaining in the cabinet while undermining the confidence of his many correspondents in the President's ability to manage the war. The humorless, self-righteous widower convinced himself that he was the strong man of the party to save the nation from ruin. A driving force behind his candidacy was his strong-willed daughter, beautiful and brilliant Kate Chase Sprague, whose consuming ambition was to reign as hostess of the White House for her father. This belle of Washington society was a shrewd, calculating manager who used every means at her command to enable her politically inept father to attain his goal. Even marriage to a millionaire Senator in 1863 was a part of the pattern.

Friends were actively at work for Chase throughout the North, but he needed a central committee at Washington. This was formed in December by Senator Samuel C. Pomeroy of Kansas, Senator John Sherman and Representative James A. Garfield of Ohio, and a number of other members of Congress, generally of radical persuasion. Two pamphlets appeared in February: one, entitled "The Next Presidential Election," savagely denounced Lincoln; the other, the better known, was "The Pomeroy Circular," which named Chase as the man of the hour. Angry at the scurrility of these attacks, Lincoln's friends struck a mortal blow at Chase's candidacy in his home state. A caucus of the Union party members of the Ohio legislature, late in February, indorsed Lincoln for another term. A few days earlier the administration men had outmaneuvered the opposition at the Indiana state convention and secured an indorsement of the President. With the Northwest refusing support, Chase withdrew his name. The professionals operating the state machines were backing a professional, and the bumbling amateur went down. But his hopes died hard. His friends talked of Lincoln's growing unpopularity and thought that the situation would eventually force his withdrawal. Chase must be in readiness. Thus the unfortunate secretary believed he was still a factor in the coming canvass.

Lincoln's control of the patronage and the party machinery was vital to his renomination, but it was not enough. Franklin Pierce and Millard Fillmore were Presidents who had failed in party conventions despite the power of their office. Lincoln had acquired what the radicals could not realize or appreciate—a hold on the hearts of the masses of voters. He had moved in step with public opinion, and his name had become the symbol of the Union cause. Except for certain big-city newspapers, his worst enemies were at Washington, where envy and hate and malodorous intrigues poisoned the air. State conventions and legislatures all over the North repudiated their Congressmen and indorsed the President for another term. His opponents could not understand it and charged that the officeholders were solely responsible. Lincoln was spineless and imbecilic, they said, and a tool of the Blairs. And yet this "awful woeful ass," as Murat Halstead of the Cincinnati *Commercial* termed him—privately, of course—checkmated such political strategists as Henry Winter Davis, Ben Wade, Thaddeus Stevens, Zach Chandler, and Horace Greeley and was nominated almost without opposition.

Postponement of the national convention was the last card of the opposition. William Cullen Bryant of the *New York Evening Post* urged it on the ground that public opinion was too disorganized for the convention to make a representative choice; much depended upon the military campaigns of the summer, and, meeting in the fall, the convention would be able to settle on a candidate that all could support. The Lincoln men, with the nomination in their hands, would not consider such a proposition, and the Union convention met on June 7 at Baltimore. When it convened, it found an anti-Lincoln candidate already nominated and in the race.

John C. Frémont, a disappointment as a soldier, nursed grudges against the President, who had removed him from command in Missouri, and against his quondam friends the Blairs, with whom he had quarreled bitterly. His radical antislavery position, adopted prior to the Emancipation Proclamation, had won the sympathy of many extremists, particularly among the liberty-loving Germans, whose good will he had fostered while at St. Louis. Missouri radicals looked upon him as a martyr and began a movement to nominate him for the Presidency. Frémont meetings were held in several northern cities in February and March, with Germans and abolitionists the active movers. Wendell Phillips, definitely anti-Lincoln, backed the movement with his fervid oratory while German newspapers, notably in the Northwest, raised the Frémont banner. At New York the *New Nation* appeared as a national organ. Calls for a national meeting resulted in a mass convention at Cleveland, May 31.

About four hundred persons—a disappointingly small number—

attended, chiefly from the Northwest and Missouri, though nearly every northern state was represented. B. Gratz Brown of Missouri and General John Cochrane of New York were almost the only leaders with pretensions to political importance in the movement. The radicals in Congress watched with interest but were not prepared to repudiate the regular convention. Frémont was named for President, and Cochrane for Vice President. The thirteen platform resolutions emphasized the need for complete suppression of the rebellion, declared in favor of free speech, free press, and habeas corpus (save in districts where martial law had been proclaimed), favored constitutional amendments to end slavery, to limit Presidents to a single term, and to provide for direct popular election, insisted that the reconstruction of the rebellious states belonged to Congress, and stated that confiscation of rebel lands would be "a measure of justice." Most of these proposals were implied criticisms of Lincoln, but there was no direct attack upon the administration.

Frémont's letter accepting the nomination rejected the proposal for confiscation of rebel lands as too vengeful, and expressed willingness to withdraw if the coming Union convention should name a proper candidate, devoted to the principles of the Cleveland meeting. He openly criticized the administration and drew the fire of leading Republican papers, which even charged that he was seeking the Democratic nomination.

The Frémont movement had little effect on the Baltimore Union convention, which was surprisingly harmonious in the face of the dissensions of the months preceding. A radical, anti-Blair delegation from Missouri contested the right of a conservative group to seats and won its fight by a near-unanimous vote. This was construed in some quarters as a slap at the Blairs but may have been merely good strategy by the Lincoln men to give the Missouri radicals no cause for bolting. The platform called for complete suppression of the rebellion and for a constitutional amendment to prohibit slavery, praised Lincoln and his policies, warned foreign powers against violating the Monroe Doctrine, and favored speedy construction of the Pacific railroad. Radicals interpreted an adroitly worded resolution in favor of harmony in the national councils to mean that Blair should go; but it could have been applied to other cabinet members equally well. The platform was a Lincoln affair, with no hint of confiscation or other drastic punishment of rebels and with complete silence on the mooted question of control of reconstruction, whether by Congress or by the President. When the vote on renominating Lincoln was taken, the Missouri delegation voted for General Grant but quickly changed to Lincoln to make the nomination unanimous.

The choice of a Vice Presidential candidate produced the only real division among the delegates. Hannibal Hamlin desired renomination, but sentiment had developed in favor of a War Democrat to give proper recognition to that element in the Union party. Anti-Seward men had been grooming former Senator Daniel S. Dickinson of New York, a "Hard" Democrat of the 1850's popularly termed "Scripture Dick," as a likely choice. Senator Sumner swung Massachusetts away from Hamlin to Dickinson, hoping to force Seward out of the cabinet. The New York delegation split between the Seward and anti-Seward men, hurting Dickinson's chances, for a formidable candidate had appeared from a slave state—Andrew Johnson, Senator from Tennessee until 1863, despite its secession, and now its military governor. As a Union man, a Democrat, and a southerner, he appealed to Lincoln as an admirable combination of qualifications. Earlier, that popular political general Benjamin F. Butler had been sounded out; but he was not receptive.

Lincoln's skill at political intrigue was revealed in his manipulations for Johnson. He had conferred separately with Simon Cameron, controlling factor in Pennsylvania politics, and Colonel A. K. McClure, an anti-Cameron man, and had won both to Johnson's support. When Cameron in the Pennsylvania delegation called on McClure to suggest a complimentary vote for Hamlin followed by a shift to Johnson, each man was surprised to find the other pledged to Johnson. They agreed on this plan of action, and the delegation accepted it in caucus though old Thad Stevens queried, "Can't you get a candidate for Vice President without going down into a damned rebel province for one?" The convention seated delegates from Tennessee, Arkansas, and Louisiana, helping Johnson, while the Seward men backed him to head off Dickinson. The first ballot gave Hamlin 150, Dickinson 108, and Johnson 200. Pennsylvania then shifted to Johnson; other states did likewise, and he was nominated without a second ballot, receiving 494 votes.

Democratic papers could call the Union candidates "a rail-splitting buffoon and a boorish tailor, both from the backwoods, both growing up in uncouth ignorance," but they appealed powerfully to the man on the street. Their vote-getting pull was underestimated by many of the party bigwigs, who were not yet ready to accept the work of the convention as final.

For three months Lincoln's reelection seemed to be in the balance. General Grant, on whose military genius the North pinned its hopes, hurled his legions against Lee; but a mounting death toll was the only result. He then settled down for his long siege of Petersburg. General Sherman was making little headway against Atlanta, and a terrible despondency fell upon the North. In July, General Early dashed up the Shenandoah valley, and for a day Washington seemed at his mercy. Greenbacks fell below forty cents on the dollar. The radicals renewed their war on the President by issuing the "Wade-Davis Manifesto," a criticism of his moderate reconstruction policy (which had been applied in Tennessee, Louisiana, and Arkansas) and a reply to his pocket veto of a radical measure of Senator Ben Wade of Ohio and Representative Henry Winter Davis of Maryland. The two vented their spleen in the manifesto with a large bloc of Republican Senators and Representatives in sympathy with them. They called the veto a "studied outrage on the legislative authority," charged that Lincoln held the electoral votes of the reconstructed rebel states at his dictation, and warned him to confine himself to his executive duties—"to obey and execute, not make the laws."

Chase had offered to resign late in June when miffed over a trivial patronage difficulty, and the President had surprised him by accepting his resignation. Now his hopes rose as defeatism threatened to engulf the North. If a new pilot was needed, he was ready. Radical leaders were not prepared to commit themselves to a particular candidacy, but in August an undercover movement centered in New York set about securing the withdrawal of both Lincoln and Frémont and the immediate calling of another national convention. Vindictive spirits like Wade and Davis, the erratic Greeley, the critical Sumner, the moderate John Sherman of Ohio, Governor Andrew of Massachusetts, the friends of Chase, and many practical politicians agreed that Lincoln must go. Even those good friends of the administration Thurlow Weed and Henry Raymond, chairman of the national committee, whose *New York Times* was the only avowed administration organ in that city, began to despair.

In the midst of this season of intrigue and gloom, the Democrats held their national convention at Chicago on August 29, with high hopes of victory and a popular candidate at hand. On the first ballot, with but slight opposition, General George B. McClellan was nominated. Military authorities credit "Little Mac" with organizing ability and a certain cautious type of generalship; but his insufferable egotism, his contemptuous attitude toward the President and the War Department, and his inability to act when action was required had caused his removal late in 1862. He had two assets, his popularity with the soldiers of the Army of the Potomac and his grievances against the administration, upon which he placed the full responsibility for his military failures. Democratic politicians, eager for a soldier candidate, found him a ready tool, and he became the party nominee on a platform that pronounced the war a failure and declared in favor of immediate efforts "for a cessation of hostilities with a view to an ultimate convention of the States, or other peaceable means" to restore the Union. Attacks upon the subversion of civil liberties, the exercise of unconstitutional powers by the administration, and military interference with elections in the border states were included in the brief platform, along with a resolution praising the soldiers and sailors and promising to protect and care for them.

The peace plank reflected the influence of the indomitable Vallandigham who had quietly returned from Canada and become a delegate to the convention from his home district. George H. Pendleton, an Ohio Congressman, was nominated to run with McClellan. The combination of a war hero and a peace platform seemed to be well contrived to attract united Democratic support for the ticket in the face of a quarreling, disunited Union party.

But on September 1 an event revolutionized the whole political situation. General Sherman captured Atlanta, key to the lower South, and broke the military backbone of the Confederacy. The Gulf states were cut off from Richmond, and Lee's fate was sealed. The tight-lipped Sherman, who had no use for politics and politicians, had inadvertently proved to be a master politician. As northern crowds cheered and rejoiced, Lincoln's star rose again, and the radicals hastened to make their peace.

All talk of a second convention was dropped. The *New York Tribune* pronounced for Lincoln on September 6. Chase, by mid-September, was ready to go on the stump. Wade and Davis, seeking a way to cover their retreat, were induced by their radical colleague, Senator Chandler of Michigan, to accept the removal of Blair from the cabinet as a peace offering. Lincoln, with the game in his hands, might have rejected Chandler's proposal, but the Postmaster General, unpopular even with many good Lincoln men, had become a liability to the administration. The President requested his resignation, and he promptly and graciously acceded, showing his loyalty to his chief by speaking soon afterward before a great Lincoln meeting in New York City. Wade and Davis, appeased, went on the stump, but it was reported that Davis would not mention Lincoln's name.

Frémont's withdrawal was almost simultaneous with Blair's resignation, and Chandler believed it was due to his own indefatigable efforts. But Frémont had already made his decision, regardless of the status of Blair. His candidacy had become hopeless, and he was seeking a way out. Efforts to sound out McClellan and possibly make a deal with him had been ignored. Sullenly acquiescing in the inevitable, this overrated man withdrew in the interest of Union success but in a final bitter fling declared that the Lincoln administration was "politically, militarily, and financially a failure," and "that its necessary continuance is a cause of regret to the country." Thus ungraciously the once popular Pathfinder passed into political oblivion.

Fate dealt Lincoln a final trump, no longer needed, in his game with the radicals: Chief Justice Taney died on October 12. Chase, eagerly desirous of Taney's office, next in importance to the Presidency itself, must have felt keenly humiliated at seeking it from the man he had so often criticized and belittled. His friends, however, ate humble pie for him and pressed his candidacy. Lincoln, amused at the situation, waited until after the election. Then he duly appointed Salmon P. Chase to the highest judicial position, and on the 4th of the following March received the oath from the solemn-visaged Jovian Chief Justice whose pettiness of spirit had so gravely marred his public career.

General McClellan, facing a united and harmonious Union party, saw his own candidacy threatened with shipwreck between the militant peace faction and the less militant war supporters. Vallandigham, still antiwar and fierce for peace, importuned the candidate not "to insinuate even a little war" into his letter of acceptance as it would cost him two hundred thousand votes in the West. He stated on September 6 at a public meeting in Dayton, Ohio, that the convention "meant peace, and it said it." But eastern Democrats, conscious of the war prosperity their section was enjoying and seeing the political appeal to the soldiers of a war stand, pressed the general to insist on restoration of the Union as a condition of peace. August Belmont, New York financier and chairman of the Democratic national committee, warned McClellan that he must emphasize this point. Bedeviled by such conflicting opinions, Little Mac wrote his letter of acceptance several times, at first with a decided swing toward the viewpoint of an armistice without conditions, then back to an unconditional Union stand. The final draft gave cold comfort to the peace men. "I could not look in the faces of my gallant comrades of the army and navy who have survived so many bloody battles," he wrote, "and tell them that their labors and the sacrifices of so many of our slain and wounded brethren had been in vain—that we had abandoned the Union for which we have so often periled our lives." The candidate had repudiated the platform, and the War Democrats were satisfied.

But the peace element, deeply disappointed, gave a grudging support or remained away from the polls. Vallandigham reluctantly stumped for the ticket, but a group of western peace Democrats attempted to put another candidate into the field. A meeting at Columbus, Ohio, chose Alexander Long, a Cincinnati member of Congress, but he refused to run.

The inconsistencies of the Democrats made their campaign a two-faced affair. A *McClellan Campaign Songster* contained both war and peace songs. To the tune of "Dixie" crowds were expected to sing:

> For rebel traitors we've a halter,
> They falsely swore at freedom's altar
> Cheer away, cheer away,
> Cheer away, cheer away.
> We've tried all means to keep 'em quiet,
> Shot and shell their only diet,
> Cheer away, cheer away,
> Cheer away, cheer away.

And on another page, to the air of "The Battle Cry of Freedom," they could chant,

> We'll extend the hand of peace,
> That this wicked war may cease,
> Shouting McClellan, boys, and freedom.

Politicians have been notoriously adept at riding two horses, but a bloody civil war compelled men to take sides. The strain on party loyalties was a heavy one. The Democratic effort to play both sides became untenable when the Union party harmonized its differences and military success cleared the air.

Democratic prospects, so bright in August, faded with the first frosts of autumn. On the heels of the fall of Atlanta came the successes of Sheridan in the Shenandoah valley while the relentless Grant's tentacles slowly extended around Petersburg without relaxing their grip. Cheered on by a season of victory in the field, radicals and conservatives alike worked for Lincoln and the Union party, and officeholders and government contractors filled Chairman Henry J. Raymond's campaign chest. On Election Day Lincoln carried all the loyal states except Kentucky, Delaware, and New Jersey. He had 212 electoral votes to McClellan's 21. The popular majority of the Union party was nearly half a million[2]—an amazing refutation of the dire predictions of radicals and Democrats but a few weeks before.

Before counting the electoral vote, February 8, Congress adopted the Twenty-second Joint Rule whereby no electoral votes objected to in joint session should be counted except by concurrent votes of both houses. This was to insure the rejection of the electoral votes of Louisiana and Tennessee, newly reconstructed under the President's plan. Elections had not been held in the other seceded states.

[2] Lincoln had 2,330,552 popular votes, McClellan 1,835,985.

13

The Politics of Vengeance

Johnson and the Radicals

In funeral sermons preached by Protestant ministers after Lincoln's death the theme frequently cropped out that God's will had guided the assassin's bullets, that a man of harder heart was needed for the work at hand. To this the radicals could have responded with fervent "Amens." Swarthy, strong-visaged, combative Andrew Johnson, whose sturdy figure impressed young and fastidious Henry Adams with his power and self-assurance, seemed better fitted to wield a whip of scorpions. Wade, Chandler, Julian, and other radical spirits, in secret caucus, agreed that Lincoln's death was "a Godsend to our cause."

To the American public Andrew Johnson was known for two things when he became President. The first was his courageous, unwavering fight for the Union. The only loyal Senator from a Confederate state in 1861, he had been driven into exile but returned to serve as military governor and be elected Vice President. The second was the drunken spectacle he had made of himself on the day he took the oath of office to preside over the Senate. The truth about his inaugural, so falsely distorted later into charges of habitual drunkenness, was simple enough. Weak from a siege of typhoid fever, he felt the need of a stimulant before the ceremony. Vice President Hamlin sent out for some whiskey, and Johnson drank more than was wise, considering that the Senate chamber was overheated and that possibly his enfeebled condition made him unduly sensitive to alcohol. In any case, he made a rambling, egotistical speech that intensely mortified his friends. A leading Democratic paper termed him "an insolent drunken brute"; but the tolerant Lincoln merely called it "a bad slip," while the elder F. P. Blair probably hit the nail on the head when he remarked that Johnson "didn't say anything that was bad sense, only bad taste."

Men in public life who drank were the rule in 1865, and Johnson was no exception; but there is no recorded instance of intemperance in his career from that day forward. Yet, whenever he publicly denounced his enemies in his forthright fashion, the whispering went round that he was drunk again. Nowhere in American history did two or three glasses of whiskey have such lasting potency.

Johnson's first impression on the radicals was favorable. His apparent bitterness toward traitors in the period of excitement following Lincoln's assassination delighted them. "Johnson, we have faith in you," exulted Ben Wade. "By the gods, there will be no trouble now in running the government." Sumner, intent on Negro suffrage for the South, mistook Johnson's friendly reception for approval of his views.

But Johnson had been a state-rights Democrat before the war. Hating secession and holding the planter aristocracy responsible, this Tennessee plebeian could talk of punishing treason without abandoning his constitutional scruples. He was not ready to grant the ballot to the poor, ignorant Negro, and he could not accept Sumner's notion that the seceding states had committed suicide or Thad Stevens's belief that the South was a great conquered province, which Congress could rule as it saw fit. Encouraged by conservative advisers, he adopted Lincoln's plan of restoration with some slight changes, had new state governments set up by the responsible whites (excluding from participation certain groups such as higher civil and military officers of the Confederacy), and thus restored the former seceded states to the Union, leaving to Congress only the question of admitting their Senators and Representatives.

The radicals saw with alarm the tendency of the North to accept this moderate policy, which made no provision for confiscation of rebel property, large-scale disfranchisement, or equal rights for the Negro. The future of the Union party seemed to be in the balance. States restored under the President's plan might vote Democratic, strengthening that party until it could turn out the radicals at Washington. The abolition of slavery added another complication. It meant the end of that provision of the Constitution which counted three-fifths of the slaves for representation in the House. Without permitting the Negro to vote, the southern whites would use the former slave population to increase their representation and electoral votes.

While this dismal specter confronted radical leaders, Johnson and his supporters, working from a different angle, seemed to be drawing together northern and southern moderates and laying the basis for a reorganization of the Union party. Former Whigs and Douglas Democrats and some of the less extreme Breckinridge Democrats of 1860 might be expected to constitute the southern wing of the party. The northern wing would consist of Lincoln Republicans and War Democrats. Both would support Johnson's policies against radical Republicans, Copperheads, and "unreconstructed rebels." In other words, a great center party might emerge in opposition to the extremists of both sections. But the skill of a Lincoln or a Clay was needed to do the welding. Johnson had courage, tenacity of purpose, and devotion to principle; but he was no political strategist.

The radicals, clearly in the minority in 1865, were cautious in avoiding a break with the President, for party conventions and committees and most of the newspapers were with him. Time was needed for such skilled politicians as Wade, Stevens, Chandler, Sumner, and Schurz to stir up unfavorable propaganda and pull the wires that controlled party machinery. Cleverly managing the Union party caucus at the opening of Congress, they committed the majority to a policy of refusing seats to the members elect from the former Confederate states until Congress could investigate. A joint committee of fifteen was appointed to report on conditions in the South. Club-footed old Thaddeus Stevens was its dominant figure, hard, bitter, cynical, partisan, not averse to loaves and fishes, hater of rebels and friend of the Negro, from which race he had selected his housekeeper and mistress. A masterful debater and a despotic parliamentary leader, he whipped the House majority into line in his duel with the President. No one of the important Senate radicals had the power and pertinacity of Stevens.

Two Presidential vetoes inaugurated the struggle. The first came when Congress passed a bill extending the life and powers of the Freedmen's Bureau. Originally a war emergency creation for humanitarian purposes, it was now to receive authority to protect the Negro against the "black codes," recently enacted by the new southern legislatures to provide some measure of control over the former slaves. The President vetoed this unprecedented extension of federal authority over the states, and the Senate sustained his veto. But he damaged his cause with the moderates by a denunciatory speech to a crowd that had paraded to the White House to express its approval.

He had not yet learned that name calling, as practiced in east Tennessee politics, was a luxury permitted only to such White House tenants as Jackson, who had acquired mastery over their parties. Stevens insinuated that Johnson had been drunk again, and the radical press assailed the veto.

The second measure rejected by the President was the civil rights bill to grant citizenship and equal protection of the laws (but not suffrage) to the Negro in every state. Though its constitutionality was questionable, political expediency required concessions to moderate northern opinion. Most of the cabinet advised Johnson to sign the bill; but his constitutional scruples weighed heavily in the scales, and he sent an able veto message to Congress. This time the moderates weakened under radical pressure, and the veto was overridden. The gap widened between the party majority and "that man at the other end of the avenue" (Stevens's designation).

Meanwhile, the joint committee on reconstruction proposed a constitutional amendment to deal with the South, which, after debate and modification by the two Houses, was finally passed as the Fourteenth Amendment.[1] Ratification was to be regarded as a condition for the readmission of Senators and Representatives from a seceded state. Only Tennessee, captured by the radicals under the notorious "Parson" Brownlow, accepted it, and her Senators and Representatives were seated. Though he could not veto it, Johnson disapproved of the amendment, and the other southern states failed to ratify. In view of what happened later, ratification might have been wiser.

The Triumphant Radicals

With control of the next Congress at stake in 1866, Johnson's friends felt that he must assume the offensive or allow the Union party to pass into radical hands. Conservatives must be rallied to his standard. Accordingly, a call was issued for a national Union delegate

[1] (1) The citizenship provisions of the Civil Rights Act were included in the Fourteenth Amendment, and states were forbidden to abridge the privileges of citizens or to deprive any person of life, liberty, or property without due process of law. (2) If any state denied any of its adult male citizens the right to vote, its representation in the House was to be reduced in that proportion. (3) Office-holding was forbidden to persons who had engaged in rebellion after having, in an official position, taken an oath to support the Constitution. (4) The Confederate debt was declared void. and any compensation for loss of slaves was forbidden.

convention at Philadelphia. This declaration of war against the radicals brought the resignation of three cabinet members; but Johnson continued to tolerate the double-dealing Edwin M. Stanton in the War Department, though he was hand in glove with the radicals. The convention, meeting on August 14, was an enthusiastic affair; all shades of conservative opinion were represented, from old Republicans such as Montgomery Blair, Thurlow Weed, and Henry Raymond to out-and-out Democrats, such as Thomas A. Hendricks, Samuel J. Tilden, Sanford E. Church, and Reverdy Johnson. Vallandigham and Fernando Wood were chosen as delegates despite the odium of Copperheadism; but they were persuaded to withdraw. The Massachusetts and South Carolina delegations walked into the hall arm in arm. This "arm in arm" convention acclaimed the statesmanship of Johnson, demanded the restoration of southern representation in Congress, and appealed to the country for support. Raymond was punished by the radicals with the loss of the chairmanship of the Union Party National Committee.

Three other conventions were held before the fall elections. The first consisted of the "loyal" men of the South, who met at Philadelphia early in September, and indorsed Negro suffrage. Northern radicals ignored this action, for Negro suffrage was unpopular in the North. Two national conventions of ex-soldiers—one conservative, the other radical—gave added political interest to an off year in politics.

More potent in molding public opinion than conventions and oratory were two developments that were to cost Johnson dearly. The first was a terrible race riot at New Orleans in July in which two hundred Negroes were killed. Radical propaganda used it, together with a bloody outbreak at Memphis in May, to show the unrepentant state of mind of southern whites and the failure of Johnson's restored state governments to protect the freedmen. In view of the sensitivity of northern opinion on the southern question, this was a powerful argument for the harsh policy which Stevens and Sumner were demanding.

The other factor was due to an unintentional piece of blundering on Johnson's own part. The dedication of a memorial to Stephen A. Douglas at Chicago in September furnished an excuse for a "swing around the circle" in which the President could present his case to the voters. With Seward and Welles of the cabinet, and General Grant, Admiral Farragut and a retinue of officers, the President went by way of Philadelphia, New York, Buffalo, Cleveland, and Detroit to Chicago and returned through Springfield, St. Louis, Indianapolis, Louisville, Cincinnati, and Pittsburgh.

Some of his wisest counselors advised him to make no extemporaneous speeches, for utterances in the excitement of the moment might be distorted and misconstrued by radical newspapers for their own purposes. But Johnson forgot this advice when he passed into enemy territory. Hecklers, planted in the crowds at Cleveland, St. Louis, and other cities, goaded him into retorts that, even if truthful, marred the dignity that is associated with the highest office in the gift of the people. At Indianapolis and Pittsburgh he was howled down by jeering radicals whose presence in the crowds was by design, and whose actions were not due to mob psychology.

A friendly press would have helped greatly by merely stating the truth about these occurrences; but Union party newspapers were mostly under radical control. Had Johnson used the patronage vigorously some months earlier, he might have developed a strong federal machine; but he had waited too long. Federal officeholders, state and local politicians, and the party press went "radical." Johnson's remarks and actions were distorted and exaggerated until thousands of voters saw him as "the drunken tailor," making a spectacle of himself in public.

Could Johnson have overcome the radicals by a different strategy? Some historians, while conceding that the cards were stacked against him, believe that he erred in not raising such economic issues as tariff, currency, the banking system, and the national debt. The war had given these matters a new significance, and old sectional alignments were showing signs of life. Agrarian Northwest and South might have been allied in his support, and war antagonisms submerged. At least, he might have shattered radical unity and acquired a body of supporters in Congress sufficient to uphold his vetoes. But Johnson held to the view that the southern question must be disposed of before other matters could be considered, because Congress, as then constituted, was not representative of the entire country. This compelled him to fight his enemies on a battleground of their own choice and with results disastrous to his cause.

He and his chief advisers failed in another respect. The Philadelphia Union convention did not organize a separate party, but left it to the conservatives in each locality to get control of the old Union party organization or make terms with the Democrats. In Ohio, Johnson men were induced to support the regularly nominated Union Republican Congressional candidates, all radical, by promises that Johnson would not be assailed. In New York, the only way in which they could support the President was by voting Democratic. Johnson lost thousands of votes because Union voters preferred radicals to Democrats of Copperhead antecedents. Instead of naming Johnson conservatives, the Democrats, with poor judgment, usually nominated straight-out Democrats.

The election was not a genuine referendum on Johnson's policies, as the voters did not have a fair chance to express themselves. Yet the margin of victory of the radicals was much narrower than their imposing majorities in the new Congress indicated. The popular vote in most northern states was reasonably close.

With the election decided in their favor, Stevens, Sumner, and their cohorts could proceed with little fear of defeat. Southern rejection of the Fourteenth Amendment furnished a sufficient pretext for harshness, and the radical program was soon enacted, beginning with the act of March 2, 1867, establishing military rule in the South and providing a method of restoring the states to the Union in which compulsory Negro suffrage and ratification of the Fourteenth Amendment were the outstanding features. Only with Negro votes could the radicals hope to get control of the southern states. Further legislation was soon found necessary, and this was also passed over the President's head. Congress was now the government.

Of more direct political import was the Tenure of Office Act, which required the consent of the Senate to removals of officials it had confirmed. Cabinet members were to hold office during the term of the President who appointed them and for one month thereafter, subject to removal only with the consent of the Senate. Congress was attempting to cripple the President's control over the federal patronage and vest in itself administrative as well as legislative powers. Though the Constitution was silent on the question, unbroken practice since 1789 upheld the unrestricted right of the chief executive to make removals.

A Congressional oligarchy, obsessed with a spirit of vengeance and a lust for power, seized control of the government, overrode all opposition, and attempted to establish a party dictatorship that would rule the North by appeals to war passions and sectional selfishness and the South by force. Even the Supreme Court did not dare to interfere. Cries of dictatorship have been raised against every strong President, but none has ever infringed upon the authority of other departments as did the radical Congress of 1867-1869. Had this trend continued, a vicious system of legislative supremacy and diffused responsibility might have resulted. The President would have become a figurehead. But in impeaching Johnson the radicals overreached themselves.

A House committee eagerly searched for grounds for impeachment in the session of 1866-1867 but found nothing even remotely resembling a misdemeanor. Only when the President removed the treacherous Stanton from the War Department in February, 1868, did an opportunity present itself. He had suspended Stanton in August, 1867, when Congress was not in session; but the Senate's refusal to agree, when it met, caused Stanton to resume his place under the terms of the Tenure of Office Act. In the second removal Johnson ignored the Senate, intending to get the question before the courts as a test of the constitutionality of the law. But the House of Representatives proceeded to impeach the President for committing a misdemeanor; and Stanton barricaded himself in his office protected by a guard of soldiers.

The Senate acting as judge and jury—or, according to radical theory, as a political body, a law unto itself and bound by no laws—tried Johnson on a number of counts. The radicals actually had no case against the President, for the Tenure of Office Act did not apply to Stanton's dismissal. He was a holdover from Lincoln's term not subject to the law, as he himself had admitted earlier. To fortify their case, the managers for the House even included some of Johnson's remarks on his "swing around the circle" and on other occasions in an effort to prove his unfitness for his high office. But only a bigoted partisan could regard such things as "misdemeanors." Every type of outside pressure was used to club doubtful Senators into voting for Johnson's removal, but seven courageous members of the majority party joined with the twelve Democrats to save him. The vote on the most important charge was 35 to 19, one short of the necessary two-thirds. The seven were assailed as traitors to the party, but they kept Ben Wade, president pro tempore of the Senate and bellwether of the radicals, out of the White House. More important than that, they kept future Presidents from becoming rubber stamps of Congressional oligarchs.

Issues and Candidates in 1868

A reaction against the radical overlords in 1867 threatened to make the coming Presidential struggle doubtful. Five states, including New York and Pennsylvania, went Democratic in state elections, and Republican margins declined generally from those in 1866. Three northern states rejected Negro suffrage at the polls. Negroes could vote in only seven northern states in 1868, and five of these were in New England. What was sauce for the southern goose would not do for the northern gander.

Another political issue rivaled the southern problem in public appeal. The greenbacks, issued without gold backing during the Civil War, had been reduced in volume, but the protests of the farmer West led Congress to stop further deflation in 1868. Pressure was even mounting for new issues of paper money to pay off the five-twenty war bonds, which were maturing and were payable in "dollars," interpreted by secretaries of the treasury to mean gold. If they were paid in greenbacks, the bondholders would receive dollars worth about seventy cents in gold. However, western farmers, holding few bonds and accustomed to the greenback currency, saw no injustice in using it to pay public as well as private debts. They also argued that more greenbacks in circulation would strengthen farm prices and make for easier credit. Many eastern industrialists felt the same way. Deflation would hurt profits.

George H. Pendleton of Ohio, McClellan's running mate in 1864, made himself the spokesman of this sentiment in 1867 by advocating the use of greenbacks to pay off bonds and to replace national bank notes—none too popular in the West. He insisted that he was opposed to both contraction and inflation, arguing that the bonds could be retired without new issues of greenbacks—a doubtful conclusion. His "Ohio Idea" won greater support among Democrats than among Republicans but was embarrassing to both parties. Two leading radical Republicans, Stevens and Ben Butler, were greenbackers. The former, burdened with debts incurred in rebuilding his ironworks, destroyed by Lee's army, had a personal interest in an easy-money policy.

The Union Republican party solved the problems of Negro suffrage and the Ohio Idea in its national convention at Chicago, May 20-21, by skillful evasions and ambiguities. Negro suffrage, the platform said, was necessary in the southern states to protect the loyal men of the South; but in the North the question properly belonged to the people of the states. This trimming of sails indicated that the radicals were well aware of northern feeling on the subject. The currency plank denounced repudiation and declared for the payment of the national debt "not only according to the letter, but the spirit of the laws." "Letter" and "spirit" were not defined, but the convention at least turned down the Ohio Idea. Eastern finance was satisfied, but Thad Stevens called the platform "tame and cowardly." Other planks denounced Andrew Johnson, upheld radical reconstruction, approved of foreign immigration and of equal rights for naturalized and native-born, and promised the war veterans that bounties and pensions provided by law were obligations never to be forgotten. The name "National Union Republican Party" appeared in the platform, but the old name "Republican" was coming into general use. All the southern states except Texas sent delegates, including several Negroes.

The candidate was named long before the convention met. Realizing the extent of General Grant's popularity, radical leaders had been working for months to draw him into their net. Originally a Democrat and a believer in a moderate southern policy, he at first supported Johnson and accompanied him on his "swing around the circle." Then, made aware of his own political potentialities by the whisperings of friends, he began to waver. An unnecessary misunderstanding with Johnson over the Stanton case, which almost convicted the general of duplicity, drove him into the arms of the eager radicals, and soon he was backing the impeachers. This conversion insured that the Republican convention would nominate him without opposition. The radicals needed him far more than he needed them. His military reputation and his political innocence gave the voters, weary of reconstruction wranglings, the feeling that here was a man who could be trusted, who stood above and beyond the selfishness of politicians. His letter of acceptance, indefinite on specific issues, sounded at the end a simple keynote that increased popular confidence in the man: "Let us have peace."

The Republican convention was enlivened by a sharp contest over the second office. Wade, disappointed by his failure to attain the Presidency through the removal of Johnson and defeated for reelection to the Senate by the new Democratic Ohio legislature, wanted the place. Several radical rivals contended with him, the most important being Senator Henry Wilson of Massachusetts, Governor Reuben

E. Fenton of New York, and the Speaker of the House, Schuyler Colfax of Indiana. Wade led for four ballots, but Colfax was named on the sixth.

Deprived of Grant by the radicals, the Democrats were confronted with a concerted movement by some elements in the party for Chief Justice Salmon P. Chase, hitherto a radical Republican and still a believer in Negro suffrage. His fine impartiality in presiding at the trial of Johnson had altered Democratic opinion of him. Treating the case as a judicial proceeding and carefully following the forms of law, he had annoyed the radicals by his rulings; and the *New York Tribune* sharply criticized him for influencing doubtful Senators to vote for Johnson. Egged on by his persistent daughter, the Chief Justice felt his old ambitions stirring and considered whether, after all, he was not really a Democrat in principles. That he had once briefly been a member of that party was in his favor, but his belief in Negro suffrage constituted a serious barrier. He would not recant on this but did couple universal suffrage with amnesty for all ex-Confederates. In a letter to August Belmont he expressed disapproval of white disfranchisement and military rule in the South. A little later he was ready to concede that, though he believed in the broad principle of equal rights, its application was a state function. That this would deprive the Negro of the vote in the South he seemed not to see—or was his Presidential yearning dimming his vision? John Van Buren, Horatio Seymour, and other eastern leaders were friendly, as were important financial interests, but the road was full of obstacles. There were more orthodox Democrats, faithful in times of trial, who were not ready to be put aside.

George H. Pendleton ("Gentleman George") was riding the Ohio Idea and gathering delegates all over the West. He held control of Ohio (though Vallandigham was secretly hostile) and prevented any Chase strength from developing there. But conservative eastern Democrats could not stomach Pendleton's financial heresies and were determined to block his nomination. From Indiana came Senator Thomas A. Hendricks, more acceptable to the East, but whose home state was committed to the Ohioan. Hendricks's friends hoped that Pendleton's strength in the convention might eventually go to their favorite. The presence of a military hero at the head of the Republican ticket, however, brought the soldier vote and the issue of Copperheadism into the picture. An orthodox Democrat of the Pendleton-Hendricks type might be too vulnerable. To fight fire with fire, a soldier candidate was uncovered, the gallant, popular General Winfield S. Hancock of Pennsylvania: his military record was good, and he had shown moderation and respect for civil authority when he commanded a military district in the South under the Reconstruction Acts.

Two men who had been in the forefront of the battle against the radicals felt that they deserved the prize. The Blair family—tired of working for other people, as one of them put it—began to push the interests of General Francis P. Blair, Jr., whose bitter quarrels with the Missouri radicals had driven him over to the Democrats. His war record and the Blair loyalty to Lincoln were in his favor; but weighing heavily against him were the family's old feuds (with Chase, for example), his outspoken denunciations of carpetbag rule and Negro suffrage, and rumors that he was a heavy drinker. A letter to Colonel James O. Broadhead, written shortly before the convention, was typical of Blair forthrightness and Blair blundering. It argued that the next President should declare the Reconstruction Acts void, disperse the carpetbag governments by force, and let the white people organize new state governments. The House of Representatives, with a Democratic majority elected along with the President, would then admit their Representatives, and the Senate would have to give in. The Republicans seized upon the letter as evidence of a Democratic intention to resort to revolution, and Blair disqualified himself for the Democratic nomination.

In the White House, reflecting over his victory in the impeachment proceedings, Andrew Johnson began to feel the need of further vindication. The Democrats, having accepted his policies, might well make him their candidate. The Tennessee and other southern delegations favored him, and his amnesty proclamation of July 4 increased their liking. But this in itself was an ill omen. The North must pick the candidate, and the Democrats of that section had scant respect for Johnson. Had he reorganized his cabinet, dispensing with Seward and McCulloch, and filled federal offices with Democrats in 1867, there might have been some response to his candidacy. Now there was very little.

The Democratic national convention, meeting at New York in the newly built Tammany Hall in midsummer, elected the handsome, popular war governor of New York, Horatio Seymour, permanent chairman and, as usual, adopted the two-thirds rule. The platform called for "the immediate restoration of all the states to their rights in the Union under the Constitution, and of civil government to the American people," amnesty for all past political offenses, and the regulation of the franchise in the states by their citizens. It indorsed the Ohio Idea of paying the bonds in "lawful money," where coin was not specified, and favored taxation of government bonds. A special resolution declared for one currency for all the people. Other sections arraigned the radicals for tyranny and oppression, declared the Reconstruction Acts "unconstitutional, revolutionary, and void," praised President Johnson, and promised the soldiers and sailors that "all the guarantees given in their favor" would be carried out.

In the balloting for President Pendleton led with 105 of the 317 votes; Johnson was second with 65, and Hancock third with 33-1/2, while favorite sons accounted for most of the remainder. Hendricks, Chase, and Blair were not formally presented. Pendleton's vote rose to 156-1/2, almost a majority, on the eighth ballot. Then eastern hostility made itself felt, and his vote declined. Hancock gained, reaching 144-1/2 on the eighteenth. Adjournment stopped the Hancock tide, and next day Hendricks had his turn, assuming the lead on the twenty-second. But on this ballot Ohio shifted to Horatio Seymour, the convention chairman. New York, which had reluctantly accepted Seymour's positive refusal to allow the use of his name, had been awaiting the right moment to present Chase; but the sudden action of the Ohio delegation upset everything. The Pendleton men did not want Chase, an Ohioan, and were only asking New York to vote for a New Yorker. Hendricks was near the nomination, and something had to be done. Seymour protested and attempted to nominate Chase; but friends pulled him off the rostrum, tears in his eyes, and hustled him away from the convention. The hot weather and the three days of fruitless balloting did the rest. The delegates stampeded to Seymour, and the harassed New Yorker was named against his will while the galleries went wild with enthusiasm.

Chase had lost the prize when it seemed to be within his grasp. The hostility of the Pendleton men in the Ohio delegation had been fatal. Daughter Kate had come to New York to manage her father's cause, but her aspirations to be First Lady were shattered by the nomination of Seymour. Had she been a delegate, the result might have been different. Yet it was well that he lost. Only by a complete sacrifice of principles could he have run on the platform adopted. As it was, he had sacrificed too much to political expediency in order to make himself available. Old friends had drawn away and he was even corresponding with the arch Copperheads, Alexander Long and Vallandigham. But everything had miscarried.

The choice of Seymour was logical enough. No Democrat was better known or commanded greater respect. Except for the financial plank, the work of Pendleton, he could stand firmly on the platform. But the convention did err badly in nominating General Francis P. Blair, Jr., for second place. His war record, his western residence, and his former Republican affiliations were assets; but a Blair was always a problem child. His Broadhead letter, widely misinterpreted to mean the violent overthrow of the new southern state governments, became a major issue. His speeches were persistently misconstrued, and his vigorous denunciation of the Reconstruction Acts was used as proof that he was a revolutionist while Grant favored peace. Chase's old dislike of the Blairs revived while the Democratic New York *World* in October demanded that Blair resign from the ticket.

A Grant Victory

The campaign of the Democrats bogged down almost from the start. Seymour and the eastern leaders did not repudiate the greenback plank, but their evasions indicated their feelings. The candidate aroused no enthusiasm in the inflationist West and the plank did not help. Although Seymour's letter of acceptance virtually repudiated Blair's Broadhead letter, it did not prevent the Republicans from playing up the issue and declaring that Blair would rule the administration if Seymour won. They even charged that the Democrats would try to pay the Confederate debt. Instead of campaigning aggressively on the reconstruction issues, the Democrats were thrown on the defensive and were unable to make headway.

Money and propaganda generally were with the Republicans, although wealthy Democrats such as August Belmont, Cyrus H. McCormick, and Samuel J. Tilden did their best. Tariff benefits, land grants to railroads, and the Republican currency position induced the Astors, the Vanderbilts, Jay Cooke, and other men of wealth to give freely to the campaign chest. The metropolitan newspapers and the leading weeklies—*Harper's*, the *Nation*, the *Independent* and *Leslie's*—were mostly Republican and conservative in their economic views, though radical enough toward the South.

Old Union party conservatives and Johnson men had to make a hard choice between the radical-sponsored Grant and the orthodox

Democrat, Seymour, whose party bore the stigma of Copperheadism. President Johnson himself tardily indorsed Seymour, though he made no speeches, and his cabinet was badly divided. Chief Justice Chase was friendly toward Seymour but hostile to Blair, and held aloof from expressions of opinion. The conservative Republican Senators who had voted for Johnson in the impeachment proceedings remained Republican despite the torrent of denunciation from party organs. Had they been forced to choose between Seymour and an out-and-out radical, many conservatives might well have preferred the Democrat; but Grant's reputation as the strong, silent soldier—he refused to make speeches—the moderation of his past views and actions, and his "Let us have peace" statement induced most of them to take him on faith.

The general trend of the October state elections toward the Republicans produced a movement, started under cover earlier, to have both Seymour and Blair withdraw. The national committee would then select a new ticket, with Chase presumably to head it. Alexander Long and some other Chase men were involved, while the New York *World* called for Blair's resignation and, by inference, Seymour's as well. But the national committee did not countenance the move, the eastern leaders were hostile, and the party newspapers disapproved almost unanimously.

One effect of the October reverses was the appearance of Seymour on the stump, actually against his wishes. He was an excellent speaker, and it was felt that he might stir the admittedly lagging spirits of the Democrats. He covered the Middle West as far as Chicago, returning through Pennsylvania. He criticized the Republicans as violators of the Constitution and emphasized the moderate, peaceful character of his own party's views. It was a fine but futile attempt to undo the damage done by Republican misconstruction of Blair's position.

The November results verified the October forecasts. Grant and Colfax had 214 electoral votes; Seymour and Blair, 80, with the popular vote running 3,012,833 to 2,703,249.[2] Seymour had New York, New Jersey, and Oregon from the North, Delaware, Maryland, and Kentucky from the border, Georgia and Louisiana from the South.

[2] Florida chose electors through the legislature; Virginia, Mississippi, and Texas, still under military rule, did not vote. Thirty-four states took part in the election.

Grant's victory rested on two pillars that Democratic campaigning could not overturn: the widespread popular confidence in the man, and the operation of radical reconstruction. The former gave him the North; the latter, the South. The effect of Negro suffrage is evident. Without the colored vote Grant would have had a smaller popular vote than Seymour, though possibly an electoral majority because of his strength in the white-voting North.

The Democratic campaign was mismanaged, but this could not explain such a decisive defeat. Nor could any other candidate have done materially better than Seymour. Pennsylvania, Ohio, and Illinois were for Grant by such majorities that it is hard to see how any Democrat could have carried them. On the other hand, Seymour won New York, which might have been lost under a different leader. Even a Democratic majority in the electoral college might not have insured victory, since the radical Congress, which counted the vote, might have thrown out the sixteen Democratic electors from the South on various pretexts and gained the day through fraud.

To Republican leaders the value of the Negro vote was clear. But it was needed in the North as well as in the South, and this required a constitutional amendment. The retiring Congress, disregarding the statement of the Republican platform that control of the suffrage in the North could be safely left to the states, passed the Fifteenth Amendment providing that the right to vote should not be denied or abridged on account of race, color, or previous condition of servitude. With Republican legislatures already chosen in the great majority of states and subject to party control, ratification was possible without giving the voters a chance to express themselves at the polls. Twelve state legislatures ratified the amendment within a month. Within a year three-fourths of the states had ratified,[3] and Negro suffrage was made compulsory everywhere with the Republican party the beneficiary.

[3] Texas, Virginia, and Mississippi were required to accept it as a condition of reconstruction. They were not readmitted until 1870.

14

The Grant Era

Old Appeals and New Leaders

When Grant entered the White House the Republican party had become an institution. It was no longer a means to an end but an end in itself. It could live on its past. A glorious tradition had been created: the party had saved the Union, struck the chains of bondage from the African, made all men equal under the Constitution and laws, and supplanted a divisive state-rights ideal with the grander conception of American nationalism. And on the more material side it could point to the boon of free lands to the landless, a Pacific railroad, a great expansion of industry, a national banking system, and an improving public credit which promised a speedy payment of the large war debt. But a list of the party's good works as recited in platforms and mouthed by campaign orators would not reveal the true source of its powerful appeal to a host of northern partisans. They voted for its candidates because of a blind mass devotion religious in its depth and intensity. Their loyalty had been christened in blood, their unity had been welded in the fires of bitter civil strife, and their faith had been hallowed by the spirit of a great humanitarian crusade. They were as likely to vote Democratic as a medieval crusader to desert to the infidels. Loyalty to the party became identified with loyalty to the Union—who served his party best served his country best; but their gaze was on the heroic past.

There was another face to Republicanism. Even before the war it had not depended on moral appeal alone. It had evolved as a partnership of antislavery crusading fervor and northern sectional interest. Now, with the retirement of the senior partner, the more practical-minded junior member was in charge. Important business interests, thriving under Republican policies, naturally supported the party in power. But the rewards had not been evenly distributed. Eastern bankers, railroad promoters, land speculators and manufacturers had gorged themselves at the federal crib; western tillers of the soil were beginning to grumble at their lean share, and only a period of hard times was needed for stirring them into action. Harassed by debts, high taxes, and falling farm prices, and disillusioned over the benefits of railroads, they were developing heretical views on economic problems.[1]

Yet the party dared not antagonize either section. Skillful evasion and the maintenance of the status quo where the issue was not too pressing afforded a partial solution; the continuance of prosperity to 1873 kept agrarian discontent from breaking the dikes, while the waving of the bloody shirt and shrewd use of Ku Klux activities in the South turned attention away from more embarrassing matters. In the main this was satisfactory to the East. It would have preferred a return to the gold standard, but this could wait. In most other policies it had already had its way. Meanwhile, the West was producing its own ranching, lumbering, and mining overlords, its large-scale farmers and petty capitalists of varied hue, to lend support to the party of business. Concessions could be made locally to western agrarian demands, but the top level of party leadership was to be found faithful to the masters of capital when the pull came. Conservatives who had looked aghast at the party's radicalism in its period of formation now pointed with pride to its humanitarian accomplishments and helped inter the crusading spirit in the grave of respectability.

Death or voluntary or enforced retirement opened the way for a new crop of leaders. Among the familiar names that disappeared from the official roster of party chieftains were such stalwarts as Stevens, Stanton, Seward, Wade, Fessenden, and Grimes. Radicals George W. Julian of Indiana and Lyman Trumbull of Illinois were soon to become party apostates, like Chief Justice Chase, who died in 1873. Sumner, sitting on the mountain of his self-esteem, continued in the Senate but was removed from the important chairmanship of the foreign relations committee in 1871 after a bitter quarrel with President Grant and Secretary of State Fish. His querulous temper and colossal ego brought about his downfall, but he no longer belonged in the political world. He was essentially the idealistic and intolerant zealot, crusading for a cause, and the cause

[1] Chapter 18 considers the third-party movements in the West as an outgrowth of this discontent.

was gone. In the sordid politics of the Grant era he was an anachronism.

The naming of a few Senatorial rulers of the Republican party in Grant's years reveals its changed character. Among the more powerful were Oliver P. Morton, once war governor and dictator of Indiana, a ruthless partisan with a vigorous mind and a paralyzed body; Roscoe Conkling, handsome, imperious, with a "majestic, supereminent, overpowering, turkey-gobbler strut" (Blaine's acid description), famed as a lawyer and orator and rapidly acquiring the mastery of New York Republicanism; Simon Cameron, seventy-year-old political despot of Pennsylvania, successively Democrat, Know-Nothing, and Republican, but always unscrupulous machine politician par excellence; and rough-mannered Zachariah Chandler, an original Republican and a Senate veteran, who was as successful in political management as he had been in the business world where he had become one of Michigan's wealthiest citizens.

In the House, where the level of ability was far lower than in the Senate, Republican soldier politicians were more conspicuous: General Benjamin F. Butler of Massachusetts, "Old Cockeye," a picturesque demagogue; General John A. Logan of Illinois, head of the Grand Army of the Republic, an expanding veterans' pressure group; and General James A. Garfield of Ohio, whose intelligence, industry, and breadth of view were walled in by his partisanship. Not a soldier but an increasingly popular idol was magnetic James G. Blaine of Maine, whose brilliant oratory and careful avoidance of extremes gained him the speakership in 1869.

The Democratic minorities in the Senate and House, deprived of southern leadership by disfranchisement and carpetbag rule, could do little. Two party stalwarts in the Senate led the hopeless fight: Allen G. Thurman of Ohio, an old-school Democrat of inflexible integrity and respected legal ability, who came to be known as "the noble old Roman," and Thomas F. Bayard of Delaware, a man of aristocratic family, distinguished appearance, and conservative principles, tinctured with a past of Copperheadism. In the House Samuel J. Randall, Democratic protectionist from Philadelphia, might expose and assail Republican corruption, but he was no enemy of business. Outside Washington, Hendricks of Indiana and General Hancock of Pennsylvania still were available for high office; but Horatio Seymour had no further ambitions. The Democratic party in New York was mired in the corruption of the Tweed Ring, and not until that was exposed and destroyed could it be a source of the leadership that the party needed.

Stigmatized by their opponents as Copperheads and rebels, the Democrats could only bide their time until new problems compelled recognition and a saner attitude pervaded the North.

The Ways of Grant

Two Grants rode through the muddy streets of the Capital on the chilly 4th of March, 1869, to take the oath of office. One was the military Grant, already almost a legendary character, known to the country as a strong, purposeful, modest, taciturn man, whose rigid jaw—concealed under a short brown beard—and stocky figure fitted the popular conception of the relentless leader of the Army of the Potomac and the generous victor at Appomattox. This was the Grant who was expected to make short shrift of politicians, reform the government and reunite the American people. The faith in him was amazing. Intellectuals like James Russell Lowell, William Cullen Bryant, and E. L. Godkin of the *Nation* looked for a new era, and even skeptical young Henry Adams had his hopes.

But there was another Grant, a concealed, enigmatic personality which the country was slow to discover. The great captain of the Civil War, now forty-seven years old, had passed forty years in obscurity, poverty, and failure. Both in the army and in the business world he had been an underdog, and deeply rooted in his personality was a sense of inferiority, which he covered with a protective silence. But the silence was an armor of weakness, not strength. Inexperienced in civil affairs, he did not invite counsel from men best fitted to give it, for this would be an admission of ignorance. Rather, he leaned on the few friends, mostly from the army, whom he had learned to trust, and presently on politicians smooth enough to gain his confidence. He knew little of political strategy and, consequently, fell back on military methods. He exacted unquestioning loyalty but returned it in full. What he did learn of political management was confined chiefly to office broking. Designing politicians like Ben Butler and General Babcock, his private secretary, had his ear, and men of wealth also found him easy of access—for the former tanner, who had never been able to make money, admired men who could. Jay Cooke, Jay Gould, and Jim Fisk entertained the President and sent gifts, and the thoroughly honest Grant was naïvely flattered. Such an attitude was not encouraging to reformers who looked to him to purge the government of inefficiency and corruption and drive the horde of lobbyists and favor seekers from the Capital. Had his tenacity of purpose been directed into the right channels, he might have made a great President. But it either lay dormant or was wasted in petty schemes like the annexation of Santo Domingo, while a carnival of corruption held sway in the government.

The inaugural, a brief collection of platitudes, was disappointing, but the original cabinet choices were amazing. With two exceptions, they were personal friends and benefactors, unfitted for their responsibilities. The exceptions, Attorney General E. Rockwood Hoar and Secretary of the Interior Jacob D. Cox, were too honest to endure the Washington smog and soon departed. Grant did blunder into an excellent appointment for Secretary of State when his original choice resigned to become minister to France. Hamilton Fish, an elderly Knickerbocker aristocrat and former Whig United States Senator, handled foreign problems skillfully and was a moderating influence on Grant and the ill assorted group around him.

The Gould-Fisk attempt to corner the gold market and the consequent "Black Friday" panic reflected on Grant's judgment and, more harshly, on the character of his brother-in-law, who was directly implicated. Indeed, Grant's problems were not made easier by the activities and importunities of a sorry lot of relatives and "in-laws," who overflowed the White House.

Civil service reform, rapidly becoming a major issue in the welter of corruption at the Capital, received Grant's approval in theory, and an act of Congress provided for a commission to prepare rules for examinations. The commission was duly appointed, but the examination system never got under way. Inadequate funds, and soon no appropriations at all, killed the reform for the rest of the Grant administrations. The President discovered that "there is a good deal of cant about civil service reform." Politicians were easier to get along with than reformers.

Grant's southern policy made a bad situation worse. When rotten carpetbag governments were threatened with overthrow by the whites organized in the Ku-Klux Klan, they appealed to the President for protection; and the influence of radical politicians of the Morton-Butler-Chandler stripe did the rest. Troops were used to support radical governments, and legislation, exemplified by the harsh "Ku-Klux Act" of 1871, made it clear that Grant had been taken into the camp of the extremists.

Tariff reform went the way of other reforms, but not without a struggle. Western farmers were anti-protectionists and had the support of Horace White of the *Chicago Tribune* and eastern intellectuals like William Cullen Bryant of the *New York Evening Post* and E. L. Godkin of the *Nation*. The Republican party had never been officially committed to a protective tariff, except in the vague plank of 1860, and it was not party treason to battle for lower rates. The protected manufacturers, however, gorged with the profits of many fat years, knew how to handle Congress. The revision of 1870 lowered rates on tea, coffee, and other non-protective articles, but the only changes affecting the protected interests provided for certain increases. On the eve of the campaign of 1872, Congress made a gesture of conciliation toward reform demands by a horizontal reduction of 10 per cent; but it was not a breach in the wall.

In the ticklish matter of the currency, the Grant forces had done nothing except insure by law the payment of government bonds in coin. This disposed of the Ohio Idea but did not solve the problem of the greenbacks. In a period of great prosperity no attempt was made to bring them to a level with gold.

As the disappointment of the reform and liberal elements with Grant turned to disgust, the regular party leaders, generally pleased with their growing ascendancy, prepared for the national convention certain that he would be renominated and his critics silenced or driven from the party. The business and financial interests were satisfied, and the storm started in Missouri might be faced with a degree of confidence.

The Liberal Uprising

Missouri had suffered from the extreme bitterness and divided loyalties of the Civil War along the border, and these carried over into the postwar years in a radical constitution excluding from the franchise persons who had served on the Confederate side, given any indirect aid or support to it, or even manifested sympathy with it. The constitution also disqualified such persons for public office, for teaching, the practice of law, and the ministry, for jury service, and for office in private corporations. The Supreme Court of the United

States had declared the stringent test oath unconstitutional in its wider application; but it remained a bar to participation in politics and government by thousands of whites. The Democratic party became a hopeless minority, and radicalism ruled for several years.

Charles D. Drake, elected to the United States Senate in 1867, was the radical leader. German-born Carl Schurz moved to Missouri and soon was a power in politics, backed by the German element. In 1869 he was elected to the Senate, but soon was ranged with Sumner against the Grant administration. In Missouri, Schurz took the lead in a movement to repeal the disabilities on white voters. The Republican state convention of 1870 split on the issue, and the Liberals broke away from the party, running B. Gratz Brown for governor against the regular candidate and electing him. The Democrats also supported Brown. At this election the hated test oath was abolished by large majorities. Grant, who had been annoyed at Schurz's hostility in the Senate, threw the administration's support against the Liberals but to no avail. The Democrats, while aiding the revolt, had got control of the legislature and now sent Francis P. Blair, Jr., to the Senate in place of Drake, who retired to a judgeship.

The anti-Grant Republicans, encouraged by the Missouri outcome, began to plan for 1872. The materials for a national movement seemed to be promising. Civil service reformers, tariff reformers, advocates of amnesty and home rule for the South, and believers in Grant's personal unfitness might well join forces against party machines and spoilsmen, radicals and their carpetbag allies in the South, and corrupt business interests which had fastened themselves on the government. Independent Republican journals such as the *New York Evening Post*, the *Springfield Republican*, the *Cincinnati Commercial*, the *Chicago Tribune*, and the *Nation* could be expected to give powerful editorial support. Senators Trumbull, Schurz, and Sumner, former Secretary of the Interior Cox, and other well known leaders were ready to act.

But this was not all. Practical politicians saw the possibilities in a reform uprising and were happy to assist. Grant's capricious rewards and punishments and his participation in factional quarrels had arrayed against him certain important state leaders who were now eager for revenge. Senator Reuben E. Fenton of New York, the anti-Cameron men of Pennsylvania, George W. Julian of Indiana, Austin Blair of Michigan, Governor John M. Palmer and Gustav

Körner of Illinois, and Governor G. C. Walker of Virginia were ready to give aid and comfort to an anti-Grant movement. In the South the Republicans were torn with dissensions and the conservatives were allying with the Democrats, since the administration backed the radicals.

The call for a national convention came from the Missouri Liberal state convention of January, 1872. Cincinnati was named as the place, and May 1 as the date. Reforming Republicans and anti-Grant politicians responded with enthusiasm, and delegates chosen in a variety of ways including self-appointment answered the call.

It had been provided that the persons in attendance from each state should designate their voting delegates. Only New York caused difficulty. A small tariff reform minority charged that the majority, controlled in the interest of Horace Greeley, had refused to give them proper representation and had tried to bind the delegation to Greeley by the unit rule. Without adopting the unit rule, the convention seated the delegates chosen by the New York majority and elected Schurz permanent chairman. He made an eloquent speech expressive of the reform purposes of the movement, and then the committee on resolutions reported the platform. The chief difficulty centered around the tariff. A small group of ardent free traders wanted an antiprotectionist plank, but Greeley had no intention of abandoning the time-honored position of his *Tribune*. The majority of the delegates were not ready to sacrifice other reforms upon the altar of free trade, and a compromise plank was worked out in committee, demanding a fair system of taxation but recognizing "in our midst honest but irreconcilable differences of opinion" with regard to protection and free trade, which it referred for decision to the voters in the Congressional districts and through them to Congress. This declaration, ridiculed by Republican regulars, was far more honest than the ambiguous tariff planks of most conventions.

On other matters there was little difficulty. Grant's administration was arraigned for its misdeeds; the equality of all men before the law was recognized, and the three war amendments were indorsed; universal amnesty was demanded for the South, along with local self-government and impartial suffrage, and the supremacy of civil over military authority; civil service reform and limitation of a President to a single term were approved; land grants to railroads were condemned; a speedy return to specie payments was urged; and the soldiers and sailors were promised the full rewards of their patriotism.

The Liberal Republicans had adopted an old-fashioned, conservative, *laissez-faire* platform. The party wanted an honest administration of the government that would eliminate corrupt politics and special privileges, and a return to local self-government as the protector of individual liberties. It failed utterly to recognize that industrialism and corporate capitalism were affecting government as well as economic life. It failed to see that political corruption and materialism were symptoms rather than diseases and could not be cured just by removing Grant and purifying the government. But the platform, even if in general negative, marked a break with the forces that had seized upon the old party, and it called for a revival of idealism as a way of salvation.

While the reformers had the platform, the practical politicians, awake to realities, took care of the candidates. The Presidential nomination was far from settled when the convention met. Charles Francis Adams had the support of the earnest reformers including the eastern intellectuals, and of the Democratic New York *World* and leading eastern Democrats, who were anxious for a Liberal whom they could support without qualification. His fine record as Minister to England during the war, his high character and unimpeachable integrity, and his refusal to bargain for the nomination fitted him admirably to lead a reform movement. Yet there were objections. He was an Adams, aloof and unemotional although more judicious than his father, and the less righteous suspected him of belonging, in the words of a fellow Liberal, to "the sneering sniffing element." His appeal was to the intellectuals, not to the masses. His letter to David A. Wells on sailing abroad to attend the Geneva arbitration must have seemed strange indeed to politicians accustomed to coy reluctance in itching candidates: In view of his isolation from all political associations, he doubted his acceptability and stated that if "the good people who meet at Cincinnati really believe that they need such an anomalous being as I am (which I do not) they must express it in a manner to convince me of it, or all their labor will be thrown away." Practical politicians could not take chances with an Adams.

The Middle West had two able contenders, but unfortunately both were from Illinois. David Davis, Supreme Court Justice by appointment of Lincoln, had strong claims. Though a Republican when appointed, he was favorably regarded by Democratic politicians and had already been named by a newly formed Labor Reform party. He was politically ambitious, but the reformers were unenthusiastic. Lyman Trumbull would have pleased them better but had to contend with Davis for support in Illinois and the Middle West. In case of a deadlock, Trumbull would have been in a strong position. Salmon P. Chase had his quadrennial attack of Presidential fever but was soon eliminated from consideration.

The strangest candidate was Horace Greeley. The veteran editor had been involved in the factional struggles in New York, had turned against Grant but looked askance at an alliance with free traders. The compromise tariff plank had been a concession to his powerful influence. At first indifferent toward the nomination, with Davis as his first choice, he was flattered at the use of his name for the Vice Presidency on a Davis ticket. But the liberal reformers, with the support of four powerful editors, Samuel Bowles of the *Springfield Republican*, Murat Halstead of the *Cincinnati Commercial*, Henry Watterson of the *Louisville Courier-Journal*, and Horace White of the *Chicago Tribune*,[2] objected so pointedly to any consideration of Davis that the politicians shifted to Greeley for first place on the ticket. The reformers realized the danger too late.

Among others considered were Governor B. Gratz Brown of Missouri, John M. Palmer of Illinois, Jacob D. Cox of Ohio, and Andrew G. Curtin of Pennsylvania. However, it seemed probable, without a long deadlock, that one of these would receive second place.

The night before the balloting, Governor Brown of Missouri arrived in Cincinnati, accompanied by F. P. Blair, Jr. Offended at Schurz because the German press had swung to Adams, they determined to throw the Missouri delegation to Greeley and secure the Vice Presidency for Brown. The first ballot gave Adams 203, Greeley 147, Trumbull 110, Brown 95, Davis 92-1/2, Curtin 62, Chase 2-1/2. Brown then appeared on the platform, withdrew his name, and declared for Greeley. The New Yorker went into the lead on the second ballot by two votes, but the Adams men, undismayed, forged ahead on the third ballot and held the lead until the sixth. Then, with the Trumbull and Davis support melting away, Greeley assumed a slight lead. This provided the opportunity for a precon-

[2] Watterson was a Democrat, but the others were Republicans. The four were termed "the Great Quadrilateral."

certed stampede, and the professionals swept the amateurs off their feet. Greeley was nominated by a large majority. The reformers had blundered in making Schurz the convention's chairman. It removed their most effective leader from the floor, where he might have controlled the inexperienced delegates in the face of an artificial stampede. Brown was named for the Vice Presidency on the second ballot.

Some leading Liberals were ready to withdraw from the movement when they contemplated the performance of the Cincinnati convention, and a public meeting at New York on May 30 of the Free Trade League, with William Cullen Bryant presiding, urged the nomination of reform candidates. But Schurz, realizing the difficulties and divisions that a new ticket would entail, helped arrange a conference of all reform groups, including Greeley men and Democrats, at the Fifth Avenue Hotel on June 20. Trumbull and Schurz spoke, urging support of Greeley as the only practical course, and all but a small minority of free traders agreed. These attempted to launch a separate ticket but failed. Except for the defection of the *Nation*, the *New York Evening Post*, and a number of German papers, the Liberal press remained loyal to Greeley.

The Republican convention at Philadelphia on June 5 aroused little interest. Grant was renominated without opposition; but Vice President Colfax was turned down, Senator Henry Wilson of Massachusetts defeating him, 364-1/2 to 321-1/2. The hostility of Washington newspapermen was said to have played a part in his defeat. The platform devoted much space to pointing with pride to the party record but offered a sop to the reformers in an indorsement of civil service reform. Resolutions denouncing repudiation of the public debt as a national crime and approving a revenue tariff, "the details of which should be so adjusted so as to aid in securing remunerative wages to labor, and promote the industries, prosperity, and growth of the whole country," took care of the business and industrial interests. A stronger commitment to the protective system was unnecessary in view of the Republican legislative record. Planks designed to appeal to the colored voters, soldiers and sailors, immigrants, capital and labor, and "the loyal women of America" were included; but labor and the women had to be content with pleasant generalities. There was approval of a recent action of Congress extending amnesty to ex-Confederates, and the Republican platform did not take clear issue with the Liberal at most points. Only

Republican approval of Grant and his southern policy indicated any real difference. But the Liberals were not deceived by Republican platform pronouncements. The apple was rotten at the heart.

For the Democrats the situation was more complex than they had expected. The way for cooperation with the Liberals had been prepared by the Missouri movement, some missionary work of Blair and other Democrats, Vallandigham's "New Departure," [3] and the failure of the party to gain ground in the local elections of 1871. "Reunion and Reform Associations" of liberals of both parties had sprung up, and a national meeting had been held at Cincinnati while the Liberal Republican convention was in session. Perplexed by the nomination of Greeley, the meeting adjourned without action. Now the regular Democrats were confronted with the same problem. Instead of Adams or Trumbull, as expected, Greeley was offered to them, a bitter potion for old-fashioned Democrats in view of his long and unrelenting criticism of their party. One of them characterized him as a "tenderhearted Moloch, whose life-long mission of hate has filled the land with fratricidal slaughter of the white race." The New York *World*, accustomed to Greeley's onslaughts, fought against indorsement by the Democratic convention; stanch party men like Charles O'Conor of New York and Thomas F. Bayard of Delaware proclaimed their opposition; but the handwriting on the wall was too plain. Defeat was certain without coalition; coalition meant Greeley.

State conventions bowed to the inevitable, and the national convention at Baltimore, July 9, voted down the bitter-enders and accepted Greeley and Brown along with the Cincinnati platform by overwhelming majorities. Southern Democrats were the most enthusiastic for Greeley. He had helped secure the release of Jefferson Davis from prison, he was now an advocate of conciliation, and, most important of all, he would draw Republican votes away from the radicals in the South and help end carpetbag domination.

But opposition did not disappear in the North after the national convention had acted. A group of anticoalition Democrats in convention at Louisville in September named Charles O'Conor of New York for President and John Quincy Adams of Massachusetts

[3] Vallandigham had offered a program before a local Democratic convention in Ohio which involved acceptance of the war and reconstruction amendments as a finality, abandonment of old issues, and indorsement of a group of reforms much like the Liberal program as a basis for future party action. The party in Ohio accepted his views, but he did not live to see the outcome.

for Vice President. A small group of Labor Reformers had already nominated O'Conor after Justice David Davis had declined their nomination. Both O'Conor and Adams refused the Louisville nominations, but the convention used their names regardless of their wishes. No Democrats of standing supported the movement; but Republican leaders looked upon it as a means of weakening Greeley and helped distribute literature for these straight-outs. Twenty-three states had O'Conor electoral tickets, but in no case was the vote large enough to affect the result. More dangerous than open defection were the lukewarm attitude of many leading Democrats toward the coalition ticket and the failure of large numbers of voters to go to the polls.

The campaign was a strange one. Never in American history have two more unfit men been offered to the country for the highest office. The simple soldier, inexperienced in statecraft, impervious to sound advice, and oblivious to his own blundering, was pitted against the vain, erratic, reforming editor whose goodness of heart could not make up for his sad lack of judgment. The man of no ideas was running against the man of too many. Intelligent voters, in perplexity, might well have preferred Grant and the evils that went with him to Greeley and evils they knew not of. But many a good American saw no problem involved in the choice. The indomitable Grant of Civil War days was resurrected by press and politicians to save the blundering, ineffectual Grant of the White House.

The legend prevailed, but not against the real Greeley. His foibles and eccentricities were exaggerated and cruelly ridiculed so that the country saw him in grotesque caricature. Thomas Nast's cruel pencil in *Harper's Weekly* held him up to ridicule in cartoons so merciless that George William Curtis, the editor, even protested. Yet it was so easy to laugh at Greeley. His appearance was anything but imposing or dignified. He was usually in a long linen duster that covered wrinkled clothes; a white hat concealed his frontal baldness but not the long silver locks at the back; metal-rimmed spectacles were hooked over his ears; and a fringe of whiskers framed his smooth round face like a miniature fur piece. A friendly observer might have detected a resemblance to Franklin, but the savage Nast cartoons made him more like a nearsighted German professor with the heavy body of a peasant, the mind of a fool, and the vanity of a child. Partisan editors dragged forth choice morsels from old files of the *Tribune* to reveal his inconsistencies and eccentricities. The courageous humanitarian editor was forgotten, and a scarecrow Greeley appeared in his place. Democratic and Liberal papers savagely attacked Grant, shouting Caesarism and corruption, but the silent soldier quietly enjoying the summer at Long Branch played the role his managers had marked out for him, without speeches. How could a caricature contend against him?

Yet even Grant could not have won in the face of a great depression. This would have torn the legend to shreds. Fortune smiled on the Republicans, however, and prosperity continued another year. Business, pleased with Grant and his party, contributed liberally to the campaign coffers. A disciplined party organization, with the patronage of the federal government and most of the states at its disposal, did the rest. The Liberals, poorly organized and embarrassed for funds, could hardly have won against such odds, even with a stronger candidate.

Greeley's strong points proved to be of slight value. His long record of friendliness to the workingman did not draw a heavy labor vote, for labor was not well organized and was politically impotent. His antislavery record and equal-rights principles failed to attract the colored vote, though Sumner gave him his blessing. Gratitude toward the Republican party and fear of the Democrats outweighed the appeals of these two veteran defenders of the black man. Greeley's efforts to bridge the "bloody chasm" were treated by exponents of the "bloody shirt" as treason to the North, and the old prejudices against the Copperhead Democracy were stirred up. Yet many Copperhead Democrats could not make themselves vote for Greeley.

The North Carolina state election in August indicated the probable defeat of the Liberals, but it remained for Pennsylvania, Ohio, and Indiana, vitally important "October states," to settle the question. Greeley went on the stump for several weeks in a remarkable oratorical campaign before large crowds. To the surprise of most people he spoke with dignity, breadth of vision, and restraint, exhibiting none of the eccentricities for which he had been lampooned. But the results were not evident on election day. Pennsylvania and Ohio went Republican, and, while Indiana elected the popular Hendricks governor, the majority of the legislature and most of the Congressmen were Republican. The Liberals lost hope, and thousands of their Democratic allies failed to vote in November.

Grant carried every northern state and most of the carpetbag South; Greeley had three border states (Missouri, Kentucky, and

Maryland), Tennessee, Texas, and Georgia. Louisiana, according to the official returning board, was apparently carried by the Liberal-Democratic coalition; but a Grant returning board reported different results, and Congress rejected both sets of electors.[4] It also threw out three Georgia electoral votes for Greeley because the electors had voted for a dead man. Arkansas, carried by Grant, was thrown out on a technicality. The coalition had made a poorer showing than Seymour in 1868. Grant's popularity seemed to be greater than ever.

For Greeley the result was fatal. His wife died October 30; he was crushingly defeated on November 5; reports came to him soon afterward of a movement to deprive him of the *Tribune;* and on November 29 he was dead. "The poor white hat!" said Harriet Beecher Stowe. "If, alas, it covered many weaknesses, it covered also much strength, much real kindness and benevolence, and much that the world will be better for."

The Liberal Republican movement disappeared with Greeley's defeat. Loosely organized and dependent upon the Democrats for most of their votes, the Liberals collapsed under the shock of a disastrous defeat. Represented in Congress by a mere handful, with no patronage to sustain them, they could not preserve their separate identity.

Despite seeming failure, the Liberal Republican movement did not live wholly in vain. It was an honest attempt to end the vexatious southern question, whose very existence imperiled any reform movement. Not until federal interference in the South ceased and local self-government was restored could the attention of the voters, northern and southern alike, be directed to the new America that had come into existence. In Grant's second term the country realized this truth, and the policy of Hayes in 1877 vindicated the Liberal position. The amnesty act of 1872 was due to Liberal pressure, and the alignment of southern conservatives in a united front was aided by the national Democratic-Liberal coalition. The Liberal movement also infused a reform leaven into the old Copperhead Democracy

[4] Greeley died before the electoral college met, and so the Liberal-Democratic electors voted for other choices. The official vote, accepted by Congress, was as follows: Grant, 286; Hendricks of Indiana, 42; B. Gratz Brown of Missouri, 18; Charles J. Jenkins of Georgia, 2; David Davis of Illinois, 1. Henry Wilson had the same vote as Grant, but the Liberal-Democratic electors scattered their votes for Vice President, Brown receiving 42, seven others dividing the remainder. The popular vote, including Arkansas and the more official of the Louisiana returns, gave Grant 3,585,444, and Greeley 2,843,563. O'Conor, straight-out Democrat, received 29,489; James Black, Prohibitionist, 5,608.

and committed it to acceptance of the finality of the war amendments, thus closing the books on the past. It loosened party ties in the West and made that section more receptive to the appeal of agrarian reformers. Perhaps the most significant accomplishment of the Liberal movement was the creation of a group of independents who, held together by a common interest in civil service reform and honesty in government, would play a notable part in the battles of the next twenty years. The Liberals had failed as party organizers, but the spirit of reform did not die with Greeley.

Republican Bankruptcy

As prosperity reached the peak, political morality sank to the lowest depths. The war and the revolutionary changes in economic life had unleashed forces that the old political system could not control. No part of the government machinery was immune. Municipal, county, state, and federal officeholders fell easy victims to the get-rich-at-any-cost philosophy. Nor were the Democrats lily-white. Though barred from federal offices, they made the most of small pickings in state and local governments under their control. In Grant's first term Boss Tweed of New York City afforded the Republicans a delightful opportunity to point the finger of scorn at the hypocrisy of Democratic reform demands. But the appalling revelations of dishonesty and corruption in the national government in Grant's second term fell upon the Republican party alone, and the country turned to the Democrats for reform.

Yet another factor buoyed Democratic hopes. Prosperity broke at last in the crash of September, 1873, inaugurated by the failure of the firm of Jay Cooke, who had been the financial angel of the Republican party with a legion of loyal politicians at his command. The panic spread rapidly, banks and business houses suspended by the hundreds, and the long depression began. Low prices, money scarcity, unemployment, farmer and labor unrest, the familiar accompaniments of hard times, soon destroyed the fiction that Republican rule was synonymous with prosperity. Not only did the party lose prestige, but the appearance of an inflationist movement threatened a sectional split. Stalwarts such as Morton of Indiana and Logan of Illinois pressed for further issues of greenbacks; and a moderate inflation bill to add $18,000,000 to the amount outstanding passed both Houses. Grant, facing a divided cabinet, unexpectedly turned down the advice of the Morton-Butler group and vetoed the bill. The pressure of eastern financial interests proved to be stronger than the appeal of party expediency.

The elections of 1874 swept the Democrats into power in New York, Pennsylvania, Massachusetts, and other Republican states and returned a House of Representatives with a large Democratic majority. The usual campaign stories of rebel outrages against the Negro in the South, touched up in lurid colors, had failed to work. Hard times and rising disgust at government inefficiency and corruption could not be answered with the bloody shirt. The southern question had been worn threadbare.

In the South itself the outraged white property owners had risen against carpetbag rule in state after state and, in spite of federal interference, had recaptured all but South Carolina, Florida, and Louisiana by 1876. The Republican party in the South was disintegrating.

Worse things marred Grant's last two years than the wreckage of his southern policy. The infamous Whiskey Ring was exposed by the reformer Secretary of the Treasury, Benjamin H. Bristow. The conspiracy even enmeshed the slippery General Orville B. Babcock, private secretary to the President, who nevertheless retained his chief's confidence after his resignation under fire. Then followed in rapid succession the Belknap scandal, involving the Secretary of War, an investigation of corruption in the Interior Department, the exposure of former Speaker Blaine's involvement in shady transactions with railroad interests, the revelation that the American Minister to England had acted as a promoter for a swindling mining scheme, and a "Not proven" verdict against a Secretary of the Navy who knew how to cover his tracks.

Grant, unable to shake off the back-stairs influence which made him see the Whiskey Ring exposure as directed against himself, developed a profound dislike for Secretary of the Treasury Bristow and forced him from the cabinet. Another reformer, Postmaster General Jewell, soon followed him into retirement. Several lesser officials who had assisted in ferreting out corruption went the way of their reforming superiors. The President had almost completely destroyed public faith in his administration and had led his party to the brink of ruin. Only a miracle could save it from defeat in 1876. The Grant legend became a poor, frayed, tattered garment, which could no longer conceal the inept wearer.

15

The Great Dispute and Its Aftermath

Hayes Versus Tilden

To offset maladministration, hard times, and carpetbag misrule the Republicans could be reasonably sure of the support of eastern business and finance. The lame-duck Congress of 1874-1875 had passed the Resumption Act to restore greenbacks to the gold level on January 1, 1879, greatly to the satisfaction of sound-money men, who felt assured that greenback inflation tendencies would be kept under control in the party. The Democrats in Ohio took an inflationist stand in 1875, when Governor William Allen, campaigning for reelection, became the protagonist of greenbackism. His defeat by Rutherford B. Hayes was an encouragement to the Republicans to hold to their conservative stand and a warning to Democrats to avoid the issue if they expected to carry any eastern states. It made the nomination of a greenbacker less likely in 1876 and helped clear the way for a reform campaign in which Republican corruption would have the leading place.

Confronted with embarrassing exposures by House investigating committees that continued even into the campaign, the Republicans had to have a candidate with an unblemished reputation, well removed from Grant and his coterie. This effectively ruled out Senators Oliver P. Morton and Roscoe Conkling, although these stalwarts continued their efforts with the disregard for the facts of the situation that sometimes characterizes politicians afflicted with the Presidential fever. Stranger even was Grant's attitude. With a blind fatuity he would have accepted a third nomination had it been offered to him. He and his family liked life in the White House and the pleasant summers at Long Branch. He had become impervious to criticism and insensible to the public reaction to his conduct. But the House by a vote of

233 to 18 declared against the third-term idea, and even Grant saw the light.

Blaine, the most popular figure in Congress, was not a member of Grant's inner circle and might have secured the nomination easily but for damaging disclosures in the Mulligan letters, made public in the spring of 1876, which involved him in shady dealings with railroad interests. His brilliant defense on the floor of the House rallied his friends, and he was still a formidable candidate when the convention met; but the reformers were adamant and Conkling, a personal enemy and heir to much of Grant's following, preferred almost any other Republican.

The reformers generally adhered to Benjamin H. Bristow of Kentucky, whom Grant's personal dislike soon forced out of the Treasury Department. A conference at the Fifth Avenue Hotel in New York of Carl Schurz, William Cullen Bryant, David A. Wells, Charles Francis Adams, and some two hundred other former Liberal Republicans issued a public declaration warning both parties against nominating any candidate who was not a thoroughgoing reformer. Bristow, while not mentioned, was obviously their choice. But eastern "silk-stocking" reformers were better at passing resolutions than at bagging delegates. Morton, Blaine, and Conkling through their control of state machines and southern carpetbag-Negro delegations placed Bristow in a hopeless position, unless his friends could effect bargains with non-reformer followers of politician candidates.

Among favorite sons were Rutherford B. Hayes, three times elected governor of Ohio, John F. Hartranft, governor of Pennsylvania, and Marshall Jewell of Connecticut, reformer Postmaster General.

The Republican convention met at Cincinnati, June 14, with the choice of a candidate uncertain for the first time since 1860. The platform caused no particular difficulties. It pointed with pride at the past but, nevertheless, promised reform in the future. Vagueness characterized most of the resolutions. Out of deference to western views, the Resumption Act was not mentioned; but "a continuous and steady progress to specie payment" was urged. The brief tariff plank implied friendliness to protection. The spoils system was condemned, and "honesty, fidelity, and capacity of the appointees" were laid down as the rule to be followed in appointments. This plank and one condemning public officers who betrayed their trusts were concessions to the reformers. The party pledged itself to protect the rights of all citizens in the South but was discreetly silent on

Grant's policy toward that section. Sectional feeling was both deprecated and stirred up in two resounding planks assailing the Democratic party for its sectionalism, its rebel sympathies, and its general incompetence and partisanship since acquiring control of the House.

Nominating speeches, now coming into vogue, were made late in the second day. One by Colonel Robert G. Ingersoll for Blaine, barely five minutes long, containing the famous "plumed knight" comparison,[1] stirred the delegates to such a pitch that Blaine's friends believed he would have been nominated had the balloting taken place at once. Defects in the lighting system—the gas supply was shut off by an anti-Blaine man, so it was charged—forced adjournment until the next morning. A heat prostration the preceding Sunday, magnified by hostile rumor into a near-fatal collapse, already had impaired his chances.

The first ballot, taken after the effect of Ingersoll's eloquence had worn off, gave Blaine 285, Morton 125, Bristow 113, Conkling 99, Hayes 61, Hartranft 58, Jewell 11, and William A. Wheeler 3. With 378 votes needed for a choice, a united opposition could defeat Blaine. But to unite the machine politicians and the Bristow reformers was not easy, and for five ballots the struggle continued, with the Blaine and Bristow votes showing little change, Morton and Conkling losing ground and Hayes rising to 104. On the sixth ballot Blaine's vote went to 308, and a stampede was imminent. The Conkling-Morton group had to choose quickly between Bristow and Hayes. Unwilling to take the reform candidate, they swung to the innocuous Hayes, whose managers had skillfully refrained from arousing antagonism and had cultivated good will in all quarters. Bristow's Kentucky delegation withdrew his name and his friends switched to Hayes, along with New York, Indiana, and part of Pennsylvania—a strange alliance of reformers and reactionaries. They were just in time. Hayes had 384, six more than he needed; but Blaine had risen to 351, and only the quick concentration of the opposition on the Ohioan defeated him.

The nomination of Hayes was not that of an obscure dark horse by an exhausted convention after a long deadlock. It was the result of a carefully planned strategy mapped out by a shrewd group of Ohio politicians, journalists, and members of Congress. Working secretly with the Bristow men to expose Blaine but building up good will and

[1] It blatantly waved the bloody shirt for Blaine and pictured him as hurling his lance against treason on the floor of the House, a reference to a recent attack on Jefferson Davis.

second-choice votes in the rival camps, they helped create a situation that fitted their man. William Henry Smith, general agent for the Western Associated Press and chief traveling salesman for the planners, confidently predicted victory to Hayes on the eve of the convention. Powerful newspaper support, the friendly atmosphere of Cincinnati, and the sharp rise in the Blaine vote—not a long deadlock—made Hayes the beneficiary of an anti-Blaine combination.

Due credit must be given to the candidate. On the reform side, the three-term governor of Ohio had a spotless reputation and the indorsement of Schurz, who had campaigned for him in 1875. Hayes preferred Bristow among the other candidates, and would have rejected second place on the ticket if Blaine had been nominated. Yet he was a faithful party man, free from the strife and bickerings of Washington, and he had proved to be Ohio Republicanism's best vote-getter. A fine Civil War record would attract soldier votes and sharpen the emotional appeal of the "rebel rule" issue. Business was pleased with his anti-inflationist stand as a candidate for governor in 1875. All in all, the Republicans had chosen wisely.

For the Vice Presidency, William A. Wheeler, a well known New York Congressman, was nominated on the first ballot.

The Democratic convention at St. Louis began two weeks later with Governor Samuel J. Tilden of New York far in the lead for the nomination. The divisions between eastern sound-money men and western greenbackers at first seemed serious; but the alluring smell of victory was in the air at long last, and a platform was drawn up that all could accept. Reform was its keynote, and reform was its refrain: reform in the administration of government to secure the country from a corrupt centralism; reform in the currency; reform in the tariff, in taxation, in public expenditures, in the public-land system; reform in immigration policies to exclude Mongolians and in foreign relations to provide treaty protection for naturalized citizens returning to their former homes; reform in the civil service and "in the higher grades of the public service." A scathing arraignment of Republican maladministration, an indorsement of the economy program of the Democratic House, and praise for the soldiers and sailors completed an unusually well written platform. It was strong in its indictment of corruption and in its program of reform but sidestepped the greenback issue. The currency section criticized Republican failure to bring about specie payment and demanded repeal of the resumption clause of the Act of 1875 as a hindrance to resumption, but was discreetly vague about what should be done. An attempt by middle western greenbackers to insert a more specific denunciation of the Republican measure was defeated on the floor of the convention by more than two to one.

The candidates presented were Tilden, Senator Thomas F. Bayard of Delaware, Governor Thomas A. Hendricks of Indiana, General Winfield S. Hancock of Pennsylvania, former Governor William Allen of Ohio, and Governor Joel Parker of New Jersey. Hendricks and Allen represented the greenback elements, but the latter was damaged by his defeat for reelection as governor the year before. Tilden had to overcome greenback distrust of his eastern viewpoint and the South's lack of acquaintance with him; but a skillfully managed pre-convention campaign did the work, and he had 417 votes on the first ballot. Hendricks received 140; Hancock, 75; Allen, 56; Bayard, 33; and Parker, 18. On the second ballot Tilden had 535 votes, well over the necessary two-thirds, whereupon the nomination was made unanimous. Hendricks was nominated for Vice President by acclamation.

Samuel J. Tilden was a veteran in New York politics, from the days of Martin Van Buren and Silas Wright; but his earlier interests were in party management rather than officeholding. Acclaimed for his part in exposing and prosecuting the Tweed Ring, he was elected governor in 1874 and showed a high order of ability as a reform administrator. That he could carry New York, essential to Democratic success, was a powerful argument for him, although Bayard, Thurman, and Hendricks were better known. Yet he was a strange choice. Sixty-two years old, unmarried, in rather poor health, this coldly intellectual, secretive corporation lawyer was far removed from the popular conception of a crusading knight of reform. Worst of all, he was a multimillionaire, having amassed his fortune in part through skill in reorganizing insolvent railroads. Such a man might give a clean, efficient administration to the country and relieve the South of carpetbag misrule, but his political and economic tenets were thoroughly conservative. The temple of business would suffer no profanation from a Tilden in the White House. He and Hayes, if not two peas from the same pod, at least gave indications of coming from the same parent vine.

The problem of the greenback Democrats, it was hoped, had been solved through the nomination of the friendly Hendricks for second place and through Hayes's outspoken stand against inflation. But, with both parties unfriendly, the extreme inflationists launched the Independent, or "Greenback," party, a threat to Democratic unity in the West.[2] Tilden's letter of acceptance, intended to harmonize differences, hurt him in the East, where concern was also expressed over the possibility that Hendricks, an avowed greenbacker, might become President if the none too robust head of the ticket did not live out his term.

Hayes, in accepting the Republican nomination, went beyond the party platform. He definitely favored resumption of specie payments, a policy of noninterference with the South, "thorough, radical and complete" reform of the civil service, and a single term for President. Republican politicians were taken aback, and Grant was annoyed at the implied criticisms of his policies; but reformers were enthusiastic. Schurz took the stump and frequently wrote letters of advice to Hayes; the former Liberal Republican organs, Bowles's *Springfield Republican*, Halstead's *Cincinnati Commercial*, and Whitelaw Reid's *New York Tribune*, extolled the virtues of the candidate in contrast with the delinquencies of Grant; and most of the Fifth Avenue Hotel conference men expressed faith in the nominee.[3] Joseph Pulitzer in the New York *World*, angry at reformer support of Hayes, could find but one reason: "Hayes has never stolen. Good God, has it come to this?"

The Conkling-Morton-Chandler group, saddled with a reformer candidate, made the best of the situation by working for party victory and ignoring Hayes, whom they did not even consult about the national chairmanship. With a better appreciation of the realities of politics, they saw that the reform issue was an admission of Republican guilt and was playing directly into Tilden's hands. A political newcomer, Colonel Robert G. Ingersoll, acclaimed for his nominating speech for Blaine, was put on the stump and drew huge crowds all the way from Maine to the Mississippi River, waving the bloody shirt as it had never been waved before and assailing the Democratic party as the party of treason and rebellion. A South Carolina riot in July in which several Negroes were slain served to point the moral of southern depravity and to show the dire consequences to be expected if the southern-controlled Democratic party came into power.

[2] The Greenback party is discussed with other agrarian parties in Chapter 18.

[3] Charles Francis Adams and Parke Godwin, however, supported Tilden. In the West, Lyman Trumbull, John M. Palmer, George W. Julian, Gustav Körner, and many other Liberals had joined the Democrats.

This stirring of old hatreds reached such a stage that late in the campaign the Democratic national chairman, Abram S. Hewitt, forced from the excessively cautious Tilden a public declaration against any payment of Confederate debts, any compensation for loss of slaves, or any recognition of damage claims of disloyal persons, a touchy point.

Republican orators assailed Tilden's private character, charging that he was a railroad wrecker, a grasping penny pincher, an income-tax evader, a sham reformer, and—Ingersoll added—a dried-up, old bachelor, as bad as Buchanan. Zach Chandler, Republican chairman, managing the Hayes campaign with no illusions about reform, collected large sums from federal officeholders and concentrated on New York and Indiana, to the neglect of other states. "A bloody shirt campaign, with money, and Indiana is safe," wrote one party leader in a letter which got into the newspapers; "a financial campaign and no money, and we are beaten." Hayes, aware of the straits of the party in these two states and even in Ohio, came down from his pedestal and urged Blaine to play up in his speeches the dread of a solid South and rebel rule to distract people's thoughts from hard times. Nor was he averse to stirring up anti-Catholic prejudices against Tilden whose record was combed to provide some evidence. The secret anti-Catholic, antiforeign "Order of the American Alliance" indorsed Hayes.

Tilden's "barrel," as depicted by the cartoonist Nast, was supposed to finance the Democratic campaign; but this was far from the case. The candidate kept a tight hold on his purse strings, offended Chairman Hewitt and the organization managers by his indifferent attitude toward their arduous work, and failed to supply funds which might have made safe the three doubtful southern states. As it was, the national headquarters centered its efforts and funds on New York and Indiana, and did a good job. The South was left to shift for itself—a fatal error.

In the October state elections Indiana was Democratic by a small margin, Ohio Republican by a slightly larger plurality. The Democrats were encouraged. Indiana, New York, and a solid South would mean victory. Betting odds favored Tilden, while Hayes calmly prepared himself for an unfavorable verdict, though worried over the possibility of a disputed outcome.

Early returns indicated before midnight of November 7 that Tilden had been elected. New York, Indiana, Connecticut, and New

Jersey had gone Democratic, and while there was some uncertainty about the "solidity" of the South, Tilden could spare two southern states and still win.[4] Republican headquarters in New York closed up, and Chairman Chandler, discouraged at reports from Louisiana and Florida, went to bed. Hayes admitted his defeat in his diary, and nearly all the Republican papers gave up hope.

The Dispute Begins

In the early hours of the morning of November 8, while the editors of the *New York Times*, stanchest of Republican organs, debated whether to concede Tilden's election, a message came from Democratic state headquarters asking for the *Times* estimate of the electoral vote. This indication of Democratic uncertainty encouraged the editorial staff to hold out a little longer. The *Times*, without basis, thereupon claimed Louisiana and South Carolina for Hayes, but left Oregon, New Jersey, and Florida in doubt. John C. Reid, managing editor, then hastened to the Fifth Avenue Hotel headquarters of Chairman Zach Chandler, picking up an ally on the way, William E. Chandler of New Hampshire, national committeeman and lobbyist. The two aroused the exhausted, uncomprehending national chairman and secured his permission to send telegrams alerting party leaders in South Carolina, Florida, and Louisiana to the fact that the national outcome depended on holding these states. Without this prod, they might have accepted as final the reported returns. Agents well supplied with money were soon heading southward, and National Chairman Chandler, belatedly aware of the situation, announced that Hayes had 185 electoral votes; Tilden, 184.

Everything seemed to depend on the official count in the three doubtful states, and both sides sent "visiting statesmen" South to watch the count.

The situation in the three states was similar. The Republicans controlled the state governments and the election machinery, had relied upon the Negro masses for votes, and had practiced frauds as in the past. The Democrats used threats, intimidation, and even violence when necessary, to keep Negroes from the polls; and where they were

[4] The popular vote is difficult to determine accurately because of disputed returns. Stanwood gives as the Republican count, Tilden 4,285,992 and Hayes 4,033,768; the Democratic count gave Tilden 4,300,590 and Hayes 4,036,298. Peter Cooper, Greenbacker, had 81,737; Green Clay Smith, Prohibitionist, 9,522.

in a position to do so they resorted to fraud also. The firm determination of the whites to overthrow corrupt carpetbag rule contributed to make a full and fair vote impossible; carpetbag hold on the state governments made a fair count impossible. Radical reconstruction was reaping its final harvest.

In Florida a small Tilden majority was wiped out by a Republican-controlled election board, and the Hayes electors received the official certificates. In South Carolina Hayes had a small margin of the popular vote, though the Democrats elected Wade Hampton governor and carried the legislature. In both states the Democratic electoral candidates claimed the election and cast their votes for Tilden, though officially the Republicans had the better case.

In Louisiana a board of four Republicans of doubtful reputation canvassed the votes. A vacancy existed—to be filled, according to the law, with a Democrat; but this had not been done. Here the discretionary power was almost unlimited. Returns from whole parishes could be thrown out if the board had reason to believe that force, intimidation, or corrupt influences had affected the result. It invited delegations from the considerable number of "visiting statesmen" in New Orleans to attend the sessions and proceeded to take testimony and examine conditions in parishes where the returns were disputed. While the Republicans had padded the registration rolls, notably at New Orleans, it was evident that violence and intimidation had been practiced by the Democrats in several parishes, in one case resulting in the reduction of a Republican vote of 1,688 in 1874 to a single defective ballot in 1876. To throw out the votes of these "bulldozed" parishes would not, however, give Hayes a majority, for the Tilden electors on the face of the returns had won without them. Other parishes had to be examined, additional irregularities uncovered, and Democratic totals reduced as a consequence until finally the lowest Hayes elector had a majority of 3,437, with a Republican governor and legislature also safely counted in.[5]

[5] Paul L. Haworth, *The Hayes-Tilden Disputed Presidential Election of 1876* (Cleveland, 1906), states that "in an absolutely fair and free election" Louisiana would have gone Republican by five to fifteen thousand, basing his figures on the numbers of colored and white voters on the registration rolls. He admits that the rolls were padded by the Republicans, but argues that they actually derived little advantage from the excess. He dismisses the census of 1880, which showed more adult white males in the state than colored, as inconclusive because "many thousands" of the whites were foreigners. If the colored voters outnumbered the whites, in "an absolutely fair and free election"—which Louisiana had not had since

The action of the board was a travesty on justice and may even have been the result of corruption. The leading member of the board, through an intermediary, offered to give the election to Tilden for $1,000,000, but the offer was not accepted. Promises by Republican visitors may have been a consideration. Three members of the board later received federal offices from Hayes. Money also went southward in discreet hands to smooth the path for Hayes.

The electors so chosen voted for Hayes. The Democratic electoral claimants, refusing to accept the board's decision, met and voted for Tilden. John McEnery, who had been kept from the governorship by federal troops since 1874, but who still claimed the office, signed their certificates. Governor Kellogg certified the papers of the Republicans.

In Oregon a peculiar situation developed which offered the Democrats a chance for an electoral vote. Hayes carried the state, but one of the three electors was disqualified by being a postmaster (no elector may hold an office of trust or profit under the federal government). Governor L. F. Glover, Democrat, gave a certificate of election to the highest Democratic electoral candidate on the theory that the disqualification of the postmaster elector made his election void. However, the two Republican electors met, received the resignation of the ineligible Republican, elected him to the vacancy (he had resigned as postmaster), and the three cast their votes for Hayes and Wheeler. Granted that Hayes was really entitled to the one disputed vote, still was not the appearance of legality with the Democrats, as in the South it rested with the Republicans? If the two Houses went behind the official certificates in one case, could they avoid doing so in the other? This contention by the Democrats explains their presentation of what was purely a technical claim to the Oregon vote.

---

reconstruction began—would some 114,000 colored voters, nine-tenths of them illiterate, have gone to the polls and voted Republican? A "fair and free election," without Republican as well as Democratic pressure and intimidation—an impossible ideal in Louisiana then—would have been marked by the absence of thousands of colored voters from the polls through sheer indifference. Carpetbag politicians played more subtly upon the ignorance, cupidity, prejudices, and fears of the Negro while the Democrats emphasized intimidation and violence. It is hard to see any difference ethically between marching ignorant colored voters to the polls with marked ballots and keeping them from voting by threats and intimidation. But, after all, the question in 1876 was not whether one party or the other had a moral right to the state of Louisiana, but which one had more votes in the ballot boxes. That the Democrats had more can hardly be questioned.

A Partisan Settlement

The Constitution states that the President of the Senate shall, in the presence of the two Houses, "open all the certificates, and the votes shall then be counted." Did this confer any power on the presiding officer to decide which votes should be counted or rejected when double sets of returns came from a state? Most authorities were inclined to answer in the negative, and this was in accord with all the precedents, though Hayes personally held to the other viewpoint. Senator Ferry of Michigan, a Republican, presided over the Senate (Vice President Wilson was dead) and would doubtless act in the interests of his party. But, granted the right of the two Houses to decide such matters, how could a Republican Senate and a Democratic House of Representatives be expected to agree?

In 1865 the two houses had adopted the Twenty-second Joint Rule providing for the rejection of the vote from any state in case either house, voting separately, objected to it. Under this rule in 1873 the electoral votes of Louisiana and Arkansas, and three from Georgia, had been thrown out. But early in 1876 the Senate refused to readopt the rule, because the House of Representatives was Democratic. Had it been in effect, the House would have rejected the electoral votes from the disputed states and Tilden would have been elected. With no rules to bind it, Congress met in December, 1876, and took up the problem. Alarmist stories in the newspapers and threats of hotheads on both sides created a tension that in the end promoted compromise. No one desired a civil war, and common sense pointed to arbitration. Most important of all, business interests put pressure on both sides to arrange a solution.

A joint committee of the two houses, after long discussion, evolved a plan for an Electoral Commission to consist of five Senators, five Representatives, and five Supreme Court Justices. The two houses were to elect their representatives (in each case, three from the majority and two from the minority); four Justices (two from each party) were designated in the bill, and they were to choose a fifth, presumably David Davis, of uncertain political affiliations. This Electoral Commission was to have final authority in the cases of double sets of electoral votes, unless both houses agreed to overrule it. The plan was accepted by large majorities, most of the opposition coming from die-hard Republicans. The Democrats felt certain that such a commission could not be so partisan as to award all the disputed votes to Hayes—and Tilden needed only one to win. Without arbitration, the cards were stacked in favor of the Republicans, who controlled the executive (and the army), the Supreme Court, and the Senate.

Democratic hopes were suddenly dashed to the ground on the very day the bill passed the Lower House. News of a startling character arrived from Springfield, Illinois. The preceding day, a coalition of Democrats and independents in the Illinois legislature had elected Justice Davis to the United States Senate, rendering him unacceptable for service on the Electoral Commission. Fortune seemed to reserve her smiles for the Republicans through these years; but in this case asinine blundering by Illinois Democrats would seem to be a more logical explanation. National Chairman Hewitt and the Congressional leaders, intent on getting the Electoral Commission bill passed, realized too late the dangers in the Illinois situation.

There was still the possibility that the judicial members of the commission would show the fair-mindedness of true judges and not the spirit of partisans. At least the fifth Justice, on whom the burden of the final decision must rest, would surely realize the gravity of his position and put aside partisan considerations. That unfortunate individual, chosen by the four Justices already on the Commission after Davis became disqualified, was Justice Joseph P. Bradley. Bradley had the approval of Democratic leaders as he appeared to be the most independent of the remaining members of the Court, all of them Republican.

The electoral count began before the two Houses on February 1, with a great crowd present in the hall of the House of Representatives. When Florida was reached, objections were raised against the certificates of both Republican and Democratic electors, and the problem went to the Electoral Commission. The first and most important matter for it to settle was whether it should go behind the returns. After long arguments by eminent counsel, it was voted, 8 to 7, that the Commission was not competent to receive evidence which was not submitted to the two houses in joint session. In other words, the regularity of the certificates would be considered, but not the proceedings and measures in Florida responsible for them. After such a decision, arguments were futile. Regularity was with the Republicans, and the Commission, 8 to 7, awarded the Florida votes to Hayes, with Bradley casting the deciding vote.

Abram S. Hewitt, Democratic National Chairman and Congressman from New York, related in his account of the Great Dispute that Justice Bradley wrote an opinion favorable to the Democrats in the Florida case, but that some after-midnight pressure from a cabinet member and a New Jersey Senator, with an assist from Mrs. Bradley, caused him to rewrite the opinion and reverse himself. Hewitt's story came from a common friend. Some months later Bradley, to quiet ugly rumors about his conduct as a member of the Commission, explained that he had written two opinions and then selected the stronger. Such an unusual procedure may be the truth; yet, if Bradley actually yielded to pressure and voted as a partisan, why should he be condemned for doing what all his colleagues did?

The Democratic House rejected the Commission's decision in the Florida case; but the Republican Senate upheld it, and so it was final according to the law. Similar verdicts in the Louisiana, Oregon, and South Carolina cases gave Hayes their disputed electoral votes. House and Senate separated to vote on each disputed state.

While the South Carolina case was under consideration, an alarming possibility developed. Democratic die-hards in the House were ready to inaugurate a filibuster that would prevent resumption of joint sessions and completion of the count before March 4. What would then happen, no one could say. Civil war might begin. But the danger was more apparent than real.

Actually, negotiations had been under way for many weeks to take care of such a situation. William Henry Smith, general agent of the Western Associated Press, acting for the Hayes inner circle, had established contacts with important southern conservatives, chiefly former Whigs, and reached a tentative agreement with them that would insure their support for the peaceful acceptance of Hayes as President. As finally worked out, the terms of the bargain included assurances that Hayes would live up to his letter of acceptance and bring to an end federal support of carpetbag rule; that at least one cabinet post, and other patronage favors, would go to southern conservatives; that Hayes would favor federal aid for education and internal improvements in the South, including a government subsidy for the Texas & Pacific Railway. The lower Mississippi valley was eager for a rail connection with the Far West, but the panic had stalled the project. Thomas A. Scott, president of the Pennsylvania Railroad, was interested in the Texas & Pacific and played a part in the consummation of the bargain.

Hayes made these commitments cautiously, through intermediaries.

In return, he received promises of equal rights and fair treatment for southern Negroes and assurances that the electoral count would proceed unobstructed. He also believed that a coalition to elect James A. Garfield Speaker of the new House might be arranged. Southern Democrats, especially those of Whig background, saw more loaves and fishes for their neglected section in a deal with the Hayes men than in a resolute stand beside their intransigent northern colleagues. Hayes had once been a Whig.

The well known conference in late February at Wormley's Hotel in Washington, long supposed to have produced the solution to the filibuster threat, actually was only a last-minute meeting to reassure worried southerners that the terms already agreed upon would be respected. A number of persons participated in the negotiations at various stages, including the indefatigable William Henry Smith, General Henry Van Ness Boynton, a Washington correspondent, Andrew J. Kellar of the Memphis *Avalanche,* Major E. A. Burk of Louisiana, Tom Scott's Pennsylvania Railroad lobby, several conservative southern members of Congress, and a group of Ohio friends of Hayes. Although not involved in the deal, Speaker Randall and National Chairman Hewitt also worked to prevent delays in completing the count of the electoral votes. In the early hours of March 2 the two Houses finished their tabulation: Hayes had 185 electoral votes; Tilden, 184.

Hayes arrived at the Capital that day and took the oath of office privately the next evening at the White House, because March 4 was a Sunday. On Monday, with due ceremony, he was formally inaugurated.

Hayes in the White House

Party strategy and the doctrine of availability have placed in the White House some strange figures, but there was nothing strange about Hayes. He seemed to be so nearly the average man that his solid merits went unappreciated. Superlatives are out of place in describing this full-bearded, pleasant-faced middle western lawyer-politician, who was merely a good soldier, a good lawyer, a good speaker, a good Congressman, a good governor, and a good husband and father. Without an ounce of brilliancy or even the slightest touch of that strange magnetism which, in a man like the eloquent Blaine, set men's blood racing, Hayes calmly set to work to be a good

President. And his equally good wife, Lucy Webb Hayes, a democratic prototype of British Victoria, proved to be a remarkably successful White House hostess, though she never deviated from her strict code of middle-class respectability. She excluded alcoholic beverages in every form from state dinners and required daily family prayers of her household, faithful attendance at church, and Sunday evenings of hymn singing, in which White House guests participated. The Grant atmosphere of whiskey and horses vanished, and the country approved of "Lemonade Lucy."

Hayes displayed his independence by naming an unusually able cabinet with small regard for party orthodoxy. The new Secretary of State was William M. Evarts of New York, who had defended Johnson in the impeachment trial and argued for Hayes before the Electoral Commission. John Sherman of Ohio, a capable financier, became Secretary of the Treasury, and Carl Schurz, civil service reformer and Liberal Republican, became Secretary of the Interior. David M. Key of Tennessee, a Democrat who had served in the Confederate Army, became Postmaster General—an appointment to which Hayes's Ohio managers had agreed during the long negotiations with southern conservatives. Both Conkling and Blaine were antagonized. Blaine even attempted to delay confirmation of the appointments; but a southern bloc supported them, and opposition dissolved.

Hayes next proceeded to end the southern question by withdrawing federal troops from South Carolina and Louisiana. The last two carpetbag governments melted away, and Democratic officials took over, pledged to equal rights for all citizens. Hayes and Secretary Sherman tried to soften the blow for their own party and carry out some earlier pledges by bestowing federal plums upon ejected Republicans and upon the members of the disreputable Louisiana returning board. But Republican Stalwarts of the Blaine-Chandler-Cameron type were alarmed at the abandonment of the southern wing of the party and became sharply critical.

And yet Democrats were equally critical, except for the southern collaborators. This group, in which Wade Hampton, South Carolina's new governor, was outstanding, found their efforts at reconciliation nullified by a faction of Bourbons who went ahead with a program of Negro disfranchisement and white supremacy. Hayes's hope of building conservative support for his party in the South faded, though he continued to work for a better understanding between the two sections. Southern rivers and harbors received more federal money than in the past, but the Texas & Pacific Railway subsidy did not carry. Northern Democrats, outraged at the "fraud" of 1876, set about proving the defective character of the title of "Old 8 to 7," aiming at a campaign of vindication in 1880. The Potter committee of the House, after an investigation, reported in 1879 that Tilden had been unfairly deprived of the Presidency; but a Republican Senate committee unearthed telegrams in cipher that implicated leading Democrats (including Tilden's nephew) in schemes to use money corruptly to secure an electoral vote. Tilden was not personally involved, but the exposure blunted the Democratic charges of fraud and corruption.

The Democrats also attacked federal supervision of Congressional elections instituted under Grant. Hayes was opposed to the use of troops at the polls but wished to continue the system under civil officials. He was forced to use the veto to prevent repeal after both houses came under Democratic control in 1879. The laws remained on the statute books, though unused for lack of funds, until Cleveland's second term. Then they were repealed.

Hayes's southern policy aroused the enmity of the Stalwarts in his party, but his attempts at civil service reform angered them even more. They dubbed him and his supporters "Half-Breeds," and the gap widened between the two factions. At his request Secretaries Evarts and Schurz drew up a set of rules to govern appointments in the various departments. With no funds to inaugurate competitive examinations, reform had to be handled departmentally. Investigations promptly begun revealed that much needed to be done, and the President took the initiative. In a drastic executive order of June 22, 1877, he laid down certain principles and made it clear that government officers were to take no part in politics other than voting. Politicians could only gasp. The millennium of the reformers seemed to be at hand.

Hayes next moved against the citadel of spoils politics, the New York Customhouse. With more than a thousand officials under his control and two-thirds of the federal revenues under his supervision, Chester A. Arthur, collector of the port, had more political power than most cabinet members. He and Alonzo B. Cornell, the naval officer, were important cogs in the Conkling machine. An investigation by a special commission in the summer of 1877 seemed to reveal enough looseness, inefficiency, and spoils politics, if not corruption, to warrant overhauling; and the President decided to replace Arthur and Cornell. Conkling had already defied the administration by having his state convention reject a resolution of indorsement. The irate Senator had called the reformers "man-milliners, the dilettante and carpet knights of politics," who forgot that "parties are not built up by deportment, or by ladies' magazines, or gush." Consequently, when the names of the Hayes appointees were submitted to the Senate, he secured their rejection by a vote of 25 to 31. Senatorial vested interests in federal patronage were at stake, and birds of a feather voted together.

But Hayes was not whipped. "I am right," he wrote in his diary, "and shall not give up the contest." After Congress adjourned he suspended Arthur and Cornell and gave their places to Edwin A. Merritt and Silas W. Burt. At the next session of Congress pressure, wire pulling and patronage were used to advantage by Secretary of the Treasury John Sherman, and the administration forces finally won the day, 33 to 24 for Merritt and 31 to 19 for Burt. Most of the Democrats, including the pro-Hayes southerners, voted favorably, but only a minority of the Republicans stood with them. The majority (including his old enemy, Blaine) voted with Conkling. The new York Colossus was not destroyed, but his power was shaken.

This was almost the only important political victory won by the reformer President. Even the veto failed him when a bipartisan coalition enacted the Bland-Allison Act in 1878 for a limited coinage of silver dollars—a concession to West and South. The return of prosperity in 1879 and the successful operation of the Resumption Act in bringing greenbacks to a gold level seemed to vindicate the anti-inflationist stand of the President. But prosperity and a record of house cleaning did not bring Hayes a second nomination. He held to his one-term pledge, and Stalwart politicians were relieved.

16

In the Doldrums—the Eighties

Grant Again?

The Stalwart leaders, scanning the horizon for a man who could recapture the White House for the true-blue Republicans and restore the happy days of Grant, found exactly the candidate for their purposes some months before the convention met: Grant himself. The Hero of Appomattox, returning in 1879 from a leisurely trip around the world, seemed to have recovered his old popularity and to be ready to reenter politics. His past blunders as President were glossed over with arguments that he was now wiser and more experienced, that he was needed to rescue the party from the well-meaning weakness of Hayes, that he would protect the Negro and revive Republicanism in the South.

Grant at first seemed to be reluctant; but he yielded to the pressure of family and friends, and presently was counting delegates and figuring his chances like any aspiring American newly stung by the Presidential bee. Conkling took charge of the movement. The New York Republican state convention not only named delegates at large pledged to vote for Grant but adopted a resolution instructing the delegates chosen at district conventions to do likewise—a high-handed attempt to shackle the large anti-Grant minority with a unit rule. J. Donald Cameron, succeeding his father as boss of Pennsylvania, had already put his state in the Grant ranks and bound the delegates to vote as a unit. John A. Logan accounted for Illinois, but a protesting minority sent anti-Grant delegates from nine districts.

Meanwhile, the opposition leaders had not been idle. Seizing upon the "No third term" argument as their best weapon, they organized clubs under that name and held a convention at St. Louis in May, 1880, under the leadership of former Senator John B. Henderson of Missouri, with fourteen states represented. But the best chance to defeat Grant lay in the strength which other candidates could muster. John Sherman had Ohio and scattered votes elsewhere; Elihu B. Washburne of Illinois had ambitions but not many delegates; Senator George F. Edmunds of Vermont had some New England support and the blessing of eastern reformers; yet neither singly nor combined could these favorite sons have stopped the Grant phalanx. Only Blaine could do that, and he was strangely irresolute. Most certainly he wanted Grant beaten and Conkling discomfited. Yet he hesitated to hurl himself into the fight, though no one was so popular with the masses of Republican voters. This gifted man seemed at times to sense the futility of pursuing his ambitions further, to have premonitions that the Presidency was never to be his. His devoted followers could not understand; but they rounded up delegates for him and made him the chief barrier in the path of Grant.

On June 2 the Republican national convention assembled at Chicago in a great barnlike building on the lake large enough to accommodate more than ten thousand spectators. It immediately became the setting for a duel between Conkling, leading the Grant men, and James A. Garfield of Ohio, who marshaled the Sherman forces but was tacitly accepted as the spokesman for all the anti-Grant elements. Garfield, a skillful parliamentary leader persuasive and courteous where Conkling was grandiloquent and overbearing, outmaneuvered the New Yorker and threw a wrench into the plans of the Stalwarts. Cameron was chairman of the national committee, and the Grant forces expected to secure the temporary chairmanship of the convention and bring about recognition of the unit rule at the very beginning of proceedings; but Garfield with the support of a majority of the committee forced the selection of an Edmunds man, Senator George F. Hoar of Massachusetts, leaving the determination of the unit rule to the convention itself.

As chairman of the rules committee, Garfield presented a rule which recognized the right of the delegates to vote individually—in contrast with the unit rule the Grant men desired, in which the majority in a state delegation cast the entire vote of the state. The acceptance of the rules committee report by the convention was fatal to Grant's chances, as it freed more than sixty members of the New York, Pennsylvania, and Illinois delegations.

The platform pointed with pride but did little else. Most of the resolutions were repetitions, rephrased, of the planks of 1876, though Chinese immigration was now specifically condemned and civil service reform was not mentioned. This surprising omission was challenged by a Massachusetts delegate who proposed a plank declaring that reform should be "thorough, radical, and complete," quoting President Hayes, and demanding legislation by Congress. There were objections, but in the end it carried without a roll call. The delegates, whatever their actual views, realized the effect of rejection on the coming campaign. Another plank lauded the Hayes administration, though nobody on the convention floor lifted a voice to suggest that his "efficient, just, and courteous discharge of the public business" might well be continued another four years.

The nominating speeches, delayed until Saturday night by wrangling over some fifty contested seats, included two notable efforts. Conkling's speech presenting Grant, regarded by Republican hero-worshipers as a convention classic and often compared with Ingersoll's presentation of the "plumed knight" in 1876, won no votes. He could not refrain from directing slurs and aspersions at Grant's rivals. Garfield's more restrained eloquence on behalf of John Sherman won votes in the end not for his candidate but for himself. Seldom has one man played such a conspicuous role in a national convention.

The first ballot revealed that Grant was doomed. He had 304 votes; Blaine, 284; Sherman, 93; Edmunds, 34; Washburne, 30; William Windom, 10. Ballot after ballot brought little change. Sherman gained part of the Edmunds vote, but no more. Conkling held out inexorably for Grant but, without the unit rule, could not obtain a majority. In the end, the Blaine and Sherman followings combined to settle the deadlock. To unite on either candidate proved to be impossible. A logical substitute was not hard to find, for Garfield had been frequently mentioned before the convention as a dark-horse contender. As Sherman's manager and Blaine's friend (oddly enough, his own district in Ohio sent two Blaine delegates to Chicago), he was satisfactory to the followers of both men. The break started on the thirty-fourth ballot when the Wisconsin delegation voted for him; the 17 became 50 on the thirty-fifth ballot, and 399 on the thirty-sixth and last. Garfield had risen to his feet in protest at the use of his name when the thirty-fourth ballot was taken but was quickly suppressed by the chairman. He had the distinction, unique among candidates, of witnessing his own nomination. There was whispering among some friends of Sherman that Garfield had had his lightning rod ready all along, but Blaine and Sherman men found consolation in Grant's defeat.

The Conkling forces, holding 306 votes for Grant to the end, now had to be appeased, and so the Vice Presidential nomination was offered them. The New York delegation suggested the deposed collector of the port, Chester A. Arthur, and he was easily nominated over Elihu B. Washburne of Illinois. It was supposed that this represented Conkling's method of securing revenge on Hayes; but, years afterward, it was revealed that the embittered boss had preemptorily ordered Arthur not to permit his name to be offered, and that the ex-collector had courteously but firmly refused to obey. Reformers and Independents were appalled at the nomination but finally consoled themselves with the thought that his "powers of mischief" would be small in the Vice Presidency.

Garfield's rise from canal boy born in a log cabin to Presidential nominee was a Horatio Alger story, and Republican propagandists made the most of it. A product of the Western Reserve with a degree from Williams College in New England, he had been a lay preacher, a college instructor and president, had studied law, and was serving in the Ohio Senate when the Civil War drew him into military service. He rose to the rank of major general but resigned his commission to enter Congress in December, 1863. Eloquent and industrious, he became Republican floor leader in 1877 and was a Senator-elect when nominated for President. Only forty-eight, he was one of the most promising younger leaders, and his unexpected nomination was well received by Republicans, except some Stalwart die-hards.

The Democratic convention met at Cincinnati on June 22 with the field wide open. Tilden was unavailable because of impaired health, Tammany opposition, and the damaging disclosures in the Senate investigation of the great dispute of 1876-77; but he left the door slightly ajar in a letter intrusted to the New York delegation. A demand that he show his hand finally produced a telegram that his decision was "well considered and irrevocable." By this time the balloting had begun.

The convention was a dull affair compared with the Republican show. There were no flaming speeches, and no candidates who evoked wild enthusiasm or bitter opposition. Thomas F. Bayard of Delaware and Allen G. Thurman of Ohio were men of high character and solid attainments, but the first was regarded as a southerner and the other was injured by a rival from his own state—Henry B. Payne, a former Congressman with Standard Oil connections, who also had the vote of the New York delegation on the first ballot. Justice Stephen J. Field of the Supreme Court received much publicity but lacked popular appeal. General Winfield S. Hancock of Pennsylvania, fifty-six-year-old professional soldier, had more elements of availability and led on the first ballot with 171 votes; but this was less than one-fourth of the total, and a long deadlock seemed to be in prospect. On this ballot nineteen candidates received votes, Bayard, Payne, and Thurman running second, third, and fourth.

On the second ballot the friends of Tilden concentrated on Samuel J. Randall, Speaker of the House, while Hancock's vote increased to 320—well under a majority and far from the necessary two-thirds. An effective opposition might have stopped him, but there was so little enthusiasm for any of his rivals that delegates obligingly changed their votes until he had 705, making a third ballot unnecessary. The nomination was his almost by default. The Vice Presidential choice proved to be equally simple. Indiana, carried by Tilden in 1876, seemed to require representation on the ticket, and former Congressman William H. English, a banker with a "barrel," was nominated without a formal ballot.

The platform, adopted before the nominations, was brief, and the most significant planks may be given verbatim:

> 3. Home rule; honest money, consisting of gold and silver, and paper convertible into coin on demand; the strict maintenance of the public faith, state and national; and a tariff for revenue only.
>
> 4. The subordination of the military to the civil power, and a general and thorough reform of the civil service.

A declaration against Chinese immigration, denunciations of the Republicans, particularly for the "great fraud" of 1876-1877, praise for Tilden, whose refusal to be a candidate was received with "deep sensibility," opposition to "centralizationism," and the usual platitudes completed the statement of party beliefs.

The convention had done a fair job with the materials at hand. Thurman or Bayard deserved the nomination on the score of fitness for high office; but a candidate was needed whose military record would match Garfield's and neutralize Republican appeals to northern sectional prejudices. The disappearance of the greenback issue with the return of prosperity made it safe to select an eastern candidate. General Hancock was a good choice.

The campaign of 1880 was barren of issues and devoid of drama. Labor troubles and farmer unrest had subsided, though the Greenback party, headed by General James B. Weaver, tried to keep the embers alive. Neither major party had a program, and only on the tariff question was there any divergence. The Republicans waved the bloody shirt rather feebly and talked of southern disfranchisement of Negroes and the power the white South would exercise in a Democratic administration. The Democrats did not overlook the "fraud" of 1876-1877 and repeated the old charges of Republican corruption, though the honest administration of Hayes gave these small weight.

The reformers, or Independents, again seemed to be in a position to decide the election. Both platforms had indorsed civil service reform, but more to the point were the records of the candidates. Here Garfield's garments were slightly spotted. As the recipient of a share of stock in the Crédit Mobilier, which had been exposed in Grant's administration, he had collected $329 in dividends. His explanations of this and of a large attorney's fee in a Washington paving contract scandal satisfied even the impeccable *Nation* and G. W. Curtis's *Harper's Weekly*. Schurz added his praises as well. But Garfield's letter of acceptance was not the positive statement on civil service reform the reformers expected, and during the campaign he seemed to cater to the machine leaders. In spite of this, the Independents turned down Hancock, with an unblemished record, apparently because of his lack of experience in government. Sneers at his imposing physique—"a good man weighing two hundred and forty pounds"—and Nast's cartoons portraying his naïve ignorance were the extent of Republican assaults on the man.

Conkling was the chief Republican problem. Arthur, Cameron, and Logan did their part but "Lord" Roscoe sulked in his tent. Garfield visited the East in August to appeal for financial support and secured Jay Gould's help. Thomas C. Platt and other New York Stalwarts conferred with the candidate and apparently received some general assurances about patronage. Conkling did not appear, but his lieutenants were satisfied and went to work. In September he went on the stump in New York for the Republican cause, if not for Garfield.

Maine startled Republican leaders by electing a Democratic-Greenback governor in September, and fears were felt for Indiana and Ohio. Conkling then went West to speak; Grant joined him, making a seven-minute speech at Warren, Ohio, and the two, with a number of retainers, were maneuvered into a brief call on Garfield in his home, at Mentor. Out of this call later grew Platt's story that the grateful candidate rushed out in the rain to embrace Conkling and pledge him control of New York appointments. Historians have given little credence to the "treaty of Mentor." Garfield was not given to making rash pledges, particularly to the domineering New Yorker.

Conkling also spoke in Indiana, where the situation was serious. Money as well as oratory flowed like water in the Hoosier State, where S. W. Dorsey, secretary of the national committee, had things in his hands. The fears of business and industrial leaders were played upon with a belated use of the Democratic "tariff for revenue only" plank. Hancock denied that the Democrats would not protect the manufacturer and declared with much truth that the tariff was "a local question." Republicans seized upon this as an example of the General's ignorance, and ridiculed his views. The Greenback character of the Maine outcome was a further argument used by Republicans to draw money from reluctant financiers, for Garfield's record was consistently anti-inflationist. At the candidate's own suggestion John D. Rockefeller was importuned to bring his Standard Oil agents into line for the Republican ticket in Indiana. In the end Republican money and organization carried the October state elections in Indiana and Ohio, foreshadowing success in November.

At this juncture appeared the forged Morey letter, a desperate attempt to turn the Pacific coast against Garfield. The letter, addressed to "H. L. Morey of the Employers' Union, Lynn, Massachusetts," and apparently signed by the Republican candidate, approved of Chinese immigration "until our great manufacturing and corporate interests are conserved in the matter of labor." Garfield learned of its existence on October 20, and at once declared it a forgery; but *Truth*, the New York paper publishing the letter, insisted on its genuineness. Doubtless it injured him in the Far West where the Chinese question was a vital issue, though every effort was made to show that the letter was simply a campaign roorback.

Democratic hopes were dashed on Election Day when the Republicans carried the entire North and West except New Jersey, Nevada, and five of California's six electors. Garfield had 214 electoral votes; Hancock, 155. However, the popular plurality was less than 10,000.[1] The Democrats took what consolation they could from the "solidity" of the South: every former slave state had voted for Hancock.

The leading factors in the Republican victory were prosperity, the support of the business and financial interests, and the improvement in reputation of the party during the Hayes administration. That it was a party victory rather than a personal one was shown by the Republican majority in the Lower House, the first in six years. In the Senate two Independents[2] held the balance of power and divided between the two parties, creating a tie on organization questions and giving Vice President Arthur the deciding vote. In effect, party government was restored in 1880 after a six-year deadlock.

Garfield and Conkling

The frail preelection harmony among Republicans ended within sixty days. Blaine was the logical choice for Secretary of State. The New York Stalwarts then demanded the Treasury Department for Levi P. Morton, a New York banker. Garfield demurred, offered him the Navy Department and when he declined made another New Yorker, Thomas L. James, Postmaster General. Conkling was not appeased, and he stormed at Garfield, charging breach of faith. He suspected—and rightly—that Blaine was pressing the President elect to conduct an undeclared war on the Stalwarts. "They must have their throats cut with a feather," Blaine suggested.

After the inauguration, the President and Conkling spent a long Sunday afternoon in conference and apparently devised a *modus vivendi.* At least the first New York nominations to federal office were Conkling men, and Half-Breeds and reformers were alike dismayed. Had Garfield surrendered to "Lord" Roscoe? "In the evening while we were at dinner Blaine came and expressed great distress at the New York appointments. . . . At 10:30 Blaine came and stayed until near 12." So runs a significant entry in Garfield's journal. Next day the blow fell and the weapon used was a bludgeon, not a feather.

[1] The popular vote was as follows: Garfield, 4,454,416; Hancock, 4,444,952; James B. Weaver (Greenback), 308,578; Neal Dow (Prohibitionist), 10,305.

[2] One of these was David Davis of Illinois. The other was William Mahone of Virginia, elected as a "Readjuster-Democrat." He had headed an insurgent movement in the party on the issue of partial repudiation of the state debt. In the Senate he voted with the Republicans and shared in the patronage.

The President sent to the Senate the appointment of William H. Robertson, a Blaine delegate in the Chicago convention and an archenemy of Conkling, to the most important federal position in the Empire State, collector of the port of New York. The vacancy was made by sending Collector Merritt, whose term had a year and a half to run, to London as consul-general. Few doubted that Blaine had a hand in the move. Yet Garfield's biographer Theodore Clarke Smith insists that the idea was the President's own; that he had determined, after giving part of the patronage to Conkling, to reward the other faction "in a conspicuous manner" (the words are Garfield's).

For once Conkling's fury seemed justified. Merritt was a good collector, civil service reformers had expected him to serve out his term, and Conkling and his new colleague, T. C. Platt, had no objections. Without warning the President had decided to defy the two Senators and apparently to build up a rival machine. Reform had nothing to do with it.

A long battle ensued in the Senate over Robertson's confirmation. In the end the Republican caucus, antagonized by Conkling's abusive threats and fury, decided to vote on the matter. Seeing certain defeat, the two New York Senators decided to resign their seats and seek vindication through reelection by their legislature. Platt first suggested this, as he had been elected with some Half-Breed support and had made pledges he could not carry out without deserting Conkling. Two days later, May 18, the nomination of Robertson was confirmed without a roll call. Garfield and Blaine had won a great victory.

Conkling, having characteristically ruined his own cause by his violence, went to Albany to work for his and "Me, Too" Platt's reelection. Vice President Arthur, cartooned by Thomas Nast as their bootblack, went along to lobby in their behalf. But the Stalwart machine was splitting apart. A moderate group was willing to make terms with the Half-Breeds, and two compromise Senators replaced Conkling and Platt. Thus passed from public life the most picturesque figure of his generation. "Lord" Roscoe quietly resumed the practice of law, and harassed Republican leaders, even his friends, sighed with relief.

In the midst of the Conkling controversy Postmaster General James, investigating his department at Garfield's suggestion, unearthed the Star Route frauds. Since Grant's administration certain mail contractors in the Southwest, in collusion with government officials, had been collecting large sums beyond their contract prices, supposedly for extra services. Thomas W. Brady, Second Assistant Postmaster General, and S. W. Dorsey, secretary of the Republican national committee, important cogs in the party machine, were deeply involved. Brady was forced to resign, but retaliated by publishing a letter Garfield had written to Jay Hubbell, chairman of the Republican Congressional committee, during the campaign, with the passage: "Please say to Brady that I hope he will give us all the assistance he can. I think he can help effectively. Please tell me how the departments generally are doing." The reference was to campaign assessments collected from government clerks and did not imply that the Star Route contractors were being milked. Yet it shocked civil service reformers and made President Garfield's professions of reform appear rather hypocritical. Brady and Dorsey thought it rank ingratitude to use their services in the campaign and then prosecute them as corruptionists. But Garfield had had no inkling of their involvements until he became President. Now he refused to let their past services protect them.

The new President was not destined to complete the Star Route prosecutions nor prove his devotion to reform. On July 2 Charles J. Guiteau, mentally unbalanced, shot him as he was about to leave Washington for the Williams College commencement. Guiteau exclaimed, after the fatal shot, "I am a Stalwart and Arthur is President now." The fact that he was a disappointed office seeker seemed to link the assassination with spoils politics and created a powerful revulsion against the whole system. Garfield died on September 19 after weeks of suffering, and Arthur became President.

Blaine's Turn

The amiable, well fed, well groomed new President, with a wardrobe that was a tailor's delight, whose coming into office was so generally deplored, dropped his role as a huckster in jobs and set about living down his past. That past was not so black as reformers and Half-Breeds had painted it, for Arthur had been unjustly judged by the company he had kept. He was not lacking in administrative ability and experience, knew from years in politics how to handle men, had both tact and good sense, and was a gentleman. In addition, he had the advantage of coming into high position by accident. Charges of broken pledges and bad faith could not dog his footsteps.

His hardest problem was to convince people that he was not the tool of the Stalwart machine. Garfield's cabinet was willing to retire, and Arthur thought it wise to relieve himself of the problem of Blaine by reconstituting the whole group, except Robert T. Lincoln in the War Department. But Conkling and Platt were not included in the administration, nor was Robertson removed from the Customhouse. The New York Stalwarts received few crumbs from their old leader, and many of them began to resent his attitude. The followers of Sherman also felt slighted, and Blaine was annoyed at the abandonment of his policies by the State Department. The Independents, though skeptical, had no reason to criticize. Arthur, the machine politician, was offending the politicos and growing in popular respect.

The chief measures of his administration, except the Tariff of 1883, showed little indication of party alignment. His vetoes were generally praised, notably that of a huge rivers and harbors bill in 1882. Yet this shining example of the "pork barrel" was passed over his head, members of both parties supporting it. The Star Route culprits were vigorously prosecuted, and it was not the government's fault that they finally escaped conviction.

Most important of all, civil service reform came to fruition under Arthur. His first message to Congress recommended legislation to set up such a system but was ignored. His second, to the lame-duck session of 1882-1883, fell on more willing ears, for the Democrats would control the next House. The time for repentance had arrived. "Voluntary contributions" from officeholders had been levied on a large scale in the Congressional campaign of 1882 and the reformers were aroused. The National Civil Service Reform League was actively at work, and Congress yielded to public sentiment. The Pendleton Act, sponsored by "Gentleman George" Pendleton of Ohio, was passed with surprising ease—38 to 5 in the Senate, 155 to 47 in the House, with many members conveniently absent. The vote was not partisan, and many who voted for it had little use for it. The act set up a commission to administer the new regulations and conduct competitive examinations, prohibited political assessments of federal officials, and provided for the immediate application of the system in certain departments. Other departments might be brought under the new rules by order of the President. This provision tested the devotion of each succeeding administration to reform. Arthur carried out the law conscientiously and deserves credit for successful institution of the merit system.

Attempts at tariff revision, badly needed and too long delayed, produced the Tariff of 1883, in utter disregard of the recommendations of a tariff commission. Swarms of lobbyists helped write a bill that gave little or no relief to the consumer and took care of every important industrial interest. One Democrat in the Senate and fifteen Democrats in the House voted with the Republicans for the bill. In the new Democratic House an attempt at a horizontal reduction of rates failed when forty-one Democrats headed by Samuel J. Randall of Pennsylvania helped the Republicans kill the bill—a significant indication of the inroads of high-tariff sentiment in the party that had declared for tariff for revenue in 1880.

The mid-term elections produced a Democratic House of Representatives and made Grover Cleveland Governor of New York. Hard times, hostility toward party machines, sentiment for reform, and local issues were involved. Arthur had not established his leadership over the party, and his desire to succeed himself won no widespread support. Many of his old Stalwart friends were hostile, the Half-Breeds were for Blaine, and the reformers preferred Senator Edmunds of Vermont. Senators John Sherman of Ohio and John A. Logan of Illinois held blocs of votes from important states. Platt of New York expressed a rather general sentiment when he remarked that Blaine's turn had come.

In the same building at Chicago as in 1880, the Republican national convention on June 3 elected John R. Lynch of Mississippi, a colored delegate, temporary chairman over former Senator Powell Clayton of Arkansas by a vote of 424 to 384—a Blaine setback. J. B. Henderson of Missouri was made permanent chairman, and the platform was adopted without opposition.

The resolutions praised the party's accomplishments and repeated the vague pledges of earlier platforms. The tariff clauses had a more definitely protective slant, though revision to correct "irregularities" and reduce the surplus in the Treasury was pledged. Better protection was promised to the raw-wool interests, angry over the duties in the Tariff of 1883. An international agreement to fix the relative value of gold and silver coinage was favored; railway regulation was indorsed; a national bureau of labor was promised; enforcement and extension of civil service reform were advocated; the improvement of the navy and the encouragement of shipping were pledged. Garfield's death was lamented, and Arthur's administration praised.

The nominating speeches aroused only perfunctory responses until

Judge William West, the "blind man eloquent" of Ohio, offered "the white plume of James G. Blaine, our Henry of Navarre." Bedlam ensued as the loyal followers of the man from Maine, encouraged by the shrieking galleries, made the gas lights tremble and the walls shake —"a mass meeting of maniacs," in the words of the disgusted *Nation*. After further speeches the exhausted delegates adjourned at 2:15 A.M. and began the balloting in a calmer frame of mind several hours later.

The first ballot gave Blaine 334-1/2; Arthur 278, Edmunds 93, Logan 63-1/2, Sherman 30, Hawley of Connecticut 13, Robert T. Lincoln of Illinois 4, General W. T. Sherman 2. Blaine was far short of a majority, and a quick concentration on Arthur might have stopped him. But the reformers were dubious about Arthur, and Senator Hoar of Massachusetts, heading the New England Edmunds bloc, had personal grievances against him. On the other hand, most of the Sherman and Logan men were ready to shift to Blaine as soon as their pledges were fulfilled. Arthur's support was too largely from the federal officeholding southern wing; the Blaine delegates came mostly from the states that normally supplied Republican electoral votes. Blaine went steadily upward and was nominated with 541 votes on the fourth ballot. Arthur had 207, and 41 die-hard eastern reformers held out for Edmunds. John A. Logan was rewarded with second place on the ticket.

That the nomination represented the wishes of the great majority of Republicans cannot be questioned. They wanted Blaine, regardless of the feelings of the "unco guid." He was their sentimental hero, and if he was prone to tilt at "rebel" windmills, they loved him for it. He had never swerved from the orthodox path, and his turn had come to lead the hosts. The heretic reformers who would revile him could go their way. Unfortunately for Blaine, they did.

Grover Cleveland

The Independents, derisively christened "Mugwumps," [3] wasted no time in repudiating the nominee. The Massachusetts Reform Club, meeting on June 7 in Boston, appealed to independent voters to aid in securing a satisfactory Democratic nomination. A public meeting on June 13 appointed an executive committee and chose delegates to

[3] An Algonquin Indian term meaning "big chief." It had appeared in 1872 but was not taken up until March, 1884, when the New York *Sun* applied it to the Independents. The name stuck.

a New York conference on the 17th. Schurz and Curtis conducted the New York conference, which called on the Democrats to name a reform ticket. Schurz favored Bayard or Governor Cleveland but expressed to the former his fear that one would be used to destroy the other and give the nomination to a man the reformers could not support.

His fear proved to be groundless. Without the Empire State the Democrats were doomed, and the New York governor had shown his running qualities in 1882. A few Tilden men indulged in wishful thinking for their old favorite, but the faithful John Bigelow induced the feeble old man to give his blessing to Cleveland. Daniel Manning, boss of upstate New York, backed the governor, and only John Kelly, Tammany czar, angry at affronts to his machine, loomed up as a dangerous obstacle. The well organized "County Democracy" under Abram S. Hewitt and William C. Whitney, favorable to Cleveland, partly curbed his power in the metropolis; but Tammany treachery, only too well known, might decide a close election. At the state convention Kelly was treated with fairness, receiving a share of the New York delegation to the national convention. Then the unit rule was clamped on to render him impotent. He was not appeased and arrived in Chicago with blood in his eye.

The argument of Kelly that Cleveland could not carry New York was of no great help to the rival candidates. Bayard was sure to be assailed for his Civil War utterances, and his Delaware residence was a great handicap; Thurman was older than Tilden and had once flirted with the greenbackers; Hendricks of Indiana was even more soft-money, and reformers looked on him as a machine politician; Samuel J. Randall of Pennsylvania was too much of a protectionist, and John G. Carlisle of Kentucky too low-tariff, besides coming from the wrong side of the Ohio River. "Cockeyed" Ben Butler of Massachusetts, demagogue extraordinary, turned up at the convention with two third-party nominations, and a mandate—self-assumed—to speak for a million and a half laboring men. But southerners, with memories of his Civil War rule of New Orleans and his part in radical reconstruction, laughed him to scorn.

A generally harmonious convention, eager for victory, assembled at Chicago on July 8. The only sour note was sounded by Tammany. Kelly and his cohorts, with anti-Cleveland support from other states, attempted to dispose of the unit rule by permitting individual voting by delegates when a state's vote was challenged. The proposal was defeated, 332 to 463, and Cleveland's home state remained solid for him.

Butler criticized the platform and offered a series of amendments; but his character and his political past defeated his proposals. The platform was far longer and consequently much more ambiguous than the succinct statements of 1880. The indictment of Republican misdeeds—it called that party "a reminiscence"—was well stated; but logic ended there, and the Democratic pledges were platitudinous and obscure. "Honest civil service reform," "honest money, the gold and silver coinage of the Constitution," "a free ballot and a fair count," and "an American continental policy," based upon "more intimate" relations with our sister republics, were among them.

Many weary hours in committee devoted to the tariff dilemma produced a verbose, ambiguous paragraph that defies analysis. That the existing tariff system was full of abuses was put clearly enough; that the Democrats would reform it "in a spirit of fairness to all interests" was as far as the platform dared go. In making reductions, "it is not proposed to injure any domestic industries, but rather to promote their healthy growth." At only one point was any definite principle suggested: articles of luxury should be taxed more heavily than articles of necessity. The Democratic position was dictated by the divisions of opinion in the party and the need to confound Blaine's efforts to shift the battle from the reform issue, where his record was vulnerable, to the tariff question where he could charge upon his enemies the heresy of free trade. With a plank acceptable to the industrial East and a candidate without a tariff record, the blunder of 1880 would not be repeated.

Tammany henchmen, Thomas F. Grady and Bourke Cockran, marred the nominating speeches with ill timed attacks on Cleveland. The hisses that greeted Grady showed the temper of the convention, and the galleries roared their approval when Bragg of Wisconsin, "grim and gray personally" but asserting his right to speak for the young men, declared, "They love him most for the enemies he has made." The first ballot gave Cleveland 392 votes, Bayard 170, Thurman 88, Randall 78, Joseph E. McDonald of Indiana 56, and Carlisle 27, with 8 votes scattered. Adjournment at 1:30 A.M. gave the anti-Cleveland men a breathing spell in which to launch a Hendricks movement. To counteract it, Daniel Manning, directing Cleveland's strategy, won Randall by patronage promises; but this was hardly necessary. The near-majority and the enthusiasm for the New

York governor made his nomination almost certain. On the second ballot he was but 72 votes short of two-thirds, and rapid changes of state after state gave him 683 to 81-1/2 for Bayard and 45-1/2 for Hendricks. Hendricks then received second place on the ticket because he was the most popular figure in a doubtful state, had been Tilden's running mate in 1876, and was a soft-money westerner. Although he was also a good machine politician and had no liking for reformers, this was of little moment: Cleveland was to head the ticket, and the Mugwumps were overjoyed.

The new leader of the Democracy was a big man with a bulky body, a sagging double chin, and an unconventional mustache in a generation of bearded statesmen. Without Blaine's personal magnetism, he never cultivated the arts of popularity; but his courage, his blunt honesty, and his healthy integrity appealed to voters in an era of corruption in public life, and he had been elected sheriff, mayor of Buffalo, and governor of New York because he regarded public office as a public trust. Having served an apprenticeship in city-ward politics, he recognized the place of the politician and was no silk-stocking reformer; but the greediness of the petty bosses annoyed him, and drew brusque treatment that often aroused bitter enmities. The bachelor Cleveland did not have the rather squeamish, middle-class, personal virtues of Hayes: he drank beer, played cards, and loved robust amusements. However, as he advanced in official life, he altered his free habits, and the Mrs. Grundys of Albany had no unfavorable comments about him. During the Civil War he had remained at home to support his widowed mother while two brothers enlisted.

The Battle of the Tarnished Warriors

The campaign for Cleveland was a double-headed affair in which the forces of darkness and of light joined hands. On the side of darkness were Daniel Manning, Democratic boss of the Empire State, William C. Whitney, a wealthy young lawyer of tremendous energy and proper Wall Street connections, and Senator Arthur P. Gorman of Maryland, an astute, hard-headed politician who headed the national executive committee (a figurehead, ex-Senator Barnum of Connecticut, was chairman of the national committee). These unregenerate partisans collected a larger campaign fund than usual from a segment of business and from Democratic state and municipal officeholders, made terms with recalcitrant or sulking local bosses, and used methods on occasion that might not have commended themselves to the candidate, had he been fully informed. Their problem was to get every real or half-hearted Democrat to the polls. On the offensive they joined hands with the Independents in vicious attacks on Blaine.

Schurz, heading a separate organization with a small, poorly manned office in New York City, conducted the Independents and the Republican bolters into battle. Among them were some of the most eminent American intellectual leaders, such as President Charles W. Eliot and almost the whole Harvard faculty, Henry Ward Beecher, James Freeman Clarke, Thomas Wentworth Higginson, and the veteran civil service reformers Godkin and Curtis. The important periodicals *Harper's Weekly*, the *Nation*, and *Puck*, and independent or Republican papers including the *Herald, Times, Evening Post* and *Telegram* in New York, the *Transcript, Herald,* and *Advertiser* in Boston, the *Springfield Republican*, the *Brooklyn Union*, the *Times* and the *Record* of Philadelphia, and the *Times* and *News* of Chicago, were anti-Blaine.

Yet many Republicans who had opposed Blaine before the Chicago convention now became mute or openly conformed. The whip of party regularity brought those looking to the future into line. Congressman Henry Cabot Lodge, young Massachusetts aristocrat, refused to sacrifice his seat to principle and stated that bolting would "destroy all the influence and power for good I possess." His fellow Harvardian Theodore Roosevelt, after weeks of uncertainty, returned from a Dakota ranch to speak for Blaine; earlier, as a New York State assemblyman, he had found much about Cleveland to commend. Senator Edmunds of Vermont was harder to move. Toward the close of the campaign he made one speech for his party but refused to mention Blaine's name. But Blaine's old enemy, Roscoe Conkling, in a reputed reply to requests for his support, was devastating: "I do not engage in criminal practice." His home county, usually Republican, was carried by Cleveland.

The Mugwump fire was centered on the Republican candidate's record, particularly the Mulligan letters. In 1869, Blaine, Speaker of the House, after helping secure renewal of a land grant for an Arkansas railroad, worked with a Boston broker, Warren Fisher, to sell its bonds. When they declined in value Blaine refunded the money to investors by secretly selling the nearly worthless bonds to the

Union Pacific at a high price. Letters supplied by Fisher's bookkeeper, James Mulligan, to a House committee in 1876 were secured by Blaine on a pretext and not returned. Instead, he read extracts to the House and made a brilliant, if disingenuous, defense. There the matter rested until Blaine's nomination in 1884 revived the old charges. Worse even was a new batch of letters uncovered during the campaign, including a draft of a letter exonerating him which he himself had written and sent to Fisher to copy and mail back. On it in his own hand was the significant request "Burn this letter." The request had not been carried out, and the draft letter had not been sent. Both now appeared in print to humiliate the candidate.

Bernhard Gillam, the cartoonist of *Puck*, who outdid Nast of *Harper's Weekly* in vindictiveness, stamped the Republican candidate unforgettably in the public mind as the "tattooed man," marked on his body with "Bribery," "Mulligan Letters," "Little Rock," and other unpleasant reminders of his record.

The unrestrained abuse of Blaine drew a savage retaliation from Republican sources that might well have been deadly, had it been better timed. In July the Buffalo *Evening Telegraph* gave the world the sordid story of Mrs. Maria Halpin. This prepossessing widow, employed in a Buflalo store in the early seventies, had been on intimate terms with several men. When a son was born to her in 1874 she named Cleveland as the father. He accepted the responsibility, perhaps to shield the others involved, and made some financial arrangements for the child. Eventually, because of the mother's misconduct, he had the boy placed in an orphanage, from which he was adopted by a good family. Few people knew of the matter until it appeared in print in 1884.

Jubilant Republican papers printed all the details, and many partisan Protestant ministers preached sermons against moral laxity and the danger of placing men of debauched character in high office. Cleveland astonished friends and enemies alike by admitting his sin and offering no excuses. His confession threw the Democratic-reformer camp into confusion. But the witty comment of a clever anonymous Chicagoan at a New York conference of Mugwumps let sunlight through the dark clouds. He argued, let Blaine, whose private life was blameless, be remanded to private life, and let Cleveland, whose public life was a model of integrity, be kept in public life. Two famous Protestant ministers, James Freeman Clarke and Henry Ward Beecher, championed Cleveland; and Republican charges of gross immorality began to lose their weight. By Election Day the Halpin affair had become no more effective than any stale gossip after the truth has been clearly revealed. Cleveland's frankness was refreshing after Blaine's dissembling evasions of the Mulligan letters.

As the contest drew to a close, Republican strategists, alarmed at the situation in the Middle West, violated Republican precedents and put Blaine himself on the stump. His tour stirred the Republican masses as he preached on the benefits of protective tariff, and dilated on his favorite theme, the dangers of rebel rule. In less spectacular fashion, Colonel W. W. Dudley, Commissioner of Pensions, and a hundred special examiners appeared in Ohio and Indiana to pressure the soldier vote.

If the Middle West, except Indiana, seemed to be safe by mid-October, New York was not, and the pleadings of Blaine's managers —or, perhaps, some inexorable fate—called him back to his destruction. The New York situation was complicated. John P. St. John, former Republican and governor of Kansas, was campaigning in New York as Prohibition candidate for President; and Frances E. Willard and the Woman's Christian Temperance Union, angry at contemptuous treatment accorded to a temperance petition at the Republican national convention, were supporting him. Temperance advocates, usually Republican in the past, might be drawn to St. John to punish Blaine just as the abolitionists had punished Clay in 1844. To offset this danger, the Republican national committee was secretly financing Ben Butler, the Antimonopoly-Greenback candidate, in an attempt to draw Democratic votes from Cleveland. John Kelly of Tammany was suspected of secret friendliness to Butler.

Tied up with the Tammany and Butler problems was the Irish vote. Blaine was of Irish descent. His mother was a Roman Catholic, a cousin was the mother-superior of a convent, and he himself had long exhibited a tendency to twist the British Lion's tail, to the edification of all good Irishmen. The *Irish Nation* and the *Irish World* of New York endorsed him, and a great meeting of Blaine Irish-Americans was held on July 28. Cleveland, son of a Presbyterian minister, had no particular appeal to the sons of Erin except as traditional Democrats. The Republicans, calling the Mugwumps and Democrats free traders, dubbed him the "British candidate," whose success would imperil American industries. The *Irish World*, speaking for the more vociferous "professional" Irish-Americans, charged that all the great British dailies were opposed to Blaine.

To New York City came Blaine with the scales so evenly weighted that a straw might unbalance them. On the morning of October 29 he spoke to a group of Protestant ministers at the Fifth Avenue Hotel. In welcoming the candidate, Samuel D. Burchard, a Presbyterian minister, carved his niche in history with one asinine sentence: "We are Republicans, and don't propose to leave our party and identify ourselves with the party whose antecedents have been rum, Romanism and rebellion." Blaine did not catch the remark, and made no mention of it in his reply. A shorthand reporter took it down, turned it in to Chairman Gorman at Democratic headquarters, and within a few hours "Rum, Romanism and Rebellion" was doing its work. Newspapers and handbills carried the story of Burchard's insult to Roman Catholics and Blaine's apparent acquiescence. No explanation could undo the damage. Enough Irish votes were probably lost to change the result in New York.

As if this were not enough for one day, Blaine was again victimized in the evening by supposed friends. Unwisely, and against Chairman Elkins's advice, he attended a dinner at Delmonico's given by the wealthiest men in the city. Present were John Jacob Astor, Jay Gould, Cyrus W. Field, Russell Sage, Levi P. Morton, and many other millionaires. The solitary reporter present (from Jay Gould's Associated Press) heard Blaine extol the tremendous increase in the country's wealth under Republican rule. Then all went into a private room (with the reporter excluded) and discussed campaign funds. Next day a New York *World* cartoon pictured "Belshazzar Blaine and the Money Kings" dining in splendor on "Monopoly Soup," "Lobby Pudding," "Navy Contract" and "Gould Pie," while a starving workingman and his wife appealed in vain for food. In a year of hard times the reaction of labor to the incident was bound to be unfavorable.

Cleveland made two formal speeches—at Newark, New Jersey, and at Bridgeport, Connecticut—and attended a great celebration at Buffalo. On the Saturday before the election he reviewed a parade of forty thousand in New York City, listening to the tramping thousands chanting "Blaine, Blaine, James G. Blaine, the Monumental Liar from the State of Maine," and "Burn this letter, burn this letter, kind regards to Mrs. Fisher," while the marchers held lighted matches to sheets of paper. Twice in this same week Blaine had had his innings when the Republican hosts paraded past him roaring "Blaine, Blaine, James G. Blaine, O-O-O-hi-O, No-No-No Free

Trade," though some were not above chorusing "Ma! Ma! Where's my pa? Gone to the White House, Ha! Ha! Ha!" Not since 1840 had Americans worked so hard at politics.

As the returns came in on the night of November 4, it was evident that New York would decide the outcome. Cleveland had the Solid South, Indiana, Connecticut, and New Jersey, a total of 183 electoral votes; Blaine had the rest, except New York, 182 in all; New York's 36 were in doubt. The weather had taken a hand at the last minute and a driving rain in upstate New York, "good weather for Democrats," made it hard for the farmers to get to the polls. Blaine was the loser thereby, for more Democrats lived in the cities.

Cleveland's plurality in New York was 1,149 in a total vote of 1,167,169.[4] The scales had indeed been tipped against Blaine by a straw. But what was the straw? Was it the much publicized Burchard remark, or the banquet of the millionaires, or Conkling's ill will, or the unexpected strength of St. John, who pulled 25,000 votes, or Butler's poor showing, or the rain of November 4, or some other fortuitous circumstance? Blaine believed that the suppression of the southern Republican vote had forced the party to depend on New York, and that the Independents, the Prohibitionists, and the Burchard remark accounted for that state. Better known is his message to Murat Halstead: "As the Lord sent upon us an ass in the shape of a preacher and a rainstorm to lessen our vote in New York, I am disposed to feel resigned to the dispensation of defeat which flowed directly from these agencies." Eloquent Colonel Bob Ingersoll, no longer a Blaine admirer, believed that he could have saved the Empire State with a speech or two, but he had been egregiously snubbed. That a preacher helped Blaine to lose when an agnostic might have won for him tickled Colonel Bob mightily.

More fundamental were two factors that accounted for heavy Democratic inroads into Republican strength everywhere in the North. One was the failure of Republican economic appeal in a year of much unemployment and business stagnation. The other was the Independent, or Mugwump, uprising. The reform groups held the balance of power in the four northern states carried by Cleveland and reduced the Republican vote in other states. But for their

[4] The popular vote was as follows: Cleveland, 4,874,986; Blaine, 4,851,981; Butler, 175,370; St. John, 150,369. In New York the vote was: Cleveland, 563,154; Blaine, 562,005; Butler, 16,994; St. John, 25,016. The electoral vote was 219 for Cleveland, 182 for Blaine.

activity in New York, Blaine would have won by such a margin that preacher, Prohibitionist, and rainstorm combined could not have changed the result.

The parties had not come to grips over economic issues. Both sides had ignored or touched lightly such matters as labor unrest, farmer problems, public-land policies, railway regulation, the growth of monopolies, and even tariff reform. The evasion was deliberate but not at all strange. Why should party leaders, whose function was to carry elections, attempt to formulate programs upon which few people were agreed? Third parties had tried and failed dismally. Reform in government thousands of honest Americans regarded as necessary before other reforms could come. For years corruption and a vicious spoils system had been undermining confidence in democratic government. The election was a contest to see whether a sentimental loyalty to a party in power which had long promised reform but had performed slowly and half-heartedly for its own Presidents, and whose candidate was now suspect, should triumph over a party whose chief pledge was a candidate of unquestioned integrity with a record to match. The majority of the voters decided that the party that had saved the Union should no longer misgovern it.

17

The Tariff Campaigns

A Man of Negative Virtues

The confident new President who calmly gave his long inaugural from memory had his reformer reputation soon put to the test. To try to please both elements in the coalition that had elected him was to undertake service to God and Mammon concurrently. Reform leaders expected him to be nobly oblivious to Manning, Gorman, and the rest; old-line Democrats wanted the loaves and fishes, and the most hardened among them even considered repealing the Pendleton Act. The President, committed to "the application of business principles to public affairs," intended that federal employees (outside the classified service), except the inefficient and offensively partisan, should serve out their terms. But such moderation put too great a strain on the ravenous Democrats. The Republicans had feasted for years; now the turn of the "outs" had come. Why should reform deny them the jobs after twenty-four years of wandering in the desert of defeat?

In the end, partisan pressure combined with the size of the task to force Cleveland to make concessions. Of the 126,000 federal offices, 15,573 were in the classified service. The rest, subject to appointment by the President or by department or bureau heads, were regarded as party spoils. Cleveland could neither give personal attention to thousands of offices nor see that his subordinates lived up to his ideal standards. Democratic appointees in important positions, particularly in the Post Office Department, took care of the problem. Republicans went out, and Democrats came in. The four-year-tenure law made vacancies where removals did not, and by June, 1887, 40,000 out of 52,609 fourth-class postmasters were changed.

Yet Republicans were kept in office in some conspicuous cases, the classified service was not disturbed, and toward the close of his term Cleveland extended it to include altogether some 27,000 places. Civil service reform had made progress, even though Schurz was offended and the *Nation* sometimes critical. These were years of experimentation under circumstances that made any advance difficult.

A conflict with the Republican majority in the Senate over the President's refusal to give reasons for the suspension of Republican officeholders ended in a victory for Cleveland. The last remnants of the old Tenure of Office Act were repealed, and the power to remove was now unrestricted. (Suspension until new appointees were confirmed had been the old rule.)

Cleveland's ability to say No was put to the test by private pension bills. He vetoed several hundred on the grounds of misrepresentation and fraud. His predecessors had been signing them as a matter of course. He also vetoed a dependent pensions bill to grant pensions for disabilities not caused by military service. The Grand Army of the Republic, the country's most powerful pressure group, was affronted. And northern breast-beating patriots set up a roar when he unthinkingly approved an order to return to their states captured Confederate battle flags then gathering dust at Washington. This order was rescinded, as he discovered that it was of doubtful legality. (Later, Theodore Roosevelt returned the flags with Congressional and popular approval.)

The two most important pieces of legislation of his term were not partisan, though they had Presidential support. These were the Dawes Act involving a fundamental change in Indian policy and the Interstate Commerce Act of 1887 which began federal regulation of railroads.

Involving the office rather than the incumbent were the Presidential Succession Act and the Electoral Count Act. Both were long overdue. A law of 1792 had provided that the president pro tempore of the Senate, and after him the Speaker of the House, should succeed to the Presidency in case both President and Vice President died or were in any manner disqualified from holding the chief office. When Garfield was assassinated the Senate did not have a president pro tempore because of a deadlock, and the House had not yet assembled. President Arthur thus had no legal successor until the Senate met in October. Early in Cleveland's term Vice President Hendricks died, making the Republican president pro tempore of the Senate second in line. Congress in 1886 fixed the line of succession through the cabinet beginning with the Secretary of State. The act was not partisan, though 75 House Republicans joined 2 Democrats in opposing it. It remained in effect until 1947 when Congress, with doubtful wisdom, restored the old system but placed the Speaker of the House next to the Vice President. In 1887 the Electoral Count Act made the state the final authority in determining the legality of its choice of electors and requiring a concurrent majority of the two Houses of Congress to reject any electoral votes.

Up to the time of his tariff message of 1887 the President was feeling his way. His practical mind, unimaginative and not very flexible, tried to meet problems as they arose. This, with a narrow conception of the President's constitutional position, led him to stand sturdily behind the ramparts and beat back his assailants. He was slow in realizing that a strong party leader must formulate policies and assume the offensive. Only when the tariff question compelled his attention did he act.

The First Tariff Campaign

Despite Blaine's efforts the Democrats had not accepted the tariff as an issue in 1884. Their ambiguous platform and their studious avoidance of the question indicated their desire not to offend the industrial interests, who already had spokesmen high in the councils of the party. Nevertheless, keen observers like Henry Adams predicted that Democratic victory would mean a step toward free trade, and most people expected some kind of tariff revision.

Cleveland moved slowly on the tariff question, because he knew little about it, and because his party was so divided that the Democratic House in 1886 defeated a bill for moderate reductions. Samuel J. Randall of Pennsylvania led a protectionist bloc, which held the balance of power. Cleveland's approach was practical. He was concerned about the surplus revenue piling up in the Treasury, an encouragement to extravagance and a deflationary factor, if not spent. The sensible solution was to get at the source. "It is a *condition* which confronts us—not a theory," he asserted in his annual message of 1887, which was devoted entirely to the tariff. He criticized the existing protective system for its bad effects on government finance and for the tax burdens it placed on the people.

Party leaders were not enthusiastic about his strong stand with a Presidential election impending, but the President cracked the patronage whip over Democratic Representatives and the House passed the Mills bill, which provided for moderate reductions. The Republican Senate prepared its own highly protective bill, and the tariff became the major campaign issue in 1888.

The task of the Democratic national convention, which assembled at St. Louis on June 5, was the easiest that had confronted the party since 1840. Presidential candidate and leading issue had been determined in advance. The resolutions committee argued whether the platform should indorse the Mills bill by name or not, and finally omitted direct mention in its report to the convention with the understanding that additional resolutions would be offered from the floor.

The finished document reaffirmed the resolutions of 1884, sang paeans of praise over the record of the Cleveland administration, and condemned the Republican Senate for blocking "a reformation of unjust and unequal tax laws." The long tariff plank emphasized the evils of the existing protective system, charging that it increased the cost of the necessaries of life, encouraged trusts and combinations, piled up a demoralizing surplus in the Treasury, and was a temptation to extravagant expenditures. However, domestic industries were assured that revision would not endanger their interests but would extend their markets. The word "tariff" was used but once in the resolution, "taxes" and "taxation" being preferred.

Three resolutions, added from the floor, indorsed the Mills bill, approved of statehood for four western territories, and expressed sympathy for Gladstone and Parnell in their contest for home rule in Ireland. The last was a bid for the Irish vote.

Governor David B. Hill of New York and Tammany Hall would have fought Cleveland's renomination, but it was evident long before the convention met that such a course was hopeless. Hill then devoted himself to his own reelection while Tammany even claimed the honor of presenting Cleveland at St. Louis. After naming its Presidential candidate by acclamation, the convention quickly nominated Allen G. Thurman of Ohio for second place over Governor Isaac P. Gray of Indiana. The choice was excellent in all respects but one. Thurman was seventy-five years old, too old to campaign actively. His popularity—he was affectionately called "the noble old Roman"—his past service in the Senate, his unblemished integrity, and his former sympathy for silver and greenbacks made him a suitable middle western partner for Cleveland, who personally favored his nomination. Thurman contributed one picturesque feature to the campaign. His use of a red bandanna handkerchief after taking his habitual pinch of snuff furnished the Democrats with a campaign emblem.

The Republicans were jubilant over Cleveland's tariff message. Blaine, interviewed by a *New York Tribune* reporter in Paris, sounded the tocsin for protection, and his friends interpreted this to foreshadow his candidacy in 1888. Suddenly and unexpectedly they were stopped by a formal declination, sent from Italy to the chairman of the Republican national committee. It gave no reason except "considerations personal to myself."

Blaine's loyal lieutenants, believing that he would not refuse a unanimous nomination, insisted on keeping his name before the public. But a flock of favorite sons accepted his withdrawal as final, and when the Republican convention met at Chicago on June 19 there was more uncertainty over the outcome than at almost any previous gathering. John Sherman of Ohio had the solid support of his home state for the first time, and had a manager of unusual acumen and considerable wealth in Marcus A. Hanna, who won southern Negro delegates by paying good prices for their extra convention tickets. Senator Matthew S. Quay, boss of Pennsylvania, was friendly. The Blaine forces were hostile, and Chauncey M. Depew, favorite son of New York, had Boss Tom Platt's backing. Senator Benjamin Harrison was Indiana's choice; ex-Governor Russell A. Alger of Michigan, a wealthy industrialist, had his home state and some southern support, reputedly by methods similar to Hanna's; Senator William B. Allison of Iowa was strong only in his own section.

Second to Sherman in initial strength but rejected by the machine leaders and put aside for Harrison by his own state was Federal Judge Walter Q. Gresham of Indiana. He was looked upon by the unbossed as their only hope, but he had no chance in such a gathering. The American Iron and Steel Association had forbidden his nomination.

The platform left no one in doubt about the tariff. It declared: "We are uncompromisingly in favor of the American system of protection. We protest against its destruction, as proposed by the President and his party. They serve the interests of Europe; we will support the interests of America." It denounced the Mills bill, opposed placing wool on the free list, and declared for the repeal of internal revenue taxes on tobacco and on spirits used in the arts and for mechanical purposes.

The widespread opposition to trusts and combinations was recognized in a plank recommending state and federal legislation to check their oppressions. Both gold and silver were favored as currency; increased appropriations were promised for navy, coast defense, pensions, and public works; the merchant marine was to be rehabilitated; civil service reform was indorsed; the western territories were to be made states; and the political power of the Mormon Church was condemned. Cleveland's policies, foreign and domestic, were criticized with particular emphasis upon his "hostile spirit" toward the veteran.

The first ballot for the Presidential nomination gave Sherman 229, Gresham 111, Depew 99, Alger 84, Harrison 80, Allison 72, and Blaine 35, with seven others dividing 120 of the 830 votes. Most of the Blaine support was under cover, awaiting developments. Through five ballots the struggle proceeded indecisively. Sherman dropped to 224, and Gresham to 87; but Alger reached 142, and Harrison 213. Platt had shifted New York to Harrison, but no one was near a majority as the convention recessed over Sunday.

It would require many pages to recount the intrigues and bargainings that went on during that hectic week end. One account has it that a group of state bosses picked Harrison at a secret meeting in the Grand Pacific Hotel on Saturday night with Platt, Quay, Elkins, Aldrich, and Clarkson present. But Governor Foraker of Ohio, long afterward, revealed that Stephen B. Elkins awakened him at two A.M., Monday, with an offer of Blaine support if he would permit his name to be used. He refused to desert Sherman. Sherman attributed Harrison's success to a bargain with Platt. Yet the Blaine men also claimed the leading role in the nomination. On Saturday, Blaine, visiting Andrew Carnegie in Scotland, twice cabled his refusal to be a candidate. A code cablegram from Carnegie to Elkins followed: "Too late. Blaine immovable. Take Harrison and Phelps."

If the state bosses had already picked Harrison, the delegates were slow in following orders, for three ballots were needed on Monday before the favorite son of Indiana received 544 votes and the nomination. Sherman had 118, Alger 100, and Gresham 59 on this ballot. Levi P. Morton was then nominated for the second office with 591 of the 830 votes.

The ticket was well chosen. Indiana, for many years a doubtful state, might be won by a Hoosier candidate. But Harrison had other assets. He was Ohio-born, had been a Civil War brigadier, was the grandson of President William Henry Harrison, had no scandals to cover up, and was a faithful Presbyterian. His austere, colorless personality offered no complications to befog the tariff issue. Morton, banker and businessman, had opened his money bags liberally in the past and would strengthen the ticket in New York.

The Republican campaign manager was Matthew S. Quay, who had succeeded the Cameron dynasty in the boss-controlled state of Pennsylvania, and whose organization methods were thorough and unscrupulous. Colonel W. W. Dudley, former head of the pensions bureau, was campaign treasurer. Money was presently raised on an unprecedented scale. John Wanamaker, Philadelphia merchant, acted as liaison officer to tap the vast resources of American business. Heading an advisory committee of businessmen, he was soon engaged in what came to be called cynically "frying out the fat." Mark Hanna, businessman-politician, raised over $100,000 in northern Ohio. A key figure was James M. Swank of Pennsylvania, head of the American Iron and Steel Association, which, with kindred organizations, sent hundreds of thousands of pamphlets to propagandize the partially industrialized Middle West on the merits of protection. No longer were officeholders expected to carry the chief burden of financing a national campaign. If businessmen felt that the security of their investments depended on Republican control, they must expect to pay a good, stiff price for it.

Harrison, a small man, aristocratic in bearing, aloof and difficult in personal contacts, called "Kid Glove" Harrison in Indiana, made surprisingly effective public addresses from his Indianapolis front porch. His good Civil War record was contrasted with Cleveland's hiring a substitute, and helped to make the G.A.R., already angry over the pension vetoes, into a Republican auxiliary. It remained for Blaine, however, to quicken Republican heartbeats with his compelling eloquence, to give to a dry tariff argument a dramatic touch, to expose the British Lion and the Confederate Brigadier hiding behind the Democratic free-trade ramparts. It was a memorable 10th of August when Blaine rode up New York harbor on a tender amid a din of whistles, horns, band music, and frantic cheers to throw his spellbinding energy into the rather apathetic campaign. Tens of thousands greeted him, and other tens of thousands fought to hear him at Indianapolis and elsewhere in the Middle West in October. Finishing in doubtful Connecticut and New York, he had done more for Harrison than he could have done for himself.

Meanwhile, what of Cleveland? With Congress on his hands all summer and far into October, he had little time for campaign matters. His one public appearance was to read his letter of acceptance. The campaign was left to his managers, William H. Barnum of Connecticut, chairman of the national committee as in 1884, and Calvin S. Brice, chairman of the executive committee, a wealthy railroad financier and Wall Street speculator with a home in Ohio. Neither had any interest in tariff reform—Barnum being a member of the Iron and Steel Association—and neither had the President's interests closely at heart. The American Free Trade League headed by David A. Wells circulated pamphlets by the thousands; the American Tariff Reform League operated after a fashion in the Middle West; Godkin, Curtis, William Graham Sumner, Henry George, and others engaged in a campaign of education; but the heavy weight of the money bags unbalanced the scales against them. Most of the old Mugwump papers remained loyal to Cleveland, but civil service reform attracted little attention. The scandal of 1884 was not revived. Cleveland had married in 1886, but stories did circulate that he beat his young wife and was drunk on the Presidential yacht.

As in 1884, New York and Indiana were the key states. In the Empire State, Governor David B. Hill, candidate for reelection and no friend of Cleveland or reform, had the strong backing of Tammany and the urban liquor interests. He was indifferent to Cleveland's fate, and Republican Boss Platt was willing to sacrifice his own party's candidate for governor, Warner Miller. A deal was apparently cooked up between three local machine leaders in the metropolis and the Republican organization. Harrison and Hill benefited at the expense of Cleveland and Miller. The *New York Times* and loyal Cleveland men charged that Hill himself was a party to the deal. The bolting of German Republicans, opposed to Miller's antiliquor position, may have been a factor. At least Harrison carried the state, and Hill won the governorship.

In New York corruption may have affected the result; in Indiana it was the deciding factor. That state no longer held its state elections in October, but a Republican poll sixty days before the November election showed the Democrats ahead. National headquarters then came to the relief of the state organization. "Divide the floaters into blocks of five," wrote Treasurer W. W. Dudley to Indiana lieutenants, "put a trusted man with the necessary funds in charge of these five and make him responsible that none get away and that all vote our ticket." This letter, put into Democratic hands by a railway mail clerk, created a sensation. Chairman Quay denounced it as a forgery and Dudley brought libel suits—later dropped—against newspapers printing it. But stories of floaters, locked up the day before the election, then marched to the polls with Republican ballots in their hands and as much as fifteen dollars each in their pockets, have been well authenticated. Never had that considerable number of poor Hoosiers who were accustomed to turning a dishonest dollar at the polling places been so well rewarded. Afterwards, an investigation was launched into Dudley's activities; but he threatened to "explode a lot of dynamite" if he were made the scapegoat, and a federal judge saw fit to dismiss the case. At all events, Indiana voted for Harrison by the scant margin of 2,348.

More widely used than direct bribery was the fear appeal. Industrialists warned employees of wage cuts and unemployment if Cleveland should win. Although he did not advocate free trade, it became the bogy of Republican orators; and such a good friend of labor as Henry George played into their hands by preaching its benefits while speaking for the Democrats.

Anti-British sentiment was stirred up by the publication of a letter from Sir Lionel Sackville-West, the British Minister, to "Charles F. Murchison" of California, favoring Cleveland over Harrison. "Murchison," a Republican, posed as a former British subject writing for advice. The stupid Minister was at once dismissed, but the episode may have cost Cleveland some Irish votes.

The election was close, but the outcome was clear by midnight. Harrison had the 36 electoral votes of New York by a margin of about 13,000. Cleveland lost Indiana but carried Connecticut and New Jersey. The rest of the North and West went Republican as in 1884, though in most cases Cleveland ran better than before and had a popular plurality of 100,476.[1] The unrepresentative electoral system gave him only 168 electoral votes to Harrison's 233.

Cleveland's courageous if inexpedient tariff stand made him the leader of his party and, in defeat, its most popular figure. He had ended its halting expediency and had given it an issue. More important, his four years in office had finally given the lie to the old cry that rebels would rule if the Democrats won. The party of the Copperheads had at last attained respectability.

[1] Another estimate puts it at 95,534. According to one set of totals, Cleveland had 5,540,329 popular votes; Harrison, 5,439,853; Clinton B. Fisk (Prohibitionist), 249,506; Alson J. Streeter (Union Labor), 146,935. A United Labor candidate polled 2,818 votes in New York and Illinois, and an "American" candidate had 1,591 in California. Socialist and scattering votes totaled 7,006. Other totals vary slightly from these.

Republican Party Rule

The party organization, not the candidate, had gained the day in 1888. Harrison, awed by his great victory and the approaching responsibilities, devoutly thanked Providence; but Quay privately expressed his disgust. "Providence hadn't a damn thing to do with it," he said. He added that the President elect would never know how near a number of men "were compelled to approach the gates of the penitentiary to make him President." The political history of Harrison's administration records this struggle between the conscience and ideals of an earnest, high-minded executive and the power and pressure of the party machine.

The cold, driving rain on Inauguration Day (from which Harrison protected himself by donning an armor of chamois leather under his clothes) was a sinister portent, for no resident of the White House has aroused so little enthusiasm. Cleveland at times angered people by his bluntness; Harrison repelled them. The benumbing frigidity with which he greeted callers, his obvious desire to have them state their business and be gone, the seeming reluctance with which he granted requests and the even more ungracious manner in which he denied them, offended politicians big and little. "During and after an interview, if one could secure it," said Tom Platt, "one felt even in torrid weather like pulling on his winter flannels, galoshes, overcoats, mitts and earlaps." Harrison probably had reason to be coldly suspicious of the New York State Boss, who was refused the headship of the Treasury; but more friendly sources reported much the same feeling.

Blaine received the State Department; but his family and close friends were annoyed at Harrison's tardiness in making the offer. Nor was he consulted about other appointments. The spoils system ran riot under Postmaster General John Wanamaker, chief campaign "fat-fryer," and his first assistant, J. S. Clarkson. Presently Clarkson, the "headsman," had to be eased out. But in appointing Theodore Roosevelt to the lethargic Civic Service Commission Harrison gave it an aggressiveness toward politicians heretofore lacking. Its rules were improved, and the President later extended the merit system in several departments—after the positions had been filled with Republicans.

In the field of legislation the administration was made notable by the power and accomplishments of the party organization. A compact, disciplined majority put the Republican program through Congress, giving the country its first real taste of party government since the tidal wave of 1874. In the years 1875-1889, not once had both Houses and the President been of the same political faith.[2] The result had been party irresponsibility, in which representative government functioned badly. Now, with small majorities in both houses and a President who was a good party man, the Republicans were put to the test. The platform had promised much to many, and industrialists, old soldiers, western farmers, and colored voters all expected to collect.

The narrow Republican majority in the House of Representatives made it possible for the minority party to delay or defeat legislation by obstructionist tactics; but the decisions of the new Speaker, Thomas B. Reed, and reforms in the House rules solved the problem. "Czar" Reed, a bald-headed, flabby-faced giant with a keen intellect and a blasting wit, used the new rules to dominate the House as no Speaker had done before him. His rather benevolent autocracy made party responsibility a fact, though the broad powers vested in his office were open to abuse in less skilled hands.

Three major pieces of legislation of a partisan character were ground through the House at this session: the McKinley Tariff Act, the Sherman Silver Purchase Act, and the Lodge Federal Elections bill. In the Senate silver Republicans, strengthened by the recent admission of four new western states, held up the tariff bill until the eastern wing agreed to do something for silver, as the platform had implied. The result was the Sherman Silver Purchase Act, which increased government purchases of silver. The House accepted it, and the Senate then passed the McKinley Tariff. Eastern Republicans had to vote for the Sherman Act to get a higher tariff and to head off free silver. Democrats of all shades of opinion opposed both measures.

The Lodge Federal Elections bill to provide federal supervision of Congressional elections squeezed through the House by six votes, but the Senate postponed action until the next session. Then a silver alliance of southern Democrats and western Republicans sidetracked it. Eastern capital, with its eye on southern investments, was also willing to have the status quo undisturbed. The proposed measure had one significant effect. It hastened the tendency in the South to disfranchise the Negro by constitutional methods such as poll taxes,

[2] Two independents held the balance of power in the Senate, 1881-1883, though the Lower House and the President were Republican.

education tests, and residence and property requirements. In theory these applied to both races alike, but in practice the colored man's road was much more difficult.

The problem of the surplus was speedily solved. The high duties and sugar bounties of the McKinley Act reduced tariff revenues, while increased expenditures for navy, coast defense, and pensions produced a record total for the Fifty-first Congress, which Democrats called the "billion dollar Congress." Republican promises to the veterans were carried out generously. Corporal James Tanner, who had lost both legs at Second Bull Run, became commissioner of pensions with the remark "God help the surplus" fastened on him by the press. He practiced it so thoroughly that he was removed from office within six months. Congress helped along the good work with the Dependent Pension bill to pension all disabled veterans and widows of veterans, regardless of cause of disability.

The Republican party had carried out most of its pledges of 1888; but the result of this "spend and elect" program was a disastrous defeat in the mid-term elections. In the new House were 235 Democrats, 88 Republicans, and 9 Farmers' Alliance men. William McKinley, victim of a gerrymander, went down with many high-tariff colleagues. A farmer uprising, product of droughts and hard times, was under way in the Republican trans-Mississippi West, but even the East went Democratic. The effect of the McKinley Tariff could not be overlooked. With consumer prices heading upward, the voters revolted at the burdens of protection, and the Democrats seemed vindicated.

The Senate was saved to the Republicans by a majority of 8, but party government came to an end. The new Democratic Lower House bombarded the Senate with popgun bills, each aimed at a particular tariff schedule; but the Upper House took no action on them. It did pass a bipartisan silver bill, but the Lower House voted not to consider it. Another campaign was under way, and neither party was prepared to assume responsibility for a silver measure.

The Second Tariff Campaign

Harrison, though cooperative with Congress on his party's legislative program, had aroused the ill will of some powerful Republican politicians, chiefly for personal and patronage reasons. Platt was unfriendly from the beginning. Quay of Pennsylvania had given up the chairmanship of the national committee after some shady dealings when he held a state office were exposed. Clarkson of Iowa also joined the opposition. Marcus A. Hanna, denied even his choice for lighthouse keeper at Cleveland, agreed with his political enemy Joseph B. Foraker in his dislike of Harrison. Reed, annoyed at patronage rebuffs, used his bitter wit in private at the austere President's expense.

But the opposition had no candidate. Platt and Quay were anxious to push Blaine; but the Secretary of State was in failing health and refused to make the race. Hanna was booming William McKinley but was aiming at 1896 rather than 1892. McKinley himself was loyal to Harrison. Platt, Quay, and Clarkson rounded up delegates for Blaine without obtaining his consent; but many of his friends did not fall for their game and supported a renomination for the President.

Three days before the convention Blaine suddenly resigned as Secretary of State. Neither he nor Harrison offered any explanation. The state of Blaine's health, the none-too-cordial relations of the Secretary (and his family) with the White House, and the use of his name by the party bosses as a potential candidate may have contributed to the break. If it was a bid for the nomination, it came too late. The administration was in control of the national convention.

The story of the Republican convention, meeting at Minneapolis in the discontented farm belt on June 7, is soon told. The platform reaffirmed the tariff position of 1888, defended the "wise revenue legislation of the Republican Congress," and criticized Democratic tariff proposals. It favored the use of both gold and silver as currency under such restrictions as to maintain the parity of the two metals. It demanded a free and honest ballot and denounced "inhuman outrages" perpetrated on American citizens for political reasons in the South. The measures of Harrison's administration, of course, were commended.

Only Harrison and Blaine were nominated, though eleven speeches were required to set forth their merits. A great demonstration for Blaine, the last time the white plume was to be waved at a national convention, did not shake the grip of the Harrison men. The President was renominated on the first ballot, receiving 535-1/6 votes out of 905. Blaine had 182-5/6; McKinley, 182; Thomas B. Reed, 4; and Robert T. Lincoln, 1. McKinley, through the effective work of Marcus A. Hanna, made a fine showing without being a candidate. Whitelaw Reid of the *New York Tribune*, long an opponent of Platt, was named by acclamation to run with Harrison. The New York boss and his friends "wrapped ourselves in overcoats and earmuffs, hurried from the convention hall, and took the first train for New York."

Among the Democrats a bitter factional fight developed, centering in New York. Governor Hill was elected to the Senate in 1891 and proceeded to set himself up as a Presidential candidate. He talked vaguely about "bimetallic coinage" for western and southern ears, but usually concealed his principles, or lack of them, under the oft repeated assertion, "I am a Democrat." Here and there, groups of protectionists, silver men, and machine politicians looked upon him with favor. At least he would carry New York. Two obstacles, however, appeared in his path. One was his reputation as a crafty politician who had used liquor licenses, street-railway franchises, and public-works contracts to advance his interests. Tammany Hall and saloon politicians running city machines might accept him as a blood brother, but this almost ruined him elsewhere. Conventions may be dominated by bosses but they do not nominate them. The other obstacle was Grover Cleveland, whose star was again in the ascendant.

The former President seemed at first to be unwilling to run. He had a good law practice, had established Wall Street connections, and was making money. But the situation and the pressure of friends overcame his reluctance. He had created the tariff issue for his party, and the elections of 1890 had been a repudiation of Republican protection. If the Presidential election was to be fought over the tariff, he was the logical candidate.

The agrarian revolt in the West and South presented some perplexities. Prophets and politicians of a new vintage were launching a third party, and the movement for free and unlimited coinage of silver had their support. Cleveland had always opposed free silver, and he repeated his hostile views in 1891 in a letter which called it a "dangerous and reckless experiment." Most of his friends felt that he was too blunt, but in the long run Cleveland had played good politics. Except for Missouri, Indiana (1876, 1884), and California and Nevada (1880), the Democratic party had not received an electoral vote from any state west of Pennsylvania since 1856. A silver candidate might gain a few western votes but would lose the fifty-two electors of New York, New Jersey, and Connecticut—all necessary to success. The better strategy seemed to call for a conservative candidate to carry the East while western Democrats made deals with the new People's party to cut into Republican strength in the farm and mining states. The South would accept any Democrat.

Eastern mercantile, banking, and railroad interests, alarmed at the farmer revolt and not concerned about the tariff, looked to Cleveland to stand stanchly against free silver and agrarian radicalism. Harrison and the Republicans had wavered on silver in passing the Sherman Act. Consequently, unlike the protected manufacturers, financial and mercantile leaders like Henry Villard, Charles S. Fairchild, and Oscar S. Straus acted with George F. Parker and William C. Whitney in promoting Cleveland's candidacy.

The New York professional politicians rallied to Hill and threatened Cleveland's success in his home state. To insure a solid Hill delegation, they called the state convention for February 22, earlier than it had ever been held. This "snap" convention was easily controlled by the Hill men, and chose Hill delegates, who were instructed to observe the unit rule. The Cleveland men late in May staged their own "anti-snapper" convention, a great demonstration of his strength, and sent a contesting delegation to Chicago.

George F. Parker managed the preliminary campaign for Cleveland, depending chiefly on little groups of loyal supporters in the various states to round up delegates. Whitney returned from Europe in May to coordinate the movement and to direct the strategy at Chicago. As between Cleveland and such possibilities as Carlisle of Kentucky, Horace Boies of Iowa, Arthur P. Gorman of Maryland, and Hill, there was but one choice. Cleveland was practically nominated when the convention met on June 21. Whitney's chief task was to smooth the way so that the nomination could be made quickly without arousing hard feelings.

The only effective speech against Cleveland was by Bourke Cockran, Tammany Hall's silver-tongued spellbinder, in a final plea for Hill. The one roll call, completed just before sunrise, gave Cleveland 617-1/3, Hill 114, Boies 103, Gorman 36-1/2, Adlai E. Stevenson of Illinois 16-2/3, and John G. Carlisle of Kentucky 14 votes. Five others received 8 scattering votes. Cleveland had 10 more than the required two-thirds.

Stevenson, a silver Democrat and former First Assistant Postmaster General, was quickly named for the Vice Presidency over Isaac P. Gray of Indiana, his chief rival.

The platform offered by the resolutions committee was not acceptable to the radical tariff reformers. It emphasized the burdens and inequalities of the existing tariff but promised revision without injury to domestic industries. Cleveland favored it as he wanted to lessen the effect of the "free trade" cry, which had played such a part in 1888. Henry Watterson and Tom L. Johnson balked at such a cautious phrasing, and secured the adoption of resolutions of a more radical stamp by a direct appeal to the convention. These denounced Republican protection as a fraud and a robbery and the McKinley Act as "the culminating atrocity of class legislation," and denied that the federal government had constitutional power to collect duties "except for the purpose of revenue only." To the tariff were attributed business distress, wage reductions, and farm-mortgage indebtedness.

The currency plank denounced the Sherman Act as "a cowardly makeshift" but otherwise was evasive, advocating use of gold and silver without discrimination and maintenance of the parity of the two metals. Trusts were attributed to high tariffs, and anti-trust legislation was approved. But for the sections devoted to the tariff and criticisms of Republican policies, the platform might have been mistaken for the Republican.

Except where agrarian discontent fed the fires of Populism, the campaign was the dullest in many years. Honest bearded Benjamin Harrison confronting honest mustached Grover Cleveland in a tariff debate was a repeat performance that did not inspire parades with torches or the chanting of campaign ditties. Neither candidate appeared on the stump, Harrison because of Mrs. Harrison's illness and death and Cleveland out of respect for his rival's sad affliction. The Democrats, out of power, could assail Republican tariff policy without clarifying their own position. Cleveland's acceptance letter made it clear that he was no theoretical free trader—a necessary precaution, as the extreme tariff plank declaring that protection was unconstitutional was a boon to Republicans picturing the dangers of Democratic radicalism. The Republicans also had to defend their spending policy against charges of waste and extravagance while the Sherman Silver Purchase Act suited neither silver men nor gold advocates.

The argument that labor benefited from protection received a stunning blow when a great strike occurred in the Carnegie steelworks at Homestead, Pennsylvania. Wage reductions were the ostensible cause, but the company's desire to break the power of the steel workers' union soon became evident. After much violence and bloodshed, the strike ended in failure; but its lesson was clear. A prohibitive tariff wall might confer huge profits on monopolistic industries, but labor would get little enough. Cleveland's letter of acceptance hammered this point home. Labor troubles in other places added to Harrison's woes.

The "fat-frying" tactics of 1888 worked poorly in 1892. Industrialists contributed to the Republican campaign, but the amounts apparently were smaller. The McKinley Tariff rates were so high that the moderate reductions to be expected from the Democrats were not alarming. Spending for corrupt purposes, however, was not much in evidence.[3] The secret Australian ballot, already adopted by thirty-three states in 1892, made vote buying more difficult. Voters might still be bribed, but it was harder to check on their fidelity.

Another aspect of this dull campaign was the lethargy of the professional politicians. Quay, Platt, and Clarkson, the active leaders of 1888, were still sulking, and did little. Hanna of Ohio worked chiefly to advertise the virtues of William McKinley by having him speak for Harrison and the tariff all the way from Iowa to Maine. Blaine, stricken by disease and the shock of the sudden death of his son Emmons, was in no condition to play his customary part. He visited Whitelaw Reid at his country estate in New York and read a ten-minute address to a crowd of citizens from the neighboring towns, his only speech of the campaign. He came to Washington shortly before the election, was cordially received by Harrison, and walked home from church with him. Within three months he was in his grave.

In the Democratic camp the indefatigable Whitney handled the campaign efficiently, without blunders. The central organization was small, and finances for a time troubled him; but his Wall Street contacts helped bring in the necessary funds. The biggest problem was Grover Cleveland. Promises of jobs and favors were foreign to his nature, and he could not forgive his enemies. In the midst of the campaign he broke with Henry Watterson, the powerful Kentucky editor; and the two were never reconciled. When Whitney undertook to gain the good will of the Hill machine, Cleveland would make no pledges as to patronage. Sensing a national victory, Hill and his cohorts fell in line and worked for the party, if not the candidate.

Whitney also advised Cleveland to take a more sympathetic attitude toward silver, as the newly organized Populists were charging him with subservience to the eastern money power. A vague sentence

[3] Tabulations of campaign expenditures since 1860 list those of 1892 as the largest in any campaign to that time. However, the estimates are largely guesswork.

in his letter of acceptance about remedying "the wants of our people arising from the deficiency or imperfect distribution of money circulation" was the limit of his concession. However, Democratic state organizations in half a dozen western states where the Republicans had the upper hand joined forces with the Populists and gave twenty-two electoral votes to Weaver, the third-party leader.

While late indications pointed to a Democratic victory, the margin was surprising. It was a near landslide. Cleveland had the South, the doubtful northern group—New York, New Jersey, Connecticut, and Indiana—and normally Republican Illinois, Wisconsin, and California (except one elector). He also had 5 of Michigan's 14 (a Democratic legislature had districted the state for electors) and one from Ohio where a Democratic elector, oddly enough, led the ticket followed by 22 Republicans. Fusion in North Dakota produced one Cleveland elector also. The totals were: Cleveland, 277; Harrison, 145; Weaver, 22. The popular vote gave the victor a substantial margin.[4] Fusion arrangements with the Populists in some states gave Weaver many Democratic votes. In New York, Cleveland had a plurality of over 45,000; but the Empire State for once did not decide the result. The Democrats would have won without it.

The verdict was too decisive to be explained by anything except a widespread revulsion against Republican policies and an abiding confidence by voters of all classes in the integrity of Grover Cleveland. Had the four years which followed brought prosperity and domestic peace, he might have retired in 1897 with the popularity of a Coolidge. But panic, business collapse, unemployment and labor troubles, farmer discontent, and the strife of classes and sections brought out in a cruel light his fundamental conservatism, the negative character of his virtues, and the inflexibility of his mind. He saw only the necessity of resisting discontent; he did not know how to allay it. In the end his party was torn apart, and his leadership repudiated.

[4] The popular vote was as follows: Cleveland, 5,556,543; Harrison, 5,175,582; Weaver, 1,040,886; John Bidwell, Prohibitionist, 255,841; Simon Wing, Socialist Labor, 21,532. Forty-four states participated in the election, six having been admitted since 1888.

18

The Great Agrarian Failure

Third-Party Movements

From 1872 down to the Democratic-Populist coalition of 1896, agrarian and labor discontent found a vent in third-party movements in every national campaign. The aggrieved farmers furnished the driving force and most of the votes; labor's role was significant but secondary. The farmers created the Patrons of Husbandry, popularly known as the Grange, and some local independent parties; the greenback movement, which penetrated both old parties to some extent and created a third party as well; and the Populist uprising, most powerful of all, which found its chief outlet in the People's (or Populist) party of the 1890's. Labor reformers furnished a third party in 1872, supported the Greenback party in the late seventies, and had two short-lived parties in the field in 1888, when no agrarian party appeared. Running through all these radical movements was the thread of protest against the growing power of big business and big finance, and the failure of the major parties to face the problem.

The Granger movement was a product of the agricultural depression in the upper Mississippi valley after the Civil War. Overexpansion of production with consequent low prices drove the farmers to organize and demand relief. The Panic of 1873 made a bad situation worse, and in 1873-1874 appeared a flock of local parties, the Grange itself being nonpolitical. The chief interest of these parties, known under such names as Anti-Monopoly, Reform, and Independent, was in railroad regulation. The stock watering, excessive rates, political activities, and monopolistic character of railroads made them natural objects of farmer resentment. These local parties, sometimes cooperating with the Democrats, carried several state legislatures, helped elect two or three "reformers" to the United States Senate, and inaugurated state regulation of railroads and grain elevators. Most of the laws were hastily drawn up, worked badly, and were soon repealed; but they established the right of the states to regulate and led to sounder legislation.

The independent parties, in eleven states, did not develop a national organization. Once the fury for reform spent itself, they disappeared. The members returned to the old parties or were drawn into the Greenback party, which appeared in the middle seventies. The first agrarian parties were not inflationist but antirailroad and antimonopoly. Otherwise they had little to offer in a program. A lower tariff, economy, civil service reform, and elimination of corruption in government exhaust their list of proposals.

The shift of interest to currency inflation was natural as the depression lengthened, and was foreshadowed by the Ohio Idea of the late sixties and the appearance of a Labor Reform party in 1872—an outgrowth of the National Labor Union, organized in 1866 to unify the work of various labor groups. It held a convention at Columbus, Ohio, February 21-22, 1872, to select a Presidential candidate. Seventeen states were represented. Justice David Davis of Illinois and Joel Parker of New Jersey were nominated for President and Vice President. The platform called for "a purely national circulating medium," to be issued directly by the government without the intervention of banks, to be legal tender for all debts, to be interchangeable at the option of the holder for government bonds bearing an interest rate not to exceed 3.65 per cent. This stand was not so much inflationist as opposed to banks and money monopoly, but it was substantially the greenback idea of the later seventies. Other planks favored taxation of government bonds, reservation of public lands for actual settlers only, the prohibition of the importation of Chinese labor, an eight-hour day for labor employed by or for the government, abolition of contract labor in prisons, payment of war costs through assessments on wealth without burdening posterity, government regulation of railroad and telegraph corporations, and revision of the patent laws in the interest of labor. The platform was more moderate than those of later third parties, and it deserved more consideration than it received.

The Labor Reform party was soon shipwrecked. Davis and Parker waited to see what the Liberal Republicans would do, and then declined the nominations; and the attempt of a poorly attended second convention to substitute Charles O'Conor was unsuccessful. O'Conor also declined a straight-out Democratic nomination, but electoral tickets were run for him in several states. He received 29,489 votes, which probably represented anti-Greeley Democrats rather than Labor Reformers. The party continued to operate locally but held no other national conventions.

The greenback idea came up again in March, 1875, when a national convention met at Cleveland to organize a new party. This was followed by a nominating convention at Indianapolis in May, 1876, which named Peter Cooper of New York for President and General Samuel F. Cary of Ohio for Vice President. Its platform called for repeal of the Resumption Act of 1875 and issuance of legal tender notes convertible into government bonds with an interest rate not to exceed one cent a day per hundred dollars. Peter Cooper, the well known philanthropist, was an odd nominee for a paper money, agrarian party; he was eighty-five years old and naturally made no campaign. The real leaders were James Buchanan, an Indianapolis lawyer, Marcus M. ("Brick") Pomeroy, editor of various newspapers and writer of tracts, and eloquent Ignatius Donnelly, former Congressman from Minnesota, who had recently been active in the Anti-Monopoly movement and who made third-party activity his life work with intervals devoted to arguing that Bacon wrote Shakespeare and lecturing on various subjects. The net result of the new party's campaign efforts was a total of 81,737 votes, most of them from Indiana, Iowa, Illinois and Michigan.

In the next two years the party grew rapidly. The depression became worse, and the year 1877 was marked by great railroad strikes, indicating that labor might be a fertile field for votes. Some Labor Reformers had aided the cause in 1876, and a conference at Toledo in February, 1878, with twenty-eight states represented, arranged a farmer-labor partnership under the name "National" party, but better known as the Greenback, or Greenback Labor, party. In the fall elections this third party won a million votes and fifteen members of Congress. However, fusion with one or the other of the old parties accounted for part of its success. The greenback views of Democratic leaders in the farm states kept many moderate inflationists from deserting that party.

Greenback hopes were high in 1880 though dissensions between radicals and fusionists caused difficulties. At the national convention in Chicago on June 9, agrarian and labor delegates, including representatives of a Socialist Labor party, started in 1876, composed their differences and adopted a farmer-labor platform. The currency planks favored complete government control of all money, abolishment of the national banking system, and unlimited coinage of silver as well as gold. Labor was recognized in a number of moderate planks similar to those of the Labor Reform party, and liberals generally were appealed to by demands for Congressional regulation of interstate commerce, the forfeiture of railroad land grants, and a graduated income tax.

The convention named for President the most solid figure the party had produced, General James B. Weaver of Iowa, Civil War veteran and former Republican, who had been elected to Congress on the Greenback wave of 1878. B. J. Chambers of Texas was named for Vice President. Weaver made an active campaign, speaking in all parts of the country and giving the party a type of leadership that it needed badly to dispel the impression that it was a refuge for crackpots and wild radicals; but the election results sorely disappointed the Greenbackers. The return of prosperity and the success of the Resumption Act removed the agrarian and labor discontent on which they built their hopes. The powerful pull of party loyalties, so evident in a Presidential election, was a further factor in blighting the bright hopes aroused in 1878. Their vote in 1880 was only 308,578.

In 1884 an Anti-Monopoly party sounded the tocsin of revolt against the "giant monopolies" which had placed enterprise under tribute and had "inflicted countless wrongs upon the toiling millions of the United States." Its national convention at Chicago on May 14 nominated General Benjamin F. Butler of Massachusetts for President and left the choice of Vice President to the national committee. Its platform was largely a duplication of the Greenback program of 1880, and fusion of the two groups seemed logical. The Greenback convention in turn, at Indianapolis on May 28, nominated General Butler and gave General Alanson M. West of Mississippi second place on the ticket. The platform was more denunciatory than in 1880, but repeated substantially the proposals of that year. Butler, intriguing with the Republicans to defeat Cleveland after his own failure to secure the Democratic nomination, was a sorry choice for the dyed-in-the-wool agrarians and obtained only 175,370 votes in November. This marked the national demise of both third parties.

The end of Greenbackism permitted labor for the moment to act as sponsor of third parties. After local successes by labor groups a Union Labor party held a preliminary conference in 1887, and then a convention at Cincinnati on May 15, 1888, with more than two hundred delegates of diverse backgrounds present from twenty states. The nominee for President was Alson J. Streeter of Illinois, who had been president of the Northwestern Farmers' Alliance and a leader in the Anti-Monopoly convention of 1884. The platform opposed land monopoly and favored public ownership of the means of communication and transportation, a legal tender currency issued directly to the people or loaned upon land security at a low interest rate, and the free coinage of silver. Its labor demands were patterned on those of earlier minor parties as were the planks favoring general reforms, such as direct election of United States Senators, an income tax, and woman suffrage. The platform was more agrarian than labor and suggests that the leaders were appealing to a wider constituency than industrial workers.

A second labor group with no agrarian leaven held a conference at Cincinnati at the same time and nominated Robert H. Cowdrey of Illinois for the Presidency. The platform of this "United Labor" convention emphasized the Henry George principle of the single tax on land, regarding other reforms as distinctly secondary. George had made a spectacular, though unsuccessful, campaign for mayor of New York City in 1886 as a labor candidate, and his followers were encouraged to extend their activities into a broader field by running him for secretary of state of New York in 1887. The result was disappointing, and George left the movement to support President Cleveland for his tariff stand; but Father Edward McGlynn, George's chief lieutenant, continued the crusade, and eighty-six delegates—forty from New York—attempted to launch a national United Labor party with the single tax as its chief stock in trade. This explains the presence of two labor parties in 1888.

The Union Labor party polled 146,935 votes, the smallest number for a farmer-labor protest party since 1876. The growing Farmers' Alliances were not ready for independent action; labor was indifferent; and most of the Union Labor votes came from the old Greenback areas. The rival United Labor party faded out with a total vote, limited to New York and Illinois, of 2,818.

The greatest of the protest movements was now about to begin. The late 1880's were hard years for western wheat and corn growers. This was especially true of Kansas, Nebraska, and the Dakotas, which had developed rapidly in the boom years before 1887 with a rush of settlers, borrowed capital, railroad expansion, and adequate rainfall.

A series of dry years from 1887 to 1897 drove many settlers out of the western parts of these states and left the middle regions seething with discontent. Unable to meet interest charges on loans, because of low prices as well as drought, the people were ripe for revolt. To a lesser degree the whole grain-growing West was burdened with mortgage indebtedness and low prices, which continued into the 1890's and grew worse after the Panic of 1893. Political action of some sort was inevitable.

In the impoverished South the masses of small farmers had become enmeshed in the crop-lien system after the war; and their burdens became heavier with declining cotton prices. Around 1890 discontent ripened into revolt. The problem was peculiarly difficult in the lower South. Here the "Bourbons" backed by businessmen, large landowners, and the professional classes controlled politics. They had overthrown the carpetbag governments, and were continued in office year after year by the grateful white voters. The widespread fear of a return of carpetbag-Negro domination was shrewdly used by Democratic politicians, who held up the division of the white vote by insurgent movements or new parties as something akin to treason. This almost compelled the dissatisfied tenant farmers to work for reform within the Democratic party where they were at a disadvantage in trying to take over the state organizations from the old leaders.

In both the South and the West the 1880's were years of activity by numerous farm organizations, which presently consolidated into two great bodies familiarly known as the Southern Alliance and the Northwestern Alliance. Efforts at merger in 1889 ended in failure, and the Southern Alliance invaded the North; but the programs of the two were substantially the same. They wanted currency expansion, regulation and possibly government ownership of railroads, and a number of other economic and political reforms which drew them inevitably into politics. In the state and Congressional elections of 1890, either through indorsement of old-party candidates or through independent tickets, the Alliance men were surprisingly successful. In the South, by capturing Democratic state and local conventions they were able to nominate and elect three governors and forty-four Congressmen, control several legislatures, and choose two or three United States Senators friendly to the farmers. "Pitchfork" Ben Tillman, organizer of the small farmers of South Carolina and now governor, and Tom Watson of Georgia, champion of southern underdogs, who went to Congress, became important leaders of the revolt.

In the West, where the Alliance men cooperated with the Democrats or ran independent candidates, the results are harder to classify. Two United States Senators, James H. Kyle of South Dakota, a young Congregational minister, and William A. Peffer of Kansas, a long-whiskered, elderly lawyer-journalist, were elected as independents, while several Alliance Congressional candidates were chosen, and a number of successful Democrats had Alliance support. Kansas, Nebraska, and South Dakota were the centers of the new agrarian uprising.

The next step was the organization of a third party, and a small group in the Southern Alliance called a convention, which met at Cincinnati, May 19, 1891, with fourteen hundred delegates present including labor representatives. Few southerners came, for sentiment in the South was against a third party because of Alliance successes within the Democratic party. The convention formed the People's party but called a conference at St. Louis to secure the cooperation of farmer, labor, and other liberal groups. The St. Louis conference, on February 22, 1892, adopted a platform, and accepted the Cincinnati proposal for a third party. A national nominating convention was called to assemble at Omaha in July.

A wildly enthusiastic convention gathered on July 2; and two days later it adopted the first platform of the People's party with a roaring forty-minute demonstration. Two-thirds of the platform was a bitter indictment of the American economic system and a condemnation of the two great parties for "a sham battle over the tariff, so that capitalists, corporations, national banks, rings, trusts, watered stock, the demonetization of silver, and the oppressions of the usurers may all be lost sight of." The rhetoric was Ignatius Donnelly's. Demands followed for a national currency issued by the government without the use of banks, the free and unlimited coinage of silver and gold at the ratio of sixteen to one, a circulating medium of fifty dollars per capita, a graduated income tax, a system of postal savings banks, government ownership and operation of railroad, telegraph, and telephone systems, and measures to end land monopoly by railroads and corporations.

Supplementary resolutions, not regarded as a part of the platform, declared for the Australian ballot, further restriction of undesirable immigration and of contract labor, rigid enforcement of the eight-hour law on government work, abolition of the Pinkerton detective system (used in labor disputes), adoption of the initiative and referendum, limitation of the Presidency to one term, direct election of United States Senators, and an end to subsidies or national aid to private corporations. There was little in the People's party program that had not been suggested by earlier third parties, but it was better synthesized; and it represented a volume of discontent that made it a challenge to the old parties in the South and West.

The choice of a candidate offered far greater difficulties than the platform. Colonel L. L. Polk of the Southern Alliance, a popular figure, had died in the spring. Judge Walter Q. Gresham of the United States Circuit Court, a nationally known independent Republican, was regarded with favor; but he decided against the use of his name. This left Senator James H. Kyle of South Dakota and General Weaver of Iowa, the old Greenbacker. Weaver was chosen over Kyle, 995 to 265, and James G. Field of Virginia, a Confederate general, was named for second place.

The spirit of the convention carried over into the campaign in the West, less so in the South. Thousands of Southern Alliance men, like Tillman of South Carolina, refused to leave the Democratic party. Only the poorer farmers accepted the third party, and logic pointed toward an alliance with the Republicans and a bid for the Negro vote. With the Democrats taking up agrarian reforms and at the same time raising the issue of white supremacy, Weaver did not secure a single electoral vote in the South, though he ran second to Cleveland in several states.

In the West a coalition with the Democrats on electoral tickets in six states resulted in victory in five, with a total of twenty-two electoral votes,[1] besides a number of state and Congressional successes. The People's party had over a million popular votes—an excellent showing for a new party. But it ran the danger of sacrificing its future independence for immediate gains. A major factor in its successes was indorsement of free silver. It carried Idaho, Colorado, and Nevada, silver states, but only Kansas and North Dakota in the farm belt. Unless the party could spread eastward, it could hardly displace either old party, despite Weaver's confident assertion that the Republican party was as dead as the Whigs in 1852.

Events in Cleveland's troubled second term made the country a

[1] Kansas, Idaho, Colorado, and Nevada chose Populist electors. North Dakota, carried by a Democratic-Populist coalition, gave Weaver and Cleveland each an electoral vote, while one Republican elector was successful. One Weaver elector was chosen in Oregon. A joint electoral ticket was defeated in Wyoming.

seething caldron of discontent. The Panic of 1893 and the great depression that followed caused further declines in farm prices; mortgage foreclosures increased, taxes went unpaid, and the currency problem took the center of the stage. Cleveland, unmoved by the growing inflationist sentiment, forced the repeal of the Sherman Silver Purchase Act and bent all his efforts toward preserving the gold standard through the maintenance of the gold reserve in the Treasury. Western and southern Democrats, embarrassed by the Populist demand for free silver, turned away from the President and unfurled the inflation banner. Labor was antagonized by the drastic actions of the federal government in the Pullman strike of 1894, and unemployment grew with the depression to add to Cleveland's burdens. Even his attempt at tariff reduction failed, for a group of conservative Senate Democrats, chiefly from the East, joined with the Republicans to amend the Wilson bill in many of its schedules to make it a thoroughly protective measure. Cleveland let it become a law, as the Wilson-Gorman Act, without his signature. This was a violation of the party platform though it did lower somewhat the extreme rates of the McKinley Act.

The Supreme Court drew a blast of criticism that was not confined to farmer and labor by a five-to-four decision that the income-tax provision of the Wilson-Gorman Act was unconstitutional. This reversal of an earlier decision, together with its sustaining an injunction in the railroad strike of 1894, brought upon it the sharpest public condemnation since the Dred Scott case. The federal government in all its branches seemed to have become the bulwark of plutocracy.

In the Congressional elections of 1894 the Republicans benefited from social unrest and Democratic dissensions. They won a large majority in the House of Representatives, but a little group of Populists held the balance of power in the Senate. The People's party seemed to have increased its vote in the West, but again fusion arrangements in various states made it difficult to estimate the total. Republican-Populist candidates in the South won several seats in Congress, carried the North Carolina legislature, and might have gained some other states but for fraudulent manipulation of returns by Democratic officials. South Carolina sent Tillman to the Senate as an anti-Cleveland Democrat. Optimistic agrarian leaders felt that the People's party might absorb the Democrats nationally by using the silver issue; but the reverse process was equally possible. Six new states, admitted in 1889-1890, had strengthened the silver cause.

Hanna

Up to the fall of 1894, Marcus Alonzo Hanna of Cleveland, Ohio, had combined business and politics to good advantage. His interests had expanded from coal, iron, and lake transportation into banking, street-railway and other enterprises, and these brought him into contact with local and state politicians. His skill as a fund raiser for campaigns gave him political stature, and he went as a delegate to the Republican national conventions of 1884 and 1888. In 1888 he managed John Sherman's unsuccessful campaign for the Presidential nomination. Seeing a better prospect in William McKinley, northeastern Ohio Congressman, lawyer, war veteran, Methodist, able speaker, and loyal party man, he helped elect McKinley governor in 1891 and held him in reserve at the 1892 Minneapolis convention in the event of a deadlock. Early in 1893, McKinley was suddenly faced with bankruptcy and possible political ruin through the failure of an industrialist friend whose notes he had indorsed. Hanna and his friends came to the rescue and raised over $100,000 to take care of the obligations. Singularly enough, this episode aroused public sympathy for McKinley and he was reelected governor by an increased majority. A post-election cartoon in the Cleveland *Leader* pictured him as the rising sun of prosperity, and from this came the slogan, "the advance agent of prosperity." His high-tariff law of 1890 was no longer a party liability, for the hard times under Cleveland could be attributed to Democratic tariff policies. Hanna was now ready to make his move as President maker.

The partnership of Hanna and McKinley was the most successful alliance of manager and candidate in American history. Weed and Seward had failed of the ultimate objective; Farley and Franklin D. Roosevelt parted when the manager tired of his role and reached for the scepter. But the two Ohioans built a relationship that withstood even the strain of McKinley's consciousness of his pedestal. It was not an intimate back-slapping "Mark-and-Bill" friendship; their letters usually began, "Dear Mr. Hanna" and "Dear Governor." McKinley did not encourage familiarities, and Hanna stood a little in awe of the sartorially correct public figure whose knowledge of the intricacies of government and political finesse had elevated him to the rank of statesman. The thick-set, round-faced capitalist brought to the partnership an ability to pick the right men for his purposes, a flexibility of mind in meeting problems, a scrupulous regard for a pledged word, a ruthlessness toward whoever and whatever blocked his path, and an honest belief that there was little that money could not buy. His colored barber, who at times also doubled as a political operative, has left this appraisal of Boss Hanna: "It was a question with him, can you do it; don't fail but do it, never mind the other fellow as long as the end justified the means. . . . There was never any question about expense; results was what he demanded, not expense accounts."

The partners' personal traits, though very unlike, complemented rather than clashed. Hanna was direct, outspoken, quick-triggered, sociable, warm-hearted. He loved cards and the theater, was a loyal, generous friend and prided himself on dealing fairly with his employees and having their good will. McKinley was unruffled, tactful, cautious, carefully cordial to everyone, adept in compromise, and wise in the ways of the politician. His dignified public front concealed an essentially kindly, tender-hearted man whose private life was marked by his devotion to an invalid wife. Her dependence upon him amounted to a gentle tyranny which must have been a heavy drain upon his time and energies. Both Hanna and McKinley came of Scotch-Irish stock; but Hanna once remarked that in disposition he had the Irish and McKinley the Scotch of the combination. In economic philosophy they agreed that stimulation of private enterprise by the government was in the public interest, that restriction normally was not. Hanna, initially at least, saw good government as one that was good to business; McKinley saw beyond that—that no government was good for business that favored business alone, that there were other plates at the table. Hanna had to learn to think, like McKinley, in terms of votes. Before 1899, his power in Ohio was repeatedly challenged with success by Joseph B. Foraker, who was twice governor in the 1880's and was elected United States Senator in 1897 in spite of Hanna.

Hanna's campaign to get McKinley the Presidential nomination began early in 1895 when he retired from business and went to Thomasville, Georgia, to escape the rigors of the Cleveland winter. He invited McKinley to visit him, and presently guests came from different parts of the South to meet the gracious governor and, perchance, to discuss politics with his host. Color was no barrier. In this way, as Hanna's biographer puts it, there was created "a species of public opinion in the South" favorable to McKinley's candidacy.

Boss Platt analyzed Hanna's hospitality more tersely: "He had the South practically solid before some of us waked up."

The old bosses "waked up" in January, 1896, when a conference of Platt, Quay, Clarkson, Joseph H. Manley and Chauncey I. Filley in New York decided to encourage favorite-son candidacies. These included Thomas B. Reed of New England, Governor Levi P. Morton of New York, Senator William B. Allison of Iowa, Senator Shelby M. Cullom of Illinois, Senator Cushman K. Davis of Minnesota, and possibly former President Harrison of Indiana. Quay himself was to be the nominal choice of Pennsylvania. The delegates from these states plus the expected southern contingent would be enough to block McKinley. The bosses' scheme went completely awry in the face of the careful planning and superior strategy of Hanna. The coalition's efforts in the South bagged exactly 26-1/2 votes. Some of the favorite sons saw the light and withdrew, while Hanna openly opposed and defeated local favorites in Nebraska and Illinois, took Vermont from Reed, and even captured some Pennsylvania votes from Quay and New York votes from Morton. Illinois's decision late in April, after a hard fight directed by young Charles G. Dawes, practically ended the battle. It had cost more than $100,000. Promises of patronage played a part though McKinley refused to permit his backer to bargain with cabinet offices. Otherwise, even Platt and Quay might have been won over.

McKinley's only serious rival had been Speaker Thomas B. Reed. This masterful man had no Mark Hanna; nor could he have attracted one. His caustic wit made most men fear him. His bluntness, his refusal to give pledges or make commitments, and his lack of funds, made worse by his hostile attitude toward large contributions, ruined his chances. But he was also borne down by his Maine residence, his undeviating hostility toward silver, and a blundering ineffectual campaign manager.

With McKinley practically nominated, the only problem at the convention in St. Louis on June 16 was the platform pronouncement on the money question. McKinley's whole Congressional record had been marked by a sympathetic attitude toward silver, and he had no wish to recant. His strongest delegate support was from areas friendly to silver, while the "gold-bugs" of the East were generally hostile. His natural inclination now was to be a "straddle-bug" —a designation credited to Reed.

Hanna played a careful game. Taking to St. Louis a somewhat

ambiguous currency resolution that represented the views of McKinley and his closest advisers, he turned it over to his chief associates for criticism and revision before the convention. Out of their conferences emerged the famous gold plank with its actual mention of the word "gold." McKinley accepted it reluctantly, but it was kept a secret until ready for submission to the resolutions committee.

Over the week end the eastern contingent of delegates began to arrive, full of fight for a positive indorsement of the gold standard. Platt and Senator Henry Cabot Lodge put pressure on Hanna, who is said to have told the lordly Massachusetts scholar-politician to "go plumb to hell." Later, according to H. H. Kohlsaat of Chicago, a member of the Hanna inner circle, the plank was shown to Lodge; he approved of it, and eventually claimed credit for it. Platt also believed that the insertion of the gold plank was "the greatest achievement of my political career," that he and Lodge had forced Hanna to capitulate. All the evidence seems to prove that the "capitulation" was prearranged. Except for slight modifications in the wording, the resolutions committee accepted the draft prepared the week before.[2] Hanna and McKinley had seemingly given in to a general demand for a moderate gold plank. Had Hanna come out publicly for the gold standard before the convention met, the McKinley forces might have split badly.

The plank, as adopted, was as follows:

> We are unalterably opposed to every measure calculated to debase our currency or impair the credit of our country. We are, therefore, opposed to the free coinage of silver, except by international agreement with the leading commercial nations of the world, which we pledge ourselves to promote, and until such agreement can be obtained the existing gold standard must be preserved. All our silver and paper currency must be maintained at parity with gold, and we favor all measures designed to maintain inviolably the obligations of the United States and all our money, whether coin or paper, at the present standard, the standard of the most enlightened nations of the earth.

[2] Former Governor William R. Merriam of Minnesota, who helped prepare the original preliminary draft, was also a member of the subcommittee of the resolutions committee, which included J. B. Foraker, chairman of the whole committee, Edward Lauterbach of New York, and Senator Lodge. Oddly enough, Foraker, as well as Lodge and Platt, claimed credit later for the plank, while H. H. Kohlsaat, Chicago publisher, says that he forced the insertion of the word "gold" in the original draft, which, according to Myron T. Herrick, had already been put in by H. C. Payne! Nicholas Murray Butler also gives the credit to Payne. Butler was one of the group that prepared the draft plank.

Superficially the party was upholding the gold standard until bimetallism could be obtained by international agreement, a position that helped mollify western Republicans. Actually it was committed to gold, for the chance of securing such an agreement was slight. The more radical silver men were not deceived, and Senator Henry M. Teller of Colorado offered a free-silver substitute on the floor of the convention. It was tabled, 818-1/2 ayes to 105-1/2 noes. Then Senator Frank J. Cannon of Utah read a protest on behalf of the silver men, after which he and Senator Teller dramatically led a group of seceders, twenty-four in all,[3] from the convention: delegations or parts of delegations from Colorado, Utah, Montana, and Idaho, and one delegate from South Dakota. Teller was leaving the party he had helped to found forty years before, with only jeers, catcalls and sarcastic "goodbyes" to mark his departure. Hanna, perspiring and happy, shouted with the rest, for the bolters were a mere handful, representing at most a baker's dozen electoral votes from the thinly populated mountain states where silver was the chief product. Only one delegate had bolted from the great grain-growing states, the centers of farmer discontent. McKinley felt that the currency question would drop out of sight thirty days after the convention was over. But he reckoned without William Jennings Bryan.

The rest of the platform aroused no controversy. It condemned Democratic policies for precipitating the panic and prolonging the depression and promised restoration of protection and reciprocity as a solution. It took seven or eight paragraphs for this general theme, relegating the brief statements on the currency to comparative obscurity in the middle of the platform. On foreign policy the imperialism of the next few years was foreshadowed by significant statements overlooked in the concern felt over the silver issue. For example, the acquisition of Hawaii, the construction of a Nicaragua canal, and the purchase of the Danish West Indies were favored; the Monroe Doctrine was reasserted, with a hope for the eventual withdrawal of European powers from the western hemisphere; sympathy was expressed for the revolting Cubans, along with a declaration that the United States should use its good offices to make Cuba independent of Spain; and the continued enlargement of the navy was approved.

The balloting for President was hardly more than a formality. McKinley had 661-1/2 votes; Reed 84-1/2; Quay, 61-1/2; Levi P.

[3] Some ten alternates accompanied them.

Morton of New York, 58; William B. Allison of Iowa, 35-1/2; J. Donald Cameron of Pennsylvania, 1. There were four blanks. With New York and Pennsylvania safely Republican, the nomination for Vice President went to a loyal member of the McKinley organization from New Jersey, Garret A. Hobart. He received 535-1/2 votes to 277-1/2 for his chief competitor, Henry Clay Evans of Tennessee.

Naturally Hanna was named chairman of the national committee to manage the campaign. He was the nearest approach to a national "boss" the country had yet seen. Platt, Quay, Whitney, and their like were state bosses who allied with others of their kind to control conventions; Hanna took the whole country for his province and made the state bosses take orders.

The bolting silver men issued an address to the public calling for a union of parties favorable to bimetallism and offering Senator Teller as a suitable candidate. If the Democrats rejected him for a straight-out Democrat, then Populists, Silver Republicans, and a recently organized National Silver party might back Teller against both old parties. The Silver Republicans had been fighting Democrats in their home states too long to feel any liking for service under an old-line partisan. Also, they wanted to preserve their identity. Optimistically they looked toward Chicago.

Bryan

"I hope that the two wings of the Democratic party may flap together," wrote William Jennings Bryan in 1891, "but I believe the time has come when the western wing shall have some say so in regard to the flapping." Turning from the tariff to silver, he became one of the leaders of the free-coinage bloc in Congress during his two terms, 1891-1895. Defeated for the Senate in 1894, he became a traveling salesman for the silver cause while acting as editor of the Omaha *World Herald*. Still in his early thirties, this clean-cut, strong-faced, well built Nebraskan was already a master of the art of public speaking. His reverberating, bell-like voice carried his words to the farthest corners of great convention halls, while his evangelistic spirit gave to every cause he advocated a religious fervor that swept all doubts away. This crusader was the prophet that the harried agrarians had been seeking; but not until that torrid day in July, 1896, was his primacy recognized. Then the East, disturbed but more amused at the vociferations and strident outcries of the Tillmans, the Leases, the Donnellys, the Weavers, and the rest of the minor prophets, suddenly grew alarmed. Was he a Moses or a Mohammed? At least he was dangerous.

Bryan, Bland, and other silver men were at work months before the Democratic convention met. Their plan was to make the Democratic party a farmer-labor vehicle instead of a Tweedledee available to the voters when they wanted to turn Republican Tweedledum out. Except for a few percentage points' difference in tariff rates, a Cleveland Democrat and an orthodox Republican viewed measures through the same spectacles. Unless the Democratic party turned to the left, Populism threatened to make it a third party in the West and endanger its hold on the South. In the East it could only play second fiddle to the dominant Republicans, with occasional New York successes as a consolation prize. The silver leaders believed that the safe course was the bold one of uniting South and West under the free-silver banner and absorbing Populism. A conference of silver Democrats at Washington in August, 1895, set up a national committee; the *National Bimetallist* was soon being published, and the American Bimetallic Union was organized in January, 1896. In state after state of the South and the West the silver forces chose the delegates to the national convention.

The Democratic national convention opened at Chicago on July 7. The national committee, hostile to silver, offered Senator David B. Hill of New York as temporary chairman; but the silver men, disregarding party custom, opposed the nomination and placed Senator John W. Daniel of Virginia in the chair by a vote of 556 to 349. The credentials committee strengthened the hold of the silver men by seating the Bryan delegation from Nebraska and by awarding four contested Michigan seats to silver men, thus giving them a majority of the delegates from that state.

The battle over the platform began in the resolutions committee and was then transferred to the floor of the convention. The majority report assailed gold monometallism for placing heavy burdens on the American people through price declines, heavy taxes and debts, the enrichment of moneylenders, and the prostration of industry. It charged that it was a British policy, "not only un-American, but anti-American." The heart of the report was this statement: "We demand the free and unlimited coinage of both silver and gold at the present legal ratio of sixteen to one without waiting for the aid or consent of any other nation." The minority report emphasized the dangers of free silver and declared for the existing gold standard until international bimetallism could be secured.

Then came the great debate. Bryan had taken no part in the preliminary work, as his delegation had just been seated. To his surprise and joy the chairman of the resolutions committee asked him to take charge of the debate for the silver men while David B. Hill acted for the opposition. He was the concluding speaker. Senator Tillman ("Pitchfork Ben") opened with a fighting speech; but his denunciations of Cleveland and the eastern Democracy won no votes for silver, and Chairman Jones of the resolutions committee took the platform to deny that his committee indorsed such a sectional argument. Then came Hill, adroit and conciliatory, followed by two other "goldbugs," who only irritated the impatient majority, eager for the vote. This was the moment for Bryan. Speaking with a voice that reached every listener in the great hall, he took command. He wasted no time on personalities or sarcastic retorts. His shells were hurled at the gold standard, and his appeal was made on behalf of "the struggling masses." He redefined "businessman" to include wage earner, country lawyer, crossroads merchant, farmer and miner, whose interests had been neglected so long.

Bryan's own description tells the story of his great effort: "The audience seemed to rise and sit down as one man. At the close of a sentence it would rise and shout, and when I began upon another sentence, the room was as still as a church. . . . The audience acted like a trained choir—in fact, I thought of a choir as I noted how instantaneously and in unison they responded to each point made." He finished with the sentence which has given the speech its name: "You shall not press down upon the brow of labor this crown of thorns, you shall not crucify mankind upon a cross of gold." Then followed a wild demonstration, as spontaneous as has ever burst forth from a great political convention. The cause had found a leader, young, dynamic, courageous, blessed with a Voice.

The speech was a dramatic performance, but it was not as extemporaneous as it sounded. Bryan had been preparing himself carefully for this opportunity. He had even tried parts of the speech on smaller audiences in pre-convention campaigning for silver. Only the arrangement, he says in his memoirs, was improvised. Yet his frequent references to the preceding speakers made it appear that the whole thing was a creation of the moment. A consummate actor as well as a trained debater, he made every line count.

The majority report was upheld, 626 to 303. A proposal to indorse the Cleveland administration was voted down, and the entire platform was then adopted, 628 to 301. In the silver majority were nearly all the delegates west of Pennsylvania and south of the Potomac, except Wisconsin, Minnesota, South Dakota, and a scattering dozen from other states.

Besides indorsing silver and condemning national bank notes, the platform advocated tariff for revenue only, though opposing further changes until the money question was settled. It criticized the Supreme Court sharply for the income-tax decision, and called upon Congress to use all power "which remains after that decision, or which may come from its reversal by the court as it may hereafter be constituted," to equalize the burdens of taxation. The labor provisions included disapproval of the importation of foreign pauper labor, indorsement of legislation for arbitration of labor disputes in interstate commerce, and sharp denunciation of the use of injunctions by federal courts and federal interference in local affairs—a reference to the recent Pullman strike. Other resolutions demanded enlargement of the powers of the Interstate Commerce Commission, condemned President Cleveland's bond sales to banking syndicates, declared for maintenance of the Monroe Doctrine, expressed sympathy for the Cubans in their struggle for independence, and opposed a third term for Presidents.

Such a platform seemed anarchistic to conservative easterners. A friend of Cleveland wrote in his diary: "Left Chicago. The platform had been announced and there was nothing more to be done—no respectable man could afford to remain." There was no formal bolt, but 178 delegates, mostly from the East and Wisconsin, refused to vote on the balloting for President.

Richard P. Bland of Missouri, veteran silver leader, had been the leading candidate, but many observers had felt that the choice would eventually fall on Senator Teller. A large field of favorite sons complicated the situation until Bryan made his electrifying speech. Then he emerged to assume the silver leadership and make himself the nominee. Bland was elderly and uninspiring; Teller was a bolting Republican; Hill and Carlisle were "goldbugs;" the various favorite sons were without national reputations. Bryan was the inspiring young leader the reborn Democratic party needed. It took five ballots to dispose of instructions and pledges.[4] On the fifth Bryan had 652 of the 930 votes in the convention, and the nomination was his. He had celebrated his thirty-sixth birthday on the preceding 19th of March.

For the Vice Presidency Arthur Sewall of Maine was named on the fifth ballot over a large field with John R. McLean of Ohio his chief competitor. Sewall, a shipbuilder, railroad director, and bank president, was an odd running mate for Bryan. Yet—a rarity among eastern Democrats—he was a free silver advocate and a believer in the income tax.

Populists and Irregulars

The thunder stealing by the Democrats gave the People's party convention a hard choice, at St. Louis on July 22. A "Middle-of-the-Road" group insisted that to ally with the Democrats would be to hand the party over to the enemy and abandon the South to the Bourbons; but expediency prevailed. To divide the silver forces would insure Republican victory. Bryan must be indorsed, and silver made the one important issue. To soften the blow, the majority agreed to make the Vice Presidential nomination first—a show of independence, as Arthur Sewall, the Democratic nominee, was unsatisfactory to hard-bitten agrarians. Thomas E. Watson of Georgia was nominated over Sewall and several others. Bryan then received the Presidential nomination by 1,042 votes to 321 for S. F. Norton of Illinois.

The platform contained little that was not found in the resolutions of 1892. Recognition of Cuban independence, employment of labor on public works in times of depression, criticism of the courts for arbitrary use of the injunction, disapproval of the Supreme Court's income-tax decision as "a misinterpretation of the Constitution," and condemnation of the "wholesale system of disfranchisement" adopted in some states covered issues that had come to the front since 1892. In conclusion, the platform affirmed the importance of the financial question and invited cooperation from "all organizations and citizens agreeing with us upon this vital question." In effect, it laid to rest the third party as a great agrarian reform move-

[4] The first ballot resulted as follows: Bland, 235; Bryan, 119; Pattison of Pennsylvania, 95; Boies of Iowa, 85; Blackburn of Kentucky, 83; McLean, 54; Matthews of Indiana, 37; Tillman, 17; Pennoyer of Oregon, 8; Teller, 8; Stevenson of Illinois, 7; Russell of Massachusetts, 2; Campbell of Ohio, 1; Hill, 1; not voting, 178.

ment and made it merely a section of the swelling chorus for Bryan and silver. The Populists thus became "Popocrats."

Two other indorsements went to Bryan. The bolting Silver Republicans, disappointed at the failure of the Democrats to take Senator Teller, reluctantly turned to Bryan. A National Silver party, sponsored by the American Bimetallic Union, held a national convention at the same time and place as the Populists. It represented silver mining rather than agrarian interests and had expected to support Teller. But when the Democrats nominated Bryan and the Silver Republicans indorsed him the National Silver party joined the coalition.[5]

The position of the Gold Democrats was an unhappy one. Outright support of McKinley meant acceptance of Republican protectionist policies, a bitter pill. Yet to take "Bryanism" meant—in the words of one of the most intelligent eastern leaders—"to leap into the foul pit of repudiation, socialism, anarchy, et cetera, temporarily called or miscalled by the grand old name Democracy." The way out was an independent movement to hold the conservatives together. As a force of irregulars under their own leaders they might accomplish more by harrying the silver crusaders than by losing their identity in Hanna's vast army.

A conference of "national committeemen" from the various states on August 7 called a convention to meet at Indianapolis September 2. On that date delegates from forty-one states and three territories assembled with ex-Governor Roswell P. Flower of New York in the chair, took the name of "National Democrats," and nominated General John M. Palmer of Illinois for President and General Simon B. Buckner of Kentucky for Vice President. One had been a Union soldier, the other a Confederate, and they came from doubtful states. The brief platform upheld the gold standard as a long-established Democratic policy, praised Cleveland's administration, and condemned all efforts to impair confidence in the Supreme Court. Cleveland, Carlisle, and most of their following indorsed the Palmer-Buckner ticket. But David B. Hill would not bolt and lose his hold on the New York organization. "I am still a Democrat," he said, "very still."

[5] Even the Prohibition party split over the silver question. The majority of the delegates to the national convention—the "narrow gaugers"—voted for a platform devoted entirely to the liquor issue. The "broad gaugers" seceded, adopted a platform of a decided Populist character, and nominated their own candidate.

The Battle of Classes and Sections

The action of the Democratic convention had upset the Republican plan of campaign. Expecting to throw the responsibility for the depression and the blunders of Cleveland's administration on the Democratic party and to advocate a return to a higher tariff as the way of economic salvation, the party of McKinley and Hanna had counted on an easy victory over a disorganized foe. But the Democrats had repudiated the Cleveland administration, had set up a standard to which all the forces of discontent were invited to repair, and were threatening to sweep the upper Mississippi valley from its Republican moorings with a far more plausible method of curing the hard times than Republican tariff policy. It was now poor strategy for the Republicans to center their guns on Cleveland as it would only antagonize the Gold Democrats whose support was worth attracting. Instead, McKinley was forced to defend the existing gold standard, for which he had little heart, and place less emphasis on protection, in which he thoroughly believed. To make concessions to silver now would only play into Bryan's hands.

McKinley determined his own role in the canvass. A fluent public speaker, he could talk generalities more impressively than any man then in public life. His formal friendliness had none of Harrison's chill, and his solid figure and careful dress—with wing collar, starched shirt, long double-breasted coat, white vest, and red carnation—convinced audiences that they were looking at a statesman before he uttered a word. As a candidate for lesser offices, he had pleaded his own cause. But a Presidential candidate, he felt, must remain in dignified waiting until the voters made their decision. He then devised a curious compromise. He might not go to the people but the people might come to him. The idea of delegations and committees calling upon the candidate was familiar enough, but the excursions to Canton in 1896 amounted to mass pilgrimages. People came by the thousands in special trains—farmers, merchants, G.A.R. posts, railroad workers, religious and racial groups, and many others, often with their expenses paid—to see McKinley and listen to a few well chosen remarks, or, in the case of large delegations, a formal address of some length. Nothing was left to chance. McKinley would have no "Rum, Romanism and Rebellion" upset his careful planning. He invited the chairman of every visiting group to Canton ahead of time and asked him to submit his remarks in writing. These were carefully edited, unfortunate or embarrassing expressions deleted, and sometimes whole sections rewritten. Then, on the appointed day, the chairman would take his delegation to McKinley's home, recite his prepared speech to the appreciative candidate, and listen to a most felicitous response on the significant issues of the campaign, particularly attuned to the interests of the group of listeners. The speeches in this "front porch" campaign of course appeared in the newspapers and added to McKinley's stature as a candidate.

Hanna's management problem was not easy. No longer was it one of raising sufficient funds to buy floaters in Indiana and deal with venal Tammany politicians in New York. The East seemed to be safely Republican, but every state west of Pennsylvania was listening to the silver siren. To win on such an extended front would require organization and propaganda on a large scale. Money must be provided by the wealthy East, if business and financial leaders wanted to save their system from the deluded "anarchists" of the midlands. The sums Hanna demanded seemed to be excessive in a period of business distress; but the wave of enthusiasm for Bryan immediately following his nomination, and the united front established by the silver groups, frightened banks and businessmen and made Hanna's task easier. James J. Hill, railroad magnate, introduced him to Wall Street, and the money began to pour in. Ability to pay, not generosity, determined the contributions. For banks the assessment was fixed at one-quarter of 1 per cent of their capital. Life insurance companies contributed liberally, as did nearly all the great corporations. The Standard Oil Company gave $250,000 to Hanna's war chest. The audited accounts of the national committee revealed collections of about $3,500,000. Charles G. Dawes, who handled all funds at the Chicago headquarters, recorded in his diary a total of $1,962,325.59 spent at Chicago. He estimated the New York total at $1,600,000.00. The wild guesses of $10,000,000 to $12,000,000 by unfriendly writers seem to be impossibly large.

Very little of this disappeared into the capacious pockets of grafting politicians. Hanna demanded results, and from the national headquarters in New York City and the well organized regional headquarters at Chicago he directed his army of workers with admirable efficiency. A group of veteran political strategists managed the New York headquarters, but he entrusted the more important Chicago center to aggressive younger men including Henry C. Payne of Wisconsin, Charles G. Dawes of Chicago, W. T. Durbin of Indiana, and Cyrus Leland, Jr., of Kansas.

Pamphlets and leaflets by the millions were sent out from Chicago, some of them in seven or eight foreign languages, to catch the interest of voters of all classes, creeds, and nationalities. Everything from boiler-plate matter for small-town newspapers to McKinley buttons for schoolboys poured out of Hanna's mill, while billboards along country roads carried the likeness of "The Advance Agent of Prosperity." Some fourteen hundred speakers were available to preach the Republican gospel in the doubtful areas.

But as the campaign grew in heat and bitterness ugly aspects appeared for which Hanna had no direct responsibility. Men of wealth, alarmed at the enthusiasm aroused by Bryan and taking at face value the extreme utterances of Populist orators, fought back with powerful economic weapons in an attempt to coerce, where persuasion might fail. Labor, the uncertain partner in Bryan's poorly constructed farmer-labor coalition, was threatened with loss of employment in case Bryan won. Buyers gave orders for materials subject to cancellation if McKinley lost. In some cases workers were told not to report Wednesday morning after election unless McKinley won. Such methods, coupled with the steady pounding away at the workingman with the prosperity argument, made of little account the efforts of those champions of the downtrodden Governor Altgeld, Eugene V. Debs, and Henry George.

In farming areas pressure of a different sort was attempted. Reports went around that agents of the great insurance companies, large holders of farm mortgages, were promising extensions at lower rates of interest if McKinley were elected. This was used to offset the boon of easier credit supposed to come when free silver went into effect.

Bryan's campaign was almost a one-man show. The "Boy Orator of the Platte" was a novelty in American politics. The "Cross of Gold" speech had made him a popular hero, and Americans clamored to see and hear him. A front-porch campaign was out of the question. The only sensible strategy was to send him around the country to carry his message to the largest possible number. There followed the most famous stumping tour in American history.

His first trip East was made early in August to receive formal notification of his nomination at New York City. The thousands that jammed Madison Square Garden wanted a fiery, fighting speech, a challenge to battle against the powers of mammon. Instead, the candidate read a carefully phrased but tiresome treatise on the economics of the currency question, while they squirmed and perspired, and some even departed. Opposition newspapers—nearly the whole metropolitan press—ridiculed the performance as a false alarm, and even the friendly *New York Journal* admitted that the audience was disappointed. Bryan had used a manuscript because he was in "the enemy country" and felt that he must make no slips in this keynote speech. This was a mistake. He had missed a great opportunity to arouse the eastern masses. Men of wealth slept more soundly after this.

The return trip provided opportunities for numerous speeches in upstate New York, Pennsylvania, and the Middle West as far north as Milwaukee. Bryan then made the most extensive trip of the campaign, a speaking tour all the way from Nebraska to Maine, and from the upper South to the Canadian border. The Middle West, the great battleground, received most attention. The trip ended at Lincoln, Nebraska, his home town, the Sunday before the election. He devoted Monday November 2 to his home state, addressing twenty-seven audiences on that day. All together, by his own estimates, he covered 18,009 miles and made some six hundred speeches to possibly five million persons. Fears that his magnificent voice would not hold out led to all manner of throat treatments—compresses, gargles, cough drops; but finally he discarded them all and found his vocal chords in fine condition at the end of his oratorical marathon.

Democratic difficulties centered around money and the fusion of the silver forces. The paltry $650,000 with which they tried to match Hanna's millions was the smallest fund since Hancock's campaign of 1880. But for the contributions of a group of wealthy silver-mine owners, the campaign chest would have been insignificant. On the other hand, donations from the Republican national committee solved in part the financial problem of those Democrats who had bolted and nominated Palmer and Buckner.

Securing the cooperation of all the silver forces was an awkward problem. Three organized parties—Democratic, Populist, and National Silver, each with its national committee—and a group of Silver Republicans were supporting Bryan and attempting to preserve their separate identities at the same time. The Populists even had their own Vice Presidential candidate, Tom Watson, and a platform which Bryan did not accept. This duality was solved by the nomination of joint electoral tickets of "Popocrats" with part of the electors apportioned to Bryan and Sewall and part to Bryan and Watson. In twenty-six states where division was agreed upon, Sewall had 198 possible electoral votes to Watson's 78. Watson naturally resented this arrangement as it rendered his defeat certain. Even if Bryan won, he would finish third and the Senate would choose from the two highest, Hobart and Sewall. Yet no other course was possible. Except in Louisiana, Arkansas, and North Carolina, the Democrats of the South rejected fusion, forcing the Populists to accept their tickets. In a few states separate electoral tickets for Bryan and Watson were nominated; but they had no effect on the election.

Fusion on state and Congressional tickets was far more complicated and was not always achieved. In the South the Populists tended to work with the Republicans; in the West, with the Democrats, though the independent Silver Republicans followed their own course and fusion became confusion in the mountain states.

The Bryan campaign headquarters, despite limited funds, sent out a considerable amount of literature. The best known piece used by either side was *Coin's Financial School.* A primer of the silver question first published in 1894 by William H. Harvey, a lawyer then living in Chicago, it recited in simple dialogue the merits of free coinage of silver, leaving the gold advocates in its pages utterly confounded. The cracker-box philosophy of the little book, like the panacea of the later Townsend Plan, struck home in a period of hard times and gave it a circulation of several millions.

Teller, Bland, Tillman, Watson, Weaver and other silver leaders also effectively presented the Democratic side in public speeches; but some of the best work for Bryan was done by "Popocrat" speakers in little schoolhouses in the depression-stricken farm belt where worn, sad-faced men and women listened to the silver gospel, sang Populist songs, and went home with spirits uplifted a little to read *Coin's Financial School* and pray for victory.

One of Bryan's greatest handicaps was lack of newspaper support in the larger cities. The Republican press, the independent journals, the influential weeklies such as *Harper's Weekly*, the *Nation,* and the *Independent,* and most of the larger Democratic papers in the metropolitan centers were against him. In New York City only William Randolph Hearst's *Journal* was loyal; even Pulitzer's *World* joined the bolters. Not again until 1936 was there such a journalistic phalanx on one side of a great political contest.

Near-hysteria seemed to grip the conservative East by autumn, and a campaign of fear and hate broke loose that outdid in vituperation the most rabid utterances of the Populists. Bryan was derided as a boy orator and a political faker; but more effective was the cartoon representation of him in *Harper's Weekly* as a huge silver dollar with Governor Altgeld of Illinois, the "anarchist," hiding behind him. Altgeld had outraged conservatives by pardoning the anarchists imprisoned for the Haymarket bombing of 1886, in Chicago. Bryan was now linked with Altgeld and Debs, the Pullman strike leader, in a trinity of subversive infamy. Theodore Roosevelt compared them in a campaign speech to "the leaders of the Terror of France in mental and moral attitude"; and he declared in an unguarded moment in a private conversation later made public that he expected to meet Altgeld and his followers "sword to sword on the field of battle." The metropolitan Protestant pulpit entered the campaign, and many eminent reverend figures, including T. DeWitt Talmage and Charles H. Parkhurst, upheld the cross of gold.

Against the tide of abuse and denunciation Hearst's *New York Journal* retaliated in kind. Its cartoonist, Homer Davenport, pictured Hanna invariably as a bloated plutocrat stamped with dollar signs, and McKinley as his puppet. Alfred Henry Lewis wrote articles so offensive that Hanna, unaccustomed to this political in-fighting, considered court action; but he decided that this might be just what Hearst wanted.

As Election Day approached, close observers could see that the result was no longer in doubt. After weeks and weeks of careful work the great Hanna organization had everything in hand. The Middle West, the battleground, was safe. Historians have usually given some credit to a fortuitous circumstance. The wheat crop of 1896 was a bumper one, yet a heavy foreign demand in the fall brought a sharp rise in price. This came without free silver and may have helped the Republican argument for gold; but the higher wheat prices seem to have benefited speculators rather than farmers, and prices of other products continued to slump.

Bryan's Failure

Before midnight November 3, Bryan knew that he was beaten. The Middle West as far as Minnesota, North Dakota, and Iowa had gone Republican, as had the East, the southern border states of Delaware, Maryland, West Virginia, and Kentucky, and California and Oregon on the Pacific coast. McKinley had 271 electoral votes to Bryan's 176. Bryan had the South and the newer western farming and mining states, admitted after 1860, except North Dakota, and also one elector each from California and Kentucky.

McKinley had 7,098,474 popular votes; Bryan, 6,379,830 including fusion electoral tickets.[6] Both Houses of Congress were Republican by safe margins. The result was decisive. Bryan's vote had failed to equal the total of the Democrats and Populists in 1892 despite a heavy increase in the votes cast. The support of the Silver Republicans had not made up for the thousands of Democrats who had supported Palmer or had voted outright for McKinley. The Republican margin was overwhelming in the East, fairly large in most parts of the Middle West (compared with Republican pluralities in 1888 and 1892), and uncomfortably close on the Pacific coast and in Kentucky, where the Gold Democrats cut sufficiently into Bryan's support to give the state to McKinley.

Bryan had failed to corral the industrial workers. The cities outside the South and the silver-mining West were nearly all Republican. Hanna had sold the prospects of prosperity and good wages to labor, though pressure and intimidation played a part. Bryan's farm vote fell short of his expectations. The debt-burdened and impoverished followed him; the better off, as so often in the past, voted Republican. The rural South and the silver-mining states did as expected, but his margin of victory in the distressed Populist belt was small, for cities and towns voted against him. In the older Middle West he shared the farm vote with McKinley, but in the rural parts of the East he failed badly. He lost every county in New England and carried but one in New York. He ran proportionately better in the seaboard cities than in the neighboring country districts. His effort to unite South and West was too late by at least two decades. Industrialism and urbanization, spreading westward, even had outposts beyond the Mississippi, while the older farm states were almost as conservative as the East.

[6] John M. Palmer, Gold Democrat, had 131,529; Joshua Levering, Prohibitionist, 141,676; Charles E. Bentley, National Party (Prohibition seceders), 13,969; Charles H. Matchett, Socialist Labor, 36,454. Bryan's total is often given as 6,467,946, or even higher, by adding in the votes cast for him on independent electoral tickets running against regular Democratic candidates. In Texas a separate Populist ticket polled 77,985 votes. For the elections 1896–1916 I have used E. E. Robinson, *The Presidential Vote, 1896–1932*, supplemented by other sources for minor parties, and for the period 1920–1964, Richard M. Scammon, *America at the Polls* (Pittsburgh, 1965).

The People's party had been swallowed by the Democratic party; but it had liberalized the older organization in the process, and while its reform program was forgotten in the din raised over silver, the best features were to be revived and accepted later by the major parties. Even free silver was vindicated in a way, for unexpectedly large increases in the world's gold supply provided the currency expansion Bryan and the "Popocrats" were demanding.

19

The Golden Age of the Grand Old Party

McKinley

Both Theodore Roosevelt and Speaker Reed are credited with the gibe that McKinley had no more backbone than a chocolate éclair, and some historians agree that the broad smooth brow and the firm jaw hid a weak-willed, kindly mediocrity who never yielded to an impulsive remark or act that might dispel the aura of the statesman. He even removed the beloved cigar from his mouth before a camera. His whole life, said caustic William Allen White, seemed to have been spent before an audience. But John Hay, who became Secretary of State in 1898, Charles G. Dawes, Comptroller of the Currency, political lieutenant and personal friend, and George B. Cortelyou, his private secretary, dissented strongly from these opinions. Cortelyou rated McKinley above Hanna in political skill, and Dawes put him above Roosevelt in statesmanship. It is no small tribute that those closest to McKinley were most aware of his merits; his critics saw only a stage figure.

The new President believed that he must try to translate the pressures directed at him and his party into the will of the American people on major issues, and formulate his policies accordingly. If he displayed a weakness, it was reluctance to resist, once he was convinced that public opinion ran strongly counter to his own opinion. This explains his last-minute abandonment of a peace policy on Cuba, when he was himself very averse to war. No President has been more successful in mirroring the composite views of the majority of voters. McKinley's success was due chiefly to adeptness at the complex game of politics. Nursing no grudges, disarming irate Congressmen by his friendliness, handling patronage with skill, he gained steadily in popular favor, and his party became united and harmonious, despite the anti-imperialism of a few old-fashioned eastern wheelhorses.

Hanna played a secondary role, both because of his inexperience at Washington and because of the President's sensitivity to the "Man of Mark" gibes in the campaign. McKinley consulted him on patronage matters but made the final decisions. Hanna might have had far more political power had he accepted the Postmaster Generalship—a natural place for a party manager. But the prestige and independence of a Senate seat appealed strongly to him. Although Ohio had no vacancy the President created one by offering the State Department to Senator John Sherman, then seventy-four years old. Sherman unwisely accepted it, and Governor Bushnell, against his will, appointed the Republican generalissimo to fill the vacancy. The next Ohio legislature elected him by a margin of one vote for the rest of Sherman's term and for a full term to start in 1899. In this bitter senatorial election insurgent Republicans and Democrats hurled charges of bribery at the Hanna forces; but the Senate Committee on Privileges and Elections found no evidence to implicate the newly elected Senator. Meanwhile, Sherman, his memory failing, was so unfit to handle the State Department that his assistant secretary, William R. Day, practically displaced him. He resigned in April, 1898, with bitter feelings toward the President.

The Senate, more swollen with importance and inclined to obstructionism than ever before in its history, looked with suspicion at McKinley's manager, and he made no attempt to act as administration spokesman and party boss. Only gradually did he make his way into the Senatorial inner circle. His power rested rather on his national chairmanship and his contacts with the world of Standard Oil and J. P. Morgan.

McKinley was fortunate in coming to the Presidency when vigorous leadership on the domestic scene was not required. To sit tight and let the economic machine right itself, helped a little by a tariff boost, was his broad policy. That it worked was his good fortune. Good crops and rising prices were stilling the tumult in the Populist areas, while new discoveries of gold and the cyanide process of extracting the metal from the ores were solving the currency problem. McKinley's party enacted the high Dingley Tariff as soon as he was in office, and duly claimed the credit for the good times that followed. The Gold Standard Act was delayed until 1900, when the Senate was no longer silver-controlled. Trusts multiplied, and big business grew bigger without any threat of governmental interference. It was the golden age of American monopolies.

The violent shift of the center of gravity of American politics from domestic problems to foreign relations in the closing years of the nineteenth century made McKinley's term of office very different from what he had expected. The Spanish-American War, the acquisition of Puerto Rico and the Philippines, the annexation of Hawaii, the Boxer Rebellion in China, and the demand for an interoceanic canal tell the story of the breakdown of isolation and the emergence of America as a world power. New problems thrust silver and the tariff into the background and made the bitter excitement of 1896 seem remote and unreal.

Cleveland had sturdily resisted demands for intervention on behalf of the rebelling Cubans, but McKinley found the pressure too great. Americans of all parties and sections clamored for war, especially after the mysterious sinking of the battleship *Maine,* and eventually the President gave way. Fearful of wrecking the Republican party, and convinced that public sentiment demanded it, he sent to Congress in April, 1898, the message that unleashed the dogs of war. The financial interests, inexperienced in the economics of war, were alarmed lest the gradual recovery of business be imperiled. Hanna was of the same mind but went along with McKinley. Speaker Reed and a few eastern Republicans tried to stem the tide and were swept aside. The newspapers of William Randolph Hearst and Joseph Pulitzer led the pack of journalists in screaming for war; Democrats and Populists of South and West, eager to make political capital out of McKinley's reluctance to act, joined with Henry Cabot Lodge and Theodore Roosevelt, vociferous big-navy disciples of Admiral Mahan, in demands for intervention in Cuba; and Americans generally seemed anxious to be distracted from domestic troubles by a new adventure in glory. Thus came the war with Spain.

Though badly managed, the war was a great success. Spain was weak and unprepared, and surrendered before the summer was over. The short war furnished plenty of glory, and was inexpensive as wars go. It added territories to please businessmen looking for trade and investments, and humanitarians and religious enthusiasts looking for backward peoples to uplift and Christianize. It made believers in manifest destiny feel vindicated and stirred the patriotic pride of Americans of all classes who saw their country as a world power.

Party politics, largely in abeyance while the war was on, burst out over the peace treaty. McKinley, after much hesitation and seeking of guidance both human and divine, decided to keep the Philippine

Islands, conquered during the war. Many Americans who approved of a war to free Cuba had grave misgivings over the acquisition of a colony on the other side of the Pacific, inhabited by a different race unfitted for self-government. Opposed to this new imperialism were men of such diverse viewpoints as Speaker Reed, Senators Hoar and Hale, Carl Schurz, Cleveland, Bryan, Andrew Carnegie, and Samuel Gompers. Anti-Imperialist Leagues appeared, and ratification of the peace treaty became doubtful.

But not all its critics agreed on the wisdom of rejecting the peace treaty. The Senate finally ratified it by a margin of two votes, most of the Republicans voting for it along with expansionist Democrats, Populists, and Independents. Bryan's course angered leading anti-imperialists. He came to Washington to urge ratification, arguing that it would be better to end the war at once and settle the problem of colonial possessions later. Critics charged that he wanted to use the issue in the campaign of 1900.

The Republican national convention assembled at Philadelphia on June 19, 1900, with everything except the Vice Presidential nomination planned in advance. The platform, adopted as presented by the resolutions committee, was a panegyric on the McKinley administration and Republican prosperity. It contrasted the distressed conditions of 1896 with the happy days of 1900. It set forth the gold standard, the protective tariff, and the Spanish-American War as the great achievements of four years of Republican rule, on which the party built its future policies. The fruits of the new imperialism appeared in resolutions upholding the acquisition of the Philippines, Puerto Rico, Hawaii, and Samoa, approving Cuban independence, favoring an isthmian canal to be built, owned, and controlled by the United States government, and extolling the Open Door in China.

With the platform out of the way the convention proceeded to the nominations. Vice President Hobart had died, and for some inexplicable reason Hanna was greatly disturbed about an office to which too little attention had been paid in the past. He wanted Cornelius N. Bliss, a close friend who had been Secretary of the Interior under McKinley, to take the place; but Bliss refused. Secretary of War Elihu Root and Senator Allison of Iowa were equally averse. Others were talked of, but Hanna's hands were tied by the refusal of President McKinley to express a preference. He insisted that the convention should be free to choose, though it was dominated by his organization. What alarmed Hanna was the rapid growth of a boom for Governor Theodore Roosevelt of New York.

Roosevelt, for a comparatively young man, had had a long official career in New York and at Washington before resigning as Assistant Secretary of the Navy to organize the "Rough Riders." He had led them triumphantly up San Juan Hill in Cuba and had emerged as a war hero. Boss Platt seized upon him as a means to save the New York organization from a merited rebuke at the polls, and Roosevelt was elected governor in 1898 by a narrow margin, chiefly because of his personal popularity and his spectacular methods of campaigning. As governor, he consulted Platt on patronage and legislation but often refused to accept his advice. The "Easy Boss" was too shrewd to break with the governor but decided that one term was enough. The Vice Presidency happily offered a solution. Platt found a powerful ally in Boss Quay of Pennsylvania, who disliked Hanna for personal reasons. The two intrigued to obtain the nomination for Roosevelt, knowing that Hanna was opposed to the "damned cowboy." But he had no candidate of his own, and the Rough Rider's popularity with the western delegates played into Platt's hands.

Roosevelt himself was in a quandary. He saw through the bosses' scheme to shelve him and was righteously indignant; but the delegates' obvious enthusiasm for him was extremely flattering. Besides, if he refused the nomination Platt might keep him from a second term as governor. He insisted publicly that he preferred the governorship, and that his friends must respect his wishes; but he did not say flatly that he would turn down the higher honor. Hanna said bluntly: "By God, Teddy, you know that there is nothing in this country which can compel a man to run for an office who doesn't want it." Roosevelt apparently agreed, and the New York delegation, after an exciting session, indorsed Timothy Woodruff; but this did not alter the situation. The western delegates were stampeding to Roosevelt, and Hanna, unable to offer a satisfactory alternative, could not stop them. He was warned by some of his close lieutenants that it might even be dangerous to attempt it, and Charles G. Dawes telephoned to McKinley, who insisted again that the convention must make the nomination. Hanna gave way, and so both McKinley and Roosevelt were named without opposition.

In the Democratic camp all the signs pointed to Bryan again. His remarkable campaign in 1896 had given him a hold on the masses of Democratic voters which the eastern conservatives could not shake. He had supported the war and had led a volunteer regiment, acquiring the title of Colonel, though there was little glory fighting the war in a fever-stricken camp in Florida. Despite his approval of the peace treaty, he was still denouncing imperialism and winning the good will of many who had differed with him on the silver question.

The only threat to Bryan's candidacy was a brief one. Admiral George Dewey, hero of the battle of Manila Bay, was so wildly acclaimed on his return from the Philippines that he finally decided in April, 1900, to be a candidate for the Presidency, though earlier he had definitely refused to consider it. Now he declared that the office of President was "not such a very difficult one to fill," and that he was willing to fill it. His popularity had already suffered because he had transferred to his wife a house given him by public subscription. His naïve announcement of his candidacy was not taken seriously, and the recent adulation turned to ridicule. In any case, his entry was made too late. Bryan already had the nomination nailed down.

The one serious problem faced by the Democratic national convention at Kansas City on July 4, 1900, was indorsement of free coinage of silver. Eastern delegates, of course, opposed, and many of Bryan's friends agreed with them. Silver no longer mattered, and to put it in the platform would antagonize many who were ready to support him on the imperialism issue. It was suggested that a simple reaffirmation of the Chicago platform without special reference to silver might solve the problem. But Bryan was unmoved. In a letter to the New York *World* appearing on July 4, he declared his willingness to go down to defeat rather than abandon his convictions. The battle continued in the resolutions committee while Bryan considered withdrawing as a candidate. After much wrangling the committee accepted the silver plank by a majority of one vote. Republicans gleefully pointed out that expansion had saved free silver, for the delegate from Hawaii had cast the deciding vote. The convention then adopted the platform without more ado.

It reaffirmed the party's faith in the Declaration of Independence and the Constitution, declared that the imposition of government upon any people by force was tyranny, and warned the American people that imperialism abroad would lead to despotism at home. It denounced the "ill concealed Republican alliance with England" and expressed sympathy for the South Africans in the Boer War. It condemned the administration's policies toward Puerto Rico, Cuba, and the Philippines, demanded immediate independence for Cuba, and pledged a stable government with ultimate independence under American protection to the Filipinos.

In the field of domestic problems, the party declared for more stringent anti-trust laws and for tariff changes to put trust products upon the free list. It charged the Republicans with fostering trusts in return for campaign contributions and condemned the Dingley tariff as "a trust breeding measure." Free silver, direct election of United States Senators, the creation of a Department of Labor, arbitration of labor disputes, and condemnation of government by injunction were bids for Populist-labor support.

Bryan was nominated with much enthusiasm, and Adlai E. Stevenson, Vice President under Cleveland, was chosen as his running mate. David B. Hill might have had the second place but withdrew his name from consideration.

Bryan already had the nomination of one wing of the Populists. Split into two groups and greatly weakened by farmer prosperity, the third party was suffering the usual fate of parties of protest. A fusion group, in convention on May 9 at Sioux Falls, South Dakota, had nominated Bryan for the Presidency with Charles A. Towne, Minnesota Silver Republican, as his running mate. Towne later withdrew in favor of Stevenson. The convention was poorly attended, and enthusiasm was lacking. The platform repeated most of the demands of the two previous conventions, but new sections denounced imperialism and the Gold Standard Act.

The more radical "middle-of-the-road" Populists, holding forth at Cincinnati on the same day, attempted to restore the party's waning strength by independent nominations. Wharton Barker of Pennsylvania was the Presidential nominee with Ignatius Donnelly of Minnesota named for second place. The platform differed from that of the fusion Populists chiefly in demanding a complete irredeemable paper currency, issued by the government, as the sole medium of exchange.

A group of Silver Republicans, meeting at Kansas City the same week as the Democrats, gave Bryan their support. There was a feeble effort to set up an anti-imperialist third party, but it miscarried. The "Liberty Congress," called by the American Anti-Imperialist League, met at Indianapolis August 15 and 16 and indorsed the Democratic candidate as the only solution. Thus Bryan had an impressive string of indorsements from various anti-McKinley groups; but the value of these could only be determined after the election.

This campaign also marked the first appearance of a significant socialist party. For many years little groups of socialists, drawn chiefly from the Germans of the larger cities, had been arousing interest in Marxist theories but had operated in politics only locally and through various working-class organizations. Efforts toward union were hampered by dissensions over methods and differences of viewpoint, but in 1876 the Working-Men's party of the United States emerged—renamed in 1877 Socialist Labor party. With a membership perhaps nine-tenths foreign-born, it seemed at times to be almost an obstacle, instead of an aid, to the progress of socialism. A loose alliance with the Greenback party in 1880 was its sole activity in national elections before 1892. The rise of anarchism in the eighties divided and weakened the socialist movement; and in the Socialist Labor party itself the question of political action caused dissensions. Under the aggressive but contentious leadership of Daniel De Leon, the party began to offer Presidential candidates, first in 1892; but many socialists refused to accept his hostility to labor organizations and were ready for a new movement.

In 1897 some western socialist groups assembled at Chicago and organized the Social Democracy of America. Their program included the establishment of a colony in some western state as the first step in the inauguration of a socialist regime. At their second convention in 1898 a minority of the delegates refused to accept the colonization scheme and bolted, forming the Social Democratic party of America with a definite program of political activity. Some local successes followed, and in March, 1900, a national convention was held. Negotiations with a seceding wing of the Socialist Labor party were begun, and Eugene V. Debs was named for President and Job Harriman for Vice President. With some difficulty cooperation of the two groups for the campaign was agreed upon; and the slow work of building up a genuinely American socialist political party was thus undertaken. Able leaders to guide the movement were found in Debs, Victor L. Berger, and Seymour Stedman.[1]

The warm-hearted, unselfish Debs, a tower of strength to his party, stumped the country in the campaign of 1900 and was rewarded with

[1] At a national convention held at Indianapolis in 1901, the name "Socialist Party" was adopted. The Socialist Labor party under De Leon continued its separate existence.

a vote of 96,116, far larger than any total yet reached by the more militant Socialist Labor party.

Imperialism and the Full Dinner Pail

Although insistent that free silver go into the platform, Bryan did not plead for it in his campaign but made imperialism the paramount issue, with the trust question second in importance. He attempted as in 1896 to make it a struggle between democracy and plutocracy, but the class and sectional appeal was less evident in 1900. He appeared rather as the defender of American liberal traditions in opposing an imperialism that would exploit weaker peoples, "civilize with dynamite and proselyte with the sword." He promised in his notification speech at Indianapolis before fifty thousand people to set up a stable form of government in the Philippines, and then to give the people independence under American protection. The strong religious strain in Bryan came to the surface repeatedly in his assaults upon the immorality of holding weaker peoples in subjection. "The command 'Go ye into all the world and preach the Gospel to every creature' has no Gatling gun attachment," he shouted. Imperialism had no warrant in the Bible, he insisted, and he flung scriptural citations at the Republicans with the fervor of a traveling evangelist.

However, the Democratic candidate began to shift his emphasis as the campaign went on. The dangers of imperialism were not arousing the voters. The woes of the little brown brothers whom unsympathetic American soldiers were "civilizing with a Krag" were not like the woes of the debt-burdened agrarians four years earlier. Then Bryan had voiced magnificently the demands of impoverished Americans for a more abundant life, and his words had struck home. In 1900 he was preaching sermons to well fed audiences on the right of self-determination for far-away Filipinos. His appeal was not much more exciting than that of a returned foreign missionary seeking funds for Christianizing the heathen. "It sounded like music, and it read like the prophets of old," was one listener's comment on a Bryan speech. But it was not stirring the masses. Bryan sensed this, and he began to play up the trust question and the need to curb special privilege. This was a note more in keeping with the Bryan of 1896 and, under more propitious circumstances, might have been powerfully effective. But Americans, relaxing from the stresses and strains of the depression years, were content for a season to enjoy the fruits of prosperity without examining too closely the warped and misshapen tree that produced them. Bryan was on the right track but he had chosen the wrong moment.

His plan of campaign, like that of 1896, involved a long speaking tour, and large crowds turned out. In the East he was particularly well received. Richard Croker, head of Tammany, had become a Bryan convert—from reading the candidate's book, *The First Battle,* so he said—and the Tammany braves made the welkin ring when the Nebraskan descended on Madison Square Garden. "Great is Tammany," said Bryan, "and Croker is his prophet." But the Gold Democrats were still hostile. Had Bryan abandoned free silver, most of them would have supported him, for nearly all were anti-imperialists. Instead, many voted for McKinley, as in 1896.

Cleveland apparently did not vote. He refused to say a word that could be construed as an indorsement of either candidate, despite all manner of requests that he commit himself. While bitter towards "Bryanism," he could not swallow "McKinleyism." Richard Olney, Judson Harmon, William L. Wilson, and J. Sterling Morton—all former members of his cabinet—and the veteran editor, Henry Watterson, chose Bryan as the lesser evil. "I am going to shut my eyes, hold my nose, vote, go home and disinfect myself," wrote Morton to his old chief.

Among Republican anti-imperialists the problem was equally difficult. Andrew Carnegie, Senators Hoar and Hale, and many other old-fashioned Republicans found Bryan's silver views and his reputation for instability sufficient justification for a vote for McKinley. Thomas B. Reed, eased out of the Speakership and now retired from politics, took refuge in a stony and embittered silence. Carl Schurz, despite his lifelong advocacy of sound money, accepted Bryan, though with a wry face. George S. Boutwell, Secretary of the Treasury under Grant and now heading the Anti-Imperialist League, and Erving Winslow, the League's secretary, gave loyal support to the Nebraskan, but Republican bolters were not very numerous. It is doubtful whether the omission of the silver plank would have drawn many of these Republican anti-imperialist conservatives to Bryan. He repelled them in too many other ways. In the end, the difficulty of uniting Gold Democrats, Bryan Democrats, Populists, Silver Republicans, and anti-imperialists on one ticket was too great to be overcome.

Hanna's management of McKinley's campaign involved fewer problems than in 1896. His organization functioned efficiently, and collected approximately $2,500,000, principally from big business interests pleased with McKinley's policies and fearful of Bryan's anti-trust program. The party machine under Hanna had become a systematic, well organized business that could be trusted to conduct a campaign honestly and efficiently. No special favors were granted, as a Wall Street group discovered when its ten-thousand-dollar contribution was returned because it had strings attached to it.

McKinley was now more than ever averse to descending from his pedestal, and so the defense of the administration was turned over to the hero of San Juan Hill—known to the average man as "Teddy," though Roosevelt thoroughly disliked the nickname. His tours were a grand success. In part, he followed Bryan's trail; and the duel of these two rabble rousers gave color to a campaign that was otherwise apathetic. Bryan preached—Roosevelt shouted. The Nebraskan quoted Scripture—the Rough Rider waved the flag. The great Democratic leader was an artist with words—his Republican rival was a better tub thumper. Roosevelt's voice, often cracking into a high falsetto, began to give way toward the end; but he waved his arms and pounded his fists and at least impressed his audiences with his tremendous vigor and his certainty as to what was right. References to "my opponent" made it almost seem as if Roosevelt himself were running for the Presidency.[2] No Vice Presidential candidate had ever before stolen the show from the head of the ticket.

Hanna had become a successful stump speaker since 1896, and the organization functioned so efficiently that he could devote some time to campaigning. People wanted to see the bloated, dollar-decorated ogre of the hostile cartoons, and there were many requests for him. Invariably he captured his audiences. A genial, unaffected soul, he spoke to a thousand in the same informal manner that he talked to three or four. He would talk on whatever came into his head at the moment, and his listeners liked it. In 1900 he confined most of his attention to South Dakota and Nebraska, home states of his particular enemy Senator R. F. Pettigrew, bolting Silver Republican, and of Bryan. His invasion of South Dakota partook of the nature of a private vendetta, for Pettigrew had attacked the validity of his election to the Senate. McKinley, dubious about the undertaking, sent an

[2] Mrs. Bryan, in the joint memoirs of her husband and herself, inadvertently refers to his defeat "by Mr. Roosevelt" in 1900.

emissary to dissuade the national chairman. Hanna, discovering who had sent his caller, answered angrily, "Return to Washington, and tell the President that God hates a coward." Sensitive over this reflection on his judgment, he considered resigning as chairman, but his old loyalty soon reasserted itself. However, he went ahead with his tour.

Accompanied by Victor Dolliver of Iowa and Senator Frye of Maine, Hanna stumped the Populist belt by special train. Large crowds gathered at every stop, and occasionally he was heckled. At one place a sign read: "*Populist Farmers, Beware! ! !* Chain Your Children to Yourselves or Put Them Under the Bed. *Mark Hanna Is in Town.*" But his good humor, his sallies of rough wit, and his blunt, straightforward style of speaking won admirers everywhere and helped dispel the bogy-man belief where it was most strongly held. It was disarming to the crowds of farmers at little railroad stations to hear the generalissimo of plutocracy in his own defense. In a tour lasting one week he made seventy-two speeches.

In declaring that there was but one issue in the campaign, "Let well enough alone," Hanna touched upon the strongest argument of the Republicans. Economic conditions were so much improved that "the full dinner pail" became the slogan of party orators and newspapers. Only in a limited sense was the election a referendum on imperialism.

The defeat of the Democrats was greater than in 1896. McKinley had 292 electoral votes to Bryan's 155, compared with the earlier 271 to 176. He added Kansas, Nebraska, South Dakota, Utah, Wyoming, and Washington to his total, more than making up for the loss of Kentucky. The silver states, Colorado, Idaho, Montana, and Nevada, remained loyal to the Democrats, but the entire agricultural West was again Republican. Bryan had the South as before, though West Virginia, Maryland, and Delaware on the border were still Republican. The popular vote was: McKinley, 7,218,491; Bryan, 6,356,734.[3] The former had exceeded his total of 1896, while Bryan had declined proportionately. Hanna was delighted. Even Nebraska was Republican and Pettigrew lost his Senate seat from South Dakota.

[3] The other candidates had these totals: Woolley, Prohibition, 209,157; Debs, Social Democratic, 94,864; Malloney, Socialist Labor, 33,432; Barker, Populist ("Middle-of-the-Road"), 50,599; Ellis, Union Reform, 5,698; Leonard, United Christian, 1,059.

"That Damned Cowboy"

For business leaders the election was a jubilee. It ended the last threat of Bryanism and Populism, and the golden age of big business flowered in giant combinations and consolidations under the beneficent McKinley-Hanna regime. There was not a cloud on the business horizon when McKinley was inaugurated on March 4, 1901.

On this occasion Roosevelt, rather than the President, was the center of interest. The crowds wanted to see the man who had led the Rough Riders up San Juan Hill, had challenged the power of Platt in the Empire State, and had outtalked Bryan. Shrewd politicians were pointing to him as the coming man, and his friends were already looking ahead to 1904. But Platt, happy at the success of his intrigue, was reported to have said that he was attending the inaugural "to see Roosevelt take the veil." For five days in March the new Vice President presided over the Senate while it handled the routine business of ratifying Presidential appointments. When it met again in December, he was President. McKinley had been shot by a half-crazed anarchist at the Pan-American Exposition at Buffalo on September 6, and died on September 14.

Roosevelt was on vacation in the Adirondacks when word came that McKinley was dying. Dashing down the mountains at night in a buckboard over mud roads with changes of horses whenever possible, he reached a railroad station at dawn; but not until the next afternoon did he arrive at Buffalo to take the oath of office. McKinley had died in the night. Roosevelt at once pledged himself in a public statement "to continue absolutely unbroken, the policy of President McKinley for the peace, the prosperity, and the honor of our beloved country." But Mark Hanna, crushed by the tragedy, is reputed to have said that he had warned McKinley against nominating that "wild man." "Now look, that damned cowboy is President of the United States." This apocryphal story may well represent the frame of mind of party bosses and their Wall Street allies, yet the "wild man" behaved very circumspectly. He retained McKinley's cabinet intact,[4] consulted freely with Hanna as to policies and appointments, wrote friendly letters to some of the elder statesmen in

[4] Within the next year, however, changes were made, and by 1909 twenty-three different individuals had served in cabinet positions under Roosevelt.

the Senate, and listened politely to representatives of J. Pierpont Morgan while they explained the views of Wall Street.

But the new President had a mind of his own. The youngest of all Presidents (under forty-three when he entered the White House), he had indeed lived "the strenuous life" that he so loved. Overcoming the handicap of a frail body in youth, he had developed a vigor and a love of sports that made him the most athletic of Presidents. His exuberant energy had found outlets in hunting, boxing, hiking, nature study, ranching, history writing, soldiering in Cuba and—his major interest—politics.[5] A succession of offices had paved the way to the Vice Presidency. He had been assemblyman from a New York City district, unsuccessful candidate for mayor (at the age of twenty-eight), United States Civil Service Commissioner in Harrison's administration, police commissioner of New York City, Assistant Secretary of the Navy, and, after his brief military career, governor of New York. He had shown reform tendencies and a commendable independence, but never once had he bolted. He had denounced bossism and corruption but had always been regular on Election Day. Swallowing Blaine in 1884 perhaps had made it easier for him to cooperate with Platt to the extent of obtaining his indorsement for the Navy appointment in 1897 and the gubernatorial nomination the next year. The rest of the story has already been told.

Whatever his intentions, Roosevelt could not have followed in the footsteps of McKinley for any length of time, for he was everything his predecessor was not. Not even the Presidency could curb his impetuous nature. He talked too freely, and was often in hot water over some thoughtless remark. On occasion, he forgot or unconsciously revised the details of some occurrence, leaving to historians the pleasant task of reconciling discrepancies. He was forever engaging in controversies: with "nature fakers," as he dubbed naturalists who disagreed with his observations; with birth-control advocates on family limitation; with educators on simplified spelling; with pacifists and nonresistants on the virtues of fighting, and so on. He was equally at home with Henry Adams, John Burroughs, and John L. Sullivan. His energy, his stocky figure, and his pugnacious face—cartooned as a double row of huge white teeth, a mustache, and a pair of eyeglasses on a black ribbon—set him apart as a President who would rule, or ruin. Americans were shocked and delighted

[5] His eyesight was always bad, and in 1908 his left eye became blind, apparently from a blow received in boxing.

with this most unorthodox chief executive. Children (six of them) and pets overran the White House, shepherded and wisely restrained by Edith Carow Roosevelt, his second wife and his balance-wheel.

Roosevelt differed from his predecessor in a more important respect than personality. The cautious Ohioan had looked complacently on the capitalist-politician partnership in the temple of government; Roosevelt, contemptuous of money-changers, longed to drive them out. "Mere wealth" aroused his resentment, though he had inherited enough for comfortable living. Criticisms of trusts and monopolies, of boss rule and corporation domination of government were appearing even in conservative quarters. Unless moderates acted to clean house, radical spirits might lay profane hands on the whole structure. The long-haired Populists had been led astray by the glitter of free silver and were no longer to be feared. But harder-headed, more farsighted leaders of middle-class background were coming to the front with proposals that invited attention. Robert M. La Follette was tackling certain aspects of the problem as governor of Wisconsin; two Ohio mayors, Tom Johnson of Cleveland and Samuel M. ("Golden Rule") Jones of Toledo, were attacking the alliance of politics and business in municipal affairs; Bryan in his organ, the *Commoner*, and Joseph Pulitzer in the New York *World* were offering reform programs that threatened to gain many adherents. These were straws in the wind. Roosevelt, a conservative reformer and an opportunist, would save his party from itself. But for the harshly reactionary character of the controlling element in Congress, he might never have been regarded as a progressive, much less a radical. Opposition aroused his combative nature and drove him to extremes he did not foresee in the beginning.

In February, 1902, he took the first step in a reform program by ordering the Attorney General to bring suit to dissolve the Northern Securities Company, a railroad merger, as in violation of the Sherman Anti-Trust Act. The Supreme Court by a five-to-four decision upheld the government's contention, and the era of "trust busting" began. More dramatic was Roosevelt's intervention in the great anthracite miners' strike of 1902. By using every type of pressure—he even threatened to operate the mines under military control—he forced the reluctant coal operators to arbitrate. His popularity soared to a new peak. Congress, at his insistence, passed the Elkins Act to strike at the evil of rebates on railroad freight rates and also created the Department of Commerce and Labor, with a Bureau of Corporations to investigate large-scale businesses. Roosevelt was putting on the armor of a reformer.

The Passing of Hanna

President Roosevelt's transcontinental journey in the spring of 1903 was actually a pre-convention stumping tour. He wanted to show himself to the voters and to defend his policies. The enthusiasm aroused was amazing and ought to have made it clear that his case was not parallel to Fillmore's or Arthur's. But he was too experienced a politician to confuse cheers with delegates and had moments of depression. Hanna had not committed himself, and Roosevelt's newly inaugurated crusade against the trusts might play havoc with campaign contributions. A well organized, well financed movement to head him off, countenanced by Hanna, might take away New York, Ohio, and possibly other machine-controlled states; and these, joined to the purchasable southern delegates, might defeat him. Even if nominated, Roosevelt's chances of election after such a struggle would hardly be good.

Yet Hanna's conduct was open and aboveboard, and he had given loyal support to the leading Roosevelt policies. He had belied his "dollar mark" reputation by showing an enlightened conservatism in the Senate, while his activities in the National Civic Federation had broadened his understanding of the problems of capital and labor and increased his respect for labor organizations. His relations with Wall Street continued friendly, and from that quarter came increasing pressure for him to enter the race against Roosevelt. At no time did he countenance such suggestions; but when he failed to declare for Roosevelt the President worried and suspicions of Hanna crept into his private correspondence.

While the President was in the West the Ohio Republican convention met to nominate a state ticket and indorse Hanna for another term. Joseph B. Foraker, Hanna's colleague in the Senate, sought to embarrass him by declaring in an interview at Washington that a proposal to indorse Roosevelt for President in 1904 was to come before the convention and he saw no reason why Ohio should turn it down. Hanna had not expected the convention to act and at once issued a statement questioning the propriety of such an indorsement. While he had no Presidential aspirations, he believed that as a candidate for reelection to the Senate and as chairman of the

Republican national committee he should avoid an expression of preference. He telegraphed an explanation to Roosevelt but received a reply that was a blow in the face: "Those who favor my administration and my nomination will favor indorsing both, and those who do not will oppose." Hanna immediately abandoned his opposition, and the Ohio convention gave its indorsement.

The President sent a conciliatory letter but wrote to Henry Cabot Lodge that he had decided to let Hanna know there was to be no more "shilly-shallying," and that he did not intend "to assume the position, at least passively, of a suppliant to whom he might give the nomination as a boon." Undoubtedly Hanna resented the humiliation; but he turned his attention to his own reelection to the Senate and outwardly continued on good terms with his chief.

The sweeping Republican victory in Ohio in 1903 increased the pressure on Hanna to seek the Presidential nomination, but he gave no signs of yielding. His health was poor, and he feared that the arduous work of a campaign would kill him. Yet he made no public statement, and newspaper rumors and tattling busybodies threatened to widen the breach with Roosevelt. Death intervened to stop the conjectures. Stricken with typhoid fever, he died on February 15, 1904. The way was now clear for the advocate of the Square Deal. Had Hanna lived, he and Roosevelt would certainly have parted company.

The two somewhat inharmonious forces that had created the party and accounted for its long years in power—middle-class humanitarian idealism and Whig regard for the interests of property—were about to clash. The latter, subverted into party domination by corrupt machines allied with privileged big business, was about to be challenged by an aroused middle class: the almost forgotten people of little business, the professions, the independent farms, the offices and stores. Equal-rights ideals were reviving. The progressive movement was getting under way. Theodore Roosevelt knew that the McKinley-Hanna equilibrium of forces was at an end.

20

The First Roosevelt

A Question of Labels

The Republican national convention at Chicago, June 21-23, 1904, was a tame affair without the physical presence of Roosevelt, though its cut-and-dried program was planned in detail at the White House. Elihu Root made the keynote speech as temporary chairman; Speaker Joseph G. Cannon took over the gavel as permanent chairman, and Roosevelt's close friend, Senator Henry Cabot Lodge, presented the platform.

The accomplishments of Republican rule and the evils of Democratic misrule were duly contrasted. For the future the platform pledged the party to uphold protective tariff, widen foreign markets (with reciprocity where consistent with protection), preserve the gold standard, encourage an American merchant marine, and maintain a big navy. It praised Roosevelt's vigorous foreign policies and his enforcement of anti-trust laws, and told capital and labor that they were subject to the laws and must not break them. It was a status quo platform. The candidate was the issue.

Roosevelt was nominated by unanimous vote of the 994 delegates, and Senator Charles Warren Fairbanks of Indiana was named to run with him, also by acclamation. Ohio-born Fairbanks was a colorless conservative and a faithful Methodist. For national chairman, Roosevelt had already selected George B. Cortelyou, his Secretary of Commerce and Labor, who was not the professional politician type but proved to be a good campaign manager.

The conservative Democrats felt that at last their hour had come. Bryanism had been tried twice and found wanting; a safe and sane easterner on a moderate platform was in order. Roosevelt had disturbed big business sufficiently to arouse Democratic hopes of business support. The minority party, with a barrel to tap and the right sort of candidate, might turn the tables on the Republicans, who were afflicted with a kind of problem child, as unpredictable as he was uncontrollable. In fact, the situation invited the return of Grover Cleveland. The dark clouds of bitterness that had surrounded him since his repudiation by the party in 1896 had been dispelled by 1904, for the course of events seemed to have vindicated his stand. Great crowds greeted him in April at the Louisiana Purchase Exposition in St. Louis, and he could have had the nomination, had he given the word. Not only old friends but former opponents, including David B. Hill and Tammany Hall, wanted him; and Roosevelt was predicting that he would run again with Wall Street support. But Cleveland had no desire to reenter the political arena. He was content to urge the nomination of any sound Democrat not pockmarked with Bryanism.

Hill, whose hold on the New York Democracy had not been destroyed by the lean years of defeat, threw his powerful support to Alton B. Parker, chief justice of the New York Court of Appeals. Parker was an able judge, but his chief qualification was the belief, fortified by his past successes, that he could carry New York. He would hardly have been a serious contender had the party not been faced with the greatest dearth of Presidential availabilities in its history. Republican successes in state and Congressional elections since 1894 had left the Democrats almost without a northern governor or Senator. This forced them to turn to the bench. Federal Circuit Judge George Gray of Delaware, a former Senator, was better known than Parker, but geography pointed to the New Yorker.

Except for two or three favorite-son movements, the chief opposition to Parker was furnished by William Randolph Hearst, once of California but now representing a New York district in Congress, who had made himself known chiefly through his sensational newspapers. Yet his reform program had much to commend it, while his wealth simplified the problem of seeking delegates. He had supported Bryan wholeheartedly in 1896, was appealing to the masses, but did not seem to fit the situation, which called for a solid, stable Cleveland Democrat to oppose Roosevelt. Nevertheless, Hearst garnered considerable support among the delegates, chiefly from the Bryan sections of the West. South and East were cold toward him and rallied to Parker to insure his defeat. Bryan, without being hostile to Hearst, hesitated to support him.

The Democratic hosts converged on St. Louis on July 6 and chose two Congressmen, John Sharp Williams of Mississippi and Champ Clark of Missouri, as temporary and permanent presiding officers. A reference by Williams to Cleveland's "dogged persistency and indomitable will" evoked a great demonstration, proof of the temper of the convention. But Bryan had not come to sit in submissive silence. His earlier pronouncements against Parker (who had not bolted in 1896) had indicated his position, and he made the most of every opportunity to embarrass or checkmate the conservative majority. His first battle—which he lost—was an attempt to unseat the Illinois delegation, controlled by Roger Sullivan, in favor of a contesting group of Bryanites. Both were pledged to Hearst, but the loyalty of the Sullivan machine was not above suspicion.

Bryan's greatest fight was over the platform. A subcommittee of the resolutions committee drafted a tentative platform without consulting him and expected to have the full committee adopt it. They reckoned without Bryan. He found much to criticize and began a sixteen-hour battle to amend it. He opposed a plank stating that gold discoveries had removed the currency problem from the field of political contention, which Hill defended. He also demanded that an income-tax resolution be included in the platform. In the end both were dropped; but Bryan secured a strong anti-trust plank. The fear that he would make a dramatic appeal to the convention if his demands were rejected brought concessions by conservatives to the man they had pronounced politically dead.

The platform upheld "the essential principles of the Democratic faith" and called for the rescue of the government from "the headstrong, arbitrary and spasmodic methods which distract business by uncertainty, and pervade the public mind with dread, distrust and perturbation." It condemned "executive usurpation," imperialism, protective tariff, and trusts as products of Republican rule. More specifically, the party confession of faith called for Philippine independence, tariff reduction, Canadian reciprocity, strict enforcement of civil and criminal statutes against trusts, and enlargement of the powers of the Interstate Commerce Commission. Bryan liberalism also appeared in planks favoring direct election of United States Senators and restrictions on the power of federal judges in contempt cases.

A night of nominating and seconding speeches produced Bryan at 4:30 A.M., July 9. Ostensibly rising to second the nomination of Senator Francis M. Cockrell of Missouri, he attempted to sway the convention against Parker. His speech assailed the militarism of Roosevelt but warned his party against choosing plutocracy as the alternative. "Must we choose between a god of war and a god of gold?" His appeal evoked a long demonstration from the galleries and a minority of the delegates, in which local pride in Cockrell's candidacy and admiration for Bryan were mixed. But Parker was nominated a few minutes later.[1] He was but nine votes short of the necessary two-thirds, and his nomination was then made unanimous.

That night former Senator Henry Gassaway Davis was nominated for Vice President on the first ballot. The wealthiest man in West Virginia, he was eighty years old—the oldest man ever nominated by a major party on a national ticket.[2] He was well enough qualified for the place, as Vice Presidents go, but age would have ruled him out if the Democrats had not been looking for a "financial angel." From Republican sources came this gibe at the Democratic ticket—"an enigma from New York and a ruin from West Virginia."

Just as the convention was ready to ballot for the Vice Presidency, with Bryan ill in his hotel room, the supposedly innocuous Parker hurled a bombshell. He telegraphed to William F. Sheehan of the New York delegation:

> I regard the gold standard as firmly and irretrievably established, and shall act accordingly if the action of the convention today shall be ratified by the people. As the platform is silent upon the subject, my view should be made known to the convention, and if it is proved to be unsatisfactory to the majority, I request you to decline the nomination for me at once, so that another may be nominated before adjournment.

Earlier Bryan had quizzed Hill about Parker's views on the gold standard and had been told that he would leave the character of the platform to the convention. Hill denied that he knew anything about his candidate's opinions on the currency question.

The Bryan men and many of the southerners, including Senator

[1] This one ballot gave Parker 658 votes; Hearst 204; Cockrell 42; Richard Olney of Massachusetts 38; Edward C. Wall of Wisconsin 27; George Gray of Delaware 8; scattering, 20. Parker had most of the East and practically all the South. Hearst's vote was mostly western.

[2] Davis actually lived to be ninety-two, dying March 11, 1916.

Tillman of South Carolina and Governor Vardaman of Mississippi, incensed at Parker's telegram, charged Hill with "peanut politics," and Bryan rose from his sickbed to lead the attack. John Sharp Williams reported to the convention a reply to Parker designed to meet the problem. It declared that the platform was silent on the money question because it was not regarded as an issue, and that there was nothing in the views expressed in the telegram which would preclude his accepting the nomination. After a spirited debate, this was carried, 785 to 190. Eastern Democratic papers praised the candidate's display of courage and independence, but the Bryan following (and the Republicans) declared that Parker would not have been nominated if he had sent his telegram earlier.

The convention had not actually healed the breach in the party. The Bryanites were angry and, without bolting, gave only a perfunctory support to Parker. Bryan took the stump, but his purpose was to retain his hold on the masses of Democrats and to recover control of the party after the election. He was shrewdly demonstrating his regularity to teach the bolters of 1896 a lesson in loyalty. Ten days before the election he announced in the *Commoner*, for many years his personal organ, his intention of reorganizing the party "along radical lines."

The general management of the Democratic campaign was in the hands of Thomas Taggart, chairman of the national committee and Indiana's shrewdest politician, with William F. Sheehan of New York at the head of the executive committee. But the hoped-for support of the business interests did not materialize. August Belmont, Thomas F. Ryan, Daniel S. Lamont, and a few other loyal Democrats helped, but Republican businessmen were not to be weaned away from the party that had protected their interests. E. H. Harriman, J. P. Morgan, George J. Gould, James Stillman, H. C. Frick, the Standard Oil interests, and a number of other wealthy corporations and individuals contributed liberally to the Roosevelt cause. The Republican candidate knew big business was supporting him; but Cornelius N. Bliss, treasurer of the national committee, kept his own books on the more than two millions he raised, and Roosevelt showed no unseemly curiosity.[3] His attitude toward the trusts had not changed, but he maintained a discreet and dignified silence dur-

[3] Not until the investigations of the Clapp Committee of the Senate in 1912 was the extent of corporation contributions revealed, although much had been surmised before this.

ing the campaign, sticking to the Presidential tradition of abstaining from speech-making. His excessively long letter of acceptance reviewed the measures and policies of his administration and invited the opposition to make them the issues.

That even a huge campaign chest could have elected Parker is highly improbable. Regardless of the fact that the Democratic platform was more liberal, the voters tended to regard Roosevelt as the dynamic progressive and Parker as the cautious conservative. Even if Parker had attempted a vigorous offensive, it would have spoiled the picture of the well balanced, dignified judge who was to save the nation from the erratic, spectacular "T. R." The Democratic candidate belonged in the Republican camp, conducting a front-porch campaign, while Roosevelt, given the leadership of the opposition, would have been freed from his inhibitions and could have assailed Wall Street, the trusts, and the corruptions of boss rule with sledge-hammer blows. The labels were mixed in 1904.

The achievements of Roosevelt were so generally popular that Democratic guns had to be leveled at methods rather than measures. Even the much criticized "rape of Panama" was an asset to Roosevelt. To the average man it meant merely that the canal, talked about for a quarter of a century, would be built at once instead of encountering further delays. Old issues were devoid of interest, while Roosevelt's trust prosecutions deprived the Democrats of ammunition in that area. Of necessity they assailed the man and his methods. Bryan attacked him for sword waving and militarism, and Henry Watterson called him "as sweet a gentleman as ever scuttled a ship or cut a throat." More staidly the Parker Constitutional Club of eminent New York lawyers pointed to Roosevelt's "arbitrary usurping of legislative functions" and his "massing enormous power in his own hands," and called for a man of "safe tendencies."

The dull campaign furnished only one lively incident, near the close. Joseph Pulitzer of the New York *World*, with his keen perception of realities, pointed to Republican Chairman Cortelyou's former headship of the Department of Commerce and Labor, containing the Bureau of Corporations, which had been strangely inactive since its creation. Did the corporations, pouring money into the campaign, assume that they were buying protection? Pulitzer called on Roosevelt to make public the contributions of big business. The Republican candidate was silent, but when Parker, rather belatedly, repeated the insinuations about Cortelyou and the Bureau of Corporations he angrily termed the charge a wicked falsehood. The campaign closed on this triumphantly righteous note.

Roosevelt did not deny the fact of corporation contributions, though not informed by Cortelyou and Bliss of their extent. In one case at least he was personally responsible. Alarmed at the prospect of defeat for the Republican state ticket (and possibly the national ticket) in New York because of local issues, he invited Edward H. Harriman, the railroad magnate, to the White House and asked him to raise funds to save the day. Harriman returned to New York and raised $250,000, which he turned over to Treasurer Bliss. Over a year later he wrote to a friend explaining his relations with Roosevelt. In April, 1907, the letter, sold by a discharged employee, appeared in the New York *World*. Roosevelt, angry over Harriman's hostility toward railroad legislation and cynical remarks about his ability to buy legislatures and courts, flamed at this revelation of their former relations. "I never requested Mr. Harriman to raise a dollar for the Presidential campaign of 1904," he stormed, insisting that the story was utterly false. The money was for the *state ticket*. Roosevelt seemed to be arguing that $250,000 spent on behalf of the state ticket would have no influence on the outcome of the national election in the Empire State.

But no revelations of corporation connection with the Republican campaign could have saved the Democrats. Roosevelt had captured the popular imagination, and nothing short of a complete economic collapse could have prevented his election. Even in that contingency he might have escaped by blaming Wall Street. Not since Jackson had there been such a popular hero. The king could do no wrong. And so Judge Parker went down to defeat on November 8 by a record-breaking margin in the popular vote. Roosevelt had 7,628,461; Parker, 5,084,223.[4] Only the South remained loyal to the Democrats—Missouri, West Virginia, and Maryland (popular vote) were lost. Roosevelt had 336 electoral votes to 140 for Parker, the largest majority since the Grant-Greeley election of 1872, when the South was under carpetbag rule. Both Houses of Congress were

[4] Maryland gave Roosevelt one electoral vote, Parker the rest. Delaware was consistently Republican from 1896 to 1936, except for 1912. The vote of the minor parties was as follows: Swallow, Prohibition, 259,257; Debs, Socialist, 402,460; Watson, People's, 114,753; Corregan, Socialist Labor, 33,724. Debs's vote had risen from 94,768 in 1900 to 402,460—a surprising increase, indicating a growing protest against the conservatism of the major parties.

Republican by large majorities. The Democratic conservatives' bid for power had been a disastrous failure.

Roosevelt celebrated his astounding triumph with an amazing blunder. On election night he issued this statement: "The wise custom which limits the President to two terms regards the substance and not the form, and under no circumstances will I be a candidate for or accept another nomination." This most energetic of Presidents, barely forty-six years of age, was relegating himself permanently to the painful estate of an ex-President at the expiration of his term. In effect, he was notifying the party leaders in Congress that his power to reward and punish was of limited duration. For so astute a politician the statement was inexcusable. Exuberance over his great victory had betrayed his judgment. The club of a possible third term (in his case actually a second elective term) would have served him well in dealing with a recalcitrant Congress in the years to follow. And in 1912 he was made painfully aware of this entirely unnecessary pledge when he chose to run again.

The Sledge-Hammer of Righteousness[5]

Roosevelt was quoted as having remarked to a friend on March 3: "Tomorrow I shall come into office in my own right. Then watch out for me." The cheering crowds, the long parade, the wild cowboy riding and yelling of the Rough Riders, the fine weather, and the boyish exuberance of the central figure combined to make it one of the gayest inaugurals the national Capital had ever witnessed. But the problem of Roosevelt was to transmute this tremendous popularity into accomplishment. At the other end of Pennsylvania Avenue sat a body of men who were not prepared to bow to this idol of the populace. Republican Presidents since Lincoln had not presumed to tell Congress what to do.

The House of Representatives was reasonably tractable at first. Many of the members had ridden into office on Roosevelt's coat tails and were quick to respond to the public opinion back of his proposals. The fundamental conservatism of the majority did not assert itself until after the business Panic of 1907. This and the

[5] "He may be figured as a Thor wielding with power and effect a sledge-hammer in the cause of national righteousness," wrote Herbert Croly in *The Promise of American Life* (Macmillan, New York, 1909), p. 174.

approaching end of Roosevelt's power to reward and punish relieved the powerful Speaker of the House, Joe Cannon, from any obligation to cooperate further. He admitted afterward that Roosevelt was one man he had really feared.

But the Senate, dominated by three- and four-term Republican oligarchs and ever jealous of its rights and privileges, resented Roosevelt's spirited leadership and, even more, the direction it was taking. The members were in large part machine leaders who had become rich or rich men who had purchased machine support. They represented railroads, steel, oil, textiles and other special interests, as these usually controlled the state legislatures which elected them. The leader of the upper house was astute, iron-willed, even-tempered Nelson W. Aldrich of Rhode Island, a multimillionaire who, for a quarter of a century, had represented the finance and factories of New England. He was a masterful parliamentary leader and had the support of an able inner circle, but he was not a party boss of the machine and ward school. He was too aloof, too closely associated with men of wealth, to work with the common herd.[6] Most people, he said, did not know what they wanted. He and his coterie did not intend to let Roosevelt Bryanize the party, though they wanted party harmony when elections were impending.

The great battle of Roosevelt's term came over the Hepburn bill to extend the powers of the Interstate Commerce Commission, and especially to give it the power to fix railroad rates. The House of Representatives passed the bill in a form satisfactory to the President; but the Senate leadership was in the railroad camp, and a long battle ensued. Roosevelt was forced to cooperate with Senator Tillman of South Carolina, with whom he was not even on speaking terms, in order to get the bill to a vote. In the end a compromise amendment saved the faces of the conservatives, and the measure passed in a somewhat weakened form. Still, it was a major administration victory and added to Roosevelt's prestige.

Some other progressive legislation encountered less opposition. The Meat Inspection Act and the Pure Food and Drugs Act of 1906 were outstanding. "Trust busting" continued, but Roosevelt became less enthusiastic over its results and moved toward regulation, rather than dissolution, of big business monopolies. His greatest achieve-

[6] Aldrich was a close friend of J. P. Morgan and other financial leaders. His daughter was married to John D. Rockefeller, Jr. His own fortune had been built up by shrewd investments in street railways and interurban lines.

ments were in the field of conservation of natural resources; but this was not a party issue. The elections of 1906 produced a few more Democrats in the House but strengthened slightly the Republican hold on the Senate. The breach in the party leadership had not appeared at the polls.

The Panic of 1907 widened the gap between Roosevelt and the powerful eastern financial interests. Using administration policies to explain the panic, they demanded a more conservative course and contributed to weaken the prestige of the President with the Congressional leadership. Roosevelt, under the immediate stress of the Wall Street crash, consented to the purchase of the Tennessee Coal and Iron Company by the United States Steel Corporation in order to save business houses loaded with the nearly valueless stock of the former concern. This helped restore confidence but later occasioned criticism when the Steel Corporation was found to have made a good bargain.

The President may have been misled for the moment by the unduly dark picture of approaching chaos on the stock market; but he did not relent in his attitude toward big business, despite letters from friends as well as hostile critics urging him in the interest of restoring prosperity to abandon his crusade for righteousness in the business world, or at least to make no more reckless utterances. Denying that he had stated that he would send "from ten to fifty capitalists to jail," or that "almost every captain of industry should be behind the bars," he angrily repelled the charges that he had caused the panic and declared that speculations of big financiers were responsible. He believed that his uncovering of rascality had brought on the trouble a year or two sooner than it would have occurred otherwise, but assailed the conservative press—"papers like the *Sun*, *Times*, and *Harper's Weekly*, read by the financial classes and I believe financed by them also"—for spreading falsehoods about him.

Two Popular Choices

Roosevelt, like Jefferson and Jackson, felt that his successor should be a man after his own heart; but his problem was more difficult. Elihu Root, Secretary of State, seemed to him to be almost ideally fitted for the highest office. He had high intelligence, untiring industry, unusual administrative ability and experience, and a cool head. He had mixed in New York politics for many years and knew how to deal with the practical politicians, including refractory Senators. His keen sense of humor eased his relations with his impetuous chief, whom he regarded with something of the affection and amused indulgence of an elder brother (he was thirteen years older than Roosevelt) for a spoiled younger one. In spite of admiring the Secretary as "the greatest living statesman," Roosevelt saw his limitations. As a former corporation lawyer, with access to the inner circles of Wall Street, Root was too vulnerable to the shafts of Bryan and Hearst; and he would not make a fighting campaign, as his age (he would be sixty-three in 1908) and temperament forbade it. Therefore Roosevelt, after much hesitation and with Root's approval, turned to William Howard Taft as the better candidate.

Secretary of War Taft was an Ohioan, a graduate of Yale, and had been successively a Cincinnati judge, solicitor general of the United States, federal circuit judge, head of the United States Philippine Commission, and first civil governor of the Philippines before entering the cabinet. His tact and skill in handling difficult administrative problems had been of value to Roosevelt. Progressive middle western Republicans had confidence in him. Yet, never having held an important elective office, he lacked experience in appealing to voters and in dealing with party leaders. His own inclinations pointed toward the Supreme Court, and Roosevelt would have been happy to gratify this ambition; but family pressure, particularly from his wife and his wealthy older brother Charles P. Taft, helped turn the balance toward the White House.

Roosevelt was troubled by outbreaks of third-term sentiment. His personal popularity was so great, despite the panic and the wrath of the rich, that there was a danger that he might be nominated in spite of himself. Unkind commentators foresaw a deadlocked convention and a stampede, manipulated by admirers, ending in a triumphant renomination. Sensitive to the charge of hypocrisy and disturbed over rumors that unscrupulous politicians might use his name merely to head off Taft, he decided late in 1907, at the suggestion of his private secretary William Loeb, to give the Ohioan not only his blessing but his active support. In the ensuing months he used the power of the administration to nominate Taft. The southern states, controlled by federal officeholders, were easily drawn into the Taft-Roosevelt fold, and a group of favorite sons in the North, often spoken of as the "Allies," offered slight resistance to the machine operated so expertly by Frank H. Hitchcock, but drawing its motive power from Roosevelt and the financial contributions of Charles P. Taft. Among the favorite sons were Governor Hughes of New York, Senator Knox of Pennsylvania, Speaker Cannon of Illinois, Vice President Fairbanks of Indiana, and Senator La Follette of Wisconsin. Senator Foraker at first had strong Old Guard support. He seized upon the Brownsville affair to attract the colored vote,[7] but failed to make any headway against Taft in Ohio, and his candidacy collapsed. The astute Senator Aldrich chose to support Roosevelt's choice.

Chicago was again the scene of the Republican national convention, on June 16, 1908. Before it met the national committee had struggled with the problem of 223 contested seats, mostly from the South. Taft delegates were usually seated over those favorable to the "Allies"—an evidence of the power of the administration. Senator Julius C. Burrows of Michigan, a veteran Republican, served as temporary chairman. Henry Cabot Lodge, as permanent chairman, summed up the achievements of Roosevelt in a speech that was interrupted by a wild demonstration lasting forty-nine minutes.

An attempt to reduce southern representation in Republican national conventions was defeated by a narrow margin, chiefly because Roosevelt opposed it (he was to regret this four years later). When the platform, drawn up in advance to suit Roosevelt and Taft, was presented the Wisconsin delegates, pledged to La Follette, offered a more liberal substitute and carried their fight to the floor of the convention; but it was voted down, 952-28. Individual proposals for publicity of campaign contributions, physical valuation of railroads for rate-making purposes, and direct election of United States Senators, were voted on separately and had more support, the last receiving 114 votes to 866 opposed.

As adopted, the party's declaration of faith was far too long for what it contained. Besides lauding Roosevelt and recording the benefits of Republican rule, it declared for revision of the tariff by a special session of Congress, strengthening of the Sherman Anti-Trust Act to provide greater supervision over large corporations and

[7] Brownsville, Texas, had been mysteriously shot up on the night of August 13, 1906, presumably by colored soldiers of a United States infantry regiment stationed there. One man was killed and another wounded. The evidence of guilt was not very clear, but the President dismissed three companies from the service on the ground that the men not guilty had refused to expose the culprits. Foraker defended the soldiers in the Senate and criticized Roosevelt. The two men clashed bitterly at a banquet of the Gridiron Club, famed Washington press club.

to secure greater publicity, conservation of natural resources and improvement of inland waterways, a more elastic and adaptable system of currency, amendments to the railroad rate law to prevent the overissue of rail stocks and bonds, and establishment of postal savings banks. A vaguely worded plank declared against injunctions in labor disputes without notice, except "where irreparable injury would result from delay." The evasive and ambiguous statements on important domestic questions represented an attempt to reconcile the progressive tendencies of Roosevelt with the conservative views of the Congressional leadership. After all, if Taft was to continue the Roosevelt policies, it mattered little what the platform said.

The balloting, on the third day, was preceded by a last-minute effort to stampede the convention for Roosevelt. The galleries, as in earlier demonstrations, contributed most of the noise, for the Taft forces had the situation well in hand. Chairman Lodge went ahead with the roll call despite the uproar, and Taft was easily nominated. He had 702 votes; Knox, 68; Hughes, 67; Cannon, 58; Fairbanks, 40; La Follette, 25; Foraker, 16; Roosevelt, 3.

The Vice Presidential nomination went to New York, and that state's delegation chose a veteran Congressman, James S. Sherman, who had 816 votes on the one ballot taken. This was almost a slap at Roosevelt, for Sherman was an extreme conservative, but the delegates had obeyed the White House on everything else.

Two weeks after the Republican convention the Democratic hosts gathered at Denver, Colorado, to name their "Peerless Leader," William Jennings Bryan. The pendulum had swung completely back since 1904. Parker's disastrous defeat had vindicated the course of Bryan. The progressive movement was under way in the West, and the Nebraskan, who claimed priority in the cause of liberalism over all crusaders, was the logical choice. The scarcity of Presidential timber in the party, so noticeable in 1904, was still only slightly relieved. In Republican Minnesota John A. Johnson, a Democrat, had attracted favorable attention as governor. Judge George Gray of Delaware, considered in 1904, again had support, but there was no available Democratic governor or Senator from an important doubtful eastern or middle western state to fit the party's needs. Grover Cleveland warned his fellow Democrats that the choice of Bryan meant defeat at the polls but died before the nomination was made. David B. Hill had retired in 1904, and no one of his political sagacity appeared to organize the conservatives.

Bryan had made one political misstep. Returning from a trip around the world in 1906, he surprised a welcoming throng in Madison Square Garden by advocating government ownership of railroads. This bold pronouncement was badly timed. The Hepburn Act had just been passed, and the policy of federal regulation was to receive a fair trial for the first time. To urge government ownership was poor politics, for it alienated many conservatives who had begun to believe that Bryan might do after all. Probably he intended the speech as a trial balloon to test public sentiment. He was anxious to prove his right to lead the liberal procession and feared that Roosevelt was stealing too much of his thunder. But he soon found it necessary to trim sails. By the summer of 1907 he was announcing in the *Commoner* that government ownership was not an issue, and that he thought it unwise to turn attention from regulation. Nevertheless, he had given a handle to his enemies, and the Republican platform charged upon his party the heinous crime of believing in socialism.

Denver welcomed its first national convention with a great display of western hospitality, including free entertainments, cowboys, Indians, snow from the mountain peaks; but it could not supply the drama of a convention battle. The decisions were made at Lincoln, Nebraska, and the delegates were as carefully coached as if their leader were present. Theodore Bell of California and Henry D. Clayton of Alabama, both loyal Bryanites, were respectively temporary and permanent chairman. When Senator Gore of Oklahoma mentioned Bryan in a speech to the convention, a volume of cheering let loose that kept up for eighty-seven minutes, a new record. Convention demonstrations were becoming artificial affairs, with newspapers reporting their length to the exact number of minutes. On this occasion the Bryanites were satisfied to have outyelled the Republicans at Chicago.

The Denver platform resembled a Bryan campaign speech. It arraigned the Republican party for misuse of power and subserviency to predatory wealth and declared the overshadowing issue to be "Shall the people rule?" Extravagance, increases in the number of officeholders, the arbitrary power of the Speaker of the House, misuse of patronage by the President in securing the nomination for President of a cabinet member, and corporation contributions to Republican campaign coffers were the chief specifications in the indictment.

On the positive side the platform promised downward revision of the tariff, more teeth in the anti-trust laws and their vigorous enforcement, wider powers for the Interstate Commerce Commission, prohibition of campaign contributions by corporations, publicity of, and limitations on, individual contributions. Other proposals differed little from Republican pronouncements, except demands for an income tax and for restriction on the use of injunctions in labor cases.

Bryan, Governor Johnson, and Judge George Gray were the only names presented. On the first and only ballot, July 10, Bryan had 888-1/2 votes; Gray, 59-1/2; Johnson, 46. For Vice President an Indiana Bryanite, John Worth Kern, was nominated without opposition. Norman E. Mack of New York became chairman of the national committee.

The usual array of minor parties presented candidates, and a new one appeared. The Socialists again offered Eugene V. Debs with high hopes of another large gain in voting strength. The Socialist Labor party named August Gillhaus and the Prohibitionists Eugene W. Chafin. The feeble remnant of Populists made their last stand, led by the veteran agrarian Tom Watson. The new party was the Independence party, a Hearst-financed, one-ring circus with Thomas L. Hisgen as candidate and Hearst as ringmaster. Its platform, occupying ground between the Democrats and Socialists, was decidedly progressive. Hearst had not yet tossed overboard the liberalism of his early years, though his recent dealings with Tammany had made progressives view him with suspicion.

Taft and Roosevelt Against Bryan

The Republican campaign got under way slowly. Taft, burdened with his judicial temperament, would have preferred a front-porch affair but was persuaded that stumping was necessary to counteract the appeal of Bryan. Frank H. Hitchcock, his manager, withheld the Republican fire for the closing weeks, and as late as September Bryan and Taft seemed to be running neck and neck. Then Taft went on the stump, Hearst attempted to expose men prominent in both parties, Roosevelt started a debate by letter with Bryan, and the tepid campaign warmed up a little.

Hearst had secured letters from the files of the Standard Oil Company revealing that Republican Senator Foraker and Governor C. N. Haskell of Oklahoma, treasurer of the Democratic national committee, had had intimate connections with the great oil trust. Foraker defended himself by showing that his dealings with Standard Oil were on a purely business basis; but the fact that a United States Senator, in a period of bitter public feeling toward trusts, had sought favors from the most hated of the species was enough to damn him. Roosevelt, with the Hepburn bill and the Brownsville affair fresh in his memory, was eager to destroy Foraker and urged Taft not to appear with him at a public meeting. Foraker solved the problem for Taft by staying away, but Roosevelt was not satisfied. "He ought to throw Foraker over with a bump," he wrote to his son-in-law. "I have decided to put a little vim into the campaign by making a publication of my own."

His "publication" was an interview attacking Bryan for retaining Haskell as campaign treasurer and showing that Taft, by contrast, had refused to have dealings with Foraker long before. Then followed a lively public controversy between Bryan and Roosevelt. Bryan went back to 1904 to show that the President's skirts were not clean of corporation assistance. He charged that the trust magnates were supporting Taft, and demanded publicity for all contributions. Charges and countercharges followed, Haskell resigning as treasurer in the midst of the controversy.

The question of publicity of campaign contributions, raised by Bryan, was an awkward one. He had announced earlier that a $10,000 limit would be placed on individual contributions, and that the names of donors of more than $100 would be made public. The Republicans were embarrassed, but Taft declared that the law of New York State, which required a statement of receipts and expenditures after the election, would be observed. This was less frank than the Democratic position but was in advance of earlier methods. Roosevelt privately protested to the Republican campaign treasurer, George R. Sheldon, against reported requests for funds from John D. Archbold of Standard Oil and Edward H. Harriman. Sheldon responded with the disagreeable information that Standard Oil money had been accepted in 1904, contrary to Roosevelt's wishes. Neither party was particularly well financed in 1908, though as usual the Republicans fared better than their rivals.

Apart from the interest injected by Roosevelt, the campaign

dragged. Trusts, tariff, and currency developed no sharp differences. Taft declared that the ambiguous Republican tariff plank meant revision downward, which seemed to place the parties rather close together on this question. Samuel Gompers, head of the American Federation of Labor, indorsed Bryan because of the anti-injunction plank in his platform, but there was little evidence of any pronounced swing of labor to the Democrats.

Bryan found that Roosevelt's liberalism had cut the ground from under his feet in the West while the East, as in his earlier campaigns, saw no reason to change its Republican allegiance. He was no longer the glamorous "Boy Orator of the Platte," but a middle-aged political preacher whose ideas, fed to Chautauqua audiences year after year, had become a familiar story. Roosevelt had altered his opinion of the Nebraskan for the better since 1896 and now spoke of him as "a kindly man and well meaning in a weak way; always provided that to mean well must not be translated by him into doing well if it would interfere with his personal prospects. But he is the cheapest fakir we have ever had proposed for President." Yet a conservative Republican of the McKinley stamp would have found this "fakir" a formidable opponent. The country was turning liberal, but Roosevelt had postponed the day of reckoning for his party by giving it the habiliments of reform.

November 3 wrote finis to Bryan's efforts to be elected President. He had 6,412,294 votes to Taft's 7,675,320.[8] His total was larger, but his percentage was slightly smaller, than in 1896 or 1900. His popular vote was far above Parker's in 1904, but his electoral defeat was almost as bad, for he had only 162 to Taft's 321. He had the usual southern bloc plus six of Maryland's eight electoral votes, Kentucky, newly admitted Oklahoma, Colorado, Nevada, and his home state, Nebraska. The rest of the North and West and Missouri, West Virginia, and Delaware went Republican as in 1904. Judged by the total vote, the Democratic party was no better off than it had been when Bryan ran before. It had merely recovered the ground lost by Parker.

But there were bright spots in the Democratic picture. Bryan's vote was less sectional and better distributed than before. In five states carried by Taft, Democratic governors were chosen. In several

[8] The minor parties had these totals: Debs, Socialist, 420,820; Chafin, Prohibition, 252,683; Hisgen, Independence, 83,563; Watson, People's, 28,131; Gillhaus, Socialist Labor, 13,825.

other states Republican state candidates ran far behind the head of the ticket. The progressive movement was spreading eastward. Unless the dominant Republicans recognized reform demands, a reviving Democracy under new leadership might serve the purpose of the progressives.

21

The Progressive Uprising

Taft Without Roosevelt

The soothsayers of Washington, recalling the pouring rain that had ushered in the term of the second Harrison, saw unfavorable omens in the sleet and snow that marred Taft's assumption of office. Was he also to be a one-term tenant of the old mansion? Already there were faint hints of an estrangement between Taft and his old chief. Whisperers said that Roosevelt was disappointed because James R. Garfield had not been retained in the Interior Department and that other requests had been ignored; that he was annoyed at Taft's emphasis on the part "Brother Charley" had played in his success. Members of Taft's family, it was said, felt that his real merits had been too long obscured by Roosevelt's shadow, that his obligations to his predecessor had been overstressed. Now he could stand on his own feet. Although the cabinet included two hold-over members, none remained from Roosevelt's inner circle. But neither the retiring nor the succeeding chief executive gave the slightest indication that the gossips were right. Roosevelt, off to Africa on a hunting trip, seemed to be eager to forget politics and departed with every show of cordiality toward his successor.

Taft as President soon disclosed weaknesses that had not appeared in his previous work. His judicial temperament made him slow in arriving at decisions, and he was perplexed and annoyed by the multitude of people insistent on conferring with him. Roosevelt had thrived under pressure that sometimes caused Taft's normally jovial disposition to grow a little frayed. Newspapermen found that they were not the welcome visitors they had been in the regime of "T. R." Taft did not like to be bothered. Neither he nor his first private secretary had any realization of the value of a good press. Yet he was thin-skinned and stopped reading newspapers that criticized him. Taft also lacked the driving energy of his predecessor. His big body demanded plenty of food, and sometimes this form of overindulgence seemed to dull his naturally keen mind and contribute to his "capacity for sleep." Golf was his chief recreation; but unfortunately this now popular sport was then regarded as a mild but rather silly exercise for the elderly rich who could afford to belong to country clubs and who found other sports too strenuous. His addiction to "cow pasture pool" had been a minor liability in his campaign.

Taft lagged far behind his predecessor in a more serious respect: he was not a politician. Without service in Congress or elective state office, he was inexperienced in dealing with the men who dealt in votes. Disliking a fight, he tended to conciliate and compromise, and sometimes to make promises which proved embarrassing later. Instead of leading his party, he was soon being led along by the Aldrich-Cannon group and later by slick politicians like Murray Crane of Massachusetts and other Roosevelt haters.

The tariff was the rock on which the Taft administration foundered. Roosevelt had steered clear of the tariff issue, but Taft, pledged to downward revision, had no choice. The House of Representatives, at the special session of Congress called to carry out the pledge, passed the Payne bill which did provide for some moderate reductions. In the Senate, Chairman Aldrich of the Finance Committee took over, and the result was practically a new bill, a revision upward. A revolt, led by Jonathan P. Dolliver of Iowa, assisted by La Follette of Wisconsin, Albert J. Beveridge of Indiana, and several other Republican Senators failed to defeat the bill but did advertise its iniquities. A conference committee accepted most of the Senate increases, and the Payne-Aldrich bill became a law, though twenty House and seven Senate insurgents voted with the Democrats. The President had tardily intervened with the conference committee to secure some reductions on raw materials, and a tax on corporate incomes was included in the bill. Though he was not satisfied with the measure he signed it, and was presently defending it. In a speech at Winona, Minnesota, he startled the country by declaring the bill the best the Republican party had ever passed. This was the final blunder.

On the heels of the tariff troubles came the Ballinger-Pinchot controversy. Gifford Pinchot, Chief Forester, charged that Secretary of the Interior Richard A. Ballinger was unfaithful to conservation in his policies with regard to certain water-power sites and mineral lands.

Pinchot went so far in January, 1910, as to write an open letter to Senator Dolliver stating his position and defending Louis R. Glavis, a discharged official of the Interior Department and a bitter critic of the Secretary. This shifted the issue from conservation to insubordination, and Taft dismissed the Chief Forester. Pinchot, convinced that the President had turned against Roosevelt's favorite policy, set out for Egypt to tell his tale to his old chief. A Congressional investigation exonerated Secretary Ballinger (the minority called it "whitewashing"), but he finally resigned in March, 1911. Taft, except for removing Pinchot, did nothing to warrant the charges of hostility to conservation. On the contrary, he did much to advance the cause both through legislation and by administrative acts; but politically it did him small good. The insurgents, hostile on other grounds, were not mollified. Former Secretary of the Interior James R. Garfield and the influential *Collier's Weekly* supported Pinchot against the administration.

The regular session of 1909-1910 produced a bipartisan uprising against Speaker Joseph Cannon. "Uncle Joe," a cantankerous, poker-playing, hard-bitten standpatter, functioned on big black cigars, appointed all committees, and ruled the House with the aid of a squad of veteran conservatives. Often he used his broad powers—inherited from Czar Reed—to punish dissenters and scotch progressive measures. A dramatic parliamentary struggle in March, 1910, led by insurgent Republicans George W. Norris of Nebraska and Victor Murdock of Kansas with Democratic support, broke the backbone of Cannon's power as Speaker through important rule changes, though he continued in office. Taft's role was passive but his chief supporters stood with Cannon, and upon the broad back of the resident of the White House went another burden—"Cannonism."

The Return from Elba

The Great Hunter, after fifteen months of slaying African lions and advising Europe's monarchs and ministers, was greeted in June, 1910, like a conquering hero. All too soon he was involved in politics despite a pledge to keep silent for two months. First, he went to the aid of Governor Hughes of New York in an unsuccessful battle for a direct primary law. Then, ostensibly to attend "Frontier Day" at Cheyenne, Wyoming, he departed on a western trip but found occasion to preach liberal doctrines en route. At Osawatomie, Kansas, he offered his

"New Nationalism," one of the best expressions of his philosophy of government. There is much evidence to show that he was trying to control the prairie fire in the West by indorsing the chief features of the progressive program.

Returning to New York, he and Root fought the machine and secured the nomination of Henry L. Stimson for governor with Taft's approval. When a Democrat defeated Stimson standpatters rejoiced, and declared that Roosevelt was politically dead. But in this same election Ohio and other Republican states went Democratic, as did the House of Representatives, while the insurgent Republicans held the balance of power in the Senate. Casualties were far heavier among standpatters than among progressive Republicans. If Roosevelt had been slapped down, so had his opponents. His relations with Taft had been strained by the growing rift in the party. He had not attacked the administration, but he had aided insurgents such as Beveridge and had been fought by standpat elements loyal to the President.

Taft's interest now centered on a reciprocity agreement with Canada providing for the removal or reduction of duties on many products by both countries. Most of the Taft Republicans and the Democrats joined forces to pass the bill over the opposition of western insurgent Republicans, representing farming and lumber interests, and some extreme protectionists including Joe Cannon. Taft's success was short-lived. Canada, at a general election, unexpectedly rejected the measure. The effect was to widen the gap in the Republican ranks. Oscar Underwood, shrewd Democratic floor leader of the new House, having aided the Taft Republicans on Canadian reciprocity, now joined with the insurgents to pass "popgun" low-tariff bills dealing with the most criticized parts of the Payne-Aldrich Tariff. The bipartisan combination also operated in the Senate, but Taft's veto killed these bills. The Democrats were profiting from Republican dissensions.

An apparent era of good feeling marked the Roosevelt-Taft relationship between November, 1910, and midsummer of 1911. They corresponded, and Roosevelt approved of Taft's annual message, supported Canadian reciprocity and other Taft policies, and seemed to be ready to go along with the administration in 1912.

Then things took a turn for the worse. Writing in the *Outlook,* Roosevelt upheld the new Arizona constitution, with a recall feature which produced a Presidential veto of statehood; and he criticized certain arbitration treaties negotiated by Taft. In October Attorney General Wickersham brought suit for a dissolution of the United States

Steel Corporation and included in the charges its acquisition of the Tennessee Coal and Iron Company in 1907. This had had Roosevelt's approval, and he regarded the suit as a piece of spite work on the part of Taft. Thenceforth reconciliation was impossible.

Yet more than personal differences were involved. Taft, it is true, had upheld most of Roosevelt's policies; but the progressives felt that more was needed: the times called for advances on many fronts, for inspirational leadership, for a new conception of the role of government. The insurgents who had battled the administration in Congress knew that the rather impressive list of progressive measures to its credit were concessions wrung from it by an aroused public opinion, that they had not had their inception in the White House. Taft was fundamentally a conservative: he cherished the sanctity of the courts, inveighed against the initiative and referendum and the recall, had little liking for the income tax, permitted Secretary of State Knox to practice "dollar diplomacy," catered to Aldrich, Cannon, Penrose, and other reactionary leaders, and gave aid and comfort to standpat opponents of insurgents in their home states. If he was a progressive he had strange ways of showing it.

The Steam Roller of 1912

Early in 1911 the leading insurgents in Congress organized the National Progressive Republican League; and they proposed Senator La Follette of Wisconsin as the candidate most likely to defeat Taft at the national convention. Organization work was carried on in a number of states, and in October a conference at Chicago indorsed La Follette. Roosevelt, while friendly, had refused to join the movement as it would have placed him openly in opposition to Taft. But it was apparent early in 1912 that La Follette could not defeat Taft. "Fighting Bob" was a courageous, uncompromising progressive; but his following was confined largely to the Middle West, and he had neither the organization nor the funds to build up support elsewhere. The growing feeling that only Roosevelt had a chance to win the nomination hurt La Follette; and after his long, rambling, repetitious speech before the Periodical Publishers Association of America at Philadelphia on February 2, unwisely undertaken under conditions of great fatigue and keen anxiety over a daughter's health, reports circulated that he had suffered a nervous breakdown. He soon recovered; but most of his support had quickly shifted to Roosevelt, who now consented to run.

By agreement among Roosevelt's closest advisers, a circular letter was prepared which seven Republican governors signed at a conference at Chicago, asking him to make the race. Before he replied Taft, in a speech at New York on February 12, attacked the "political emotionalists or neurotics" who were trying to pull down "the pillars of the temple of freedom and representative government." Roosevelt, aroused by the attack, told a reporter at Cleveland on February 21: "My hat is in the ring." That same day he addressed the Ohio Constitutional Convention at Columbus on "A Charter of Democracy."

The Columbus speech, one of Roosevelt's greatest efforts, outlined the progressive creed, including the initiative and referendum, the recall of elective officials, and a curbing of the power of the courts. As a substitute for the recall of judges he offered the recall of judicial decisions on constitutional questions—really a popular vote to determine whether they should stand oı be reversed. This would, of course, apply only to state courts, but it alarmed many of his followers and some of the faint-hearted deserted. Yet it was perfectly in keeping with his views, long held, on the conservatism and rigid legalism of the courts. If state constitutions could be amended by popular vote, why not the interpretation of them as well?

On February 24 he announced that he would accept the nomination, and the greatest pre-convention struggle in American history was on. Taft's control of the national committee and of the vast body of federal officeholders made it certain that most of the southern rotten boroughs would send Taft delegates to the national convention. Roosevelt had used the federal machine to name Taft in 1908; now he became the victim. Taft seemed to have the advantage in the East and the Middle West, where most of the state machines lined up for him; and among the state bosses on his side were Crane of Massachusetts, William Barnes, Jr., of New York, Penrose of Pennsylvania, James E. Watson of Indiana, and Reed Smoot of Utah.

But there was a fly in the ointment. The direct primary was coming into use, giving voters the right to express preferences directly for delegates to the national convention. In the past these had been elected by state or district conventions of delegates from local conventions. The voters, who took part only in primary meetings in wards and townships, were too remote to have much influence on the ultimate selections. The direct primaries gave Roosevelt his chance. In twelve states the results were overwhelming: Roosevelt had 278 delegates; Taft, 48; La Follette, 36. The great Republican states of Pennsylvania, Illinois, and Ohio, were among the Roosevelt successes. These were due in part to the activities of such practical politicians as Walter Brown and Dan Hanna of Ohio, William Flinn of Pennsylvania, and Governor Deneen of Illinois. Where the convention system prevailed, Taft had the advantage, though wherever possible the Rooseveltians sent contesting delegations, charging fraud and trickery, sometimes on flimsy grounds. In some southern states separate conventions were held. Altogether, 254 of 1,078 seats were in dispute for one reason or another.

Both candidates took an active part in the pre-convention battle, with speech-making tours on an unprecedented scale. Taft, deeply hurt by his old friend's challenge, could not contain himself and let loose an amazing torrent of recrimination at Roosevelt in a speech at Boston. "This wrenches my soul," he almost sobbed. The enraged Roosevelt struck back the next day at Worcester charging that Taft was the tool of the bosses and the great privileged interests and was biting the hand that had fed him. For the Ohio primaries both men covered the state, with a climax of name calling that included "demagogue," "fathead," "Jacobin," "apostate," and "brawler." A genuine difference of principles had degenerated into a cat-and-dog fight of personalities.

Control of the national convention depended on the decision of the national committee as to the contested seats. If it seated the Taft contestants until the convention could elect its officers, and gave them the right to vote on these preliminaries, the Taft forces would get control and, through the committee on credentials, would award the disputed seats permanently to their partisans. There were precedents aplenty for such action, but the number of seats at stake was exceptional. The national committee, chosen in 1908 by the delegates from each state, had a two-thirds Taft majority, though it had ceased to represent the sentiment of the party. By "steam-roller" tactics, as the Roosevelt men described its operations, it manufactured a majority for Taft by giving 235 of the 254 contested seats to the Taft claimants. Granted that many of the Roosevelt contests had an unsubstantial basis and were made for effect, it still seems reasonable to conclude that at least fifty Roosevelt delegates were unfairly deprived of seats.

Victor Rosewater of Nebraska, chairman of the national committee, called the convention to order on June 18 at noon in the Coliseum at Chicago. Refusing to hear any motions affecting the temporary roll, he proceeded, amid disorder and confusion, to hear nominations for temporary chairman. Elihu Root was presented as the committee's choice and was elected over Governor Francis E. McGovern of Wisconsin, offered by the Roosevelt men to get the La Follette support, by a vote of 558 to 501.[1] The Rooseveltians carried their fight for seventy-four of the disputed seats to the floor of the convention; but the "steam roller," operated by the outwardly imperturbable Root, rolled over them with a display of plausible precedents and, when necessary, brute force. Squads of police were present to uphold the rulings of the chair when violence threatened or disorders developed. Few present knew of the concealed barbed wire under the decorations around the railings to the rostrum. Every evening Root, Watson, Penrose, Crane, and two or three others planned the next day's proceedings, including the motions to be made and the rulings to be handed down by the chair.

Excitement was all the more intense from the presence of Roosevelt himself in Chicago. A last-minute decision brought him to the scene of battle to direct the strategy in person. Cheering mobs greeted him to roar approval at every opportunity. "I'm feeling like a bull moose," he said to a reporter, and forthwith the "Bull Moose" became the symbol of his cause. A brilliant speech at a great public meeting on Monday night June 17 ended in a note of stirring, almost mystical, idealism: "We stand at Armageddon," he said, "and we battle for the Lord."

The rough-and-tumble fighting in the convention was hardly Armageddon. Governor Hadley of Missouri, boyish, handsome, intelligent, self-possessed, the idol of the galleries, acted as floor leader for the Roosevelt men but failed to secure the substitution of Roosevelt contestants for Taft delegates in the disputed cases. A motion that delegates whose seats were disputed should not vote on any disputed cases was voted down, 567 to 507. The committee on credentials, elected by the Taft majority, went through the usual forms of hearing contests and then gave the Taft men permanent seats; the convention's "steam-roller" majority accepted these decisions in case after case, while the pro-Roosevelt galleries jeered and made noises in imitation of a steam roller in action. At this juncture Henry J. Allen of

[1] Fourteen La Follette delegates voted for other candidates; five did not vote.

Kansas announced that the Roosevelt men would no longer participate in the work of the convention, as it did not represent the voters of the Republican party: they would not leave but would sit in silent protest. He read a statement from Roosevelt advising this action.

Compromise was an impossibility. Taft had ceased to matter to the standpat leaders, who were merely using him to preserve their hold on the party machinery. They knew he could not be elected, but they were determined to defeat Roosevelt. Some among them—Watson of Indiana, for example—would have switched to the popular Governor Hadley as a compromise choice in the hope of yet saving the party, but neither camp seriously considered the proposal.

The rest of the convention proceedings were a formality. The platform was reported by Fairbanks of Indiana and it was adopted, 666 to 53, with 343 delegates not voting. Then Taft was nominated by Warren G. Harding, who with fatuous eloquence referred to him as "the greatest progressive of the age" and to his critics as "inspired by pap rather than patriotism." La Follette was nominated by Michael B. Olbrich of Wisconsin, his handful of delegates refusing to bolt. The vote was as follows: Taft, 561; Roosevelt, 107; La Follette, 41; Cummins, 17; Hughes, 2; not voting, 349; absent, 6. Vice President Sherman was then renominated, and the farce was over. The Taft margin of control had been a narrow one. Had Roosevelt received even half of the fifty contested seats that probably belonged to him, he might have been nominated. The slippery southern delegates would hardly have remained loyal to Taft when the band wagon hove in sight. The Old Guard leaders were even fearful that the convention might be prolonged over the week end, leaving them short of funds to pay the extra expenses of their southern following. These might then have gone home or have been enticed into the Roosevelt camp by the reputedly well filled moneybags of George W. Perkins (of the house of Morgan), Frank Munsey, and others.

The platform was on the whole rather liberal. It defended the integrity of the courts and opposed the recall of judges but favored a simplification of the process by which a judge could be removed from office. It favored legislation to clarify the anti-trust law and proposed a federal trade commission, without being definite as to its functions. It defended protective tariff but admitted that some existing rates were too high. It praised the Tariff Board as a scientific method of correcting injustices and condemned the Democrats for not providing funds for its continuance. It advocated a scientific inquiry into the high cost of living, a better banking and currency system, easier credit facilities for farmers, prohibition of corporation contributions to campaign funds, publicity for all contributions, continuance of conservation of natural resources, establishment of a parcel-post system, and an adequate navy and merchant marine.

As soon as the Republican convention adjourned the Roosevelt men held a mass meeting in Orchestra Hall to protest against its action and to plan for the future. Roosevelt promised to continue the fight and urged his followers to organize public sentiment for the progressive cause. The bolting delegates set up a committee, which announced a convention to meet in Chicago on August 5. The call of the Bull Moose was sounding through the land.

Many of the progressive group did not heed the call. The Senate insurgents were badly divided. Cummins of Iowa, Borah of Idaho, and Bourne of Oregon favored Roosevelt but not a third party. La Follette, Gronna of North Dakota, and Works of California eventually decided for Wilson. Dolliver of Iowa was dead. Six of the seven governors who had signed the call for Roosevelt to run against Taft backed away from the new party. Hadley was among them. But the bolters included Dixon, Bristow, Clapp and Poindexter of the Senate insurgents, former Senator Beveridge, Gifford and Amos Pinchot of Pennsylvania, William Allen White, fighting Kansas editor, Judge Ben B. Lindsey of Colorado, James R. Garfield, and a host of others. Lugging the moneybags were George W. Perkins and Frank Munsey.

The Battle of Baltimore

Now came the turn of the jubilant, yet worried, Democrats. They had been the real victors in the Chicago battle, which that eminent working journalist William Jennings Bryan had watched with interest from a press seat. The very next week he was in the thick of the fight as general of the Democratic progressives in the battle of Baltimore. The division was like that in the Republican party, but the long years of desert wanderings made both groups willing to forbear and to forgo much with the promised land in sight. Bryan was ready to stand at Armageddon, but a less advanced position might be acceptable; and at least he was not a candidate.

The party was overblessed with candidates in 1912. Democratic victories in 1910 had produced an unusual crop of state governors and had opened the way for two Congressional leaders by giving the party control of the House. Well in the lead in delegates was Speaker Champ Clark of Missouri, whose years of party regularity and faithful service in Congress seemed about to be rewarded. His House record, his western residence, and strong support from that section seemed to certify to his liberalism; but he had conducted a cautious campaign, and the conservatives were prepared to accept him if their first choices failed to reach the goal. He spoke the language of the party workers and understood their ways, and state machines tended to line up for him. William Randolph Hearst's newspaper support was a more dubious asset. Former Governor Joseph W. Folk had been regarded as Missouri's choice until Clark had entered the race and captured the state organization. Bryan, friendly to the progressive Folk, had doubts as to Clark's liberalism but did not openly oppose him. Oscar Underwood of Alabama, floor leader in the House, became a candidate despite Clark's seniority. His well planned strategy on reciprocity and the tariff, 1911-1912, had added to his reputation; but his southern residence and generally conservative principles did not suit progressives, and Bryan was hostile.

Among the governors Woodrow Wilson of New Jersey was outstanding. Called from the presidency of Princeton University by the New Jersey machine to give it the cloak of respectability, he had dumped the bosses overboard, assumed control of his party, and put through an unusual group of reform measures. He had also ditched his first sponsor, Colonel George Harvey of *Harper's Weekly*, whose contacts with the world of finance might have proved embarrassing. Without the enmities or vulnerable spots that go with a long career in politics, Governor Wilson ranked next to Clark in delegate strength. He was not a politician's candidate, and his chief managers were amateurs; but he had strong popular support and had aroused enthusiasm wherever he appeared. There was one awkward moment when a passage from a private letter he had written in 1907 was made public: "Would we could discover something at once dignified and effective to knock Mr. Bryan into a cocked hat." Friends of both men worked to undo the damage, and cordiality ruled at the Jackson Day banquet in January, 1912, when Wilson paid a graceful tribute to the Nebraskan in a speech that sent him far along the road toward the nomination. Bryan was pledged by his state's primary vote to support Clark, but preserved a friendly attitude toward both men.

Of the other governors, only Judson Harmon of Ohio was more than a favorite son. Attorney General under President Cleveland

and twice governor of Ohio, he was a man of sturdy qualities who would have made a strong candidate if conservatism had been in order. But Bryan was fixed in the determination that Harmon should not be named, and even in Ohio there was opposition to him from Newton D. Baker and a liberal group, who voted for Wilson in the national convention after the unit rule had been rescinded for states using direct primaries. Four governors, Thomas R. Marshall of Indiana, John Burke of North Dakota, Simeon E. Baldwin of Connecticut, and Eugene N. Foss of Massachusetts, were favorite sons, resting their hopes on a deadlock but willing to accept second place on the ticket.

Before the convention met Bryan gave notice that he would leave no stone unturned to defeat the "reactionaries." In a dramatic speech at the opening session, he opposed the choice of the national committee, Judge Alton B. Parker, for temporary chairman. Unable to find an acceptable alternative, he let his own name be used. Parker won by 579 votes to 508. Ollie James of Kentucky, satisfactory to Bryan, was then elected permanent chairman. The Nebraskan agreed to serve on the resolutions committee and helped write the platform, which was not adopted until after the nominations were made. But he was not mollified and his next move, after the preliminary work of the convention was completed, was an amazing one. He offered a resolution that the convention declare itself "opposed to the nomination of any candidate for President who is the representative of or under obligation to J. Pierpont Morgan, Thomas F. Ryan, August Belmont,[2] or any other member of the privilege-hunting and favor-seeking class." The suggestion for such a resolution had originated with his brother Charles, but the decision to propose it was his own. After great uproar and confusion, with some excited delegates demanding his head, the declaration was adopted by a large majority: 883 to 201-1/2. It meant little, but it served to smear the conservatives with the tar of Wall Street and keep Bryan before the country in his favorite role of guardian of the liberal temple.

The rest of the Thursday night session was consumed with interminable nominating and seconding speeches and with "spontaneous" applause, carefully measured in minutes and reported in the press.

At seven o'clock, Friday morning, the first ballot was taken. It gave Clark 440-1/2, Wilson 324, Harmon 148, Underwood 117-1/2, Marshall 31, Baldwin 22, Sulzer 2, Bryan 1, not voting 2. There was little change until the tenth ballot. Then Boss Charles Murphy shifted

[2] Belmont was a delegate from New York; Ryan, from Virginia.

the ninety votes of New York from Harmon to Clark. The ballot was delayed an hour while the Missouri delegation led a Clark parade, believing that it was all over. Their candidate had a majority and traditionally should receive the necessary two-thirds. The Wilson-Underwood lines held firm, however, and the break did not come, though Clark reached 556, eleven more than a majority.

Behind the scenes the Wilson and Underwood managers had reached an agreement to stand together against Clark. If Wilson withdrew, Underwood was to get his delegates. But Wilson's manager, William F. McCombs, became panicky and telephoned to Wilson for permission to release his delegates. The governor agreed and was about to send a congratulatory message to Clark when William G. McAdoo and other resolute lieutenants persuaded him to hold out. Aid came to the hard-pressed Wilsonians on the fourteenth ballot, on Saturday afternoon. Bryan stepped into the breach with a statement explaining his intention to change his vote from Clark to Wilson. He declared that he would not be a party to the nomination of any man who might be under obligation to the interests represented by Murphy and his New York delegation. Nebraska, accordingly, shifted to Wilson. The convention was in an uproar as the Clark men attacked Bryan; but their candidate's vote receded, and at adjournment on Saturday night Clark had 463-1/2; Wilson, 407-1/2.

The situation was almost without precedent. Not since Van Buren's failure in 1844 had a candidate failed to receive the required two-thirds after obtaining a majority. Clark rushed to Baltimore to defend himself before the convention but arrived after it had adjourned. He charged that an outrageous aspersion had been cast upon his character and demanded a retraction. Bryan answered that he had not criticized Clark for acting wrongfully but for failing to act.

Bryan's strategy was almost Machiavellian. He was climbing down from the Clark band wagon because Tammany Hall and Wall Street were getting on. Presumably Clark must do what no aspirant—Bryan included—had ever done before: tell delegates not to vote for him. The Clark men charged that the Commoner wanted to prolong the deadlock and get the nomination for himself.

Yet Bryan had a case. If Clark was a progressive, why had his friends lined up state machines, accepted Hearst's support, elected the conservative Parker temporary chairman, and thrown their hats in the air at Boss Murphy's significant shift? Could Clark, with the best intentions in the world, free himself from the obligations necessarily incurred? What a mark he would have made for Roosevelt, then organizing the Progressive party! Bryan realized the danger and struck at the forces behind Clark with deadly skill. Perhaps the blow was below the belt; but Bryan had received many such, and he knew the crowd he was dealing with.

That Sunday saw a wave of progressive sentiment demand the nomination of Wilson. Thousands of telegrams poured into Baltimore. The balloting on Monday reflected the change. On the twenty-eighth ballot Wilson passed Clark; but the deadlock continued into Tuesday. Then, influenced by the July heat, the strain on their pocketbooks, and the shift of Roger Sullivan, boss of Illinois, to Wilson, the anti-Wilson groups began to give way. On the forty-fifth Wilson had 633 votes, and the end was at hand. Underwood's lieutenants were ready to quit. On the next ballot all the candidates but Wilson withdrew; only the Missouri and California delegates and a scattering few from other states still voted for Clark, as a sentimental gesture. Senator Stone of Missouri then moved that the nomination be made unanimous—about 3:30 P.M. on the seventh day of this remarkable convention.

Underwood, whom Wilson preferred as a running mate, would not accept, and Governor Marshall was nominated by acclamation after two trial ballots put him well in the lead. Governor Burke was his chief competitor.

The platform, ready for several days, was adopted before the balloting for Vice President. Much of it repeated previous declarations. It demanded immediate downward revision of the tariff and assailed the Republican system of protection. It declared for the enforcement of criminal as well as civil law against trusts and trust officials and demanded additional legislation to put an end to private monopoly. Other planks were: ratification of the proposed constitutional amendments for an income tax and direct election of United States Senators; publicity for campaign contributions; Presidential preference primaries; a single term for President; and prohibition of corporation contributions to campaign funds. The work of the Democratic House was duly praised, and Republican extravagance condemned.

The platform favored regulation of railroads, express companies, and telegraph and telephone lines in interstate commerce, based in part on physical valuation of their property by the Interstate Commerce Commission. It advocated banking reform while condemning the Aldrich plan for a central bank. On labor, it simply repeated the declarations of 1908.

The platform was silent on the initiative and referendum and the recall. It recognized the need for reforms in the legal system to eliminate "delays, expense and uncertainties," but was cannily noncommittal as to the nature of the reforms. The traditional doctrine of state rights received the customary approval; but the rest of the platform was a practical denial of its existence.

The Bull Moose Bolt

On August 5, 1912, the newly formed Progressive party held its national convention at Chicago. Never had the Windy City witnessed such scenes in a convention: spontaneous, almost religious enthusiasm; delegates and galleries singing "Onward, Christian Soldiers" and the stirring "Battle Hymn of the Republic"; a score of women sitting as delegates; the awed professional politicians far outnumbered by the crusaders; and eloquent speeches that did not evade or point with pride but planned for the future. The chieftain of the Bull Moosers was there to inspire the mighty host of more than two thousand delegates, representing every state except South Carolina.

Albert J. Beveridge, whose devotion to Roosevelt had cost him his seat in the Senate, presided as temporary chairman and made an eloquent keynote speech. Roosevelt, appearing on the second day, received an hour-long demonstration, and then gave his "Confession of Faith," a detailed exposition of his program and a condemnation of the old parties as boss-controlled and incapable of serving as instruments of reform. Again he stood at Armageddon.

On the third day the convention took the name "Progressive" for the party, adopted the platform, and nominated Roosevelt for President and Governor Hiram Johnson of California as his running mate. Jane Addams of Hull-House fame made one of the seconding speeches —a recognition of the new party's liberal views toward women's rights. The convention adjourned in the spirit with which it had opened, singing the "Doxology."

The platform was the most comprehensive and detailed ever offered by an American party. Its aim was "to destroy this invisible government, to dissolve the unholy alliance between corrupt business and corrupt politics," through a host of reforms the progressive movement had spawned or inherited, including the initiative and referendum, direct primaries, direct election of United States Senators, the recall of elective officials, the recall of judicial decisions of state courts, and woman suffrage. It offered labor a broad program of social and industrial justice ranging from protective legislation in the interests of safety and health to social insurance against sickness, unemployment, and old age. Big business was to be regulated by a federal commission, the tariff was to be lowered, the currency was to be made more elastic, and income and inheritance taxes were approved. This was a middle-class reform program designed to cope with all the evils sprouting from the industrial revolution and to restore government to the people. It was not socialistic, as conservatives charged, but an antidote for socialism. It was Populism broadened and made respectable.

The Triumph of Wilson

The campaign of 1912 really ended with the three conventions. Woodrow Wilson's liberal views and aggressive campaigning soon made it clear that he would poll the normal party vote; and it would be sufficient to elect him, regardless of any other consideration. Had the Democrats nominated a conservative, a Progressive tidal wave might have carried Roosevelt to victory. Fortunately they had named their strongest man. Wilson, an easterner and once a conservative, had won the liberals by his courageous course as New Jersey's governor and had received the blessing of Bryan. Yet he steered clear of extremes and conducted a campaign that kept him safely between the conservatism of Taft and the radicalism of Roosevelt.

To nullify the fiery aggressiveness of Roosevelt, Wilson was put on the stump. Curiosity drew many to see what a professor-politician was like, and they were pleasantly surprised. The tall, homely, long-jawed candidate was no owlish, dry, remote scholar but a skillful phrase maker, occasionally witty, always clear and convincing, who knew what he wanted to say and said it well. In dealing with issues he dwelt on tariff and trusts; but he was more concerned with the regeneration of politics through a spiritual awakening. This sometimes worried his friends. Like the evangelist's appeal to "get right with God" and thus solve all mundane problems, it hardly seemed to come to grips with the hard facts of life. Roosevelt battled with devils and had a weapon to slay each one. Wilson's faultless sentences pleaded for a "new freedom," but his listeners too often were more inspired and uplifted than enlightened. Rather naïvely, he proposed to destroy private monopoly and restore competition, thus making business free and giving to every man the just rewards of his talents. Roosevelt termed such ideas "rural toryism." The Progressives' program of government regulation was more realistic. Yet, as President, Wilson came far nearer the Progressive position than his speeches forecast.

Samuel Gompers supported Wilson. The anti-injunction plank in the Democratic platform pleased him, and he also developed a great admiration for the candidate. The appeal of the Progressives' program of social justice failed to overcome union labor's doubts of Roosevelt himself and the segment of big business in his camp.

The party campaigns were managed much as in the past. William F. McCombs, manager of Wilson's pre-convention campaign, became Democratic national chairman. Suffering from ill health, he had to leave much of the work to William G. McAdoo, with whom he often disagreed. Henry Morgenthau handled Democratic finances efficiently, ending the campaign with a cash balance. Nearly ninety thousand persons contributed $1,159,446.33. Wilson warned the party treasurer not to accept contributions from certain dubious sources, and one gift was returned to avoid embarrassment to the candidate.

The Progressive chest was better filled than a third party had any right to expect.[3] Supporting Roosevelt were a few men of wealth such as Frank Munsey, magazine publisher, and George W. Perkins, once a partner of J. P. Morgan and an important figure in the International Harvester Company and other large corporations. Without their financial backing Roosevelt might have refused to run. Perkins, chairman of the executive committee, managed the campaign. Senator Joseph M. Dixon of Montana, although chairman of the national committee, was relegated almost to a figurehead role. The Democrats accused Roosevelt of favoring the International Harvester Company and the United States Steel Corporation during his Presidency by not prosecuting them under the Sherman Act, and much was made of his intimacy with Perkins.

Charles D. Hilles, Taft's private secretary, was chairman of the Republican national committee, and George R. Sheldon, a New York banker, was treasurer. Business, angry at Taft's trust prosecutions,

[3] The national committee reported receipts of $676,672.73, disbursements of $665,500.00, and liabilities of $5,714.31.

gave niggardly.[4] Taft made few speeches, as his cause was recognized as hopeless. In his acceptance speech he made an able defense of his administration but revealed his essential conservatism by picturing the dangers of socialism and the destruction of American institutions if either of his opponents triumphed.

The Republican split occasioned serious problems for the organization. Many Roosevelt men nominated for office or serving on committees resigned to join the Progressives, creating vacancies to be filled. In a few cases, the state organizations and candidates supported Roosevelt. In California and South Dakota the Republican electoral tickets were pledged to Roosevelt, and the Taft men played the unhappy role of bolters. In many states where the organization forced pledges of loyalty to Taft upon state and Congressional candidates, separate Progressive tickets appeared. Fusion arrangements were sometimes made whereby Republican candidates adopted a policy of neutrality to save their necks. The Progressives, confronted with the problem of organizing a great national party between June and November, preferred to concentrate on the head of the ticket and make terms with the Republicans on many lesser offices or let them go by default. This explains the small number of Progressive Congressmen elected in proportion to the total Presidential vote.

The usual third parties appeared: the Socialists with Debs again as candidate; the Socialist Labor group with Arthur E. Reimer; and the Prohibitionists with Eugene W. Chafin. The Socialists, despite dissension at their national convention between conservatives and direct actionists, conducted an aggressive campaign. The unrest that had produced the progressive movement in the old parties helped their cause, and a number of victories in local elections encouraged them to believe that 1912 would bring a great increase in their vote, even though the new third party would attract many radicals.[5]

The campaign drew to its close without the excitement that the convention struggles had seemed to foreshadow. The most dramatic incident occurred on October 14 in Milwaukee when an insane man attempted to assassinate Roosevelt. The bullet entered the right side

[4] Receipts were reported at $1,076,391.51; disbursements, $1,076,548.57. These and the figures reported for the other parties were filed with the clerk of the House of Representatives in accordance with the act of 1910.

[5] Milwaukee had a Socialist mayor and a Socialist Congressman, Emil Seidel and Victor Berger, elected in 1910. In 1912 it was estimated that 1,141 Socialists held elective offices in the nation.

of his chest and lodged in a rib. Showing his usual fortitude, Roosevelt delivered his scheduled speech without medical treatment. Although the wound proved to be not too serious, it ended his speaking tour. Both Taft and Wilson telegraphed their regrets and suspended campaign activities until he recovered. On October 30 he addressed a great New York gathering at Madison Square Garden, where the faithful showed their loyalty in the shadow of defeat.

On November 5 the Democrats were successful for the first time since 1892. Wilson had 435 electoral votes; Roosevelt, 88 (Michigan, Minnesota, Pennsylvania, South Dakota, Washington, and 11 of California's 13); and Taft, 8 (Utah, Vermont).[6] Wilson polled 6,296,547 popular votes, to 4,126,020 for Roosevelt and 3,486,720 for Taft. This made Wilson a minority President; but it would be a mistake to assume that he would have lost if he had had only one major opponent. In the two-party battle of 1910 the Democrats had won a majority in the House and had elected governors in several Republican states. The tide had not changed in 1912, and Wilson was to be victorious in 1916 when conditions were much less favorable.

The surprising increase in the Socialist vote from 420,820 in 1908 to 897,011 gave clear proof of the country's swing to the left. The liberalism of Roosevelt and Wilson kept the Debs total from being greater. The Prohibition vote, which had been around 250,000 for two campaigns, dropped to 209,923 in 1912. Reimer, Socialist Labor, had 29,079.

The new Congress was Democratic: the Senate 50 to 44, not counting one Progressive and one vacancy; the House 291 to 144. Of the 144, only about 15 were Progressives though many others had been elected with Progressive assistance. The situation was much the same in the various state legislatures, thus placing the new party under a serious handicap. With few officeholders and almost no patronage, it was not in a good position to establish itself as a major party. But much depended on what happened to the Democrats under Wilson's leadership.

[6] Vice President Sherman, running with Taft, died on October 30. The eight Republican electors cast their Vice Presidential votes for Nicholas Murray Butler.

22

The Rule of Wilson

The Party and the Man

Three major elements made up the Democratic party that prepared to feast at the federal crib after sixteen lean years. In the East and the Middle West its backbone consisted of foreign-born and second generation Americans, centered in the cities and under the control of such bosses as Charles Murphy of Tammany, Thomas Taggart of Indiana, and Roger Sullivan of Illinois. Reform to these politicos was weighed in the scales of success at the polls. In the rural South, the dominant leadership was conservative and state-rights. Lower tariff rates and anti-trust legislation were acceptable enough; but the social justice doctrines of the progressives did not appeal to the ruling groups in a region where poverty and illiteracy were widespread and the race question was ever present. In the Bryan West the party was agrarian-liberal, and a reform administration would have strong support. Unfortunately, western Democratic members of Congress were mostly newcomers, lacking in experience, and by the seniority rules in the two Houses, could not claim important chairmanships, which went southward. The new President was confronted with a situation requiring the most skillful handling.

Heredity and environment combined to produce in Woodrow Wilson a strong will, deep convictions, a high sense of duty, and "a single-track mind," as he put it. Scotch-Irish on his father's side, Scotch on his mother's, this son of a Presbyterian minister was brought up on a Calvinist intellectual and moral diet that strengthened the tough Scotch fiber of his character. He was born in Virginia, though his parents came from the North, and lived his boyhood and youth in a Presbyterian manse, first at Augusta, Georgia, and then at Columbia South Carolina His education divested him of any provincialism. He did his undergraduate work at Princeton, studied law at the University of Virginia, and received his graduate training in the study of politics at Johns Hopkins. Years of teaching and scholarly writing led to a professorship at Princeton and then to the presidency of that university. Here he received a certain practical training in petty politics in his dealings with trustees and faculty and alumni donors to endowments. Halted by opposition in the faculty and the board of trustees in his efforts to democratize aristocratic Princeton, he accepted nomination for the New Jersey governorship from the state bosses and continued his political apprenticeship in a wider field.

A strong believer in executive leadership, fitted by temperament and training to lead, Wilson took control of the Democratic party and used the caucus to produce unity and enforce discipline in Congress. But a more important weapon was public opinion. From his limited political experience he realized that his greatest strength lay in appealing to the voters. Party organizations could be whipped into line, lobbyists confounded, and legislators put on the right track by the pressure of an aroused public. His early successes led him to believe that the people would understand and uphold unfailingly his own uncompromisingly righteous principles whenever he chose to present his case to them. In the end, his faith in the power of his rhetoric led to his undoing. A master politician needs to know how to handle every weapon in the arsenal of politics.

Patronage matters wearied Wilson. In cabinet appointments he leaned heavily on Colonel Edward M. House of Texas, adviser and friend, and Joseph P. Tumulty of New Jersey, his shrewd private secretary. Bryan in the State Department, Josephus Daniels of North Carolina, Secretary of the Navy, and Postmaster General Albert S. Burleson of Texas were able politicians and helped the President with "the men on the Hill." Bryan's appointment was a pledge of faith to the progressives. There were fears that these two strong-willed men would soon clash, but Bryan, vastly pleased with his high office, interested himself chiefly in making "cooling-off" treaties with other nations, banning alcoholic drinks from his official dinners, and rewarding deserving Democrats with jobs. When the Mexican situation and World War I produced crises, Wilson wrote the key notes, and Bryan merely signed his name. After the sinking of the *Lusitania*, Bryan was disturbed by the administration's strong stand against submarine warfare and took the honorable course of resigning in June, 1915.

Far closer to the President than any member of the cabinet was Colonel House, a wealthy man with a flair for politics and a distaste for the limelight. This self-effacing, shrewd man of the world attached himself to the Wilson cause in 1911, swung the forty Texas delegates to him at Baltimore, and became his most trusted adviser. He slipped in and out of the White House with messages from politicians, business leaders, and diplomats, serving as a confidential agent and unofficial contact man for the aloof, idealistic President; but he reflected, he did not determine, his chief's viewpoints.

Joseph P. Tumulty had come from New Jersey with Wilson. His Irish geniality and his skill at the game of politics were invaluable to his chief in dealing with press and politicians. The President found the majority of Washington correspondents interested in "the personal and trivial" rather than policies. His press conferences were a bore to him.

The New Freedom in Operation

Two constitutional amendments, ratified in 1913, made Wilson's path easier. Both were products of the progressive upsurge. The Sixteenth Amendment, authorizing taxes on incomes, simplified tariff reduction; the Seventeenth, providing for popular election of United States Senators, weakened the Senate as a citadel of reaction and obstructionism by making the members directly responsible to the voters.

President Wilson's program, which he effectively presented to Congress in person—a return to the Washington-Adams precedent of "the speech from the throne"—included tariff revision, a new banking and currency system, reforms in industry and agriculture, and the conservation of human as well as natural resources. When Congress hesitated overlong, the former schoolmaster used the whip.

By October, 1914, after months of arduous work under Presidential pressure, Congress had completed significant reform legislation in three important fields. The Underwood-Simmons Tariff Act provided substantial reductions in tariff rates and included an income tax. The Federal Reserve Act gave organization and an elastic currency to the national banking system and put it under public control. The Clayton Anti-Trust Act and the Federal Trade Commission Act attempted to define business practices which tended to produce private monopoly, and to curb their use. The Clayton Act also declared that strikes, picketing, and boycotts did not violate federal laws, and limited the use of the injunction in labor disputes. Because of the complex problems involved, neither act lived up to the expectations of its proponents; but both were forward steps of major importance.

Other reform acts voted by this and the following Congress in the fields of farm credit, seamen's welfare, agricultural education, conservation, and child labor furnished further proof of the liberalism of the administration. Wilson's ascendancy over his party evoked comparisons with Jackson and Jefferson. Nor was it merely a matter of bills passed. He freed the Democratic party from its worship of the state-rights fetish, held its discordant elements together in a program of reform, gained the confidence of farmers and organized labor, and refused to let the opposition of big business deter him from his chosen course.

But there were breakers ahead. A business recession in the spring of 1914 was attributed to an overdose of reform. Conservative newspapers, hoping that a reaction against liberalism was at hand, began to attack the administration. In midsummer Europe suddenly exploded into World War I. American business and finance turned panicky; imports fell off, and new excise taxes were levied to furnish needed revenue. This atmosphere of worry and uncertainty drew attention away from the solid achievements of the administration in the domestic field, and the fall elections brought a Republican revival. The Democratic margin in the House fell to 29, though the party gained two seats in the Senate. New York and Ohio elected Republican governors. The Progressive party's vote fell to less than half the total of 1912, and it elected only seven members of the House. The bolters were going back to the old party. Yet the Democrats could console themselves that they had retained control of Congress in what was virtually a two-party battle with conditions less favorable than in 1910 and 1912.

The years 1914-1916 were utterly different from the first months of Wilson's term. In becoming President he had not expected foreign complications to interfere with his domestic reform program; and he had not prepared himself specifically to deal with them. Almost at once he was confronted with problems of dollar diplomacy in China, revolution and civil war in Mexico, a proposed protectorate over Nicaragua, friction with Colombia over the "rape of Panama," difficulties with Japan over the treatment of Japanese in California, and a dispute with England over the exemption of American coastwise shipping from tolls on the Panama Canal. These were only partially solved when war in Europe dwarfed all other issues, foreign and domestic.

World War I brought troubles and burdens like those of Jefferson a century before. President Wilson's plea to Americans to be neutral in thought as well as in deed fell on deaf ears. The German invasion of Belgium, stories of German atrocities, the sinking of the *Lusitania*, and other incidents and influences made the great majority of Americans pro-Ally while German-Americans and a small but vociferous group of British-hating Irish-Americans took the other tack. Wilson's handling of neutral rights drew fire from both extremes. Roosevelt, who had become a bitter critic of the Kaiser and all his works, charged the President with spinelessness after the sinking of the *Lusitania* and declared that he was the worst chief executive since Buchanan. Eastern Republican newspapers took the same line in their editorials. Roosevelt also assailed the President for tardiness in advocating military preparedness. The ever present militarism in Roosevelt's make-up made him one of the war's first victims. Largely forgotten was his progressivism; and he resumed friendly relations with Root and other conservatives. Patriotic and preparedness organizations, financed and run by men high in the business world who disliked Wilson, were looking with favor on the radical of 1912.

Yet at the other extreme were the pacific-minded and the "hyphenated Americans" who felt that the President was moving toward war. Their viewpoint was reflected by Bryan's resignation during the *Lusitania* crisis, by German-American charges that Wilson was pro-British, and by the attempt of a group of western and southern Congressmen to pass the Gore-McLemore Resolutions forbidding Americans to travel on belligerent merchant ships. Altogether, Wilson was placed in an unhappy situation; yet it seems to be certain that his moderate policy had wide support outside the pro-British East and certain German-American centers. Neutrality, though it was working in one-sided fashion in practice, was definitely preferred to war. This was the situation when the campaign of 1916 began.

Republican Reunion

The Old Guard Republicans, in control of the party machinery and much encouraged by the elections of 1914, were prepared to welcome back the Progressive bolters without insisting upon sackcloth and ashes, provided only that Roosevelt be eliminated as a candidate. To facilitate their return the Republican national committee in 1913 revised somewhat the basis of representation in national conventions to correct in part the overrepresentation of the South, which had enabled Taft to win the nomination in 1912. This also reduced the number of potential purchasables in conventions.

Roosevelt was the major problem of the Republicans. He had stumped for Progressive candidates in 1914 but had no illusions about the party's future. He deplored its lack of practical men and the "well-meant extravagances" of its reform enthusiasts. Clearly he was not made for lost causes. But the very existence of the party was a threat to Republican success, and Roosevelt and practical George W. Perkins realized its bargaining value. The shift of public interest to war problems and national defense offered a bridge by which the Roosevelt following might return to the old party if proper terms were offered. But this raised the question of a suitable Presidential candidate. Roosevelt denied that he would try for the Republican nomination and declared that it would be a mistake to name him unless the country had in its mood "something of the heroic." This left the door quite ajar. The Progressives assembled at Chicago on June 7, at the same time as the Republicans, determined to nominate him; but Perkins came to negotiate.

The search for a suitable Republican candidate produced a flock of favorite sons of doubtful availability. Elihu Root reluctantly consented to the use of his name and was supported by eastern Republican notables with strong business backing; but his seventy-one years were an almost insuperable barrier, even if the Progressives could have forgotten his Wall Street connections and his role in the bitter Chicago battle of 1912. Other possibilities were Senators John W. Weeks of Massachusetts, Albert B. Cummins of Iowa, and Lawrence Y. Sherman of Illinois, former Senator Theodore E. Burton of Ohio, and former Vice President Fairbanks of Indiana—all respectable but undistinguished conservatives except Cummins, who did not suit the Old Guard. Not one of them fitted the situation. A man was needed who had not been involved in the split of 1912, who had not offended Roosevelt, and whose record was completely blank on every significant question. Such a paragon of negation could be found only in the political vacuum in which the Supreme Court is supposed to function.

The availability of Supreme Justice Charles E. Hughes was high. He had been in the judicial cloister, protected from the sins of politics, since 1910—when the Republican party was in power, the Bull Moose known only as a lubberly beast of the northern woods, and wars regarded as Balkan pastimes. Remembered as the high-minded reform governor of New York, he might suit progressives without alarming conservatives. Old Guard leaders of New York, with unpleasant memories of him as a hard man to handle, preferred Elihu Root and divided their delegation; but he had strong support from the unpledged of other states and was a second choice of many favorite-son backers. In keeping with the traditions of the court Hughes preserved a sphinxlike silence as to the nomination and refused to enter the primaries; but Governor Whitman of New York, W. Murray Crane of Massachusetts, and other astute leaders took care of his interests. It was Hughes against the field when the Republican convention assembled on June 7 in the Coliseum at Chicago.

The convention was unusually dull. The oratory was uninspired, and enthusiasm was lacking except when the galleries yelled for "Teddy." Senator Warren G. Harding was duly cheered when he made an old-fashioned flag-waving speech as temporary chairman, but attracted more attention by his good humor and little pleasantries after being chosen as permanent presiding officer also. The Wisconsin delegation stirred up some ill feeling by offering a radical substitute for the report of the resolutions committee, but it was shouted down without a roll call.

The platform assailed Wilson's foreign policy as one of "shifty expedients" and "phrasemaking," and promised an "honest neutrality" and the protection of the rights of American citizens at home and abroad. It denounced the administration's handling of Mexican problems at some length but was conveniently vague as to the Republican position. A strong national defense plank, criticisms of Democratic policies toward business, denunciation of the Underwood Tariff, and indorsement of woman suffrage by state action covered other issues of political significance.

The platform was markedly negative in character and it made only vague commitments on the troublesome issues of foreign relations. It strove to please equally Theodore Roosevelt and the members of the German-American Alliance. To the candidate was left the impossible problem of clarification.

The Progressives still hoped to force Roosevelt upon the Republicans. Their convention went ahead with a fine display of enthusiasm that deserved a better fate than was meted out to it. It adopted a platform suspiciously like the Republican and then listened to speeches while a committee conferred with a Republican committee as to candidates; but agreement proved to be impossible. The Republicans would not take Roosevelt; the Progressives had no alternative, though willing to consider Republican suggestions. Finally, the obvious solution, a telephone call to Roosevelt, discreetly aloof at Oyster Bay, produced an astonishing proposal—Senator Henry Cabot Lodge. To ask the Progressives to take the archconservative Massachusetts Brahmin was an insult to their principles and to their intelligence. The Republican conferees were equally aghast, then proposed Hughes.

By this time the Republican convention had begun to ballot. The first trial, taken Friday night, gave Hughes 253-1/2, Weeks 105, Root 103, Cummins 85, Burton 77-1/2, Fairbanks 74-1/2, Roosevelt 65, Sherman 66 and several others smaller numbers. On the second ballot Hughes had 328-1/2. Adjournment overnight did not help the efforts of certain organization leaders to head off this "Wilson with whiskers," and the third ballot ended the opposition. Hughes got 949-1/2 of the 987 votes. Former Vice President Fairbanks, also bewhiskered, was named to run with him.

Meanwhile, what of the Progressives? Their convention had spent a weary time, restrained with difficulty by George W. Perkins and other compromising leaders, while negotiations were conducted with the Republicans. Finally, learning that Hughes was nearing the Republican nomination, the delegates broke loose, rejected Perkins's proposals of Lodge and Hughes with hisses and jeers, and nominated Roosevelt just before the Republican roll call was completed. John M. Parker of Louisiana was selected for Vice President. Most of the delegates hopefully awaited word from Oyster Bay that the battle was on. But the reply of Roosevelt was a conditional refusal; his final decision would be determined by the attitude of Hughes on the vital questions of the day. A wave of anger swept over the convention at what seemed like a betrayal by its trusted leader. The delegates adjourned in bitterness and defiant resentment, leaving to the national committee the determination of the party's future course.

When, after a conference with Hughes, Roosevelt announced his definite withdrawal, the Progressive national committee voted 32 to 15 against a separate ticket. However, the Vice Presidential nominee, John M. Parker, remained in the race for a time and eventually turned to Wilson, as did many others who felt that the bitterest enemies of the things they stood for were in the Republican camp. Generally, the pro-Hughes Progressives were the personal following of Roosevelt and the political professionals, not the ardent believers in progressive principles or the advanced social reformers. The conglomeration of materials in the third party had been held together by the magic of Roosevelt's name. When that was removed they fell apart. Blind adoration of a magnetic leader is no substitute for organization and planning. The Progressives had not envisioned a future without Roosevelt. Those who would have kept up the fight had no one to lead them.

If Roosevelt had declined the Progressive nomination earlier, the core of genuine believers might have determined on a course of action to preserve the party for future usefulness. It might have served as a supporting left wing for Wilsonian progressivism or as a refuge for liberals if both the old parties turned conservative. But Roosevelt, unconcerned about the fate of Progressive principles with the drums of war throbbing in his ears, saw in the third party only an instrument to be used against the man he had come to hate. When it ceased to have value for bargaining purposes, he killed it. But thousands of Progressive voters who would follow Roosevelt the crusading liberal would not follow Roosevelt the warmonger. Their weight was felt in November, 1916.

The Democratic convention, meeting at St. Louis on June 14, was a ratifying rather than a nominating body. Wilson, of course, was renominated,[1] and, while rumors persisted that he preferred another running mate, Vice President Marshall was renominated by acclamation and with his complete approval. The keynote speech, by former Governor Martin Glynn of New York, played unexpectedly upon the peace theme and created much enthusiasm with a defense of Wilson and his policy of avoiding war. Senator Ollie James of Kentucky, permanent chairman, began his speech with domestic policies, but stirred the delegates most when he talked of the triumphs of peace. "Who would say that we can afford to swap horses while crossing a bloody stream?"

The platform, most of it the work of Wilson himself, caused some difficulty in committee. Senators William J. Stone and James A. Reed of Missouri thought the plank on Americanism too strongly worded

[1] One delegate from Illinois opposed the motion to name Wilson by acclamation, and so the chair proclaimed him nominated by a vote of 1,092 to 1.

for states with large German populations. But word from the White House was sufficient to prevent any changes. A southern bloc opposed the plank recommending woman suffrage by state action on the floor of the convention; but it was upheld, 888-1/2 to 181-1/2.

A large part of the platform, longer even than that of 1912, recited the accomplishments of the Wilson administration and defended its policies, domestic and foreign. It indorsed a tariff commission bill pending in Congress, favored preparedness measures, assailed as disloyal all groups and organizations promoting the interests of a foreign power, and expressed the view that the United States should assist the world in securing settled peace and justice.

A significant statement commended "the splendid diplomatic victories of our great President, who has preserved the vital interests of our Government and its citizens, and kept us out of war." Without any pledge for the future, the inference from platform praise and convention oratory was that Wilson was a peace President and would continue to be one. Americanism, or national unity, as opposed to the disloyalty of "hyphenated" groups, was foremost in Wilson's thoughts, and he wanted this theme stressed at the convention. But the delegates yelled loudest and longest when Glynn and James and Bryan (who was invited to the platform) contrasted peaceful America and war-torn Europe and praised Wilson for the victories of peace. Here was a clue to the feeling of the large part of the nation that lived away from the Atlantic seaboard, and the Democratic strategists were quick to see the value of such an appeal.

Three other parties put candidates into the field. The Socialist Labor group named Arthur Reimer of Massachusetts; the Prohibitionists, former Governor J. Frank Hanly of Indiana. The Socialists, using a referendum instead of a convention, nominated Allan L. Benson of New York when Debs refused to be a candidate.

"He Kept Us Out of War"

Hughes, asserting his prerogative as the party's nominee, selected as campaign chairman William R. Willcox of New York City, a man not well known to party leaders. Cornelius N. Bliss, Jr., served as treasurer of the national committee. Wilson displaced William F. McCombs with Vance McCormick of Pennsylvania as chairman of the Democratic national committee, while Henry Morgenthau looked after finances and Robert W. Woolley directed publicity. On the whole the Democratic campaign was handled much better than the Republican, although it was not so well financed.

Hughes was one of the country's finest legal minds, but the task assigned to him was an impossible one. A man of force and sincerity, he was not gifted in equivocating; but any other course would cost votes. His dilemma on the major issues of foreign policy was a cruel one. He had to criticize Wilson's handling of Mexican difficulties and his failure to compel respect for American rights at sea. This provoked Democratic charges that Hughes's more vigorous policy might lead to wars with Mexico and Germany, which, of course, he must disprove. German-Americans and many pacifists believed that Wilson had dealt too harshly with Germany; the friends of the Allies, as represented by Roosevelt, charged him with spinelessness. Hughes had to satisfy both groups. The Democrats could insist that Wilson had preserved peace; no one knew what Hughes might do. On preparedness the Republican candidate was more effective, for Wilson had been tardy in advocating defense measures. But his conversion and the steps taken satisfied most voters. Americans were not military-minded, and in some quarters the Hughes-Roosevelt position smelled of the militarism charged against the Kaiser.

Among domestic questions, only the tariff offered a safe issue, for Wilson's accomplishments in other respects were hard to attack. But a war boom had ended the recession of 1914, and Republican warnings of bread lines to come under the Underwood Tariff fell flat. Hughes blundered in criticizing the Adamson Act to authorize an eight-hour day for railway trainmen, enacted in September, 1916, at Wilson's suggestion to avert a nation-wide rail strike. Without opposing the eight-hour day in principle, he assailed Wilson for submitting to a pressure group. His forthright stand was taken in speeches in Ohio, headquarters of the Railway Brotherhoods. Organized labor, already suspicious of Hughes, swung sharply to Wilson, and Ohio proved to be a crucial state.

An inadvertent blunder probably cost him the vote of California. Here Governor Hiram Johnson, Roosevelt's running mate in 1912, was a candidate for the Republican nomination for United States Senator and was bitterly opposed by an Old Guard faction headed by National Committeeman William H. Crocker. Johnson of course was supporting Hughes and, as governor, might have been expected to preside at a Hughes meeting or confer with the candidate when he arrived in California in August. Crocker, however, made all the arrangements and kept the two men apart, even though at one time they were in the same hotel. This unnecessary snub was repaid in full when Johnson won the senatorial nomination and was elected in November by 300,000 votes, while Hughes lost the state by 3,773. Like the Reverend Mr. Burchard in 1884, Crocker achieved the unenviable distinction of defeating his own candidate. But Hughes ought to have realized the dynamite in the situation and made it a point to conciliate Johnson.

Despite the bogging down of the Hughes campaign shown by the decline in betting odds from two to one to ten to seven, the Republicans expected to win. The return of the Progressives, and German-American and Irish-American resentments toward Wilson, seemed to insure Democratic defeat.

But the Democratic strategy was to write off the East as lost and center their efforts on the states west of Pennsylvania. They had two powerful appeals. One was Wilson's progressive accomplishments. Progressives who put principles ahead of loyalty to Roosevelt came trooping into the Wilson camp, especially west of the Mississippi.

The other appeal was, "He kept us out of war," one of the most effective slogans ever used in a campaign. It did tremendous damage to Hughes away from the eastern seaboard, particularly in farming sections with pacifist and isolationist leanings, and in the woman suffrage states of the West. Roosevelt became a Democratic asset in this connection. His belligerent utterances were quoted and coupled with a statement of Hughes that he and Roosevelt were in complete accord. A pre-election Democratic paid advertisement carried this appeal:

You are working, not fighting!
Alive and happy, not cannon-fodder!
Wilson and peace with honor?

Or

Hughes with Roosevelt and war.

This must have been galling to Roosevelt, who was not happy in his support of the "bearded iceberg" and was reported to have remarked that Hughes was the kind of man who would vote for Wilson.

Wilson, with Congress in session all summer, could not campaign then. Later he yielded to party leaders and spoke at Omaha, Indianapolis, Chicago, and Cincinnati, key points in Democratic strategy.

Speeches at Buffalo and New York City just before the election were concessions to the feeling that New York must not be abandoned without a struggle. A great parade headed by Sheriff Alfred E. Smith preceded the final rally at Madison Square Garden, where thousands, unable to get in, clamored for a sight of the President. The enthusiasm was metropolitan only; the state voted for Hughes.

The campaign closed with the Democratic candidate much stronger than at the beginning but with Wall Street still betting on Hughes. The returns up to midnight, November 7, bore out this view. Even the Democratic papers in the East conceded defeat. As the returns from the Middle West came in with only Ohio for Wilson, the President privately admitted to a feeling of relief that the great burden of office had been lifted from him. A great Democratic "victory" banquet given by Henry Morgenthau for party leaders and cabinet members at the Biltmore Hotel in New York that night was a "morgue-like" affair while rejoicing Republicans serenaded Hughes at the Astor with two bands. Toward morning, as word came from the West, doubt succeeded certainty. Minnesota and California were the last to report, and not until Thursday afternoon was it known that Wilson had the latter state. This elected him, regardless of Minnesota, which finally went to Hughes by a plurality of fewer than four hundred votes.

Wilson had 277 electoral votes, Hughes 254. The popular vote was in Wilson's favor, 9,127,695 to 8,533,507.[2] The new House of Representatives was almost evenly divided between Republicans and Democrats, while the new Senate was Democratic by ten votes, instead of the former sixteen. Clearly it was a Wilson rather than a Democratic party victory. His liberalism and his avoidance of war received a vote of confidence. Other factors were incidental. Among them were the failure of the Republicans to get a solid German-American vote, the poor strategy of Hughes and his managers, the swashbuckling of Roosevelt, the effect of the Adamson Law, the apparent swing of the Mormon voters of Utah and neighboring states to Wilson, the peculiar California situation, and the support given to Wilson by the woman suffrage states of the West.

The alignment was singularly like that of 1896 with one or two

[2] The minor parties were as follows: Benson, Socialist, 585,113; Hanly, Prohibition, 220,506; Reimer, Socialist Labor, 13,403. The sharp decline in the Socialist vote was due probably to the party's extreme antiwar position, which was confused in the popular mind with pro-Germanism, and to the attractions of Wilsonian liberalism for many radicals and pacifists.

significant exceptions. Wilson had the solid South and the border states except Delaware and West Virginia (which gave Hughes 7 of its 8 votes); all the trans-Mississippi West except Oregon, Minnesota, South Dakota, and Iowa; and Ohio and New Hampshire east of the Mississippi. Hughes had the remaining area from New England westward to South Dakota, including the great industrial and older farming sections. He carried substantially the McKinley states of 1896 with two fatal exceptions, California and Ohio.

Hughes and the Republicans in a sense were fortunate in defeat. The Democrats had to bear the chief responsibility for American entry into the war. If Hughes had won, he could scarcely have avoided doing what Wilson did in 1917. Yet the Democrats then could have thrust upon him and his party the blame for what followed. It might have given the war a partisan aspect and engulfed the Republicans in the great revulsion of 1920. Luck was really with them in 1916, for to the successful peace candidate fell the momentous decision to make war.

Politics Adjourned for the War?

Members of Congress, regardless of party, supported the President in his break of diplomatic relations with the German government after it inaugurated unrestricted submarine warfare, and only "a little group of willful men, representing no opinion but their own," filibustered in the Senate long enough to prevent the passage of his bill to arm merchant ships.[3] The situation grew rapidly worse as American ships were attacked, and Wilson finally reached the fateful decision to declare war. The new Congress, called into special session on April 2, 1917, heard the President's solemn message and voted its approval, the Senate 82 to 6, the House 373 to 50. Political considerations played no part; the declaration of war was approved by both parties.

With politics adjourned for the war, votes in Congress had slight political significance. Republicans supported war measures as strongly as Democrats, and Wilson ignored politics in drawing leaders of the business world into government service. Yet criticisms of mismanagement and inefficiency in the conduct of the war presently found vent in Congress, and politics inevitably came into the picture.

[3] Twelve Senators were opposed, eleven taking part in the filibuster. The bill passed the House, 403 to 13.

Roosevelt, disappointed at the administration's refusal to let him lead a volunteer division overseas, saw only muddling and mismanagement through the distorting lenses of his emotions. He was an ardent supporter of the war, and Republican leaders realized the soundness and political strength of his position. He was urged to run for governor of New York, but he refused. The Presidential nomination in 1920 seemed to lie ahead for him, when death suddenly intervened on January 6, 1919.

In the state and Congressional elections of 1918 the political truce broke down. The Republicans, while vigorously proclaiming their support of the war, struck oblique blows at the administration through conventions and party newspapers. In the western farm belt, southern domination of Congress was charged upon the Democrats, and the administration's failure to fix the price of cotton, booming because of a crop scarcity, was contrasted with its actions with regard to wheat, wool, and other products. Embarrassed by such tactics, Democratic candidates looked to the White House for support. Wilson responded on October 25 with an appeal to the country to return a Democratic Congress. The Republicans then proclaimed that he had broken the party truce. Actually it had been undermined long before. The election produced Republican margins of forty-five in the House and two in the Senate. The gains were chiefly in the Middle West—proof of the success of the sectional appeal in an area where there was a large amount of under-cover opposition to the war.

The blow was a severe one. Had Wilson kept silent, the result would have been much the same; but at least he could have met his fellow diplomats at Paris in the far stronger position of a nonpartisan President. As it was, he seemed to have been repudiated by the voters just as he was preparing to translate into action his ideal of world cooperation to make war impossible.

President Wilson has been much criticized for attending the peace conference in person. A more serious error was his failure to take along some eminent Republican leader—Root or Hughes or Taft—and a United States Senator or two. Colonel House, Secretary of State Lansing, and Henry White, despite their qualifications as diplomats, had no political value in the battle that would have to be waged at home. Wilson underestimated the importance of politics in the field of diplomacy. He had been too successful in the grand strategy of appealing to public opinion in the past to appreciate the value of clever tactics and a little guile. Then, too, he found it troublesome to work with men of great prominence whom he did not completely trust. Even Lansing felt snubbed by his chief, and before the conference was over the faithful House was under a cloud. Neither man was ever in the President's confidence again. It is significant that the second Mrs. Wilson confirmed him in his growing distrust of both men.

In the Senate battle over the Treaty of Versailles, Wilson might have built up a two-thirds majority from both parties if he had permitted some amendments to the most criticized clauses; but he was adamant. Possibly Senator Lodge, majority leader and bitter opponent of Wilson and the League of Nations, would have proposed other changes if Wilson had yielded. His craftiness, the able and unrelenting opposition of a group of extreme irreconcilables led by Borah and Johnson, and Wilson's breakdown on a speaking tour to arouse sentiment for the League defeated ratification, though a majority on both sides favored it in some form. After the final vote the sick man in the White House asked that the coming election be "a great and solemn referendum" on the question.

23

The Conservative Reaction

An Ohio Editor

The years 1919-1920 were years of turmoil. The economic machine, geared to the needs of a great war, threatened to fly apart when suddenly shifted to peacetime needs. Capital, gorged with war profits, and labor, enjoying wages undreamed of in 1914, seemed ready to fly at each other's throats as their poorly kept war truce ended and good times seemed about to vanish. The middle class, groaning under the tremendously increased cost of living, was aroused against both. For the farmers, suddenly deprived of war markets, readjustment was most difficult of all, since production could not be controlled as prices fell. Eager to take advantage of the widespread unrest and stirred by the success of the Bolshevik revolution in Russia, radicals began to organize for a social revolution. The reaction against their activities turned into a hysteria of "Red-baiting," with Attorney General Palmer leading the hue and cry. Deportation of aliens, convictions for sedition, and suppression of freedom of speech were the order of the day.

These same years brought a shift of leadership in the major parties that augured ill for an intelligent solution of such problems. The American people were in for a season of mediocrities as the generation of party notables of the progressive period faded out of the national picture and lesser men filled their shoes. Roosevelt and Aldrich had died; Cannon was a kind of emeritus member of the House; Taft and Hughes were elder statesmen with distinguished judicial careers still ahead but without political influence; Root had retired from public life; La Follette was still active but burdened with the opprobrium of opposition to a victorious war. In the Democratic camp

Bryan had lost caste after his resignation from the cabinet in 1915, and Wilson's collapse had left the party leaderless.

Strangely enough, the war had not produced a single military hero with political possibilities. General Pershing, the outstanding military figure, seemed to possess the glamourless efficiency that attaches to the head of a great business organization. He was a professional soldier with no interest in politics. In the field of wartime civilian activities one man stood out. First as director of Belgian relief and later as food administrator, Herbert Hoover, a mining engineer, had acquired a reputation that pointed toward a brilliant political career, if he so willed; but he was not a party man. His popularity, while widespread, had no organization behind it, and politicians were cold toward him. Liberals, intellectuals, and the *Saturday Evening Post* gave him aid and comfort but few delegates.

The absence of dynamic figures and the reaction against the wartime rule of Wilson seemed to call for the nomination of second-rate men. This was the situation in both parties. Americans had had enough of progressivism, of making the world safe for democracy, of self-denial and sacrifice, of crusaders and prophets. They were done with wheatless days, meatless meals, gasless Sundays, and all the restraints and controls of war-time. Rampant individualism and greedy materialism asserted themselves. The business of making money and enjoying life had never seemed so important. Widespread apathy toward politics gave the politicians a free hand.

The Chicago Republican gathering of June 8-12, 1920, was under Senatorial domination. Fresh from their triumphant rejection of Wilson's League of Nations, the Republican Senators chose to regard the party as their personal property. Yet the best of them were second-rate politicians and did not quite know what to do with the power that was theirs by default. They were not agreed on the League of Nations and they made no plans to break the deadlock over the nomination which everyone saw developing. Smoot of Utah and Lodge of Massachusetts were relics of the Old Guard of Aldrich's day, but they had had more experience in taking orders than in giving them. Penrose of Pennsylvania was too ill to attend the convention. Watson of Indiana, Curtis of Kansas, Brandegee of Connecticut, and other junior members of the Senatorial inner circle lacked the power and skill of the old-time state bosses. Another element also appeared in force. That veteran convention delegate and newsman, William Allen White, wrote that he had never seen a national convention so dominated by predatory economic forces; that oil, railroads, steel, and other interests had men in every delegation. Yet whatever their influence it was not concentrated behind any one candidate. That matter remained to be worked out.

Lodge, eager for his quadrennial exposure to the limelight, took for himself the temporary chairmanship, and then was continued as permanent chairman, with Watson of Indiana as head of the resolutions committee. Senator Borah of Idaho, strongly anti-League, made trouble for the committee until a vague, meaningless plank was devised by Colonel George Harvey, once a Democrat and always close to Wall Street, that approved the Senate's rejection of the League and pledged the Republican party to "such agreements with other nations of the world as shall meet the full duty of America to civilization and humanity, in accordance with American ideals, and without surrendering the right of the American people to exercise its judgment and its power in favor of justice and peace." This could mean anything and was acceptable to everyone.

The rest of the long platform did little more than assail Wilson and his works and promise to restore constitutional government. It favored an executive budget, simplification of the taxation system, reorganization of federal departments, and protective tariff. White, Borah, and other liberals on the resolutions committee secured indorsements of collective bargaining for labor and federal child-labor legislation. Everyone favored the pending woman suffrage amendment. Other planks took care of agriculture, conservation, reclamation, and highway construction in sympathetic terms. The platform was quickly adopted after a Wisconsin minority report had been voted down with scant courtesy.

Three men, all objectionable to the Old Guard leadership, had conducted extensive campaigns for the nomination—two of them expensive. General Leonard Wood, rejected for active service in France by the administration and General Pershing, was highly regarded for his administrative ability, was an old friend of Roosevelt, had broken with his early organization supporters, and was amply financed by William Cooper Procter, wealthy soap manufacturer, in a campaign for primary support. Old Guard leaders feared he would be hard to handle; not all the Roosevelt men would accept him to fill the shoes of their idol, and the doughboys of 1917-1918 were cold to an advocate of universal military training in peacetime. Yet Wood had moderate success in state primaries, and he led in delegates when the convention met. Revelation by a Senate investigation that his backers had spent $1,500,000 was one of the strongest arguments against his nomination.

Governor Frank O. Lowden of Illinois was Wood's chief rival. Outstanding among Republican governors, he was well located geographically and seemingly well qualified as a candidate. He had married into the wealthy Pullman family, and his campaign also was well financed. This, unfortunately, contributed to his undoing. Money unwisely spent in Missouri, without his knowledge, led to charges that he was buying up delegates; and it besmirched the most promising candidacy in a mediocre group.

Senator Hiram Johnson lacked the funds of his rivals but made up for this in part by vigorous campaigning and appeal to old Progressives and isolationists. A *Literary Digest* poll and the primaries he entered revealed that he was stronger with the voters than with the practical politicians, who were not ready to forget the curious outcome of the election of 1916 in California. His extreme "irreconcilability" toward the League of Nations further injured his chances.

Some ten or twelve favorite sons, seeing a deadlock in prospect, hopefully set up their lightning rods. Governor William Sproul of Pennsylvania had the support of its large delegation, but the tendency of Republican conventions to take the Keystone State's steady Republicanism for granted and look for candidates elsewhere worked against him. Senator Boies Penrose, still boss of Pennsylvania, ill and unable to go to Chicago, had slight influence on the convention, though he was favorable to Senator Harding in private and hostile to Wood. Nicholas Murray Butler, president of Columbia University, served as the nominal choice of New York. Massachusetts offered Governor Calvin Coolidge, but he was no favorite of Senator Lodge.

Far better situated was Warren G. Harding, Senator from Ohio. Residence in the state that had tilted the balance to Wilson in 1916 was in his favor. Blessed with a pleasing personality and a handsome figure, he also had a shrewd campaign manager: Harry M. Daugherty, lobbyist-lawyer, who was well acquainted with various state politicians and carefully built up good will for his favorite as a second and third choice.

Harding was hampered at the outset by a poor showing in the preconvention struggles. Wood had entered the Ohio primaries and had taken nine of the forty-eight votes. In other states the Ohio candidate had only a handful of pledged delegates; and political experts gave him a low rating. But Daugherty refused to be discouraged. He revealed his hopes in an inadvertent and somewhat facetious remark to a skeptical New York reporter that the nomination would be made in a smoke-filled hotel room "about eleven minutes after two o'clock" in the morning by a group of some fifteen leaders after the delegates became hopelessly deadlocked. Harding would then be the lucky man. This statement received much publicity and was both ridiculed and condemned.

In two respects the convention broke with precedent. Nearly all the candidates were in Chicago to work for the nomination. The coy reluctance of other days vanished in 1920. The presence of several women delegates was also an innovation. The Nineteenth Amendment needed the ratification of but one more state to make it a part of the Constitution, and women were already participating actively in party affairs.[1]

The nominating and seconding speeches consumed much time without evoking much spontaneous enthusiasm. The sweltering galleries cheered loudest for Hoover. The early ballots ran true to the predictions of most observers. On the first, Wood had 287-1/2 votes; Lowden, 211-1/2; Johnson, 133-1/2; Sproul, 84; Butler, 69-1/2; Harding, 65-1/2; Coolidge, 34; several others, smaller numbers. After four ballots on Friday afternoon with Wood reaching 314 and Lowden 289,[2] Chairman Lodge, on the motion of Senator Smoot, declared the convention adjourned until the next morning, although a majority seemed to have voted "No." The leaders wanted time for consultation. A long deadlock might create bad feeling and possibly produce a nominee unacceptable to the party bigwigs. The Senatorial group prepared to guide the nomination to one of their own kind.

The long conference—or succession of conferences—that night did the work. The "smoke-filled room" became a reality, though Daugherty was not admitted by the inner circle of the party's sages. His prediction had become an embarrassment. Senators Lodge, Curtis, Brandegee, and Colonel Harvey discussed the nomination at dinner in Harvey's suite. Afterward Watson of Indiana, James W. Wadsworth of New York, and several other state leaders

[1] Tennessee ratified in the summer, and women voted in the Presidential election.

[2] Harding had dropped to 58-1/2 on the third ballot and 61-1/2 on the fourth. Not until the fifth ballot next day did his votes exceed his first ballot total.

dropped in or were summoned. There was no agreement at first. Senator Knox of Pennsylvania, Chairman Will H. Hays of the national committee, and Charles E. Hughes were considered and dropped. Harding was discussed, but nobody showed any enthusiasm. Significantly enough, however, his name stirred up no antagonisms. The more he was considered, the more innocuous and available he appeared. By about "2:11 A.M." the weary conferees were ready to give him his chance.

Harding, who earlier had almost given up hope, was summoned before this self-constituted board of directors of the Republican party and quizzed like a suitor of uncertain reputation seeking the hand of an only daughter. Was there anything in his past, inquired the magisterial Harvey (who had assumed the role of spokesman for the group), that might embarrass the party or disqualify him as a candidate? He must answer on his conscience and before God. Harding took ten minutes to think it over alone and then answered that there was no impediment. This settled it. Word went out quietly that Harding was to be the man. The deadlock would be permitted to continue a little longer to convince both Wood and Lowden of the hopelessness of their chances; then the Senate cabal would end the struggle.

That Harding submitted to such treatment at the hands of the party chieftains is a sufficient commentary on the character of the nomination. One can imagine how Charles E. Hughes, Theodore Roosevelt or Woodrow Wilson would have reacted to a demand from such a source for a certificate of good character. In fact, Wilson had dispensed with Harvey's services before 1912. But the Senatorial clique wanted a man who was pliable, unassertive, deficient in ideas, and who would be grateful to his benefactors. In a not particularly distinguished Senate Harding had been one of the rank and file, content to vote with his party, and to utter occasional sonorous speeches with much feeling but little filling. Had the nomination been decided by a slip drawn from a hatful of Republican Senatorial names, the result might not have been any worse, and might have been a great deal better.

Proceedings next day went as planned. The deadlock continued for a few ballots; Lowden passed Wood—a compliment to the Illinois governor—and slowly the shift toward Harding started. On the tenth ballot he was nominated with 692-1/5 votes. This was late Saturday afternoon.

After Harding was nominated Daugherty and others close to the candidate denied the importance of Senatorial backing and magnified their own roles. There is even some evidence that Colonel Harvey and possibly some others of the inner circle wanted Will Hays, after they had used Harding to head off Wood and Lowden, but could not stop the band wagon. But the hard fact remains that the conferences in the "smoke-filled room" had put the Ohioan on the track that led to the nomination. Otherwise, his chances would have been as slim as he had believed them to be a few hours earlier.

Hiram Johnson could have had second place but resented the suggestion, and the Senatorial overlords then passed the word that Senator Irvine Lenroot of Wisconsin was their man. The delegates gagged at this final example of Senatorial dictation and, in their one and only display of independence, followed the lead of an aggressive Oregon delegate who nominated Governor Calvin Coolidge of Massachusetts. With 674-1/2 votes Coolidge became the nominee. Lodge disliked him, but his role in putting down a Boston police strike and his telegram to Samuel Gompers—"There is no right to strike against the public safety by anybody, anywhere, any time"—caught the public imagination in a year of labor disputes and social unrest. Had the voters been consulted, they might have reversed the names on the ticket.

Another Ohio Editor

A leaderless Democratic convention met at San Francisco on June 28 to solve the problem that had faced the Republicans at Chicago. The Titans had passed on. Except for 1904, three strong men—Cleveland, Bryan, and Wilson—had monopolized Democratic Presidential nominations since 1884. Now the invalidism of Wilson left the party leaderless. Three front runners and a group of favorite sons offered themselves, but none aroused much enthusiasm. William G. McAdoo, lately resigned as Secretary of the Treasury, was the best known, but, as Wilson's son-in-law, would carry much of the opprobrium cast upon the administration. A few days before the convention met he announced that he was not a candidate; but he was voted for, nevertheless. Attorney General A. Mitchell Palmer, "Red-hunter" extraordinary, was backed by federal officeholders but had little popular strength and no attractions for liberals. More available but little known outside his home state was James M. Cox, three times governor of Ohio, who had no Wilson administration burdens to carry. Edmond H. Moore, one of Ohio's shrewdest politicians, managed his campaign. Among the lesser local favorites were Governor Alfred E. Smith of New York, Secretary of Agriculture E. T. Meredith, and John W. Davis of West Virginia. None of the candidates had the stamp of Wilson's approval, not even McAdoo. The President was playing with the idea of a third nomination.

Bryan attempted to chart the party's course by offering a strong antiliquor plank and a compromise on the League of Nations, but lost out both in committee and on the floor of the convention. Thereupon he took a walk that lasted throughout the campaign.

The long platform ignored the new Eighteenth Amendment and indorsed Wilson's course on the League of Nations, though it did not oppose clarifying reservations. It defended his conduct of the war and blamed the Republican Congress for the nation's post-war troubles. Most of the remaining sections recited the administration's accomplishments with only vague suggestions for the future. Woman suffrage and Philippine independence were at least definite. The platform and the keynote speech of Homer Cummings, temporary chairman, indicated that the party would stand on the record of its stricken leader. Bainbridge Colby, Secretary of State and a delegate to the convention, misled by the enthusiasm, at one stage sent a message to his chief that he intended to present his name and that the convention would then draft him. Wilson sought the opinions of Josephus Daniels and Newton D. Baker at San Francisco, and their answer squelched the foolish proposal.

The first ballot for President gave McAdoo 266 votes, Palmer 256, Cox 134, Smith 109, Meredith 72, and minor candidates the rest. Ballot after ballot went by, with Cox gaining steadily. New York, Illinois, and Indiana, controlled by Charles F. Murphy, George Brennan, and Thomas Taggart respectively, swung to his support. He was in the lead when the deadlocked convention recessed on Saturday night. On Monday, Palmer withdrew after the thirty-eighth ballot; and on the forty-fourth Governor Cox was nominated, at 1:40 A.M., Tuesday.

Stocky, energetic James M. Cox was probably as good an answer to the Democratic problem as could have been found, after Herbert Hoover had eliminated himself by revealing that he was a Republican. He was not connected with the Wilson administration, and he was on good terms with the northern Democratic state bosses. He had carried one of the most important middle western states in 1918 in the face of a strong Republican trend. When the Republicans named an Ohioan, shrewd politicians saw in Cox the proper antidote. He had established a reputation as a reform administrator and a cautious liberal in implementing Ohio's new constitution and in dealing with the wartime problems of a large state with a diversified economic life. As to the liquor question, he was a "wet" and might draw a heavy urban vote.

The Vice Presidential nomination was quickly disposed of. New York seemed to require representation on the ticket, and Franklin D. Roosevelt, thirty-eight-year-old Assistant Secretary of the Navy, was named by acclamation. He was Cox's own choice. A popular figure in the Wilson administration and earlier an anti-Tammany reformer, he had no liabilities and had two political assets, his state of residence and a vote-getting name.

Both Cox and Harding had entered politics by way of the newspaper business. Cox had risen from reporter to publisher of the *Dayton Daily News* and the *Springfield Press-Republic* before he was elected to Congress in 1908. Harding had literally grown up with the *Marion Star*, a feeble local sheet when he purchased it at the age of nineteen that prospered with the community into one of the most substantial of Ohio's smaller-city papers. Both men had been drawn into local politics and had risen to prominence in their state organizations. Neither at the time of his nomination was well known outside Ohio. It was odd that their backgrounds, if not their personalities, were so much alike.

The Socialists, suffering from the loss of a prowar group in 1917 and a left-wing faction in 1919, held their convention in May at New York with their veteran leader, Eugene V. Debs, confined in the federal prison at Atlanta for utterances in opposition to the war. Nevertheless, the delegates nominated him for President on a platform assailing the Wilson administration for "undermining the very foundation of political liberty and economic rights," and demanding a complete reorganization of the economic system upon the basis of public ownership of public necessities. The old Socialist Labor party preserved its separate existence by running its own candidate. Some extreme leftists, taking their cue from Lenin and Trotsky, attempted to organize for revolutionary action but wound up with a "Communist Party" and a "Communist Labor Party," each claiming the mantle of red orthodoxy. Neither played any part in the campaign.

Labor radicals who could not stomach the doctrinaire positions of the above groups, bolting liberals and progressives from the old parties, and the Nonpartisan League,[3] a well organized farmer movement in the Dakotas and Minnesota, attempted to appeal to city workers, discontented agrarians, and homeless liberals with a Farmer-Labor party. But the ingredients would not mix. A labor group of a somewhat radical complexion took control of the national convention, meeting at Chicago in July, and nominated Parley P. Christensen of Utah for President and Max Hayes of Ohio for Vice President on a platform not unlike that of the Socialists. The "Committee of Forty-eight," representing the liberal groups, and the Nonpartisan League abandoned the movement, and it polled only 265,000 votes at the election.

The Prohibitionists, refusing to regard their work as completed by the passage of the Eighteenth Amendment, centered their efforts on the enforcement and the maintenance of prohibition and nominated —naturally enough—an Ohioan, A. S. Watkins, for the Presidency. Had Bryan consented he would have been the choice.

Democratic Debacle

The Republican campaign as managed by the efficient and tireless national chairman, Will H. Hays of Indiana, was a model of vote-catching banality. "Americanism" and "Getting back to normalcy" constituted its sum and substance. The first—which no one has ever been able to define—implied that Wilson had put the rest of the world ahead of his own country. The Republicans would reverse this. The second nostalgically promised a return to some less troubled past, though no one could be sure just when Americans had lived in a state of "normalcy." At least Harding was the ideal candidate to present this dose of soothing syrup to an angry and disillusioned electorate. Modest, unassuming, given to making speeches that consisted of "an army of pompous phrases moving across the landscape in search

[3] The Nonpartisan League, organized by Arthur C. Townley in 1915, had captured control of the Republican party in North Dakota and had carried the state in 1916. Its program of a state bank and state-owned grain warehouses, elevators, and flour mills, operated in the interest of the farmers, was put into practical effect in 1919; but the collapse in farm prices wrecked its plans, and a conservative reaction followed. The League also operated in several other states but only in Minnesota was it very successful. Here it joined with organized labor to set up a state Farmer-Labor party, which became an important factor in Minnesota politics.

of an idea," he seemed to the typical good resident of small town and countryside to be a man who understood the ways of his fellow men and would work with them to find solutions for their problems. Except for a few carefully prepared major speeches which skillful ghost writers provided, he campaigned from his front porch at Marion, Ohio, uttering pleasantries to visiting delegations after the McKinley pattern but less studied, more informal, more human.

One problem stumped Harding and almost baffled his speech writers. This was the League of Nations. He had voted for the League with the Lodge reservations attached, and this position was supported by Hughes, Taft, Root, Hoover, and other party bigwigs in varying degrees. But the Borah-Johnson irreconcilables had blood in their eyes and demanded repudiation of the League. Harding tried to emulate the vagueness of the platform; but the task proved to be far too great for his powers of circumlocution, and George Harvey and Richard Washburn Child came to the rescue. The result was a long and involved speech in which the candidate seemed to favor a world court of justice and an "association" of nations for conference in place of the Wilsonian League. Even these vague proposals were not to be final, for he promised to consult "the most experienced minds of this country" before presenting his plans to other nations. Late in the campaign, still confused, the candidate seemed to wobble more to the isolationist side, though thirty-one distinguished Republicans signed a public appeal urging his election as the only way to bring the United States into "an effective league."

A 1923 magazine article, written with White House approval, stated that Harding had never had any intention of having the United States enter the League of Nations. Apparently he had convictions and was merely concealing them during the campaign.

Lesser Republican speakers, unable to follow their leader along the tight wire, felt free to flay Wilson's League as a superstate dangerous to American sovereignty. Voters of Irish, German, and Italian ancestry, hostile to the Treaty of Versailles for various reasons, joined in the clamor against American involvement. In the upper Mississippi valley, where the peace appeal had worked for the Democrats in 1916, isolationism was now rampant.

Cox put up a brave battle against heavy odds. Soon after the nomination he and his running mate, Franklin D. Roosevelt, called upon the pathetic figure in the White House and assured him they would stand with him on the League. As Cox had not been involved in the Senate battle, such a pledge seemed to be inexpedient; but he refused to be a trimmer. Then he went on the stump, speaking in all parts of the country. He attempted to revive the progressivism of the prewar days, in which he had played a notable part in his home state; but the country was in no mood for reform. George White, Democratic national chairman, was hampered by finances and apathy in building up an effective organization. The Democratic national committee spent $1,470,000 compared with the Republican $5,417,000; but no amount of money could have saved Cox. The swing was to the right.

In this campaign appeared the first large-scale attempt to poll the electorate in a Presidential election. The *Literary Digest,* a well-known weekly devoted to presenting newspaper opinion in digest form, undertook the task through millions of postcards.[4] Its methods overemphasized middle-class sentiment, but this was not evident when the Republican trend was so general.

The whispering that sometimes disgraces a Presidential campaign appeared in 1920. The most sensational story was the allegation that Harding had Negro blood. Circulars purporting to prove it by affidavits and a family tree appeared mysteriously on doorsteps and even in the mails. The authorship could not be clearly established. It had an Ohio origin but was widely circulated shortly before the election.

On November 2 a tidal wave engulfed the Democratic party. Harding carried the entire North and West including Oklahoma; the border states of the South except Kentucky; and Tennessee from the Solid South—its first lapse from Democratic orthodoxy since 1872. He had 404 electoral votes to Cox's 127. The popular vote was divided as follows: Harding, 16,153,115; Cox, 9,133,092; Debs, Socialist, 915,490; Christensen, Farmer-Labor, 265,229; Watkins, Prohibition, 189,339; Cox, Socialist Labor, 30,594. With more than 60 per cent of the total vote and a plurality of 7,000,000, Harding shattered all records. In the new House of Representatives, more than 300 of the 435 members were Republicans. In the Senate 59 were Republicans, and only 37 Democrats.

In 1920, it has been said, the voters voted their resentments. Champ Clark, defeated after twenty-eight years in Congress from Missouri, snarled one word at a newspaperman who asked the cause

[4] It sent out 11,000,000 postcards before the conventions to test the popularity of various candidates. During the campaign certain states were polled as a basis for estimating the outcome of the election.

of the landslide: "Wilson!" It was not the broken man in the White House that the voters were repudiating but Wilson as the symbol of things they wanted to forget. The intoxication of patriotic sacrifices for high ideals and the exhilaration of war prosperity were over. The year 1920 was the morning after. The world was out of joint, and the American people, in their disillusionment, sought a victim. The election was not, as Wilson had hoped, a "great and solemn referendum" on the League. Without the League as a factor, the result would have been much the same. Americans were homesick for the hopeful, sane, and secure world of 1914. Perhaps an average man like Harding could restore that "normalcy." But the President elect was looking beyond that. He wanted to go back to McKinley.

Harding's Two Years

Harding was perhaps the most distinguished-looking man in public life. In his fifty-sixth year when inaugurated, he had not permitted his girth to dwarf his breadth of shoulders and thickness of chest. Tennis, pingpong, and golf had given him an appearance of physical fitness that many a younger man might have envied. The thick gray hair and the handsome, rather heavy features in his formally posed photographs conveyed an impression of severity; and on the platform he was the perfect picture of the dignified statesman. Off stage he was the friendliest of men, kindly and well disposed toward everyone. These two factors had much to do with his success: his appearance and his friendliness. Unfortunately the Presidency requires more than good looks and a kind heart.

Harding's amiability was his greatest virtue and his worst fault. The White House needed his warm, receptive spirit within its portals to remove the atmosphere of inaccessibility and gloom that had settled there during Wilson's long illness. Even before his breakdown, many had felt that the war President was too aloof, too guarded and suspicious, too flintlike in his *No*'s. But if his nature prevented him from giving the soft answer that turneth away wrath, his successor had this virtue in too great abundance. Wilson had become almost fearful of friendship lest it mislead him; Harding blundered headlong into the morass of trusting everybody. He couldn't be an ingrate, he remarked when warned against yielding to the importunities of a particular friend.

Harding liked to think of himself as a second McKinley whose task was to harmonize and conciliate, leaving to Congress the initiative in policies; but the soft-hearted McKinley had a hard head and a fund of worldly wisdom while Harding, for all his experience as a politician, was a lamentably poor judge of men, and far too easily swayed by the last man to talk to him. Inexperienced in administration, unintellectual, and indolent by nature, he found that the Presidential harness chafed and burned. There was too little time for golf, poker parties, and the other diversions of a good fellow. After a year he commented at a Press Club dinner on the inability of a President "to be a human being." The consciousness of his own unfitness for the great office seemed to grow upon him. The testimony of such friendly critics as Nicholas Murray Butler, James Watson, and Mark Sullivan bears on this.

Always at Harding's side was his wife, Florence Kling Harding, who watched over him with a devotion almost maternal. Several years his senior and childless, she had more ambition for him than he had for himself. Her advice and judgment, sometimes dictated by personal feelings, were not always sound; but her persistence did not disturb her easy-going husband.

Harding's cabinet of "best minds" included Charles E. Hughes as Secretary of State, Andrew Mellon of Pittsburgh, one of the nation's wealthiest men, as head of the Treasury, Herbert Hoover as Secretary of Commerce, and National Chairman Will Hays as Postmaster General. The other department heads were less exalted, and the appointment of one of them, Attorney General Harry M. Daugherty, was regarded in some quarters as questionable. Only Harding's insistence on rewarding his old friend and pre-convention manager secured his confirmation. A worse choice, as it turned out—Senator Albert B. Fall, an anticonservationist, to head the Interior Department—aroused no opposition in the friendly Senate.

In the Harding-Daugherty retinue were some Ohio émigrés who received lucrative federal posts, for Harding did not forget old friends. The damning "Ohio Gang" label was applied later when certain shady characters among them were exposed. These camp followers used their influence, real or supposed, as a source of revenue, though the extent of their under-cover dealings is still a mystery.

Harding, both by inclination and out of regard for the forces that nominated him, let the leadership the American people had come to associate with his office pass over to a Congress that lacked an Aldrich or a Czar Reed to guide it. The results in legislation were not impressive: large increases in the tariff, tax reductions, though not as much in the large income brackets as Secretary Mellon desired, and some farm-relief legislation for which a bipartisan Farm Bloc could claim the credit. In foreign relations, isolationism triumphed, though the Washington Conference on limitation of naval armaments and Pacific problems involved commitments that proved the futility of trying to ignore the rest of the world. Senator Borah and Secretary of State Hughes, rather than Harding, were responsible for these steps.

The Harding administration, on the whole, was conservative, friendly to business, indifferent to the farm problem, hostile to labor, unpopular with veterans (Harding vetoed a soldiers' bonus). That it was also mired in corruption was still unknown when the mid-term elections occurred.

The Congressional elections of 1922 were a sharp rebuke to the confused, leaderless administration. The huge Republican margin in the House was reduced to fifteen.[5] In the Senate the nominal majority of six actually gave control to the opposition, for the liberal La Follette and Norris group cooperated more often with the Democrats than with the administration. Minnesota sent a Farmer-Laborite, North Dakota a Nonpartisan League adherent, and Iowa a Republican radical to the Senate. Farmer discontent in the grain-growing sections and labor unrest—this was the year of the miners' and railroad shopmen's strikes—accounted in part for the election results.

The impact of economic group interests upon party loyalties was tending to break down party government in Congress—a situation that continued through the rest of the 1920's. Farm organizations, labor unions, the American Legion, the Anti-Saloon League, and business groups operated on Congress, and votes reflected such pressures rather than party affiliations. This situation left the Republican ship at the mercy of the prevailing winds. A conservative captain stood on the bridge; but he was confused, the course was poorly charted, and the crew refractory. The drift was to the right, but the much sought port of normalcy was never attained, if indeed it even existed. And now, in the midst of the voyage, the captain was suddenly stricken dead.

[5] The House contained 225 Republicans, 207 Democrats and 3 Independents. In the Senate there were 51 Republicans, 43 Democrats, 2 Independents.

24

The Yankee Politician and the Great Engineer

Calvin Coolidge

In June, 1923, President Harding set out on a transcontinental trip that would take him to Alaska. Plausible Charles R. Forbes, whom he had appointed to head the Veterans' Bureau, had resigned in February under attack for a carnival of waste and corruption. Charles F. Cramer, general counsel under Forbes, had committed suicide in March. Then came the death of Jess Smith, the fidus Achates of Daugherty and long-time friend of the President. Smith shot himself under mysterious circumstances in the Attorney General's apartment. Nicholas Murray Butler, who talked to Harding before he left Washington, and William Allen White, who saw him in Kansas, both felt that he had something on his mind he could not reveal.

Daugherty, Senator James Watson, and Dr. Sawyer, his physician, were disturbed by his poor physical condition, which was made worse by the arduous trip with its numerous speeches, dinners, and other functions. He came back from Alaska to Seattle, became ill, was removed to San Francisco, and died suddenly on August 2 with Mrs. Harding at his bedside, when apparently recovering from what was said to be bronchial pneumonia. Later, murder and suicide were brought into the picture by rumor mongers, when revelations of corruption at Washington were expanded and distorted into a sensational literature of exposure. It is much easier to believe that the strains of office, both mental and physical, made Harding an easy victim for the grim reaper.

Calvin Coolidge, visiting at his father's little Vermont farm twelve miles from a telegraph office, was awakened after midnight and informed that he was President. By lamplight he took the oath of office from his father, Colonel John Coolidge, a notary public, with eight persons as witnesses—in its sheer simplicity as dramatic an induction into office as any President has ever had. This was Friday morning August 3, 1923. The new President's first thought, as he related it afterward, was: "I believe I can swing it."

Coolidge had passed his fifty-first birthday on the Fourth of July. Born and reared in rural Vermont, graduated from Amherst College, and admitted to the bar at Northampton, Massachusetts, he had slowly ascended the ladder of political preferment without missing a rung, learning, as he climbed, the ways by which men get ahead. Successively he was elected member of the city council, city solicitor, member of the lower house of the legislature, mayor of Northampton, state senator, lieutenant governor, and governor, adding a little to his reputation in each post. His connection with the suppression of the Boston police strike won national acclaim, and the nomination for Vice President followed. Invited to sit in Harding's cabinet, he attended faithfully but said little.

This spare, unimpressive man of medium height had political perspicacity in a high degree; but outwardly he repelled rather than attracted men. Sour-faced and tight-mouthed, he was a poor mixer, was often regarded as a "queer fish," and occasionally was labeled as "dumb." Yet his silent shrewdness, his party regularity, and his faithful work as a member of Murray Crane's Massachusetts machine paid better dividends than being a good fellow. The business and financial overlords of the Bay State took under their collective wing this dependable, plodding lawyer-politician whose personal rectitude did not impel him to pry into their methods and measures.

Coolidge was one of the most conservative of Presidents. His economic philosophy was simple and firmly fixed, coming down from his Puritan forebears: Success came to those who, like himself, worked hard, practiced frugality, economy, and personal honesty, and had an eye for the main chance. Investments represented savings and self-denial; government restrictions and taxes penalized the thrifty. Completely provincial in his outlook—he boasted that no Coolidge had ever gone West—he had slight appreciation of the problems of western farmers, southern sharecroppers, or immigrant steelworkers. They were beyond his horizon. His individualistic faith required that men save themselves, that economic ills be remedied without government meddling; and it seemed to be justified by the rocketing prosperity of his Presidential years. If Coolidge was one of the most conservative of Presidents, he was also one of the luckiest. The depression of the early 1920's lifted, and business boomed. The negative viewpoint of the President fitted the situation exactly. All that he needed to do was to reduce taxes and to sit tight. The accelerating roar of the business machine was drowning out discontent. The apostle of nonaction arrived at exactly the right moment.

The new President kept Harding's cabinet intact, as he knew the members already and was not inclined to make changes without good reason. With an eye on the 1924 convention, he made C. Bascom Slemp, a former Congressman from Virginia, his private secretary. Slemp, a practical politician, served as contact man with party workers and knew how to distribute patronage to advantage, particularly in the South. Coolidge had neither a Colonel House nor a Daugherty; but in Frank W. Stearns, Amherst alumnus and wealthy Boston merchant, he possessed a patron and faithful friend who had thought of him as a Presidential possibility as early as 1915 and had contributed money and effort to his advancement without thought of reward. Several years older than the President, he was a kind of father confessor who listened to confidences or shared silences, without giving advice.

Even Grace Goodhue Coolidge, the White House mistress, had never been taken into her husband's confidence on public matters. These, he felt, were outside her sphere, though she was a university graduate. Yet no wife did more to make a President's career a success. Her gracious friendliness eased the social atmosphere when the unsociable President fell into one of his silences. She understood his moodiness and his occasional irritability, and appreciated his virtues. The death of their younger boy, Calvin, Jr., in 1924 was a terrible blow, but Mrs. Coolidge bore up bravely and did not permit this sorrow to alter the social life of the executive mansion.

Coolidge's most serious problem was to clean up the mess created by the oil scandals and other revelations of corruption under Harding. A Senate committee with Senator Thomas J. Walsh as chief investigator discovered that Secretary of the Interior Fall had received large sums in cash and bonds for leasing the naval oil reserves at Elk Hills, California, and Teapot Dome, Wyoming, to Edward L. Doheny and Harry F. Sinclair respectively, two of the largest oil producers in the country. Sinclair had also set up a dummy corporation, part of whose profits had gone in Liberty bonds to Fall and part to the Republican national committee to pay a campaign deficit. Another Senate committee, investigating the Attorney General's office, raised more questions than it answered;[1] but the smoke around Daugherty became so thick that Republican leaders in Congress urged the President to remove him. Secretary of the Navy Denby, who had innocently transferred the naval oil reserves to the Interior Department without looking into the matter, resigned under pressure, but Daugherty refused to quit under fire, even when Chief Justice Taft suggested it.

Coolidge, ever slow to commit himself, said nothing during the weeks of exposures except that the guilty must be punished. Fall had long since departed from the cabinet, and was not a problem. The President appointed two special prosecutors for the government in the oil cases, in itself a mark of lack of confidence in the Attorney General; but not until Daugherty refused a Senate committee access to certain files in his office did Coolidge see fit to act. Then he asked for the resignation of Harding's devoted staff officer. Harlan F. Stone, a friend of Coolidge from his Amherst days, became the new Attorney General. The next year he was made an associate justice of the Supreme Court.

Congress was refractory enough to pass a soldiers' bonus bill—in the form of paid-up insurance certificates—over the President's head and to disregard his wishes by including a Japanese exclusion clause in the immigration restriction bill; but Coolidge was borne along by a wave of popularity toward the Republican nomination and no Senatorial clique could stop him. The Harding scandals had not touched his garments, and the "Ohio Gang" was gone. The peculiar quirks of his character made him strangely popular, and humorous stories (most of them sheer inventions) went around about his parsimony, his sparing use of words, and his dry wit. He seemed to be a reincarnation of the shrewd, thrifty, horse-and-buggy, small-town Yankee of long ago, called forth to exemplify to his people the old-fashioned virtues of America's youth. If they refused to follow his precepts, at least they liked to feel that their government was in safe hands. After Harding, that was something.

William M. Butler, Massachusetts textile manufacturer and leader of the old Crane machine, took charge of Coolidge's candidacy and

[1] In 1927 Thomas W. Miller was found guilty of accepting money as Alien Property Custodian to approve a claim for the return of alien property. Daugherty also had been indicted. Jess Smith had received a large fee in connection with this same claim. Miller was convicted and sentenced to eighteen months in prison. Daugherty strangely refused to testify, and the jury disagreed in his case. The destruction of certain ledger sheets of a Washington Court House, Ohio, bank controlled by his brother added to the mystery.

directed affairs at the national convention in Cleveland on June 10. Everything was cut-and-dried. Congressman Theodore E. Burton of Ohio was temporary chairman and delivered a carefully worded keynote speech which evoked mild applause.[2] Former Congressman Frank W. Mondell of Wyoming, another party veteran, was permanent chairman, and Charles B. Warren of Michigan was chairman of the resolutions committee. Marion L. Burton, president of the University of Michigan, presented Coolidge's name to the convention. Not one of the Senatorial overlords who had run the show in 1920 received any consideration in the Coolidge scheme of things. Coolidge, snubbed in the past by Lodge and annoyed at the Senate leader's treatment of his measures, saw to it that no honors went to him.

The platform, tailored to the Coolidge pattern, pointed with pride to the administration record of economy and tax reduction and promised more of the same. The farm and labor planks recognized that problems existed in both fields but offered few concrete recommendations. A perfunctory indorsement of the World Court and a strong stand against the League of Nations continued the Republican retreat into isolationism on foreign policy. Near the end the platform declared that the recent exposures of corruption in government affected men of both parties and demanded punishment of the guilty; but it condemned attempts "to besmirch the names of the innocent and undermine the confidence of the people in the government under which they live," especially for partisan purposes. In this oblique way nosy investigators were slapped for their zeal and doubts cast upon their motives.

The one ballot for President gave Coolidge 1,165 votes, La Follette 34 (Wisconsin's votes plus 6 from North Dakota), Hiram Johnson 10 (South Dakota).

Coolidge favored Senator William E. Borah for the Vice Presidential nomination. He had developed a liking for the independent, outspoken Idaho Senator, whose views were so at variance with his own, but Borah flatly refused the nomination. When the convention balloted, former Governor Lowden of Illinois led. William S. Kenyon of Iowa, judge and former Senator, was second, and General Charles G. Dawes of Illinois was third. On the second ballot Lowden received a majority. He promptly rejected the nomination, and the convention reassembled and quickly nominated Dawes. He had been purchasing

[2] Radio broadcasting was used for the first time at this convention, although receiving sets were still crude.

agent for the American Expeditionary Forces during the war and had fathered a plan by which Germany was to pay reparations to the victors. A banker and the first director of the budget, he had been in politics since the McKinley-Hanna days. He had a gift for vigorous, expressive English and was known as "Hell 'n Maria" Dawes, from his favorite expletive.

The convention completed its work in three days without discord and with a minimum of enthusiasm. Coolidge's name had been cheered for four minutes when he was put in nomination. "Uncle Andy" Mellon received a rousing welcome when he appeared on the platform, but the rest of the show was perfunctory. The convention had applied the campaign slogan of 1924, "Keep cool with Coolidge."

Even the Cleveland weather did its part. But there was an undercurrent of pessimism in some quarters. Teapot Dome was the reason.

The Madison Square Garden Fiasco

The Democrats seemingly had an issue made to order in the scandals of the Harding administration. But it was spoiled by unforeseen factors. Instead of being outraged by the exposures, people seemed to be callously indifferent in this postwar atmosphere of disillusionment and cynicism. In some quarters, notably among businessmen, there was actual resentment at the investigations, echoed in metropolitan journals. Just when profits were rising, snooping pseudo-reformers were trying to shake people's confidence in sound government. Some believed the Communists were involved. Anyhow, it was better to let well enough alone. Exposures were unwelcome guests at the prosperity feast.

A second factor was the death of Harding and the accession of Coolidge. The sourly honest New Englander was above reproach. All the attacks on Republican corruption left him untouched. He had eliminated the rascals and replaced them with good men. What more could the Democrats do? Harding had been imposed upon, but Coolidge was of sterner stuff. Why experiment when the man in the White House had demonstrated his fitness?

The third factor was the cat-and-dog fight at the Democratic national convention, in Madison Square Garden, New York, on June 24. The slim chances of the Democrats were wrecked by the bitter dissensions that blazed up here. The contenders were the urban machines of the East and the rural Democracy of South and West. The alignment was old, but the issue was not.

The Ku Klux Klan provided the new issue. Taking the name and much of the paraphernalia of the secret night riders of Reconstruction days and expanding upon their intolerance, it appealed especially to culturally retarded and economically thwarted small-town and rural folk of older native stocks. These found compensation for their frustrations by participating in its secret ritual, its hooded parades, its mysterious burning of fiery crosses on hilltops at midnight, and its cult of Nordic Protestant supremacy. Lynchings, whippings, riots, and other acts of violence were more sinister outlets. Coating itself with that favorite whitewash of bigotry, the preservation of "Americanism," the Klan was antiforeign, anti-Catholic, anti-Jewish and anti-Negro, depending upon the locale. Its slick organizers, who made fortunes from membership dues and other graft, saw opportunities in politics, and soon candidates for office in many communities, outside the urban East, were joining the Klan or coming to terms with it.

The Republicans, with their predominantly Protestant and middle-class dependence, quietly accepted the white-sheeted brotherhood as an auxiliary where it was strong but otherwise ignored its existence. There was no mention of it at the Cleveland convention.

The Democrats were less fortunate. The Klan had infiltrated the party in many sections of the rural hinterlands; but in the urban centers of East and Middle West, where their voters were largely of immigrant stock and under Irish Catholic leadership, it was extremely unpopular. The issue seemed bound to explode at the national convention. But there was the matter of candidates also at stake. These plebeian city Democrats felt that proper recognition in the first echelons of party leadership had been denied to them in the past. Tammany in particular had been treated at times like a family alcoholic who could neither be cast off nor be reformed. Metropolitan city halls and sometimes a state capital were suitable rewards for such Democrats. But by 1924 they were ready to demand their place in the sun. From their ranks had emerged a man of national stature. Governor Alfred E. Smith of New York was the idol of this eastern Democracy. He was anti-Klan, antiprohibition, a Tammany product and a Catholic, of immigrant parentage. The Klansmen saw in his candidacy an amalgam of all their fears and hates.

Out of the West came their choice, a somewhat tarnished Lochinvar wielding the lance of Wilsonian liberalism and resolved to save the Madison Square Garden maiden from the eastern bosses. William Gibbs McAdoo of California, son-in-law of Woodrow Wilson and once his Secretary of the Treasury, had in his camp Bernard Baruch and other stanch Wilsonians, the railway brotherhoods, many rural dry Democrats, some assorted liberals, and a corps of former federal officeholders. McAdoo was well in the lead when the Walsh investigations revealed that he was a legal advisor to Edward L. Doheny, wealthy oil man involved in the Fall bribery disclosures. Though ignorant of Doheny's under-cover manipulations, he was sufficiently splattered with oil to dampen his usefulness as a crusader against Republican corruption. His eastern opponents now charged that he was the Klan favorite. He was no believer in the hooded order, but many of his delegates had its blessing; and he chose to overlook this blight. This was in sharp contrast with the positions of Governor Smith and Senator Oscar Underwood of Alabama. Underwood's anti-Klan stand wrecked his chances in his own section.

The liquor issue widened the sectional breach. Smith and Underwood were wet; McAdoo was dry. Under the circumstances the national committee blundered in holding the convention in New York City—wet, anti-Klan, and pro-Smith. The attitude of the galleries and the metropolitan press angered the McAdoo delegates and closed their ranks into an unyielding phalanx. This city-country struggle all but blotted out the faint liberal-conservative division between McAdoo and anti-McAdoo forces.

The convention opened in Madison Square Garden on June 24 and elected Senator Pat Harrison of Mississippi as temporary chairman and keynote orator and Senator Thomas J. Walsh, investigator extraordinary, as permanent chairman. Both stressed Republican corruption in their speeches; but this was soon forgotten in the bitterness of the Smith-McAdoo battle. Nominating speeches, made before the adoption of the platform to save time, produced a large field of favorite sons, because the impending deadlock pointed to a compromise solution. Perhaps the most effective speech was made by Franklin D. Roosevelt, the stalwart Vice-Presidential nominee of 1920, in nominating Governor Smith. Recently stricken by infantile paralysis, he was a pathetic figure leaning on his crutches; but his captivating voice overcame his infirmity.

While the demonstrations that greeted the speeches for Smith and McAdoo revealed the angry spirit of their supporters and the violent partisanship of the galleries for Smith, the climax came when the committee on resolutions, badly divided over denouncing the Klan by name, reported its problem to the convention. The difference in wording of the two proposed resolutions seemed to be trivial; but behind it was the swelling bitterness of the contending groups. Bryan and Bainbridge Colby led the debate on the issue. The former, now a delegate from Florida, was no defender of the Klan; but he objected to exaggerating its importance by specific mention in the platform. While the unmannerly galleries interrupted with jeers and catcalls, he pleaded for harmony and elimination of the religious issue. Colby, in biting words, denounced the Klan and demanded its repudiation by name. The vote favored the Bryan-McAdoo forces, 546.15 to 541.85. A plea by Newton D. Baker for a plank indorsing the League of Nations failed by a vote of 742-1/2 to 353-1/2.

Other resolutions, which carried, denounced Republican corruption, the Fordney-McCumber Tariff, and the Mellon plan of taxation, and attributed the ills of the farmer to Republican policies. Yet, except for a lower tariff, the farm proposals were as indefinite as the Republican promises.

A law enforcement plank pledged the party to enforce "the Constitution and all laws," and criticized the Republican administration specifically for failure to enforce prohibition. Pious hopes for world peace were expressed, and the Republicans were derided for having no foreign policy. A referendum of the American people was proposed as a settlement of the question of American membership in the League of Nations. Like the Republicans, the Democrats promised to draft other resources as well as man power in case of war.

The first ballot for the Presidential nomination followed the adoption of the platform. It gave McAdoo 431-1/2 votes, Smith 241, former Governor Cox of Ohio 59, Pat Harrison 43-1/2, and Underwood 42-1/2, with fourteen other persons dividing the rest of the votes. Then followed the longest deadlock in convention history. The McAdoo forces, hoping to break down the field, held on and prevented a choice. Smith was willing to abandon the fight if his chief rival would withdraw, but McAdoo refused. He hoped to reach a majority, expecting then that the Smith forces would concede the two-thirds. On the 69th ballot he had 530 votes, just 20 short of a majority; but this was his peak.[3] Underwood might have been named if the South had shifted to him, for the Smith forces were friendly; but this was impossible because he was wet and anti-Klan. At last

[3] Bryan had tried to swing the convention to McAdoo after the 37th ballot.

the convention voted to release the delegates from their instructions. Smith passed McAdoo on the 87th ballot, but his 368 votes were barely one-third of the total. McAdoo withdrew after the hundredth ballot. John W. Davis of West Virginia then went into the lead, and on the 103rd he had 844 votes and the nomination.

Since Davis was an eastern conservative, a western liberal was nominated for Vice President, Governor Charles W. Bryan of Nebraska, brother of William Jennings. Thus ended the battle of Madison Square Garden. It had lasted from June 24 to July 9.

Out of all the smoke and fury and bitter passions had emerged a rather colorless conservative, an able lawyer nominally from West Virginia but practicing in New York City, who had been a member of Congress, solicitor general, and ambassador to Great Britain. Among his clients was J. P. Morgan & Company.

"Keep Cool with Coolidge"

Dissatisfied liberals, seeing an opportunity for a farmer-labor movement, turned to Senator Robert M. La Follette, who had at last decided to break with the Republican party. A gathering of farmer, labor, and liberal groups at Cleveland on July 4 named him for President and Burton K. Wheeler, Democratic Senator from Montana who had conducted the Daugherty investigation, for Vice President. The platform, prepared by La Follette, declared that the great issue before the people was the control of government and industry by private monopoly. It favored public ownership of the nation's water power, important natural resources, and railroads, reduction of taxes on moderate incomes but large increases in inheritance-tax rates on large estates, constitutional amendments to permit Congress to reenact a law over a judicial veto and to provide for popular election of federal judges, farm-relief measures, abolition of injunctions in labor disputes, ratification of the pending child-labor amendment, direct nomination and election of Presidents, a popular referendum on declarations of war, outlawry of war, and a drastic reduction of armaments.

The Conference for Progressive Political Action, active since 1922, launched the La Follette candidacy, and it had the support of the American Federation of Labor, the railroad brotherhoods, the Socialist party, and other left-wing farmer and labor groups, as well as intellectuals of liberal stamp as represented by the *New Repub-*

lic and the *Nation*. La Follette and Wheeler made an active campaign; but there was no party organization and little money back of them, and labor did not prove to be of much assistance. Their chief hope was to carry enough states in the upper Mississippi valley, where farmer discontent centered, to throw the election to the House.

The Republicans, blessed with a campaign fund of more than $4,000,000, a popular candidate, an able manager and organizer in the person of William M. Butler, and a return of prosperity—even farm prices went up in 1924—had no very serious problems. A fear that La Follette's strength in the farm states might prevent an electoral majority led the party leaders to center their attack on the independent candidate. They played up his economic radicalism and his proposal to take away the judicial veto of the Supreme Court in order to frighten conservatives into voting for Coolidge rather than Davis, thus making certain that the election would not go to the House. Prosperity and satisfaction with the status quo made Republican success almost certain in any case. Had Harding lived, the exposures of corruption might have been awkward to meet; but with Coolidge in office the situation was completely changed. The slogan "Keep Cool with Coolidge" expressed the sentiments of a majority of the electorate.

The Democrats, having used up their energies at the convention, had none left for the campaign. Clem Shaver of West Virginia became national chairman at Davis's request, but he was not well known to party leaders and was hampered by lack of funds and by organization problems. Expenditures were about $1,100,000. Davis went on the stump and made able speeches assailing Republican corruption, but could not overcome Democratic lethargy or draw Republican fire. Labor was cold toward the Wall Street lawyer, and the Bryan West refused to be stirred by the speeches of the aging Commoner. The Klan question drifted into the background and had slight effect on the election. Prohibition had become a matter of law enforcement, and both major parties, of course, gave it lip service.

The *Literary Digest* poll predicted a Coolidge victory, and the prediction was more than verified in November. Coolidge had 382 electoral votes; Davis, 136; La Follette, 13 (Wisconsin). West Virginia, Kentucky, Missouri, Maryland, and Delaware followed the lead of the entire North and West in going Republican. Only the South (including Oklahoma) was Democratic. Coolidge's popular vote was 15,719,921; Davis had 8,386,704; La Follette, 4,832,532. Several minor-party candidates polled insignificant votes.

The outcome was less sweeping than in 1920 but still decisive enough. Both houses of Congress were Republican by safe majorities. La Follette had run second in eleven western states. He had been favored by those farmers who were not satisfied with Coolidge prosperity, and his antiwar stand had not been forgotten in German communities. In California and the Pacific Northwest, thousands of liberal Democrats preferred him to Davis. East of the Mississippi, liberal, labor and socialist support accounted for a heavy urban vote. But admiration for the Wisconsin veteran and disgust with the old parties could not, of themselves, create a new party. The basic groundwork of local organization was not laid, and the Progressive movement of 1924 passed into history.

This campaign marked the last stumping appearances of two old warriors of liberalism, La Follette and Bryan. Both died in 1925. La Follette bequeathed his Wisconsin organization and his principles to his sons, but Bryan had all but blotted out the memory of his battles against plutocracy by his later crusades against the liquor traffic and the teaching of evolution.

The Passing of Coolidge

Coolidge's politics underwent no change as he assumed the Presidency in his own right. Lodge died the day after the election, and Curtis of Kansas succeeded to the Senate leadership. But administration views were more often presented by William M. Butler, Republican national chairman, who succeeded Lodge in the Senate. The western liberal group continued to make trouble by coalitions with the Democrats. Such a coalition rejected the President's nomination of Charles B. Warren as Attorney General—a snub without precedent since Andrew Johnson's troubled term. Coolidge, unwilling in most cases either to fight or to make concessions, withdrew into the recesses of the executive offices and let the Congressional leaders wrestle with party problems. "I have never felt that it was my duty to attempt to coerce Senators or Representatives, or to make reprisals," he wrote afterward.

His plans for tax reduction, especially for the higher incomes, prepared by Secretary Mellon, encountered opposition from Democrats and liberal Republicans and were greatly altered in the bills eventually passed. Farm relief, in the form of the McNary-Haugen bill, twice encountered Presidential vetoes. The vigor, even irritation, exhibited by Coolidge's veto messages, reflected the narrowness of his economic and political philosophy. Protective tariffs and subsidies for the good of business, he regarded as natural and normal; farm relief of a similar pattern, he assailed as unsound economically and as unconstitutional.

Coolidge also vetoed the Norris plan for government operation of water power at Muscle Shoals on the Tennessee River. This was perfectly consistent with his general attitude toward expansion of governmental functions and invasion of what he regarded as the sphere of private business. Far more serious than any legislation or Presidential vetoes was the complacent attitude of the administration toward the orgy of speculation that marked the late 1920's. The amazing shortsightedness of Secretary Mellon—and of the President, who followed his lead—in approving the upward surge of the stock market was to wreck the reputation of both men for sagacity in a field in which Mellon at least was supposed to be an expert. Business leaders who were to be so alarmed in the next decade at the mounting burden of public debt regarded the great increases in private debts in the 1920's with complacency, as merely symptoms of unusual prosperity.

Yet, as Coolidge's term drew to a close, the political skies were not unclouded for the Republicans. The Congressional elections of 1926 reduced the Republican majority in the House and produced a Senate almost evenly divided between the two parties. The President's close friend, William M. Butler, was among the defeated. The Norris-Borah group held the balance of power in the Senate. The divided character of the majority party and the weakness of White House leadership were painfully apparent. But in spite of this the organization headed by Butler began to prepare the way for another term for Coolidge. Renomination seemed certain, for the business world wanted him and his personal popularity was still great.

Coolidge upset their plans with a startling message of renunciation. From his summer residence in the Black Hills of South Dakota this brief sentence went flashing over the wires on August 3, 1927: "I do not choose to run for President in 1928." His intimates were taken by surprise and refused to believe that the statement was final.[4]

[4] He had consulted only with Everett Sanders, his private secretary. Not even Mrs. Coolidge had been informed of his decision.

Efforts to get him to amplify it failed, and a "draft Coolidge" movement showed signs of getting under way. He would not refuse if the nomination were tendered, it was argued, and no less a person than Chief Justice Taft tried to secure some encouraging word. But the object of these solicitations only became more clamlike. Except for a brief reference to his decision in a speech to the Republican national committee in December, he made no more public statements; and his advocates grew discouraged.

In the Senate opponents attempted to spike a third-term movement by passing a resolution sponsored by Robert M. La Follette, Jr., that "any departure from this time-honored custom [no third term] would be unwise, unpatriotic and fraught with peril to our free institutions." For the resolution were 18 Republicans, 37 Democrats, 1 Farmer-Labor; against it were 22 Republicans and 4 Democrats.

The way was now open for Secretary of Commerce Herbert Hoover. He had been making plans for a long time, and soon his personal organization was engaged in an active delegate hunt. His reputation as a great organizer, won by his handling of Belgian relief and his work as food administrator in the war years, had not suffered from his service in the cabinet. Though the Secretaryship of Commerce was not a major administrative post he had enlarged its functions and had made the most of its possibilities. The Great Engineer, a new type to be seeking the Presidency, was easily the outstanding figure in the administration; and the withdrawal of Coolidge at once made him the leading contender for the nomination. His organization spent nearly $400,000 in his pre-convention campaign.

But he lacked the President's blessing. The relations of the two men were almost coldly formal. Hoover did not consult with his chief about his candidacy and went ahead bagging delegates in state after state with no help from such administration stalwarts as Charles D. Hilles of New York or Secretary Mellon. A very mediocre crop of favorite sons offered themselves, including Senators Frank B. Willis of Ohio, James E. Watson of Indiana, Charles Curtis of Kansas, and Guy D. Goff of West Virginia. Willis died just before the Ohio primaries, in which his slate of delegates was badly defeated by a Hoover group. A more serious candidacy was that of former Governor Lowden of Illinois, who won support in the farm belt by indorsing the McNary-Haugen bill. But he did not make an active campaign for delegates as he had done in 1920, and had few outside his home state. Vice President Dawes was regarded as a possibility but chose to support Lowden. The Nebraska Presidential primaries expressed a preference for the veteran Senator Norris, but part of the delegation refused to be bound by such instruction.

The only worry in the Hoover camp was over the attitude of the White House. Chairman Butler, Hilles, and Mellon were reported as hopeful that a last-minute word from the President would enable them to form an anti-Hoover bloc, deadlock the convention, and then renominate their chief. Hoover was disturbed at such rumors, but in the end Coolidge's inaction removed the chief danger.

The convention met at Kansas City on Tuesday June 12, with the nomination practically settled. The day before, William S. Vare, ruling Philadelphia boss, had declared for Hoover and wrecked any last hope that the powerful Pennsylvania delegation would join a coalition movement. Mellon saw his own following climbing on the band wagon and perforce went along. A rush to Hoover followed, and only the feeble favorite-son opposition remained in his path.

The convention was opened with a keynote speech by Senator Fess of Ohio, which reached thousands of listeners over the air waves through nine microphones arrayed around the speaker's desk. Senator George H. Moses of New Hampshire, choice of the Hoover forces, became permanent chairman. Senator Reed Smoot of Utah, chairman of the resolutions committee, brought a draft platform with him but the problems of prohibition and farm relief had to be settled by the committee.

Long hours of discussion produced a lengthy review of the Republican record of friendliness to agriculture with certain promises for the future, including creation of a federal farm board to help control surpluses, adequate tariff protection for the farmer, "a federal system of organization for cooperative and orderly marketing of farm products," and the broadening of export markets. The plank was too vague to suit the advocates of the McNary-Haugen bill, and they carried the fight to the floor of the convention while a group of farmers armed with rakes and hoes demonstrated outside. Senator Borah, leading figure of the convention, used his powerful voice in favor of the platform as reported by the committee, and the delegates of the farm bloc went down to defeat, 807 to 277. Lowden then withdrew as a candidate.

The prohibition question caused less difficulty. Borah, ardently in favor of upholding the Eighteenth Amendment, had written in February asking Hoover's views on the matter, and he had answered declaring for the "efficient, vigorous and sincere enforcement" of the prohibition laws. He concluded with this statement: "Our country has deliberately undertaken a great social and economic experiment, noble in motive and far-reaching in purpose. It must be worked out constructively." Hoover's "noble experiment" evoked groans and jeers from the thirsty, but it satisfied the dominant drys. The platform plank accordingly committed the party to the "observance and vigorous enforcement" of the Eighteenth Amendment, and included appropriate quotations from Washington and Lincoln upon the sacredness of observing and enforcing the Constitution. Nicholas Murray Butler, president of Columbia University, spoke for the eastern wet Republicans in opposition to this plank, but his proposal for the repeal of the Eighteenth Amendment was defeated without a roll call.

The rest of the platform was hardly more than a recital of the accomplishments of the party during the Harding-Coolidge years, accompanied by pledges to continue along the same lines in the future. The water-power issue was treated evasively, and the Norris proposal for the Tennessee valley was ignored. Labor was saluted with declarations for "freedom in wage contracts," the right of collective bargaining, and a suggestion that abuses in the use of injunctions "have given rise to a serious question for legislation." Existing high wages were attributed to Republican tariff and other policies.

The only ballot for President gave Hoover 837 votes, Lowden 74, Curtis 64, Watson 45, Norris 24, Goff 18, Coolidge 17, others 5. A motion to make the nomination unanimous then carried. The opposition to Hoover had consisted chiefly of die-hard party regulars who would not accept the Great Engineer as a genuine Republican. Curtis in particular had assailed him, demanding a candidate for whom no apologies would be required. His reward was the Vice Presidential nomination with 1,052 of the 1,089 votes. Borah, after finding that Norris would not consider second place, had insisted that Curtis be named. He was satisfied with the Kansan's attitude toward prohibition and thought that his corn-belt background would help appease farmer discontent.

The Republicans had named their strongest man. Hoover in the popular mind was the one heroic figure in the Grand Old Party, and the objections of the old-line politicians only added to his popularity. That he would lead and control the party was taken for granted. Harding and Coolidge, as stock figures in an era of good times, had suited the temperament of the average American; but even among satisfied Republicans there was a vague feeling that if conditions changed for the worse a more resourceful man than Coolidge might be useful to have around. And "Constitutional" Presidents get rather tiresome; the prospect of dynamic leadership was a welcome relief in 1928.

"The Happy Warrior"

The Democrats were now ready to take Alfred E. Smith, four times elected governor of New York. Born in the shadow of Brooklyn Bridge,[5] this son of a boss truckman was forced by the death of his father to leave school before he was thirteen and assist in supporting the family. Newsboy, clerk in a fish market, shipping clerk, and holder of minor political offices, Smith emerged from his Tammany background to become governor of his state in 1918 after making a fine record as assemblyman, member of the New York State constitutional convention, and sheriff. Defeated for reelection as governor in 1920 by the Harding landslide, he returned to office in 1922 for three more terms, while the Republican tide was sweeping all before it in most of the northern states.

"Al" Smith, on whom Franklin D. Roosevelt bestowed the title "Happy Warrior" at the national convention of 1924, was a strong and able governor and was in line for the Presidential nomination that had come to Samuel J. Tilden and Grover Cleveland. His ever present brown derby hat, his expressive speech with a Manhattan flavor, and his refreshing candor and democratic spirit had made him the idol of the city Democracy of the East. Nurtured by Tammany and tolerant of its ways, he had outgrown its selfish limitations and had become the master of his party in New York State. He had made his declaration of independence in 1922 when he uncompromisingly resisted nomination by the party of William Randolph Hearst for United States Senator, despite strong Tammany backing of the newspaper magnate. Hearst withdrew, and the Tiger retired to its metropolitan confines, leaving Smith unchallenged in the state. Businessmen liked his careful management of state business; social reformers found him sympathetic, for his own humble beginnings had given him an intimate knowledge of urban social problems; and party politicians knew that "Al" knew how organizations are run and

[5] His mother's parents came from Ireland, but he knew nothing about the ancestry of his father, who died in 1886.

elections won. Governor Smith seemed to be ready for a second try at national leadership in 1928.

At first sight the obstacles were serious. Smith was a Roman Catholic, a pronounced wet—even, to the drys, a nullifier—and a Tammany product. To many voters of rural and small-town America he seemed to be thrice disqualified. But this was not all. In the American tradition, the path to the White House for the poor lad had led from log cabin or humble village home; the sidewalks of New York were something else. The belief, nurtured in nativism, that the great metropolis was alien to the spirit of America found utterance when this son of the city sought the highest office.

How did Governor Smith overcome all obstacles to the nomination? One factor was his powerful support in the East by certain wealthy Democrats and by city-controlled state organizations. Donations of more than $150,000 enabled his supporters to set up Smith organizations all over the country and to corral delegates from favorite sons. The backing of the urban Democracy insured him practically all the North, east of the Mississippi River. Ohio and Indiana gave a nominal support to favorite sons, but the New York governor was a strong second choice in both states.

Another factor was the lack of a strong candidate to draw together the hostile elements in the West and South. McAdoo was unwilling to engage in another Madison Square Garden brawl. Elderly Thomas J. Walsh, exposer of Republican corruption under Harding and, like Smith, a Roman Catholic though a dry, refused to let his name go before the convention. Fiery Senator James A. Reed of Missouri campaigned actively but in the end had few votes outside his home state. Old Wilsonians remembered his bitter hostility toward the League of Nations, and his opposition to prohibition made the drys regard him as little better than Smith. Kansas and Nebraska offered local favorites, William A. Ayres and former Senator Gilbert M. Hitchcock, but otherwise the West fell to Smith. In the South attempts were made to rally the rural Democracy against the New York candidate; but only Senator Walter F. George of Georgia, Representative Cordell Hull of Tennessee, and Jesse H. Jones of Texas were presented to the convention.

The convention, drawn to Houston, Texas, by the money and efforts of Jesse Jones and the desire of the Smith men to appease the South, opened on June 26 with a brilliant keynote address by Claude G. Bowers, historian and editorial writer for the New York

World. Senator Joseph T. Robinson of Arkansas was made permanent chairman and Senator Key Pittman of Nevada headed the resolutions committee.

The awkward prohibition issue was solved in committee by a plank criticizing the Republican party for inconsistency between its record and its pledges, and promising "an honest effort to enforce the Eighteenth Amendment." Senator Glass wrote the plank, and the Southern drys accepted it, though some would have preferred a more positive statement.

Farm relief received more space than any other subject. The chief proposals were to grant federal loans to cooperatives, to create a farm board to assist the farmer in marketing his products, to work through proper government agencies to reduce the spread between the prices of producer and consumer, and to give consideration to agriculture in formulating financial and tax measures. An obscurely worded sentence seemed to indorse the Coolidge-vetoed McNary-Haugen bill.

The tariff plank promised to reduce monopolistic and extortionate rates, but would measure duties by the actual difference between the cost of production at home and abroad with adequate safeguard for the wage of American labor. The Republican position was more emphatic, but the difference was not marked. The Democrats were tossing overboard their low-tariff tradition.

The Democratic platform recognized the growing problem of unemployment, which the Republicans had ignored. The Houston plank favored adoption by the government of a "scientific plan" of appropriations for public works during periods of unemployment, which would be scaled down during good times. In other respects there was little difference between the two platforms.

For the third time Franklin D. Roosevelt of New York presented Governor Smith's name to a national convention; and this time success crowned his effort. The roll call was hardly more than a formality. It gave the Happy Warrior 724-2/3 votes, 10 votes short of the necessary two-thirds. Ohio at once changed from its nominal choice, Atlee Pomerene, to Smith; other states did likewise, and the revised ballot finally read: Smith, 849-2/3; George, 55-1/2; Reed, 52; Hull, 50-5/6; Jesse Jones, 43, and some others scattering support.

The next day Senator Robinson, permanent chairman of the convention and minority leader in the Senate, received an almost unopposed nomination for the Vice Presidency. The choice was natural because the South needed to be conciliated and he was one of its best known leaders. As a dry and a Protestant he balanced the ticket. And it was a belated recognition of the faithful support given to Democratic candidates by the South without representation on national tickets since 1860.

Governor Smith startled the convention in its closing moments with a telegram expressing the belief that there should be "fundamental changes in the present provisions for national prohibition," based on the principles of Jeffersonian democracy. While these changes could be made only through the elected representatives of the people, he felt it was his duty to point the way to a sane, sensible solution of the problem. The drys regarded this virtual repudiation of the platform plank as a challenge to battle in the coming campaign.

The minor parties presented candidates as usual, but only Norman Thomas, named by the Socialists, was in a position to cut into the major party vote. A man of high intelligence and fine character and a forceful speaker, he had naturally inherited the mantle of Debs and could appeal to dissatisfied liberals; but, as the campaign went on, most of these turned to Smith, and Thomas had a disappointingly small vote.

Prosperity, Prohibition, and the Pope

The Republican organization was quickly set up. Dr. Hubert Work of Colorado resigned as Secretary of the Interior to be national chairman and Joseph R. Nutt of Ohio was treasurer. Jeremiah Milbank, a New York banker, served as contact man with Wall Street. A huge campaign fund was raised, and the national committee spent more than $6,000,000, a record-breaking total; but the general prosperity made collecting money less difficult than in some other campaigns.

Hoover's acceptance speech, delivered in the stadium of Leland Stanford University, played up Republican accomplishments and the prosperity issue. In this and later speeches he talked optimistically of the coming abolition of poverty and want, praised rugged individualism, and opposed state socialism. His radio addresses, solid, humorless, and often boring, reiterated his basically conservative tenets.

Charles E. Hughes in the East and Senator Borah in the midlands displayed more voter appeal than the candidate. Hughes stuck to prosperity and Republican achievements in the East where prohibition was unpopular. Borah, the bellwether of the Republican progressives, used prohibition, farm relief, and Tammany Hall in the depressed farm belt and did much to allay farmer discontent. Only Senator Norris, the veteran Nebraska progressive, and the La Follette group in Wisconsin refused to follow him. Norris, satisfied with Smith's stand on government operation of hydroelectric power at Muscle Shoals, bolted Hoover in a speech which also paid his respects to the religious intolerance that was engulfing all other issues.

Smith was his party's most dynamic figure and its best campaigner. After a set acceptance speech at Albany on August 22, he took to the road and covered a large part of the country with major addresses. Radio enabled him to reach a nation-wide audience without exhausting his voice in short speeches at a series of train stops. Disdaining careful preparation, he spoke from notes scrawled (but well organized) on the backs of envelopes. Each speech was confined to a particular subject, designed for a particular locality: for example, farm relief at Omaha; prohibition at Milwaukee; religious intolerance at Oklahoma City. His captivating personality, his ready wit, his pungent expressions, and his brown derby won the visible audiences and stamped him as one of the most colorful campaign speakers in the history of American politics. An old popular song, "The Sidewalks of New York," was revived to add the final touch. Not one serious slip did he commit through his free, extemporaneous method of speech. Unfortunately, he was less successful over the radio—or "raddio," as he called it. His voice had a rasping quality, and listeners caught occasional grammatical lapses while missing the appeal of his personality.

Smith's campaign was the best financed in Democratic annals. John J. Raskob of Delaware, lately a Republican but a personal friend of the Democratic nominee, managed it. An official of General Motors and a millionaire, he gained business support for the party; but he lost some votes, for he was both Catholic and wet. Senator Peter G. Gerry of Rhode Island helped direct the political strategy. James W. Gerard, ambassador to Germany under Wilson, was treasurer of the national committee. A Wall Street banker, Herbert H. Lehman, acted as chairman of the finance committee and was aided by Jesse Jones of Texas. This set-up enabled the national committee to collect and spend $5,342,000. But clearly the election was not determined by the size of the war chests. Had Raskob spent twice what he did, the result would have been much the same. The Democrats were faced with an impossible problem.

Boiled down to its lowest terms, the difficulty was twofold: to combat the prosperity appeal, and to overcome the triple objections to Smith, namely, his "wetness," his religion, and his Tammany associations. In the wet East, when Smith attempted to appeal to antiprohibition feeling, he was confronted with the prosperity argument. In the farm belt, when he pointed to the depressed condition of the farmer and virtually indorsed the McNary-Haugen plan, Borah answered with charges of "wetness" and Tammany and promises that Hoover, the miracle man, would come nearer to solving the farm problem than the inexperienced city politician. Thus prosperity served the Republicans where it existed; where it fell short, emotional appeals to bigotry and prejudice took its place.

In the Democratic South the Republicans kept in the background and let the anti-Smith Democrats, or "Hoovercrats," fight their battle. The real force in the anti-Smith movement was Bishop James Cannon, Jr., of the Methodist Episcopal Church South, who appealed to his large following to vote against rum, Romanism, and Tammany, and helped organize the rural South for Hoover. A certain Colonel Horace Mann operated in the background with funds from Republican sources. The Anti-Saloon League, the Woman's Christian Temperance Union, the Ku Klux Klan, and other dry or Catholic-baiting organizations joined in the hue and cry.

Though Smith boldly met the religious issue in his Oklahoma City speech and attempted to bring his accusers into the open, he could do little to combat the "whispering" which made the campaign one of the dirtiest in American history. Tales went around of Catholic projects to bring the Pope to the United States to reside if Smith were elected, and pictures of the governor at the entrance of the new Holland Tunnel under the Hudson were circulated in the rural South with the amazing explanation that the tunnel was to be extended under the Atlantic to the basement of the Vatican! A story was fabricated that Smith was so drunk on a certain public appearance that it took two men to support him, though different versions made the occasion of this lapse vary considerably. Evidence pointed to a common source for this invention but denials of authorship met his efforts to run it down.

In the East liberals without party affiliation who had followed La Follette in 1924 tended to swing to Smith, as he clarified his views by his speeches in contrast with Hoover's more evasive but generally conservative attitude. The *Nation* and the *New Republic* and Professor John Dewey spoke for this group. The Scripps-Howard League of independent newspapers expressed a preference for Hoover at the start of the campaign but grew more lukewarm toward the close, though nominally for him. Labor, to judge from the expressions of its leaders, was divided though Smith seemed to have more indorsements.

On November 6 this bitter campaign ended in another great Republican victory. Hoover had the East with two exceptions, the entire West, the border South, and Texas, Florida, North Carolina, Tennessee, and Virginia from the old "Solid South." He had 444 electoral votes; Smith had 87, carrying but eight states: Massachusetts and Rhode Island, where his antiprohibition stand and his religion were assets, and South Carolina, Georgia, Alabama, Mississippi, Louisiana, and Arkansas. Even New York was lost by more than 100,000 votes. He had persuaded Franklin D. Roosevelt to help the Democratic cause by running for governor. The latter surprised by carrying the state in the face of the tremendous Republican sweep.

The popular vote was nearly 8,000,000 above that of 1924. Hoover received 21,437,277; Smith, 15,007,698. The vote of the minor parties was unusually small. The Socialist vote for Thomas was but 265,583, the poorest showing since 1900.[6] Smith had the consolation of knowing that he had polled the largest vote ever given to a Democratic candidate, and that, despite the electoral vote, he had run far better than Cox in 1920 or Davis in 1924. He had received a large urban vote, carrying New York, Boston, Cleveland, St. Louis and San Francisco, and running well in other large cities. A dry Protestant candidate would have held the southern electoral votes but would have done far worse than Smith in the East and probably but little better in the West. No Democrat could possibly have won, and none but Smith could have gained such a large popular support.

The Democrats could thank their lucky stars for the defeat of 1928. Had they won, the Great Depression would have descended upon them as relentlessly as it did upon Hoover, and the Republican dogma that prosperity was a G.O.P. monopoly would have become

[6] The others were as follows: Foster, Workers', 48,896; Reynolds, Socialist Labor, 21,585; Varney, Prohibition, 20,101; Webb, Farmer-Labor, 6,390.

so established in the popular mind that no Democrat could have overcome it for another generation. The Great Engineer was the unfortunate man in 1928, not his defeated opponent. The Happy Warrior would not have remained happy very long in the White House after 1929.

25

The Second Roosevelt

The "Hair Shirt"

With Mellon continued in the Treasury Department and the stock market rocketing to new heights, the business world listened with satisfaction to Hoover's inaugural keyed in a note of practical optimism as to America's future. The new President, true to Borah's promise, called Congress into special session to deal with the farm problem, the sagging timber in the structure of prosperity. Congress promptly set up a Federal Farm Board to reduce marketing costs and to control surpluses through loans to cooperative associations and stabilization corporations. Senator Borah, favoring an export bounty plan, was dissatisfied; but Hoover was opposed to subsidies and the proposal was killed. Whereupon the disappointed Idaho Senator resumed his accustomed role of administration critic, joining Norris, the bolter, in opposition to the man he had helped elect as a friend of the farmer.

The tariff widened the breach still further. Borah had assumed that tariff revision, promised by Hoover, would be confined to schedules affecting the farmer. The House of Representatives, however, voted general increases all along the line, with manufacturers the chief beneficiaries. A long deadlock ensued in the Senate; but ultimately, in June, 1930, the Smoot-Hawley Tariff carried by two votes. It was popularly dubbed the "Grundy Tariff" because of the lobbying activities of Joseph R. Grundy, president of the Pennsylvania Manufacturers' Association and collector of funds for Republican campaigns, who became a member of the Senate by appointment of Governor Fisher while the tariff bill was still pending.

Hoover signed the bill, though a thousand economists, many prominent industrialists, and the American Bankers Association opposed it. He believed that it would relieve business uncertainty, and that he could readjust unfair rates under a flexible provision of the law. The ten liberal Republicans led by Borah and Norris who had opposed the bill in the Senate took this as a Taft surrender. The parallel with the Payne-Aldrich fiasco was striking. The economic effects were far worse. Foreign trade was damaged by the higher tariff barriers and the Great Depression, already slowing down industrial production, was only aggravated. The feud in the party was made worse by the sneer of Senator Moses at the insurgents as "sons of the wild jackass" and Senator Fess's charge that they were "pseudo-Republicans."

Hoover's answer to the great stock-market crash of October, 1929, and the decline in business which followed was to treat it as a speculators' panic and to insist that economic conditions were fundamentally sound. Secretary Mellon and leading financiers sang the same song and predicted a speedy recovery. The trouble was merely "psychological." Months went by without any action by the government. A great drought in the summer of 1930 made the farmer's lot all the harder. As the difficulties multiplied, Hoover wrote that the Presidency was like "wearing a hair shirt."

The Congressional election of 1930 reflected both disappointment with Hoover and discontent with economic conditions. It was not a violent repudiation of the administration; but it indicated a loss of confidence in the President and his party, a disillusionment after the glittering promises of 1928. The House was Democratic, 219 to 214; the Senate contained 48 Republicans, 47 Democrats, and one Farmer-Laborite. Several new Democratic governors assumed office, and Franklin D. Roosevelt was reelected governor of New York by a record-breaking margin.

As the depression deepened, President Hoover abandoned nonaction and recommended to Congress in December, 1930, an enlarged public-works program and loans through the Farm Board for drought relief. Both recommendations were adopted, but the President frowned on the La Follette-Borah-Norris idea of direct relief to individuals. It smacked too much of the English dole. He conferred with industrialists and tried to get them to cooperate in preventing further unemployment and wage cuts; but the situation grew steadily worse.

In December, 1931, he was ready to use government aid to prop the tottering structure of private credit. The most important step was creation of the Reconstruction Finance Corporation to make emergency loans to banks, railroads, insurance companies, and other businesses. Indirect credit relief was also offered to farmers and home owners by other measures, but the President still held out against direct relief to the unemployed. Eventually he yielded sufficiently to accept a bill for loans to states and municipalities for public works and relief.

The government now began to pay the penalty for the tax reductions of the Coolidge-Mellon regime in the form of growing Treasury deficits as the depression dried up revenues. A new tax bill, passed after a bitter struggle, imposed higher income taxes and a number of new excises, but failed to solve the problem. Matters were made worse by the importunities of former servicemen. Suffering from the effects of the depression, they now demanded that the government allow them to borrow on their adjusted-service certificates, granted in 1924 and payable in twenty years. Congress gave in and, over Hoover's veto, allowed loans up to 50 per cent of the face value of the certificates in 1931. Within a few months many were demanding full payment in cash; and an "expeditionary force" of several thousand assembled in Washington in the summer of 1932 to put pressure on Congress. They failed in the effort, but the President's use of military force to drive them from their camps on government property aroused a wave of indignation and accelerated the demand for cash payment of the bonus.

How far Hoover might have succeeded as President had the depression not occurred may only be conjectured. Far superior to Harding and Coolidge in intelligence, industry, and grasp of public affairs, he had shown political ineptitude in the first year of his administration; and both party regulars and insurgents were displeased with him. Watson, the genial Republican floor leader of the Senate, found that the round, cherubic face concealed "a man of extreme reserve," who neither told nor seemed to appreciate humorous stories and witticisms. He fumbled when he tried to play politics and impressed Old Guard leaders with the notion that his organization was his own and not the party's. Like Taft his experience in office had been by appointment, not election; and he lacked the intimate contacts with party workers and voters that come with campaigning, legislative service, and holding elective positions. Newspapermen disliked his aloofness and gave him a poor press.

While the regulars found fault with the man and his methods, the liberals disliked his policies. He stood with the eastern industrialists on the tariff. He vetoed the Norris plan for public operation of Muscle Shoals. He gave scarcely half a loaf to the agricultural interests. He objected to direct federal relief for the unemployed, though he would bolster private credit with federal funds to save business and banks from collapse. And what he did, his critics charged, was always too little and too late. His prediction that prosperity was just around the corner became the butt of vaudeville jokes. The "Hoovervilles" of the unemployed that rose along railroad tracks and on city dumps were devastating to Republican hopes.

Yet neither old-line politicians nor progressives believed that he could be defeated for renomination. There was some whispering that Coolidge might be offered to the convention, but the idea was soon dropped. The party had to stand or fall on the record Hoover had made. His friends controlled the party machinery, and a fight would be hopeless.

The Republican convention met at Chicago on June 14 in the huge new stadium, arranged to seat 19,000 persons. It was artificially cooled, but there was little reason for excitement. The temporary chairman was Senator L. J. Dickinson of Iowa, and the permanent officer Representative Bertrand H. Snell of New York. The platform, as reported by James R. Garfield of Ohio, aroused no opposition except for its statement on prohibition. The long majority plank, after admitting that differences of opinion existed among Republicans over the Eighteenth Amendment, recommended that the people be given an opportunity to pass upon a proposed amendment allowing the states to deal with the problem, reserving to the federal government the power to protect dry states and "safeguard our citizens everywhere against the return of the saloon and attendant abuses." Senator Bingham of Connecticut offered a minority report favoring outright repeal, and he and Nicholas Murray Butler made a hard fight for its adoption. Ogden Mills, who had replaced Mellon as Treasury head, marshaled the administration supporters against it, and it was defeated, 681 to 472. The ambiguous and evasive character of the plank adopted aroused much unfavorable comment. The tide was running strongly against prohibition, and the platform only half-heartedly recognized the fact.

The platform attributed the continuance of the depression to events in Europe, eulogized Hoover's leadership, and duly praised his measures. Various planks hopefully called the attention of the farmers to the higher tariff rates on agricultural products and the work of the Farm Board, promised support for any plan to help balance production against demand, "provided it is economically sound and administratively workable without burdensome bureaucracy," and suggested the importance of "control of the acreage of land under cultivation, as an aid to the efforts of the farmer to balance production." In view of the policy later adopted by the Roosevelt administration, this statement has a peculiar significance. Most of the long document was devoted to a defense of the party's record, the customary criticism of the Democrats, and repetition of planks of other years, reworded to fit the situation in 1932.

There was little comfort in all this for the western progressives. Indeed, insurgents were gently reminded that it was the duty of members of Congress to abide by the will of the majority on general policies. But this mattered little, for they were practically in revolt.

Hoover was nominated almost without opposition, receiving 1,126-1/2 votes to 13 for Senator Blaine of Wisconsin (11 from Wisconsin and 2 from South Dakota), 4-1/2 for Calvin Coolidge, 4 for former Senator Joseph I. France of Maryland, 1 for Charles G. Dawes, and 1 for James W. Wadsworth of New York. France was thrust from the platform when he tried to withdraw in favor of Coolidge. Vice President Curtis was opposed for renomination by many delegates who wanted new blood on the ticket, and five rivals were formally put in nomination against him while some others received votes on the one ballot taken. Colonel Hanford MacNider, who had been national commander of the American Legion, General James G. Harbord of New York, former Governor Alvan T. Fuller of Massachusetts, and Congressman Bertrand Snell of New York were his chief opponents; but he was only 19-1/4 votes short of a majority on the first ballot, and Pennsylvania then changed to him, making his total of 634-1/4 votes, well over the line. Word came that the White House wanted Curtis, and that settled it.

The Man with the New Deal

The optimistic Democrats had been smelling victory ever since the Congressional overturn of 1930. The party management had been conducting a remarkably effective "Smear Hoover" campaign through the "Executive Committee" of the Democratic national committee headed by Jouett Shouse, for which Charles Michelson, an experienced newspaper writer formerly of the New York *World*, handled publicity. Supplied with funds by Chairman Raskob, who wanted to rehabilitate the party he had led to such a disastrous defeat, Michelson performed one of the most skillful jobs of destructive criticism in the history of American politics. From his relentless mimeograph machine poured forth a steady stream of anti-Hoover material; his bureau even furnished editorials for newspapers, and statements and speeches for prominent Democrats to give to the world as their own. Newspapers and press associations carried a great deal of his propaganda, for it often had news value. Republican efforts were feeble by comparison, partly because Hoover failed to realize the value of favorable publicity. He writhed under Michelson's attacks but took refuge in a dignified silence.

Candidates for the Democratic nomination were numerous enough, but destiny was pointing in one direction months before the convention met. Governor Franklin Delano Roosevelt, a New York country gentleman of Dutch descent and a distant relative of Theodore Roosevelt, combined assets that almost insured his nomination. His feat in carrying New York in the face of the Hoover landslide of 1928 had made him a marked man, and reelection in 1930 by a majority greater than any amassed by Alfred E. Smith was an argument no rival could meet. Blessed with a winning personality and a gift for making friends, he was skilled in the ways of the politician and had a wide acquaintance with party leaders all over the country. Though crippled by infantile paralysis in 1921, he had fought bravely against his handicap and had recovered sufficiently to walk with the aid of canes and steel braces. He had a fine stage presence and an unusual command of language. His private secretary, frail, wizened Louis Howe, was a shrewd and devoted adviser. Not the least of Roosevelt's assets was his manager, James A. Farley, a big genial Irishman who never forgot a face, and who established friendly contacts with hundreds of local leaders all over the West and South.

Roosevelt had a record that was difficult to attack. He had begun as an anti-Tammany member of the legislature, had served as Assistant Secretary of the Navy under Wilson, had been Vice Presidential nominee in the forlorn fight of 1920, and had established a reputation in the governorship as a progressive leader that appealed strongly to the West. Senator Norris liked his attitude on electric power and made little concealment of his willingness to support him against Hoover. The depression-stricken farmers were ready to revolt against Republican rule; and, in the absence of a western candidate, Roosevelt was the answer. In the South, he was well known and popular from his sojourns at Warm Springs, Georgia. Unlike Smith, he was Protestant and anti-Tammany; and his antiprohibition views mattered little to southerners in 1932, when the depression overshadowed all other considerations.

The chief opposition to Roosevelt at first came from local favorites. Speaker John N. Garner of Texas was the strongest, for he had had the help of William G. McAdoo and William Randolph Hearst in adding the California delegation to his Texas support. A straight-out party man, he had no special appeal to liberals and independents. The chief claim of Governor Albert C. Ritchie of Maryland was an unwavering opposition to prohibition; former Governor Harry Byrd of Virginia enjoyed a local popularity; James A. Reed was again Missouri's choice; Illinois offered a prominent Chicago bank president, Melvin A. Traylor; and Ohio supported Governor George White. There was much talk that former Secretary of War Newton D. Baker of Ohio or Owen D. Young, chairman of the board of General Electric Company and author of a well known plan for German reparations, might be chosen, particularly in case of a deadlock.

However, the opposition to Roosevelt made little headway until Alfred E. Smith entered the race. He had declared after his defeat in 1928 that he would never run for office again; but the pressure of certain eastern leaders and a desire to see Roosevelt defeated changed his mind. Most observers felt that he had no chance for the nomination; but his strength in the East was used in an effort to stop Roosevelt. Why Smith turned against the man he had persuaded to run for governor in 1928 has not been made clear. At the time there were no sharp divergences over policies, indicating that personal considerations may have played a major part. The Smith-Raskob leadership set out to retain control of the party and rounded up a bloc of delegates from New England, New Jersey, and New York, leaving Roosevelt but a minority from his home state. The troubles which the governor was having with Tammany also complicated the New York situation.[1] He was thus compelled to depend chiefly upon the West and the South for his delegate support.

On June 27, 1,154 enthusiastic Democratic delegates and a great

[1] The Seabury investigation of corruption in the New York City government resulted in Roosevelt's removal of Sheriff Thomas M. Farley and Mayor James J Walker in the summer of 1932.

crowd of well wishers assembled at Chicago and heard Senator Alben W. Barkley of Kentucky deliver the keynote speech as temporary chairman. The spirit of victory was in the air; but the harmony so desirable for winning elections was lacking the next day. The anti-Roosevelt forces offered Jouett Shouse, choice of the national committee, for the permanent chairmanship but the Rooseveltians supported Senator Thomas J. Walsh of Montana. Walsh was elected, 626 to 528—an indication that control rested with Farley's cohorts, but that the two-thirds rule might be a serious obstacle. There had been talk that it might be abrogated but the rules committee merely recommended that it be abandoned in 1936.

The platform recommended unequivocally repeal of the Eighteenth Amendment and immediate legalization of the manufacture and sale of beer. The drys attempted a substitute but were defeated, 934-3/4 to 213-3/4. The widespread feeling that repeal would add to government revenues and create jobs made this platform statement a big vote-getter.

The other features of the platform were less candid, though the brevity of the document was impressive. The customary promise to reduce expenditures went along with a balanced budget, a sound currency, and "a competitive tariff for revenue." Reciprocal tariff agreements and an international economic conference to restore international trade and facilitate exchange took issue with Republican economic nationalism. To meet the depression the platform favored extension of federal credit to the states for unemployment relief, an expanded public-works program, reduction in hours of labor, and unemployment and old-age insurance.

To the farmer it talked vaguely of better financing of mortgages, extension of cooperatives, control of crop surpluses, and every other measure necessary to raise prices above cost of production. Of broader appeal were promises to enforce anti-trust laws, conserve and use water power in the public interest, and regulate public utilities, holding companies, and exchange trading in securities and commodities—a sore spot after the collapse of 1929.

While the platform attacked Republican policies with convincing severity, most of its counterproposals were cautiously qualified. Yet the overtones of a resurgent liberalism were present, and it challenged the basic tenets of Hoover's rugged individualism.

Hours of oratory and sustained applause on June 30 delayed the balloting so that an all-night session was necessary to complete three ballots. The first one told the story of all three. It gave Roosevelt 666-1/4, Smith 201-3/4, Garner 90-1/4, and the favorite sons the rest. Roosevelt went up to 682.79 on the third, Garner to 101-1/4, while Smith dropped to 190-1/4. Since 770 votes were necessary under the two-thirds rule, Roosevelt was but 88 votes short of his goal, and all precedents pointed toward his nomination when the convention met the next evening. Yet there was considerable discouragement in his camp. His managers had hoped that his showing on the first ballot would start the band wagon; but the favorite sons were still holding on, while the Smith-Tammany group seemed to be more determined than ever. Fears were expressed that some of the Roosevelt delegates might desert if the deadlock went on. But the weariness of the all-night struggle probably made the situation appear darker than the facts warranted. A candidate so near two-thirds was not likely to be stopped, particularly when the opposition groups lacked a popular figure on whom they could concentrate. Party leaders were concerned at preventing another Madison Square Garden brawl, and most important of all, Farley had the Vice Presidency as trading stock to draw in the necessary votes. The Texas and California delegations were ready to go to Roosevelt when Garner consented to take second place.

When the convention met again, William G. McAdoo of California, amid the jeers of the pro-Smith galleries, announced the shift of the Garner forces to Roosevelt. The delegates demonstrated for ten minutes, and then the ballot was completed, giving Roosevelt 945, Smith 190-1/2, and four others 13 votes in all. Garner received the Vice Presidential nomination unopposed the next day.

Then followed an unprecedented action by the head of the ticket. Coming by plane from Albany, he appeared before the delegates to accept the nomination the day after it was made. His speech was aggressively liberal as he pledged himself to a "new deal" for the American people. Except for a remnant of embittered Smith men, Democrats generally were greatly pleased with their candidate. His apparent physical vigor despite his affliction, his fine voice, his warm personality, and his liberal creed seemed to mark him as the man of the hour. Liberal Republicans and independents were more skeptical. Though Norris was friendly, most of them regarded the New York governor as a pleasant gentleman with a keen sense of political values and a milk-and-water progressivism that remained to be tested.

The Battle of '32

Depressions produce a bumper crop of protest parties and extremist movements, some of which never get beyond the name stage. In 1932 twenty-one different parties had their names on the ballots in various states, and several others claimed an existence that was not in evidence on Election Day. In the end none of the new movements reached the strength of the older third parties, all of whom offered candidates as usual.

Of the others that did not expire before Election Day, Coin Harvey's "Liberty" party made the best showing. Harvey, forgotten since 1896, raised the inflationist banner again, but few flocked to it. However, he had a larger total than that once famous leader of the jobless of the nineties, General Jacob S. Coxey of Massillon, Ohio. Coxey, candidate of a Farmer-Labor remnant, did not get on the ballot in most of the states. Some other protest parties were confined to a single state.

The Democratic campaign was well planned and well managed. James A. Farley naturally became national chairman and handled affairs from his New York headquarters directly through the state organizations, without special regional or branch headquarters. Charles Michelson took care of publicity. An efficient corps of assistants worked with Farley, and the "brain trust"—experts selected for their knowledge of public problems but lacking in political experience—came on the scene to advise the candidate and help him in the preparation of important addresses. The charter members were Raymond Moley, Rexford G. Tugwell, and Adolf A. Berle, Jr., all from Columbia University, and Justice Samuel I. Rosenman. According to Moley, the group was concerned exclusively with policy-planning and had nothing to do with campaign management or tactics. Roosevelt's major speeches were prepared from materials compiled and interpreted by this "brain trust." That a candidate should seek guidance from unbiased experts on difficult problems, chiefly economic in character, was indeed an innovation in a political campaign. Unlike Harding, Roosevelt did not recite what others had written. He used the ideas of others but, according to Charles Michelson, was a better phrasemaker than anybody around him.

Roosevelt conducted a vigorous offensive, with twenty-seven major addresses from coast to coast. His purpose was not only to give the lie to whispers about his physical condition but, more important, to play the role of a New Deal Messiah, particularly in the midwestern farm belt where riots against mortgage foreclosures and forced sales indicated the temper of farm voters.

His sympathetic approach attracted George N. Peek, Henry A. Wallace, and other farm leaders to his camp and was a factor in the bolt of Senators Norris, Hiram Johnson, Bronson Cutting of New Mexico, and Robert M. La Follette, Jr. Norris was more interested in his friendliness toward public ownership of electric power. Borah preserved a sullen silence toward both candidates.

In the East the conservative Smith-Raskob wing of the party had to be conciliated. Roosevelt and Smith cooperated in obtaining the nomination of Herbert Lehman for governor of New York, and then the man with the brown derby went on the stump to make antiprohibition speeches. Tammany also fell in line, and the urban East seemed united behind Roosevelt.

The Republican organization was headed by Everett Sanders, former Indiana Congressman and secretary to President Coolidge. As in 1928, Joseph R. Nutt and Jeremiah Milbank handled finances. Hoover had intended to make only three or four set speeches, but alarming reports of Republican defections—Maine went Democratic in September—forced him to take the stump. In ten major speeches and many brief talks at train stops he exhibited a sturdy fighting spirit, in contrast to his ignoring of Smith in 1928. Despite fears of his advisers, he was treated everywhere with respect, except in Detroit, where there were some catcalls and boos from the sidewalks.

Republicans hoped that the depression would begin to lift and prosperity peep around the corner in time to save them, but Fortune refused to favor them this time. There was left only the argument that things would be worse if the Democrats won. "Grass will grow in the streets of a hundred cities," warned Hoover in his final speech in a moment of emotional strain unusual with him. But the old fear argument had lost its potency. With better psychology his opponent was offering the more abundant life to the forgotten man.

Neither party was blessed with a huge campaign chest. The Republicans as usual were better off, but the depression had reduced some of their chief sources of revenue. At one time Hoover had to take personal direction of the job of collecting funds to stave off a financial breakdown. About $2,900,000 was spent, against receipts of $2,650,000. The Democrats collected $2,379,000 and spent $2,246,-

000, without allowance for a large deficit incurred in the preceding four years. Both national committees continued heavily in debt after the campaign was over.

Radio was a more powerful factor in 1932 than in 1928. The major speeches of both candidates and many broadcasts by lesser figures reached millions of listeners and challenged the significance of newspapers and other forms of publicity. The direct appeal of candidates to voters sitting in their homes and unmoved by crowd psychology compelled greater care in the preparation of speeches and a special technique in presentation. Here the Democrats showed to advantage. The heavy, monotonous seriousness of Hoover's speeches made listening an effort. Roosevelt, by contrast, was at his best when heard over the air. The deep mellow tones of his voice, a cheerful warmth of personality, and a skill in interjecting light, humorous touches into his speeches made his broadcasts the most effective type of propaganda the Democrats used.

The result was almost foreordained. Republican money, organization, and propaganda could not meet the deadly realities of the Great Depression. The difference between the two candidates was not so much in specific issues as in methods of approach. Hoover stood on his record and could promise little more than continuance along the same lines. Roosevelt, critical of the President's conservatism, could offer an open mind and a willingness to try new paths. The country had soured on Hoover, and felt that any change would be for the better.

On November 8 the Republicans went down to a crushing defeat. Roosevelt had 472 electoral votes; Hoover, 59. Pennsylvania, Delaware, Maine, New Hampshire, Vermont, and Connecticut constituted the Republican total. In the popular vote Roosevelt had a plurality of more than 7,000,000.[2] The Democrats had more than 70 per cent of the House and a margin of twenty-two votes in the Senate. Such Old Guard leaders as Watson of Indiana, Smoot of Utah, and Moses of New Hampshire were defeated. As in 1920 the voters had voted their resentments; but this time the Republicans were the victims. The Socialist vote approached the total Debs had received in 1920; but on the whole the minor parties made a poor showing for a depression year. The discontented had chosen the Roosevelt road,

[2] Roosevelt, 22,829,501; Hoover, 15,760,684; Thomas, Socialist, 884,649; Foster, Communist, 103,253; Upshaw, Prohibition, 81,872; Harvey, Liberty, 53,247; Reynolds, Socialist Labor, 34,043; Coxey, Farmer-Labor, 7,431.

which offered some hope of immediate relief, rather than unfamiliar third-party bypaths and blind alleys. It remained for the Democrats to prove that they had made no mistake.

Liberalism in Power

The dark winter of 1932-1933 brought the nation nearer to economic and psychological demoralization than at any time in its history. Unemployment reached the staggering figure of fourteen or fifteen millions and local governments were being bankrupted by relief expenditures. As the Hoover administration ended the banking system was collapsing like a house of cards. The depression seemed at last to have struck rock bottom. The country was prostrate, and the way was clear for a great emergency program of recovery and reform. In keeping with the gay spirit of the bands in the inaugural parade as they played "Happy Days Are Here Again," the cheerful, confident air of the new President, in sharp contrast with Hoover's chronic gloom, created a favorable reaction at once. A few days later he gave his first "fireside chat," in which he explained the measures taken to meet the banking problem. Roosevelt's warm reassuring voice, as much as his words, helped to dispel fear. Faith in the new Moses grew by leaps and bounds. The close-mouthed, fearsome attitude of Hoover was replaced by the sometimes too buoyant enthusiasm of the Knight of the New Deal, who boldly challenged the powers of darkness and invited them out into the light. It was good medicine for the American people, after months of hearing that prosperity was just around the corner only to see business continue its downward spiral. What was needed first of all was a return to a sane perspective on depression problems and a recovery of morale; and Roosevelt performed a notable service here.

But more than a healthy attitude was needed. The situation called for dynamic leadership and drastic action, and the man who was regarded in some quarters as a water-gruel liberal assumed the role of democratic dictator. At his request the new Congress enacted a series of far-reaching laws that gave him the widest powers ever conferred on a President in time of peace. In rapid succession legislation on currency and banking, agricultural relief, industrial recovery, loans to home owners, railroads, public works, unemployment relief, conservation, the Tennessee valley, and the liquor question went through Congress, usually with slight opposition from the Republican minority. The Borah-Johnson-McNary group of western liberals generally supported the administration, while Norris and La Follette became practically identified with it.

Refusing to separate reform from recovery, Roosevelt drove through the major points of his program before the conservatives in both parties had time to rally their forces. Fundamentally he was reviving the old progressive movement that had withered away in the searing heat of the war years of 1914-1918 with much of its task unfinished. The liberals of 1910-1914 had been more engrossed with boss rule, machine politics, and the restoration of popular government; the New Deal drove ahead in economic and social reform. Business was to be subjected to drastic regulation; farmer and labor, long neglected, were to have the first seats at the table; and the most imposing body of humanitarian legislation in the country's history was enacted in this high tide of liberalism. This brief survey of the political aspects of the New Deal program will not attempt to evaluate it. It is enough to say that it was boldly conceived and was carried through on the impetus of a wave of reform sentiment swelling from a depression psychology, and that its sponsor did not make the mistake of waiting for times to improve. However, there was too little real planning, much improvising, and some blundering. The people were not always certain which way they were going; but they were relieved to be on their way.

The new administration represented an odd combination of orthodox Democrats and partyless liberals, held together by the leadership of Roosevelt and his unexpectedly powerful appeal to all classes of Americans. The cabinet, as a whole, was not distinguished. Roosevelt passed over Smith, Davis, Cox, and Baker. Cordell Hull, an old-fashioned, low-tariff southern Democrat, became Secretary of State. Farley was Postmaster General, and the others included four party regulars, two former Republicans, William H. Woodin, Secretary of the Treasury, and Henry A. Wallace, Secretary of Agriculture, and two political orphans, Harold L. Ickes, Secretary of the Interior, an old Progressive, and Miss Frances Perkins, Secretary of Labor. Thomas J. Walsh was to have been Attorney General but died just before the inauguration. Harry Hopkins, who became relief administrator, exercised far more power than most members of the cabinet.

Mrs. Eleanor Roosevelt was an important influence in strengthening the liberal viewpoint of the President. This remarkable woman found time, despite her social duties, to lecture, speak over the radio, conduct a newspaper column, attend numerous conventions, chiefly of a social welfare or humanitarian character, travel about the country, and in other ways display an intense interest in the welfare of her fellow Americans. The more conventional-minded lifted their eyebrows, but the majority came to admire this most unusual White House hostess, even when they disagreed with her freely expressed views on public matters.

The "brain trusters" of the 1932 campaign continued as palace advisers for a time; but their influence declined, and two of them, Raymond Moley and General Hugh S. Johnson, ended up as sharp critics of administration policies. A new crowd was emerging, the "New Dealers," who held key positions in administrative bodies and wrote much of the new legislation enacted by Congress. Among them were protégés of Felix Frankfurter, professor of law at Harvard and friend and adviser of Roosevelt, who elevated him to the Supreme Bench in 1939. Thomas G. Corcoran and Benjamin V. Cohen were at first the best known and most influential of the group. Two of the New Dealers, Robert H. Jackson and William O. Douglas, followed Frankfurter to the Supreme Court.

To the general public the New Deal meant the policies of the Roosevelt administration, and the term "New Dealers" had a broad application. But primarily they were the more independent and liberal spirits, scattered through the administration, who cooperated to combat Bourbonism and to give meaning to the vague reformist ideals of the groups that followed Roosevelt. This injection of new blood into the veins of that torpid creature of the post-Wilsonian years, the Democratic party, which had survived chiefly in metropolitan city halls and southern state capitals, gave it a sudden vitality that at times caused it to perform strange gyrations; but no one could deny that its potentialities were tremendously increased.

The Republican party was in the worst plight of its long history. Its defeat in 1932 was due not to factionalism or schism, as in 1912, but to failure to meet the country's problems. With the Republican prosperity myth destroyed, and the Hoover leadership discredited, a new deal was badly needed in the party; but the reins were still in conservative hands, and the prospect of Democratic defections encouraged the die-hards. A Liberty League backed by the Du Ponts and other men of wealth appeared in 1934 to checkmate radicalism and defend private property. Alfred E. Smith, who had become an open critic of the New Deal, and John W. Davis, Democratic standard-bearer of 1924, were on the Liberty League's board of directors; but it was badly timed. Resentment against the "money-changers," a powerful factor in the election of 1932, had not subsided, and the League in its brief existence only provided the Democrats with ammunition. The mid-term elections of 1934, instead of producing the usual reaction against the party in power, reduced Republican strength in the House from 117 to 103 and in the Senate from 36 to 25. The Senate minority consisted of half a dozen conservatives from rural New England, two or three stray survivors from the middle regions, and a group of trans-Mississippi westerners of uncertain regularity and various shades of liberalism. The Old Guard of the 1920's had disappeared, a consolation to those who saw the need of reorganizing the party on more liberal lines. Most of the states chose Democratic governors, even Pennsylvania succumbing. From the seaboard to Kansas reached an unbroken Democratic waste.

26

The New Deal Landslide

The Convention of '36

Despite the setback in the elections of 1934, the Republicans began to recover hope as 1936 approached. Millions were still unemployed; lavish government expenditures had not restored prosperity; the budget was unbalanced, and the national debt was mounting; taxes and government restrictions alarmed businessmen; many conservatives saw constitutional government in danger. There were signs also of restiveness in Congress. While the passage of a comprehensive social security act marked the high-water mark of the reform program, Roosevelt suffered his first defeat in the Senate when his proposal for American entry into the World Court failed by seven votes to attain the required two-thirds. A Coughlin-Hearst clamor stirred up the isolationists. The Wheeler-Rayburn bill to regulate public utilities had its drastic "death sentence" provision for holding companies modified because of conservative pressure, though in the main the administration was satisfied with the measure. These straws seemed to indicate a weakening of the Roosevelt magic and a possible conservative revival.

The Republican problem was to find a suitable candidate. Hoover was a liability; the Senate Old Guard had been almost wiped out; the insurgents were generally disqualified as bolters in 1932 or supporters of New Deal measures; hardly a Republican governor of a strategically important state was left. Never had the material been so unpromising. Three names were considered: Charles L. McNary and Arthur H. Vandenberg, Senators from Oregon and Michigan, and Alfred M. Landon, Governor of Kansas. Neither Senator was well known outside his home state; NcNary was badly located geographically, and both had voting records that indicated liberal tendencies.

The party regulars found Landon the most suitable. The Kansas governor had been an oil producer—a fact which would appeal to businessmen. He had twice carried an important farming state and presumably would run well in the farm belt, where Republican losses had been heavy. He had once followed Theodore Roosevelt and was regarded as mildly progressive, which would suit the liberal element. A group of Kansas friends, including John D. M. Hamilton, national committeeman, Roy A. Roberts of the *Kansas City Star*, and William Allen White, provided backing and publicity, and the Hearst papers began to praise him.

Who else was there? Colonel Frank Knox, publisher of the *Chicago Daily News* and an old Bull Mooser, jumped into the race and showed plenty of energy but aroused no popular support. Belatedly and unexpectedly Borah decided to run, but the regulars would not even consider him.

The Landon backers, playing up their candidate as a western reincarnation of Calvin Coolidge, mellowed by a progressive heritage and a Kansas environment, came to the Republican national convention at Cleveland on June 9, 1936, with the nomination sewed up. Senator Frederick Steiwer of Oregon was temporary chairman of the convention, and Congressman Bertrand H. Snell of New York, permanent chairman. Hoover aroused the most enthusiasm with a speech which emphasized the dangers threatening the American way of life and the need for the party to conduct "a holy crusade for liberty."

The platform required a great deal of work to satisfy conflicting interests. Borah adopted a threatening attitude with demands for liberalism on domestic policies and isolationism in foreign relations. Herman M. Langworthy of Missouri for the resolutions committee reported a compromise platform, and it was adopted without opposition.

It began with the solemn preamble: "America is in peril. The welfare of American men and women and the future of our youth are at stake. We dedicate ourselves to the preservation of their political liberty, their individual opportunity and their character as free citizens, which today for the first time are threatened by government itself." Then followed an indictment of "the New Deal administration" (all through, the term "New Deal" was used instead of "democratic") for misdeeds and usurpations. All Americans, irrespective of parties, were invited "to join in defense of American institutions."

The preservation of constitutional government and the American system of free enterprise came first in the list of pledges. Then followed statements of policy on various problems.

Unemployment was to be solved by encouragement of private business and removal of hampering government regulations; relief was to be returned to local control with federal grants-in-aid; more adequate old-age pensions were offered in place of the social security act; protective tariff with flexible provisions to promote international trade was recommended; further devaluation of the dollar was opposed, New Deal finance condemned, and a balanced budget promised. A thirteen-point agricultural section of the platform accepted, with some qualifications, most of the administration farm program, and even insisted that the New Deal had taken over the Republican policy of soil conservation and land retirement. Collective bargaining in labor disputes was promised, and state laws and interstate compacts to protect women and children in industry. Extreme isolationism characterized the statements on foreign relations. Even the World Court was condemned.

On the whole, it was superior to recent Republican convention pronouncements in length and in clarity of phrasing. In places its positive commitments were cautiously hedged in with qualifications and conditions; and it was glaringly inconsistent in advocating drastic economy and a balanced budget, and at the same time a program of farm aid, old-age security, unemployment relief, and other policies involving heavy expenditures. But the party out of power can afford to be both evasive and inconsistent. The Democrats had played this game in 1932.

The convention cheered for half an hour a telegram from Governor Landon approving the platform but favoring a constitutional amendment to permit states to enact legislation necessary to protect women and children as to hours, wages, and working conditions, if this could not be attained within the Constitution (a Supreme Court decision setting aside a New York minimum wage statute had aroused a storm of criticism). Landon also declared himself for a stable currency expressed in terms of gold, and for the application of the merit system to all administrative positions below the rank of assistant secretary. This display of independence received generally favorable comment, though Borah, who had left the convention, was displeased with the gold-standard pronouncement.

Landon was nominated almost without opposition after half a dozen nominal favorite sons released their delegates.[1] He received 984 votes; Borah, 19 including 18 of Wisconsin's 24. Knox's preconvention campaigning won him the Vice Presidential nomination when Senator Vandenberg refused to be considered. John D. M. Hamilton of Kansas, who had presented Landon's name to the convention and had managed his delegate hunt, naturally was chosen for the post of national chairman.

Landon's acceptance speech, at Topeka on July 23 before 50,000 persons, was preceded by a picturesque pageant of frontier days, emblematic of the candidate's background; and an enthusiastic and apparently united party approved of the general tenor of his remarks. But the pageant, not the candidate, provided the color. He appeared as a sincere, uninspiring conservative, rather than as the wielder of the sword of Theodore Roosevelt. It remained for the Republicans to prove that the country needed his type, an average man of substantial virtues without Coolidge's narrowness or Franklin Roosevelt's dangerous "charm."

The Democratic convention, at Philadelphia in the Municipal Auditorium, June 23-27, 1936, was an utterly useless performance, except for the hotels, restaurants, and stores of the Quaker City. Platform and candidates were predetermined, and the delegates came merely to ratify; yet the program was spread over five days. Chairman Farley called the convention to order and gave the opening address; Senators Alben W. Barkley of Kentucky and Joseph T. Robinson were the presiding officers. The most significant action taken was the abrogation of the century-old two-thirds rule, as recommended by the convention of 1932. The only opposition was in the rules committee, where the vote was 36 to 13.

Senator Robert F. Wagner presented a White House platform that paraphrased the Declaration of Independence with its self-evident truths, proclaiming that farmers, workers, businessmen and the youth of the nation had been returned to the road to freedom and prosperity, and promising, "We will keep them on that road." A recital of accomplishment was offered as evidence.

Unemployment was declared to be a national problem, to be met

[1] These were Senator Vandenberg, Senator L. J. Dickinson of Iowa, Governor Harry W. Nice of Maryland, Frank Knox, Robert A. Taft of Ohio, and Walter E. Edge of New Jersey.

in a national way. While more than five million had found employment through "our stimulation of private enterprise," a continuation of work relief was promised where needed. Republican proposals to solve national problems by state action were derided. The Democrats promised to deal with them by federal legislation within the Constitution or, if this proved impossible, by a "clarifying amendment" to give Congress and the states the necessary powers, within their respective jurisdictions. The financial measures of the administration were defended, and a balanced budget was promised at the earliest possible moment, as relief requirements declined and national income increased.

The party pledged itself to continue the "Good Neighbor" policy in foreign relations, to take the profits out of war, and to guard against involvement in any war anywhere. The World Court and the League of Nations were not mentioned. The platform closed by defining the issue as one between a party that would regiment the people in the service of privileged groups and an administration dedicated to the establishment of equal opportunity for all.

After the adoption of the ready-made platform came a marathon of oratory. To make the convention last, Farley had planned that each state, territory, and dependency should have a seconding speaker after Judge John E. Mack had presented the President's name. Over the air waves, hour after hour, flowed a seemingly endless stream of banal oratory which listeners could tune off, but which the delegates had to endure. Forty-nine men and eight women participated. At the end Roosevelt and Garner were safely nominated without opposition. The enthusiasm for Roosevelt was tremendous but the oratorical relay was indefensible.

At Franklin Field that night, June 27, President Roosevelt delivered his acceptance speech to an assemblage estimated at one hundred thousand, while the whole country listened in. Though for the most part he spoke in terms of exalted idealism, his denunciation of "economic royalists" sounded the keynote of a campaign that was to carry the war into the enemy's country.

While Roosevelt's course as President had made him the man most hated by archconservatives, certain radical groups were creating a diversion on the left. The old minor parties were no more active than in 1932; but three new prophets arose to gain a hearing where Socialists and Communists had failed. The first combined the arts of the demagogue with the practical skill of the machine politician and the ruthlessness of a dictator; the second was a radio voice; and the third was an elderly physician with a startlingly simple plan to solve America's economic ills.

Huey P. Long, of Louisiana, a rabble rouser of the Tillman-Vardaman-Blease school, rose to be governor by appealing to the prejudices and discontents of the poor whites. Once in office, he established a machine so powerful that when he went to Washington as United States Senator in 1932 he was absolute dictator of the state with every official including the governor at his beck and call. He supported Roosevelt in that election but soon broke with the administration, chiefly over patronage, and began a savage warfare against it. His legislative accomplishments in Louisiana gave him a certain claim to the support of the common man, and soon he was heading a "Share-the-Wealth" movement to give every American family five thousand dollars a year. In September, 1935, when he was preparing to invade Arkansas and Mississippi in an attempt to defeat administration Senators he was assassinated. None of his henchmen was strong enough to take over his power; but the Reverend Gerald L. K. Smith attempted to lead the "Share-the-Wealth" groups into a third party movement.

Father Charles E. Coughlin, a Roman Catholic priest, speaking Sundays on problems of the hour from a Detroit radio station, had acquired millions of listeners. Assailing communism and international bankers with equal vigor, he pleaded fervently for social justice, and the National Union for Social Justice appeared in 1935 as his special vehicle. His program, eloquently indefinite, seemed to favor complete government control of currency and credit, much after the old Populist fashion.

An even more popular figure, Dr. Francis E. Townsend of California, inaugurated a movement for federal monthly pensions of two hundred dollars to be paid to non-workers over sixty years of age on condition that the money be spent in the month in which it was received. The impoverished and dependent elderly flocked to his banner, and thousands of Townsend clubs were soon in existence. While individual Congressmen gave lip service to the Townsend Plan, neither party dared indorse such an extreme proposal, and some of the Townsendites began to look toward the Coughlin and Smith groups.

Congressman William Lemke, a Nonpartisan League Republican from North Dakota, announced his Presidential candidacy on a "Union Party" ticket June 19 with Thomas C. O'Brien, a Boston lawyer, as his running mate. On the same day Father Coughlin gave his support. On July 14 the Townsendites assembled in large numbers at Cleveland and listened to Lemke, Townsend, Gerald L. K. Smith, and Father Coughlin, who outdid himself in abusing the President. No formal nominations were made, but Dr. Townsend indorsed Lemke. Coughlin's National Union for Social Justice also met in convention at Cleveland on August 15, adopted a platform of its own, and accepted Lemke and O'Brien, though refusing to indorse the Union party or its platform. In such left-handed fashion these groups from the cave of Adullam launched their third party.

There were practically three platforms: the Townsend Plan, the original Lemke proposals, and the Coughlin planks. The second and third emphasized federal control of currency and credit but were too vague about most other matters to attract liberal support. Lemke's background was radical agrarian, but Coughlin was regarded as leaning toward Fascism. The combination did not inspire confidence, and most of the Townsendites rejected Lemke. Although the leaders claimed millions of supporters, they found that organizing a third party was difficult, and their campaign languished.

The other minor parties were still active. The Socialists nominated Norman Thomas of New York; the Communists, Earl R. Browder of New York; the Socialist Labor party, John W. Aiken of Massachusetts, and the Prohibitionists D. Leigh Colvin of New York. None of these played any significant part in the campaign. The Communists, following the "party line"—later changed—of a united front against Fascism, assailed Landon, Hearst, and the Republicans and showed an embarrassingly friendly attitude toward Roosevelt.

More important than these minor parties in voting strength were three state parties, the Farmer-Labor party of Minnesota, the La Follette Progressive party of Wisconsin, and the new American Labor party of New York. All three supported Roosevelt, giving him large blocs of votes in three important states.

A national conference of liberals and progressives at Chicago on September 11 also indorsed Roosevelt. Senator La Follette, Mayor La Guardia of New York, John L. Lewis, and other liberal and labor representatives attended. Frank P. Walsh of New York was made head of an executive committee.

The Roosevelt Tidal Wave

The campaign soon revealed that the country was dividing less along traditional party lines and more according to economic groups than at any time since 1896. The leaders of the American Federation of Labor and its new rival, the Committee for Industrial Organization, supported Roosevelt. In the political field their support was made effective by an organization known as Labor's Nonpartisan League. John L. Lewis, though not the official head, was its real organizer. The farmers, less united in sentiment, seemed to be still favorable to the New Deal in the great grain-growing regions, once Republican strongholds. The La Follettes, Norris, the Minnesota Farmer-Laborites, and other western progressives cooperated with the Democrats on the Presidential ticket, while Senators Borah and McNary campaigned for themselves, not for Landon. Thus the party of Roosevelt appeared as a farmer-labor combination, as Bryan had attempted to make it in 1896, and as it had been in Jackson's day, though the labor partner then was a pygmy compared with 1936.

Backing the Republican cause was big business as represented by the Liberty League, the National Association of Manufacturers, and other organizations, numerically small but financially powerful. There was general expectation among Republicans that the smaller businessmen and the professional groups—the upper middle class—would be with them as in the past. Dislike and fear of New Deal spending and regimentation were evident here. The conservatism of the party also drew Democratic allies, unable to stomach New Deal liberalism. These conservatives, calling themselves "Jeffersonian Democrats," [2] included such impressive names as John W. Davis, Alfred E. Smith, James A. Reed of Missouri, Bainbridge Colby (Wilson's Secretary of State), and former Governor Joseph B. Ely of Massachusetts. Unfortunately for the Republicans, these figures were hardly more than museum pieces, imposing to gaze upon but useless as vote getters. In fact, the Toryism of the Republicans cost them far more votes through defections on the left than were gained from recruiting on the right.

The Republican management seemed to be liberally supplied with funds, though it ended the campaign with a budget badly out

[2] A conference of bolting conservative Democrats, held at Detroit on August 7, took this name.

of balance. It spent nearly $9,000,000—a new record for campaign expenditures. This did not include sums raised and spent by the Liberty League and by state committees. Such names as Hearst, Guggenheim, Rockefeller, Du Pont, Pew, and Vanderbilt among Republican contributors indicate the party's financial backing.

Yet money alone could not solve the problem. A strategy had to be devised to recover the populous East and Middle West, long Republican but rendered doubtful by the popularity of the New Deal with labor and farmer. Relying upon the past conservatism of this area, the Republican general staff began a vigorous assault upon the New Deal and all its works. Criticisms of its spending policy, its farm-relief measures, its attitude toward business, its currency program, its disregard of the Constitution, and Roosevelt's violation of his platform of 1932 filled Republican newspapers, were the meat of hundreds of speeches, and reached millions of voters over the air waves. These attacks were made more pointed by charges that the New Deal was collectivistic and even Communistic.

Toward the close of the campaign a concerted attempt was made to use the Social Security Act against Roosevelt. To alarm wage earners, the act was assailed as a "pay reduction" measure. Many employers assisted the Republican cause with explanations designed to influence their employees. Some used bulletins in factories and slips in pay envelopes, reminiscent of the tactics of 1896. The net effect was to sharpen the class alignment, and make labor more resentful toward such pressure and more pro-Roosevelt than before.

The Republican organization functioned badly. Chairman Hamilton, inexperienced in national politics but filled with enthusiasm for his task, found the state and local organizations in bad shape, their morale broken by the succession of defeats since 1930. The national chairman, assuming the role of a traveling salesman, went around the country making the acquaintance of local leaders, stirring them to action, and delivering speeches for Landon at the same time. The national headquarters at Chicago became a huge propaganda machine manned by supersalesmen, and pouring forth every possible type of publicity for the Republican cause. Much of this was wasted because of bad management and bungling tactics.

Chairman Farley's Democratic machine reached its peak in 1936. Fortified by victory and the possession of offices, and stimulated by the chairman's unceasing vigilance, the Democratic organizations, national, state, and local, left nothing to chance. Numerous reports from party workers to the New York headquarters, tabulated, checked, and analyzed by Emil Hurja, gave the national chairman a clear picture of the battle at every stage and enabled him to adapt his tactics to the immediate situation.

The hostility of big business reduced the number of large contributors and compelled the Democrats to rely upon a larger number of small gifts than in the past. Half a million individuals gave to the Democratic campaign fund, more than a third of the total amount being accounted for by gifts of less than $100. Labor organizations—a hitherto untapped source of funds—were heavy contributors. A new device, continued after 1936, was the holding of Jackson Day dinners all over the country on January 8, with tickets selling as high as $100 a plate but graded down to fit the pocketbooks of the faithful who attended in the provinces.[3] The campaign expenditures by the national committee amounted to $5,194,000. Like the Republicans, the Democrats had the assistance of auxiliary organizations whose outlays added materially to the total cost.

The Democratic strategy was not cautiously defensive but a vigorous assault on the forces of reaction. The "economic royalists" and "Tories" behind Landon, "the straw man," received the major brunt of the attack. The support given by Hoover, Hearst, former Governor Smith, and the Liberty League was offered as concrete evidence of the reactionary character of the opposition.

But the strongest argument in the Democratic repertory was the contrast between 1932 and 1936. Even conceding that the glittering prosperity of the 1920's had not returned, they argued that conditions had improved immeasurably under Roosevelt, that old abuses had been removed and confidence had been restored, and that farmer, laborer, and businessman were better off. Against this the Republican cry that the Constitution and the American way of life were in danger fell flat.

Both candidates took the stump. They centered their attention on the Middle West but appeared also in the East, and Landon made a foray to the Pacific coast. Roosevelt aroused far greater mass enthusiasm. At Chicago five miles of streets were almost impassable for the Presidential car, and a hundred thousand people packed the stadium to hear him. His oratorical cleverness and his role of crusader against

[3] Another device, much criticized, was the sale of the *Book of the Democratic Convention*, with the President's autograph, at $100 or more per copy. Its sale was continued after the campaign to help pay off the national committee's deficit.

plutocracy made him the greatest political attraction since Theodore Roosevelt and Bryan had charged and countercharged. Landon, utterly lacking in magnetism and mediocre as a speaker, did not appear to advantage on the stump; and he was further handicapped by a poor radio voice.

The power of radio to overcome unfavorable newspaper publicity was clearly shown in this campaign. No candidate since Bryan in 1896 had had to fight such a powerful array of newspapers as confronted Roosevelt. To the normal Republican journalistic preponderance outside the South were added the Hearst chain, the *Baltimore Sun*, and the *St. Louis Post-Dispatch*. In the fifteen largest cities the newspaper alignment was 71 per cent for Landon, as measured by circulation figures. In Chicago it was eight to one in his favor, but Roosevelt's majority was almost two to one. The press, with its savage editorial denunciations of the New Deal—comparable to the anti-Bryan violence of 1896—its warped news stories, and its misleading headlines, played a rather sorry part in the campaign.

The whispering, or under-cover, campaign that has so often disgraced American politics appeared chiefly in the form of stories about the President's sanity. In 1932 it was his physical condition; in 1936, his mental state. It was "whispered" at country clubs and across bridge tables that his mind had been affected by his siege of infantile paralysis; and medical authorities were cited to prove that his symptoms foreshadowed mental collapse. The divorces in the Roosevelt family and Mrs. Roosevelt's manifold activities offended the sensibilities of middle-class Roosevelt haters and were used as propaganda wherever possible. Among the overly well fed the most astonishing reason offered for opposing the President was that he was a traitor to his "class."

The various polls, with one notable exception, pointed toward a Roosevelt victory. But the huge postcard poll of the *Literary Digest*, so successful in its prophecies in the past, indicated a large Landon electoral majority. Its failure to give due weight to the different groups and classes in the voting population was its undoing. On the other hand the careful "sampling" methods of the American Institute of Public Opinion, headed by Dr. George Gallup, and similar techniques used by *Fortune* magazine and by Archibald M. Crossley were completely vindicated by the result in November. They underestimated the size of the Roosevelt victory, as did all the polls and the major prophets except Chairman Farley. With Emil Hurja's figures before him, he created amusement among Republicans by extravagantly claiming all the electoral votes for Roosevelt except those of Maine and Vermont.

On November 3 he was found to be exactly right. Roosevelt had 523 electoral votes; Landon, 8 (Maine and Vermont). Not since Monroe had a winner come so near to a clean sweep. Roosevelt's share of the popular vote, 60.8 per cent, was slightly over Harding's in 1920; but his plurality was the largest ever recorded, eleven million votes.[4] Lemke's poor showing indicated the end of the Union party. Father Coughlin's German and Irish Catholic isolationists had provided much of his support. The Townsendites and Huey Long's old following had gone elsewhere. The other minor parties likewise had fared badly. The Socialist vote was the smallest since 1900.

The House had 333 Democratic members out of the total membership of 435; the Senate, 75 Democrats out of 96; and a host of Democratic candidates for state and local offices rode to victory on Roosevelt's coattails. In 1932 the verdict had been anti-Hoover; in 1936 it was pro-Roosevelt. The New Deal's good works had built up a powerful farmer-labor-Negro coalition and had cut heavily into Republican middle-income strength. Urban solidarity for Roosevelt was without precedent. The Democratic tide had receded somewhat in the trans-Mississippi West, and nationally the Republicans carried more counties than in 1932. But the loss of the cities was fatal. Labor, whether of native or of immigrant stock, voted its economic interests.

The result was a complete repudiation of the Toryism that had governed the Republican party's strategy despite the new leadership. The old myths and the old slogans had failed to convince. Standing by the Constitution, defending the American way of life, and calling New Dealers Communists would not supply food for the unemployed, higher farm prices for debt-burdened agrarians, or security for the wage-earners. So the masses of voters had seemed to reason. No Republican could have defeated Roosevelt, but a more intelligent leadership in the years before 1936 might have averted the complete debacle. This was the lesson for 1940. The emaciated frame of the Grand Old Party needed both vitamins and calories.

[4] Roosevelt had 27,757,333; Landon, 16,684,231; Lemke, Union, 892,267; Thomas, Socialist, 187,833; Browder, Communist, 80,171; Colvin, Prohibition, 37,677; Aiken, Socialist Labor, 12,829.

The Master Politician Slips a Little

The second Franklin Roosevelt administration began on January 20, 1937,[5] with inauguration ceremonies marred by a cold, drenching rain. The President served notice in his address that the New Deal was not completed, that much remained to be done while one-third of the American people were "ill-housed, ill-clad, ill-nourished." The era of good feelings that followed his nearly unanimous electoral victory was a mirage that vanished with the meeting of the new Congress. Harmonious inaction had no place in the Roosevelt lexicon. The New Deal was to be implemented further by reform legislation dealing with the still difficult problems of economic maladjustment.

But a serious obstacle to reform was the conservative Supreme Court, without a single Roosevelt appointee. Six of the nine members were past seventy, making it the oldest Supreme Court in American history. In the preceding two years it had overturned seven basic New Deal laws, usually by split decisions based on "personal economic predilections," according to Justice Stone. Roosevelt, strengthened by the popular verdict of 1936, now proposed to liberalize the Court by adding a justice for each justice past seventy. The result was the bitterest battle of his career. A group of conservative Senate Democrats charged him with "court packing" to build up his own power, and defeated the proposal with Republican support. However, during the struggle the Court, influenced by Chief Justice Hughes, began to uphold New Deal social legislation; and the resignation of conservative Justice Van Devanter broke the hold of the septuagenarian majority. Politically Roosevelt had suffered a major setback. The Court issue had split the Democratic party in Congress, and the effects were evident later at the polls, even though most of his domestic program fared well enough. Acts affecting labor, farmers, and housing rounded out his reform program.

More serious in general effects than the Court fight was a business recession in 1937-1938. It produced an increase in federal spending and gave weight to the charge that the New Deal had failed to bring about a sound recovery. An epidemic of sit-down strikes by unions

[5] The change from March 4 was effected by the Twentieth Amendment, the work of Senator Norris, which eliminated the lame-duck session of Congress by fixing January 3 as the date for each new Congress to begin to function, and set January 20 as the date for the new President and Vice President to be inaugurated.

under the newly organized Committee for Industrial Organization alarmed businessmen and farmers over the radicalism let loose by the New Deal.

With the political skies more clouded than at any time since 1932, Roosevelt set out to punish the conservatives in his own party in the primaries of 1938. In this "purge," he went on the stump in several states to bless for renomination Senators who had stood with him and to defeat those who had opposed his measures. His failure to defeat Millard E. Tydings of Maryland and Walter F. George of Georgia was a blow to his political prestige.

The elections of 1938 produced a Republican revival. Eighteen states turned against the Democrats, and increased the Republican membership in the House of Representatives from 89 to 170 against 262 Democrats, and in the Senate from 17 to 23 against 69 Democrats.[6]

A bipartisan conservative bloc could now offer an effective opposition. One of its achievements was the Hatch Act of 1939 prohibiting political activities by federal administrative officials, except a few top-ranking ones. In 1940 a more stringent act included state officials paid wholly or in part with federal funds and limited a party's campaign expenditures to $3,000,000.

But foreign problems now overshadowed domestic issues. Hitler had invaded Poland in September, 1939. World War II had begun.

[6] There were 3 independents in the House and 4 in the Senate.

27

"That Man" Again

The Philadelphia Miracle

American politics, for nearly two decades, had been more isolationist than American policies. Since 1920, foreign problems had not entered into Presidential elections, and had not divided the parties in Congress. Though the United States participated actively in various international conferences, it drew back from cooperation with the League of Nations when aggression threatened war. A series of drastic neutrality acts in the 1930's, backed by both parties, attempted to insulate the nation from foreign wars by cutting off American arms, loans, and shipping from all belligerents, with the unintentional effect of encouraging aggressors. Roosevelt was not satisfied with this solution, but public sentiment was against him. Domestic questions were far more pressing, in any case.

At the outbreak of World War II Americans were strongly anti-Hitler; but not until the collapse of France in June, 1940, was there alarm at the prospect of a dictator victory. All aid for England short of war and an immediate American rearmament program were major policies on which Roosevelt and most Americans agreed. But Republicans soon realized that this might mean a third term for him, and the hostility of some turned from the New Deal to his "warmongering." A convention divided in opinion on foreign policy and uncertain as to its nominee for the first time since 1920 gathered at Philadelphia in late June.

The elections of 1938 had produced a new crop of hopefuls, though nearly all were too untried and inexpert to do battle with the master politician in the White House. Senator Robert A. Taft of Ohio and District Attorney Thomas E. Dewey of New York City were the leading contenders. Senator Taft, son of a President, had a sharp mind, came from an important doubtful middle western state, and had the assistance of a wealthy family; but he was a colorless, uninspiring speaker, too orthodox to attract independents and liberals, and seemed to be reaching for the grand prize before he had won his spurs in the Upper House. Nevertheless, by avoiding primaries and working with the practical politicians, he bagged a goodly number of delegates and had strong second-choice support. Dewey's aggressive handling of the district attorney's office in New York and his close race against Governor Lehman marked him as a man with a future. He showed surprising strength in several state primaries, but it was freely predicted that his delegate support would melt away after the early ballots. Aspiring New Yorkers, by tradition, should reach the White House by way of Albany.

Among favorite sons, Charles L. McNary of Oregon, Senate floor leader, and Arthur H. Vandenberg, Senator from Michigan, had the most experience. They did not attract much outside support, though a deadlock might enhance their chances.

A few days before the convention a great deal began to be heard about Wendell L. Willkie. Indiana-born and formerly of Ohio, he lived in New York City and had made his way in the business world through his ability as a utilities lawyer until in 1933 he became head of Commonwealth & Southern Corporation, a large holding company. Long opposed to the federal Tennessee Valley Authority, he had finally sold a subsidiary company in that area to it and declared a truce with the government. He had been a Democrat until 1938 and had even served on a Tammany Hall committee, but had never held public office. At first sight this was not a promising background for an aspirant for the Republican Presidential nomination.

But Willkie had assets that his rivals lacked. A big tousle-headed man in the prime of life—he was forty-eight—he had a dynamic personality, supreme self-confidence, a wise-cracking sense of humor, skill in extempore speaking, a disarming frankness, and an ability to win friends. Of small-town upbringing, he had the look of the stalwart middle western self-made man that old-fashioned Americans had long regarded as one of the most wholesome products of their land of opportunity. That he was no politician was entirely in his favor. Business and professional men, wearied of the New Deal and dubious over the ability of any politician candidate to defeat Roosevelt, trooped into the Willkie camp, for here was one of their own sort. Big business approved but wisely kept in the background, for its support would be a liability.

Who first suggested Willkie's name is a matter of dispute; but the men who organized his candidacy were Oren Root, Jr., a young lawyer and a grandnephew of Elihu Root, and Russell Davenport, managing editor of *Fortune* magazine. Blank petitions were sent out to be circulated, Willkie clubs sprang up in different parts of the country, literature about the new man was soon in demand everywhere, and the encouraging popular response made his backers redouble their efforts. Delegates already elected were made aware of the Willkie candidacy by the pressure of business and professional men in their own communities, who were organizing Willkie clubs and creating a backfire hard to resist with a barrage of last minute letters, telegrams, and declarations for Willkie.

The "amateurs," as his backers proudly called themselves, did an excellent job of selling their man, and the galleries soon gave evidence of pronounced Willkie sentiment. Charges were made afterward that they were packed by the use of forged tickets, but in any case they correctly reflected the growing desire of voters opposed to the New Deal for a non-politician candidate. Taft, Dewey, and the rest of the field aroused no enthusiasm. Willkie could appeal, as they could not, to conservative Democrats and independents. Perhaps labor and farmer votes might be attracted to the standard of a man who was not embarrassed by Bourbon Republican connections or a partisan public record. The fact that his views on foreign policy were much like Roosevelt's would tend to controvert charges of "isolationism" and "appeasement."

But the regular Republicans were not ready to hand over the party leadership to a man whose coating of Republicanism had hardly had time to dry. A hundred Congressmen representing some twenty states held a caucus and demanded that the convention name a man "whose personal views and public statements present an opportunity for a clear-cut vote on foreign and domestic issues in harmony with the Republican record in Congress." His utilities record was played up as a grave liability, and a strong isolationist group objected to his support of Roosevelt's foreign policy. There was much talk of a "Stop Willkie" movement, and a Taft-Dewey ticket was rumored as the solution.

The youthful Governor Harold E. Stassen of Minnesota opened

the convention at Philadelphia on Monday June 24, 1940, with a stirring keynote speech assailing the Roosevelt administration for its failure on the fronts of national preparedness, "fifth column" activities, domestic economic welfare, and governmental effectiveness and integrity. Joseph W. Martin, Jr., of Massachusetts, Republican floor leader in the House of Representatives, as permanent chairman followed with another assault on the New Deal record. On Tuesday night former President Hoover had his moment of glory; but the hopes of friends that he might stampede the delegates and win the nomination were dimmed by his performance. He was still the Hoover of old. He was warmly applauded and then dropped from consideration as a candidate.

The battle over the platform was fought out behind the scenes. A 35,000-word report by Dr. Glenn Frank for the program committee, set up two years before, supplied the resolutions committee with the material for the platform; but the rapidly shifting character of foreign problems made an enunciation of policies here difficult. A group of out-and-out isolationists offered an antiwar plank in such positive terms as to arouse the opposition of believers in extending all aid to England short of war. In the end a compromise was arranged, but the isolationists had somewhat the better of it.

The platform, much briefer than usual, began with an arraignment of the Roosevelt administration and then pledged the Republican party to "Americanism, preparedness and peace." It promised an adequate national defense and condemned the "explosive utterances" of the President as imperiling peace. The controversial plank on aid to Britain promised "the extension to all peoples fighting for liberty, or whose liberty is threatened, of such aid as shall not be in violation of international law or inconsistent with the requirements of our own national defense." This statement left the candidate plenty of leeway later.

Unemployment was to be solved by encouraging private enterprise; relief was to be turned over to the states with federal grants-in-aid; social security was to be extended to groups not yet covered, with the states controlling the administration. The right of free organization and collective bargaining was guaranteed to labor, but the National Labor Relations Act was to be amended to provide "true freedom for, and orderliness in, self-organization and collective bargaining."

The farm planks, as in 1936, received much attention. In effect, they promised to continue existing benefit payments until expanding business and greater consumer buying power took care of overproduction. Easier credit, encouragement of cooperatives, better tariff protection, and a condemnation of reciprocal trade agreements were also thrown into the agricultural hopper. Business was wooed with promises of economy, encouragement of investment, an end of the President's control of the currency, and a minimum of federal competition. A constitutional amendment limiting a President to two terms was also indorsed.

The general tone was friendly to business, but the party asked to be taken on faith. Other than currency control, no pledge was made to repeal or modify seriously any major acts of legislation of the Roosevelt administrations.

With the platform out of the way on Wednesday afternoon, the nominating speeches were in order. In a flood of oratory, Dewey, Frank E. Gannett of New York, Taft, Willkie, Hanford MacNider of Iowa, Vandenberg of Michigan, H. Styles Bridges of New Hampshire, McNary of Oregon, Governor Arthur H. James of Pennsylvania, and Governor Harlan J. Bushfield of South Dakota were placed in nomination. When Representative Charles A. Halleck of Indiana offered Willkie the galleries shrieked approval; but whistles, boos, and heckling from delegates pledged to other candidates indicated a resentment at the outside pressure for the "utilities tycoon." This hostility grew more intense as the balloting went on and threatened to bring about a coalition movement in favor of a true-blue Republican.

The first ballot, on Thursday afternoon, ran almost as predicted. Dewey led with 360; Taft had 189; Willkie, 105; and eleven others divided the rest of the thousand votes.[1] The next three ballots saw Dewey's support decline to 250 votes, while Taft went up to 254 and Willkie to 306. On the fifth ballot, Willkie reached 429 and Taft 377, while Dewey, who had released his delegates, dropped to 57. With the shift of Kansas and most of New York to Willkie on this ballot the band wagon hove in sight. Desperately the Taft leaders tried to rally the straight-out party men; but the avalanche of letters and telegrams, the excellent publicity for the businessman candidate, and the roars of the galleries had done the work. The "amateurs" were

[1] These were as follows: Vandenberg, 76; James, 74; Chairman Joseph Martin, 44; MacNider, 34; Gannett, 33; Bridges, 28; Capper, 18; Hoover, 17; McNary, 13; Bushfield, 9.

cleverer than the politicians. When Vandenberg released the Michigan delegates on the sixth ballot and they shifted to Willkie, the battle was practically over. Pennsylvania then decided for him, and other delegations changed their votes before the count was officially announced, to make the nomination unanimous.

Next day, after several of the Presidential aspirants refused to be considered, second place on the ticket went to Senator McNary, who reluctantly accepted. His western residence, his post as floor leader in the Senate, and his liberalism as attested by his support of a number of New Deal measures made him an excellent choice.

Willkie, who had been in Philadelphia conducting his own campaign—as had his chief rivals—came before the convention and was received like a conquering hero. Overnight the old-line politicians forgot their bitterness and began to sense that the delegates might, after all, have done a shrewd piece of work. As a businessman Willkie would have the backing of the financial overlords, which meant a well financed campaign; as an ex-Democrat he was satisfactory to Democrats opposed to the New Deal and to a third term; and his middle western background might help the party where help was badly needed. His vulnerable spot—his record as a utilities lawyer and official—might be offset by the argument that he was an able administrator, and that he had not amassed a great fortune by dubious practices. Had the Republicans at last found a challenger who could fight it out on even terms with the "champ" himself?

The Chicago Anticlimax

That the 1,094 delegates who assembled at Chicago on Monday July 15 would nominate President Roosevelt for a third term was a foregone conclusion. For several months the "Draft Roosevelt" movement had been eliminating any possible competitors. The President's silence had had a sharply deterrent effect on candidacies, and the few primaries where opposition showed itself indicated an overwhelming sentiment for the man in the White House. The liberal groups had no alternative. No one in the administration had developed any degree of popular strength, and, if Roosevelt refused to run, the choice promised to fall upon an old-line Democrat, such as Hull, Farley, or Garner. But there was another angle. Mayor Kelly of Chicago, Mayor Hague of Jersey City, and other local organization leaders, in bad repute with liberals, saw in the President their best bet to save their state and local tickets. In state after state the organizations lined up for the man on whose coattails they had been riding to victory since 1932. Only he could check the Republican tide that had swept away several states in 1938 and was threatening to engulf even more in 1940.

Vice President Garner, refusing to await the President's decision, let it be known in December, 1939, that he would be a candidate. In March, Postmaster General Farley, apparently no longer in the President's confidence, announced that his name would be presented in the Massachusetts primaries, though it was not clear whether the Farley delegates would remain loyal if Roosevelt decided to run. Senator Wheeler of Montana and Senator Tydings were regarded as potential anti-Roosevelt candidates, but neither had any strength outside his own state. Secretary of State Cordell Hull was popular among the rank and file and might have been named if Roosevelt had withdrawn. But there was no strictly New Deal candidate except the President himself. He had failed to groom a successor.

The Chicago convention opened with the stage set for the President's renomination. Harry Hopkins established headquarters at the Blackstone Hotel to direct proceedings, but the regulars resented his presence and almost got out of hand on the final day, when the balloting for Vice President began. Speaker William B. Bankhead delivered the keynote speech as temporary chairman, and Senator Barkley was chosen as permanent chairman. Both were good party men, loyal to Roosevelt, and their speeches were strong defenses of the administration's foreign and domestic policies.

Barkley closed his speech with a message from the President—a tense moment, for some believed he would yet renounce the nomination. But the words from the White House merely indicated that the President had no wish to be a candidate again, that "all the delegates are free to vote for any candidate." This did not change matters, and the forty-five-minute demonstration that greeted Barkley's announcement indicated clearly what the convention would do.

The resolutions committee, headed by Senator Robert F. Wagner of New York, had some difficulty with foreign affairs, but ended with a watered-down compromise pledging the party against participation in foreign wars or sending military forces to fight outside the Americas except in case of attack. This was a concession to Senator Wheeler and the isolationists. Stressing the problems created by the world crisis, the platform contended that the Roosevelt administration had strengthened democracy by taking defensive measures against aggression, by increasing economic efficiency, and by improving the welfare of the people. Aid to Britain was promised in a plank that pledged "all the material aid at our command consistent with law and not inconsistent with the interests of our own national defense" to peace-loving and liberty-loving peoples wantonly attacked by ruthless aggressors.

The sections dealing with agriculture and labor recited the accomplishments of the preceding seven years with pledges to continue along the same general lines. The platform took direct issue with the Republicans by opposing local control of federally financed work relief. It promised to extend the Social Security Act to cover new groups and to strengthen the unemployment insurance system.

A long section on "capital and the businessman" was chiefly a defense of New Deal policies. Electric power received separate consideration because of the Republican candidate's record as a utility executive and an opponent of public power. The Tennessee and Columbia River projects were offered as proof of the success of hydroelectric plants under government ownership and operation.

A brief flurry occurred when Congressman Elmer J. Ryan of Minnesota offered a resolution against a third term. A roar of boos and shouts of disapproval from the delegates turned it down without a roll call. The platform was then accepted as presented by the resolutions committee.

As soon as it was out of the way on Wednesday night, Senator Lister Hill of Alabama presented the name of President Roosevelt in a dramatic speech. A sweaty demonstration twenty-three minutes long ensued, with the cheers led by one of Mayor Kelly's henchmen from a basement microphone. The venerable Senator Carter Glass of Virginia then nominated James A. Farley; but his remarks were none too well received, particularly his reference to Jefferson's refusal of a third term. Maryland offered Senator Tydings and Texas Vice President Garner, while the delegates and galleries listened with ill concealed impatience. Senator Wheeler's name was not presented, though he had established headquarters at Chicago. On the first ballot Roosevelt had 946-13/30 votes; Farley, 72-9/10; Garner, 61; Tydings, 9-1/2; Cordell Hull, 5-2/3. Before the result was announced, the nomination of Roosevelt was made unanimous. Farley received a great ovation as he withdrew his name, as it was known that he planned to resign from the cabinet and from the national chairmanship.

Next day, unexpectedly, there broke out the only real battle of the convention. From Washington came the word that Secretary of Agriculture Henry Wallace was the President's choice for second place on the ticket. Smoldering dissatisfaction blazed into open revolt. Primarily it was directed at New Deal control of the convention, and the rebels were orthodox, old-line regulars. They resented the prominence of Hopkins and others and refused to believe that Wallace, once a Republican and reputed to be a star-gazing idealist, was a proper choice. Southern Democrats of conservative cast wanted a southerner on the ticket and friends of Farley and Garner saw an opportunity to strike a blow at the New Deal crowd. The galleries, eager for a fight, cheered for the insurgents, who presented Speaker Bankhead of Alabama. A movement for Paul V. McNutt, social security administrator and former governor of Indiana, stalled when the tall, handsome favorite of the crowd withdrew his name in the face of roars of "No" and declared for Wallace. One ballot unofficially gave Wallace 627-7/10 votes, Bankhead 328-2/3, and McNutt 66-19/30, and several others scattering support. The nomination of Wallace was then made unanimous.

The Secretary's Iowa residence and his responsibility for the administration's farm policies were regarded as assets in appealing to the farm belt, long Republican but pro-Roosevelt since 1932. The Republican revival of 1938 seemed to require that the Democratic Vice Presidential nominee be from this region.

The last act of the delegates was to listen to a calming radio address by the President, delivered just after midnight of the long Thursday session. He declared that he had not desired a third term but insisted that the world crisis forced personal considerations into the background. He would not have time, he said, because of the pressure of his work, "to engage in purely political debate," but would "never be loath to call the attention of the nation to deliberate or unwitting falsifications of fact, which are sometimes made by political candidates."

The Battle of America

Willkie's acceptance speech, delivered on August 17 before a huge crowd at his old home in Elwood, Indiana, shocked right-wing Republicans. He accepted the major objectives of the Roosevelt foreign and domestic policies and confined his criticisms chiefly to methods. He advocated an economy of production as opposed to one of scarcity, which he charged upon the New Deal, without calling for the repeal of any significant New Deal measure. On foreign policy he rejected isolationism and promised to "outdistance Hitler in any contest he chooses."

On the whole, Willkie's strategy was sound. The Toryism of 1936 would not be repeated in 1940; nor would he accept the equally fatal position of the isolationists, which would have opened the way to Democratic charges of appeasement and Hitlerism. His courageous indorsement of the pending selective service law, opposed by the majority of Republicans in Congress, was a case in point. Ambiguous silence or open opposition would have pleased the party regulars, but he refused to compromise with his convictions. Thus the issue was eliminated from the campaign.

Willkie also indicated his intention of controlling the management of his campaign by relegating Chairman Hamilton of the national committee to a post of executive secretary and placing in the chairmanship Joseph W. Martin, Jr., who had presided over the convention. Martin's task was not easy. The untamed candidate often ignored the professionals and listened to the amateurs, and the campaign broth had too many cooks. Raising funds was turned over to a leading industrialist, Tom M. Girdler, head of Republic Steel Corporation, who had the confidence of business but had an antilabor record that was a source of embarrassment in the campaign. Willkie announced at the outset that his campaign expenditures would be kept strictly within the $3,000,000 limit prescribed by the new Hatch Act.

The first speech was on September 17 at Coffeyville, Kansas, where Willkie had once taught school. The "battle of America" was his theme—the battle to save democracy at home against concentration of power in one man. Then followed as arduous a campaign as any since Bryan's famous stumping tours. Covering thirty-four states, he traveled an estimated 30,000 miles by rail, air, and automobile to deliver 540 speeches. Perhaps 12,000,000 people turned out to see and hear him. His deep voice grew strained and husky, but he never spared it. He was the despair of his throat specialist, for he held forth in his private car between platform appearances. His inexperience in politics cropped out sometimes in indiscreet statements that had to be qualified or explained away afterward. But his unfailing good humor, his abundant vitality, and his vigorous style of speech were increasingly effective in arousing enthusiasm as the campaign progressed and he developed greater adeptness in presenting his case. Over the radio he was a better speaker than Landon; but a sloppiness of diction and a clumsiness of phrasing reduced the effectiveness of his appeal somewhat.

The Republican organization was assisted by several auxiliary groups, separately financed, the most important being the "Associated Willkie Clubs" and the "Democrats for Willkie." Thousands of "amateurs" gave their services to Willkie Clubs to prepare and mail literature, telephone to voters, and perform other political labors usually left to the professionals. Middle-class housewives, discovering a sudden interest in politics, worked in relays at the telephones in Willkie headquarters to warn women voters about the dangers of war and the third term. The "Mothers of America," financed by the Republican national committee, presented emotional radio appeals on behalf of Willkie and peace.

In some of the more doubtful states local Republican organizations raised and spent large sums, ostensibly for state and local tickets, thus evading the limitations of the Hatch Act. In Pennsylvania, for example, a survey after the election revealed that the Republicans had spent $2,500,000 through state and local organizations and volunteer clubs, an astonishing amount even for a state accustomed to freehanded spending in primaries and elections. Wide use of every form of political advertising and propaganda testified to the size of the Republican party's war chest and the elaborateness of the Willkie set-up.

Meanwhile, the Democrats were having their troubles. The coldness of many regulars toward the New Deal element made the problem of a successor to Farley as national chairman an awkward one. But Roosevelt found a reasonably satisfactory solution. He chose Edward J. Flynn of New York, a successful lawyer of independent means and for years boss of the Bronx. He had long been close to both Roosevelt and Farley, who was to continue as state chairman. Thus it was hoped that the soreness in evidence at Chicago might be removed. Flynn lacked his predecessor's wide acquaintance among politicians of the hinterland, and did not essay the role of traveling salesman; but he managed the campaign competently from his New

York headquarters. In any case, the grand strategy was in the hands of Roosevelt.

That some conservative Democrats would repudiate the New Deal leadership seemed to be certain, and with the no-third-term tradition as a convenient bridge, a long procession was soon crossing over to the Willkie camp. The wisdom of naming a former Democrat as Republican standard-bearer seemed to be amply justified; but observers pointed out that nearly all of the more prominent bolters were either former "greats" or lame ducks who had lost influence in the party. Among them were former Governors Smith of New York, White of Ohio, and Ely of Massachusetts, former Senator Reed of Missouri, former Representative John J. O'Connor of New York, and Senator Edward R. Burke of Nebraska, who had just been defeated for renomination. Such Senate conservatives as Glass and Byrd and Tydings, and the isolationists Wheeler of Montana and Bennett Champ Clark of Missouri silently acquiesced in the Roosevelt candidacy, Clark even giving a half-hearted indorsement of the national ticket in a belated radio speech. Vice President Garner neither spoke nor voted.

In every locality newspapers carried stories of lifelong Democrats who were repudiating the national ticket. These were usually business or professional men and not active figures in the party organization. Despite the heat and the bitterness of the struggle, Democratic insurgency was far less extensive than in the Hoover-Smith campaign of 1928. Among the rank and file it was more in evidence in rural than in urban districts.

As a partial offset to conservative defections a group of liberals set up a committee of "Independent Voters for Roosevelt." The veteran progressive, Norris of Nebraska, and Mayor La Guardia of New York were the leaders, with Thomas G. Corcoran the chief organizer. Willkie's headship of a great utilities holding company and his battle with the Tennessee Valley Authority made him anything but satisfactory to Norris and the friends of public power. Mayor La Guardia, Fusionist opponent of Tammany, threw his fiery energy into the Roosevelt cause. The American Labor party of New York also indorsed the President. In Wisconsin, Robert M. La Follette, Jr., who had cooled toward the administration and was opposing its foreign policy, ran for reelection to the Senate with his state Progressive party's backing. Fighting for his political life against a Republican trend, he decided for Roosevelt on domestic issues and won the backing of liberal Democrats. Dorothy Thompson, influential woman columnist, who had been critical of the New Deal, supported Roosevelt on foreign policy.

The President in his acceptance speech had indicated the line of argument to be followed in the campaign, but the brunt of the battle was to be left to the Vice Presidential candidate. Wallace centered his attention on the doubtful farm belt; but the growing enthusiasm aroused by Willkie required that the Democrats play their trump card, and so Roosevelt went before the voters to inspect national defense projects from Maine to Virginia and west to Dayton, Ohio. Though his brief remarks were in a nonpartisan key, huge crowds turned out at all stops to cheer him. Republican newspapers frothed at this further evidence of Rooseveltian hypocrisy.

In the closing days of the campaign the President threw off all disguise and made five major political addresses in key cities of the East and the Middle West. His entry into the campaign did much to restore Democratic morale, which had been shaken somewhat by the Willkie trend of some of the polls and by the tremendous barrage of Republican propaganda.

Equaling the Civil War and free-silver campaigns in bitterness and emotional pitch, the struggle of 1940 tended to become one of highly charged appeals to prejudices, traditions, class hatreds, and partisan bigotry. Sound and fury made rational discussion of concrete issues impossible.

Magnifying Roosevelt's refusal to respect the no-third-term tradition into an assault upon constitutional government, Republican newspapers and orators proclaimed that dictatorship was imminent and democracy itself in dire peril. Willkie himself solemnly declared that if the administration was restored to power for a third term, "our democratic system will not outlast another four years." Obsessed with dislike of the man in the White House, Republicans forgot that they would have rejoiced if Calvin Coolidge had consented to stand for another term in 1928, and that in their ranks were many old-timers who had done their best to put Theodore Roosevelt in the White House for a third term in 1912. Several Democratic Senators and the Progressive La Follette found themselves compelled to eat their own words, as they had supported a resolution against a third term in 1928.

The Democrats met the third-term argument with much talk about the grave emergency and the dangers of swapping horses "until we reach the clear sure footing ahead"—as Roosevelt phrased it in his Cleveland speech. Hurling back at his critics the dictatorship cry, he attacked the "unholy alliance" of Communists and "Girdlers" who were trying to weaken democracy in America and "to destroy the free man's faith in his own cause." The Democrats invoked Washington's authority to offset Republican quotations of Jefferson's familiar anti-third-term sentiments. Had not the Father of His Country once written that he saw no reason for "precluding ourselves from the services of any man, who on some great emergency shall be deemed universally most capable of serving the public"? Yet the third-term issue was a difficult obstacle for the Democrats to hurdle. Americans are pronounced traditionalists in their political thinking, and the Republicans were defending an old tradition. Their appeal was simple and emotional and irrational, and therefore all the more difficult to combat.

In the closing stages of the campaign the Republican offensive centered on the war issue and the closely related problem of national defense. Willkie had indorsed the Roosevelt policy of all possible aid to the democracies, and favored immediate rearmament and the compulsory military service law. Both candidates declared that they would not send American boys to Europe to fight except in defense of American liberty. Republican propaganda, however, charged that Roosevelt was the war candidate, and used the air waves and the newspapers to appeal to the mothers of America to save their boys from slaughter on foreign battlefields by voting Republican. Roosevelt partisans denied that he was a warmonger and countercharged that leading Republicans were isolationists and Hitler appeasers. As to national defense, the pot called the kettle black by pointing to the spots on its record.

A dramatic incident of the campaign was John L. Lewis's radio address on October 25 urging labor to vote for Willkie and pledging himself to retire from the headship of the C.I.O. if Roosevelt won. He charged that the Democratic party had broken faith with labor, that Roosevelt was aiming at war and dictatorship, that the administration had failed by every test, and that Willkie's election was imperative to the country's welfare.

Lewis's plea won support from some left-wing leaders in the C.I.O.

including Harry Bridges, under fire as a Communist; but the heads of the larger unions generally repudiated his stand and reaffirmed their support of Roosevelt. Most of the leaders of the rival American Federation of Labor, then bitterly hostile to Lewis, were already strongly pro-Roosevelt. The presence of Tom Girdler, Ernest T. Weir, and other antiunion industrialists in the Willkie camp detracted from the effectiveness of the Lewis appeal to labor.

Minor parties received slight support from labor and farmer in 1940. The crazy-quilt Union party of 1936 had not survived. Father Coughlin tried to take his following over to Willkie; but his support was regarded as a liability. The Republican candidate denounced racial and religious intolerance and offered cold comfort to budding Fascist groups. The Socialist party convention at Washington in April adopted a strongly isolationist and antiwar platform, opposing even economic aid to any belligerent. Norman Thomas was again its nominee.

The Communist party, weakened in membership and even more in prestige by the Stalin-Hitler pact of 1939, offered Earl Browder for President. It declared against any participation in the "imperialist war," opposed military preparations, and in general followed the party line laid down from Moscow. Browder, sentenced to prison for misuse of a passport, was out on bail; but his campaign activities were sharply circumscribed.

The Socialist Labor and Prohibition parties also nominated candidates but attracted little attention and few votes.

The Verdict

The polls, scientific and otherwise, which attempted to predict the result, were in such sharp disagreement that even veteran political analysts were bewildered. The American Institute of Public Opinion—the Gallup poll—issued a final statement on the eve of the election giving Roosevelt 198 electoral votes, Willkie 59, but leaving 274 doubtful! Roosevelt, it conceded, might have 52 per cent of the total popular vote, but because of the heavy concentration of Democratic strength in the South this might not mean electoral success. *Fortune* magazine's survey gave Roosevelt 55.2 per cent of the popular vote but admitted that Willkie might squeeze through with an electoral majority. Two other nation-wide samplers of opinion predicted a decisive Willkie victory. Chairman Flynn's claim of 427 votes for Roosevelt seemed to be the customary exaggeration of a party manager.

But the verdict on November 5 went beyond even Flynn's expectations. Roosevelt had 449 electoral votes to Willkie's 82. The Dakotas, Nebraska, Kansas, Iowa, Colorado, Indiana, Michigan, Maine, and Vermont constituted the Willkie total. Roosevelt's popular vote was 27,313,041; Willkie's 22,348,480.[2] The victor's 54.7 per cent of the popular vote was lower than it had been in 1932 (57.4) and 1936 (60.8). The Democrats added slightly to their House majority but lost three Senate seats.

Isolationist Republicans took the election of seventeen Republican governors in thirty-four state contests as proof that Willkie was weaker than his party. But the Republican representation in the House was proportionately less than its Presidential vote, though in many states the arrangement of districts overrepresented the rural voters.

Willkie ran better in the western wheat and corn states than anywhere else. His persuasive philosophy of an expanding economy, with farm subsidies if needed, struck the right note. Farmers, unhappy over government restrictions even with benefit payments, complained about laborers loafing on the W.P.A. while farm workers were hard to get, were alarmed at continuing Treasury deficits, and, especially in German-American localities, suspected Roosevelt of maneuvering to involve the nation in the war.

But the Democrats retained most of their urban support. Republican charges that reliefers decided the election ("You can't beat Santa Claus") were apparently refuted by the equally heavy Roosevelt vote of employed labor. Prolabor policies and various New Deal benefits weighed heavily with the city voters. The swing of Polish-American, Jewish, and other anti-Hitler elements to Roosevelt overcame losses among voters of German and Italian ancestry, where emotions overruled economics.

The role of the press came in for much comment. Roosevelt lost the *New York Times*, the Cleveland *Plain Dealer*, the Scripps-Howard chain, and other supporters of 1936, while some nominally Democratic organs were lukewarm. Yet in the face of a heavy Republican journalistic preponderance, he had carried every city of

[2] Minor party totals were: Thomas, Socialist, 1,116,410; Babson, Prohibition, 58,708; Browder, Communist, 46,529; Aiken, Socialist Labor, 14,892; others, 63,471.

more than 400,000 population except Cincinnati, sometimes without a single friendly newspaper. Was it radio? or popular feeling that urban journalism, having evolved into a few big business corporations, reflected its corporation character? Or was Roosevelt too overshadowing to be much affected by editorial arrows or editorial praise?

28

And Again

Wartime Politics

President Roosevelt, fortified by his great victory at the polls, continued and extended his policy of making the United States the arsenal of democracy. Though supported by Wendell Willkie, he encountered a growing isolationist opposition from men of such divergent views as Senator Burton K. Wheeler, Democrat, of Montana, Senator Gerald P. Nye, Republican, of North Dakota, Robert E. Wood and Robert Young of the business world, John L. Lewis of the United Mine Workers, Charles A. Lindbergh of aviation fame, Colonel Robert R. McCormick of the *Chicago Tribune,* Norman Thomas, Socialist leader, and the La Follettes. Most of them were affiliated with an America First Committee. Embarrassingly friendly to them were the followers of Father Coughlin and Reverend Gerald L. K. Smith, and for a time, the Communists.

Roosevelt's major Congressional victory came over his proposal to lend or lease war materials to any nation whose defense the President deemed vital to the defense of the United States. A few isolationist Democrats and the great majority of Republicans in Congress opposed the measure; yet the alignment was as much sectional as partisan. The upper Mississippi valley, represented largely by Republicans, was more isolationist than other sections.

Hitler's attack on Russia strengthened the isolationists for a time. England, it seemed, was now safe from invasion, and Americans felt a sense of relief. When the President sent American forces to occupy Iceland and used the navy to patrol the western Atlantic in order to protect Lend-Lease shipments against submarine attacks, America Firsters sharply criticized him for drawing the nation closer to the abyss of war. In Congress the opposition to extending the one year of service of drafted men was so great that it carried in the House by the bare margin of one vote. Yet by November the President was able to secure the passage of a measure freeing American merchant ships from the restrictions of the Neutrality Act and authorizing their arming. The final House vote showed 53 Democrats and 137 Republicans in opposition. Attacks upon American destroyers had altered the situation. Aid to England was too vital to American defense to permit pretensions to neutrality to stand in the way.

The Japanese attack upon Pearl Harbor on December 7 closed the mouths of administration critics. The war came to America, and from an unexpected quarter. The long months of negotiation with Japan had not prepared Americans for a Pacific war. Politics had not been involved, and isolationists had been strangely indifferent to the dangers in the Far East. The tardiness of the administration in stopping shipment of war materials to Japan had evoked as much criticism from its friends as from its foes. Consequently, when the blow fell at Pearl Harbor, isolationists and interventionists joined forces in support of the war, though a few of the former felt that Rooseveltian diabolism was behind the whole thing. As in 1917, politics was adjourned.

The months of discouragement and defeat made 1942 another 1862. The war machine was slow in getting under way, and criticisms of men and methods, of wartime restrictions, of price controls and labor difficulties, appeared in Congress and in the newspapers. With the allies everywhere on the defensive in the summer, except in the Solomon Islands, where progress was dishearteningly slow, the war seemed to stretch endlessly into the future. Roosevelt was berated as a dictator and was berated for not using his vast powers more effectively.

The mid-term elections aroused slight interest, and political analysts predicted little change in the composition of Congress. They were wrong. The Republicans gained ten seats in the Senate and forty-seven in the House, which they almost captured.[1] New York, Ohio, Pennsylvania, Michigan, Minnesota, and California elected Republican state tickets. In a light vote the nation had almost repudiated the administration.

[1] The House had 222 Democrats, 209 Republicans, 2 Progressives, 1 American Labor, 1 Farmer-Labor. In the Senate were 57 Democrats, 38 Republicans, 1 Progressive.

One effect of the setback was the organization by C.I.O. leaders of a Political Action Committee in July, 1943, with Sidney Hillman in charge, to get labor to the polls through organization and propaganda at the household level. It soon showed its power in state primaries, even in the conservative South. The P.A.C. was a virtual Democratic auxiliary.

The swing to the right in 1942 was reflected in the relations of the President and the new Congress. The administration had its way on Lend-Lease renewal, extension of the Reciprocal Trade Agreement Act, war appropriations, and other non-domestic measures; but taxation, food subsidies, antistrike bills, soldier voting, and proposals to do away with poll taxes provoked sharp controversies, in which the wishes of the White House were often ignored or overridden. A bloc of southern conservatives led by Senator Harry F. Byrd of Virginia usually voted with the Republicans.

The administration's efforts to provide a federal ballot for soldier voting were blocked by the coalition majority in Congress. A state-rights bill became a law without the President's signature. It permitted the use of a federal ballot by absentee voters in the armed services who wished to vote for Presidential electors, Senators, and Representatives and who had applied for and failed to receive a state ballot by October 1, provided that the governor of their state had certified that the federal ballot might be used in his state. The act contained such severe restrictions on the circulation of political propaganda that it deprived the soldiers of information essential to intelligent voting, and it had to be amended in August, 1944. The governors of twenty states accepted the federal ballot; but the others, for various reasons, did not permit its use. Administration advocates charged that its enemies sought to keep soldiers from voting because most of them would favor the reelection of Roosevelt; and they made much of an alleged statement of Senator Taft that men in the armed services were out of contact with developments at home and might not vote intelligently. Both sides realized that the election might be decided by the soldier vote, and both proclaimed that their purpose was to secure the largest possible poll. While the defeat of the federal ballot plan may have cost the Democrats some votes, it supplied them with a piece of campaign propaganda to hurl at the Republicans.

Dewey and Bricker

The elections of 1942 provided the Republicans with three possibilities for President in 1944, all governors of states: Thomas E. Dewey of New York, John W. Bricker of Ohio, and Harold E. Stassen of Minnesota. Bricker and Stassen were reelected, but Dewey's victory was his first. A fourth availability was General Douglas MacArthur, in command in the Southwest Pacific. Over all these hung the shadow of Wendell Willkie, whose ambitions had not been destroyed by the verdict of 1940, and who seemed at first to be in a strong position to determine the future course of the party.

Dewey, well known since the 1940 convention, added to his popularity by the leadership he displayed at Albany. He avoided campaigning and primary battles by refusing to announce his candidacy, though delegates pledged to him were generally successful in state primaries. A public address in April made it clear that he had abandoned his earlier isolationist views and favored a strong United Nations to prevent future wars. When the convention met, MacArthur and Willkie were already eliminated, and the only remaining opposition was from Bricker and Stassen.

The MacArthur movement had never got beyond the talking stage. The general was regarded as willing but organization and popular support failed to materialize. The publication of some correspondence with a Nebraska Congressman brought from MacArthur a statement that he was not a candidate for the nomination; but this did not eliminate the possibility of a draft. On April 30, 1944, when the Dewey band wagon had begun to roll, a second statement withdrew his name with finality.

Wendell Willkie was the problem child of the G.O.P. The party regulars had never accepted him as a genuine Republican, and they blamed him for the 1940 defeat. The isolationists had never liked him, and his support of Lend-Lease in 1941 brought forth a chorus of denunciation. The *Chicago Tribune* charged that international bankers, together with the "champagne and caviar liberals of the East," had brought about his nomination. Willkie visited England during the "blitz," endeared himself to the British, and in 1942 made a trip around the world as an unofficial emissary of President Roosevelt. His book describing the journey, *One World*, was an immediate best-seller; but it damned him for the more orthodox Republicans, who resented both his internationalism and his increasingly liberal viewpoint. Although critical of New Deal methods, he seemed to be determined to liberalize the Republican party by committing it to New Deal objectives.

Willkie's downfall was due in part to his rashness—or courage—and in part to his lack of political skill. His enemies were strongest in the isolationist Middle West; yet he decided to risk his candidacy for the Republican nomination by entering his name in the Wisconsin, Nebraska, and Oregon Presidential primaries. Confident that the voters were with him, he went to Wisconsin and conducted an aggressive campaign. The primary election, on April 4, was a major defeat for him, Dewey's supporters sweeping the field. Before the Nebraska primaries, Willkie announced his withdrawal from the race. He had lost not only the nomination but his influence in shaping party policies. A series of newspaper articles in which he advocated a decidedly liberal platform received no consideration in the national convention. He was not even accorded the courtesy of an invitation to address the delegates, a snub that many of his supporters answered with Roosevelt ballots in November.

Stassen and Bricker did not profit from Willkie's withdrawal. The party regulars who had backed Dewey to kill off the 1940 standard-bearer now found the New Yorker too far in the lead to be stopped. Stassen had entered the United States Navy, but Senator Joseph H. Ball, an anti-isolationist from his own state, conducted a campaign to draft him for the nomination. Poor showings in Wisconsin and Nebraska practically eliminated him. Bricker, the only remaining avowed candidate, crossed the country in a quest for delegates, hammering hard at New Deal bureaucracy and mismanagement but suggesting an alternative only in general terms. An aura of old-fashioned Republicanism emanated from the broad-shouldered, handsome Ohioan, and Old Guardsmen and isolationists took him to their hearts. William Allen White caustically called him "an honest Harding" (a gibe that he credited to Alice Roosevelt Longworth); but his friends saw a kinship with McKinley in his cautious party regularity and his ability to work with the men who ran the organizations. Party leaders liked him, and business approved; but Dewey seemed to be stronger with the voters.

The Republican convention, held in Chicago June 26-28, was marked by the utmost harmony. The 1,057 delegates listened t Governor Earl Warren of California, the temporary chairman, the first night session and elected Joseph W. Martin, Jr., of Massachusetts permanent chairman the next day. The platform, presented by Senator Taft of Ohio, had been in preparation since September, 1943, when a preliminary meeting of party leaders at Mackinac, Michigan, had organized eight committees to study different aspects of party policy and offer recommendations. The resolutions committee of the convention was thus in a position to write the platform with commendable speed. The delegates accepted it unanimously.

This rather lengthy document committed the party to a prosecution of the war to total victory and promised "responsible participation by the United States in postwar cooperative organization" to maintain peace, with the qualification that any agreement or treaty should receive Senate approval. A section on domestic policy pledged the party to end government competition with private industry, to promote stable employment through private enterprise, and to avoid regulation of farmers, workers, businessmen, and consumers; it warned the country that four years more of New Deal policy would centralize all power in the President and endanger the Republic. A broad social security program was indorsed, with emphasis on federal aid and state or local control.

As in 1940, the labor and farm pronouncements did not take issue with the New Deal measures but criticized methods and administration. A special bid for the Negro vote appeared in planks favoring a fair employment practices commission, anti-lynching legislation, and a constitutional amendment abolishing poll taxes. Equal rights for women and the opening of Palestine to unrestricted Jewish immigration were other vote catchers.

The Dewey leaders sought to give Governor Warren of doubtful California second place on the ticket but struck a snag when he positively refused it. This opened the way for Governor Bricker, and before the balloting began he appeared before the delegates to in-
orse Dewey and withdraw his name from consideration for first
ce. He was warmly applauded. Senator Ball withdrew Stassen, and
y, placed in nomination by Governor Dwight R. Griswold of
ka, became the convention's all but unanimous choice—one
Wisconsin delegate insisted on voting for MacArthur.
hose popularity had been steadily mounting, then re-
ice Presidential nomination. Dewey came at once to
ccepted the honor of leading the Republican forces.
most efforts to winning the war and declared against

any change in its military conduct, but assailed the incompetence of the administration and charged that it was unfit to achieve a lasting peace. His reference to "stubborn men grown old and tired and quarrelsome in office," sounded the keynote of his acceptance. He minimized the differences between isolationists and internationalists and emphasized the "broad area of agreement" between the two extremes of isolation and a superstate.

The convention was a cut-and-dried affair. The delegates showed little spontaneous enthusiasm as they listened to the customary partisan oratory, high-lighted by Herbert Hoover's quadrennial appearance as the prophet of gloom and Mrs. Clare Boothe Luce's emotional interpretation of the feelings of "G.I. Joe" and "G.I. Jim." The drafting of Dewey was carefully prearranged by his board of strategy, and the delegates chose him not from any personal attachment to a magnetic leader but from the belief that the shrewd, competent New York governor was their best bet. The candidate knew that he would be drafted and carefully prepared his acceptance speech in advance. He made a good impression, and the delegates adjourned in an optimistic mood. From the outside came one discordant note. Wendell Willkie did not like the platform. Some Republicans began to wonder if they hadn't slapped him down too hard. He still had a following.

Truman or Wallace?

The Democratic picture was not encouraging in the early months of 1944. Conservative southerners could not defeat Roosevelt's fourth nomination, but there was a danger that they might withhold their support at the polls. Party conventions in Texas, South Carolina, and Mississippi named electoral tickets that were not pledged to the national nominees. Demands were made for the restoration of the two-thirds rule, the elimination of Wallace for Vice President, and the recognition of white supremacy. Senator Byrd was the dissenters' favorite for the Presidential nomination.

For the great majority of Democrats, Roosevelt was the only choice. New Dealers and machine politicians were agreed on this point, and public opinion polls offered further proof. The new national chairman, Robert E. Hannegan of St. Louis, secured a statement from the President, made public before the convention met, that he would accept another nomination. This left only the question of his running mate to be settled.

Chicago also entertained the Democratic convention. The 1,176 delegates assembled on July 19, with Governor Robert S. Kerr of Oklahoma as temporary chairman delivering the keynote speech. He charged the Republicans with isolationism and Old Guard domination and answered Dewey's "tired old men" charge by citing the ages of Stalin, Churchill, and top-ranking American military leaders. Senator Samuel D. Jackson of Indiana succeeded Governor Kerr in the chair. Two delegations from Texas created a problem, which was solved by seating both and dividing the vote. Thirty-three delegates and alternates of the "regulars," who were anti-Roosevelt, walked out, but many later returned to their seats.

The platform of 1,360 words, less than one-third the length of the Republican, cost the drafting committee many hours of labor to iron out difficult points but was generally acceptable in the end. It declared that the Democratic party stood on its record in peace and war, and summed up the major accomplishments. It pledged American membership in an international organization with the power to use armed force to prevent aggression and to preserve peace. It indorsed an international court of justice, the Good Neighbor policy, the administration's trade policies, the Atlantic Charter, and the opening of Palestine to unrestricted Jewish immigration. These commitments on foreign policy were more definite than the Republican stand, but there were no sharp differences. A postwar domestic program was outlined to appeal to ex-servicemen, farmers, labor, and businessmen; but this was hardly more than an assurance that all would be well with all of them.

In one respect the Democratic platform fell short of the Republican. The race relations declaration was watered down to a vague statement that "racial and religious minorities have the right to live, develop and vote equally with all citizens and share the rights that are guaranteed by our Constitution," and that Congress should protect these rights. The poll tax and the fair employment practices commission were not mentioned.

The much advertised southern revolt began to peter out. Senator Barkley presented Roosevelt's name, and a Florida delegate offered Senator Byrd for the nomination. The one ballot gave Roosevelt 1,086 votes, Byrd 89, and James A. Farley 1. Most of the Byrd vote was from seven southern states, and even there it was only a minority.

Twelve of the Texas "regulars" voted for Roosevelt, despite the "walkout" of their faction. The victor was nominated by a larger margin than in 1940. He was so obviously the choice of both party leaders and Democratic voters that the cry of "synthetic draft" fell flat. Roosevelt accepted by radio from a Pacific coast naval base, emphasizing the dangers of entrusting the government to "inexperienced and immature hands," and to those who had opposed Lend-Lease and international cooperation, and who had led the American people down to "the abyss of 1932."

The real drama of the convention came next day when the Vice Presidential nomination was made. Henry Wallace seemed to be the popular choice in 1944. By his speech seconding the nomination of Roosevelt he won the admiration of galleries and radio listeners alike; but he hurt his own chances by his declarations against the poll tax and for educational and economic equality "regardless of race or sex." Roosevelt earlier had given Wallace the kiss of death by expressing a preference for him but a readiness to let the convention decide about second place. National Chairman Robert E. Hannegan, after the convention met, made public a letter from the President approving either Senator Harry S Truman of Missouri or Justice William O. Douglas for second place. War Mobilization Director James F. Byrnes of South Carolina had wanted to run, but he suited neither the Political Action Committee nor Roosevelt. Northern state machines were lining up for Truman, and southern conservatives preferred him to Wallace. The convention, after Roosevelt's acceptance speech, showed signs of getting out of hand and possibly stampeding to Wallace when Chairman Jackson adjourned it until the next day at Hannegan's insistence. Behind Wallace were the labor leaders Philip Murray and Sidney Hillman, Senators Guffey of Pennsylvania and Pepper of Florida, and Governor Arnall of Georgia, a southern liberal.

The outwardly confused situation brought out twelve nominations. The first ballot gave Wallace 429-1/2 votes and Truman 319-1/2, while a flock of favorite sons held the rest. On the second ballot Truman reached 473 and Wallace, 477-1/2; but before the result could be announced Alabama and Indiana dropped their favorites for Truman, and a procession of other states followed suit until his total reached 1,031 of the 1,176 convention votes. His victory was a triumph for the organization men as opposed to the liberal-labor group. Yet Truman was at least acceptable to Hillman and his labor following, and had the support of southern conservatives who wanted Wallace stopped.

The southern dissenters had actually lost their fight. The two-thirds rule had not been restored; white supremacy was not recognized; and the South was unrepresented on the national ticket. But most of the dissatisfied stayed regular. Their plan to have southern electors withhold their votes from the national candidates collapsed. Wherever electoral candidates refused to support Roosevelt, they were forced to resign or were ousted by state committees. Seven were dropped in Louisiana. In Texas the "regulars" were deposed and became an ineffectual third party. In South Carolina a conservative third party also appeared but had almost no support. An increased Republican vote in the South was one result; but most of the rank-and-file Democrats voted for the national ticket as usual. Senator Byrd took refuge in silence.

The minor parties appeared as usual, but radical reforms aroused slight interest in wartime. The Socialist, Socialist Labor, and Prohibition parties nominated candidates[2] as in the past, but the Communists, who had abandoned their opposition to the war after Hitler attacked Russia, dissolved as a party in May, 1944, and formed the Communist Political Association. In New York they formed a segment of the American Labor party. A seceding conservative wing of that party formed the Liberal party; but both groups supported Roosevelt, as did the Farmer-Labor party of Minnesota, which joined forces with the Democrats in that state. An America First party held a convention at Detroit on August 30 and nominated Gerald L. K. Smith for President and Governor Bricker for Vice President. Bricker indignantly rejected the dubious honor, for Smith had shown Nazi sympathies, and the platform was anti-Jewish, anti-Negro, and extremely isolationist. In most states the America Firsters did not appear on the ballot.

The War Election

Both campaigns were managed by newcomers; but they were not amateurs. Democratic Chairman Robert E. Hannegan had lined up the organization leaders in the Vice Presidential battle at Chicago,

[2] The Socialists nominated Norman Thomas of New York; the Socialist Labor party (also called the Industrial Government party), Edward A. Teichert of Pennsylvania; and the Prohibition party, Claude A. Watson of California.

and he worked with them in the campaign. Hillman, Murray, and the labor group continued the P.A.C. but allied with it a "National Citizens Political Action Committee" appealing to liberals of all shades and not limited in its spending by the Smith-Connally Act. The P.A.C.'s most effective work was in getting the labor vote to the polls. A series of simple leaflets, prepared by writers and artists at its New York headquarters, appealed to the workers to register and vote. Some of these abandoned any pretense of nonpartisanship, and one, entitled "Lest We Forget," contained a photograph of an unemployed man selling apples in front of a "Hoover Club" in 1932, with an inset showing a large red apple and a picture of Dewey conferring with Hoover. Nearly 10,000,000 such leaflets and pamphlets went out every week in the closing stages of the campaign to C.I.O. unions and through their 14,000 locals to the members. Clubs, speeches, radio programs, and even doorbell ringing helped arouse labor from the lethargy of high wages and war prosperity. Democratic organization leaders welcomed the P.A.C. as an ally and worked with it.

Herbert Brownell, Jr., manager of Dewey's campaign for governor, handled his pre-convention campaign with assistance from Edwin F. Jaeckle, New York state chairman, and J. Russel Sprague, national committeeman from New York. These three continued to direct the national campaign, Brownell heading the national committee. John Foster Dulles was Dewey's adviser on foreign policy. This grandson of a Secretary of State had had considerable diplomatic experience in his earlier years, and his law practice had had international connections. Republican contacts with the business world were maintained through James S. Kemper, chairman of the finance committee and a former president of the United States Chamber of Commerce, who had shown marked isolationist sympathies.

The moneybags of business were opened to the Republicans as in 1936 and 1940. The legal limitation of national campaign expenditures to $3,000,000 did not prevent heavy contributions to state campaigns and independent organizations. The totals, according to the Senate Campaign Expenditures Committee, almost equaled the record level of 1936. The United Republican Finance Committee for Metropolitan New York collected $1,629,451 and spent $1,260,593; the Pennsylvania Republican Finance Committee, $1,252,700 and $939,934. The P.A.C.'s receipts for the entire country were $1,405,120; its expenditures $1,327,775. The Du Pont and

Pew families together gave more than $200,000 to the Republican chest. The Democrats collected $22,000 from the Marshall Fields and $20,680 from the Andrew J. Higgins family of New Orleans. The Republicans spent nearly twice as much as the Democrats, with expenses of local candidates not reported to the Senate committee.

The campaign opened late and was comparatively brief. Much depended, as in 1864, on the military situation. A summer of victories in France was followed by an autumn stalemate but with ultimate allied victory not too far off. This was probably more favorable to Roosevelt than to Dewey. It was no time to swap horses.

Dewey's speechmaking began at Philadelphia on September 9, and covered a large part of the country outside the South. He made no platform appearances, kept secret the exact train route on his western swing, and aimed his brief, well phrased speeches at the radio rather than the visible audiences. His general themes were a more efficient administration, an end to the quarreling and bickering of the "tired old men," better relations with Congress, a durable peace settlement, and jobs for all through the stimulation of private enterprise. He assailed the administration for inadequate preparedness, for burdening labor, agriculture, and business with unnecessary and conflicting restrictions, for planning to keep men in military service to prevent unemployment, and for consorting with Communists.

The last charge was the basis for an eleventh-hour fear campaign. Sidney Hillman of the P.A.C. was linked with Earl Browder, Communist leader, as "Hillman, Browder, and Co.," a Communist conspiracy controlling the P.A.C. The attacks upon Hillman as "foreign-born" and "Russian-born" came close to anti-Semitism, as when a leading New York newspaper referred to his "rabbinical education." The admonition, "Clear it with Sidney," was the favorite Republican slur, for Roosevelt had allegedly made this remark with regard to the Democratic Vice Presidential nomination before the Chicago convention. It became a stock gibe in Republican campaign speeches, and Hearst newspapers had "Sidney" limerick contests. This concentrated asault on an important labor leader, with its scarcely veiled Ku-Kluxism, gave Roosevelt the opportunity in his final speech to slash at the Republicans as enemies of the foreign-born, and gave the P.A.C. a publicity that probably helped it in getting lethargic labor to come to the polls.

Roosevelt limited his campaign to two dinner addresses and three public speeches, all broadcast, and three special radio talks. Rumors about ill health seemed to be disproved by the vigor of his campaigning.

On foreign policy the two candidates were close together. Both upheld the Dumbarton Oaks plan for a world security organization, and both favored empowering the American representative on a security council to act in an emergency to enforce peace. But Dewey was embarrassed in his criticisms by his party's record on defense and foreign policy and by the isolationism of a considerable segment. Though he courageously repudiated the candidacy of Hamilton Fish for reelection to Congress from New York, he had to accept the support of the *Chicago Tribune* and its middle western satellite papers and to indorse his party's candidates generally, despite their deviations from his stands on major policies.

On October 8 Wendell Willkie died suddenly without revealing how he intended to vote. Some of his Republican and independent sympathizers announced for Roosevelt. These included Russell Davenport, his 1940 pre-convention manager, Bartley C. Crum, head of the California Willkie Committee, Gifford Pinchot of Pennsylvania, Daniel A. Poling, nationally known Baptist minister, and Walter Lippmann, columnist. A surprise bolter was Senator Ball of Minnesota, a Stassen supporter at the Republican convention. Although the newspaper preponderance was heavy for Dewey, two independent newspapers that had been hostile in 1940, the *St. Louis Post-Dispatch* and the *New York Times*, favored Roosevelt.

As in Roosevelt's earlier campaigns, the Democrats depended on radio to offset newspaper hostility; but Dewey's deep voice and clear diction made him the strongest opponent the old Democratic master of air technique had faced.

The two second-place nominees concentrated on doubtful areas. Bricker thundered at bureaucrats and "Hillman, Browder, and Co.," and worked to keep the party regulars in line. Truman's plain, uninspired speeches were helpful in appeasing the Democratic disgruntled. Henry Wallace also stumped for the ticket and was especially effective with the Negro voters.

Political forecasters and professional takers of polls had a hard time. The size of the soldier vote, the number of disfranchised migratory workers, and the apparently narrow margins between the candidates in the large states forced them to hedge their predictions with many qualifications, so that they had slight value. The usual conclusion was that Roosevelt had a narrow popular lead, but the electoral vote might go otherwise. Unusually heavy registration in several large cities dampened Republican hopes somewhat.

The early returns on November 7 indicated another Roosevelt sweep, which became greater as the urban vote was reported. The electoral landslide—432 to 99—represented a popular plurality of approximately 3,600,000 votes in a total vote of 47,976,870. Despite the fact that several millions in the armed services had not been able to vote, the total was surprisingly near the 1940 vote of 49,900,418. The percentages of the popular vote were 53.4 (25,612,610) for Roosevelt and 45.9 (22,017,617) for Dewey.[3] Roosevelt's plurality was 1,370,000 less than in 1940, when he polled 54.7 per cent of the total vote.

Dewey carried Ohio, Wisconsin, and Wyoming, which had gone for Roosevelt in 1940. He lost Michigan, which Willkie had carried, but won the other Willkie states: Maine, Vermont, Indiana, Iowa, the Dakotas, Kansas, Nebraska, and Colorado. Both houses of Congress were Democratic by substantial margins.

Roosevelt's greatest losses in the popular vote were in the South, where they did not matter. He ran better than in 1940 in the important states of New York, Illinois, Michigan, and Minnesota. His electoral vote in the North and West was so large that he could have won without the South, as in his other victories.

The soldier vote was not a decisive factor. In the few states that tabulated it separately it was more heavily pro-Roosevelt than the civilian vote, giving point to the earlier fears of some Republicans that a uniform federal ballot would work to their disadvantage. The Republican radio appeal, "End the war quicker with Dewey and Bricker," may have influenced civilian voters, but soldiers on the fighting fronts had little interest in politics, and many who could have voted did not.

Roosevelt retained most of his labor and urban Negro support in the North but lost ground in the farm belt. The draining away of farm labor by industry and the draft, difficulties in getting machinery, rationing requirements, price ceilings, and other restrictions angered individualistic farmers, who felt that labor was pampered by the government. In Kansas, Nebraska, Iowa, and the Dakotas,

[3] Minor parties polled 0.7 per cent of the total: Thomas, Socialist, 79,003; Watson, Prohibition, 74,779; Teichert, Socialist Labor, 45,191; others (mostly bolting Democrats), 147,470.

where Hoover's name still aroused bitter memories, farmers were now almost as critical of his successor. In some communities this was an expression of a latent anti-war feeling.

Political observers noted one striking fact about the election. This was the devastating blow dealt to isolationism. Senator Nye of North Dakota, Representative Hamilton Fish of New York, and several others went down to defeat while Republicans of internationalist views survived the Roosevelt sweep. The Republican *New York Herald Tribune* declared that the records of leading Republicans were a millstone around Dewey's neck, and that the candidate had been too laggard in taking an advanced stand on foreign policy. Yet Colonel McCormick of the *Chicago Tribune* wanted to chart the party's course in the opposite direction. Dewey, he insisted, had made the mistake of adopting the "coloration of his opponent" and not presenting the foreign policy issue in sharp opposition to Roosevelt's position.

The fundamental explanation of Roosevelt's fourth victory was the war. The majority felt that it was too great a risk to drop the pilot. "Without a doubt the desire to play it safe was the determining factor in the election," stated a leading Republican newspaper. "Roosevelt's leadership represented a known quantity which had every prospect of going on to victory." "He would have won," commented another, "if we had never heard of the P.A.C. and if Dewey had received the solid Republican vote."

In spite of his fourth sweeping victory, Roosevelt soon encountered trouble in the new Congress. The Senate held up his appointment of Henry Wallace as Secretary of Commerce in place of Jesse Jones until the lending powers of the Reconstruction Finance Corporation were separated from the Commerce Department. Certain southern Democrats, angry at the removal of Jesse Jones, were again cooperating with the Republicans.

In foreign relations, however, the President's leadership was unchallenged. He played his cards skillfully, including leading Republicans in the American delegation to draw up a United Nations charter. Arthur Vandenberg, once an isolationist, was a delegate and helped steer his Republican colleagues in the Senate to acceptance of American support of a world organization for peace. But Roosevelt did not live to attain his objectives. On April 12, 1945, with military victory in sight, he was stricken by a cerebral hemorrhage and died.

29

The Great Surprise

"Left of Center"

Like Harding, Harry S. Truman had come to the Presidency from the Senate and was a party regular; but the resemblance went no further, in spite of his unpromising background as a cog in the notorious Pendergast Kansas City machine. Eight years as presiding judge of the Jackson County Court and his Pendergast connections had helped him to the United States Senate in 1934. In 1940, after the boss and his chief henchmen had been sent to prison, he won renomination in the primary only after a bitter fight and rode to victory in the election on Roosevelt's coattails.

The early Senate record of the modest, earnest, industrious Missourian, whose personal integrity was untouched by his political background, was that of an undistinguished administration supporter. In 1941 Senator Truman, disturbed at evidences of waste in the government's construction program for the new army, secured the creation of a special Senate committee to ferret out graft and inefficiency in the huge national defense program. The committee, headed by Truman and assisted by an able young attorney, Hugh Fulton, did its work so well that the mild-mannered, colorless Senator's reputation was made.

After the numbing shock of personal loss that swept the nation at Roosevelt's death had passed, many reasoned that it was all for the best. Roosevelt was the crisis statesman, a man fitted to meet great emergencies; his successor, an average man, might handle more effectively the prosaic but difficult tasks that would come with peace. Then, too, the bitter enmities that F. D. R. had aroused might now be stilled; no one held any grudges against Truman.

The new chief executive set about taking advantage of his political honeymoon. As Senator and Vice President, Truman had been disturbed at the widening gap between White House and Capitol Hill. Now he was in a position to do something. Cooperation was to be his keynote. Personalized government was at an end. He expected to operate through the established departments, not through "palace" advisers, and to consult the wishes of Congress. An era of good feelings seemed at hand. Little parties with Senate cronies were in order.

Cabinet changes, however, were soon found desirable. Stettinius, Miss Perkins, Morgenthau, and Ickes were replaced by Truman appointees. Henry Wallace resigned in September, 1946, after a speech criticizing the "get-tough-with-Russia" policy of the State Department. The departure of these Rooseveltians seemed to symbolize the declining New Deal influence in the administration.

In policies, the President was happily tagged as "a little to the left of center." He would try to harmonize the party by following a middle course of moderate liberalism without abandoning the major Roosevelt objectives. On foreign policy he was at first quite successful. Congress accepted the Bretton Woods pact for an international bank and the United Nations Charter in the summer of 1945 with but slight isolationist opposition. A year later the British loan agreement carried, but 155 votes were cast against it in the House, chiefly by Republicans. Generally speaking, on international issues the Democratic majority held together fairly well; the Republicans were divided, with a varying group of isolationists opposing administration measures. The role of Senator Vandenberg, now committed to international cooperation, was increasingly important in holding Republicans in line.

On domestic questions, the President soon discovered that Roosevelt's policies, rather than his methods, had created the coalition of Republicans and southern Democrats. Appeasement did not work. When he pressed for action on public housing, extension of the Office of Price Administration, full employment, a permanent fair employment practices commission, and other Rooseveltian proposals, he was checkmated by the bipartisan alliance that had blocked his predecessor on so many occasions. The battle against inflation was lost when the President, after one veto, was forced to accept an unworkable OPA that virtually ended price control. Administration bills, when not defeated outright, were killed in committee or by filibuster, or were passed in mangled form. Truman's honeymoon had ended.

Industrial unrest—the product of rising prices, postwar maladjustments, and labor's fears of losing its "top-dog" position—produced an epidemic of strikes and, consequently, demands for antistrike legislation. President Truman estranged labor by a proposal to draft strikers during the brief railroad strike of May, 1946; but later he vetoed the sharply restrictive Case bill, passed by the coalition in Congress.

This year of turmoil turned into the year of jubilee for the Republicans. Shortages of consumer goods, soaring prices, inability of returning veterans to find homes, anger of farmers and businessmen at the remaining controls, labor resentments and unrest, middle-class fears of Communism, all went into the brew the Republicans were concocting. "Had enough?" was their slogan. It was more than enough. No program was necessary. The voters were looking for a scapegoat, and the Truman administration was it. The meat shortage—really a strike of livestock interests and meat packers—became so acute that President Truman lifted all controls in October. It made little difference. The Republican sweep could not be checked. When the votes were counted on November 5, the G.O.P. had a margin of 28 in the House and 2 in the Senate and had nearly all the governorships outside the South. Even Missouri elected a Republican Senator and turned down the President's choice for the House from his home district. The Republicans could now legislate to "end controls, confusion, corruption, Communism," as they had promised.

The rejoicing Republican majorities placed experienced leaders in charge of Congress. Joseph W. Martin, Jr., became Speaker, and Charles A. Halleck of Indiana Republican floor leader of the House, and hard-boiled conservatives became committee chairmen according to the rule of seniority. Arthur H. Vandenberg became president pro tempore of the Senate and remained the guide on foreign policy; Taft headed the steering committee, which planned party strategy, and took for himself the chairmanship of the Labor and Public Welfare Committee. The bipartisan line on foreign policy was continued, though restive Republican isolationists voted against aid to Greece and demanded an end to loans to European nations. Economy and tax reduction ran into the threat of Russian expansion in Europe and Asia.

The dire economic situation of western Europe and the growing American fear of Russia led Congress to accept the administration's plan to aid economic recovery, proposed by Secretary of State George Marshall. Only a little group of isolationists rejected Senator Vandenberg's pleas and voted against it. On other matters, as the 1948 election approached, President and Congress battled for political advantage. Six Presidential vetoes were overridden by the Eightieth Congress. The Republicans could boast of tax reduction, a cut in the budget, and the Taft-Hartley Act restricting labor; Truman could blame Congress for the failure of his civil rights and anti-inflation proposals, and could point to Congressional inaction on housing, minimum-wage extension, and other social welfare measures. The fact that many southern Democrats had followed the Republican line made no difference to the President. He calculated shrewdly that the administration must stay left of center and play up Republican Toryism in order to hold together the Roosevelt liberal-labor following. Safe seats and seniority had placed in key positions standpat Republicans who saw no need to make concessions to reform; and Truman made the most of this. He called the Eightieth Congress the worst in American history.

Dewey's Comeback

Meanwhile Presidential candidates were trooping across the stage. Governor Dewey, triumphantly reelected in 1946, had the edge in popularity among the voters in the public opinion polls; but isolationists were hostile, and party regulars preferred Senator Taft. Taft's leadership in Congress had enhanced his reputation. More in the nature of liabilities were his generally conservative and isolationist record, his forthright but sometimes inept publc utterances, the pronounced opposition of organized labor, and his lack of voter appeal. Harold E. Stassen of Minnesota, the first to announce his candidacy, appealed to the more liberal elements, the internationalists, and the younger voters, especially the war veterans; but the men who ran the state machines were unfriendly to him. Vandenberg did not avow his candidacy but was regarded as a "draft" possibility if a deadlock occurred. Earl Warren, governor of California, was popular on the Pacific coast and was in the favorite-son category. Two war heroes were mentioned: General Douglas MacArthur, military administrator of Japan, and General Dwight D. Eisenhower, chief of staff, who was soon to become president of Columbia University. A "Draft Eisenhower" movement seemed to be stirring some popular interest, but he disposed of it in January, 1948, with an unequivocal refusal to run. General MacArthur took the other tack. In March he announced that he would accept any public duty to which he might be called. A MacArthur organization was soon engaged in an active delegate hunt.

Party organizations dominated the choice of delegates in the majority of states; but where Presidential primaries existed the results were surprising. Stassen captured 19 of Wisconsin's 27 delegates and polled more than 40 per cent of Nebraska's vote. MacArthur, winning only 8 delegates in Wisconsin and ranking fifth in Nebraska, was finished as a contender. The support of Hearst newspapers, of some top figures in World War I veterans' organizations, and of a few men of wealth had done him more harm than good.

Governor Dewey, who had taken Stassen too lightly, now turned his attention to the Oregon primary and devoted three weeks to arduous campaigning in that state. The result, late in May, was an impressive victory. Stassen, already damaged by his failure to break Taft's hold on Ohio, was relegated to third place. There seemed to be a genuine possibility that the front runners would kill each other off.

An enthusiastic horde of Republicans converged on Philadelphia late in June to see "the next President" nominated, while millions of Americans across the country listened in and other millions along the eastern seaboard watched the proceedings through the miracle of television. Dwight H. Green, governor of Illinois, gave the keynote speech as temporary chairman, and Speaker Martin followed him in the chair. Speeches from party notables included, as in previous conventions, the wise-cracking sarcasms of Mrs. Clare Boothe Luce and the portentous solemnities of Herbert Hoover.

Long hours of committee wrangling produced a platform sufficiently innocuous to suit all elements in the party. A group of isolationists lost the fight to tone down the strong internationalist section, which had Vandenberg's approval. It indorsed collective security and support of the United Nations and approved of the bipartisan foreign policy. It upheld aid to peace-loving nations "within the prudent limits of our own economic welfare"—a virtual indorsement of the Marshall Plan. A cautiously qualified statement in favor of federal aid for slum clearance and low-rent housing dealt with a problem upon which Congress had refused to act. The Taft-Hartley Act was called "a sensible reform of the labor law," but another paragraph pledged "continuing study to improve labor-management legislation." On civil rights the platform was emphatic—it favored legislation against lynching and poll taxes and for "equal opportunity to work."

Other planks condemned the mismanagement of the Truman administration and praised the record of the Republican Congress but proposed no important changes in government policies. The philosophy of the New Deal was attacked, without recommendations for repeal of specific measures. Men and methods were criticized.

In seven hours of oratory, parading, and carnival revelry the names of all the candidates were presented to the convention. The Taft demonstration was the longest; the Stassen parade, the most colorful; but the Dewey band-wagon drive did not depend on ballyhoo. Behind the scenes the efficient Dewey managers rounded up the votes. Senator Edward Martin of Pennsylvania announced for the New York governor on Tuesday, carrying with him a majority of that state's delegates. Representative Halleck then followed suit with Indiana, and rumors of other defections in favorite-son delegations multiplied. In alarm Taft, Stassen, and representatives of Vandenberg and Warren tried to arrange an anti-Dewey coalition before the balloting; but the Dewey blitz forged ahead. Senator Leverett Saltonstall withdrew as the choice of Massachusetts, and New Jersey was reported as ready to join Dewey on the second ballot.

The first ballot revealed that Dewey had 434 of the necessary 548 votes. Taft had 224; Stassen, 157; Vandenberg, 62; Warren, 59; and there were half a dozen others. The second ballot showed results of the careful work of the Dewey machine. The New Yorker gained most of New Jersey, a majority from Iowa, and stray votes from other states to reach 515, just 33 short of a majority. A recess, conceded by the confident Dewey forces, revealed the hopelessness of the coalition efforts. Before the third ballot, all the other candidates withdrew in favor of Dewey, who then received a unanimous nomination. He accepted soon afterward in a brief speech evidently prepared well beforehand.

A night of conferences by Dewey and invited supporters produced a decision to name Governor Warren for Vice President. Warren was reluctant but agreed after promises that the office should have more authority than in the past. The delegates obeyed the mandate from Dewey headquarters and Warren was named by acclamation. The nomination of the big friendly California governor seemed to insure Republican success in the Far West and recognized that section's growing importance in national elections. Yet it was a snub for the Middle West, which had been accustomed to representation on Republican national tickets since the days of Lincoln. Warren's views on public questions were close to Dewey's, and the work of the convention was a bitter disappointment to old-fashioned Republicans whose opinions were well voiced by Colonel Robert McCormick and the *Chicago Tribune.*

Dewey's success had been a compound of the skillful work of his general staff and the inept tactics of his rivals. Before the convention many shrewd observers had predicted a deadlock and the nomination of Vandenberg. But the Dewey machine, with its carefully compiled information about individual delegates, overlooked no type of persuasion or pressure to pick up a vote. Its carefully timed announcements of new adherents, and its rumor factory with stories of other prospective defections, created a band-wagon psychology that drew in the hesitant and demoralized the opposition. Yet a coalition might have stopped him, had not jealousies and mismanagement delayed cooperation until too late. Stassen had taken nine Ohio delegates from Taft in the primaries, and each candidate probably preferred Dewey to the other. Supporters of Senator Vandenberg disliked Taft's isolationist leanings and thought Stassen should yield to a more experienced man. They were hampered by Vandenberg's reluctance to become an active candidate. Torn between a natural desire for the great honor of a nomination and fear that heavy burdens entailed would be too much for him, the sixty-four-year-old Senator let his chances slip away. Taft was the victim of inept management. His supporters arrived with a baby elephant and a theme song and seemed to feel that they could ballyhoo into the nomination a man whose solid merits deserved different treatment; but he could hardly have won in any event, with a record that was so vulnerable on both domestic and international issues.

Truman and Barkley

Democratic prospects seemed to be so hopeless in the early summer of 1948 that a concerted movement developed to put aside Truman for Eisenhower. City bosses, disgruntled New Dealers, discouraged labor leaders, and southerners angry over civil rights agreed on one thing—the certainty of defeat if Truman ran. Only Eisenhower was thought to be popular enough to stem the Republican tide. Hoping against hope, they pressed the case for the hero of World War II up to the week before the convention. Then Eisenhower settled the matter with a positive refusal. Some turned to Justice Douglas of the Supreme Court; but when he was equally adamant opposition to Truman evaporated, except from some die-hard southerners who intended to go down fighting and who already were considering a bolt.

The Philadelphia convention met on July 12, with two problems: a running mate for Truman, and a civil-rights plank. The first was solved without much difficulty. The President preferred Justice Douglas, a decided New Dealer. When Douglas would not permit his name to be offered Senator Alben W. Barkley, the temporary chairman, came into the picture. The seventy-year-old Kentucky spellbinder settled the matter by his keynote address, a homely, fighting speech that shook the convention out of its lethargy and produced a spontaneous demonstration that lasted for half an hour. After that, no one else was considered for Vice President. President Truman, New Dealers, and southerners were in accord. Barkley would be a decided asset in a slugging campaign.

After electing Sam Rayburn of Texas permanent chairman and listening to an array of speakers, the delegates considered the platform. It contained a rather vague indorsement of equal rights for racial minorities, to be guaranteed by Congress to the limit of its constitutional powers. This started the fireworks. A southern state-rights minority report, two other southern amendment proposals, and a stronger civil-rights statement drafted by Hubert H. Humphrey, Jr., mayor of Minneapolis and candidate for the United States Senate, were offered from the floor. A bitter debate followed. As was expected, the southern proposals were beaten overwhelmingly. More surprising, with the eloquent Humphrey leading the battle, the strongly worded northern substitute plank carried by a vote of 651-1/2 to 582-1/2. New Deal liberals, determined to take the party "out of the shadow of states' rights and into the sunlight of human rights," and northern state machines, concerned over possible Negro defections, joined forces to put it over. In effect, the convention repudiated the southern conservatives who had been making common cause with the Republicans in Congress on domestic questions for many years.

From the purely political angle, the decision was sound. The party could not afford to risk the populous northern states in order to hold in line the electoral votes of two or three, or at most half a dozen, southern states. After all, most of the southerners were not going to bolt, though the issue was a touchy one. Nor were all of them die-hard conservatives. When the shouting was over, only Mississippi and half of the Alabama delegation walked out, defiantly waving a Confederate flag.

In addition to the strong civil-rights statement the platform incorporated the chief recommendations of President Truman which Congress had largely ignored: measures to control inflation, federal housing and education programs, national health insurance, increased social security benefits, repeal of the Taft-Hartley Act, and retention of price supports for farm products.

Then followed the nominations. Truman had 947-1/2 votes on the only ballot for President; Senator Richard Russell of Georgia, 263; Paul V. McNutt, 1/2. Barkley had no opposition for second place.

President Truman came from Washington to accept the nomination, and delivered a militant speech shortly before two A.M. which did much to dispel the defeatism that had enshrouded the convention. He announced that he was calling "that worst Eightieth Congress" into special session to give the Republicans a chance to carry out their platform pledges.

Two more conventions named candidates that month. The anti-Truman southerners, denying that they were bolters, met at Birmingham on July 17 and nominated Governor J. Strom Thurmond of South Carolina for President and Governor Fielding L. Wright of Mississippi for Vice President on a state-rights and anti-race-equality platform. In spite of appeals to the emotions and prejudices of the white South, these sectionalists—called Dixiecrats—drew in few nationally important southern Democrats. But the bolters had control of the state organizations in several states and could compel the regular Democratic Presidential electors to support Thurmond. This would force the Truman electors to run as independents with slight chance of success. The Dixiecrats aimed to defeat Truman, even though Dewey's civil-rights position was just as unsatisfactory.

While the Dixiecrats preempted the extreme right, a new party appeared on the left—not a wing of seceding Democrats but a hybrid of radicals and non-party liberals of all shades of opinion. In December, 1947, Henry Wallace had accepted the invitation of a group called the Progressive Citizens of America to run for President. A national convention, meeting at Philadelphia on July 22, organized the Progressive party and nominated Wallace and Senator Glen Taylor of Idaho as its candidates. Wallace appeared at a great mass meeting at Shibe Park to accept the nomination on a platform that attacked the Marshall Plan, called for disarmament and the destruction of atomic-bomb stockpiles, and demanded equality of treatment for all minority groups. It was a gathering, in large part, of idealistic young voters who, gazing through the tinted glasses of peace and equal rights and alarmed at the cold war and the revival of the draft, could not see the Communist pattern of the platform and the skillful management of the party-liners in the convention's proceedings. Early in August a Communist party convention indorsed Wallace and adopted a platform very similar to that of the Progressive party.

Congress, called into special session by Truman, refused to act on most of his program. The Republican majority denounced his action as a political move—which it was—and adjourned after passing weak housing and anti-inflation bills that were hardly more than gestures for campaign purposes. The cast-iron conservatism of the House leadership played into Truman's hands. He could now go on the stump and repeat his charges against the Eightieth Congress with even more emphasis.

But Truman's plight seemed to be hopeless. The Dixiecrats were certain to win some southern electoral votes. Wallace would cut into Democratic strength in New York and possibly other states of the East and the Middle West. If Dewey polled the normal Republican vote he would move into the White House. And there was no evidence that the Republican trend of 1946 had been reversed. As a result, the Democratic leadership fell into a defeatist lethargy, and Truman and a few loyal supporters had to bear the brunt of the campaigning. The national chairman, J. Howard McGrath, was confronted with a lack of funds and a disorganized party, and had one of the most difficult tasks a campaign manager had ever faced.

Truman, undaunted by the odds against him, traveled 31,000 miles in a "whistle-stop" campaign and spoke to some 6,000,000 people. He hammered away at the record of the Eightieth Congress, blaming it for price and rent rises and the housing shortage (an appeal to salaried workers and veterans) and for the Taft-Hartley Act (an appeal to labor). For farmers, he pointed to years of prosperity under Democratic rule and warned of the dangers of an end of price supports if the Republicans won. For the conservation-minded West, he emphasized the benefits of a liberal federal policy and the threats to reclamation projects from Congressional cuts in appropriations. Thus he offered both performance and promise. Late in the campaign, he shifted to the civil-rights issue in speeches in the East and the

Middle West where large minority groups—Negroes, Jews, foreign-born—were tempted by the Wallace lure. This put a strain on southern Democrats, but traditional party loyalty had to take care of the Thurmond threat.

The President's speeches were homely, down-to-earth, hard-hitting talks of an average man aimed at the average man. A little group of faithful aides assisted him, and their planning belied the caustic comment of a newspaperman: "With Truman's staff, Robert E. Lee couldn't carry Virginia." All the working journalists were puzzled by the large crowds that turned out to see the President, and wondered at the apparent warmth of their greeting. But did this mean votes? or merely admiration for a little guy who didn't know when he was licked?

On the Republican side the campaign was managed by the same efficient methods that had brought Dewey the nomination. Representative Hugh D. Scott, Jr., of Pennsylvania was national chairman, but Governor Dewey and his experienced general staff directed the strategy. Dewey's speeches stressed the need for an administration that would promote national unity and the cause of world peace. He promised to "work for peace through the United Nations and by every honorable means wherever the peace is threatened." At home, he would promote both social progress and individual freedom. He avoided concrete commitments which might create trouble in his own party and might prove embarrassing after election. His task, with victory seemingly assured, was not to win friends but to keep from alienating people. His deep voice, excellent for radio, poured out polished, faultless sentences, correctly inflected and uttered with a confident assurance that carried conviction. Truman appeared as an inept fumbler beside him; but the Republican candidate's speeches seemed to flow over his audiences, not into them. He seemed to be the cool, cautious champion; Truman, the fighting challenger. Dewey chose to let his wild-swinging opponent defeat himself, rather than to take chances by trading punches; but it made the campaign singularly dull. Dewey was a machine with a cellophane cover, said one observant critic.

In the South the Dixiecrats conducted a vigorous campaign. They controlled the state committees in Alabama, Mississippi, South Carolina, and Louisiana, where their electors ran as the regular Democratic candidates. In Alabama the ballot listed no Truman electors. In other parts of the South Thurmond-Wright electoral candidates ran as independents and threatened to give Virginia, Florida, and Tennessee to the Republicans. Loyal Truman Democrats believed that the Southern Rights movement had financial support from northern business interests with southern connections, and that state rights, rebel yells, and Yankee dollars worked in harmony for Republican victory.

Henry Wallace provided the thunder on the left. His invasion of the South to preach equal rights produced some acts of rowdiness where it defied Jim Crow regulations, but his political importance was in the urban sections of the East and the Middle West. Wherever his name appeared on the ballot, it lessened Democratic chances of victory. Likewise, it pointed up the Communist issue for the major parties. The Un-American Activities Committee of the House of Representatives, under Republican control, unearthed sufficient evidence of Communist espionage and other operations to create a good deal of concern, and Republican speakers made much of Communist infiltration. Dewey, however, opposed outlawry of the Communist party. Truman criticized the inquisitorial methods of the investigators and called their allegations "a red herring" to divert attention from more important matters. Wallace's candidacy actually did the Democrats a good turn. It attracted radicals of all shades and freed Truman of the taint of their support. But there were fears that he would need these votes to win the close states.

All the leading polls, the political analysts, and the important newspapers predicted a Dewey victory, though some conceded that Truman's fighting campaign had stirred lagging Democratic spirits, and that control of the next Senate was in doubt. The cautious *New York Times*, on the basis of reports of its correspondents, gave Dewey 305 electoral votes, Truman 105, and Thurmond 38, with 43 votes doubtful. The President himself forecast in mid-October: Truman, 229 votes; Dewey, 109; Thurmond, 8; doubtful, 189.

On the night of November 2 the early returns put Truman in the lead, but Republican headquarters remained optimistic. These were urban votes that would be nullified by later returns from rural districts. Quite the reverse happened. Truman's popular lead increased as the western states reported, but there was uncertainty about the electoral votes. The election might go to the House. Not until 11:14 A.M. on Wednesday, after California and Ohio had gone into the Truman column, did Dewey concede defeat. The electoral results were 303 votes for Truman, 189 for Dewey, 39 for Thurmond.

Dewey had carried Maine, New Hampshire, Vermont, Connecticut, New York, Pennsylvania, New Jersey, Maryland, and Delaware in the East, Michigan and Indiana in the Middle West, North Dakota, South Dakota, Nebraska, and Kansas in the farm belt, and Oregon on the Pacific coast. Thurmond had South Carolina, Alabama, Mississippi, and Louisiana, and one Tennessee elector who violated his Truman pledge. Truman carried the remaining twenty-eight states.

The states from Ohio westward and the upper South provided most of his votes, but the surprising thing was the wide distribution of his strength. But for the Wallace candidacy he might have carried New York, Michigan, and Maryland; and Thurmond certainly cost him 39 electoral votes in the South. Dewey's percentage of the popular vote (45.1) was a little under that in 1944 (45.9). Truman had 49.6 per cent; the minor parties, 5.4 per cent.[1]

Various explanations were offered for the incredible result: farm prosperity and farmer distrust of Easterner Dewey; labor's weight in the cities; Truman's whistle-stop campaign, stressing the record of the Eightieth Congress; Dewey's failure to come to grips with the issues; Republican overconfidence and consequent failure to get out a full vote; an unusually strong crop of Democratic candidates for the Senate and for state governorships, which aided the national ticket; the failure of Thurmond and Wallace to do what the pollsters had predicted.

Samuel Lubell has argued convincingly that the very instability of a majority coalition may be a source of strength. Disaffection on the left may strengthen loyalties on the right, and vice versa. In 1948 the Wallace candidacy took the blight of radicalism off Truman's shoulders and eased the return to the fold of some isolationist and other anti-Roosevelt groups such as farm-belt German Catholics and urban Irish. The Democratic Catholic vote in some areas exceeded the turnout for Al Smith in 1928. The Dixiecrat seceders also did Truman a good turn by proving to northern Negroes that he was sound on civil rights. But the urge to preserve, if not to advance, the various gains of the Roosevelt years was basic in the Democratic miracle, and Truman made the most of it. In a sense Roosevelt won his greatest victory after his death.

The most heartening thing about the election was the stubborn

[1] The popular vote was as follows: Truman, 24,179,345; Dewey, 21,991,291; Thurmond, 1,176,125; Wallace, 1,157,326, Thomas, Socialist, 139,572; Watson, Prohibitionist 103,900; Teichert, Socialist Labor, 29,241; Dobbs, Socialist Workers, 13,614.

independence of the voting majority in defying the band-wagon psychology created by polls, newspaper opinion, and the near-unanimous verdict of the political pundits. These samplers of opinion were quite crestfallen, and the laughter over their discomfiture tempered the disappointment of the defeated. Never again would an election be regarded as settled until the votes were counted.

One other lesson was not so well learned. For a few hours after the polls closed on November 2 it had seemed possible either that Dewey would have a majority of the electoral votes, though second in the popular vote, or that the election would go to the House of Representatives for lack of an electoral decision, with the ultimate verdict in doubt. Fortunately, later returns ended the danger of a perversion of the popular will. But in Congress down to 1957 efforts to alter or abolish the antiquated, undemocratic electoral college produced only debates and disagreement. Liberals and conservatives in both parties were badly divided over the merits of several reform proposals.

The Fair Deal Fails

Truman had been triumphant running on his "Fair Deal" program, and with both houses again Democratic he had the right to expect the legislators to register the verdict promptly. But the old pattern reappeared. Republicans, despite their platform pledges, aided the antiadministration southern Senators in blocking civil-rights legislation. The story was repeated with other administration measures, and the fruits of the great victory of 1948 were lost. Particularly bitter to Truman supporters was their inability to repeal the Taft-Hartley Act, as pledged to labor in the campaign. On this issue the coalition won in both houses. While the President failed to secure enactment of a large part of his domestic program, he did secure the renewal of the reciprocal trade agreements, continued appropriations for the European Recovery Program, and ratification of the North Atlantic Security Pact. Senator Vandenberg lined up most of the Republican Senators for the bipartisan foreign policy. But the victory of the Communists in China in 1949 and the outbreak of war in Korea in June, 1950, saddled the administration with a set of liabilities so potent that Republican hopes rose to a new high by 1952.

The North Korean Communist invasion of South Korea produced a temporary united front against aggression in Congress, but this soon broke down. The initial United Nations failure in stemming the

North Korean sweep, the glaring unpreparedness of the American military arm, the nullification of General MacArthur's later successes by Communist China's entry into the struggle, the long stalemate that ensued, the heavy American casualties and increased defense expenditures, the removal of MacArthur by President Truman for alleged interference in policy matters, and a widespread belief that past State Department blunders in China were responsible for the Communist triumph in that country were factors that did not need Republican oratory to raise doubts in the minds of many Americans as to the wisdom of administration policies. The war also created a state of alarm in which fears of the Communist menace within the United States mounted. Even before the Korean crisis Alger Hiss had been convicted of perjury for denying that he had used his position in the State Department in the late 1930's to further Communist ends. Other cases involved leading Communists in conspiracy charges, and some underlings were caught betraying atomic energy secrets. This helped set the stage for Congressional investigations to determine the extent of Communist infiltration in government departments. Republican Senator Joseph R. McCarthy of Wisconsin made the headlines by blanket charges that the State Department harbored Communists.

Secretary of State Dean G. Acheson became McCarthy's chief target, and other Republicans soon joined in the hue and cry. Although President Truman had instituted a system of loyalty checks of administrative employees, Red-hunting critics were not appeased; and the Communist issue loomed large on the political horizon with the Korean War a constant reminder of the ever present Russian menace.

On the domestic front the administration struggled with increased consumer prices, ineffective controls, heavier tax burdens, wage freezes and labor unrest, the slow pace of rearmament, and presently, exposure of corruption in governmental departments. The last was, politically, far and away the most serious. Congressional investigations dug out details of shady deals, of activities of influence peddlers, of tax frauds, and of other unsavory transactions by officials in the Bureau of Internal Revenue, the Justice Department, and the Reconstruction Finance Corporation. "Mink coats," "deep freezers," and "five per centers" hit the newspaper headlines and were used in Republican campaign propaganda to remind the voters of the "mess in Washington." Unlike the Harding scandals, the Truman frauds were entirely below the cabinet level, though some top officials were guilty of bad appointments and of woeful blindness to the doings of responsible subordinates. Truman was compared with Harding in his inclination toward "government by crony" and in his slowness to see the faults in his friends. His belated housecleaning did little to undo the political damage resulting from the exposures.

The mid-term elections, before the full impact of exposures of corruption and Communism had been felt but after reverses in Korea, brought a decided slap at the administration. Gains put the Republican party within two seats of control of the Senate, and the Democratic majority in the House was greatly reduced. The Democrats were better off in Congress than in 1946, but there were ominous aspects. Among the defeated in the Senate were Scott W. Lucas of Illinois, majority leader, Francis J. Myers of Pennsylvania, majority whip, and two long-time important committee chairmen, Millard Tydings of Maryland and Elbert Thomas of Utah. Tydings' defeat was attributed chiefly to the tactics of Senator McCarthy in the Maryland campaign, later the subject of a Senate investigation. Most significant of the Republican victories was that of Senator Taft, who was reelected by a landslide in the face of labor opposition. After this resounding popular indorsement, "Mr. Republican" could not overlook the White House in his plans for 1952.

30

I Like Ike

Republican Rivals

Senator Taft announced in September, 1951, that his intentions were serious and embarked upon as strenuous a delegate hunt as a candidate had ever undertaken. The sparse-haired, bespectacled, scholarly-looking Ohio statesman with the dry, metallic voice was not a good rabble rouser, but in his own way was an effective campaigner. His intelligence, earnestness, command of facts, and unrelenting partisanship made sympathetic listeners overlook his lack of humor and imagination. Believing that the party had lost too many times with "me too" candidates, he took issue with every major Truman policy and gave the voters his version of true Republicanism. To his standard came party wheelhorses, courthouse politicians, isolationists, Asia Firsters, and small-town and country tories, especially the elderly. Middle western state machines and the southern skeletons, as before, lined up for "Mr. Republican." Where the party was well intrenched—New England excepted—and where it was weakest, Taft was favored.

But internationalists and liberals could see no hope in Taft's line. He was calling the primitive Republicans to arms; but independents and anti-Truman Democrats would look askance at a man who had been an isolationist, a defender of McCarthy, a critic of organized labor, and an extreme conservative. The East, doubtful Michigan and Minnesota, and the farther West were at stake. Truman's humorous comment that Taft was his favorite Republican candidate had a point. The anti-Taft forces, however, were at a disadvantage within the Republican party, where independents and Democrats had no voice. Only an outstanding man would have a chance against him.

And so General Dwight D. Eisenhower ("Ike") was urged to make the race.

This popular leader in World War II, after a brief tenure as president of Columbia University, had been placed in charge of the European defense system of the North Atlantic Treaty nations. A nominal Republican, he had, like Grant, a popularity that transcended party lines. A group of anti-Taft Republicans—Governor Dewey, Senators James H. Duff of Pennsylvania, Frank Carlson of Kansas, and Henry Cabot Lodge of Massachusetts—launched a "Draft Eisenhower" movement to put pressure on the reluctant general, who was still in Europe. In January, 1952, he permitted his name to be entered in the New Hampshire primary, and an organization headed by Senator Lodge undertook to transmute popularity into delegates. Financial backing was expected from big-business sources. Metropolitan newspapers and the largest news weeklies were friendly.

Two lesser figures also offered themselves. Harold Stassen decided to try his luck again, and Earl Warren, elected for a third term as governor of California, was the Pacific coast's choice. Here and there a voice was lifted for General MacArthur after his dismissal by President Truman, but his "martyrdom" served his party's interests better than his own.

The preferential primary results were indecisive and somewhat sectional. New Hampshire, voting first, gave Eisenhower a clear margin over Taft and Stassen, but direct clashes between the two top candidates were avoided in most of the other primary states. Sometimes "write-in" campaigns were attempted to show popular support. Stassen and Warren also complicated matters. In general, Taft showed greater strength in the Middle West although he lost six Wisconsin delegates to Warren, and Eisenhower ran better in the East, although he almost took Minnesota from Stassen by write-in votes.

Eisenhower, at the insistence of his managers, resigned as NATO commander and returned home in June to strengthen his cause by direct appeal. His first speech was at Abilene, Kansas, his boyhood home. After this initial plunge, he began to act more like a candidate. Speeches and conferences with party leaders and delegates in key states followed. His statements on issues drew the fire of the Taft men —"five star generalities," the *Chicago Tribune* called them—but the warmth and sincerity of his personality meant more for his cause than what he said. He was still a tyro in politics; but the voters more than once have favored a candidate unsoiled and unspoiled by the evils of politics. His propaganda played him up as the people's choice, Taft as the politicians', and pointed to opinion polls as proof.

Though the Eisenhower movement made surprising headway, Taft led in pledged delegates when the convention met in International Amphitheater at Chicago on July 7, 1952. But the uncommitted delegates, including Michigan and Pennsylvania, the contested seats from the South, and the Warren and Stassen blocs held the answer for the two front runners. Taft had one decided advantage—control of the national committee. That body chose Walter S. Hallanan of West Virginia as temporary chairman of the convention, former Speaker Martin as permanent chairman, General MacArthur as keynoter, and Herbert Hoover for an evening address. Not one of them favored Eisenhower. More important was the power of the national committee to rule on contested seats, and then to make up the temporary roll. A situation like that of 1912 seemed to be shaping up, for some seventy seats were in dispute.

Taft's Final Try

The national committee, with television cameras carefully excluded, heard arguments over the contested seats. Georgia, Louisiana, and Texas were the key states. Here the Republican organizations were, in effect, closed clubs which hand-picked delegates to national conventions and controlled the patronage when there was any. These had been lined up for Taft, and it was assumed that local and state conventions would be the usual cut-and-dried affairs. Unexpectedly, Eisenhower Republicans had turned up in force at the local primary meetings or caucuses, and in many instances had elected their slates of delegates to district and state conventions. Charging that these interlopers were not true Republicans, the Taft regulars sometimes had walked out and chosen their own delegates at closed caucuses. The party committees, being pro-Taft, denied recognition to the Eisenhower delegates whenever Taft claimants appeared. Such tactics split state and district conventions, and produced two sets of delegates to Chicago. The national committee, after wrestling with various compromise proposals, ended by giving a large majority of the disputed seats to Taft. This was 1912 again.

The matter now came before the opening session of the national convention on a routine motion to adopt the rules of the 1948 convention. This would have permitted the delegates from each contested state occupying temporary seats to vote on all matters except their own seats. The Eisenhower strategists countered with a substitute that delegations opposed by more than one-third of the national committee should not vote on the credentials of any other delegation. The key vote came on a proposal to exempt seven Louisiana delegates from the operation of the rule. After a bitter two-hour debate, the Taft forces lost by a margin of 110 votes. The substitute then carried.

The credentials committee, under Taft control, now heard all contests for seats in the glare of television cameras. This exposure of southern dirty linen did the Taft cause no good. The convention rejected the committee's report on the Georgia contest, 607 to 531, and the Eisenhower delegates were then seated in all cases. The bitterness displayed in the debate by the usually well-mannered Republicans was almost unparalleled. At one stage impassioned Senator Everett M. Dirksen of Illinois, pointing at Governor Dewey, in the New York delegation, assailed him for leading the party down to defeat in the past. This produced a roar of boos. The internationalist East and the isolationist Middle West were locked in a battle for control. To a degree, it was the large urban centers versus the smaller places and the countryside.

While the credentials committee struggled over the contested seats, the convention endured speech after speech by Taft-selected party celebrities, high-lighted by the oratory of General MacArthur and Herbert Hoover at evening sessions. MacArthur's dramatic passages did not quite meet expectations; Hoover, now seventy-seven, was more appealing with his jeremiads than in the past. Before the balloting he indorsed Taft.

After voting on the contested seats the convention received the platform with such noisy inattention that Chairman Martin had to take a hand with a sharp reproof. The resolutions committee had ironed out the controversial issues, and the convention accepted the result with a voice vote. The document of six thousand words contained mostly denunciations, with some carefully qualified pledges as to future action. The foreign relations plank, written by John Foster Dulles, rejected both isolationism and the Truman policy of containment of Communism, accepted collective security and foreign commitments with the reservation that they should not endanger the economic health of the United States, and promised equal treatment of Asia and Europe. It spoke of making the nation again a "dynamic, moral and spiritual force" and ending "the negative, futile and immoral policy of containment."

Communism and corruption in the administration were condemned, and an improved national defense was promised with economy and tax reduction. A long section on agriculture covered "a farm program aimed at full parity prices." A civil-rights section was a little less emphatic than in 1948, putting more weight on state action. Except for approval of the extension of social security, the platform leaned strongly toward state rights and opposed government in business. It favored eventual local control of federal water projects, opposed "Federal socialistic valley authorities," declared for state ownership of lands and resources beneath offshore waters, and proposed changes in public-land policy in favor of individual and local interests. It condemned federal compulsory health insurance and upheld the Taft-Hartley Act, but left the door open for possible amendments to improve it.

The votes on the contested seats had foreshadowed defeat for Taft. The unpledged Pennsylvania and Michigan delegations, controlled by Governor John S. Fine and National Committeeman Arthur E. Summerfield respectively, had voted with the Eisenhower forces. The Stassen and Warren blocs were also anti-Taft and seemed certain to go to Eisenhower on the Presidential balloting if he should come close to a majority. The result of the one ballot for the nomination was even more favorable than the strategists for Eisenhower had expected. He had 595 (9 short of a majority); Taft, 500; Warren, 81; Stassen, 20; MacArthur, 10. Minnesota, which had already cast 9 votes for Eisenhower, now added the rest of its votes to his total; other states followed until he had 845. Taft had 280; Warren, 77; and MacArthur, 4. Senator Bricker of Ohio then sorrowfully moved that the nomination be made unanimous. Taft's third and last attempt had fallen short.

In a sense Taft had defeated himself. He had relied too much on party regulars and organizations, and these had overreached themselves in the South. The time-honored, if shabby, methods of corralling delegates there gave the Eisenhower leaders an opportunity to occupy high moral ground in refusing to compromise with sin. When the television cameras invaded the hearings of the credentials committee, they confirmed—to the uninitiated—the villainies of the hardened professionals in delegate grabbing. A crusade against Democratic corruption by a candidate nominated through such methods would have been unconvincing. Yet there were hardened professionals and shrewd manipulations on the victor's side. Governor Dewey, still a power, was unrelentingly anti-Taft. Herbert Brownell, Jr., who had directed Dewey's campaigns, pulled the strings behind the scenes at Eisenhower headquarters. Senator Lodge, Governor Adams of New Hampshire, and others handled floor tactics far better than the bungling Taft lieutenants. If Taft could have been his own floor leader, he might have done better—but the historian can multiply the *if*'s that seem to explain his defeat. The nomination of Taft would have violated the doctrine of availability which most Republican conventions have respected. The candidates are not taken from the conservative right.

The Vice Presidential choice of the Eisenhower high command was Senator Richard M. Nixon of California. The selection recognized the youth movement in the party—he was thirty-nine—and acknowledged the importance of the Pacific coast. It was designed also to point up the Communism-in-government issue, because Nixon, as a member of the House Un-American Activities Committee, had played a major part in exposing Alger Hiss. In other respects the nomination was highly unorthodox for the Republicans. It denied the Taft minority a customary consolation prize and departed from the usual practice of choosing among important state governors or Senate veterans. Nixon was a junior Senator as obscure as the Truman of 1944 and far more inexperienced; but he was a fluent speaker who appeared to advantage on television, and his attractive wife was not the least of his campaigning assets.

The Stevenson Draft

President Truman's decision not to run again, announced in early April but made long before, opened the way for a free-for-all battle for the Democratic nomination. Though the civil-rights issue was present, there was not the sharpness of alignment and consequent bitterness of the Republican struggle. The Democrats, chronically inharmonious, expected a fracas over candidates or platform planks or both.

Senator Estes Kefauver of Tennessee was the most persevering of the active candidates, and the leader in pledged delegates. The lanky Tennessean had become a national figure by heading a special Senate committee to investigate crime, whose televised proceedings made him a popular hero; but he had incurred some enmities by exposing the tie-up of certain local politicians with gangsters and gamblers. Also, his early announcement of his candidacy without consulting party leaders, at a time when Truman was still expected to run, did him no good with organization men, and his New Deal and Fair Deal record kept southern conservatives away. Lacking money and organization, he conducted an informal but extensive street-corner and hand-shaking campaign, assisted by his prepossessing wife, and won a number of surprising primary successes. His reforming record, his coonskin-cap emblem, his opposition to boss rule, and his vague liberalism attracted young voters, moral reformers, antiorganization men, small-town Democrats, and some liberals. Opponents charged that his primary victories were won over weak candidates or organization unpledged slates.

A more openly anti-Truman candidate was Senator Richard Russell, a highly respected Georgia conservative who was backed by state-rights southern Democrats and Dixiecrats. He rallied southerners who wanted to force concessions from the northern liberal majority.

Among favorite sons were W. Averell Harriman of New York, Senator Robert S. Kerr of Oklahoma, and Vice President Alben W. Barkley. Harriman, millionaire son of E. H. Harriman of railroad fame, was a Roosevelt-Truman loyalist who had served capably in several administrative posts, had strong labor backing, but was inexperienced in politics, with New York his only large bloc of votes. Senator Kerr, a wealthy oil man, was an administration supporter in most respects; but northern liberals were cold toward him, and a setback at Kefauver's hands in Nebraska left him with only scattered support outside Oklahoma. A late entrant was the beloved "Veep," Alben Barkley, who was informed that the Truman administration was ready to take him, as none of the other possibilities fitted the situation. He could easily have been nominated had he been ten years younger, but labor leaders turned him down flatly because of his age, seventy-four.

The most suitable candidate from availability angles was Governor Adlai E. Stevenson of Illinois. His public career included service in responsible posts with the Navy and State departments before Colonel Jacob M. Arvey, shrewd Chicago party head, spotted him as a fine prospect to recapture the state house from the Republicans. He had won by a landslide in 1948, running ahead of Truman in Illinois. His record as governor, working with a Republican legislature, added to his reputation. Also in his favor were his middle western roots, a grandfather who had been Vice President with Cleveland, and brilliant public speeches studded with apt quotations and clever quips. His Ivy League education (Princeton was his alma mater) recommended him to "high and middle brows," if not to the commonalty. His recent divorce and a deposition he had once signed attesting to Alger Hiss's good character were not regarded as serious drawbacks.

But Stevenson refused to run. He insisted that a second term as governor was his only ambition. A strong movement in the Truman administration and in important state organizations to line up delegates for him was stalled. A group of Illinois admirers, including members of the University of Chicago faculty, refused to be discouraged and set up Stevenson headquarters to keep the door open for a draft. As the national convention was about to open, Mayor David L. Lawrence of Pittsburgh and other influential state leaders threw their support to the Draft Stevenson movement. It gained momentum hourly and the governor, apparently torn by conflicting emotions, could not stop it.

The convention opened two weeks after the Republican conclave in the same International Amphitheater, with 1,230 delegates present. Governor Paul A. Dever of Massachusetts was temporary chairman and keynoter and veteran Sam Rayburn, Speaker of the House, succeeded him in the chair. At the opening session a "loyalty" pledge was put through by a northern liberal bloc requiring all delegates to agree to use all honorable means to get the nominees of the convention on the state ballots as Democrats. In view of the misuse of the electoral system by the Dixiecrats in 1948, this mild proposal seemed to be quite in order. Southern opposition to a specific pledge flared up, however, with Senator Byrd of Virginia, Governor Byrnes of South Carolina, and Governor Kennon of Louisiana representing the die-hards, who would not sign the pledge. Finally, on the fourth day, the convention voted, 615 to 529, to seat the Virginia delegates without the pledge. Assurance was given that Virginia laws covered the matter. Then South Carolina and Louisiana were also seated, without a roll call. The vote on the Virginia case showed that the southern contingent had the backing of important northern machine leaders against a Harriman-Kefauver liberal bloc. Harmony had triumphed over party discipline.

Rather surprisingly, the platform caused no difficulty in the convention. The troublesome civil-rights statement of 1948 was virtually repeated in demands for federal legislation to secure equal rights for all with regard to employment, security of persons, and political life. It was not opposed except by Mississippi and Georgia, which were recorded as voting against the platform as a whole. The Republican plank, with its specific mention of anti-lynching and anti-poll-tax legislation and an end of segregation in the District of Columbia, possibly made the Democratic position appear milder to the southern wing. In the civil-rights section was a statement favoring an end of Senate filibusters, long a weapon of the southern minority.

Other planks defended the Truman foreign policy of resisting Communist aggression through collective security; commended Congressional exposures, under Democratic leadership, of dishonesty and disloyalty in the public service; favored tax reduction, but only when defense requirements would permit it; upheld the Truman loyalty program for government officials; promised the farmer 90 per cent of parity; and, for labor, favored the repeal of the Taft-Hartley Act.

The Democrats were generally as immune to political spellbinding as the Republicans, but they did demonstrate warmly for two party veterans, Vice President Barkley and Mrs. Franklin D. Roosevelt. One other speaker, Adlai E. Stevenson, in his brief address of welcome as governor of Illinois, was highly effective and gave a strong impetus to the draft movement he had disavowed.

Hours of nominating speeches for eleven men, and the battle over the loyalty pledge, delayed the balloting until Friday afternoon. The first ballot gave Kefauver 340 votes, Stevenson 273, Russell 268, Harriman 123-1/2, Kerr 65, Barkley 48-1/2, and eight others scattering votes. On the second ballot Stevenson went up to 324-1/2 and Kefauver to 362-1/2 as the favorite sons began to drop out. The third ballot produced a general shift to Stevenson. He had 617-1/2 votes, Kefauver 275-1/2, Russell 261, and Barkley 67-1/2. The Stevenson draft had succeeded.

The nominee appeared before the convention, was introduced by President Truman, who had arrived from Washington, and delivered a moving acceptance speech whose exalted, idealistic tone and expressive phraseology made it a classic of convention oratory. Quite in contrast was the down-to-earth fighting speech of Truman which ended the session. Unfortunately for the Democrats, most Americans had gone to bed and did not hear the two speeches that presented the party's case most effectively.

Next day, the convention nominated Stevenson's choice for Vice

President, Senator John J. Sparkman. The big, curly-haired likable Alabaman, fifty-two years old, was a liberal, though opposed to civil-rights legislation, had fought the Dixiecrats, and had compiled a good record in his sixteen years in the House and Senate. He had also been a delegate to the United Nations General Assembly. Southern conservatives were cold toward both nominees but at least gave no consideration to the idea of separate Dixiecrat candidates, as in 1948.

Both conventions came in for a good deal of criticism from watchers at TV sets. The noisy inattention of delegates, the artificial demonstrations (the Republicans even had paid performers), the banal oratory, the parliamentary tangles and public quarreling, the mysterious deals and shiftings of votes behind the camera's eye, the "show-off" delegates who demanded polls of their delegations just to give themselves a brief television appearance, the hectic carnival atmosphere—all were disillusioning to citizens who, before the television era, had thought of a convention as a kind of deliberative assembly. Radio had revealed unlovely aspects, but the camera was devastating. Thoughtful observers wondered about substitutes such as a national primary which would let the voters nominate. The skeptical pointed to the enormously expensive sales campaigns necessary to win votes, which might make the nominee the one with the slickest publicity men. At least the convention system had produced two excellent candidates in 1952; and by and large it had not worked badly. If it had rejected front runners in favor of a Pierce or a Harding, it had also produced a Lincoln and a Wilson, both availabilities. Where the public voice was clear, it had responded. Grant, Cleveland, the Roosevelts, and Hoover were popular choices, whatever their merits as chief executives.

The Eisenhower Sweep

In the Republican camp Arthur Summerfield, who had swung unpledged Michigan to Eisenhower at Chicago, became national chairman and campaign manager. Governor Sherman Adams of New Hampshire was personal adviser to the candidate. A Citizens Committee for Eisenhower, which had worked for his nomination, continued its separate organization and aimed its propaganda at independents and Democrats. Stevenson chose Stephen A. Mitchell, a Chicago lawyer whose experience was more legal than political, but who brought new blood into the organization, and Wilson W. Wyatt of Kentucky, a founder of the liberal Americans for Democratic Action, to handle his campaign, with Mitchell as national chairman. Both had had experience in Washington positions. Sinclair Weeks handled finances for the Republicans, Beardsley Ruml for the Democrats.

The big Republican problem was Taft's attitude. The boos that had greeted Eisenhower when he called at Taft headquarters just after the nomination indicated the feelings of the Taft men. Taft himself formally indorsed the nominee, then left for his summer home in Quebec. Apparently he was prepared to sit out the campaign, and his devoted following might do likewise. They regarded Eisenhower as the tool of the "Dewey people" and another "Me, too" candidate. Not since the Taft-Roosevelt feud of 1912 had there been such fratricidal strife in the party. Eisenhower moved to heal the breach by inviting Taft to his home on Morningside Heights. They conferred on September 12, and a manifesto written by Taft was accepted with only slight changes by the candidate and made public. It committed him to the orthodox (to Taft) position on all major points, except for some "differences of degree" on foreign policy, and promised equality of treatment for Taft supporters as to offices.

This "surrender," as Democratic critics termed it, brought the Ohio Senator into the fold; his lieutenants went to work, and party unity seemed to be assured. Eisenhower appeared with Senators Jenner in Indiana and McCarthy in Wisconsin, though Jenner had called his old mentor and friend, General George C. Marshall, "a front for traitors" and "a living lie," and McCarthy had been equally harsh. Possibly, Eisenhower was thinking that he would need support from the Taft wing, so powerful in Congress, if he won in November. In any case, Republican nominees for office received pats on the back wherever the head of the ticket appeared.

Stevenson's troubles lay southward. There the conservatives were unhappy over the civil-rights issue, and Texas, Louisiana, and Florida had a special grievance—Truman's vetoes of bills giving title of offshore lands to the states. The candidate refused to back away from his platform. Referring to civil rights, he told a Richmond (Va.) audience: "I should justly earn your contempt if I talked one way in the South and another way elsewhere." Later, in Texas, he upheld federal control of offshore lands and damned himself with the oil interests and with state-rights men generally.

These issues and the widespread dislike of southern conservatives for the Truman administration caused bolting to Eisenhower that was like the Hoovercrat revolt against Alfred E. Smith in 1928. Governors Byrnes of South Carolina, Kennon of Louisiana, and Shivers of Texas led the rebels, while Senator Byrd of Virginia criticized Stevenson without announcing for Eisenhower. Most members of Congress were loyal, but many gave the ticket lukewarm support. Several important newspapers led by the *Atlanta Journal* came out for Eisenhower. The loyalty pledge of the Democratic national convention was observed everywhere, and Stevenson electors ran as Democrats. To avoid the Republican imprint, Eisenhower Democrats offered independent electoral tickets in South Carolina and Mississippi. Eisenhower campaigned vigorously in the South and drew large crowds. And sentimental southerners did not forget that he was born in Texas.

Using train and plane, the two rivals displayed their bald heads all over the continent. Important addresses in key cities were televised. This meant a different speech for each occasion, and a corps of skilled phrasemakers supplied much of the ammunition. This was particularly necessary in Eisenhower's case. Not well informed on domestic questions, nor blessed with the gift of eloquence, and inexperienced before the television camera, he had much to learn about campaign spellbinding. But his technique improved under coaching, and his audiences liked him for his sincerity, his humanness, his informal presence and folksy ways. They were not too concerned about what his advisers put into his set speeches. In his whistle-stop appearances, when he talked in familiar, if hackneyed, terms about his middle-of-the-road philosophy with Mamie waving at the cheering throngs, he was at his best. He was not a good partisan, he had no grudges, he chose to attack the "administration" rather than Truman, and his Communism, Korea, and corruption lacked personal devils. Yet, while he had trouble acting like a strong party man, he belonged in the Republican party. Fundamentally, he was a conservative.

Stevenson was a surprising discovery to most Americans. This not very impressive man with a receding hair line and a slightly paunchy middle immediately moved into the front rank of American political orators of all time. He had a good voice, but his speeches read even better than they sounded. He had a gift for the telling phrase, a probing wit, a keen mentality, and a challenging, if troubled, idealism that sometimes emerged in passages of moving eloquence. The intellectuals that had enlisted with F. D. R. in the depression years, but had found themselves pushed aside by the "cronies" under Truman, thronged into the Stevenson camp, for they saw him as one of their own kind. But these "eggheads" were not all gain. In the climate of anti-intellectualism engendered by fears of Communist infiltration and McCarthy accusations, many voters confused loyalty with conformity and suspected men who thought too much. The Wisconsin Senator went on the air to smear Stevenson and his personal staff, and Senator Nixon echoed McCarthy that Stevenson had never expressed one word of indignation at Alger Hiss's treachery. Leftists were not to be trusted.

While Ike was a world figure, the Democratic candidate was virtually unknown when nominated. Even at the campaign's end, he was still, to many voters, an uncomfortable type of party leader. He was almost too clever, too witty, too abstruse. Ike's platitudes and homilies, they understood and accepted. More important, the supreme commander of World War II seemed to be better equipped to end the stalemated Korean War. His master stroke of the campaign, suggested by a shrewd journalist, was the eleventh-hour announcement that, if elected, he would go to Korea in person. Stevenson, carrying the weight of Truman's Korea burdens, could only reply that Moscow, not Seoul, held the key to peace.

The most dramatic development of the campaign involved Nixon, the Republican choice for Vice President. In late September, the *New York Post* featured a story that, as Senator, he had been subsidized by a secret fund set up by California millionaires. Nixon, then campaigning in the West, admitted that the fund had existed, but asserted that it had been used for purely political expenses and involved him in no obligations to his benefactors. The fund treasurer opened its books, which revealed expenditures of about $18,000 in a year and a half for such expenses as trips to California, printing and mimeographing, and radio and television appearances. The dubious ethics of a public career financed by men of wealth, the size of the fund, and the concealment of its existence seemed to provide the Democrats with an answer to the Republican reiteration of "mink coats" and "deep freezers," symbols of exposures at Washington. Republican newspapers, in alarm, debated whether Nixon should be dropped from the ticket; Eisenhower and his advisers were equally perturbed, but final action was held up until the California Senator had offered his defense on television.

That defense saved his public career. Skillfully shifting from the fund issue, where he was vulnerable, to a defense of his reputation for honesty and integrity, he related the history of his personal finances from youth on. It was the story of the honest poor boy's rise to fame through his own efforts with no ill gotten gains to smooth his path. His wife (who was with him), her "respectable Republican cloth coat" (not mink), and their children's dog were brought into his affecting story. He invited his listeners to send their opinions to the Republican National Committee, which would decide his case. The result was a deluge of approving messages, and he went East to be greeted by Eisenhower as a man of courage and honor who had been subjected to "a very unfair and vicious attack." Democratic critics called his performance "ham acting" and "a financial strip tease," but he had emerged as a popular hero.

To blur the fund issue still further, Republican sources unearthed a fund which Stevenson had used for political purposes, so it was charged. Stevenson then was forced to explain that he had collected money—part of it a state campaign surplus—which he used to supplement the salaries of certain administrative state officials who, he felt, were underpaid. He supplied names and amounts. He and Sparkman then made public their income-tax returns for the preceding ten years, and Eisenhower followed suit.

As partisan fury increased, old combatants jumped into the fray to do the kind of slugging that the heads of the ticket could not or would not attempt. President Truman put on another whistle-stop tour; Senator Taft was happy again assailing Trumanism; and his party rival, Governor Dewey, appeared in a television series for Eisenhower.

The Republicans kept pounding away at their trinity of Democratic failures: blunders in foreign policy, the "mess" in Washington, the Communist danger within. Other issues were peripheral, but all fitted the slogan, "It's time for a change." As the party of the outs, they could promise much and specify little. The hard-pressed Democrats had to defend and condone—an admission that all was not well. And so they turned to a weapon that had worked well in the past, and proclaimed that good times would end if the Republicans won. Prosperity and the social gains of the New Deal were in danger. "Don't let them take it away" and "You never had it so good" were their war cries. This was effective enough to cause the Republicans to promise that nothing would be taken away; things would only be made better. For instance, Eisenhower told the Minnesota farmers that they were entitled to 100 per cent of parity instead of the Democratic 90 per cent, and in New England he promised full employment and an extension of social security.

Public opinion polls indicated an Eisenhower victory, as the trend everywhere was strongly in his favor; but the percentage of undecided was still large enough to hold the balance in many states, and pollsters, after having burned their fingers in 1948, were duly cautious. That Eisenhower seemed to be much stronger than his party was a safe conclusion.

They were too cautious this time. It was an Eisenhower, if not a Republican, landslide. With a total of 442 electoral votes, he had the entire North and West; Virginia, Tennessee, Florida, and Texas in the South; and Maryland and Missouri in the border area. Stevenson, with only 89 electoral votes, carried the rest of the South and Kentucky and West Virginia—nine states in all. Eisenhower had surpassed Truman in 1948 and Roosevelt in 1944, and was two votes short of Hoover's total of electors in 1928. He had repeated Hoover's victories in the South, except for North Carolina. His popular vote was 33,936,234 (55.1 per cent) to Stevenson's 27,314,992 (44.4 per cent). The record total vote was 61,550,918. In contrast to 1948, the minor parties were unimportant.[1]

The country had voted overwhelmingly for Eisenhower but hesitatingly for his party. His coattails did not carry into office the usual proportion of Congressional and local candidates. In the House were 221 Republicans, 213 Democrats, and 1 independent; in the Senate, 48 Republicans, 47 Democrats, and Wayne Morse, Oregon Republican who had bolted and was now an independent. His vote enabled the Republicans to organize the Upper House. The defeat of three extreme isolationist Senators, and the fact that McCarthy of Wisconsin, Jenner of Indiana, Bricker of Ohio, and Malone of Ne-

[1] The older third-party votes are as follows: Vincent Hallinan, Progressive, 140,023; Stuart Hamblen, Prohibition, 72,949; Eric Hass, Socialist Labor (Industrial Government in some states), 30,267; Darlington Hoopes, Socialist, 20,203. Other splinter parties had smaller totals. In Mississippi, an independent Eisenhower ticket had 112,966. There was no Republican ticket. In South Carolina a similar ticket polled 153,289 of the Eisenhower total of 168,082.

vada ran far behind Eisenhower indicated that many independents and Democrats had liked Ike but rejected his party.

Eisenhower's victory was a vote of confidence in the man himself but also in his party's somewhat fictionized picture of him, which assured troubled Americans that he had the answers to all the nation's problems. His appeal was like Harding's return to normalcy. Korean bloodshed, tax burdens, inflation, subversives, corruption—all would yield to the skill of the soldier statesman, and happier days would return.

Stevenson had much less to offer in his person and in his program. He seemed at times more in the mood of Churchill's blood, sweat, and tears as he told Americans there was no easy way—"Your salvation is in your own hands"—and that he could not promise miracles.

Stevenson had two major assets—his brilliant campaigning and his party's claim to a patent on prosperity. He presented his case eloquently, but he had to defend an unpopular administration; and, unlike Truman in 1948, he had no Republican Congress to use as a whipping boy, though the last two were Democratic in name only. His situation was made worse by the more than four-fifths hostile press. The most partisan newspapers not only blacked out the Stevenson side on the editorial page but played down Democratic publicity by poor space allocation and used biased headlines. The larger news weeklies were mostly pro-Eisenhower or slanted in that direction.

The prosperity appeal seemed to be about played out. The Hoover Depression had served the Democrats well for twenty years, just as the bloody shirt had once carried the Republicans to victory after victory. But references to bread lines and apple selling meant little to a young generation facing more immediate problems such as military service or the payments on a new car or the purchase of a home in the suburbs. Prosperity was a habit.

The defeated candidate was still his party's strongest figure. Seldom has an also-ran survived such a defeat with so little loss of prestige and so little criticism. Outside the South, he was the opposition leader and its early choice for 1956.

31

Ike Again

Republicanism on Trial

Washington thronged with Republican men and women of distinction when their Homburg-hatted leader—top hats and tail coats were banned—was inaugurated. His idealistic and inspirational address revealed little about policies, but his cabinet choices told more—"eight millionaires and a plumber" was a sardonic characterization. George M. Humphrey, Secretary of the Treasury, and Charles E. Wilson, Secretary of Defense, were outstanding examples of the President's reliance upon the business world for administrative talent and guidance. Most of the new appointees had had slight experience in politics and Secretary Wilson's celebrated remark—"What's good for General Motors is good for the country"—seemed to illustrate their political naïveté. More orthodox were the selections of Herbert Brownell, Jr., of the Dewey inner circle to be Attorney General and Arthur Summerfield, national chairman, to be Postmaster General. The new Secretary of State John Foster Dulles, long the party's expert on foreign affairs, was a logical appointment.

The President set up an efficient executive staff headed by former Governor Sherman Adams of New Hampshire as Presidential Assistant. This taciturn Yankee was presently tabbed as one of the most influential figures in the administration. James C. Hagerty, veteran newspaper man, handled press relations. Vice President Nixon was included in the cabinet group and was especially useful as a party harmonizer and as a good-will ambassador to other lands.

Eisenhower's conception of his office followed the pattern of most Republican Presidents—cooperation with Congress and a careful regard for its prerogatives. Dynamic leadership was out; teamwork was stressed. This was good political strategy as well, for the suspicious

Taft wing, dominating Congressional committees, needed to be mollified. An Eisenhower program was still in the formative stage.

This situation and the President's military experience explain his heavy reliance upon staff advisers and administrators. Dulles in foreign affairs, Humphrey in Treasury matters, Benson in agriculture, McKay in conservation, and others not only administered but in large measure developed policy. Naturally enough, they—and not their chief—caught the brickbats. His extensive delegation of authority evoked from unfriendly sources a comparison with a constitutional monarch who reigned but did not govern.

The high level of public esteem for Ike owed something at first to editorial friendliness. In sharp contrast with their acid treatment of Truman, news weeklies of large circulation seemed to have rediscovered some long unused adjectives for syrupy descriptions of the doings of Ike and Mamie. The editorial comments and the columnists of the 80 per cent friendly press were more restrained, but even isolationist misgivings over policies usually absolved the President from any blame.

At his press conferences, though there were moments of constraint and tension at first, Eisenhower soon handled himself with skill and poise. After all, he was hardly a novice in dealing with newspaper men. A notable innovation was the occasional admission of television and newsreel cameramen, though all film was screened by Secretary Hagerty before its release. The President's television technique for nation-wide telecasts was made more folksy and relaxed under the direction of actor Robert Montgomery, who became a White House staff member.

Taft, miffed because he had not been consulted about cabinet appointments but determined to have the new administration succeed, assumed the post of Senate leader. Eisenhower's skill as a conciliator and Taft's influence with the Republican right wing operated to keep the majority reasonably harmonious in the first session of Congress. Whether the Eisenhower-Taft alliance could have held up under the stresses and strains of the McCarthy controversies will never be known. The Senate's dominating figure died, a cancer victim, on July 31, 1953. His personal selection, William F. Knowland of California, became majority leader. Knowland was not an ideal choice for administration men, but Democratic votes were usually available to make up for Republican defections.

Many pages could be filled with the doings of Senator McCarthy but the long-time political implications seem too slight to warrant anything but a brief reference. His investigations of disloyalty in the government reflected on the vigilance of the Eisenhower administration as well as its predecessors, and ultimately brought him into a head-on conflict with Secretary of the Army Robert T. Stevens, who charged that McCarthy and his chief counsel, Roy Cohn, had sought favored treatment for Cohn's assistant, G. David Schine, recently inducted into the army. The nation watched on television screens the Senate investigation of the charges and counter-charges. Later, a select committee headed by Senator Arthur Watkins of Utah investigated McCarthy's methods and conduct and the result was a censure resolution passed by the Senate by a vote of 67 (44 Democrats, 22 Republicans, and one Independent) to 22 (all Republicans). Knowland, majority leader, voted against censure. With the loss of his chairmanship in the new Democratic Senate, McCarthy disappeared from the headlines. The press relegated his intermittent sniping to the inside pages. He died in 1957, completely discredited.

Campaign pledges were carried out by a bill returning the tidelands oil reserves to the states and by some modest tax reductions; but the budget could not be balanced until 1955-1956, and foreign-aid requirements continued high. The most notable administrative achievement was the ending of hostilities in Korea. In Indo-China, where the President refused to intervene with armed forces, France yielded the northern provinces to the Communists. Taft Republicans had rejoiced over the "unleashing" of Chiang Kai-shek on Formosa and Dulles's warning of American "massive retaliation" against aggressors, but presently had to support the administration in following what was virtually a continuation of the Truman-Acheson foreign policy. Isolationists and conservatives had to swallow the defeat of a proposed constitutional amendment, offered by Senator Bricker of Ohio, to restrict the treaty-making powers of the President. Eisenhower was disappointing the extremists, and his popularity was undiminished.

The approaching mid-term elections of 1954 forced Republicans of all viewpoints to fall in line behind the President. Maine elected a Democratic governor in September; a mild business recession affected employment in some industrial centers; signs of dissatisfaction with Secretary of Agriculture Benson's farm policy appeared in the western farm belt; and certain local situations seemed to favor the Democrats. To counteract this Democratic swing, the cries of Communism and corruption were revived, and Vice President Nixon, campaigning in the doubtful states, arraigned the Democratic party for harboring Communists and subversives. Whether he called the Democratic party the party of treason was a matter of controversy later, but thereafter he was political enemy number one for loyal Democrats.

Even Eisenhower was drawn into active, last-minute campaigning with peace and prosperity his themes, but the Democrats captured the Senate, 49 to 47, and the House of Representatives, 232 to 203. Seven close states, including New York and Pennsylvania, elected Democratic governors. The voters had slapped down the Republican party, if not the President.

The Preliminaries of 1956

The aftermath was anything but the "cold war" Eisenhower had predicted if the Democrats controlled Congress. Committee chairmanships went largely to southern conservatives who agreed with his position on most domestic matters. Nearly all the Democrats stood with him on foreign policy where his own party sometimes wavered. His preference for the soft answer over the big stick and his past annoyance—expressed in private—at the Republican right wing, made it easy for him to work with Senator Lyndon Johnson of Texas, now majority leader, Senator Walter George of Georgia, foreign affairs chairman, Speaker Rayburn, and others.

The results were creditable: foreign aid on a somewhat reduced scale, a fifty-billion-dollar highway construction program, a liberalization of social security benefits, a soil bank plan to reduce farm surpluses. Federal aid for school construction lost in the House of Representatives when an anti-segregation amendment, added by a Republican-liberal Democratic coalition, caused southern Democrats to join Republicans in opposing the bill. The administration won a victory in the Senate when a bi-partisan combination defeated a proposal for a government-financed dam in Hell's Canyon on the Oregon-Idaho border. The President vetoed a bill to exempt natural gas producers from federal regulation, passed by another bi-partisan alliance, when unsavory lobbying activities were exposed.

A Senate investigation discredited and killed the administration's Dixon-Yates contract, a bungling attempt to subsidize a private power company at the expense of the Tennessee Valley Authority.

Other investigations produced a few cases of "conflict of interest" by holders of important federal offices—who apparently had synchronized their public and private interests to assist the latter—and an instance of influence peddling by a former campaign manager of Vice President Nixon. On the whole, Eisenhower fared well at the hands of the Democratic Congress.

The President's popularity zoomed to new heights after the Big Four summit conference at Geneva in July, 1955, which had lessened the tensions of the cold war. Then Fate dealt a cruel blow. While on a Colorado vacation in September, he suffered a serious heart attack. It was soon evident that he would recover, but his steady improvement still left in doubt his future physical fitness. If he retired, a bitter intra-party conflict would break out and Republican chances for victory might be wrecked. The problem was solved finally in March when, after a favorable report by medical specialists, he announced that he would run again, although he would have to restrict his activities to the primary duties of his office. Republicans all but danced in the streets on the night of his acceptance telecast.

Then, on June 8, came a second blow. The President suffered an attack of ileitis and an emergency operation was necessary. His recovery was fairly rapid, however, and he soon resumed his duties. But the health issue and the importance of Vice President Nixon were already grist for the Democratic campaign mill.

The situation had its humorous aspects. It was 1944 in reverse. The Republicans now had the indispensable man and the Democrats were shaking their heads about his uncertain health and his approaching sixty-sixth birthday.

Meanwhile, an unexpected battle for the Democratic nomination —conceded earlier to Adlai Stevenson—began when Senator Kefauver announced that he would contest important primaries. Favorite sons, smelling the possibility of a deadlock, displayed signs of receptivity, with Averell Harriman, elected governor of New York in 1954, the most receptive. A further complication was an upsurge of race antagonism in the deep South over the implementation of the Supreme Court's pronouncement against segregation in the public schools. State sovereignty, next to "Americanism" the last refuge of intolerance, was hauled out and southern Democratic politicians harked back to John C. Calhoun, its patron saint, to justify their yielding to white supremacy extremists. In the North, urban Democratic tacticians, long aware of the voting weight of minority groups, took strong anti-segregation stands. Governor Harriman spoke their language. Stevenson favored moderation in reaching a solution, and party leaders friendly to him sought to avert a southern bolt. Kefauver refused to sign a manifesto of southern Senators against desegregation.

The early primaries did not clear the Democratic picture. Kefauver, past master of the art of personal solicitation, carried New Hampshire and Minnesota. The Minnesota result shocked the Stevenson forces. Their favorite had campaigned in person with Senator Humphrey's backing. Yet the indefatigable Tennessean, by promising more farm relief, shaking more hands, and drawing Republican votes into the Democratic primary (so the Stevenson men charged), had scored an upset victory.

But Minnesota was Kefauver's zenith. New Jersey rejected him for Governor Meyner's slate, and Stevenson, copying his rival's tactics, won in the Florida, California, and Oregon primaries. In states using the convention system the organizations named delegates hostile to Kefauver. On August 1 he acknowledged defeat by withdrawing in favor of Stevenson, though he had bagged 165 delegates.

Worried Stevenson partisans and some more objective commentators sharply criticized the primary system for putting a premium on sales skills and irrelevant personality traits at the expense of statesmanship and national fitness. The shades of the old standpatters of the Progressive Era must have listened with sardonic amusement; but those scarred battlers for the direct primary, Theodore Roosevelt and Bryan, would not have been amused at these revisionist liberals.

Democratic Repeat Performance, 1956

Both parties held their 1956 conventions unusually late. Only the Civil War Democratic convention of 1864 had been later. Air transport, radio, and television had made short intensive campaigns possible, and early nominations unnecessary and even unwise. A late August convention could come closer to anticipating and expressing the voters' November moods than a June one.

On August 13 Democratic delegates casting 1372 votes assembled in the air-conditioned International Amphitheater at Chicago. The keynote speech by young Governor Frank Clement of Tennessee was a crowd-pleasing performance of alliterative jibes and perfervid denunciations and pleas that ranged from Bryanic heights to the levels of a backwoods camp meeting. Stern-faced Sam Rayburn, House Speaker, took command as permanent chairman on the second day with a more sober attack.

The general expectation that it would be a dull week had already been upset by the early arrival of former President Truman and his announcement on Saturday afternoon that Governor Harriman had his support for the Presidential nomination. The wealthy New York governor had become an active candidate some weeks earlier with Carmine De Sapio, astute head of Tammany, as his strategist. His strong civil-rights stand had antagonized the South, but he had corralled some delegates in the mountain states and had Governor Raymond Gary of Oklahoma as his manager. The Truman blessing put new life into his campaign and Harriman backers proclaimed that Stevenson was stopped.

Most of the favorite son contingent now became active. Those with pledged delegates included Governors Frank J. Lausche of Ohio, Albert B. ("Happy") Chandler of Kentucky, and G. Mennen ("Soapy") Williams of Michigan, Senators Lyndon Johnson of Texas and Stuart Symington of Missouri, and Representative John McCormack of Massachusetts.

The smoothly running Stevenson organization, headed by a skilled Philadelphia professional, James A. Finnegan, worked to counteract Truman's announcement. Stevenson, feeling, he said ruefully, like a prize Angus bull on exhibit, visited delegation after delegation; Mrs. Franklin D. Roosevelt staunchly supported him with her customary reasoned and temperate arguments; and Truman did not help Harriman by blasting Stevenson as a conservative and a defeatist who lacked fighting qualities and who would carry no more states than in 1952. In a convention talk, Mrs. Roosevelt indirectly struck at the former President by calling for a young, forward-looking leadership and a turning away from old attitudes and old issues.

Stevenson's lines held firm, and Governors Williams of Michigan and Meyner of New Jersey added their delegations to his total. Most of the candidates had their names presented to give nominators and seconders some platform publicity and to let the demonstrators have some fun, but the battle was over. When the roll call on Thursday reached Pennsylvania, Governor Leader jubilantly announced that its vote was putting Stevenson over the top. The final count gave him 905-1/2 to Harriman's 210, with seven others dividing the rest of the 1372 votes.

Then followed a surprising pronouncement from the winner. Coming to the convention platform, he stated that he was leaving the choice of a running mate to the delegates. Important leaders and some of his closest advisers were against such a step. The result was too unpredictable. But it proved to be both shrewd politics and popular. It relieved the candidate of a disagreeable responsibility, it was a demonstration in democracy, and it gave Democrats a chance to taunt the Republicans with the cut-and-dried character of the approaching San Francisco choice of Nixon.

The night of Thursday, August 16, produced some of the wildest politicking in convention annals. A group of promising young bloods, including Senators Hubert Humphrey of Minnesota (a candidate before the convention met), John Kennedy of Massachusetts, Kefauver and Albert Gore of Tennessee, and Mayor Robert Wagner of New York, went the rounds of the delegations pleading for support. On the first ballot on Friday afternoon Kefauver had 483-1/2, Kennedy 304, Gore 178, Wagner 162-1/2, Humphrey 134-1/2. Kefauver, opposed by his own section and by most of the organization leaders elsewhere, had powerful farmer and labor support in the middle and farther West. To stop him, most of the South and the East concentrated on Kennedy, who went into the lead as the second ballot moved along. But last-minute changes from Humphrey and Gore to Kefauver put the lanky Tennessean across. As finally recorded the vote was 755-1/2 to 589. Kennedy then moved that the nomination be made unanimous.

The most surprising feature of the sharp contest had been the large vote given young Kennedy, an Irish Catholic, by southern states. In part it was anti-Kefauver, but it did suggest that the religious barrier to national preferment might not be as insurmountable to a personable, Harvard-educated scion of a wealthy family as it had been to that ex-clerk in a fish market and Tammany politico, Alfred E. Smith.

The platform, adopted before the nominations, did not produce the expected civil-rights melee. Representative John McCormack, heading the platform committee, worked tirelessly to preserve harmony. The civil-rights statement in the final draft displeased some southerners who kept silent and some liberals who presented a minority report. A thirty-minute debate, with Truman induced to speak for the majority version, ended in a voice vote upholding it. Chairman Rayburn's gavel cut off a demand for a roll call. Neither extreme had much stomach for an all-out struggle. The losers were talking for home consumption and the southerners did not want to bolt.

The civil-rights plank promised to continue efforts to eradicate discriminations of all kinds. It recognized the importance of recent decisions of the Supreme Court on segregation and accepted them as the law of the land, but rejected "all proposals for the use of force to interfere with the orderly determination of these matters by the courts." There was no pledge to implement desegregation.

The rest of the 12,000-word platform attacked, deplored, and viewed with alarm the Eisenhower policies. It charged that the administration had injured America's standing with other nations, fraternized with the Communists, increased the risk of war, and weakened national defense. It had failed to provide adequately for farmers, small business, low-income workers, and the elderly. The long farm plank offered 90 per cent price supports on basic crops as opposed to the Benson flexible plan, and suggested a number of measures to handle the problem of surpluses. Labor was promised the repeal of the Taft-Hartley Act and a minimum wage of $1.25 an hour; and state right-to-work laws were opposed. Tax reduction for people with small incomes and a $200 increase in income-tax exemption, a balanced budget, better protection and conservation of natural resources, and government plants for the production of atomic power were other major stipulations.

Republican Repeat Performance, 1956

Vice President Nixon announced late in April that he would seek a renomination. He had refused the President's offer of a cabinet post as an alternative, and support in the party seemed to assure him an uncontested nomination. Four weeks before the national convention was to meet, Harold Stassen, now disarmament adviser to the President, announced at a news conference that Nixon's name on the ticket would reduce the Eisenhower vote some 6 per cent—he had done some polling—and that Governor Christian A. Herter of Massachusetts would make a stronger candidate. This startling pronouncement was made with the knowledge, but not the approval, of the President who assumed a hands-off attitude. Soon afterward it was reported that Herter had agreed to place Nixon in nomination.

Stassen insisted that Herter could be drafted, and took a month's leave of absence from his office to head an Eisenhower-Herter movement. Pledges of support for Nixon and denunciations of Stassen by party leaders, big and little, and the hostility of the Republican press soon made it evident that his cause had slight support. If any prominent Republicans sympathized with him, they did not dare to reveal it, for he was being branded a traitor to his party.

The Republican national convention met at San Francisco's Cow Palace, August 20-23. Delegates and visitors were there to enjoy themselves, for all the business of the convention was prearranged, and, except for the Stassen flurry, there was not merely harmony but unanimity. The television watchers, consequently, found little to interest them. Governor Arthur B. Langlie of Washington gave the keynote address, a sober pointing-with-pride presentation—"We have come a long way in a short time." Senator Knowland, temporary chairman, and former Speaker Martin, permanent chairman, hammered harder at the Democrats but the angry vehemence of 1952 was missing. General MacArthur and Senator McCarthy were conspicuously absent. Dewey, booed in his seat four years ago, now had a speaking role and was warmly received, even by old enemies. One veteran reappeared—for the seventh time. Herbert Hoover, though still warning against dangers to personal liberty, was more optimistic and mellower than in the past and drew an impressive ten-minute tribute.

Seventeen candidates for Senate and House from close states, fourteen women speakers—carefully rehearsed and timed beforehand—and paid entertainers tried to hold the attention of the delegates when headliners were not performing. Organized squads of Young Republicans, imported from all parts of the country, provided numbers and snake dances whenever needed, both inside and outside the convention. California hospitality took care of the evenings, as there were no night sessions. Governor Goodwin Knight's "champagne supper" for 11,000 invited "guests" amazed even veteran journalists.

The Stassen insurrection against Nixon provided materials for news stories and television interviews, but was kept alive only by the remote possibility that Eisenhower might yet proclaim a "free-for-all" on the Vice Presidential choice. Without indorsing Nixon, he had expressed himself as "delighted" if the convention should renominate him. Governor Knight of California was reportedly opposed to the Vice President; Governor Theodore McKeldin of Maryland and one or two others were mentioned as possible candidates; and Nixon himself declared for an open convention and canvassed the various state delegations. But the temper of the delegates was shown by threats that Stassen would be denied unanimous consent to address the convention, since he was not a delegate, and by reports that a walk-out might occur if he appeared. He was even booed by Young Republicans during a television interview. President Eisenhower, who arrived Tuesday night, refused to change his position, and next morning announced in a televised press conference that Stassen had decided to support Nixon and would even second his nomination.

Stassen's capitulation made the nominating session a formality. Representative Charles A. Halleck of Indiana nominated Eisenhower and Governor Herter presented Nixon's name. Eight seconding speakers followed Halleck, and six, Herter. A Nebraska delegate tried to nominate "Joe Smith" for the Vice Presidency, but the chairman had the sergeants-at-arms escort him from the convention. He insisted later that his fictitious character was "a symbol of a wide-open convention," but Joe Smith got no votes. This was the only bit of unplanned business during the entire convention, and the newspaper men at least welcomed it.

At the final session on Thursday decorous unanimity turned into a tumultuous welcome for the nominees with parading delegates jamming the aisles and a barrage of Ike and Dick balloons let loose overhead. In his acceptance speech, Eisenhower called the Republican party the party of the future, "of long-range principle, not short-term expediency," and he used the broad policies of his administration to prove his case. The tone of the address was idealistic, middle of the road, optimistic, as he lifted examples and quotations from one hundred years of Republican party history. His ideas were in accord with those of a recent book, *A Republican Looks at His Party*, by Arthur Larson, Under Secretary of Labor, who had upheld the thesis of Republican progressivism, now called "new Republicanism."

The platform, presented by Senator Prescott Bush of Connecticut, chairman of the resolutions committee, had been adopted before the nominations by a unanimous vote. It was even longer than the Democratic declaration, but not unlike it in many of its positive commitments. On the touchy farm problem, the Republican plank upheld the administration's "versatile flexible program" and promised continued efforts to help farmers get full parity. The Democrats had offered rigid price supports at 90 per cent of parity. On civil rights the Republicans went a little farther than their opponents in accepting the Supreme Court decision for desegregation in the schools and favoring "all deliberate speed" in carrying it out, but opposing the use of force. The Republican platform also declared for tax reductions (the budget permitting); development of natural resources through partnership agreements between the federal government and lesser agencies; revision and improvement of the Taft-Hartley Act; a strong national defense which already had "the strongest striking force in the world"; and a federal aid program for schools.

The foreign policy plank credited the administration with reducing the threat of global war and checking the advance of Communism. It favored collective security, a strong United Nations, aid for underdeveloped countries, and other features of the Eisenhower-Dulles program. It made no concessions to isolationist sentiment. The President's acceptance speech was even stronger. He called it "madness" to suppose that the United States could be "an island of tranquillity" in a "sea of wretchedness and frustration." He even held out the hope of a peaceful coexistence with a more conciliatory Communist world, a far cry from the plank of 1952 denouncing the "immoral policy of containment."

Minor parties—some seventeen with eleven separate tickets, according to the *New York Times*—struggled for places on the ballot; but only one caused more than a ripple of interest. A States Rights gathering named for President T. Coleman Andrews, formerly President Eisenhower's Commissioner of Internal Revenue and a sharp critic of the income tax. Former Republican Representative Thomas H. Werdel of California was his running-mate. A Constitution Party and a For America Party also backed them.[1] This ticket represented a protest movement against both major parties by extreme conservatives, isolationists, segregationists, and state-rights reactionaries. There was a remote possibility that it might draw enough votes in one or two southern states to hold the balance of power. The older third parties had their candidates at the starting gate as usual, but, as usual, they were left at the post.

Ike Versus Issues

Stevenson appointed James A. Finnegan, his pre-convention strategist, as his campaign manager with Paul Butler continuing as chair-

[1] State-rights tickets, unpledged or favoring Senator Byrd of Virginia, ran in some states.

man of the national committee. A separate organization, the Volunteers for Stevenson-Kefauver, was designed to operate outside the party fence. It tapped the enthusiasm and energy of the younger voters.

In early September the Democratic nominees attended a series of regional meetings with party leaders and state and local candidates to coordinate the different levels of the campaign. To offset the personal popularity of Eisenhower, Stevenson needed to activate party loyalties and to make common cause with strong local vote-getters—coattails in reverse, it was dubbed. Nine eastern and middle western states had elected Democratic governors since 1952. Their aid and the voting pull of popular candidates for the Senate might swing close states. Kefauver was to center his efforts in the western farm belt where he had never lost a primary, where the rural voters liked his homespun personality. After joining with Stevenson in the television opening of the campaign at Harrisburg, Pennsylvania, he embarked on his canvass of the common man.

The Democratic campaign was given a sudden lift on September 10 when traditionally Republican Maine reelected its popular Democratic governor, Edmund S. Muskie, and for the first time in twenty-two years sent a Democrat to Congress from one of its three districts. Maine had been an uncertain barometer in past Presidential elections, but the size of the Democratic victory there could not be overlooked in the crystal balls of the forecasters.

Stevenson set out to show himself to as many voters and to shake as many hands as possible. He directed his talks at ordinary folk, ever suspicious of highbrow candidates with flashing rapiers. Consequently, he was less witty, more down-to-earth than in 1952. Major addresses were televised. From friendly quarters came occasional expressions of disappointment that he was not projecting his speeches well, that his perfectionist concern with the text did not include its delivery, which sometimes left the impression that he was still pondering over his sentences. His technique improved toward the end but his appeal was rational, not emotional. Yet he had attracted a devoted personal following centering in the Volunteers for Stevenson who too often had to take over registration drives, circulation of campaign literature, telephone canvassing, and other tasks when party organizations were dragging their feet or pushing only local candidates.

The Republican campaign, directed by Leonard W. Hall, national chairman since 1953, was planned to start late, use Nixon for heavy barnstorming, and call upon Eisenhower only for a token trip or two to demonstrate his physical fitness. But the Maine outcome, the early burst of Democratic energy, disaffection in the Republican farm belt, and pleas for the use of his coattails by hard-pressed Senatorial candidates—several of them his personal selections—drew the President into making some half a dozen forays that reached nearly all of the key states. But for the Near East crisis, he would have spent most of the final week on the trail. He drew larger crowds than Stevenson and helped mightily to restore party morale.

The Republican appeal added peace and prosperity to "We Like Ike." The administration had ended the Korean War and had stabilized prosperity without war and inflation. "America is happier than it was four years ago," said Eisenhower again and again, and crowd responses to his smiling face and confident voice made his discussion of issues almost a waste of time.

The Democrats answered that the prosperity was inherited, that Stalin's death had made possible the Korean truce, that Democrats in Congress had done more for Ike than his own party. Stevenson tried to draw his opponent into debates on specific policies but had only limited success. His problem was to find vote-getting issues and to break through Nixon, Dulles, Benson, and the rest of the White House cordon to battle with the chief himself. Foreign policy, farm problems, national defense, conservation, aid for public schools, and the broader questions of Eisenhower's past conception of his office and his fitness for future leadership, with Vice President Nixon's role a major consideration, all were legitimate subjects for party debate, but the Democratic candidate could not stir a complacent electorate. Attacks on the Dulles foreign policy were shrugged off so long as the nation was at peace. Farmers were dissatisfied, but, outside certain western drought areas, not distressed, and the Democratic offer of 90 per cent parity was viewed with mixed feelings, even by the considerable number who disliked Secretary Benson's flexible price supports and his soil conservation plan.

Stevenson threw national defense into the campaign hopper by suggesting the possibility of an end to the draft system, and later by proposing that the United States offer to join with Russia in stopping hydrogen bomb tests. Both propositions met with Republican charges that they would weaken national defense, and Eisenhower's stand carried special weight here, though the proposed ban on bomb tests did provoke discussion and disagreement among scientists as to the health hazards involved in repeated testing.

"Give-away" charges leveled at the administration's partnership policy toward power projects had some effect in the Pacific Northwest and entered into the defeat of former Secretary of the Interior Douglas McKay by Senator Wayne Morse for the Senate seat from Oregon. The fact that in Congress a number of Democrats had voted with Republicans on the Hell's Canyon, school-aid, and natural-gas regulation bills made it difficult for Stevenson to use these issues, about which few of his listeners were well informed or felt much concern, in any case.

The Democratic candidate put the greatest emphasis on the failure of Eisenhower to provide strong leadership. The President, he charged, "has never had the inclination and now lacks the energy for full-time work at the world's toughest job." A man whose age and state of health were serious voter considerations became a more doubtful risk, Democrats argued, when the Republican Vice Presidential choice was evaluated. Kefauver was expected to carry more than his weight, Nixon less than his. No Republican name called forth such roars of boos at Democratic rallies. The "hatchet man" tactics of past campaigns and his popularity with right-wing Republicans made "this man of many masks" (Stevenson's characterization) the one personal devil all Democrats could assail.

The Vice President's answer was to conduct a campaign to sell a "new Nixon." His speeches dealt with the accomplishments of the administration—"the best four years of our lives"—and the commanding stature of the President. Skilfully intermingling statistics with praise and pleas, he answered Democratic charges by comparing the records of Eisenhower and Truman, and the merits of Ike and Adlai. The slashing partisanship of 1952 and 1954 was missing and personal attacks upon him were not answered in kind. While he disappointed the McCarthy following by ignoring the Communist issue, the new Nixon filled more effectively the role of the second in command. His strenuous barnstorming—42,000 miles—was a model of efficient management. He consulted with local leaders, eulogized local candidates, fitted his remarks to his audiences, and was especially effective in appealing to women and young voters. At his side was Mrs. Pat Nixon with an appeal of her own. Yet, to the end of the campaign, Democrats saw only the horns of the old Nixon.

One issue was not emphasized on the national level—segregation in the schools. Eisenhower insisted that it made no difference whether or not he indorsed the Supreme Court decision, that the question must be handled on a state and local basis, that his record in the army and as President spoke for itself. Stevenson upheld the Supreme Court but agreed with his party's platform in rejecting the use of force to interfere with the orderly determination of such matters by the courts. Senator Eastland of Mississippi, an active segregationist and chairman of the Senate Judiciary Committee, was an embarrassment to northern Democrats, for Republicans charged that he would block all civil-rights legislation with the support of other southern Democrats. Congressman Adam Clayton Powell, Jr., of New York, a Negro Democratic leader, after an interview with the President, announced that he was supporting him. Several Negro newspapers and a number of prominent professional men were reported as turning to the Republicans.

Organized labor—now the united AFL-CIO—through its executive council voted to indorse Stevenson, although 8 of the 22 members were against any indorsements. Walter Reuther, head of the United Automobile Workers, led the Stevenson forces and was the most active labor leader in the campaign both for the national ticket and for other candidates. In states where labor indorsed senatorial or gubernatorial candidates, as in Michigan and the Pacific Northwest, doorbell ringing by union workers increased Democratic registration and insured a heavy vote.

Secretary of Labor James P. Mitchell, popular in labor circles, worked strenuously to convince the rank and file that the administration was friendly to labor and that southern Democrats would, if Congress was Democratic, block pro-labor and social welfare measures. The peace-prosperity theme was used in urging workingmen to discard their old distrust of the Republican party.

With no burning issues to stir a complacent electorate, Stevenson and Kefauver could not overlook the old battle cry that the Republicans favored big business, the Democrats were for the little people. "It is time to take the government away from General Motors and give it back to Joe Smith," declared Stevenson. Eisenhower defended his appointees from the business world as men who had demonstrated administrative fitness. His party, he said, supported social welfare measures but would do for the people only what they could not well do for themselves; the Democrats would guide and direct from Washington.

The campaign on the national level was singularly devoid of mudslinging, hate mongering, smear tactics, and whispered stories. F. D. Roosevelt, and Truman—to mention only the most recent cases—had been objects of every type of verbal missile, guided or misguided. Genial Ike increased no blood pressures by utterances or actions and his family life was above reproach. The sharp attacks on Nixon represented a Democratic desire to get even with him for past thrusts and to show up his political inconsistencies rather than a bitter hatred of the man. Stevenson and Kefauver were not subjected to personal attacks, although Stevenson's divorce was a silent factor in the campaign, according to samplers of opinion. Religious scruples, a Victorian code of personal conduct, or a feeling—even among the less strait-laced—that the White House family should be a model of domestic felicity entered into this reluctance to vote for a divorced person. Stevenson's three sons and an attractive daughter-in-law appeared in public with him as a silent reminder that he was a good family man and just before the election a grandson arrived in time to add his testimony.

In the final two weeks of this lethargic contest American voters were shaken out of their complacency by the news of a bloody revolt against Communism in Hungary, which required Russian tanks to suppress, and an Israeli invasion of Egypt followed immediately by Anglo-French military intervention at the Suez Canal. The American government supported the United Nations in condemning aggression in both areas and this course did not draw direct partisan fire. But Stevenson, who had been attacking the Dulles "brinkmanship" policy for its failure to checkmate Communism, its lack of direction, its rose-tinted view of the world's problems, now saw in these eruptions "the total bankruptcy of the administration's foreign policy." "The NATO alliance is crumbling," he charged, "the Middle East is in shambles"; Communism had benefited, and the United States had been cut off from its old friends.

Eisenhower, in the one speech he made after the Suez crisis, discussed only the broad principles of American policies. He said that he was undisturbed by "the strident voices of those who seem to be seeking to turn world events to political profit"—his only reference to his critic. The election was too near for these explosions abroad to have much effect on the voters. Their minds were already made up.

The 1956 Paradox

The first returns on the night of November 6 pointed to an Eisenhower victory which soon became an avalanche surpassed only by the Roosevelt sweep of 1936. The President polled 457 electoral votes and 35,590,472 popular votes to Stevenson's 73 and 26,022,752.[2] One electoral vote went to Judge Walter B. Jones of Alabama from an Alabama elector who violated his party pledge.

Of the Eisenhower states of 1952, only Missouri shifted to Stevenson; but Kentucky, West Virginia, and Louisiana left the Democratic column, which consisted of only North Carolina, South Carolina, Georgia, Alabama, Mississippi, Arkansas, and Missouri. The explanation was simple. The nation voted its confidence in an experienced leader whose administration had a peace-and-prosperity record, whose middle-of-the road policies fitted the mood of the American people, and whose services, despite his age, seemed indispensable with external dangers mounting. Generally, except in the western farm belt and California, his margins were larger than in 1952. His best showings were in the urban East, where foreign problems mattered most, and in the South, where apparently a shift of Negro voters swelled his totals.

Nevertheless, the nation elected a Democratic Congress, the Senate 49 to 47, the House 234 to 201. This was unprecedented. The Whigs had elected Zachary Taylor in 1848 without carrying Congress, but both Whigs and Democrats were in a minority in the House of Representatives where thirteen Free Soilers held the balance of power. In 1860 the Republicans failed to carry the House for Lincoln, but the secession of the South reduced the opposition to a minority. The disputed Hayes-Tilden election of 1876 produced a Democratic House and a Republican Senate. In 1916, Wilson's party did not win a majority in the House but organized it with the support of a group of independents. The Senate was Democratic. In every other Presidential election the victors carried the House of Representatives. In decisive elections, prior to 1952, the majority party had shown proportionately greater strength in the House than the Presidential winner in the popular vote. Single-member districts do not permit proportional representation. This pattern had been

[2] Minor parties polled 413,684 votes, three-fourths of the total going to various state-rights tickets.

broken in 1952 when Eisenhower's 55 per cent of the popular vote brought his party less than 51 per cent of the membership of the House. In 1956 a more sweeping victory had resulted in the loss of both Houses, an astonishing setback.

Why Eisenhower's coattails pulled so badly was hard to understand, in view of his pleas and his party's well filled coffers. It was conjectured that party lines had come to mean little, that voters were picking candidates on their merits or personalities. One would need to conclude that the Democratic party had more meritorious or personable candidates, both in 1954 and in 1956, not to mention the near Congressional stalemate of 1952. Personalities have always been important in politics, and the lines dividing the parties become blurred in good times; but to assume a heavy Democratic preponderance in talent is at least doubtful. One might more logically conjecture that voters tended to vote with their party for Congress and state offices, but large numbers transcended party lines at the top. Eisenhower's past actions in office and his "modern Republicanism" were proof that he was far less the partisan than Republican candidates for other offices. Thousands of Democrats and independents supported him because they liked Ike and in spite of his party.

Organized labor activity, certain issues of local significance, and strong Democratic state organizations were offered as explanations for particular Republican defeats, but these were largely offset by Republican advantages such as larger campaign funds, the lethargy of Democratic urban machines, and the rapid growth of suburbs where social pressure produced Republicans.

Viewed in its immediate aftermath, the election, then, was actually a vote for a bi-partisan administration—a President of one party, a Congress of the other—a perplexing verdict for believers in party or parliamentary government. But the voters certainly wanted peace and prosperity continued and this was their solution. They trusted Eisenhower to preserve the one, the Democratic party to safeguard the other. In 1956, this seemed to make sense.

32

The Kennedys Take Over

Eisenhower's Assertion of Leadership

President Eisenhower became more directly involved in major decisions of foreign policy after the death of John Foster Dulles from cancer in the spring of 1959. Undersecretary Christian Herter, who became Secretary of State, did not carry foreign policy around in his portfolio, as had Dulles.

The President also lost, by resignation, efficient but none too popular Sherman Adams, his administrative assistant, in the midst of the Congressional campaign of 1958. Adams had unwisely accepted gifts —the most publicized a vicuña overcoat—from a free-handed Massachusetts industrialist, Bernard Goldfine, who was in difficulties with the government over some of his business practices.

Eisenhower did well enough legislatively with the two Democratic Congresses of his second term. Measures that were non-political or cut across party lines included reciprocal trade extension, reorganization of the Department of Defense, establishment of a National Aeronautics and Space Administration, a National Defense Education Act, an act for further relaxation of farm controls and reduced parity payments, and the admission of Alaska and Hawaii as states.

Congress in September, 1959, passed a labor reform bill for stricter federal regulation, particularly in requiring financial accountability of labor officials and guaranteeing to union members a more democratic control of their organizations. This was an Eisenhower victory, gained after a television appeal for a stronger measure than Democratic liberals wanted. The groundwork for it was laid by a Senate investigating committee under Senator John McClellan of Arkansas, which had unearthed evidence of gangster associations and misuse of union funds, reflecting especially on James Hoffa, head of the

International Brotherhood of Teamsters. Robert Kennedy, attorney for the committee and brother of Senator Kennedy of Massachusetts, was Hoffa's chief critic.

For the Negro, the 1950's were the years of promise rather than fulfillment. Integration in southern schools made slow progress in the face of legal delays, mob outbreaks, and the closing of public schools in some localities. President Eisenhower met the issue at Little Rock, Arkansas, with federal troops to enforce judicial process when Governor Orval E. Faubus attempted to block Negro enrollment in a high school. Virginia's "massive resistance" laws broke down in the face of a series of federal and state court rulings, and in 1959 integration began in the Old Dominion without violence. The lower South, the heartland of segregation, continued to hold out. White Citizens' Councils, reminiscent of Ku Klux days, manned the barricades of intolerance.

Negroes, backed by the National Association for the Advancement of Colored People, began to use economic boycotts, sit-in demonstrations at lunch counters, and other passive resistance tactics to end discrimination in public transportation facilities, shopping centers, and drugstores. Successes were most marked in the larger cities.

A civil rights act in 1957, the first since Reconstruction days, created a Civil Rights Commission, and was designed to protect the Negro's voting rights. A stronger act, passed in 1960, strengthened the enforcement machinery, but did not greatly alter the situation in the lower South in the national election. Negro voters were a small minority or non-existent in many areas.

The mid-term elections produced one of the sharpest rejections of an administration in many years. A business recession in 1957–1958, the worst since World War II, was chiefly responsible. Eisenhower, concerned about inflation, rejected pump-priming proposals, as mounting defense and other expenditures were already producing a huge deficit. He attacked the Democrats as spenders, and Vice President Nixon, carrying the brunt of the campaign, hammered away at this theme and the radicalism of the Democratic left. But farmers were angry at Secretary Benson's farm policy, and northern Negroes remained Democratic. Labor turned out in large numbers to fight anti-union, right-to-work laws, generally sponsored by Republicans, in half a dozen states.

Senator Bricker was defeated for reelection in Ohio, and Senator Knowland lost his bid for California's governorship. Conservatives up for reelection generally fared badly. Almost the only exception was Senator Barry Goldwater of Arizona, right-wing, anti-Eisenhower Republican. The one significant Republican gain was in New York where liberal, personable Nelson Rockefeller defeated Governor Averill Harriman, candidate for reelection, in spite of the Democratic landslide.

The Democrats had 64 votes in the Senate and 283 in the House, after Alaska had voted in late November. Thirty-five states now had Democratic governors. President Eisenhower was surprised and dismayed at the verdict. He could not see that he had done anything to cause such a complete reversal of the sweep of 1956.

Democratic leadership in the experienced hands of Lyndon Johnson in the Senate and Speaker Sam Rayburn in the House followed a middle-of-the-road policy very much as in the preceding Congress. Liberals, as represented by the Democratic Advisory Council, a policy-making body outside the Congressional halls, were reported as dissatisfied with the lack of a forward-looking program after the decisive November verdict, but the majority in Congress could not function as a unit.

Eisenhower, no longer faced with elections and now acting more as his own chief of staff, worked with new leaders in Senate and House, Everett Dirksen and Charles Halleck, and had his way on major fiscal policies. Conservative Democrats provided the margin of victory in most cases, and kept the majority from overriding his vetoes, which were chiefly of bills involving increased expenditures and expanded federal authority. He brought the budget into balance, but a return of prosperity had added to government receipts. Visits to eleven Old World nations and Latin America were further evidence of a more dynamic leadership in the White House.

His worst setback was the Senate's rejection, in June, 1959, of the nomination of Lewis Strauss to be Secretary of Commerce. Strauss, chairman of the Atomic Energy Commission, had aroused enmities by his aggressive actions, but the vote became a test of Democratic leadership. Forty-seven Democrats and two Republicans voted against Strauss's confirmation as opposed to thirty-one Republicans and fifteen Democrats in his favor. Not since 1925 had a cabinet appointee been rejected.

The Cold War continued its tortuous course in different parts of the globe, but adjustments, if not solutions, and postponements where action was not required kept crises from reaching the ultimatum stage. Tensions relaxed sufficiently for Khrushchev to visit the United States in 1959. This was to be followed by a summit meeting next year at Paris and an Eisenhower visit to Russia. But just before the conference was to open, a U-2 reconnaissance plane was brought down on Soviet soil in May, 1960, and the Russian premier angrily refused to negotiate further with Eisenhower.

Defense matters took on a political cast. Russia's apparent lead in the exploration of space with its Sputniks upset American pride, and raised American fears that in the field of nuclear weapons the nation was lagging behind its Communist rival. Administration critics could charge that budget balancing had overruled defense needs.

Relations with the Latin American nations, which had deteriorated to a low point in 1958, were improved by measures to provide economic assistance and strengthen economic and political ties, but Cuba was an unexpected exception. Fidel Castro, who had overthrown the corrupt Batista regime in 1959 with American approval, proceeded to set up a Communist-oriented dictatorship, and moved toward close relations with Iron Curtain countries. Expropriation of American property and other unfriendly acts led President Eisenhower to stop imports of Cuban sugar, and finally to break diplomatic relations. Liberal Cubans by the thousands fled to neighboring Florida. When Castro received military equipment and advisers from Communist nations, Cuba became a political as well as a diplomatic and defense problem.

The Kennedy Machine

The Presidential sweepstakes on the Democratic track had four strong contenders, with entries expected from the usual number of favorite sons. Strangely enough, all four were members of the Senate. Democratic governors, with New York now Republican, were overshadowed by Senatorial aspirants in a period of grave national problems.

Majority leader Lyndon B. Johnson of Texas had been as successful in managing his badly divided, sectionally minded following as any of his predecessors, and, if Congressional support could have nominated, would have won handily. But he could not escape the deadly embrace of the conservative segregationist South, even though civil rights legislation had had his strong backing. Nor was his Texas upbringing an asset. Even with Speaker Sam Rayburn's support, Johnson's candidacy seemed to present a typical Texas image with its oil politicos, ten-gallon hats, and beautiful girls chanting "All the Way with L. B. J." Johnson's formal entry came late, after the primaries had been held. But he was the strongest southern Democratic candidate since ante-bellum days, and in a deadlocked convention might draw heavy second-choice support.

Hubert Humphrey, for twelve years the voice of farmer-labor Minnesota, suited the liberals in his votes and speeches, but was a little too left-of-center and too much the representative of his section to appeal to the large-state leaders. Humphrey was an able debater, and his rapid-fire fluency appeared to advantage on the stump. Hampered by lack of funds, he still had to make a strong showing in the primaries to shorten the long-shot odds against him. Probably he was more nearly Stevenson's heir than any of his rivals, and had hopes that a liberal coalition might look in his direction if the balloting was prolonged.

Stuart Symington of Missouri had left a successful business career during the war to take high administrative office, then had won election to the Senate, where he became a leading authority on national defense. His general record was satisfactory to almost every segment of the party outside the South, but his rather colorless personality lacked voter appeal, and his reputation was confined chiefly to Washington and Missouri. He was a good compromise solution. He had Truman's endorsement.

John F. Kennedy, reelected to the Senate from Massachusetts in 1958 by a landslide, had more assets and heavier liabilities than any of his rivals. Son of Joseph P. Kennedy, Roosevelt's isolationist ambassador to England before World War II, he had on the credit side a keen mind, family wealth, good looks, a Harvard education, a record of heroism as a naval officer in the war, authorship of a best-seller book, and a very attractive young wife and small daughter. During his Massachusetts battles he had drawn to him a young and very able group of organizers headed by his brother Robert. Also, the devoted Kennedy family was a host in itself. The Senator's mother (daughter of John F. Fitzgerald, once a Boston mayor and Congressman), his two brothers and three sisters, and the in-law contingent were active wherever their services could be used. The elder Kennedy preferred to remain in the background where his millions and presumably conservative views would not embarrass his son. The candidate's wife, Jacqueline Bouvier Kennedy, also was not on political display. A second child expected in the fall was reason enough.

But a heavy liability, which had been an asset in his rise in Massachusetts politics, was Kennedy's Roman Catholic religion. Even his co-religionists among party leaders were not convinced that a Catholic, even if nominated, could be elected. Against Kennedy also was his comparative youth—he was approaching forty-three—his lack of administrative experience, and a not particularly outstanding record in Congress, although it was acceptable to labor and liberal groups. There was also some question as to whether he had sufficiently recovered from a back injury and operations to correct it to undertake the burdens of campaigning. A story was even circulated that he was a victim of Addison's disease.

Kennedy necessarily had to take the primary route to show that he had the qualifications of a winner. In a few instances favorite sons were accepted as Kennedy stand-ins. Only Humphrey chose to contest with him.

New Hampshire's primary came first. Kennedy had no opposition, but was complimented by a large vote. Wisconsin, in Humphrey's territory but with a large Catholic population, voted next. The result was indecisive. Kennedy had six of the ten districts, and led on the state-wide vote, but it was charged that Catholic Republicans had crossed over to vote in the Democratic primary for him. West Virginia was a better test of his strength. It lay on the edge of the Bible Belt where anti-Catholic prejudice was strong. Kennedy met the issue head-on, and won by a wide margin. Superior organization and use of television, and the necessary funds for both, played an important part in selling the Harvard candidate in the land of the hillbillies. Humphrey's withdrawal followed his defeat. The remaining primaries, largely uncontested except for Senator Wayne Morse's candidacy in Oregon and Maryland, gave the Kennedy cause a momentum that weakened the neutrality of the uncommitted large states.

If either Adlai Stevenson or Estes Kefauver had waited until 1960 for his second run, Kennedy would have found the primary road a difficult one. Stevenson was still not entirely out of the picture. His devoted following talked of a Stevenson-Kennedy ticket as the ideal solution. He was out of the country for several weeks during the preconvention struggle, and kept out of the battle for delegates. On his return he refused to endorse any candidate, and a movement to draft him showed signs of life. It had a good deal of support in California, but it was fragmentary elsewhere, although Gallup polls rated him second only to Kennedy as a popular choice.

The tide was running strongly for Kennedy when the delegates assembled in the new Sports Arena at Los Angeles on July 11. All the candidates were present, and were expected to visit and display their talents to state caucuses, much like bathing beauty contestants. Large-state leaders from New York, Illinois, and Pennsylvania, however, committed their states to Kennedy before the first session. Governor Edmund G. Brown of California could not overcome strong Stevenson support, and his delegation was badly divided. The Kennedy board of strategy had a superb organization with helpful information compiled on every delegate. Robert Kennedy was his brother's manager, but he had a veritable army of operatives.

This first national convention in Los Angeles history departed from tradition by beginning its sessions in late afternoon to suit the convenience of eastern viewers. At 7:15 P.M., eastern time, Chairman Paul Butler rapped for order, and introduced Archbishop Francis Cardinal McIntyre who gave the invocation. Thereafter the convention went the noisy, inattentive way of so many of its predecessors. Youthful-looking Senator Frank Church of Idaho sounded the keynote with a recital of the derelictions of the Republican "tranquillizing" administration. Genial Governor LeRoy Collins of Florida took over as permanent chairman next day, and had his difficulties. Speaker Sam Rayburn had preferred to lead the Lyndon Johnson supporters instead of presiding.

Two speakers held the attention of the convention and the TV listeners. Senator Eugene McCarthy of Minnesota, in nominating Adlai Stevenson, made a brilliant and impassioned appeal for the idol of the liberal wing. Mrs. Eleanor Roosevelt was accorded a great ovation on her convention appearance, and was listened to with the respect due her attainments. The rest of the oratory was largely wasted. Delegates and outsiders milled in the aisles, and television interviews added to the confusion on the floor.

Stevenson was the local crowd favorite. An endless chain of Stevenson paraders marched outside the convention hall, and his loyal following ruled the galleries. Their hero was almost mobbed by his admirers on the second day when he entered the hall and attempted to reach a seat with his delegation. Next day his supporters, after his name was presented for the nomination, again staged a wild demonstration, but the paraders in the aisles included few delegates, and much of the noise came from upstairs. By various maneuvers, his local retainers had acquired a disproportionate share of admission tickets, not the first time gallery packing has occurred. But this sound and fury did not signify votes.

The platform as presented by Chairman Chester Bowles of Connecticut had been long in preparation. Preliminary work by the Advisory Council to the Democratic National Committee, appointed in 1956, was followed by hearings for interested groups in different parts of the country. The convention viewed a film showing how this was done. In the platform committee, the civil rights issue had produced a sharp division between the liberal majority and a southern minority. Outvoted 66 to 24 in the committee, the minority carried the fight to the floor of the convention, but were defeated by a voice vote after a rather mild debate.

The civil rights plank was a declaration for "equal access for all Americans to all areas of community life including voting booths, schoolrooms, jobs, housing and public facilities." It called for federal action to ensure the right to vote, and favored a federal fair employment practices commission to end job discrimination. The South was asked to achieve "first step compliance" with school desegregation by 1963. Negro Congressman Adam Clayton Powell of New York approved the plank, but angry southern spokesmen said that it would lose the party most of the South.

The "Rights of Man" sections called for a broad program of public welfare measures to bring about full employment, decent living for the farmer through price supports of 90 per cent of parity, an expanded federal housing program, and medical care for the aged based on the social security system. The Eisenhower administration was charged with failure to promote the growth of the national economy and with an exaggerated concern over balancing the budget.

On foreign policy the Democrats promised more vigorous action along all lines, coupled with a diversified national defense program sufficient in quantity and quality to deter aggressions, both limited and general.

Nominating speeches were scheduled for the third day. Two favorite sons, Governor Herschell C. Loveless of Iowa and Governor George Docking of Kansas, yielded to Kennedy persuasion, but Governor Meyner of New Jersey held out. Nine candidates were put in nomination. After the usual demonstrations, supposed to be limited to ten minutes but running far over, the balloting began. When Wyoming was reached, Kennedy needed eleven votes for a majority. That state then provided fifteen. The official roll call showed Kennedy had 806, Johnson 409, Symington 86, Stevenson 79-1/2, others 140-1/2. Missouri's Governor James Blair moved that Kennedy be nominated by acclamation, and this was done.

Failure of a first ballot nomination might have been serious for Kennedy. Several states, voting under the unit rule, were held by thin margins. A few defections might have stalled the steamroller.

The big surprise of the convention came next day when Kennedy announced that Lyndon Johnson was his choice for running mate. Negotiations in the night had done the work. Liberals of the Americans for Democratic Action protested that Johnson was too conservative, and would cost the party labor and Negro votes. Many Middle Westerners were disappointed. They had expected a Protestant from the farm belt to balance the ticket. Symington would have suited both groups.

But the Kennedys were realists, and saw that Johnson could do more than any other man to hold the wavering South in line. Hard-headed northern party leaders also saw the light. Southern die-hards from the lower South, angry over the civil rights plank, were upset at Johnson's acceptance. Why the latter chose to give up his vote for a gavel—which he had said he would never do—occasioned much comment and conjecture. Apparently the honor associated with the second highest office, where he might still exercise influence without the heavy burdens of floor leadership, was more appealing than he had realized earlier. And most commentators seemed to have forgotten that no candidate with a real chance for first place would admit beforehand that he would settle for second.

The opposition could find no one willing to come out against Kennedy's choice. After a nominating speech by Governor David Lawrence of Pennsylvania and enough seconding speeches to present a picture of unanimity, Johnson was nominated by acclamation, although a good many noes were ignored by the chairman.

The Friday acceptance ceremonies, held in the Los Angeles Coliseum, overflowed with harmony and good will. Kennedy reached a high note of idealism when he called upon Americans to conquer the New Frontier of the 1960's, "with its unknown opportunities and perils . . . It sums up not what I intend to offer to the American people but what I intend to ask of them."

Nixon in Charge

In spite of the Democratic sweep of 1958, Republicans remained hopeful about 1960. A Presidential election has different conditioning factors, as both Truman in 1948 and Eisenhower in 1956 had shown following party mid-term reverses. The country still liked Ike, if not Ike's party, and the potency of his victory magic might save the White House for his heir apparent, although both Houses of Congress would almost certainly be Democratic. Then, too, there was a fair prospect that the Democratic convention would concoct such a bitter brew out of religious differences, liberal-conservative feuding, desegregation, personal ambitions, and sectional differences that the party would defeat itself.

The one bright spot in the Republican picture in 1958, the victory of Nelson A. Rockefeller in New York, had created an unexpected problem for Nixon. Here was a possible rival for the nomination. The Rockefeller family had long since lived down the robber baron reputation of its Standard Oil progenitor, and was respected for its leadership in the business world and its philanthropic interests. The New York governor had served in various capacities under three Presidents, was especially concerned about international problems, and had left Washington in 1956 both because he was unhappy over the direction of administration policies, as was indicated by his later public pronouncements, and because he was not making headway in politics. He had surprised the New York party regulars by taking the gubernatorial nomination away from former National Chairman Leonard Hall, and then defeating Governor Harriman by an impressive margin. He had much to recommend him—an engaging personality, a handsome profile, a familiar name, a grasp of public affairs, financial independence, and demonstrated organizing ability.

Rockefeller added to his reputation by his early accomplishments as governor. He was clearly a man with a future in national politics. Presently he set up an organization to sound out party sentiment and measure his chances as a Presidential aspirant. He also made trips to different parts of the country to see for himself. The results were not encouraging. People were interested in meeting him, but the delegates were another matter. The resurgent Taft regulars could not stomach his internationalist outlook and his domestic liberalism, and the Eisenhower men were satisfied with Nixon. To enter the primaries would place the challenger in the role of critic of the administration, and win few delegates. And so Rockefeller announced, late in 1959, that he would not be a candidate, without, however, indorsing Nixon. This oversight occasioned a good deal of comment. Was the door left ajar for a draft?

The Vice President, with Leonard Hall directing his forces, might have relished a battle for the nomination. It would have meant an easy victory with plenty of favorable publicity. With the Rockefeller threat removed, however, the proper strategy was to favor the New Yorker for second place. This would ensure harmony and a balanced ticket. But the lesser post had no appeal for the Governor. He not only declined to be considered, but countered, early in June, a time of growing international tensions, with an amazing statement. It criticized the party leadership and the "leading candidate" for not offering a definite program, in view of the serious problems confronting the nation, and proposed, under nine headings, courses of action that covered every major aspect of national policy.

The immediate effect of this insurgent outburst was a belated draft-Rockefeller movement. It stirred up a flurry of letters, telegrams, and columnist comments, but not much more. For the national convention to ignore his program was another matter, however, particularly if he chose to fight.

Charles H. Percy, a Chicago businessman of middle-of-the-road views, had been working for months as chairman of a committee to devise a forward-looking program, and he was accorded the honor of heading the Republican convention's platform committee. It began operations a week ahead of the national convention, had a White House draft to guide it, and worked out a set of statements that tried to embrace enough of the Rockefeller position to prevent a fight.

The Governor was not satisfied, and said so publicly. Nixon then took the initiative. He arranged for a secret meeting in New York where the two men ironed out their differences. He honestly did not believe they were very far apart. He had tempered his views in the interest of party harmony and loyalty to Eisenhower, and may have welcomed the opportunity to clarify his position. But the result seemed to be a surrender, on his part, on basic points, particularly civil rights and national defense. When the members of the platform committee, which was predominantly conservative, learned of this cavalier treatment of their labored handiwork, they vented their indignation in cries of "dictatorship" and "Munich surrender," and threatened to ignore the terms of the Nixon-Rockefeller compact. But the Vice President, arriving in Chicago on Monday, by using both diplomacy and pressure, won a majority of the committee to his position on the all-important civil rights plank and secured a national defense statement that was acceptable to both Rockefeller and Eisenhower. This averted a bitter convention battle that might have left its mark in November.

The twenty-seventh Republican convention opened in the Chicago International Amphitheatre on Monday, July 25, with National Chairman Thruston Morton wielding the gavel. Proceedings went strictly according to script. Mindful of the roving television eye, the managers saw to it that delegates behaved and listened, and camp followers did not clutter up the aisles. With its decisions preordained, the convention became a series of pep rallies with the pep ebbing out as repetitious and generally dull speakers used up their allotted time.

At the Monday evening session ex-President Hoover humorously made his customary farewell speech, and Senator Goldwater, a convention favorite, was warmly received. Representative Walter Judd of Minnesota, a veteran of the lecture platform, made the keynote speech. It was a rabble-rousing recital of past Democratic misdeeds of foreign policy with the audience roaring approval at each stab. Representative Charles Halleck of Indiana took over as permanent chairman on the second day, which was highlighted by President Eisenhower's appearance. He was given a great ovation, and responded with a review and defense of his administration.

The convention performed its important functions on Wednesday. The platform was presented with a film accompaniment, as in the case of the Democrats. It was adopted unanimously.

The controversial civil rights plank was a little more general than the Democratic statement, omitting any mention of a fair employment practices commission, but was satisfactory to the Rockefeller liberals, and angered the helpless southerners. The platform walked a tightrope on defense. It claimed that America was the world's strongest military power, but added that expanded production and new defense efforts might be needed. In dealing with domestic problems, the party conceded that the pace of economic growth must be quickened, but insisted that the private sector of the economy must be chiefly responsible. The farm plank made general promises without commitments as to price support levels.

The central theme of the Republican document was the danger of Communist imperialism and the need for responsible and mature leadership to meet it. The Eisenhower administration had provided such leadership, and Nixon would continue it.

The platform satisfied Rockefeller who appeared wearing a Nixon-for-President ribbon and hatband. But the conservatives were unhappy. After Governor Mark Hatfield of Oregon had placed Nixon's name in nomination, Governor Paul Fannin of Arizona offered Senator Goldwater as his state's choice. In spite of the chanting demonstrators, the popular idol of the right wing withdrew his name and appealed to conservatives to follow Nixon. Ten Louisiana delegates refused, and voted for Goldwater. Nixon had 1,321 votes. The Arizona chairman then moved that the nomination be made unanimous.

The Vice Presidential choice was made by Nixon before the Thursday session. After consulting with party leaders, he named Henry Cabot Lodge, ambassador to the United Nations and former Massachusetts Senator, as his choice. Middle westerners were disappointed that their section was overlooked, but Lodge's selection pointed up the issue of foreign affairs. The delegates ratified Nixon's choice.

The convention closed with the acceptance speeches of the nominees. Nixon's reemphasized the theme of the platform, "the race for survival" and the need to meet Khrushchev's challenge by developing a world-wide strategy for peace and freedom.

The Campaign of the Great Debates

Senator Henry Jackson of Washington succeeded Paul Butler as Democratic national chairman, but the young Kennedy organization, much expanded, planned and directed the strategy. Lawrence F. O'Brien, chief Kennedy organizer in Massachusetts and in the primary states, became director of organization for the national committee. Byron ("Whizzer") White of Colorado, a past football all-star, looked after the National Citizens for Kennedy-Johnson, designed to operate outside the party lines. Closest to the candidate was his manager and brother, Robert F. Kennedy. Pierre Salinger, press secretary, Kenneth P. O'Donnell, in charge of scheduling, Theodore C. Sorenson, policy adviser and brain trust director, and Louis Harris, chief pollster, were other key figures. A squad of Harvard professors headed by Archibald F. Cox supplied materials for speeches, and made suggestions on policies.

The candidate, delayed by the fruitless summer session of Congress, took to the hustings on September 2, and opened the campaign formally at Detroit on Labor Day, September 5. Thereafter his jet plane carried him on a carefully planned but exhausting campaign that overlooked no section of the nation, although it did concentrate to a degree on the large key states of the East and Middle West.

Nixon had announced in his acceptance speech that he would begin his campaign at once, and that he would go into every one of the fifty states. His organization was also headed by a United States Senator as national chairman, Thruston B. Morton of Kentucky, a stanch Eisenhower supporter. Former Chairman Leonard Hall, who had managed Nixon's pre-convention campaign, and Robert Finch, a Los Angeles lawyer, played major roles in directing the Nixon strategy. Charles S. Rhyne headed the Volunteers for Nixon-Lodge. The National Committee created a special advertising agency, "Campaign Associates," with Carroll Newton and Edward A. Rogers in charge, to handle publicity. A brain trust of economic and governmental specialists included two Harvard professors. The Vice President believed that a campaign should build up gradually to reach a peak just before the election, and that too rigid planning was unwise, as it left no room for maneuver when circumstances might require it.

Unfortunately, an unkind fate dealt the Republican nominee the first of a series of blows that planning could not avert. In August, trips to North Carolina, Alabama, and Georgia drew such huge and demonstrative crowds, particularly at Atlanta, that even the skeptics in his newspaper entourage wondered if the Confederacy's heartland was wavering. But on the North Carolina trip the candidate struck his knee against a car door, presently had to be hospitalized with an infected kneecap, and lost two weeks of campaign coverage. He was left in poor physical condition to endure the stresses and strains that a visit to every state forced upon him.

The climactic event of the campaign was the series of four television debates between the rivals, held on September 26, October 7, 13, and 21. The three great national networks arranged the details with the candidates' managers, and some seventy million Americans tuned in. The first debate centered on domestic questions, the second on foreign policy, the others on miscellaneous issues with a good deal of repetition evident toward the end. The first and fourth debates followed debating procedure with opening and closing speeches, but with questions in between from four news representatives. The second and third used a quiz show format with both candidates answering each question from the newsmen. The results were no Lincoln-Douglas classics. The rivals battled for points and displayed their skill in fast exchanges and sharp returns, with occasional misses. Performance overshadowed content.

Kennedy drew first blood, although he had been given the underdog rating. Various explanations were offered for Nixon's poor initial showing before the relentless TV camera—bad lighting, bad makeup (it was even charged that a Democrat had done the job), campaign weariness, the disconcerting self-possession of his supposedly immature rival, or some other less tangible factor. Whatever the reason, his past mastery of television seemed to have departed at the outset, and he appeared haggard, ill at ease, perspiring with nervousness, and on the defensive. Kennedy, more photogenic, projected to the viewers the image of a coolly confident, highly articulate, quick-witted antagonist who measured up to the requirements of national leadership. The immaturity charge lost its momentum.

Nixon was more like himself in the later debates, and scored effectively, especially in the area of foreign relations, but the effect of the first encounter could not be undone. People forgot the arguments, and remembered what they saw. This may have been the turning point of the campaign. After the first debate the Kennedy forces were buoyed up by favorable polls and the mounting size and enthusiasm of his crowds. Ten of eleven southern governors attending a conference fell in line and sent a telegram of congratulations.

On the campaign trail the two candidates, with much repetition, developed the major issues. Kennedy's program of expanded federal action included the fields of public education, housing, medical care for the aged, farm relief, and aid for depressed areas. Positive measures were needed to strengthen the American economy, which, he charged, had undergone three recessions in six years, and was still stagnating. Nixon held to the orthodox Republican view that federal power should be used only to stimulate private enterprise and to deal with situations where local solutions had failed. He pointed to the nation's economic progress under Eisenhower, and warned that Kennedy's proposals would lead to extravagant spending, burdensome taxes, inflation, and large increases in the national debt.

Foreign problems produced another sharp divergence of views. Kennedy assailed the administration for following a policy of drift and stagnation, which was not checking the inroads of Communism, and which had caused a serious loss of American prestige abroad. He promised to revitalize both domestic and foreign policies to make America move again.

Nixon answered that his opponent was downgrading his own country, and thereby encouraging Khrushchev, whose presence and actions at the session of the United Nations in the midst of the campaign made public displays of disunity particularly unwise. He defined the administration's policy as one of peace without surrender of principle, and emphasized the experienced leadership in the Republican camp as contrasted with the immaturity and irresponsibility of Kennedy.

On two specific points, the rivals argued until their forensics became problems in semantics. In the second television debate, Kennedy, defending his Senate votes on American policy toward the Chinese offshore islands of Quemoy and Matsu, stated his belief that they were indefensible, and that the United States should not be committed to protect Nationalist China's hold on these outposts. Nixon answered that their defense was a matter of principle, and charged that Kennedy's policy would lead to war and surrender. Kennedy, shifting ground somewhat, insisted that he favored defending the islands if the Communist attack was directed at Formosa, and that his stand was, after all, the administration policy. Nixon called this a change of position, and continued to press the issue during the rest of the campaign.

Relations with the Castro regime in Cuba provided Kennedy with ammunition. He blamed the administration for permitting a Communist outpost to rise only ninety miles from the United States, and called for more aggressive actions. When an embargo on exports was declared in October, he said that it was too little and too late, that we should consider more stringent economic sanctions, strengthen anti-Castro elements in Cuba and in exile, and attack the problem of Communism in the hemisphere. Nixon struck back by charging that Kennedy's proposal to aid anti-Castro forces would violate treaty obligations and "be an open invitation for Mr. Khrushchev to come in." He called his opponent "dangerously irresponsible." Kennedy had termed him "trigger-happy" as to Quemoy and Matsu. To the voters was left the puzzle as to which one was more anti-Communist.

The religious issue was threatening, in September, to blanket the campaign in a poisonous fog of prejudice and bigotry which would stifle any sane discussion of national problems. Undercover at first, it was brought into the headlines by a secret meeting of a hundred and fifty Protestant ministers and laymen at Washington on September 14, called by the Reverend Norman Vincent Peale of New York, a nationally syndicated columnist and author and a Nixon supporter.

These "Citizens for Religious Freedom" listened to speeches warning of the dangers of Vatican control of the government under a Catholic President, and issued a manifesto of similar tenor. Sharp denunciatory responses came from eminent Protestant divines, but the most effective answer was from Kennedy himself.

Speaking before the Greater Houston Ministerial Association, he declared in favor of absolute separation of church and state and against "unconstitutional aid to parochial schools," and pledged himself to make decisions in accordance with his conscience and "without regard to outside religious pressure or dictates." He would resign from office before he would violate his conscience or the national interest. He answered pointed questions without evasion, and impressed his auditors with his sincerity. The Kennedy managers sent taped recordings of the Houston performance to all parts of the country. Dr. Peale soon expressed regret over his involvement in the controversy, and the Citizens for Religious Freedom called Kennedy's Houston stand "complete, unequivocal and reassuring." The upper air of the campaign was cleared for more vital issues, but there were lower levels where the miasma of ancient prejudices could not be dispelled.

While Kennedy was confronted with the religious problem, Nixon ran afoul of the race question. The strong civil rights plank of the Republican platform, largely his work, not only angered southern racists and conservatives, but was not used effectively to draw Negro support in the big northern states. An incident involving the South's outstanding Negro leader, the Reverend Martin Luther King, gave Kennedy an opportunity that Nixon missed. Arrested for participating in a "sit-in" attempt in an Atlanta restaurant, King was sentenced in late October to serve a prison term at hard labor. Kennedy, advised of the situation by watchful members of his staff, telephoned Mrs. King to offer his sympathy and support, and next day his influence operated to help secure King's release on bail. His quick action, contrasted with Nixon's silence, accelerated a Negro swing to Kennedy, which may have accounted for Democratic victories in five or six states.

In the South, however, the major factor in combatting Republican appeal was the campaign activity of Lyndon Johnson. He whistle-stopped his way across the old Confederacy on the L. B. J. Victory Special, "the grandson of a Confederate soldier," who talked the language of his listeners and who knew how to stir up the lagging loyalties of the party regulars who would get out the vote. His most effective work—and Speaker Rayburn assisted here—was done in Texas, twice carried by Eisenhower. The struggle was a bitter one. Late in the campaign the Vice Presidential candidate and Mrs. Johnson were booed, jostled, and shoved around by a group of well-dressed Nixon supporters when leaving a Dallas hotel for a public meeting. This treatment of a distinguished native son exceeded in political stupidity the acts of some Michigan irresponsibles who hurled eggs and tomatoes at the Nixon entourage, and a Milwaukee woman who threw a glass of whiskey into Kennedy's face. But only the Dallas episode backfired seriously in terms of votes.

Lodge had already contributed to Nixon's southern dilemma by asserting in New York's Harlem that a Negro would be appointed to a cabinet post if the Republicans won. Nixon repudiated the pledge, for it was both improper and inexpedient.

Only in the final week did President Eisenhower take to the stump, although an earlier non-political tour was reminiscent of some of F. D. Roosevelt's subterfuges. The Nixon strategy was to build up the campaign to a grand finale with Eisenhower the great drawing card the last week. In metropolitan New York, accompanied by Nixon, and at Pittsburgh and Cleveland, the President extolled the merits of the experienced Republican candidates who could be depended upon to keep the peace and prevent inflation. He called Kennedy "this young genius" who lacked the knowledge, wisdom, and experience necessary for a President.

Earlier in the campaign Nixon had sought to dispel any impression that he was an apron-string candidate. He wanted to project the image of a leader who would stand broadly for the basic policies of the administration, but who was prepared to offer new programs where needed. But now, with the election a toss-up, the voters needed to be reminded that they still liked Ike, and that Nixon was Ike's choice. The President was warmly greeted by his usual large and enthusiastic crowds, but some hindsight Republican critics thought that Nixon waited too long to use him, and wasted his help in states that did not prove to be close.

A Hairline Decision

Early returns on November 8 pointed toward a Kennedy sweep of the coastal east by large majorities. In the lower South he seemed to be holding much of the normal Democratic strength, although Virginia, Kentucky, and Tennessee were evidently repeating the defection of 1956, and unpledged electors were ahead in Mississippi and Alabama. But early talk of a Kennedy landslide subsided when the Middle West reported. Ohio and Wisconsin soon were conceded to Nixon—Kennedy's biggest disappointments—and the western agricultural states were almost solidly Republican. The election turned into one of the closest in American history. In four states—Illinois, Michigan, Minnesota, and California—early Kennedy leads were being whittled away by a heavy Republican non-urban vote. Nixon needed all four to win an electoral majority; Kennedy needed two. Mississippi's eight unpledged electors and Alabama's six (Kennedy had the remaining five) could play a decisive role if neither candidate had a majority.

Before noon on Wednesday, the four doubtful states fell into the Kennedy column, and Nixon formally conceded his defeat. Later, a surprisingly large number of absentee ballots in California, counted after the election, shifted his home state to Nixon. Little Hawaii's three votes were not finally determined for Kennedy until the electoral college was meeting. This made his total 303 electoral votes to Nixon's 219. Senator Byrd was the choice of the eight unpledged electors of Mississippi and the six of Alabama, and also of an Oklahoma Republican who defected from Nixon.

Republican charges of fraud in Texas and Illinois lacked sufficient evidence to warrant the prolonged court battles that would ensue if the official count were questioned. Kennedy's margin in Illinois was 8,858 votes, in Texas 46,233.

By the tabulation of the clerk of the House of Representatives, Kennedy had 119,450 more popular votes than Nixon in a total of 68,836,385, a difference of one-tenth of 1 per cent. Other tabulations differ slightly from this. The mixed result in Alabama is the chief complicating factor. This was the closest voter verdict since 1880. Minor parties and unpledged electors accounted for enough popular votes to put both major party candidates below 50 per cent of the total.[1]

[1] Scammon, *America at the Polls*, gives the following totals: Kennedy, 34,226,-731; Nixon, 34,108,157; Louisiana independent electors (credited to Faubus in some tabulations), 169,572; Mississippi unpledged, 116,248; Haas, Socialist Labor, 47,522; Decker, Prohibition, 46,203; Faubus, National State Rights, 44,977; Dobbs, Socialist Workers, 40,165; others, lesser numbers. If Kennedy is given only five-elevenths of the Alabama popular vote, his total falls below Nixon's.

Both Houses of Congress were Democratic as expected, the Senate 64 to 36, the House of Representatives 263 to 174. The Republicans had gained two Senators and twenty-one Representatives. In state legislatures there were further evidences of Republican recovery from the near-debacle of 1958. The elections of state governor put fifteen Democrats and twelve Republicans in office, a net gain of one Republican.

The Presidential results had revealed a clear sectional pattern. Except for upper New England, the East was Kennedy's heartland, industrial, an ethnic mosaic, largely Catholic in the urban centers, controlled by machines and responsive to group loyalties. The big cities of the Middle West were much like those of the East, but Democratic machines had more difficulty matching Republican strength in suburbs, smaller cities, and countryside. Catholic voters were less numerous, and, in the more rural German sections, less committed to a co-religionist who was eastern, Irish, liberal, and educated and accented by Harvard. Wisconsin, Ohio, and Indiana gave Nixon solid majorities; Michigan, Minnesota, Illinois, and Missouri went for Kennedy by much slimmer margins.

In the South, Kennedy had the Carolinas, Georgia, Arkansas, Louisiana, Texas, and five Alabama electors. Nixon actually improved on Eisenhower's 1956 popular vote (although not on his percentage of the total), but lost Texas and Louisiana. He carried Kentucky, Tennessee, Virginia and Florida, all Eisenhower states. The result was a vindication of Kennedy's choice of Lyndon Johnson to run with him.

The great West, north and west of Texas, gave Kennedy a bare handful of electoral votes (four from New Mexico and three from Nevada), a great disappointment to his managers. Iowa and the tier of states from North Dakota to Oklahoma turned in heavy Republican majorities. The margins grew thinner in the states to the westward, and Nixon barely squeezed by in California. Dissatisfaction with Benson's farm policies was more than offset by the Republican peace-prosperity appeal and the distrust rural and small-town Protestants felt toward this urban Catholic, eastern candidate.

There can never be a definitive conclusion as to the importance of the religious factor on the outcome. Neither statistics nor methods of measurement are sufficiently reliable.[2] It seems likely that Ken-

[2] For analyses of the election, see Theodore H. White, *The Making of the President 1960* (New York, 1961); Paul T. David, ed., *The Presidential Election*

nedy's Catholic gains were largely from defecting Eisenhower Democrats who were now reviving their old loyalties. But his religion repelled many more, in heavily Protestant areas, who might otherwise have voted Democratic. With local situations and personality factors operating in state and Congressional elections, results frequently run counter to national trends, and 1960 had more than its share. Yet the loss of Democratic seats in the House and the fact that few of his party's candidates were helped by his coattails suggest that Kennedy's religion was a serious obstacle. Otherwise, his youthful vigor, crowd appeal, excellent organization, and skillful strategy might have gained a more decisive popular verdict. In any case, the fact did stand out that the nation had elected a Catholic President and that well over half of his votes came from Protestants.

The closeness of the outcome again drew attention to the defects in the electoral system. Unpledged electoral tickets, as used in the South, might prevent either major party candidate from obtaining a majority of the electoral votes, and throw the election to the House of Representatives. This would mean a two-months interregnum in a period of grave international problems and a tarnished title for the victor when the House did elect. But agreement on what changes should be made in the old system seemed as far away as ever.

Campaign finances had become the most serious problem in party management. The rising costs of transportation, advertising, registration drives, polling, and other indispensables of an intensive struggle for votes made the campaign of 1960 the most expensive in history. On the national level the major parties spent over $25,000,000 as compared with a total of $17,200,000 in 1956. Unlike 1952 and 1956, the Democrats, if labor disbursements are included, spent slightly more than the Republicans nationally, although the former ended up with a huge deficit. Victory gave its customary stimulus to post-election fund raising, and saved the party's credit. If the expenditures at state and local levels are added, the grand total has been estimated at $175,000,000.[3] To meet such outlays, fund-raising dinners, large contributors, and state quotas, which passed the burden on to local organ-

and Transition, 1960–1961 (Washington, D.C., 1961); Philip E. Converse, Angus Campbell, Warren E. Miller, Donald E. Stokes, "Stability and Change in 1960: A Reinstating Election," *American Political Science Review*, Vol. 55, June 1961, pp. 269–280.

[3] The above are the estimates of Herbert E. Alexander, "Financing the Parties and Campaigns," in David, *The Presidential Election and Transition, 1960–1961*, referred to earlier.

izations, were the chief sources, but these were in danger of being wrung dry by election day. A partial solution pointed toward some form of government subsidy.

The newspapers and the magazines of opinion, as in the past, displayed a heavy Republican editorial preponderance, but narrow partisanship in the form of slanted news stories and misleading headlines seemed to be less marked. The press in the many one-paper or one-ownership cities in the main recognized its responsibility to give equal space to and objective presentation of campaign activities of both parties. The working journalists who followed the campaign trail were charged by the Nixon staff with a Kennedy preference which, it was alleged, infiltrated their news stories. Certainly, the Kennedy entourage included a more sympathetic journalistic retinue, and the Democratic candidate achieved a rapport with press representatives that Nixon did not.

But contributing to the decline of newspaper editorial influence was the wide use of television. It provided candidates with direct contacts with the voters, who could see and hear them at close hand, and judge accordingly, if often irrationally. Kennedy demonstrated his maturity and increased his public stature by his television performances, particularly in the great debates. He believed that they made victory possible. Most political experts agreed with him.

The Kennedys in Charge

President Kennedy put aside political considerations in several of his cabinet choices. Dean Rusk came from the Rockefeller Foundation to head the Department of State. Douglas Dillon, Eisenhower's Under Secretary of State, became Secretary of the Treasury, and Robert S. McNamara, president of Ford Motor Company, transferred his managerial talents to the Secretaryship of Defense. A brilliant labor lawyer, Arthur Goldberg, became Secretary of Labor, but was soon appointed to a Supreme Court vacancy. Under Johnson, he became American ambassador to the United Nations.

Most criticized was the choice of Robert Kennedy for Attorney General. The new President's desire to have his campaign manager and closest adviser in this key post outweighed objections based on family influence and the appointee's limited legal experience. Adlai Stevenson, regarded in many quarters as the logical choice for the State Department, accepted the post of ambassador to the United Nations.

Kennedy's aides in the executive offices came chiefly from his campaign staff with some additions from the Harvard faculty such as McGeorge Bundy and Arthur M. Schlesinger, Jr. The presence of so many Harvard men in various key posts evoked both humorous quips and caustic comments from the various molders of opinion. "Kitchen Cabinets," rather than the official body, advised and helped shape policies.

Kennedy believed strongly in exercising Presidential leadership. With one exception he followed the traditional methods of publicity, persuasion, and pressure to achieve the goals of the New Frontier. The deviation was the admission of live television cameras to his news conferences. Held in an auditorium before several hundred newsmen, they conveyed to the millions of Americans watching on their screens the image of the "cool, businesslike manager of the national enterprise," as one observer aptly described him. He displayed intellectual keenness, unusual mastery of factual information, skill in phrasing, and a refreshing humor which displayed itself especially in turning embarrassing questions to his advantage.

Mrs. Kennedy, youngest and most beautiful White House hostess since Frances Folsom Cleveland, added to Kennedy appeal by her gracious personality and her cultural interests, shown particularly in her efforts to refurnish the old mansion to fit its historical traditions. Her entertainments also emphasized her artistic interests, and artists, musicians, writers, and exponents of cultural New Frontiers enjoyed White House hospitality as never before. Two small children provided material for human interest news stories.

President Kennedy's campaign promises to provide leadership that would get the country moving again struck snags in both of his Congresses. His New Frontier legislation advanced along some lines such as social security extension, foreign trade expansion, aid for depressed areas, and national defense involving especially the missile race. He also created a Peace Corps of American volunteers to do humanitarian and cultural work in more backward nations, and an Alliance for Progress to aid Latin American nations in making social and economic reforms. But he suffered defeats on medicare (financing of hospitalization through social security), the creation of a department of urban affairs, reform of the complex tax structure, aid for schools, and a revision of the farm price supports program.

The bipartisan bloc of northern Republicans and southern Democrats operated much as it had in the Roosevelt-Truman years. The seniority system kept in key positions men reelected continuously, more often from conservative rural areas, and gave a disproportionate share of committee chairmanships to southerners. The elevation of Lyndon Johnson to the Vice Presidency and the death of Speaker Rayburn weakened party leadership. Their successors, Mike Mansfield and John McCormack, could not function as effectively as their experienced predecessors.

The Cuban question continued to plague the Kennedy administration as it had the Eisenhower. An attempted invasion of Cuba by anti-Castro exiles in April, 1961, had administration approval but insufficient material support. This "Bay of Pigs" fiasco gave the Republicans a promising issue for the Congressional election of 1962, but the edge was dulled by a surprise retreat on Khrushchev's part just before the election. It had become clear that Russian missile bases were being set up in Cuba. To meet this next-door threat, Kennedy moved to establish a naval quarantine to keep offensive weapons from being landed. To avoid an armed clash, the Russian chief of state then yielded and agreed to remove such weapons and stop building bases. The President's firmness in the crisis did much to restore his prestige, although skeptics questioned whether Russia had lived up to the terms of the agreement. Kennedy's Cuban policy seemed certain to draw heavy Republican fire in 1964.

In other troublesome areas of international tensions—East Berlin, Laos, the Congo, Viet Nam—a measure of bipartisanship prevailed. Any worsening of a situation in their cases or anywhere else would inevitably bring American policy under review and make it an issue on the campaign trail. Expenditures for foreign aid were running into increasing Congressional opposition, as shown by Congressional reductions of administration estimates. Grave doubts were also raised about expenditures of the project to send astronauts to the moon.

A strong conservative movement in the Republican party, born in the prosperity of the post-war years, swung more sharply to the right after Nixon's defeat. Right wing Republicans, strong in state legislatures of the less populous states, were joined by segregationist southern Democrats in attempts to exhume state sovereignty through a group of constitutional amendments designed to limit drastically the powers of the federal government. The Supreme Court was especially under fire for its civil rights decisions, its banning of official religious exercises in the public schools, and its decision in *Baker* v. *Carr* requiring redistricting by state legislatures where apportionment of seats disregarded population. This last struck at overrepresentation of rural voters in legislative bodies, long a bulwark of conservatism. The initiated amendments harked back, in certain aspects, to the government of the Articles of Confederation of the 1780's. Seventeen state legislatures approved one or more of these proposals in 1962–1963.

This revolt of the right was carried further by more extremist groups concerned primarily with anti-Communism. The best known was the John Birch Society, founded by Robert H. W. Welch, Jr., a retired candy manufacturer, who once called President Eisenhower a "dedicated, conscious agent of the Communist conspiracy." It soon had a considerable middle-class membership and seemingly a good deal of millionaire money. Operating in secret, it projected to its followers a Communist menace honeycombing government, higher education, churches, and every organization of even a mildly liberal character. Washington was viewed as a center of subversion. There were no shades of good and evil, only reds and whites. Other rightist groups including veteran anti-Semitic guerrillas found the water and the funds to their liking, and soon fright-peddling lecturers, "seminars," propagandist bookstores, and a mass of exposure literature offered baits for the credulous and the frustrated.

The program of the "radicals of the right" included American withdrawal from the United Nations and its withdrawal from the United States, the impeachment of Chief Justice Earl Warren and possibly his associates of the "Communistic" Supreme Court, an end of diplomatic relations with Communist nations, drastic limitations on federal authority and a restoration of state sovereignty, and a wide range of repressive anti-subversive activities at the community level. Desegregation was labelled as Communistic by southern rightists.

Drawing their strength, outside the South, from the Republican party, these extremists aimed to commit its candidates to their program wherever possible. The danger to genuine conservatism and to party unity was so evident that Richard Nixon, Governor Rockefeller, Senators Thomas H. Kuchel of California and Jacob Javits of New York, and other moderates voiced strong disapproval of any association with this "lunatic fringe." Senator Goldwater, however, said that the Birchers he knew were "good people," that while "you can argue with their methods . . . that doesn't mean you have to condemn them." Instead he denounced the radical left as the real danger.

The midterm elections of 1962 brought little comfort to conservatives. Instead of the expected gains for the out-of-power party, the

Republicans lost four Senate seats, and added only four to their House minority. A third Kennedy joined the clan in Washington when Edward won the Massachusetts seat in the Senate once held by the President.

In state elections where local issues predominated, the Republicans did better. They captured the governorships from the Democrats in Michigan, Ohio, and Pennsylvania, and Governor Rockefeller was reelected in New York. These gains were partially offset by Richard Nixon's defeat by Governor Edmund Brown in California. Of the newcomers, George Romney of Michigan, former head of American Motors, and William Scranton of Pennsylvania, member of an old, well established family of that state, attracted attention as possibilities for 1964.

Governor Rockefeller, an early favorite, now raised doubts about his availability by marrying a divorcee after a divorce from his first wife. It was evident from the tide of criticism that the New York governor had lost ground.

The most striking development in Republican ranks was the Goldwater boom. Frank and forthright in speech and actions, this son of a Jewish father and Protestant mother had become the voice of the booming Southwest that accepted government aid but resented government controls. Attractive in appearance, his gray hair set off effectively by his dark-rimmed glasses, the Arizona Senator offered a simple, unabashed conservative philosophy through speeches and writings, including a popular book, *The Conscience of a Conservative.* At various times he committed himself against the graduated income tax, farm subsidies, medicare, compulsory social security, the Tennessee Valley Authority, and the whole fabric of the welfare state. He questioned the final authority of the Supreme Court—certain decisions were "jackassian"—and opposed civil rights legislation except possibly where voting and interstate travel were involved. He favored state right-to-work laws in the face of labor hostility.

His foreign policy ideas included a hard, even interventionist, line toward Castro in Cuba, an end to diplomatic relations with Iron Curtain countries, a drastic reduction of foreign aid, and, in general, a return to a more nationalistic, even isolationist position. His critics belittled Goldwater as a simple romantic of the nineteenth century, but his admirers saw in him the Moses who would lead the nation back to true, old-fashioned Americanism.

The Goldwater corps included old Taft politicos, young businessmen, suburban housewives, new millionaires, segregationists, Birchers, and miscellaneous rightists. Planning the strategy was an astute political technician, F. Clifton White of New York, a business consultant who had won his political spurs some years before as a leader of the Federation of Young Republicans. With a number of associates from different states, he had been organizing a draft movement for several months before it generated a spontaneity of its own.

But moderates argued that a Goldwater nomination would carry too heavy liabilities. Eastern Republicans would risk the loss of both electoral and state tickets. Labor, racial minorities, internationalists, and independents would go all the way with the Democrats. The support of fanatic rightists would drive away many Eisenhower Republicans. And fears of nuclear war might well be aroused by Goldwater's anti-Communist, anti-Castro belligerency.

Goldwater enthusiasts saw his candidacy in a different light. They argued that a real conservative would draw to the polls thousands of voters who had not turned out in the past because of the "neutralism" of Republican candidates. They offered statistics to show that Goldwater would have almost a solid South, the farm and mountain West, and most of the Middle West. This would leave Kennedy only his eastern bloc and a scattering of electoral votes elsewhere. If the race issue dominated, white racism, not confined to the South, would provide more votes than a Negro equality stand. The charge that the party was selling its birthright for southern votes could be met by the argument that the Negro had deserted the Republican party. Why not come to terms with the old Confederacy on a states rights platform?

Nor was the southern Republican party attracting only embittered segregationists. In the cities in particular were business and professional men, including many non-southerners, who were economic conservatives drawn to the party and to Goldwater for the same reasons that moved their kind outside the South. The Eisenhower-Nixon vote in three national elections was largely their contribution. Goldwater would accelerate the trend.

As election year began, Goldwater seemed to be shifting ground toward a more moderate and less consistently rightist position in his numerous speaking engagements. Rockefeller, trying to improve his own position, challenged Goldwater to a debate on party policies, but the latter refused, as this would only headline their differences.

Meanwhile, Nixon, now a New York resident, was making public appearances as an administration critic, and while denying any interest in another nomination, was not overlooked by political pundits as a strong contender if the liberal-conservative strife threatened party unity or the convention deadlocked.

Governors Romney and Scranton and Senator Thruston Morton of Kentucky, former national chairman, were also available choices still in the favorite son category.

In the Democratic party earlier optimism as to Kennedy's reelection faded with the rising tensions over race relations. Although peaceful demonstrations and non-resistance generally marked the course of the Negro's struggle for equal rights, many sympathetic whites criticized the leadership for moving too far and too fast. The northern metropolitan centers felt the increased frictions between Negroes and lower-income whites, particularly over jobs and housing. Would Kennedy lose votes from a "white backlash" because of his civil rights stand?

Racial clashes and bombings in Birmingham and certain other southern centers showed what white supremacists thought. In some instances school desegregation in the South required federal intervention through court processes enforced by federal marshals, and, at the University of Mississippi, by the use of troops to put down a riotous outbreak. Attorney General Robert Kennedy bore the brunt of responsibility and criticism for these steps. Attempts of Negroes to register for voting made slight headway in Alabama and Mississippi in the face of local hostility. Existing legislation was ineffective. President Kennedy secured bipartisan backing for a strong civil rights bill, but the measure was stalled in committee as the session of Congress ended.

Governors George Wallace of Alabama and Ross Barnett of Mississippi and other segregationist leaders planned to preempt the Democratic emblem for unpledged electoral tickets wherever possible in the coming Presidential election. This would force Kennedy to run as an independent, if he ran at all, in the states using this device. Alabama and Mississippi had chosen thirteen unpledged electors in 1960. This scheme might give the unpledged the balance of power in the electoral college and enable them to determine the outcome of the election. These segregationists had no desire to join the Republican party. They controlled Congressional seats and state and local offices, and disloyalty to the Democratic national ticket carried no penalties for them.

In addition to his efforts for a stronger civil rights law, Kennedy offered two other major proposals as his administration neared the home stretch. One was a treaty with the Soviet Union banning atmospheric nuclear tests. It won Senate approval, 80 to 19. Its wide appeal and the support of both Senate party leaders, Mansfield and Dirksen, overcame the conservative opposition led by Senators Russell and Goldwater. On top of this, the administration approved the sale of large quantities of surplus wheat to Russia. This was generally accepted as good business in conservative circles.

The second proposal called for a sharp reduction in federal income taxes. Such a bill passed the House in September, 1963, with some Republican support, but Senator Byrd, chairman of the Finance Committee, bottled up the measure in the Senate until the next session.

On the business front Kennedy came under fire because of large-scale spending, unbalanced budgets, the continued outflow of gold, and the feeling that he relied on economic advisers who were impractical Keynesian doctrinaires. Business leaders regarded the President's intervention by denunciation to stop a proposed increase in steel prices in April, 1962, as an example of his anti-business viewpoint. A sharp slump in the stock market in May did not help matters.

But the sluggish economy gradually improved, White House pressure averted a railway strike, a tax cut seemed likely, and in late 1963 the stock market hit record levels. Business in certain major areas including automobiles reached near boom proportions, employment went up to almost seventy millions, and unemployment fell off slightly. If no bad slump occurred and no new crisis developed with the Iron Curtain countries, the Kennedy ship could unfurl all its sails for a peace-and-prosperity campaign.

But the ship was never to sail for the port of a second term. An assassin's bullet struck down the captain just as the promise of greater achievements seemed near to fulfillment. The grief and horror of the nation obliterated party lines. Even the voices of the extreme Kennedy haters were stilled, and their propaganda of smear and venom, prepared for the coming campaign, became a liability.

33

L.B.J. All The Way

Primaries and Conventions of 1964

Lyndon Johnson came to the Presidency with the best preparation of any Vice President suddenly elevated to the highest office. While not a member of the Kennedy inner circle, he had participated in the deliberations of the cabinet and the National Security Council, and had played an active part in other top-level matters, including the exploration of space. He had gone abroad as a good-will salesman for his country, and his range of greetings encompassed rulers and camel drivers.

The tall Texan, possessed of superabundant energy, self-assurance, a rather sharp temper, and an instinct for politics, lacked Kennedy's intellectual interests and gift of speech, but he was a skilled tactician in the art of the possible who operated best through personal contacts, and he had an unsurpassed knowledge of the men and methods of Capitol Hill. He had outgrown his Texas territorialism, and was strongly committed to civil rights legislation and other major Kennedy measures.

That he would be nominated at the 1964 Democratic national convention was taken for granted, presumably with a liberal from the East or Middle West as his running mate. But to win in November he needed to convince the urban Kennedy strongholds that he had no southern sectional spots on his national toga.

The new President, operating with a practiced hand in the legislative field he had ploughed so often, secured the passage of the long-delayed tax reduction measure and a stronger civil rights bill than the original Kennedy measure. A bipartisan combination backed the civil rights measure with Senate Republican leader Everett Dirksen leading the conservatives of the midlands to its support after securing some clarifying amendments. Senator Goldwater was one of six Senate Republicans who voted against it. He called certain provisions unconstitutional and feared their enforcement would produce "a police state" and "an informer psychology." The Senate passed the bill on June 19. Goldwater was already well in the lead for the Republican Presidential nomination.

In the early spring the contest for the Republican prize had seemed invitingly open. The New Hampshire primary of March 10 produced a surprise result. A well-organized write-in campaign for Henry Cabot Lodge, ambassador to Vietnam, put him ahead of Goldwater, Rockefeller, Nixon (also a write-in choice), Senator Margaret Chase Smith of Maine, and Harold Stassen.

Down to the California primary the Republican voters confused the experts with their own confusions. Candidates avoided direct primary battles where the results appeared doubtful, voters used write-ins frequently, and favorite son figureheads enabled some states to postpone commitments. In the convention states of the South and West Goldwater zealots were capturing the delegates. Rockefeller won a surprising victory in the Oregon primary over Lodge, which practically eliminated the latter. Goldwater wisely had abandoned Oregon to his rivals. But contrary to pollster predictions he carried California over Rockefeller by a 68,350 margin in a total vote of 2,172,456. This meant eighty-six delegates. Later conventions, which included Texas, added enough, by his supporters' claims, to give him the 655 votes needed for the nomination.

Republican moderates, in alarm, looked to Eisenhower to encourage a stop-Goldwater movement, as the former President had made statements about the need for a candidate in the mainstream of Republican thinking. But, when no help came from Eisenhower, Governor William Scranton of Pennsylvania announced his intention to run and set about belatedly to win the uncommitted and the loosely committed delegates to his support. The prepossessing forty-six-year-old governor, who smiled easily and spoke fluently and with serious conviction, argued that Goldwater's votes and utterances were out of line with past Republican platforms. Could the party, he asked, "stand with one foot in the twentieth century and one in the nineteenth?"

Rockefeller, Romney, and Lodge were ready to help, and Lodge joined Scranton on a western delegate hunt, but the results were not encouraging.

The convention opened at San Francisco's Cow Palace on July 19 with National Chairman William Miller presiding. Governor Mark Hatfield of Oregon, in his keynote speech, emphasized the humanitarian heritage of the party. When he castigated extremists and lumped together the John Birch Society, the Ku Klux Klan, and the Communist party, there were ill-concealed murmurs of disapproval. Next day when Eisenhower spoke on the same general theme, an incidental reference to "sensation seeking columnists and commentators" produced a roar of approval and an eruption of fist shaking directed at the occupants of television booths and press seats. This showed the temper of the majority, convinced of the bias of eastern news media.

The platform committee, headed by Representative Melvin Laird of Wisconsin, had met the week before the convention opened to hear speakers for all manner of causes. The finished product did not suit the liberals. Senator Hugh Scott of Pennsylvania, Scranton's manager, offered three amendments: a repudiation of extremists with the John Birch Society mentioned by name; a reassertion of Presidential control over nuclear weapons (not giving commanding officers in the field an option as to nuclear tactical weapons, as Goldwater had suggested); and a stronger statement for enforcement of the civil rights law. All were voted down, as were similar amendments offered by Governor Romney. But the most astonishing incident of the convention was the treatment of Rockefeller when he tried to speak for the first proposal. From the galleries came boos and hisses and cries of "We Want Barry," and Chairman Thruston Morton had great difficulty getting order for the grim-faced governor to speak for his allotted four minutes.

The platform on key points was a Goldwater textbook. Its central themes were the dangers to liberty at home from an expanding federal power, and the need for a dynamic strategy against Communism to secure victory for freedom "every place on earth." Democratic failures and weaknesses in both areas were cited at length. The touchy civil rights question was disposed of with a promise of full implementation of the Civil Rights Act of 1964 and continued opposition to discrimination, with the qualification that the elimination of such discrimination is "a matter of heart, conscience, and education, as well as of equal rights under law." Endorsement was given constitutional amendments to permit religious exercises in public places and to enable states having bicameral legislatures to apportion one house on a basis other than population.

At the Wednesday evening session, nominating speeches provided eight candidates. The customary demonstrations followed, with most of the sound and fury for Goldwater, nominated by Senator Dirksen. The one ballot gave Goldwater 883 votes; Scranton, 214; Rockefeller, 114; Romney, 41; Mrs. Margaret Chase Smith, 27; Walter Judd of Minnesota, 22; Hiram Fong of Hawaii, 5; and Lodge, who had withdrawn, 2. Scranton moved that the nomination be made unanimous.

The ticket was completed with the nomination of Congressman and National Chairman William Miller of New York for Vice President. Although geographically and in religion—he was a Roman Catholic—he seemed to give balance to the ticket, Miller was a conservative, had slight strength in his home state, and was better known to party professionals than to the rank and file of party voters.

In his acceptance speech Goldwater offered no olive branch to the defeated. He reiterated his conservative creed and stirred his listeners with his challenging statement: "Extremism in defense of liberty is no vice . . . moderation in pursuit of justice is no virtue." The counterrevolution had been successful, and the Eastern Establishment had been toppled in the dust, even stamped upon.

The Goldwater forces took control of the Republican National Committee immediately after the convention. Dean Burch, a thirty-six-year-old Phoenix attorney who for several years had been a member of the Senator's Washington staff, became national chairman. Denison Kitchel, a Harvard-educated lawyer, was Goldwater's personal manager. A long-time friend, he had taken over direction of the pre-convention campaign but preferred to work in the background. The southern Goldwater forces were represented by John Grenier of Alabama, who ranked next to Burch in authority. Ralph Cordiner, former chairman of the board of General Electric, handled finances.

Old professionals, such as former national chairman Leonard Hall of New York and Ohio state chairman Ray C. Bliss, were ignored as much as used for advisory purposes. The committee organization was staffed by the "Arizona Mafia" in all important positions. A new crowd was running the show, and the preliminary planning was done efficiently, on paper.

The Democratic national convention met at Atlantic City on August 24 with everything planned in advance by President Johnson, although he withheld the name of his running mate until the time came for nominations. Governor Wallace of Alabama had upset pre-convention harmony by entering the primaries in Wisconsin, Indiana, and Maryland against favorite son stand-ins for Johnson. He won no delegates but polled a considerable vote with his racist appeal, getting forty-three per cent in Maryland where white resentment against Negro militancy was especially strong.

A revised formula for apportionment of delegates provided for 2,316 convention votes as against 1,521 in 1960 and the 1,308 voting delegates to the 1964 Republican convention. In all, 5,260 officially accredited Democrats came to Atlantic City. Of these, 2,944 were delegates, 108 were the voting members of the national committee, and 2,208 were alternates.

Senator John Pastore of Rhode Island offered a slashing keynote address, sprinkled with jibes at Goldwater's irresponsible utterances, and presided as temporary chairman. He was succeeded in the chair next day by House Speaker John McCormack.

The credentials committee was faced with the problem of two Mississippi delegations, a regularly elected one and a contesting "Freedom" group. The convention adopted a solution that gave seats to the regulars on the condition that the delegates take a pledge to support the ticket, and allotted two seats at large to the Freedom claimants. Only three signed the loyalty pledge, and the Freedom group rejected the compromise. The Alabama delegates were also asked to take a similar pledge, but only eleven complied and were seated.

The lengthy platform, presented by Representative Carl Albert of Oklahoma, promised "unflagging devotion to our commitments to freedom from Berlin to South Vietnam," the further isolation of Castroism, and a continued resolve, under tested leadership, to use every resource to find the road to peace. On the domestic front it offered a broad federal program of social and economic welfare measures covering education, Medicare, civil rights, the war on poverty, farm policies, urban improvement, and conservation. Labor was promised repeal of the Taft-Hartley Act. The Ku Klux Klan, the Communist Party, and the John Birch Society were condemned as extremist organizations. Thirty-eight citations from the platform of 1960 were followed by the accomplishments of the Kennedy-Johnson administration in each case.

The nominating session was a formality. President Johnson surprised everyone by coming to the convention, accompanied by his family, to announce that Senator Humphrey would be his running mate, which was no great surprise in itself. Senator Eugene McCarthy, also of Minnesota, had been regarded as the only other possible choice, with Robert Kennedy eliminated earlier by Johnson's politic decision not to take anyone from the cabinet. Kennedy was taken care of by an invitation from a New York group to run for the Senate from that state. Humphrey, a Middle Western liberal, had tempered his early crusading zeal into a more realistic willingness to work for the possible, had demonstrated his skill as party whip in the Senate, was a popular figure outside the lower South, and had no peer as a rapid-fire, extemporaneous speaker. Both Johnson and Humphrey were nominated by acclamation.

At the closing session on Thursday, tributes were paid to three deceased party notables. John F. Kennedy was eulogized by his brother Robert, who was given a moving thirteen-minute ovation; Mrs. Eleanor Roosevelt by Adlai Stevenson; and Sam Rayburn by James Farley. Acceptance speeches by Humphrey and Johnson followed. The former shook the convention out of its Kennedy nostalgia with a stirring recital of Goldwater's negative Senate votes until his listeners began to chant with him "—but not Senator Goldwater." Johnson offered no flaming battle cries but pictured the nation on a course of peace and prosperity moving toward "the Great Society." "Let us be on our way," he ended.

The Atlantic City gathering had been a party jamboree, with a good time had by all, in spite of complaints about the resort city's not very modern host city facilities. The delegates had come merely to ratify and the performance satisfied its director.

The Consensus Campaign

Before beginning his campaign, Goldwater conferred with Republican notables including governors and gubernatorial candidates at Hershey, Pennsylvania. He tried to restore unity by clarifying his views on major issues to show that he was repudiating extremism of both the left and the right. Most of those present expressed approval of his explanations.

But the cleavage was too deep to be repaired in this fashion. Disaffection developed on a scale unequalled since the Bull Moose split of 1912. Among candidates who refused to indorse the Goldwater-Miller ticket were Senator Keating of New York and Governor Romney of Michigan, while several others, including Senator Hugh Scott of Pennsylvania, Robert Taft, candidate for the Senate from Ohio, and Charles H. Percy, running for governor in Illinois, conducted virtually independent campaigns. Senators Case of New Jersey, Kuchel of California, and Javits of New York, not up for re-election, withheld indorsement. Governor Rockefeller gave a nominal support to the ticket. Of the better-known figures only Nixon and Scranton went on the campaign trail.

In the South, Governor Wallace dropped the idea of an independent candidacy but refrained from any indorsement to avoid embarrassing Goldwater, he said. He supported his unpledged electoral ticket. But in South Carolina Senator Strom Thurmond, a segregationist and a conservative, joined the Republican party.

Prominent Republican business and financial leaders and several Eisenhower officeholders, including four former cabinet members, took the bolters' path. The larger metropolitan pro-Republican and independent newspapers and periodicals were almost a unit in support of Johnson. In terms of circulation, the press was heavily anti-Goldwater, an unprecedented situation for a Republican candidate. Members of the working press in the Goldwater entourage were sometimes greeted with boos and insulting remarks. The Republican candidate, feeling that he had been the victim of misinterpretations of off-the-cuff remarks in the past, dispensed with formal press conferences and presented his case in prepared speeches and television appearances.

In one respect, the war of paperbacks, the Goldwater attackers far outdistanced the Johnson defenders in verbiage and venom. Right-wing organizations circulated thousands of copies of this hate literature, whose authors foot-noted one another to prove that the nation was in the clutches of a conspiracy of subversion, with the particular devils varying according to the speciality of the author.

Citizens' organizations appeared outside the regular party fences, aimed at bolters and independents. Citizens for Goldwater-Miller and National Citizens for Johnson and Humphrey led the procession, but auxiliaries and subdivisions for various professions and skills multiplied until the Republicans were accredited with thirty, the Democrats with twenty-eight, according to press reports. Here the advantage lay heavily with the Democrats, for the masses of Republican bolters could find congenial company in citizens' committees for Johnson, while Democratic bolters were lonesome outcasts, outside the South.

Goldwater opened his campaign formally on September 3 at Prescott, Arizona, the starting point for his two Senatorial campaigns. He attributed to the administration "the way of the regimented society," "the way of mobs in the streets," appeasement in foreign affairs, unilateral disarmament in the face of militant Communism, and a low tone of morality in the public service. He emphasized his own devotion to peace through strength. These themes he returned to repeatedly in later speeches, with the need for morality in public life getting more and more attention toward the close of his campaign.

The slogan of the Republican campaign, "In Your Heart You Know He's Right," appeared in every kind of publicity put forth by the Goldwater supporters. It was easy to parody, and its interminable repetition possibly was a mistake.

The Democrats made sure that Goldwater's utterances before he became a candidate would return to plague him. He was called trigger happy because of his statement that the field commander might have the option of deciding when to use tactical atomic weapons, and the horrors of nuclear war were pictured in paid television propaganda. He was charged with hostility to social security because of a remark, before the New Hampshire primary, that it should be made voluntary, and he made matters worse by attacking Medicare. A television picture of a social security card torn in two was an effective Democratic rejoinder. His vote against the Civil Rights Act of 1964 blotted out the memory of his support of the earlier acts. His campaign declarations against both forced segregation and forced integration appealed only to the South.

The issue of morality in government became Goldwater's strongest weapon. Two cases, both close to Johnson, came to light. Bobby Baker, Senate majority secretary and once a protégé of Johnson, had been forced to resign the preceding year while under investigation for possible conflicts of interest. The Rules Committee reported in July, 1964, that he was guilty of "gross improprieties" but left the question of law violations for the Justice Department to handle. Republicans charged that the report was a whitewash, that prominent Democrats were involved, and demanded that the Baker case be reopened. Unanswered questions about various Bobby Baker deals provided Republicans with excellent campaign ammunition.

Late in the campaign Walter Jenkins, long a confidential assistant to Johnson, was convicted on a morals charge. He was at once dismissed and placed in a hospital. The effects would have been more damaging but for startling news from abroad: Khrushchev had been deposed and Red China had detonated a nuclear bomb. The Jenkins affair was overshadowed by these developments, although not forgotten.

The Baker and Jenkins cases became Republican evidence of "a cloud over the White House" and "a mess in Washington." Immorality and loose standards at the top were trickling down to infect the nation, Goldwater asserted. But he rejected as racist a documentary film entitled "The Choice," which was designed to depict moral rot and violence in the streets. He refused to permit its use in the campaign.

The Democratic campaign management was headed by Chairman John Bailey, a professional who depended on professionals, but Johnson did his own planning; tactics and itineraries were changed on short notice. His personal control rested on groups of overlapping staff specialists—speech writers, television publicity men, campaign planners, directors of voter registration, citizens' committees, and minorities, and a flock of others. Several key members of the 1960 Kennedy team held important posts, notably Lawrence O'Brien and Kenneth O'Donnell.

The President began his campaign in Cadillac Square in Detroit on Labor Day. His theme then, and later, was national unity on a program of prosperity, justice, and peace. He set up the Great Society as his goal, with unemployment and poverty eliminated and equal opportunities for all. In the final weeks of the campaign he was on the stump almost as much as his rival and far excelled him in handshaking, crowd mingling, and folksy speeches. Although buoyed up by the favorable reports of the polls, he wanted to win by a landslide and set out to cover every section of the country. Critics dismissed his extemporaneous remarks largely as homilies and hokum, but he knew how to please the huge crowds and did not let some heckling, most evident in his own South, disturb his happy front. Both Mrs. Ladybird Johnson and Senator Humphrey had encountered some hostile treatment in tours of the race-conscious southern states.

Humphrey's long record as a battler for liberal causes and his membership in the Americans for Democratic Action labeled him as a Socialist in Republican propaganda and as a Communist in extreme rightist nomenclature. Miller, termed the hatchet man and the bantam gut fighter by hostile sources, confined his stumping chiefly to the smaller cities. Unlike the polyloquent Humphrey, he settled down to one basic speech which he could fit to different audiences with minor changes.

Smear tactics were used with little restraint on both sides, with hate more in evidence in extreme Republican propaganda and fear in Democratic. Bruce L. Felknor, executive director of the Fair Campaign Practices Committee, said that it was "the most vicious and bitter campaign I've ever seen, or for that matter, heard tell of."

Republican efforts to arrange some type of televised debate by the two major party candidates ran into snags in Congress and in the White House. The Senate on August 18 killed a proposal to suspend the section of the Communications Act which prevented such confrontations. Senator Dirksen and most of the Republicans were in the minority. The National Broadcasting Company offered to arrange for joint appearances of the candidates in a series of news interview programs but President Johnson declined to participate. Cries of "chicken" from the Republicans were ignored. Before his nomination, Goldwater had refused to debate with Rockefeller and Scranton but now was ready to meet Johnson. Observers above the partisan smoke questioned whether it was in the national interest for an incumbent President to become involved in a forensic duel while handling delicate matters of foreign policy on which he could not speak freely. Johnson, at least, believed it was not in his own interest.

Minor parties played insignificant roles. The veteran Prohibition, Socialist Labor, and Socialist Workers parties made their quadrennial appearances, with E. Harold Munn, Sr., Eric Hass, and Clinton DeBerry as their respective candidates. Less well known were some six or seven other candidacies, mostly of recent vintage. Three on the extreme right regarded Goldwater as too liberal. Of the ten or more minor candidates (some self-nominated), six were on the ballots in a total of 22 states, according to a *New York Times* tabulation.

The popular verdict on November 3 was more decisive than the Harding and Roosevelt landslides. Johnson received 43,129,484 popular votes to Goldwater's 27,178,188; in percentages 61.1 to 38.5.[1]

[1] Minor parties and independent tickets polled 336,838 votes. Of these, the Alabama unpledged electors had 210,732 votes.

The electoral votes were 486 and 52. Goldwater's electoral votes came from Arizona and five southern states— South Carolina, Georgia, Alabama, Mississippi, and Louisiana. The Senate was Democratic, 67 to 33; the House of Representatives, 295 to 140. In the governors' races the Republicans won only eight of twenty-five contests. Romney's success in Michigan kept him in the picture for 1968.

To defeat an incumbent riding a prosperity-peace horse has been proved an impossible task in the past, but the race would have been closer if a less vulnerable candidate had been named. An "echo" would certainly have run better than the "choice." At least the mortality percentages for lesser offices would have been reduced. The Goldwater record and bad strategy, which gambled too much on the white backlash, were the major causes of the debacle.

Goldwater's victories in the deep South added seven Republican members to the House of Representatives. These were elected as segregationists and only complicated matters for the party in the North. It was an anomalous situation for the party of Lincoln to have received nearly all of its electoral votes from the former Confederacy. Goldwater did not carry a state that had voted for Lincoln, Theodore Roosevelt, Hoover, or Eisenhower except Arizona in the last two cases and Louisiana in Eisenhower's second election.

The debacle produced an outburst of angry recriminations in Republican ranks. Goldwater loyalists blamed the defeat on the failure of the moderates to give the ticket united support and contended that their idol's conservative philosophy had been approved by twenty-seven million voters. Opponents countered that the majority of these were loyal Republican regulars who would vote for any party candidate, and that the swing to the right had driven away the moderates and the independents who had been so responsible for past Republican successes. The restoration of some degree of unity was the Republican goal and problem for the immediate future.

Both parties' expenditures set new records. On the national level, total spending for the campaign was nearly $35,000,000, divided among a large number of committees of both parties. The Republican total was over $17,000,000, the Democratic $12,000,000, but the Democrats benefited also from the independent spending of labor and other Democratic-oriented groups. The 1964 campaign was unusual in the increased number of large givers to the Democratic campaign, notably in the case of the President's Club, which consisted of some 4,000 donors of $1,000 or more to Johnson's election. In the Republican camp, money came from more small contributors than in the past, largely as a result of direct mail and television solicitation. Goldwater's special appeal to middle-class business and professional people and the zeal of his workers, mostly amateurs, further explain this broadened financial base. Actors Ronald Reagan and Raymond Massey were especially effective at television solicitation.

The grand total of all election expenditures, national, state, and local, from pre-convention to final accounting, has been estimated at $200,000,000.[2] This exceeded by $25,000,000 the former record set in 1960.

The election of 1964 was marked by an improved method of reporting the returns, which was used again in 1968. A centralized system, the National Election Service, set up by the three national television networks and the two major press associations, provided quicker service at lower cost than the old competitive methods. Thousands of workers at the precinct level reported returns to state centers for tabulation. As these reports were analyzed, reasonably safe predictions could be made as to trends and outcomes. A more sophisticated tool for rapid prediction and analysis of election outcomes was Vote Profile Analysis, set up by the Columbia Broadcasting System and two other sponsors. It was used in 1962, and in primaries and elections in 1964 with apparent success. However, this early forecasting of final results aroused criticism in several quarters. Voters in areas where the polls were still open, it was charged, were thus being told that the battle was over and their participation would have no effect. Pre-election polls also came in for unfavorable comments for affecting rather than reflecting voting trends.

The Aftermath of 1964

President Johnson, assured of the support of a strongly liberal Congress, set about to reap the fruits of his great victory. In the two sessions of the Eighty-ninth Congress, platform promises in the more important fields were carried out by the enactment of a far-reaching program of legislation, notably with regard to Medicare for

[2] See Herbert E. Alexander, "Financing the Parties and Campaigns," in Milton C. Cummings, Jr., ed., *The National Election of 1964* (Washington, D.C. 1966), pp. 158–198.

the elderly, aid to education, federal supervision of voting rights, urban problems, air and water pollution, automobile safety, and the war on poverty. But widespread opposition to open housing and outbreaks of racial violence in several cities dampened the prospects of further civil rights legislation, and labor was denied the repeal of the right-to-work section of the Taft–Hartley Law.

The most serious problem for the administration was in Vietnam, where the bombing of the Communist North brought only limited military gains and seemed to promise a further escalation of the war. Opposition to the Johnson policy found vent in public anti-war demonstrations and in Senate criticisms, notably by Chairman William Fulbright of the Foreign Relations Committee and Wayne Morse of Oregon, both of whom won some degree of support from a number of their colleagues. The terms "hawks" and "doves" came into the political vocabulary as applied to supporters and opponents of Vietnam escalation. The President was relying too heavily on two cabinet "hawks," Secretary of State Dean Rusk and Secretary of Defense Robert McNamara, according to his "dovish" critics. Republicans, with a few exceptions, were "hawkish," calling for even more vigorous measures against the Communist aggressors.

On the economic front, heavy military expenditures, the costs of the war on poverty, the threat of inflation, and the prospect of tax increases disturbed business and middle-class friends of the administration. Labor pressures for wage increases added to fears that the prosperity machine was grinding to a halt.

Negro militancy caused in part by the limited practical gains in the civil rights struggle led to outbreaks of violence in the black ghettos of Los Angeles, Atlanta, Cleveland, and several other cities in 1965–66. The rise of a "Black Power" leadership in certain Negro protest groups and a white backlash reaction seemed to threaten an increase in racial tensions, especially where open housing and school bussing as a desegregation tactic were issues.

These various discontents commingled to create a national mood of insecurity and dissatisfaction with things as they were and affected the midterm elections of 1966. The old political axiom that unhappy voters take it out on the party in power operated in favor of the Republican "outs." They reduced the Democratic majorities in Congress by 47 seats in the House of Representatives and three in the Senate, and won eight additional governorships to bring their total to twenty-five, which included five of the seven largest states.

Improving Republican prospects foreshadowed a sharp struggle for the Presidential prize at the convention of 1968. The early listing of possibilities included George Romney, returned to Michigan's governorship by a landslide; Charles Percy of Illinois, elected to the Senate over veteran liberal Paul Douglas; Ronald Reagan of California, former movie favorite, who had defeated Governor Edmund G. Brown in the latter's try for a third term; James A. Rhodes of Ohio, reelected governor by a record margin; and Richard M. Nixon, who built up good will by campaigning in 1966 wherever Republican candidates could use his services. Governor Rockefeller of New York ruled himself out of the contest, but his impressive victory for a third term in New York could not be overlooked. Only Reagan wore a conservative collar, although Nixon had made himself acceptable to the right wing. Retiring Governor Scranton of Pennsylvania declared himself no longer available for public office.

In the Democratic ranks, President Johnson seemed assured of a renomination, even though his escalation of the American military commitment in Vietnam had antagonized liberal groups which had supported his domestic policies. News media criticisms that he was withholding information on important matters from the public and creating a communications gap further depressed his poll popularity. The much publicized rift between the President and Senator Robert Kennedy seemed to be largely personal, but shades of difference over policies might sharpen as tensions increased. Kennedy's aim seemed directed toward a nomination in 1972.

In Alabama, George Wallace, whose wife Lurleen had succeeded him as governor, was planning an independent candidacy for the Presidency if the old party nominations did not conform to his state sovereignty views. This threatened to confuse further the party situation in the deep South, where the Republicans had captured two governorships in 1966 and almost won a third in Georgia—where the legislature voted in the Democratic contender, a racist, in a contested outcome. The once Democratic South was becoming incorrigibly wayward.

34

Nixon and Agnew

Unforeseen Events and Upsets

The reforming tide that followed President Johnson's consensus victory of 1964 ebbed in the Congress elected in 1966 but was still strong enough to bring about a continuance of the Great Society program, a civil rights bill for open housing and better protection of voter rights,[1] and some other regulatory measures less political in character. To check inflationary pressures and strengthen the dollar internationally, in 1968 Congress reluctantly levied a ten per cent surtax on incomes but attached requirements for a heavy reduction in federal spending.

A crime control bill containing a prohibition of the interstate sale of handguns, passed after the assassination of Robert Kennedy, was followed late in the session by one which regulated the sale of long guns but did not require registration or licensing. The sharp controversy over these measures carried over into the campaign of 1968.

The most widespread racial violence in the nation's history scarred the American image in 1967. Federal troops were required to quell the disorders in Detroit, but Newark and many other cities were afflicted only in lesser degree. The President appointed a special advisory commission on civil disorders which reported on March 2, 1968. It called for drastic measures to be taken in the areas of employment, education, welfare, and housing. With a national election impending, neither Congress nor the President was inclined to press for action. Rioting in the wake of the assassination of the

[1] The Supreme Court on June 17, 1968, expanded the act's provisions by applying the Civil Rights Act of 1866 to bar all racial discrimination in the sale and rental of property.

Reverend Martin Luther King and a six-weeks encampment of poor people, mostly blacks, in "Resurrection City, U. S. A.," Washington, D.C., did not help the cause of racial reconciliation.

Meanwhile, the growing opposition to the Vietnam war and the draft boiled up in demonstrations on campuses, at induction centers, and wherever pro-administration speakers were scheduled to appear. A national gathering of various anti-war and left-wing organizations at Washington in October, 1967, required special marshals and military units to protect the Pentagon from the more activist demonstrators.

But the various peace groups were too splintered and politically impotent to be considered a threat to the renomination of President Johnson until Allard K. Lowenstein, a former president of the National Student Association and a liberal whose restless energies drove him away from university teaching positions, began to organize the dissenters. Using student groups and his connections with the Americans for Democratic Action, he launched a "Dump Johnson" movement with an evangelical fervor that took him wherever a peace dove cooed. His "Concerned Democrats" group attracted support, but his search for a candidate was fruitless until he used his persuasive eloquence on Senator Eugene McCarthy of Minnesota.

In late November McCarthy announced that he would contest certain Democratic primaries with President Johnson or whoever ran as stand-in for him. He would run as an anti-war candidate, although critics conjectured that other motives were involved. The tall, sharp-witted, soft-speaking Senator, philosophical and reflective in temperament rather than self-assertive, more popular outside the upper house than in it, took upon himself the role of crusader in the cause of peace with little hope of being nominated but to demonstrate through the primary route the strength of the peace marchers. Such seedling groups as the Dissident Democrats and the National Conference of Concerned Democrats indorsed him, and a flock of anti-war groups soon established McCarthy-for-President clubs, but money and organization on any considerable scale were lacking. Unfriendly critics suggested that McCarthy might be a stalking horse for Robert Kennedy, but the two had not been particularly close in the past and Kennedy gave no indication of approving this surprise candidacy.

The course of events helped McCarthy's cause. Secretary of Defense Robert McNamara resigned and was succeded by Clark Clifford, one-time Truman assistant and a trusted advisor of Johnson, who was reputedly more inclined than McNamara toward a hard line policy on Vietnam. Before he took office, the Viet Cong offensive during the Lunar New Year celebration on January 31 altered the military situation for the worse, increased American casualties, and made the war an even more divisive political issue.

McCarthy, with limited funds and a makeshift organization, went into New Hampshire to oppose the regular party organization which was backing Johnson with a write-in program. The long-shot contender whose calmly reasoned speeches did not dramatize his cause found eager listeners in the liberal students of eastern schools—idealistic, anti-draft, and unhappy with the world of their parents. Busloads of these students poured into New Hampshire in the closing days of the campaign to lick envelopes, ring doorbells, and try to sell their candidate by personal persuasion. Beards, shaggy locks, and too abbreviated mini-skirts were ruled out for the door-to-door solicitors of votes. The hippie image would damage the candidate with staid Yankees. McCarthy was developing the "egghead appeal" of Adlai Stevenson.

The result was a surprising McCarthy vote. He had 42.2 per cent of the Democratic preference vote to 49.4 for Johnson, but captured twenty of the state's twenty-four delegates. More important, he had badly damaged the President's standing with politicians and voters generally.

The New Hampshire vote brought Robert Kennedy into the race. Explaining that the party was already badly divided and that Johnson's policies had met the nation's crises with "too little and too late," he announced his candidacy on March 16 in the Senate Caucus Room, where his brother had taken the same step in 1960. Kennedy's late start had kept him from entering the early primaries, but he indicated his readiness to help McCarthy in Wisconsin, Pennsylvania, and Massachusetts, although he made it clear he intended to run against him in later tests. McCarthy rejected the offer. In New Hampshire he could have used Kennedy's help. Now he no longer needed it.

McCarthy's expected victory in Wisconsin against a disorganized Johnson following suddenly was deprived of its importance by an astonishing development. Addressing the nation in a television broadcast on Sunday night, March 31, President Johnson announced that American bombing raids on North Vietnam would be ended except for defense purposes in certain contingencies. This unexpected shift of policy, which pointed toward negotiations with Ho Chi Minh, was overshadowed by his concluding sentences in which he announced that he would not seek and would not accept a nomination for another term. The reason he gave was "the divisiveness among us all tonight." With America's future under challenge at home and the world's hopes for peace in the balance, he did not want the Presidency involved in partisan divisions.

Johnson's abdication coup produced a revolution in American politics. He had deprived his critics of their chief issue and of their personal devil. The chant of anti-Vietnam marchers—"Hey, hey, L. B. J., how many kids have you killed today?"—ceased to be heard, and the number of anti-war demonstrations abated. In the score sheets of the pollsters, the President's popularity zoomed upward. Kennedy and McCarthy had to revamp their strategies, and party regulars and others who had been lukewarm toward Johnson but not attracted to the dove-leftist orientation of his opponents now rediscovered his merits and looked around for a pro-administration candidate.

Vice President Hubert Humphrey was the immediate and almost the only choice. His experience in national affairs, his domestic liberalism, his loyalty to the President, especially on Vietnam, his strength with labor, and his reputation as a campaign exhorter were all in his favor. Paradoxically, in the South this veteran champion of civil rights was developing strength with conservatives who had no use for Kennedy and who could not stomach McCarthy's peace stand. The Vice President delayed announcing his candidacy, kept out of the primaries, and let state organizations and favorite sons try to block the Kennedy-McCarthy drives. Finally, on April 27, when his organization and financing had been set up, he hoisted his standard at Washington and pledged himself to a campaign of moderation and restraint with party unity his goal. Senators Walter F. Mondale of Minnesota and Fred Harris of Oklahoma were his joint managers.

As predicted, McCarthy carried Wisconsin over Johnson, 57 per cent to 35 per cent, two days after the latter had announced his withdrawal as a candidate. An army of Middle Western collegians provided enthusiasm and doorbell ringing, a following which was better organized than the administration forces. But the gloss of New Hampshire was missing. He had defeated a non-candidate.

Although their appeals on major issues were not substantially different, Kennedy and McCarthy battled for delegates in Indiana, Nebraska, Oregon, South Dakota, and California. The assassination of the Reverend Martin Luther King on April 4 and the rioting that followed made civil rights problems even more pressing. Kennedy's record was better in this area and his name meant more to ghetto dwellers and other underdogs. He had more experienced aides, funds for all purposes, and the prestigious Kennedy clan in his corner. Only Oregon, without ethnic blocs and serious urban problems, went for McCarthy, who drew more upper-middle-class support. This was the first defeat for a Kennedy in a primary since John F. had set out to run for office in Massachusetts.

This setback made the California primary a make-or-break test for Kennedy. Both candidates had only a week after Oregon for intensive stumping but did appear together on a television panel, which revealed no clear differences on any important issues.

By midnight of June 4, the nation's most populous state registered a safe but not overwhelming margin for Kennedy, 46 per cent, as opposed to 42 per cent for McCarthy and 12 per cent for an uncommitted group. That same evening, South Dakota gave Kennedy fifty per cent of its total, with Humphrey and McCarthy dividing the rest. But what started out as a night of victory turned into a night of anguish. An assassin's bullet cut down a second Kennedy just when his primary appeal had reached a new peak.

Kennedy's leaderless forces continued to offer slates of delegates who would uphold his principles in the remaining states. They would not accept McCarthy, and Humphrey's Vietnam stand repelled them, although the Kennedy field marshal, Lawrence O'Brien, moved into the Vice President's camp and took over direction of his strategy. Senator George McGovern of South Dakota offered a solution by a belated announcement of his candidacy just two weeks before the date of the convention. Anti-war and a liberal on domestic policies, he drew in a considerable number of Kennedy political orphans. But Humphrey was apparently too far in the lead in delegate count to be affected by this late candidacy.

Among the Republican possibilities, Governor George Romney was off to an early start by an announcement of his candidacy on November 18, 1967. A western tour and some other public appearances seemed to reveal a haziness on major issues that was made worse by some inept extemporaneous utterances. In answer to a question in a television interview about his shift of views on Vietnam, Romney stated that he had been "brainwashed" by administration experts at the time of his earlier stand. Some other off-the-cuff answers to newsmen's questions further damaged his public image.

Romney's apparent decline was accompanied by a rise in the poll popularity of two non-candidates, Governor Ronald Reagan of California and Governor Rockefeller of New York, now in his third term. Reagan, attractive in appearance and skilled in audience appeal, was the conservative choice to wear Goldwater's mantle, but insisted he was only California's favorite son. Rockefeller, committed to Romney and faced with the hostility of the Goldwater alumni, resisted the pressure of liberals and independents to become a candidate. Senator Charles Percy of Illinois remained in the Polk–Pierce category.

Romney made a trip around the world to gain insight into foreign policy and entered the New Hampshire primary to contend against Richard Nixon, who declared his candidacy on February 1, 1968. Both Romney and Nixon campaigned for the Granite State's delegates, but the former's balloon had so shrunken that he suddenly announced his withdrawal on February 28, less than two weeks before election day. Nixon secured the state's eight delegates by default, polling seventy-eight per cent of the Republican preference vote to eleven per cent for Rockefeller, for whom a belated write-in campaign had been started after Romney dropped out. The more liberal Republicans increased the pressure on the New York governor, and he weakened enough to say that he would not refuse the national convention's call if its voice was clear. This was ten days after New Hampshire voted.

But the shifting political winds of this unpredictable April soon blew Rockefeller's non-candidacy from its moorings after President Johnson's withdrawal. Senator Thruston Morton of Kentucky and William Miller, Goldwater's running mate in 1964, began to operate a draft-Rockefeller movement. Governor Reagan was showing signs of extending his favorite son role to include California's neighbors, which could cut into Nixon's western support. In several other states, such as Ohio, favorite sons were holding out to help create a deadlock. With Nixon vague and vulnerable on Vietnam and ghetto problems, Rockefeller saw the opening widening for a liberal opponent. On April 30, he announced that he would run. It was now too late to enter the remaining primaries.

The New York governor had to sell himself through personal appeal and large-scale organized efforts as the one Republican candidate who could capture the Democratic liberals and independents so necessary for electoral success. Too many of the delegates were already chosen and committed, which made it harder to shake Nixon's hold. Rockefeller offered a fresh approach, a "New Politics," stressing his handling of urban problems in New York and outlining a four-point program on Vietnam in contrast with the cautious Nixon who, after a sweeping victory over Reagan in Oregon, ceased to campaign actively.

Robert Kennedy's death had a significant impact on the Republican situation. Rockefeller, using his talents as a crowd pleaser, spoke of the similarity of his program to the deceased senator's, and the "Rocky" badges and youngsters clamoring for autographs suggested that if he was not capturing some of the Kennedy youth contingent, at least he was drawing a G.O.P. adolescent legion who could provide enthusiasm if not votes. Whether the crowds that surrounded him and his heavy spending for television and newspaper advertising could produce much of a delegate shift was doubtful, but opinion polls kept him optimistic, and he campaigned up to the date of the national convention.

Nixon's Second Chance

In choosing a southern meeting place for the Republican national convention, the national committee seemed to break with tradition, but Miami Beach had far greater kinship with the affluent North than with the old Confederate South. Several considerations explain the choice, but the beach city's island location, which insulated it from neighboring Miami with its ghetto problems, insured the convention against the pressures from outside demonstrators that might have occurred if Chicago's bid had been accepted. But the local security authorities took no chances. A six-foot chain-link fence surrounded the convention hall, and police were stationed at all key points. Delegates, newsmen and spectators had to provide proper credentials at every turn.

Some members of the Poor People's Campaign staged brief demonstrations in the convention area, and a group attended the Tuesday session on guest tickets, but delegates were hardly aware of their presence or of the violence that erupted in the Miami ghetto on two nights of the sessions.

The Twenty-ninth Republican National Convention began its deliberations on Monday, August 5, with 1,333 accredited delegates present and National Chairman Ray C. Bliss presiding. Introduction formalities, organization matters, the usual platform exposures of miscellaneous minor celebrities and candidates, and speeches brimming with confidence occupied the two sessions. The first evening's oratorical festival headlined former President Eisenhower, who was heard from via a brief inspirational message recorded at Walter Reed Hospital where he had been confined by a heart attack; Senator Edward Brooke of Massachusetts, temporary chairman; Barry Goldwater; and Governor Daniel Evans of Washington, who gave the keynote address. All the main speakers adhered to the theme of restoring national unity with new leadership and new programs. Not one touched on the current prejudices and hates or anything else likely to inflame the emotions of the listeners.

On the second day, after accepting committee reports and listening to Thomas E. Dewey and Representative Gerald R. Ford of Michigan, permanent chairman, attack the Johnson administration, the delegates were presented with the platform. The show was then taken over by Senator Everett Dirksen, chairman of the platform committee, whose unruly gray hair, rumbling voice, dark-rimmed glasses, and old-fashioned oratory had given him status as a television personality in addition to his minority leadership in the Senate. His denunciation of rioting and crime and his references to the unsafe streets of Washington and Cleveland captured his audience as the liberal pronouncements of the preceding night had not.

The moderately long (11,500 words) platform was presented in summarized form by several speakers, each dealing with one section. Dirksen took over again at the end. A week of hearings before subcommittees and the full committee had produced a platform whose chief planks had been worked out in a form acceptable enough to prevent floor fights. Urban problems and Vietnam were the original apples of discord, but, as the party out of power, the Republicans could attack, generalize, and evade as the administration party could not. Differences were easier to resolve.

A preamble viewed with alarm the dire state of the nation, called for new leadership, and set forth the party's aims and pledges. A special section headed "Crisis of the Cities" began with a promise to "transform the blighted areas into centers of opportunity and progress, culture and talent." Then followed a list of broad proposals with emphasis upon federal support of state and local programs and "a greater involvement of vast private enterprise resources." Measures to alleviate and remove the frustrations that contribute to riots were advocated along with the support of "decisive action to quell civil disorders."

A special section of the platform was devoted to crime. Improved law enforcement was to be promoted in a number of ways, but the enactment of gun control legislation was to be a state responsibility with only such federal laws as might be necessary to "better enable the states to meet their responsibilities" recommended.

Welfare and poverty programs were to be overhauled, tax credits were proposed for employers who would provide job training, and local ownership of businesses in depressed areas would be encouraged by state and community development corporations and other aids. Youth was given a special section which included a recommendation to the states to consider giving eighteen-year-olds the right to vote and promises to liberalize the draft system with a volunteer military force a future possibility. Education was covered in a detailed list of proposals, with federal assistance in the form of grants and loans to states and individuals a leading feature. In general, the document was liberal and forward-looking on domestic affairs and had fair words, if not many specific proposals, for taking care of every important element of American life.

On Vietnam the platform committee had been pulled between the hawkish views of Reagan and the dovish inclinations of Nixon and Rockefeller. A carefully worded compromise proved surprisingly acceptable, with the doves having the better of the solution. The final version criticized administration policies as political, military, and diplomatic failures and called for new leadership and a strategy concentrating on the security of the Vietnamese population and the development of a greater sense of nationhood along with "a progressive de-Americanization of the war." A fair and equitable settlement was promised—"Neither peace at any price nor a camouflaged surrender of legitimate United States or allied interests"—and a willingness to pursue peace negotiations "as long as they offer any reasonable prospect for a just peace." Neither a bombing halt nor possible further escalation of military activity was mentioned.

Other aspects of foreign relations and national defense were covered in generalities and ambiguities on the positive side, although Israel was promised "countervailing help" to offset the imbalance created by Soviet military build-up in the Middle East. The strong anti-Communist tone of the 1964 platform was absent from the 1968 party pronouncement.

The platform was adopted without opposition, although a North Carolina delegate was prevented by a dead microphone from offering as an amendment a stronger plank on Vietnam.

Nixon, last of the candidates to appear on the scene, arrived on Monday evening to find his carefully planned organization functioning smoothly. Rockefeller and Reagan, who announced his candidacy Monday afternoon, had been presenting their cases to state delegations and key individuals, but Nixon held open house in his Hilton Plaza headquarters while his hundreds of workers looked after his interests from branch centers in various hotels. A communications network coordinated activities. All indications pointed toward his nomination if his lines held firmly.

At the nominating session on Wednesday, August 7, twelve candidates were put in nomination, with speeches and demonstration ceremonies consuming over seven hours. Two favorite sons, Governor Walter J. Hickel of Alaska and Senator Strom Thurmond of South Carolina, heard their merits recited, then withdrew in favor of Nixon. The balloting, completed at 1:52 A. M., gave Nixon 692 votes, Nelson Rockefeller 277, Reagan 182, Rhodes 55, Romney 50, Senator Clifford P. Case of New Jersey 22, Senator Frank Carlson of Kansas 20, Governor Winthrop Rockefeller of Arkansas 18, Senator Hiram L. Fong of Hawaii 14, Harold E. Stassen 2, Mayor John V. Lindsay of New York 1. Wisconsin's 30 votes had given Nixon the 667 votes necessary for the nomination. Changes of votes added to his total but Governor Reagan's motion to make the nomination unanimous seemed to have been overlooked by Chairman Ford.

After many hours of consultation with party bigwigs and selected lesser lights, Nixon chose Governor Spiro Agnew of Maryland as his running mate. He arrived at this solution by a process of eliminating names of the too liberal and too conservative possibilities, such as Mayor Lindsay and Senator Hatfield of Oregon on the left and Reagan and Senator Tower of Texas on the right. He had promised Senator Thurmond, his southern spokesman, that he would not name a man objectionable to the South, which virtually ruled out a northern choice. It has been asserted on good authority that Nixon would have chosen his close friend, Lieutenant Governor Robert Finch of California, but the latter refused to be considered.

Agnew had had a satisfactory civil rights record as governor until the Baltimore riots when he angered Negro leaders with his criticisms of their attitudes and his defense of strong measures to put down rioting. Of Greek ancestry (his father's name had been Anagnostopoulous), the tall, broad-shouldered governor had a direct, forceful manner of speech and promised to be an effective campaigner. Although he had originally favored Rockefeller, he had switched to Nixon and had made the nominating speech for him.

When the delegates reassembled at the final session on Thursday night, liberals objecting to the southward slant of the choice tried to stir up a revolt. However, Rockefeller refused to help, Lindsay refused to run, and the remnant of dissidents ended up voting for Governor Romney, who was nominated by a Nevada delegate. He received 186 votes to Agnew's 1,119, with 28 scattered or not voting. The vote for Agnew was then made unanimous.

Vice Presidential candidates many times have been lifted out of a contemporary anonymity to provide sectional or factional balance to tickets. The Theodore Roosevelts and the Lyndon Johnsons are far outnumbered by the Fillmores, the Hobarts, and many others who may not have lacked merit but who certainly were short in political stature. Governor Spiro Agnew was one of these running-mate dark horses. But Nixon himself had been an unknown quantity to most of the voters in 1952.

Nixon's acceptance speech was one of his best. Most of it was an old story to reporters who had followed him on the campaign trail, but to national television audiences it revealed the new Nixon whose vigor in denunciation was balanced by a forward-looking idealism and warm personal touches, and whose skillful appeal to "the forgotten Americans, the non-shouters, the non-demonstrators" seemed to strike the right chord for the campaign ahead.

Tumult and Strife at Chicago

President Johnson and Mayor Daley were given the credit for the Democratic National Committee's choice of Chicago as the site of the party's 1968 convention. This was on October 9, 1967, but already Black Power and anti-Vietnam extremists were talking of making the city the scene of mass demonstrations aimed at disrupting the convention and preventing the renomination of Johnson. Mayor Daley's assurances that security would prevail helped counteract the arguments for Miami Beach, already the Republican choice.

The mayor lived up to his promises by turning International Amphitheatre into a fortress protected by seven feet of barbed wire, an army of security guards, and electronic credential scanners at check points. The Chicago police force of nearly 12,000 was put on twelve-hour shifts, and 5,600 national guardsmen and 7,500 federal troops were being kept in reserve for riot duty. President Johnson's withdrawal as a candidate had changed the situation but there was still the possibility that he might visit the convention. In any case, anti-administration demonstrations which might lead to rioting were to be expected.

Members of the National Mobilization Committee to End the War and the Youth International Party (the "yippies"), groups of McCarthy's collegians (who came against his wishes), and various New Leftist militants made up the army of protesters who assembled at Chicago expecting to vent their frustrations and disenchantments in mass demonstrations. They were refused permission to parade and were dispersed when they tried to camp overnight in Lincoln Park. Although disappointed at the small total of visiting dissidents, the leaders nevertheless were determined to provoke confrontations with the police. Even though the fear of an outbreak there was one reason for the presence of federal troops, the city's black ghetto gave almost no support to the "whities." In the end, the security forces seemed to have outnumbered the demonstrators.

The Thirty-fifth Democratic National Convention, a body of 3,099 delegates casting 2,622 votes, opened its proceedings on Monday evening, August 26. It engaged in acrimonious debates interspersed with frequent roll calls for four days and ended its work on Thursday in an atmosphere of angry recriminations. Senator Daniel K. Inouye of Hawaii was temporary chairman, Representative Carl Albert of Oklahoma permanent chairman. The latter presided during the most tumultuous periods.

The first two sessions were largely taken up with the reports of the credentials and rules committees. The former had been confronted with seventeen contests from fifteen states. Racial imbalance was the issue involved in the challenges in several southern states.

In each case, the committee's recommendations, presented by its chairman, Governor Richard J. Hughes of New Jersey, were accepted, but several required roll calls. The Georgia decision was to seat both claimants and divide the vote equally, a solution rejected by Governor Lester G. Maddox who earlier had announced his candidacy for President. In the case of Mississippi an insurgent "loyal" delegation was seated. The regular Alabama group was accepted after a party loyalty declaration had been required of each delegate.

The convention voted to abolish the venerable unit rule, obsolete in most states, and to forbid the use of a unit rule in any stage of the delegate selection process in the future. The national committee was also instructed to make sure that all Democrats in a state should have meaningful and timely opportunities to participate in the selection of delegates.

The platform was presented by Representative Hale Boggs of Louisiana at the Tuesday session. A week of hearings at Washington and Chicago before four panels, a report by a Democratic Congressional Platform Hearing Committee, and, reportedly, some strong suggestions from the White House produced a reasonable consensus on all matters except Vietnam. Consideration of a minority report on this issue was postponed to the next day.

The majority report generally upheld the administration policy on the Vietnam war. It favored a total bombing halt only when this would not endanger the lives of troops in the field but promised negotiations with Hanoi for an immediate end of hostilities and the withdrawal of foreign forces. The minority plank represented a consensus of all shades of "dovishness." It called for an unconditional end to all bombing, negotiations for a mutual withdrawal of United States and North Vietnamese troops, and the encouragement of negotiations by the South Vietnamese with the National Liberation Front (the Viet Cong) with a view toward the creation of a broadly representative government for South Vietnam.

The debate, with each side allotted an hour to present its case, was conducted on an unusually high intellectual level for a convention floor battle. Over thirty speakers shared the rostrum.[2] The

[2] Among the better known speakers were the following: For the majority report—Senators Edmund S. Muskie (Me.), Gale W. McGee (Wyo.), and Frank Moss (Utah); Representative Wayne Hays (O.); Governor Warren E. Hearnes of Missouri, Wilson W. Wyatt of Kentucky; and Representative Boggs, chairman of the platform committee. For the minority report—Senators Wayne

minority report lost by a vote of 1041¼ to 1567¾. The platform was then adopted by a voice vote.

Its 18,000 words reaffirmed the party's position on most foreign and domestic questions and reiterated its object "to march at the head of events," although "we candidly recognize that the cost of trying the untried, of ploughing new ground, is bound to be occasional error." It took pride in the ninety months of recession-free prosperity under Democratic administrations. Accomplishments in such fields as education, health, civil rights, and housing were catalogued and contrasted with the negative attitude of the Republicans toward reform.

The Democrats went beyond the Republicans in declaring for a constitutional amendment lowering the voting age to eighteen. The Peace Corps and other youth programs were praised and their expansion promised. Soviet aggression against Czechoslovakia was condemned, and American contributions to the solid achievements of the free world praised with due credit to Democratic policies. A strong and balanced defense establishment and a strengthening of the ties of the North Atlantic Community were pledged along with praise for the limited Nuclear Test Ban Treaty, the Non-Proliferation Treaty, and the treaty barring the orbiting of weapons of mass destruction.

Continued progress in the removal of trade barriers was advocated along with provisions to remedy unfair and destructive import competition. Other advanced nations were expected to share in foreign aid development programs in greater degree. The United States was pledged to continue to accept world responsibilities but would not try to mold the world in its own image.

At the nominating session on Wednesday evening, five candidates were put in nomination—McCarthy, Humphrey, McGovern, Governor Dan Moore of North Carolina, and Reverend Channing Phillips, a Negro humanitarian leader from Washington, D. C. Governor Maddox of Georgia had ceased to be a candidate and had gone home. A movement to draft Senator Edward Kennedy aborted

---

Morse (Ore.), Vance Hartke (Ind.), Albert Gore (Tenn.), Joseph Tydings (Md.), and Claiborne Pell (R.I.); Representatives John Conyers (Mich.), Henry Reuss (Wis.), and Phillip Burton (Calif.), who had charge of the minority speakers; Senatorial candidates Paul O'Dwyer of New York and John J. Gilligan of Ohio; Kenneth O'Donnell of Massachusetts; Pierre Salinger of California; and Governor Phillip Hoff of Vermont.

when Mayor Daley committed Illinois to Humphrey and Kennedy sent word to the drafters to desist.

Meanwhile, leftist dissidents who had been engaging in skirmishes with the Chicago police for three days in Lincoln and Grant Parks attempted to mobilize in front of the Conrad Hilton hotel for a march on the convention hall. Exacerbated by the dissidents' tactics of planned provocation and their refusal to disperse, the police charged upon the jeering demonstrators and proceeded to club indiscriminately whoever happened to be caught in their onslaught net, whether demonstrators, male or female, newsmen, photographers, or more-or-less-innocent bystanders.

In the amphitheatre angry anti-Humphrey delegates, appalled by the televised pictures of police violence, made Mayor Daley, in a front seat, the particular object of their denunciations and jeers. Senator Abraham Ribicoff of Connecticut used his nominating speech for McGovern to deliver a direct attack upon the mayor for his "Gestapo tactics." Other hostile speakers played upon the same theme, and a Wisconsin delegate tried to interrupt the roll call to move an adjournment to another city.

The balloting produced no surprises. It gave Humphrey 1,760¼ votes, McCarthy 601, McGovern 146½, Phillips 67½, Moore 17½, Kennedy 12¾, Paul Bryant 1½, James H. Gray ½, George Wallace ½, with 14 abstentions. A voice vote made the nomination unanimous, as the chairman ignored a scattering of boos. The galleries, reportedly packed with Mayor Daley's retainers, yelled their approval.

The Thursday session began with a tribute to Robert Kennedy, consisting of a taped speech by Edward Kennedy from Cape Cod and a film eulogy. Delegates sang the Battle Hymn of the Republic, and some of the angry minority attempted to continue repeating the chorus to delay convention proceedings. A tribute to the Reverend Martin Luther King ended the song filibuster.

Senator Fred Harris of Oklahoma, runner-up on the Humphrey list for the second office, presented Senator Edmund S. Muskie of Maine as the nominee's Vice-Presidential choice. Wisconsin put in nomination Julian Bond of Georgia as a gesture of dissent, but Bond withdrew, since he was only twenty-eight years old, and could not constitutionally qualify. Muskie received 1,922½ votes, Bond 48½, several others 26¾ in all, with 199¾ not voting or not recorded. The nomination was then made unanimous.

The tall, rugged-faced Maine Senator was not a surprise choice. Nine years on Capitol Hill after two terms as governor of his state had established his reputation as a working Senator, an authority on urban problems, and a liberal with an independent spirit and little taste for power grabbing and self-aggrandizement. A Roman Catholic and son of a Polish immigrant, (Marciszewski had been shortened to Muskie) he overbalanced Republican Agnew's voting pull in Democratic books, for Polish voters outnumbered Greek by a considerable margin. A Phi Beta Kappa key established his rapport with the intelligentsia.

Humphrey's acceptance speech, a masterpiece of his skill at conciliation, expressed regret at the tragic events of the week but warned that violence breeds violence, and assured his listeners that the policies of tomorrow need not be limited by the policies of yesterday. A standing ovation unmarred by boos followed his concluding appeal for unity. President Johnson, with much of the blame for the party's troubles put at his door, celebrated his birthday in Texas, and watched the convention proceedings on television.

Humphrey announced that his campaign manager and the new national chairman would be veteran professional organizer Lawrence F. O'Brien, who had served both John F. and Robert Kennedy, had been Postmaster General under Lyndon Johnson, and had joined Humphrey's camp as national campaign coordinator after Robert Kennedy's death. Senator McGovern, candidate for reelection from South Dakota, appeared on the platform with Humphrey but McCarthy remained at his headquarters. Later, in a valedictory in Grant Park he advised his followers to work for peace candidates but refused to indorse the national ticket.

Charges that the convention had been rigged and the minority suppressed reflected the bitterness of the defeated rather than the actual situation. Mayor Daley's too rigid security measures, some gallery packing, and the handling of some matters of convention procedure had angered the minority but did not affect the major decisions. They had been made on the floor of the convention after open debate and sometimes acrimonious exchanges, with the whole world watching on television, as the street dissidents chanted in front of television cameras. If the game had been played unfairly, the rigging had been done back in the states where the old rules had been followed in electing the delegates. McCarthy admitted later that he could not have been nominated at Chicago even if his supporters had not been given the Daley treatment. Charges of majority rigging are an old story in convention history.

A Choice of Evils?

Nixon opened his campaign at Chicago on September 4 with a ticker-tape-and-confetti motorcade witnessed by several hundred thousand cheering curbside admirers, followed by a televised question-and-answer session with a local panel, which was beamed at a regional audience. Visits to San Francisco, Pittsburgh, and Houston followed. The candidate was breaking ground for an intensive campaign to capture the large swing states necessary for victory.

Nixon's efficient pre-convention organization carried over into the campaign, although it was necessarily expanded, and some personnel shifts were made. John N. Mitchell, a law partner, continued as his manager. Mitchell's wide experience in the financial field of state and municipal bonds had given him contacts that made up for the handicap of a late entry into politics. A carefully charted division of labor and a staff largely of younger men not associated with the 1960 struggle relieved the candidate of the heavy burdens of planning and decision-making except at the top levels. Electronic aids and gadgets of every type made the communications setup a marvel of speed and efficiency.

Working with the newer men were such old friends and associates of the Eisenhower days as Maurice Stans, heading the Republican finance committee, Charles S. Rhyne, a law-school friend, in charge of the United Citizens for Nixon-Agnew, Herbert S. Klein, a San Diego editor, who became director of communications, and Robert Finch, lieutenant governor of California, an old friend and closest to the candidate personally. Former Governor William Scranton of Pennsylvania was sent on a scouting trip to Europe and served as a roving foreign affairs adviser. National Chairman Ray Bliss was outside the Nixon orbit and dealt with state and local politicos and their candidates.

Dropping the plane-hopping and whistle-stopping methods of 1960, which exhausted the candidate physically and mentally, the New Nixon limited the number of major addresses, had one basic speech for ordinary party jubilees, followed a carefully timed schedule, and used all the resources of television and radio to present his case. In answering questions from selected panels or telephoned in by interested listeners, he sought to match Humphrey's skill in extemporaneous speech without the latter's volubility. In his appearances in motorcades and at open meetings he was bothered very little by hostile demonstrators and hecklers who found better game elsewhere. Only near the end of the campaign did he resort to some old-fashioned barnstorming and stumping, mostly in Ohio and Pennsylvania.

The New Nixon offered the country a new leadership and a new approach. Assailing administration policies and Humphrey as a responsible formulator of policy, he summed up his campaign appeal in an oft-repeated key statement: "I say the man who helped us get into trouble is not the man to get us out." He broke with the traditional Republican concept of the Presidency, to which Eisenhower had adhered, by taking an activist view of the office whose occupant must provide leadership above all else. He called for an "open administration"—a thrust at the credibility gap charged against Johnson.

On Vietnam Nixon was carefully noncommittal. He explained that he did not want to say anything to undercut the Paris negotiations with North Vietnam or to reveal his hand as to the policy he might follow as President. He held the administration responsible for the war but he did not pinpoint its mistakes. The Soviet invasion of Czechoslovakia, he felt, justified a postponement of ratification of the nuclear nonproliferation treaty. He would strengthen national defense to eliminate the "security gap" that the Johnson-McNamara policies had permitted to develop.

On domestic issues, the Republican candidate called for reduced federal spending, a balanced budget, and other measures which might be found necessary to combat inflation and strengthen the dollar. He sent a letter to two thousand leaders in the business of handling securities in which he denounced the Democrats for heavy-handed regulatory schemes and promised an independent, comprehensive study of the entire role played by financial institutions in the economy. Nixon denied Humphrey's charge that he was opposed to social security and Medicare and promised to make them work better for the people they were supposed to help.

On the problems of the ghetto Nixon held to the platform pledge to encourage the private sector of the economy through tax incentives and other aids to create employment and to develop "black capitalism." Little effort was made to win Negro votes. Few blacks came to Nixon meetings; neither Nixon nor Agnew campaigned in person in the urban ghettos; and Agnew was reported to have commented, "When you've seen one [ghetto], you've seen them all." There is evidence that late in the campaign a little-publicized effort was made by spending money and sending out field workers to build up Nixon as a friend of the black man, but it came too late to get results or to disturb his rapport with the Thurmond South.

Nixon, like Wallace, who accused him of thunder-stealing, got the most mileage out of the law-and-order issue. He warned of the ominous increase in crimes of violence, deplored the failure of the administration—and Attorney General Ramsey Clark in particular—to use federal power to curb rioting and lawlessness, and promised the "forgotten people"—the law-abiding middle class citizens—that the streets would be made safe for them and their children. In his southern forays the New Nixon did not repudiate desegregation but spoke out against the use of federal grants to force compliance on school districts and, while favoring open housing, implied that it might be handled better at state and local levels.

Vice President Humphrey, after a brief Minnesota vacation, came to Washington to address a B'nai B'rith convention on Sunday, September 8. Then on Monday he began at Philadelphia his first campaign trek, which took him across the large industrial states. With much of the South abandoned to Wallace, the Democrats had to reinvigorate the loyalties of city ethnic groups, propitiate anti-war defectors, and work with organized labor leaders to offset the pull of the Alabama governor on the blue collar workers of the North.

Humphrey's campaign encountered heavy weather from the beginning. Peace extremists and other anti-administration dissidents organized demonstrations to disrupt his meetings with hecklings, anti-war chants, and walkouts. When he appeared with Humphrey at a political rally in his home city of Boston, even Senator Edward Kennedy was shouted down. With the organization still being structured, financing unsettled, and local disaffection a drag on party energies, the Democrats seemed to be facing a November disaster. But Chairman O'Brien presently got his house in order and made some changes in publicity arrangements. With campaign consultant Joseph Napolitan as director of advertising, the Democrats put on a belated but effective television blitz which hurled spot commercials at the enemy, presented Humphrey to advantage in a documentary, and showed him at his extemporaneous best in selected film clips. Financing improved with the Democratic candidate's rise in poll percentages but remained a problem to the end.

At first Humphrey tried to reach too many people in too short a time. He could not keep to his planned schedules. Sometimes he overtalked to the point of blurring rather than clarifying his stands, and, when he was not too ebullient, was too vehement and too denunciatory. Presently hoarseness, frayed nerves, pressure from his advisers, and evidence of growing party unity helped to tame down somewhat this battler for a seemingly lost cause in his attempt to emulate Truman's feat of 1948.

President Johnson at first took an aloof and almost disparaging attitude toward his Vice President, as, for example, when he openly contradicted Humphrey's overoptimistic prediction that a beginning of troop withdrawal from Vietnam might come in late 1968 or early 1969. But on October 10 he gave a fifteen-minute indorsement of Humphrey intermixed with slams at Republican "reaction and inaction" and Wallace's "empty rhetoric and violent appeals to emotion." On later occasions he spoke out wholeheartedly for the candidate and appeared with him before a capacity crowd in the Houston Astrodome at a final rally. However, he did his party's cause the most good when he announced a bombing halt in Vietnam just before the election.

Humphrey's early campaign speeches followed the pattern of his liberal past. He pointed to the years of prosperity under Democratic rule but said he was looking forward to a new day of equal rights for all, and promised a national attack on the problems of poverty, health, and education. Nixon he called a social reactionary. The lukewarm responses of his audiences and the widespread concern over rioting and increases in crimes of violence compelled him to shift his emphasis to the law-and-order issue, which he coupled with justice for all. Toward the campaign's close he was promising federal funds and other aids to strengthen and improve local law-enforcement agencies, legislation to deal with guerrilla bands and vigilantes, and a firearms registration law. He accused Nixon and Wallace of stirring up fears and emotions without offering programs and of ignoring the need to combat poverty, despair, and alienation. He also denied that court decisions were a factor in the crime increase.

Labor's leadership backed Humphrey solidly and pressured the rank and file to resist the Wallace lure. The Alabama governor's record was combed for evidences of anti-labor views and acts, which were then cited in pamphlets circulated by the thousands by the A.F.L.–C.I.O.'s Committee on Political Education.

Humphrey's stand on Vietnam bombing was his and the party's most difficult problem. In a nationwide televised address on foreign policy given at Salt Lake City on September 30, the candidate teetered in the balance by promising to end the bombing while at the same time saying that he "would place key importance on evidence—direct or indirect, by deed or word—of Communist willingness to restore the demilitarized zone between North and South Vietnam." Otherwise, bombing might be resumed.

On October 8, before an editors' group Humphrey invited the Soviet Union to take the responsibility for seeing that Hanoi did not show bad faith once the bombing had been stopped. This implied that he was now committed to an unconditional bombing halt. But not until President Johnson did declare an unconditional bombing halt just before the election did the candidate get completely out of the Vietnam jungle.

Senator McCarthy had left Chicago without indorsing Humphrey and remained inactive until he returned from a trip to Europe. Then he began to campaign for Senatorial peace candidates and, although he gave Muskie a verbal pat on the back, he still insisted certain conditions he had laid down before he would support his party's candidates had not been met. But the pressure for party unity was pulling most of the McCarthy and McGovern dissidents into the path of orthodoxy, particularly those who were themselves running for office. McCarthy finally fell in line with a half-hearted indorsement of the national ticket a week before the election but confirmed it more warmly on a Humphrey telethon on election eve.

George Wallace announced on February 8 that he would run for President as the candidate of the American Independent party. The energies of his volunteer workers at first were directed to solving the problem of getting his name on the ballots of the different states with their hodgepodge of requirements. Finally, they succeeded, but it required a decision of the United States Supreme Court setting aside Ohio's stiff requirements to put the third party candidate on the ballot of the fiftieth state.

In the deep South Wallace's new party drew in the conservative racist Democrats, who took over the regular organization and name in his home state. In this area most of the Democratic candidates for

Congress and state offices supported Wallace or preserved a careful neutrality.

Outside the South the third party was a Presidential candidacy, not a party. It offered only a national ticket. The Presidential candidate had no running mate until October 3 when he introduced General Curtis E. LeMay, former Air Force Chief of Staff, as his choice before television cameras at a Pittsburgh hotel.

John Birchers, White Citizens' Councils, and various radical rightist splinters helped the American Independent party with money and workers, although these were disruptive assets in some states. But it was Wallace's appeal to the dissatisfied that gave his candidacy its vitality and threatened to make serious inroads into strongholds of the old parties. His simplistic approach to national problems drew into his net blue-collar industrial workers, small business men, urban ethnic groups of recent European origin, particularly those living on the edges of Negro neighborhoods; small town and rural little people worried over rioting, student violence, and Vietnam; well-to-do Birchers from suburbia; and racists wherever found. Money came in from many sources, much of it in small amounts, by mail or collected at his rallies, but reports that "fat cats" were helping out in his own section and westward were not verified.

Wallace offered the voters an anti-federal government, pro-state rights, and law-and-order package with racism underneath the wrapper. His major points included complete community control of public schools (federal aid would be acceptable if unaccompanied by desegregation guidelines), the repeal of open housing and voting rights legislation, the shunting of welfare to the private sector, reduction of foreign aid, and the preservation of law and order at all costs, with jail treatment for radical agitators, anarchists, and Communists, and the use of troops to patrol city streets to make them safe. He announced himself as opposed to gun control bills and derided or assailed "pointed heads" (intellectuals), beatniks, the Supreme Court, bureaucrats, school bussing, tax free foundations, "national liberal parties," pollsters, and national news media generally—with the *New York Times* given special treatment (it had called his movement "an evil phenomenon").

Using substantially the same speech with slight alterations and an occassional change of quips, the bantam battler "who told it like it is" often excelled his major party rivals as a crowd attraction. He also got more audience participation, both friendly and hostile.

He termed all disturbers "anarchists" and "Communists" and insisted that his altercations with hecklers gained him votes.

On the subject of Vietnam Wallace was a moderate hawk. He would end the war quickly either by negotiation or, if that failed, by letting the joint Chiefs of Staff take over. He blamed the old political parties for the war and the failure to bring it to an end. Although he carefully disclaimed any intention of using nuclear weapons, his choice of General LeMay to run with him proved embarrassing. In accepting the nomination, the former Air Force Chief of Staff repeated his long-held view that he would favor using such weapons if necessary although he was careful to state that he did not believe the Vietnam situation required such drastic action.

The major party candidates for Vice President were comparatively unknown outside their home states at the time of their nominations, but they were not long in developing contrasting images. Agnew, as Maryland's governor, had affronted Negro civil rights leaders, and his blunt law-and-order campaign speeches did nothing to mollify them. He was only following Nixon's lead in trying to counteract the Wallace pull. But his forthrightness and inexperience in national politics led him to make loose statements in his extemporaneous remarks that had to be explained away or retracted, to the embarrassment of the Nixon high command. Among them were his comment that Humphrey was "soft on Communism," his casual use of the belittling terms "Jap" and "Polack" for citizens of Japanese and Polish origin, and his sharp criticisms of the Special Advisory Commission on Civil Disorders. But his propensity to put his foot in his mouth was offset to a degree by the evident fact that he was a man who spoke his honest convictions in language the voters could understand.

Senator Muskie was the surprise of the campaign. He spoke with tolerance and restraint, insisted that law and order would mean little without justice, and praised the McCarthy youth for their involvement in politics. He respected their right to dissent but warned them that they could not expect instant results. He answered hecklers rationally and without heat and, on several occasions, invited them to share the platform with him to present their views. He urged Polish audiences to recall their own past and to reject those who clothed discrimination and prejudice with law-and-order appeals. Better informed and more experienced in the national arena than Agnew, he was a campaign asset and a good balance wheel for his more voluble, more outgoing chief. His height and craggy features were in the Lincoln mold and added to his crowd appeal.

Dissatisfaction on the left did not jell into a party for lack of a national candidate. When McCarthy refused to let his name be used, some of his following decided to organize a New Democratic Coalition to back local peace candidates and work to get control of Democratic state organizations for future battles, while sitting out the Presidential election. Other groups of dissatisfied leftists called themselves the New Party but solved the candidate problem by accepting black splinter party nominations or voting for McCarthy without his consent.

A Peace and Freedom party, at a national convention in August, nominated extremist Black Power author Eldridge Cleaver of California as its Presidential candidate. A more moderate faction backed Dick Gregory, well-known entertainer, who ran as a Freedom and Peace and New Party choice in five states, mostly in the East. Cleaver, a Black Panther leader in California, drew most of his support in that state.

The older minor parties, the Prohibition, Socialist Labor, and Socialist Workers, also offered candidates as usual, and a woman, Mrs. Charlene Mitchell, ran as a Communist candidate in Minnesota and Washington; she was the first Communist Presidential candidate since 1940. Some overlapping of indorsements by splinter parties and some ballot write-in candidates added to the complexity of tabulating minor party votes.

Unlike the anti-Goldwater line-up of 1964, the press was largely pro-Republican in 1968, as it had been in the Roosevelt–Truman years. The Republican Goldwater defectors returned to their old faith. The Scripps–Howard newspaper chain represented the most significant shift from its 1964 policy when it declared for Nixon. The more liberal independent papers inclined toward Humphrey, with the *New York Times* his outstanding supporter. Most striking was the lack of enthusiasm for either of the major party candidates and the almost universal hostility toward Wallace. But newspaper editorial indorsements carried little weight compared with the direct appeal of candidates through television.

The closing session of the Ninetieth Congress had campaign repercussions. A virtual filibuster prevented action on President Johnson's nomination of Justice Abe Fortas to succeed Chief Justice Earl Warren, who had offered to resign. Conservative dislike of the

Warren Court and Republican arguments, supported by Nixon, that a lame-duck President should leave such an important vacancy to be filled by his successor seemed to account for the rejection by non-action of Fortas.

The Senate also refused to act on a House measure to suspend the provision of the Communications Act that required equal treatment of all candidates by the television networks. This would have permitted the three candidates to debate before a nationwide audience, like the Kennedy-Nixon confrontation of 1960. It was Senator Dirksen who prevented action on the proposal. Nixon felt that he had nothing to gain in a triangular free-for-all and did not relish getting involved in a law-and-order melee with Wallace which would sharpen the line between them.

Republicans answered Humphrey's charge that Nixon was afraid of a duplication of the Kennedy-Nixon affair of 1960 by pointing to Johnson's failure to take on Goldwater four years earlier and Humphrey's refusal to lock horns with McCarthy during the recent Democratic primary battles. The Democratic candidate offered to share with his rivals an hour of Sunday evening prime time but Nixon ignored the invitation, although Wallace was willing. Humphrey then used the hour, on October 20, for a program of his own. In his later speeches, he referred to Nixon as "Richard the Chicken Hearted." All three candidates made final television appearances on election eve, Humphrey and Nixon in live question-and-answer sessions, Wallace with a taped speech.

A Hairline Decision

Last minute poll predictions of a close election were borne out by early returns on November 5. Humphrey was running surprisingly well in the East and was in a close battle for the Middle West. Nixon was sweeping the upper South and most of the trans-Mississippi West. Not until shortly before noon on Wednesday, when three large doubtful states, California, Ohio, and Illinois, were accredited to Nixon, was it certain that he had won.

Nixon carried Tennessee, Kentucky, Virginia, the Carolinas, and Florida in the South, the West except for Texas, Washington, and Hawaii, and the Middle West except for Michigan and Minnesota. In the East, New Hampshire, Vermont, New Jersey, and Delaware were the only Republican states. The rest of that section plus West

Virginia, Maryland, and the District of Columbia constituted a contiguous Humphrey electoral bloc. Humphrey and Muskie had carried their home states; Nixon and Agnew had lost theirs. Wallace had only the 1964 Goldwater South—Georgia, Alabama, Mississippi, and Louisiana, with Arkansas instead of South Carolina.

Nixon received 301 electoral votes, Humphrey 191, and Wallace 46. One North Carolina Nixon elector defected to Wallace. The final tabulation of the popular votes gave Nixon 31,770,237 (43.4 per cent), Humphrey 31,270,533 (42.72 per cent), Wallace 9,897,141 (13.53 per cent), others 239,910 (.35 per cent).[3] The American Independent candidate had received the largest vote ever cast for a third party choice, and only Theodore Roosevelt in 1912 and LaFollette in 1924 had greater percentages of the popular votes.

The closeness of the contest after the landslide predictions of early autumn caught political pundits and commentators by surprise. The late shiftings, as shown by the final polls, had given them no time to attempt new diagnoses. Most of the post-mortems offered several explanations for the hairline outcome: the exertions of labor leaders to keep blue-collar admirers of Wallace in the Democratic fold; the courageous battle Humphrey had waged against apparently overwhelming odds; the failure of Nixon to debate with Humphrey; Agnew's slips; the unexpected popular appeal of Muskie; and President Johnson's last minute announcement of a bombing halt which may have helped bring dove holdouts into line for Humphrey. It is also to be remembered that the fires of party insurgency tend to abate with the approach of November, the more so if the alternatives are unattractive. And the decrepit old Roosevelt coalition of interest groups had more vitality than the experts suspected.

If Nixon's strategy did not secure the mandate he wanted, at least it had paid off in giving him an electoral majority. The nomination of Agnew and the support of Strom Thurmond had saved the Carolinas and the upper South from Wallace. Nixon's exploiting of the law-and-order theme, his avoidance of a Vietnam commitment, and his emphasis on administration failings, domestic and foreign,

[3] Minor party candidates received the following votes: Hennings Blomen, Socialist Labor, 52,588; Fred Halstead, Socialist Worker, 41,300; Dick Gregory, New Party and Freedom and Peace, 47,097; Eldridge Cleaver, Peace and Freedom, 36,385; E. Harold Munn, Sr., Prohibition, 14,519; Charlene Mitchell, Communist, 1,075. Although not a candidate, Eugene McCarthy received 25,858 votes in five states. Write-in votes for other candidates totalled 19,608 and for the New Party without candidates 1,480.

and the need for a change kept the party unified and worked well enough outside the East.

In the Congressional races, the voters seemed to have resolved their perplexities by voting for familiar names. Incumbents were generally successful, regardless of party, and Democratic majorities held up. The Republicans netted only four more seats in the House of Representatives and five in the Senate. The new line-up in the House was 243 Democrats and 192 Republicans; in the Senate, 58 and 42. These results did not reflect as much of a swing to the right as the Presidential vote seemed to indicate. In the state elections the Republicans did somewhat better. With victories in thirteen of twenty-one governorship contests, they now had control of the statehouses in thirty-one states, although Agnew's resignation returned Maryland to the Democrats.

In the South the spread of the Republican party and the intransigent racism of Wallace's American Independent party had created the incongruity of a three-party system in national elections and a two-party line-up at the lower levels. Many Democratic candidates for state and local offices indorsed Wallace or came to terms in some fashion with his supporters to save themselves. If he and his following continued to dominate the old cotton South, it seemed fated to remain a racist enclave with its own type of politics.

From all quarters came a demand for an end to the old electoral system which, for a few hours on election night, held over the country the danger of a constitutional crisis and an interregnum that could possibly end with a subversion of the popular will. The nation might not be so fortunate next time.

President and Mrs. Johnson did their part to make the transfer of authority and responsibility to the new administration one of the smoothest on record for a party change. With the books closed on the Johnson years, commentating journalists, donning the garb of Clio, and impatient historians, in their concern for posterity and profit, were offering their ratings of the proud controversial Texan. The most objective felt that Johnson's consensus had foundered on Vietnam; although he had been remarkably successful in the field of domestic legislation, he had contributed to his difficulties with the press and public by a deviousness and lack of candor (the "credibility gap"), and excessive personal vanity and a display of quirks of temperament and temper had further flawed his Presidential image.

Not to be minimized is the hard fact that from the moment of his accession to the Presidency, Johnson had had to contend with a Kennedy myth and a Kennedy cult, too ready to downgrade his performance. Yet, in the company of the activist reforming Presidents, he might well rate a place in the front row.

Selective Bibliography

The following titles do not constitute a bibliography of materials consulted in the writing of this book, but are rather intended to assist the interested reader in exploring further. A reasonably comprehensive bibliography of books on past politics would require a large volume in itself.

Space limitations have ruled out general American histories; most of the numerous studies of regional and state politics; all but a representative group of biographies, autobiographies, and journals; books of a contemporary rather than historical interest; commentaries on government and political theory; and campaign lives and other propaganda publications.

The alphabetical arrangement used in the two preceding editions of this book has been replaced in this edition by a more usable grouping of titles under six major headings. The biographical section, it should be emphasized, is intended to be representative of the many individuals who played significant roles in influencing the course of national politics, either in public capacities or behind the scenes. Multivolume lives and the collected works of eminent figures have been ruled out, as well as biographies of statesmen whose careers were on the periphery of politics or who were drawn in only briefly.

For readers who wish to delve more deeply into the subject of this volume, the books listed here should be helpful.

I. General Accounts and Reference Works

American Heritage History of the Presidency, The. New York, 1968.

American Heritage Pictorial History of the Presidents of the United States, The. 2 vols., New York, 1968.

BAIN, RICHARD C., *Convention Decisions and Voting Records.* Washington, D.C., 1960.

BINKLEY, WILFRED E., *American Political Parties: Their Natural History.* New York, 1947.

BURNHAM, W. DEAN, *Presidential Ballots, 1836–1892.* Baltimore, 1955.

BURNS, JAMES M., *The Deadlock of Democracy: Four-Party Politics in America.* Englewood Cliffs, N.J., 1963.

CHAMBERS, WILLIAM N. and BURNHAM, WALTER D., eds., *The American Party Systems: Stages of Political Development.* New York, 1967.

Congressional Quarterly Service. Various publications on politics and government, especially semi-annual *Guide*. Washington, D.C.

DAVID, PAUL T., GOLDMAN, RALPH M., and BAIN, RICHARD C., *The Politics of National Party Conventions*. Washington, D.C., 1960.

DAVIS, JAMES W., *Presidential Primaries: Road to the White House*. New York, 1967.

EATON, HERBERT, *Presidential Timber: A History of Nominating Conventions, 1868–1960*. New York, 1964.

EWING, CORTEZ A. M., *Presidential Elections: From Abraham Lincoln to Franklin D. Roosevelt*. Norman, Okla., 1940.

FORD, HENRY JONES, *The Rise and Growth of American Politics*. New York, 1898.

KENT, FRANK R., *The Democratic Party: A History*. New York, 1928.

LORANT, STEFAN, *The Presidency: A Pictorial History of Presidential Elections, from Washington to Truman*. New York, 1951.

———, *The Glorious Burden: The American Presidency*. New York, 1968.

MCKEE, THOMAS H., *The National Conventions and Platforms of All Political Parties, 1789–1905*. Baltimore, 1906.

MAYER, GEORGE H., *The Republican Party, 1854–1964*. New York, 1964.

MINOR, HENRY A., *The Story of the Democratic Party*. New York, 1928.

MOOS, MALCOLM, *The Republicans: A History of Their Party*. New York, 1956.

MYERS, WILLIAM STARR, *The Republican Party: A History*. New York, 1931.

NICHOLS, ROY F., *The Invention of American Political Parties*. New York, 1967.

PETERSEN, SVEND, *A Statistical History of the American Presidential Elections*. New York, 1963.

POMPER, GERALD, *Nominating the President: The Politics of Convention Choice*. Evanston, Ill., 1963.

PORTER, KIRK H., and JOHNSON, DONALD BRUCE, eds., *National Party Platforms, 1840–1964*. Urbana, Ill., 1966. Supplement, 1968.

ROBINSON, EDGAR E., *The Evolution of American Political Parties*. New York, 1924.

———, *The Presidential Vote, 1896–1932*. Stanford University, Calif., 1934.

———, *They Voted for Roosevelt*. Stanford University, Calif., 1947.

SCAMMON, RICHARD, compiler, *America at the Polls* (covers 1920–1964). Pittsburgh, 1965.

STANWOOD, EDWARD, *A History of the Presidency*. 2 vols., Boston, 1916.

STODDARD, HENRY L., *Presidential Sweepstakes: The Story of Political Conventions and Campaigns*. New York, 1948.

WOODBURN, JAMES A., *American Politics: Political Parties and Party Problems in the United States.* New York, 1914.

II. Histories of Conventions, Campaigns, Elections

BAGBY, WESLEY M., *The Road to Normalcy: The Presidential Campaign and Election of 1920.* Baltimore, 1962.

BRYAN, WILLIAM J., *The First Battle: A Story of the Campaign of 1896.* Chicago, 1896.

CHESTER, LEWIS, HODGSON, GODFREY, and PAGE, BRUCE, *An American Melodrama: The Presidential Campaign of 1968.* New York, 1969.

CLANCY, HERBERT J., *The Presidential Election of 1880.* Chicago, 1958.

COLEMAN, CHARLES H., *The Election of 1868: The Democratic Effort to Regain Control.* New York, 1933.

CRENSHAW, OLLINGER, *The Slave States in the Presidential Election of 1860.* Baltimore, 1945.

CUMMINGS, MILTON C., JR., ed., *The National Election of 1964.* Washington, D.C., 1966.

DAVID, PAUL T., ed., *The Presidential Election and Transition of 1960–1961.* Washington, D.C., 1961.

DONAHOE, BERNARD F., *Private Plans and Public Dangers: The Story of F. D. R.'s Third Nomination.* Notre Dame, Ind., 1965.

FITE, E. D. *The Presidential Campaign of 1860.* New York, 1911.

GAMMON, SAMUEL R., JR., *The Presidential Campaign of 1832.* Baltimore, 1922.

GLAD, PAUL W., *McKinley, Bryan, and the People.* Philadelphia, 1964.

GUNDERSON, ROBERT G., *The Log-Cabin Campaign.* Lexington, 1957.

HALSTEAD, MURAT, *Three against Lincoln: Murat Halstead and the Caucuses of 1860.* Ed. by William B. Hesseltine. Baton Rouge, 1960.

HAWORTH, P. L., *The Hayes-Tilden Disputed Presidential Election of 1876.* Cleveland, 1906.

JONES, STANLEY C., *The Presidential Election of 1896.* Madison, Wis., 1964.

KNOLES, GEORGE H., *The Presidential Campaign and Election of 1892.* Stanford University, Calif., 1942.

LUTHIN, REINHARD, *The First Lincoln Campaign.* Cambridge, Mass., 1944.

MACKAY, KENNETH C., *The Progressive Movement of 1924.* New York, 1947.

MOORE, EDMUND A., *A Catholic Runs for President: The Campaign of 1928.* New York, 1956.

NICHOLS, ROY F., *The Democratic Machine, 1850–1854.* New York, 1923.

PARMET, HERBERT S., and HECHT, MARIE B., *Never Again: A President Runs for a Third Term.* New York, 1968.

PEEL, ROY V., and DONNELLY, THOMAS C., *The 1928 Campaign.* New York, 1931.

———, *The 1932 Campaign.* New York, 1935.

REMINI, ROBERT V., *The Election of Andrew Jackson.* Philadelphia, 1963.

ROSS, IRWIN, *The Loneliest Campaign: The Truman Victory of 1948.* New York, 1968.

THOMAS, H. C., *The Return of the Democratic Party to Power in 1884.* New York, 1919.

THOMSON, CHARLES A. H., and SHATTUCK, FRANCIS M., *The 1956 Presidential Campaign.* Washington, D.C., 1960.

WARREN, SIDNEY, *Battle for The Presidency* (ten elections). Philadelphia, 1968.

WESTON, FLORENCE, *The Presidential Election of 1828.* Washington, D.C., 1939.

WHITE, THEODORE H., *The Making of the President, 1960.* New York, 1961.

———, *The Making of the President, 1964.* New York, 1965.

———, *The Making of the President, 1968.* New York, 1969.

ZORNOW, WILLIAM F., *Lincoln and The Party Divided.* Norman, Okla., 1954.

III. Books on Periods and Other Special Aspects of Party History

BEARD, CHARLES A., *Economic Origins of Jeffersonian Democracy.* New York, 1915.

BOWERS, CLAUDE G., *Jefferson and Hamilton: The Struggle for Democracy in America.* Boston, 1925.

———, *Party Battles of the Jackson Period.* Boston, 1922.

———, *The Tragic Era: The Revolution after Lincoln.* Boston, 1929.

CARMAN, H. J. and LUTHIN, R. H., *Lincoln and the Patronage.* New York, 1943.

CARROLL, E. MALCOLM, *Origins of the Whig Party.* Durham, N.C., 1925.

CHAMBERS, WILLIAM N., *Political Parties in a New Nation: The American Experience, 1776–1809.* New York, 1963.

CHARLES, JOSEPH, *Origins of the American Party System.* Williamsburg, 1956.

COLE, ARTHUR C., *The Whig Party in the South.* Washington, 1914.

CRANDALL, A. W., *The Early History of the Republican Party.* Boston, 1930.

CUNNINGHAM, NOBLE E., JR., *The Jeffersonian Republicans: The Formation of Party Organization, 1789–1801*. Chapel Hill, N.C., 1958.

———, *The Jeffersonian Republicans in Power: Party Operations, 1801–1809*. Chapel Hill, N.C., 1967.

DAUER, MANNING J., *The Adams Federalists*. Baltimore, 1953.

DUNN, A. W., *From Harrison to Harding*. 2 vols., New York, 1922.

FISCHER, DAVID H., *The Revolution of American Conservatism: The Federalist Party in the Era of Jeffersonian Democracy*. New York, 1965.

HECHLER, KENNETH W., *Insurgency: Personalities and Politics of the Taft Era*. New York, 1940.

HOFSTADTER, RICHARD, *The Age of Reform: From Bryan to F. D. R.* New York, 1955.

HOLLINGSWORTH, J. ROGER, *The Whirligig of Politics: The Democracy of Cleveland and Bryan*. Chicago, 1963.

JOSEPHSON, MATTHEW, *The Politicos, 1865–1896*. New York, 1938.

———, *The President Makers . . . 1896–1919*. New York, 1940.

KEY, V. O., *Southern Politics in State and Nation*. New York, 1949.

KURTZ, STEPHEN G., *The Presidency of John Adams: The Collapse of Federalism, 1795–1800*. Philadelphia, 1957.

LAMBERT, OSCAR D., *Presidential Politics in the United States, 1841–1844*. Durham, N.C., 1936.

LIVERMORE, SHAW, *The Twilight of Federalism: The Disintegration of the Federalist Party, 1815–1830*. Princeton, N.J., 1962.

LYNCH, WILLIAM O., *Fifty Years of Party Warfare*. Indianapolis, 1931.

MCCORMICK, RICHARD P., *The Second American Party System*. Chapel Hill, N.C., 1966.

MERRILL, HORACE S., *Bourbon Democracy of the Middle West, 1865–1896*. Baton Rouge, 1953.

MORGAN, H. WAYNE, *From Hayes to McKinley: National Party Politics, 1877–1896*. Syracuse, N.Y., 1968.

PAUL, JAMES C. N., *Rift in the Democracy* (1841–1844). Philadelphia, 1951.

SCHLESINGER, ARTHUR M., JR., *The Age of Jackson*. Boston, 1945.

SIMMS, HENRY H., *A Decade of Sectional Controversy, 1851–1861*. Chapel Hill, N.C., 1942.

WOODWARD, C. VANN, *Reunion and Reaction: The Compromise of 1877 and the End of Reconstruction*. Boston, 1951.

IV. Third Parties and Insurgent Movements

DONOVAN, H. D. A., *The Barnburners*. New York, 1925.

DURDEN, ROBERT F., *The Climax of Populism: The Election of 1896*. Lexington, Ky., 1965.

Fine, Nathan, *Labor and Farmer Parties in the United States, 1828–1928*. New York, 1928.

Haynes, Fred E., *Third Party Movements Since the Civil War*. Iowa City, 1916.

Hicks, John D., *The Populist Revolt*. Minneapolis, 1931.

Hillquit, Morris, *History of Socialism in the United States*. New York, 1910.

Kipnis, Ira, *The American Socialist Movement, 1897–1912*. New York, 1952.

McCarthy, Charles, *The Anti-Masonic Party, 1827–1840* (American Historical Association Report, 1902, I). Washington, 1903.

McCoy, Donald R., *Angry Voices: Left-of-Center Politics in the New Deal Era*. Lawrence, Kan., 1958.

MacKay, Kenneth C., *The Progressive Movement of 1924*. New York, 1947.

Nash, Howard P., *Third Parties in American Politics*. Washington, 1959.

Nye, Russel B., *Midwestern Progressive Politics: A Historical Study of Its Origins and Development, 1870–1950*. East Lansing, Mich., 1951.

Overdyke, W. Darrell, *The Know-Nothing Party in the South*. Baton Rouge, 1950.

Quint, Howard H., *The Forging of American Socialism: Origins of the Modern Movement*. Columbia, S.C., 1953.

Ross, Earle D., *The Liberal Republican Movement*. New York, 1919.

Shannon, David A., *The Socialist Party of America: A History*. New York, 1955.

Smith, Theodore Clarke, *The Liberty and Free Soil Parties in the Northwest*. New York, 1897.

Stedman, Murray S. and Susan W., *Discontent at the Polls: A Study of Farmer and Labor Parties, 1827–1948*. New York, 1950.

V. Political Biographies, Autobiographies, and Personality Studies

Adams, Samuel Hopkins, *The Life and Times of Warren G. Harding*. Boston, 1939.

Alexander, De Alva S., *Four Famous New Yorkers: The Political Careers of Cleveland, Platt, Hill and Roosevelt*. New York, 1923.

Baringer, William, *Lincoln's Rise to Power*. Boston, 1937.

Barnard, Ellsworth, *Wendell Willkie, Fighter for Freedom*, Marquette, Mich., 1966.

Barnard, Harry, *Rutherford B. Hayes and His America*. Indianapolis, 1954.

Bemis, Samuel F., *John Quincy Adams and the Union*. New York, 1955.

BENTON, THOMAS H., *Thirty Years View*. 2 vols., New York, 1854–1856.
BLUM, JOHN M., *The Republican Roosevelt*. Cambridge, Mass., 1954.
———, *Woodrow Wilson and the Politics of Morality*. Boston, 1956.
BORDEN, MORTON, *The Federalism of James A. Bayard*. New York, 1955.
BOWERS, CLAUDE G., *Beveridge and the Progressive Era*. Boston, 1932.
BRODIE, FAWN, *Thaddeus Stevens, Scourge of the South*. New York, 1959.
BURNS, JAMES M., *Roosevelt, the Lion and the Fox*. New York, 1956.
CAPERS, GERALD M., *John C. Calhoun, Opportunist: A Reappraisal*. Gainesville, Fla., 1960.
———, *Stephen A. Douglas, Defender of the Union*. Boston, 1959.
CHAMBERS, WILLIAM N., *Old Bullion Benton*. Boston, 1956.
CHESSMAN, G. WALLACE, *Theodore Roosevelt and the Politics of Power*. Boston, 1968.
CHITWOOD, OLIVER P., *John Tyler, Champion of the Old South*. New York, 1939.
COIT, MARGARET L., *John C. Calhoun, American Portrait*. Boston, 1950.
COX, JAMES M., *Journey Through My Years*. New York, 1946.
CROLY, HERBERT D., *Marcus Alonzo Hanna*. New York, 1912.
CURRENT, RICHARD N., *Old Thad Stevens*. Madison, Wis., 1942.
EATON, CLEMENT, *Henry Clay and the Art of American Politics*. Boston, 1957.
ELLIS, ELMER, *Henry Moore Teller, Defender of the West*. Caldwell, Ida., 1941.
FARLEY, JAMES A., *Behind the Ballots: The Personal History of a Politician*. New York, 1938.
———, *Jim Farley's Story: The Roosevelt Years*. New York, 1948.
FLICK, ALEXANDER C., and Lobrano, G. S., *Samuel Jones Tilden*. New York, 1939.
FLYNN, EDWARD J., *You're the Boss*. New York, 1947.
GARRATY, JOHN A., *Henry Cabot Lodge: A Biography*. New York, 1953.
———, *Silas Wright*. New York, 1949.
GINGER, RAY, *The Bending Cross: A Biography of Eugene V. Debs*. New Brunswick, N. J., 1949.
GLAD, PAUL W., *The Trumpet Soundeth: William Jennings Bryan and His Democracy, 1896–1912*. Lincoln, Neb., 1960.
GOEBEL, DOROTHY B., *William Henry Harrison: A Political Biography*. Indianapolis, 1926.
GOLDWATER, BARRY, *The Conscience of A Conservative*. Shepherdsville, Ky., 1960.
GOSNELL, HAROLD F., *Champion Campaigner: Franklin D. Roosevelt*. New York, 1952.
HAMILTON, HOLLMAN, *Zachary Taylor: Soldier in the White House*. New York, 1951.

HANDLIN, OSCAR, *Al Smith and His America*. Boston, 1958.

HOWE, GEORGE F., *Chester A. Arthur*. New York, 1934.

ISELY, JETER A., *Horace Greeley and the Republican Party, 1853–1861*. Princeton, 1947.

JAMES, MARQUIS, *Andrew Jackson: Portrait of a President*. Indianapolis, 1937.

JOHNSON, DONALD BRUCE, *The Republican Party and Wendell Willkie*. Urbana, Ill., 1960.

KLEIN, PHILIP SHRIVER, *President James Buchanan: A Biography*. University Park, Pa., 1962.

LA FOLLETTE, BELLE CASE and FOLA, *Robert M. La Follette, June 14, 1855–June 18, 1925*. 2 vols., New York, 1953.

LOWITT, RICHARD, *George W. Norris: The Making of a Progressive*. Syracuse, 1963.

MCCORMAC, EUGENE I., *James K. Polk: A Political Biography*. Berkeley, Calif., 1922.

MCCOY, DONALD R., *Calvin Coolidge, the Quiet President*. New York, 1967.

MILTON, GEORGE FORT, *The Age of Hate: Andrew Johnson and the Radicals*. New York, 1930.

———,*The Eve of the Conflict: Stephen A. Douglas and the Needless War*. Boston, 1934.

MITCHELL, BROADUS, *Alexander Hamilton*. 2 vols., New York, 1957–1962.

MORGAN, H. WAYNE, *Eugene V. Debs: Socialist for President*. Syracuse, 1962.

———, *William McKinley and His America*. Syracuse, 1963.

MOWRY, GEORGE E., *Theodore Roosevelt and the Progressive Movement*. Madison, Wis., 1946.

MUZZEY, DAVID S., *James G. Blaine*. New York, 1934.

NEVINS, ALLAN, *Grover Cleveland*. New York, 1932.

NICHOLS, ROY F., *Franklin Pierce*. Philadelphia, 1931.

PARKS, JOSEPH H., *John Bell of Tennessee*. Baton Rouge, 1950.

PRINGLE, HENRY F., *The Life and Times of William Howard Taft*. 2 vols., New York, 1939.

———, *Theodore Roosevelt*. New York, 1931.

REMINI, ROBERT V., *Martin Van Buren and the Making of the Democratic Party*. New York, 1959.

RUSSELL, FRANCIS, *The Shadow of Blooming Grove: Warren G. Harding in His Times*. New York, 1968.

SCHACHNER, NATHAN, *Aaron Burr: A Biography*. New York, 1937.

———, *Alexander Hamilton*, New York, 1946.

SCHRIFTGIESSER, KARL, *The Gentleman from Massachusetts: Henry Cabot Lodge*. Boston, 1944.

SELLERS, CHARLES G., JR., *James K. Polk, Jacksonian: 1795–1843*. Princeton, N.J., 1957.

———, *James K. Polk, Continentalist: 1843–1846*. Princeton, N.J., 1966.

SHENTON, JAMES P., *Robert J. Walker: A Politician from Jackson to Lincoln*. New York, 1961.

SIEVERS, HARRY J., *Benjamin Harrison: Hoosier Statesman. From the Civil War to the White House, 1865–1888*. New York, 1959.

SIMKINS, FRANCIS B., *Pitchfork Ben Tillman, South Carolinian*. Baton Rouge, 1944.

SIMMS, HENRY H., *Life of Robert M. T. Hunter*. Richmond, 1935.

SMITH, ELBERT B., *Magnificent Missourian: The Life of Thomas Hart Benton*. Philadelphia, 1958.

SMITH, WILLIAM E., *The Francis Preston Blair Family in Politics*. 2 vols., New York, 1933.

SORENSON, THEODORE C., *Kennedy*. New York, 1965.

SPENCER, IVOR D., *The Victor and the Spoils: A Life of William L. Marcy*. Providence, 1959.

THOMAS, LATELY (ROBERT V. STEELE), *The First President Johnson*. New York, 1968.

TREFOUSSE, H. L., *Benjamin Franklin Wade*. New York, 1963.

TRUMAN, HARRY S., *Memoirs*. 2 vols. Garden City, N. Y., 1955–1956.

VAN DEUSEN, GLYNDON G., *The Life of Henry Clay*. Boston, 1937.

———, *William Henry Seward*. New York, 1967.

———, *Thurlow Weed, Wizard of the Lobby*. Boston, 1947.

VON ABELE, RUDOLPH, *Alexander H. Stephens: A Biography*. New York, 1946.

WALTERS, EVERETT, *Joseph Benson Foraker*. Columbus, Ohio, 1948.

WALTERS, RAYMOND, JR., *Albert Gallatin*. New York, 1957.

WEISENBURGER, FRANCIS P., *The Life of John McLean: A Politician on the United States Supreme Court*. Columbus, O., 1937.

WHITE, WILLIAM ALLEN, *Autobiography*. New York, 1946.

WHITE, WILLIAM S., *The Taft Story*. New York, 1954.

WOODWARD, C. VANN, *Tom Watson, Agrarian Rebel*. New York, 1938.

ZAHNISER, MARVIN R., *Charles Cotesworth Pinckney: Founding Father*. Chapel Hill, N. C., 1967.

VI. Miscellaneous

BROWN, W. BURLIE, *The People's Choice: The Presidential Image in the Campaign Biography*. Baton Rouge, 1960.

BAILEY, THOMAS A., *Presidential Greatness: The Image and the Man from George Washington to the Present*. New York, 1966.

BILLINGTON, RAY A., *The Protestant Crusade, 1800–1860: A Study of the Origins of American Nativism*. New York, 1938.

DEARING, MARY R., *Veterans in Politics: The Story of the G. A. R.* Baton Rouge, 1952.

DESANTIS, VINCENT P., *Republicans Face the Southern Question: The New Departure Years, 1877–1896*. Baltimore, 1959.

HAMMOND, BRAY, *Banks and Politics in America from the Revolution to the Civil War*. Princeton, N.J., 1957.

HATCH, LOUIS, C., *A History of the Vice-Presidency of the United States* (rev. and ed. Earl L. Shoup). Chicago, 1934.

HEARD, ALEXANDER, *The Costs of Democracy* (election expenses). Chapel Hill, 1960.

HESS, STEPHEN, and KAPLAN, WILLIAM, *The Ungentlemanly Art: A History of American Cartoons*. New York, 1968.

HYMAN, SIDNEY, *The American President*. New York, 1954.

NEVINS, ALLAN, and FRANK WEITENKAMPF, *A Century of Political Cartoons*. New York, 1944.

OVERACKER, LOUISE, *Presidential Campaign Funds*. Boston, 1946.

PEIRCE, NEAL R., *The People's President* (electoral college). New York, 1968.

POLLARD, JAMES E., *The Presidents and the Press*. New York, 1947.

SMITH, JAMES MORTON, *Freedom's Fetters: The Alien and Sedition Laws and American Civil Liberties*. Ithaca, N. Y. 1956.

STONE, IRVING, *They Also Ran*. New York, 1943.

WILLIAMSON, CHILTON, *American Suffrage from Property to Democracy, 1780–1860*. Princeton, N. J., 1960.

WILMERDING, LUCIUS, JR., *The Electoral College*. New Brunswick, N. J., 1958.

YOUNG, DONALD, *American Roulette: The History and Dilemma of the Vice Presidency*. New York, 1965.

Index

Acheson, D. G., 506
Adams, C. F., 140, 227-229, 241 n.
Adams, John, quoted, 6; elected Vice President, 16; writes essays, 26; re-elected in 1792, 27-28; elected President, 33-35; as President, 35-38; in election of 1800, 38-44; leaves Washington, 48
Adams, John Quincy, supports embargo, 71; Secretary of State, 75; in 1824 election, 79-80, 83-84; elected by House, 84-86; corrupt-bargain, 87-88; as President, 89-90; defeated, 91; member of House, 92
Adams, Samuel, 3, 4, 6, 7, 8, 11, 12
Adams, Sherman, 517, 524; resigns, 543
Agnew, Spiro, 595-596, 601, 604, 608, 611, 612
Aiken, J. W., 452
Albert, Carl, 576, 597
Alger, R. A., 279-280
Allen, H. J., 363-364
Allen, William, 136, 236, 240
Alliance for Progress, 565
Allison, W. B., 279
Altgeld, J. P., 318
America First party, 486
American Federation of Labor, 415, 453, 474, 539
American Independent party, 606-607, 611, 612. *See also* Wallace, George
American Labor party, 452, 471, 486
"American" party, 159-160, 164, 166, 173, 174, 176
American Republican party, 132
"American System," 78-79
Antifederalists, 11-12, 16, 24
Antimasons, 101-103, 105, 110, 111
Anti-Monopoly party, 296
Arthur, C. A., 251, 252, 256, 262-264
Atchison, David, 150-151
Ayres, W. A., 423
Bache, B. F., 31, 33, 40
Baker, Bobby, 579, 580
Baker, N. D., 367, 414, 436
Baker v. *Carr*, 566
Ball, J. H., 481-482, 489
Bank of the United States, first, 19, 64; second, 73-74, 103-104, 109
Bankhead, W. B., 466, 468
Banks, N. P., 160, 164
Barbour, P. P., 99
Barker, Wharton, 327
Barkley, A. W., in Democratic conventions, 437, 449, 466; Vice Presidential nominee, 499-500; in 1952 convention, 514-516
Barnett, Ross, 570
Barnum, W. H., 268, 282
Baruch, Bernard, 413
Bates, Edward, 179, 187
Bayard, J. A., 45-47, 51
Bayard, T. F., 221, 240, 256-257, 267-268
Bell, John, 176, 180-184
Bell, Theodore, 351
Benson, Allan L., 384
Benson, Ezra, 525, 526, 532, 534, 537, 544, 562
Benton, T. H., 109, 116, 128-129, 135, 141, 164
Berle, A. A., Jr., 439
Beveridge, A. J., 357, 359, 365, 370
Birney, J. G., 131-133
Black Panther party, 209
Black Power, 584, 596, 609
Blaine, J. G., Speaker, 221; corruption charges, 235; candidate, 1876, 237-239; candidate, 1880, 254-256; Secretary of State, 260-261; nominated for President, 264-265; in campaign of 1884, 269-274; declines to run again, 279-280; speaks for Harrison, 281; Secretary of State, 284, 287; at Republican convention, 1892, 287; role in 1892 campaign, 291

Blair, F. P., Jr., 193, 214, 216-217, 225, 228
Blair, F. P., Sr., edits *Globe*, 94, 97; and Van Buren, 128, 129; estranged from Polk, 135; and Free Soilers, 141; joins Republicans, 160; and Bates, 179; quoted, 203-204
Blair, James, 551
Blair, Montgomery, 187, 190, 193, 199-200
Bliss, C. N., 324, 342, 344, 384
Bliss, Ray C., 575, 593, 602
Boies, Horace, 289, 311 n.
Boggs, Hale, 598
Bond, Julian, 600
Borah, W. E., and Roosevelt, 365; in Republican conventions, 393, 410, 420-421, 447-448; opposes League of Nations, 390, 393; and Hoover, 420-421, 425-427, 430-431, 440
Bovay, A. E., 153
Bowles, Chester, 550
Bradley, J. P., 247-248
Breckinridge, J. C., 164, 175
Bricker, John W., 480-483, 486, 489, 512, 526, 544
Bristow, B. H., 235, 237-238
Brooke, Edward, 593
Brooks, Preston, 165
Broom, Jacob, 154
Browder, E. R., 452, 474, 488
Brown, B. Gratz, 196, 225, 228-229
Brown, Edmund G., 549, 568, 585
Brownell, Herbert, Jr., 487, 513, 524
Bryan, C. W., 367, 415
Bryan, W. J., silver leader, 307-308; first nomination, 309-312; campaign of 1896, 313-319; favors peace treaty, 1898, 324; second nomination, 325-328; campaign of 1900, 329-332; in 1904 convention, 339-342; third nomination, 350-352; campaign of 1908; 352-355; in 1912 convention, 365-369; Secretary of State, 376; in 1924, 414; death, 417
Bryant, Paul, 600
Bryant, W. C., 195, 229, 237
Buchanan, James, Presidential aspirant, 128, 137, 145; nominated, 163-164; campaign of 1856, 163-167; as President, 168-173, 180-184
Buckner, S. B., 312
Bundy, McGeorge, 565
Burch, Dean, 575
Burleson, A. S., 376
Burr, Aaron, elected to Senate, 24; considered for Vice President, 27; in election of 1796, 34-35; in election of 1800, 41-42, 44-47; in Federalist schemes, 54-55; duel with Hamilton, 55
Burton, T. E., 380, 410
Bush, Prescott, 534
Bushfield, H. J., 464
Butler, Ben, 197, 212, 221, 222, 235, 266-267, 271, 296
Butler, Paul, 535, 555
Butler, William M., 409-410, 416, 417, 418
Butler, William O., 137
Byrd, Harry, 436, 479, 484, 515, 519, 535 n., 571
Byrnes J. F., 485, 515, 519

Calhoun, J. C., War Hawk, 66; Secretary of War, 75; in 1824 election, 80, 83; reelected Vice President, 91; breaks with Jackson, 95-99; in Senate, 108, 109; supports Van Buren, 117; Secretary of State, 127-128; opposes compromise, 143
Cameron, Simon, 166, 179, 187, 197, 221
Cannon, F. J., 306
Cannon, James, Jr., 427
Cannon, Joseph, Speaker, 346, 350, 358
Carlisle, J. G., 266, 289, 312
Carlson, Frank, 595
Cary, S. F., 295
Case, Clifford, 578, 595
Cass, Lewis, 127-128, 137-138, 141-142, 145
Castro, Fidel, 546, 558, 568, 576
Caucus, Congressional, in 1796, 33; Federalist, 1800, 38; Republican, 1800, 42-43; policies, 51; Republican, 1804, 55-56; Republican, 1808, 59; War Hawks control, 1812, 68; Republican, 1816, 74; in 1820, 75; in 1824, 83
Chafin, Eugene W., 352, 373
Chambers, B. J., 296
Chandler, A. B., 530
Chandler, Z., 199, 221, 241-243
Chase, Salmon P., antislavery leader, 131, 140, 142, 147, 151; elected governor of Ohio, 158; Presidential

Chase, Salmon P. (*cont.*)
aspirant, 1860, 178; and Lincoln, 187, 193-194, 198-200; Presidential aspirant, 1868, 213-216
Chase, Samuel, 40, 52
Christensen, P. P., 400
Church, Frank, 549
Civil Rights Act of 1964, 572-573, 574, 579, 584, 586
Civil Rights Commission, 544
Civil service reform, Grant and, 223; in 1872 campaign, 225-226, 229; in 1876 campaign, 237, 239, 241; Hayes and, 241, 251-252; in 1880 campaign, 255, 257, 258; Pendleton Act, 263; in 1884 campaign, 264, 267; Cleveland and, 275-276; Harrison and, 284
Clark, Champ, 366-369, 402-403
Clark, Ramsey, 604
Clarkson, J. S., 284, 287, 304
Clay, Henry, War Hawk, 66; early career, 66-67; Speaker, 67, 75; American System, 78-79; in 1824 election, 79, 83; in House election, 84-88; in Adams administration, 89-90; nominated for President, 1832, 100-101; defeated, 104-105; compromises nullification, 108-109; anti-Jackson, 109; defeated by Harrison, 118-120; breaks with Harrison, 123; and Tyler, 124-125; Whig leader, 125; nominated for President, 1844, 129-130; in campaign of 1844, 130-133; opposes expansion, 137; defeated in Whig convention, 1848, 139; and 1850 Compromise, 143-144
Clayton, H. D., 351
Cleaver, Eldridge, 609
Clement, Frank, 529
Cleveland, Grover, elected governor, 264; in 1884 election, 265-274; as President, 275-277; in 1888 election, 278-283; in 1892 election, 288-292; supports Gold Democrats, 312; refuses to run again, 339
Clifford, Clark, 587-588
Clinton, De Witt, 59-60, 68-69, 81-82, 89, 90
Clinton, George, 11, 16, 24-25, 27-28, 55-56, 59-60
Cobb, Howell, 142, 165
Cockran, Bourke, 267, 289
Cockrell, F. M., 341
Cohen, B. V., 444
Cohn, Roy, 526
Colby, Bainbridge, 398, 414, 453
Colfax, Schuyler, 213, 229
Collins, Leroy, 549
Colonial period, politics of, 2-7
Committee for Industrial Organization (later, Congress), 453, 473-474, 479, 539
Communications Act, 581, 610
Communist party, 441 n., 452, 457 n., 477, 486, 500-501, 503, 609, 611 n.
Compromise of 1850, 143-145
Confederation period, 9-12
Conkling, Roscoe, Stalwart Republican, 221; Presidential aspirant, 237-238; opposes Hayes, 250-252; backs Grant, 253-256; in 1880, 258-259; and Garfield, 260-261; and Blaine, 269
The Conscience of a Conservative (Goldwater), 568
Constitution of United States, 10-14; movement for, 10-11; ratification of, 11-12; and parties, 12-14
Constitutional Union party, 176, 180-184
Conventions, national nominating, first, 98-99, 100-101, 102-103; origins of, 105-107; criticisms of, 517. *See also* Elections, Presidential
Cooke, Jay, 194, 234
Coolidge, Calvin, in 1920 Republican convention, 394-397; becomes President, 406; characterized, 407-408; policies, 408-409; nominated, 1924, 409-411; second term, 416-419
Cooper, Peter, 295
Copperheads, 191 n., 190-192, 199, 200-202
Corcoran, T. G., 444, 471
Cordiner, Ralph, 575
Cortelyou, G. B., 321, 338, 343-344
Corwin, Tom, 133, 137, 141
Coughlin, C. E., 451-452, 457, 474, 477
Cowdrey, R. H., 297
Cox, Archibald, F., 555
Cox, James M., 397-400, 400-403, 414
Coxey, J. S., 439
Crane, W. M., 357, 361, 381
Crawford, W. H., 24, 79, 82-84, 86, 89, 96
Crittenden, J. J., 176, 185
Crocker, W. H., 385

Crockett, Davy, 114
Cummings, Homer, 398
Cummins, A. B., 364, 365, 380
Curtin, A. G., 179, 228
Curtis, G. W., 178, 231, 258, 269, 282
Cushing, Caleb, 173, 175

Daley, Richard, 596-597, 600, 601, 602
Dallas, G. M., 104, 129
Daniels, Josephus, 376
Daugherty, H. M., 394-397, 404, 406, 408-409
Davenport, Russell, 462, 489
Davis, David, 179, 228-229, 231, 246-247, 294
Davis, Garret, 160
Davis, Henry Gassaway, 341
Davis, Jefferson, 143, 150, 173, 183
Davis, John W., 398, 415-417, 444-445, 453
Dawes, C. G., 304, 315, 321, 410-411, 420
Dayton, W. L., 162-163
DeBerry, Clinton, 581
Debs, Eugene V., 315, 318, 328-329, 373, 399
Democratic party, origins, 93-99. *See* Elections, Presidential, and names of chief figures for later history
Denby, Edwin, 409
Depew, C. M., 279
De Sapio, Carmine, 530
Dewey, George, 326
Dewey, Thomas E., 593; as aspirant, 460-464; as candidate, 480-483, 486-491, 495-498, 501-504; backs Eisenhower, 509, 511-513, 521, 533
Dickinson, D. S., 145, 150, 197
Dickinson, L. J., 433
Dillon, Douglas, 564
Dirksen, E. M., 511, 545, 571, 573, 575, 581, 593, 610
Dixiecrats, 500, 502-504
Dixon, J. M., 372
Docking, George, 550
Doheny, E. L., 408
Dolliver, J. P., 357, 365
Donelson, A. J., 94, 160
Donnelly, Ignatius, 295, 299, 327
Douglas, Paul, 585
Douglas, Stephen A., and Compromise of 1850, 143; Presidential aspirant, 145-146, 163-164; and Nebraska bill, 150-151, 154; and Buchanan, 170-171; debates with Lincoln, 171-172; nominated for President, 173-175; campaign, 180-184; supports Union, 185, 188
Douglas, W. O., 444, 485, 498-499
Dred Scott decision, 168-169
Dudley, W. W., 271, 281-283
Dulles, J. F., 487, 511, 524, 526, 540; death, 543

Earle, Thomas, 131
Eastland, James O., 539
Eaton, John H., 81, 94, 95-96, 98
Edmunds, G. F., 254-255, 264-265, 269
Eighteenth Amendment, 398, 400, 413-414, 420-421, 424-425, 427, 433, 437
Eisenhower, Dwight D., refuses to run, 495, 498; nominated, 509-513; in 1952 campaign, 517-523; as President, 524-528, 603; nominated, 533-535; in 1956 campaign, 535-542; in 1964 campaign, 573, 574; in 1968 campaign, 593; leadership, 543-546, 552, 553, 554
Elections, Congressional: (1789) 16; (1794) 32-33; (1810) 64-66; (1846) 136; (1854) 153-154, 157; (1858) 172-173; (1862) 190; (1866) 209; (1874) 235; (1882) 264; (1890) 286, 298-299; (1894) 301; (1910) 359; (1914) 378; (1918) 389; (1922) 405; (1926) 418; (1930) 431; (1934) 444-445; (1938) 459; (1942) 478; (1946) 494; (1950) 507; (1954) 526-527; (1960) 560-563; (1964) 582; (1966) 584, 586; (1968) 612
Elections, Presidential: (1789) 15-17; (1792) 26-28; (1796) 33-35; (1800) 38-39, 41-47; (1804) 55-56; (1808) 59-61; (1812) 68-69; (1816) 74-75; (1820) 75-76; (1824) 79-88; (1828) 89-91; (1832) 98-105; (1836) 111-113; (1840) 117-123; (1844) 127-134; (1848) 137-142; (1852) 145-148; (1856) 159-167; (1860) 173-184; (1864) 193-202; (1868) 211-218; (1872) 225-234; (1876) 236-249; (1880) 253-260; (1884) 264-274; (1888) 277-283; (1892) 286-292; (1896) 301-320; (1900) 324-332; (1904) 338-345; (1908) 347-355; (1912) 360-374; (1916) 379-

Elections (*cont.*)
388; (1920) 391-403; (1924) 409-417; (1928) 419-429; (1932) 433-442; (1936) 446-457; (1940) 460-476; (1944) 480-491; (1948) 495-505; (1952) 508-523; (1956) 527-542; (1960) 543-571; (1964) 572-585, 609; (1968) 586-611
Electoral Commission, 246-248
Electoral Count Act, 276
Elkins, S. B., 280, 335
Ellmaker, Amos, 103
Emancipation Proclamation, 190
English, W. H., 257
Evans, Daniel, 593
Evarts, W. M., 250
Everett, Edward, 176

Fairbanks, C. W., 338, 350, 364, 380
Fair Campaign Practices Committee, 581
Fall, A.B., 404, 408-409
Farley, James A., in 1932 campaign, 435-442; in 1936 campaign, 449-450, 453-457; as aspirant, 466-467; eulogy of, 577
Farmer Labor party (1920), 400; (1932), 439
Farmers' Alliance, 286, 298-300
Faubus, Orval, 544
Federalists, as supporters of Constitution, 11-12; in election of 1792, 26-28. *See also* Elections, Presidential (years are indicated), and chief figures
Felknor, Bruce L., 581
Fenno, John, 25-26, 33
Fenton, R. E., 212, 225
Fess, S. D., 420, 431
Field, S. J., 257
Fifteenth Amendment, 218
Fillmore, Millard, 133, 139, 143-145
Finch, Robert, 556, 596, 602
Fine, John S., 512
Finnegan, J. A., 530, 535
Fish, H., Secretary of State, 223
Fish, H., Congressman, 489, 491
Fitzgerald, John F., 547
Fitzpatrick, Benjamin, 175
Flynn, E. J., 470, 474
Fong, Hiram L., 575, 595
Foraker, J. B., 280, 287, 303, 305 n., 336, 349, 353
Ford, Gerald R., 593, 595
Fortas, Abe, 609-610
Fourteenth Amendment, 206, 209
Frankfurter, Felix, 444
Free Soil party, 140-142, 147-148, 152-153
Freedom and Peace party, 609
Frelinghuysen, Theodore, 130, 132
Frémont, J. C., 161-163, 164-167, 195-196, 200
Freneau, Philip, 25-26
Fugitive Slave Law, 143-144, 146-147, 169
Fulbright, William, 584
Fuller, A. T., 434

Gallatin, Albert, Republican leader, 41, 42, 45-46; Treasury head, 51; relations with Madison, 63-64, 69; named for Vice President, 82-83
Gannett, F. E., 464
Garfield, James A., in Congress, 221, 249; nominated for President, 254-256; in 1880 campaign, 258-260; and Conkling, 260-261; assassination, 262
Garfield, James R., 356, 358, 433
Garner, John N., 436, 438, 450, 465-467, 471
George, Henry, 282, 283, 297, 315
George, Walter F., 423, 459, 527
Gerry, Elbridge, 37, 68
Giddings, J. R., 140-141, 147, 151, 178
Giles, W. B., 51, 63
Gilhaus, August, 352
Gillam, Bernard, 270
Girdler, T. M., 460, 473, 474
Glavis, L. R., 358
Glynn, Martin, 383
Godkin, E. L., 224, 269, 282
Goff, G. D., 419
Gold Democrats, 312-313, 316, 319, 330
Goldberg, Arthur, 564
Goldfine, Bernard, 543
Goldwater, Barry M., 554, 555, 591, 593, 610, 611; as Senator, 545; as 1964 Presidential candidate, 573-575, 577-579, 579-580, 582-583; views of, 567, 568-569, 573, 579
Gompers, Samuel, 324, 354, 372
Gorman, A. P., 268, 272, 289, 301
Grady, T. F., 267
Graham, W. A., 145
Granger, Francis, 101, 113

Grant, Ulysses S., in 1864 convention, 197; and Johnson, 207, 212; nominated for President, 212; elected, 216-218; character, 222; policies, 223-224; second election, 231-233; second administration, 234-235; and third term, 236, 253-256; speaks for Garfield, 259
Gray, George, 339, 341 n., 350, 352
Gray, Isaac P., 278
Gray, James H., 600
Great Society, 577, 580, 586
Greeley, Horace, as editor, 144, 147, 153, 162, 171, 178-179, 185, 198; as aspirant, 226, 228-229, 230-234
Green, Duff, 91, 97
Green, Dwight H., 496
Greenback party, 271, 273, 295-296
Gregory, Dick, 609
Grenier, John, 575
Gresham, W. Q., 279-280, 300

Hagerty, J. C., 524, 525
Hale, J. P., 139-140, 147
Hall, L. W., 536, 552, 556, 595
Halleck, C. A., 464, 534, 545, 554
Hamilton, Alexander, in election of 1789, 16-17; measures, 18-19; ideas, 20-21; in newspaper war, 25-26; and Burr, 27, 42, 44-47, 55; and foreign policy, 30-32; in 1796 election, 33-35; and Adams, 36-39; and House election, 44-47; duel and death, 55
Hamilton, J. D. M., 447, 449, 454, 469
Hamlin, Hannibal, 180, 197
Hammett, W. H., 127
Hammond, Charles, 90
Hampton, Wade, 224, 250
Hancock, John, 11
Hancock, W. S., 214-215, 240, 257-260
Hanly, J. F., 384
Hanna, Mark, backs Sherman, 279; opposes Harrison, 287; and McKinley, 287, 291, 302-304; in 1896 Republican convention, 304-307; in 1896 campaign, 313-319; in Senate, 322; in 1900 convention and campaign, 324-332; and T. Roosevelt, 333, 336-337
Hannegan, E. A., 136
Hannegan, R. E., 483, 485, 486-487
Harbord, J. G., 434
Harding, Warren G., convention delegate, 364, 381; in 1920 Republican convention, 394-397; in campaign, 400-403; as President, 403-405; death, 406; corruption exposures, 408-409
Harman, Judson, 366-368
Harriman, E. H., 344, 353
Harriman, W. A. 514-516, 528-530, 545, 552
Harris, Fred, 589, 600
Harris, Lou, 555
Harrison, Benjamin, nominated for President, 279-280; campaign, 281-283; as President, 284-286; renominated, 286-287; defeated, 290-292
Harrison, Pat, 413, 414
Harrison, William Henry, Presidential aspirant, 112-113; nominated, 119-120; campaign, 120-123; as President, 123
Hartranft, J. F., 237, 238
Harvey, George, 366, 393, 395-396, 401
Harvey, W. H., 317, 439
Haskell, C. N., 353
Hass, Eric, 581
Hassaurek, Friedrich, 177
Hatfield, Mark, 555, 574, 595
Hay, John, 321
Hayes, Lucy W., 250
Hayes, Max, 400
Hayes, Rutherford B., nominated for President, 237-239; campaign, 241-243; disputed election, 243-246; elected President, 246-249; administration, 249-252
Hays, Will H., 396, 400, 404
Henderson, J. B., 253-254, 264
Hendricks, T. A., 213, 215, 240, 267-268, 276
Henry, Patrick, 6, 11, 16, 33
Herter, Christian A., 532, 534, 543
Hewitt, A. S., 242, 247-249, 266
Hickel, W. J., 595
"Higher law" Whigs, 147
Hill, David B., 278, 282, 288-289, 291, 309, 312, 327, 339-342
Hill, Lister, 467
Hilles, C. D., 372, 419-420
Hillman, Sidney, 479, 485, 487, 488
Hisgen, T. L., 352
Hiss, Alger, 506, 513, 515, 520
Hitchcock, F. H., 348, 352

Hitchcock, G. M., 423
Hoar, G. F., 254, 265, 324
Hobart, G. A., 307, 324
Hoffa, James, 543-544
Homestead policy, 140, 147, 152, 156, 161, 177, 181, 188
Homestead strike, 290
Hoover, Herbert, in 1920 Republican convention, 392, 395; Secretary of Commerce, 404; nominated for President, 419-422; campaign, 425-429; administration, 430-433; renominated, 433-434; defeated, 439-442; in later conventions, 463, 483, 496, 511, 533, 554
Hopkins, Harry, 443, 466, 468
House, E. M., 376, 377, 389-390
House election of Presidents: Jefferson, 44-46; J. Q. Adams, 84-86
Houston, Samuel, 160, 176
Howe, Louis, 435
Hughes, Charles E., Presidential aspirant, 349-350; nominated, 1916, 380-382; campaign, 384-388; Secretary of State, 404; speaks for Hoover, 425-426; as Chief Justice, 458
Hughes, R. J., 598
Hull, Cordell, 423, 443, 466
Humphrey, G. M., 524
Humphrey, H. H., Jr., 499, 529, 531; as LBJ's running mate, 577, 580-581; in 1964 election, 547, 548; as 1968 candidate, 589, 590, 599-602, 603, 604-606, 608, 609, 610
Hunter, R. M. T., 174
Hurja, Emil, 455

Ickes, Harold L., 443, 493
Independence party, 352
Independent Treasury, 114-117, 124, 135
Ingersoll, R. G. 239, 241, 273
Inouye, D. K., 597
Internal improvements, opposed by Monroe, 76; as sectional issue, 77-79; in 1824 election, 79-81; in 1828 election, 89-90; Maysville Road veto, 95; in 1832 election, 100, 101; in 1840 Democratic platform, 117

Jackson, Andrew, in 1824 election, 80-84; in House election, 84-86; charges corrupt bargain, 87-88; campaign slanders, 1828, 90-91; inauguration, 92-93; begins spoils system, 93-94; relies on Kitchen Cabinet, 94-95; vetoes Maysville Road bill, 95; and Eaton affair, 95-96; break with Calhoun, 96-98; renominated, 98-99; opposes U.S. Bank, 103-104, 109; reelected, 105; tariff and nullification, 108-109; achievements, 113; opposes Harrison, 121; and Polk, 128, 129
Jackson, Henry, 555
Jackson, Robert, H., 444
Jackson, Samuel K., 484
James, Arthur, H. 464
James, Ollie, 367, 383
Javits, Jacob, 567, 578
Jay, John, 8, 17, 27, 31-32, 42
Jefferson, Thomas, in Virginia assembly, 6; bargains with Hamilton, 18-19; philosophy of, 22-23; as politician, 22-24; opposes Federalists, 25-31; in election of 1796, 33-35; as Vice President, 39-41; in election of 1800-1801, 41-47; first term, 48-54; reelection, 55-56; second term, 56-61
Jenkins, Walter, 580
Jewell, Marshall, 235, 237-238
John Birch Society, 567, 574, 576, 607
Johnson, Andrew, 174, 197, 203-210, 213-215, 217
Johnson, Cave, 128
Johnson, Herschel V., 175
Johnson, Hiram, 370, 385-386, 390, 394, 397, 410, 440
Johnson, John A., 350, 352
Johnson, Lyndon B., 527; as Senate leader, 545; in 1960 Presidential race, 559-562; as Vice President, 566, 572; as President, 572-573, 583-585, 612-613; in 1964 Presidential race, 576-577, 580, 581; in 1968 campaign, 585, 593, 596-597, 601, 603, 605, 606, 609; withdrawal of, 589, 591, 597; and Kennedy myth, 613
Johnson, Mrs. Lyndon B., 560, 580, 612
Johnson, Richard M., 66, 112-113, 117, 123, 128
Johnston, William F., 144, 160, 162-163
Jones, Jesse H., 423, 424, 426, 491
Judiciary Act of 1801, 51-52

Judd, Walter, 554, 575

Kane, J. K., 132
Kansas-Nebraska Act, 151
Keating, Kenneth, 578
Kefauver, E., 513-516, 528-529, 531, 536, 548
Kendall, Amos, 94, 99
Kennedy, Edward, as Senator, 568; in 1968 campaign, 599-600, 604
Kennedy, John F., 531, 590, 601, 610, 613; as Senator, 544; in Presidential race, 547-564; and Nixon in TV debates, 556-558; election returns for, 561-563; as President, 564-571, 572; assassination of, 571; eulogy of, 577
Kennedy, Mrs. John F., 547, 565
Kennedy, Joseph P., 547
Kennedy, Mrs. Joseph P., 547
Kennedy, Robert F., 577, 585, 601; assassination of, 586, 590, 592; as Attorney General, 564, 570; and Hoffa investigation, 544; in JFK's presidential campaign, 547, 549, 555; in 1968 campaign, 587, 588, 589, 590; tribute to, 600
Kern, R. S., 484, 514, 516
Khrushchev, N., 545-546, 555
King, Leicester, 139
King, Martin Luther, 559, 600; assassination of, 587, 590
King, Preston, 136
King, Rufus, 24, 56, 60, 68-69, 74, 77
King, W. R., 146
Kitchel, Denison, 575
Klein, Herbert S., 602
Knight, Goodwin, 553
Knowland, W. F., 525, 533, 544
"Know-Nothing" party, 154-160, 166
Knox, Frank, 447, 449
Knox, Henry, 18, 37
Knox, P. C., 349, 360, 396
Kremer, George, 87
Kuchel, R. H., 567, 578
Ku-Klux Klan, 223, 412-414, 574, 576
Kyle, J. H., 299

Labor Reform party, 231-294-295
Labor's Nonpartisan League, 453
La Follette, R. M., progressive, 335, 349, 360-361; in 1912 Republican convention, 363-365; as aspirant 410, 415-417
La Guardia, F. H., 452, 471
Laird, Melvin, 574
Landon, A. M., 446-449, 453-457
Lane, Henry S., 160, 179
Lane, Joseph, 175, 183
Langdon, John, 68
Langworthy, H. M., 447
Lansing, Robert, 389-390
Larson, Arthur, 534
Lausche, F. J., 530
Law, George, 159
Lawrence, David, 551
League of Nations, 390, 393, 398, 401, 414
Lecompton Constitution, 170
Lee, Richard Henry, 8, 11
Leggett, William, 116
Lehman, H. H., 426, 440, 461
LeMay, Curtis, 607, 608
Lemke, William, 452, 457
Lenroot, Irvine, 397
Lewis, John L., 452, 473-474, 477
Lewis, Samuel, 131
Lewis, W. B., 81, 94, 96, 103, 135
Liberal party, 486
Liberal Republican movement, 224-234
Liberty League, 444, 453
Liberty party, 131-133, 139
Lincoln, Abraham, Vice Presidential aspirant, 162; seeks senatorship, 171-172; nominated for Presidency, 178-180; campaign of 1860, 180-184; develops policies, 186-188; and slavery, 189-190; and radicals, 193-194; renominated, 194-197; campaign, 198-202
Lindsay, John V., 595, 596
Livingston family, 5, 24-25
Lodge, Henry Cabot, 269, 285, 305, 338, 349-350, 382, 390, 393, 395-396, 410, 417
Lodge, Henry Cabot, Jr., 509, 513, 560; as Nixon's running mate, 555; in 1964 campaign, 573, 574, 575
Lodge Federal Elections bill, 285
Logan, John A., 189, 221, 253, 264-265
Long, Alexander, 201
Long, Huey P., 451
Lovejoy, Owen, 131
Loveless, Herschell C., 550
Lowden, F. O., 393-397, 420-421
Lowenstein, Allard K., 587

Lowndes, William, 66, 80
Luce, Clare Boothe, 483, 496

McAdoo, W. G., 368, 372, 397-398, 412-415, 438
MacArthur, Douglas, 480, 495-496, 506, 511
McCarthy, Eugene, 549; in 1964 campaign, 577; in 1968 campaign, 587-588, 589-590, 597, 599, 600, 601-602, 606, 609, 610
McCarthy, Joseph R., 500, 507, 518, 520, 525-526
McClellan, George B., 198-202
McCombs, W. F., 368, 372
McCormack, John, 530, 531, 566, 576
McCormick, Robert, 477, 498
McCormick, Vance, 384
McGlynn, Edward, 297
McGovern, F. E., 363
McGovern, George, 590; in 1968, 599, 600, 601, 606
McGrath, J. Howard, 501
McHenry, James, 33, 38
McIntyre, Francis Cardinal, 549
McKay, Douglas, 538
McKeldin, Theodore, 533
McKinley, William, and tariff, 285, 286; and 1892 convention, 287; and Hanna, 302-304; in 1896 convention, 304-307; in 1896 campaign, 313-315, 318-319; as President, 321-324; second nomination, 325; in 1900 campaign, 331-332; death, 33
McKinley Tariff Act, 285, 286
McLean, John, 89, 102-103, 112, 140, 161-162, 179
McLean, John R., 311
McNamara, Robert S., 564, 584, 587, 588, 603
McNary, Charles L., 446, 461, 465
McNary-Haugen Farm bill, 418, 420, 427
MacNider, Hanford, 434
McNutt, Paul V., 468
Mack, John E., 450
Mack, Norman E., 352
Macon, Nathaniel, 57, 58
Maddox, Lester G., 598, 599
Madison, James, on parties, 13; elected to Congress, 16; opposes Hamilton's measures, 18-19; in newspaper debates, 25, 31; Secretary of State, 51; elected President, 59-61; sketch of, 62-63; difficulties of, 63-64; renominated, 68; second election, 69; and War of 1812, 69-70, 72-74, 76
Mangum, W. P., 113
Manning, Daniel, 266, 268
Mansfield, "Mike," 566, 571
Marcy, W. L., 116, 134, 145
Marshall, George, 494, 496
Marshall, John, 37-38, 41, 52, 74
Marshall, Thomas R., 367, 369, 383
Martin, Joseph W., Jr., 463, 469, 482, 494, 496, 510, 533
Massey, Raymond, 583
Mellon, Andrew, 404, 411, 417, 418, 420
Meredith, E. R. 398
Meyner, R. B., 529, 530, 550
Michelson, Charles, 434, 439
Milbank, Jeremiah, 425, 440
Miller, William, 574 as Goldwater's running mate, 575, 578, 579, 581; in 1968 campaign, 591
Mills, Ogden, 433
Mitchell, Charlene, 609
Mitchell, John N., 602
Mitchell, Stephen A., 517
Moley, Raymond, 439, 444
Mondale, Walter F., 589
Mondell, F. W., 410
Monroe, James, 16, 58-60, 64, 74-76
Moore, Dan, 599, 600
Moore, E. H., 398
Moore, Ely, 115
Morey letter, 259
Morey letter, 259
Morgan, William, 101
Morgenthau, Henry, 372, 384, 387
Morris, Thomas, 131
Morse, Wayne, 522, 538, 548, 584
Morton, Levi P., 260, 280, 394
Morton, Oliver P., 221, 236-238
Morton, Thruston, 554, 556, 570, 574, 591
Moses, G. H., 420, 431
Mugwumps, 265, 269-274
Mulligan letters, 237, 269
Munn, E. Harold, Sr., 581
Munsey, Frank, 364, 372
Murchison letter, 283
Murdock, Victor, 358
Murphy, Charles, 367, 398
Muskie, Edmund S., 536; as Humphrey's running mate, 600, 601, 606, 608-609, 611

Napolitan, Joseph, 604
National Association for the Advancement of Colored People, 544
National Citizens for Johnson and Humphrey, 578
National Citizens Political Action Committee, 487
National Election Service, 583
National Mobilization Committee to End the War, 597
National Republican Party, 99 n., 100, 101, 103-105
National Silver party, 312
National Student Association, 587
National Union for Social Justice, 451
Native Americanism, 132, 154
Negro suffrage, 209, 211-212, 213, 218, 285
Negro militancy, 576, 584. *See also* Black Power
New Democratic Coalition, 609
New England, "courts of election," 2; radicals of, 8; becomes Federalist, 22; and the West, 53, 65; secession movement, 54; opposes embargo, 58; and War of 1812, 70-73; alteration of, 78
New Party, 609
Newspapers and periodicals, 5, 25-26, 31-33, 34, 40-41, 60, 107, 149, 171, 181, 216, 222, 224, 225, 228, 229, 230, 231, 241, 243, 258, 265, 269, 272, 276, 283, 316-318, 343, 347, 366, 394, 402, 415, 416, 428, 456, 475, 477, 480, 489, 498, 509, 609
Newton, Carroll, 556
Nicholson, A. O. P., 138
Nicholson, J. H., 45, 47, 58
Nixon, Richard M., 513, 520-521, 523-534, 538, 567; as Vice President, 544; in 1960 presidential race, 552-553, 556-561; at Republican Convention, 553-555; and Kennedy in TV debates, 556-558; election returns for, 561; defeated in California gubernatorial race, 568; in 1964, 570; in 1964 campaign, 578; as 1968 Presidential candidate, 573, 585, 591, 592-596, 602-604, 605, 608, 610-612
Nonpartisan League, 400
Non-Proliferation Treaty, 599, 603
Norris, G. W., 358, 418, 420, 426, 430-431, 438, 453, 471
"North Americans," 160, 162-163
Northwestern Alliance, 298
Nuclear Test Ban Treaty, 599
Nutt, Joseph R., 425, 440

O'Brien, Lawrence F., 555, 580, 590, 601, 604
O'Brien, Thomas C., 452
O'Conor, Charles, 230-231, 294-295
O'Donnell, Kenneth, 555, 580
"Ohio Idea," 211
Order of the Star-Spangled Banner, 155
Ostend Manifesto, 161
Otis, H. G., 69, 72
Otis, James, 3, 6

Palmer, A. Mitchell, 391, 397-398
Palmer, John M., 228, 312
Panics: 1837, 114; 1857, 172-173; 1873, 293; 1893, 292, 301; 1907, 347
Parker, Alton B., 339-345, 367
Parker, George F., 289
Parker, Joel, 240
Parker, John M., 382
Parties, political, 2-8, 9-14, 18-20, 24. *See also* Elections, Presidential, and names of parties
Pastore, John, 576
Payne, Henry B., 174, 257
Payne-Aldrich Act, 357
Peace Corps, 565, 599
Peace Democrats, 190-193, 199-201
Peale, Norman Vincent, 558, 559
Peffer, W. A., 299
Pendleton, G. H., 199, 211, 213-215, 263
Pennington, William, 173
Penrose, Boies, 361, 392, 394
Pension bills, 276, 281, 286
People's party, 299-301, 311-312, 316-317, 320, 327, 352
Percy, Charles, 553, 578, 585, 591
Perkins, Frances, 443
Perkins, G. W., 364, 372, 380, 382
Pettigrew, R. F., 331-332
Phillips, Channing, 599, 600
Phillips, Wendell, 195
Pickering, T., 33, 38, 54-55, 72
Pierce, Franklin, 146-148, 149-151, 155, 163
Pike, J. S., 169
Pinckney, C. C., 43, 56, 60

Pinckney, Charles, 43
Pinckney, Thomas, 33-35
Pittman, Key, 424
Platt, T. C., 258-259, 261, 279-280, 282, 284, 287, 304-305, 325, 333
Plumer, William, 53, 54, 67, 71, 75
Political Action Committee, 479, 485, 487, 488
Polk, James K., named for President, 128-129; campaign, 132-134; as President, 134-137; death, 142
Poor People's Campaign, 592-593
Populists. *See* People's party
Powell, A. C., Jr., 539, 550
Presidential Succession Act, 276
Progressive party (Bull Moose), organized, 365, 370-371; in 1912 campaign, 371-374; in 1914 election, 378, 380; in 1916, 381-383
Progressive party (1924), 415-417; (1952), 500-501, 503-504, 522 n.
Pugh, George E., 174
Pulitzer, Joseph, 241, 317, 335, 343

Quay, M. S., 279-283, 284, 286, 304, 325

Randall, S. J., 221, 257, 266-267, 277
Randolph, Edmund, 18, 33
Randolph, John, 51, 57-59, 67, 108
Raskob, John J., 426-427, 435, 436-437
Rayburn, Sam, 499, 515, 527, 530, 577; as Speaker, 545, 546, 560; backs Johnson, 549; death, 566
Raymond, Henry, 158, 198, 202, 207
Reagan, Ronald, 583; as Presidential aspirant, 585, 591, 594, 595
Reed, James A., 383, 423, 453, 471
Reed, Thomas B., 285, 287, 304, 323
Reid, Whitelaw, 241, 287
Reimer, Arthur E., 373
Republican party (antislavery), origins, 152-154; in 1855, 158-159; first national convention, 160-163; first campaign, 164-167; 1964 split in, 577-578, 582. *See also* Elections, Presidential and important figures
Republicans (Jeffersonian), origins of, 18-19, 22-25; in election of 1792, 26-28. *See also* Elections, Presidential and important figures
Resumption Act, 236, 237, 239, 241, 252
Resurrection City, U.S.A., 587
Reuther, Walter, 539
Revolution, American, 7-9
Rhodes, J. A., 585, 595
Rhyne, Charles, 556, 602
Ribicoff, Abraham, 600
Ritchie, Albert C., 436
Ritchie, Thomas, 122, 127
Rives, John C., 97
Rives, William C., 115
Robertson, W. H., 261
Robinson, J. R., 424-425, 449
Rockefeller, J. D., 259
Rockefeller, Nelson M., 567; elected governor of New York, 545; as Nixon rival, 552, 553; reelected governor, 568; and Goldwater, 569; in 1964 Presidential race, 573, 574, 575, 578, 581; in 1968 Presidential race, 585, 591-592, 594, 595
Rockefeller, Winthrop, 595
Rogers, Edward A., 556
Romney, George, 568, 570; in 1964 Presidential race, 574, 575, 578; in 1968 Presidential race, 582, 585, 590-591, 595, 596
Roosevelt, F. D., named for Vice President, 399; nominates Governor Smith, 413, 424; governor of New York, 428, 431; nominated for President, 435-438; 1932 campaign, 439-442; first administration, 442-446; second nomination, 449-450; 1936 campaign, 453-457; second administration, 458-460; third nomination, 465-468; 1940 campaign, 470-476; wartime policies, 477-479; fourth nomination, 483-486; 1944 campaign, 486-491; final acts, 491
Roosevelt, T., and Blaine, 269; on civil service commission, 284; in 1896 campaign, 318; nominated for Vice President, 325; in 1900 campaign, 331; becomes President, 333; analyzed, 334-335; policies, 335-336; and Hanna, 336-337; renominated, 338; 1904 campaign, 342-345, second administration, 345-347; backs Taft, 348-350; opposes Taft, 358-360; 1912 Republic convention, 360; 1912 Republican convention, 370-371; in 1912 campaign, 371-374; criticizes Wilson, 379, 389; ends Progressive party, 380-383; in 1916, 385-386; death, 389

Root, Elihu, 338, 347, 363, 380-382
Rosenman, S. I., 439
Rusk, Dean, 564, 584
Russell, Richard, 500, 514, 516, 571
Ryan, Elmer J., 467

Sackville-West, Sir Lionel, 283
St. John, John P., 271, 273
"St. Tammany Society," 41-42
Salinger, Pierre, 555
Schine, G. David, 526
Schlesinger, Arthur, Jr., 565
Schurz, Carl, 177, 181, 225-229, 239, 241, 250, 251, 258, 266, 269, 324, 330
Scott, Hugh, 574, 578
Scott, Winfield, 119, 138-139, 145, 146-148
Scranton, William, 568, 585, 602; in 1964 Presidential race, 573, 574, 575, 578, 581
Sergeant, John, 101
Sewall, Arthur, 311, 317
Seward, W. H., favors Antimasons, 101, 103; in 1848 election, 141; and Taylor, 143; and Clay's compromise, 144; supports Scott, 145-147; joins Republicans, 158-159, 161; on Dred Scott decision, 178-180; in 1860 campaign, 181-182; Secretary of State, 186-187; radicals oppose, 193; and Johnson, 197, 207
Seymour, Horatio, 190, 213-218
"Share the Wealth" movement, 451
Sheldon, G. R., 353, 372
Sherman, James S., 350, 374 n.
Sherman, John, 173, 194, 250, 252, 254-256, 264-265, 279-280, 322
Sherman Silver Purchase Act, 285
Sinclair, Harry F., 408
Slemp, C. Bascom, 408
Smith, Alfred E., 398
Smith, Caleb, 179, 187
Smith, G. L. K., 451-452, 477, 486
Smith, Gerrit, 139 n., 151, 164
Smith, Jess, 406
Smith, Margaret Chase, 573, 575
Smith, Robert, 63-64
Smith, Samuel, 47, 63
Smith, William, 113
Smith, William Henry, 239, 248-249
Smoot, Reed, 361, 420, 441
Smoot-Hawley Tariff, 430
Snell, Bertrand H., 433
Social Democratic party, 328-329. *See also* Socialist party
Social Security Act, 454
Socialist Labor party, 295, 328, 352, 373, 374, 384, 399, 428 n., 581, 609
Socialist party, 328-329, 344 n., 352, 373, 374, 384, 399, 415, 425, 441, 474, 486, 490 n., 504 n., 522 n.
Socialist Workers party, 581, 609
"Soft-shells" (New York), 150, 163
Soldier voting, 479, 490
Sorenson, Theodore C., 555
Southern Alliance, 298-299
Spalding, R. P., 162
Spanish-American War, 323-324
Sparkman, J. J., 517
Special Advisory Commission on Civil Disorders, 608
Spoils system, under Jackson, 93-94, 107. *See also* Presidents
Sprague, Kate Chase, 194, 215
Sproul, William, 394
Stalwarts (Republican faction), 250, 253, 260-261, 262, 263
Stans, Maurice, 602
Stanton, Edwin M., 187, 207, 210
Stassen, H. E., 462, 480-482, 495-498, 509, 512, 532-534, 573, 595
Sterns, F. W., 408
Steiwer, Frederick, 447
Stephens, Alexander, 134, 137, 143, 146
Stevens, Robert T., 526
Stevens, Thaddeus, 103, 110, 166, 205-206, 209-210, 211
Stevenson, Adlai E., Vice President, 289, 327
Stevenson, Adlai E., Presidential candidate, 577, 588; in 1952 convention, 514-517; in campaign, 517-523; in 1956 convention, 528-531; in campaign, 536-542, 548, 549, 564; in Presidential race, 547, 548, 549, 550
Stimson, Henry L., 359
Stockton, Robert, 159
Stone, Harlan F., 409
Strauss, Lewis, 545
Sullivan, Roger, 340, 369, 375
Summerfield, A. E., 512, 517, 524
Sumner, Charles, 140, 147, 151, 164-165, 193, 197, 204-205, 209, 220, 232
Symington, Stuart, 530, 547, 550

Taft, Charles P., 348
Taft-Hartley Act, 576, 584
Taft, Robert, 578
Taft, Robert A., seeks Presidency, 1940, 460, 464-465; Senate Leader, 494; seeks Presidency, 1948, 495-498; reelected Senator, 507; loses Presidential nomination, 508-513; and Eisenhower, 518, 521, 525, 552
Taft, William Howard, nominated for President, 348-350; in campaign, 352-355; as President, 356-360; 1912 struggle, 360-365; in campaign, 372-374; favors League of Nations, 401; as Chief Justice, 409, 419
Taggart, Thomas, 342, 375, 398
Tallmadge, N. P., 115
Tammany Tweed Ring, 221, 240; opposes Cleveland, 266-267, 271, 282, 289; supports Bryan, 330; in 1912 convention, 367-368; Al Smith and, 412, 422-423; F. D. Roosevelt and, 435, 436; backs Harriman, 530
Taney, Roger B., 104, 109, 168
Tariff: of 1816, 73-74; as sectional issue, 77-79; in 1824 election, 79-81; in 1828 election, 89-90; and nullification, 108-109; of 1842, 125; in 1844 election, 130, 132; of 1846, 135-136; in 1852 election, 147-148; of 1857, 152-153; Republican stand, 1860, 177, 181; in Johnson's term, 208; in Grant's term, 224; Liberal Republicans and, 226; issue in 1880, 257, 259; of 1883, 254; Democratic plank, 1884, 257; Cleveland's attitude, 277-278; Republican plank, 1888, 279; in 1888 campaign, 281-283; McKinley Act, 285-286; in 1892 campaign, 287, 289-291; Wilson-Gorman Act, 301; in 1896 campaign, 306, 310, 313; Dingley Act, 322, 324, 327; in 1908 campaign, 349, 352, 354; Payne-Aldrich Act, 357-358; Canadian reciprocity, 359; in 1912 platforms, 364, 369, 371; Underwood-Simmons Act, 377; in 1916 campaign, 381, 384, 385; Fordney-McCumber Act, 405, 414; in 1928 platforms, 420, 424; Smoot-Hawley Act, 430-431; in 1932, 430-431; in 1932 platforms, 433, 437; Republican plank, 1936, 448; Republican plank, 1940, 464
Taylor, Glenn, 500
Taylor, John, 57, 60
Taylor, Zachary, 138-139, 141-144
Tazewell, L. W., 123
Teapot Dome, 408-409
Teller, Henry M., 306, 307, 310, 312
Tenure of Office Act, 209-210, 276
Thomas, Norman, 425; 441 n., 452, 475 n., 477, 486 n., 504 n.
Thurman, A. G., 221, 256-257, 266-267, 278-279
Thurmond, J. Strom, 500, 502-504, 578, 595, 611
Tilden, S. J., 239-249 (disputed election), 251, 256-257, 266
Tillman, Ben, 298, 300, 301, 309, 341-342, 346
Tompkins, D. D., 74, 75 n.
Toombs, Robert, 143, 146, 165
Tories, 7, 10, 30
Towne, Charles A., 327
Townsend, Francis E., 451
Truman, Harry S, named for Vice President, 485-486; as President, 492-495; nominated, 1948, 498-500; in campaign, 501-505; in second term, 505-507, 513; in 1952, 530-531; after 1960, 547, 552
Trumbull, Lyman, 171, 228, 241 n.
Tumulty, Joseph P., 376-377
Twenty-second Joint Rule, 246
Tydings, Millard E., 459, 467, 507
Tyler, John, 108, 113, 120, 123-126, 127, 129

Underwood, Oscar, 359, 366, 368-369, 377, 413-414
Union Labor Party, 296
Union Party (Civil War), 188-189, 193-202, 203-212. *See also* Elections, Presidential (1864, 1868)
United Labor, 297
U-2 overflight, 546

Vallandigham, C. L., 192, 199, 200-201, 207, 216, 230
Van Buren, "Prince John," 136, 140, 213
Van Buren, Martin, supports Crawford, 79; and House election, 86; and Jackson, 93-98; minister to England, 98; nominated for Vice President, 99; elected, 105; elected President, 112-113; policies, 114-117;

Van Buren, Martin (*cont.*)
renominated, 117; not reelected, 122-123; not nominated, 1844, 127-128; nominated by Free Soilers, 140-141
Van Rensselaer, Stephen, 86
Vandenberg, A. H., 446, 449, 461, 464-465, 491, 494, 495-498, 505
Vietnam, 576, 584, 585; Humphrey's views on, 606; and 1968 election, 587-588, 590, 591, 592, 593, 594, 595, 596, 598, 605, 607, 611, 612; Nixon's views on, 603, 611; Wallace's views on, 608
Virginia–New York Alliance, 24-25, 27, 34-35, 42-43, 55-56, 59, 68, 74
Virginia Resolutions of 1798, 41
Vote Profile Analysis, 583
Votes, electoral and popular (1789) 16; (1792) 28; (1796) 34-35; (1800) 44; (1804) 56; (1808) 60; (1812) 69; (1816) 74-75; (1820) 75; (1824) 83-84; (1828) 91; (1832) 105; (1836) 112-113; (1840) 122-123; (1844) 133; (1848) 141-142; (1852) 148; (1856) 166-167; (1860), 183-184; (1864) 202; (1868) 217; (1872) 232-233; (1876) 243-249; (1880) 259-260; (1884) 273; (1888) 283; (1892) 292; (1896) 318-319; (1900) 332; (1904) 344; (1908) 354-355; (1912) 374; (1916) 387-388; (1920) 402-403; (1924) 416-417; (1928) 428-429; (1932) 441-442; (1936) 457; (1940) 474-475; (1944) 490-491; (1948) 503-505; (1952) 522-523; (1956) 541-542; (1960) 560-563; (1964) 581-582; (1968) 610-611

Wade, Ben, 179, 193, 198, 199-200, 204-205, 210, 212-213
Wagner, Mayor Robert, 531
Wagner, Robert F., 449, 466-467
Walker, Robert J., 128-129, 134-135, 169-170
Wallace, George C., 570; and 1964 campaign, 576, 578; as 1968 Presidential candidate, 585, 600, 604, 606-607, 608, 609, 610, 611
Wallace, Lurleen, 585
Wallace, H. A., 440, 443, 468, 472, 485-486, 489, 493, 500-501, 503-504
Walsh, T. J., 408, 413, 423, 437, 443
Wanamaker, John, 281, 284
"War Hawks," 66-68. *See also* "Young Republicans"
Warren, Charles B., 410, 417
Warren, Earl, 481-482, 495-498, 509-512, 567, 609
Washburne, E. B., 254, 256
Washington, George, inaugural, 1; views on parties, 1-2, 17, 26; elected to House of Burgesses, 4; favors Federalists, 17-18, 33; reelected, 28; foreign problems, 29-32; Whiskey Insurrection, 32; retirement, 33; favors Hamilton to command army, 37-38
Watkins, Aaron S., 400
Watkins, Arthur, 526
Watson, James E., 361, 364, 392-393, 395, 419, 432, 441
Watson, Tom, 298, 311, 316-317, 344 n., 352
Watterson, Henry, 228, 290, 291, 330, 343
Weaver, J. B., 292, 296, 300
Webster, Daniel, backs J. Q. Adams, 85, 86; National Republican leader, 100; and Jackson, 108, 109; Presidential candidate, 111, 113; in 1840 campaign, 121; Secretary of State, 123; relations with Tyler, 124, 125; favors Clay, 129; criticizes Taylor, 139; backs Clay's Compromise, 143; in Fillmore's cabinet, 144; loses Whig nomination, 1852, 145; death, 147
Weed, Thurlow, in 1824 election, 83; organizes Antimasons, 101-102; opposes Clay, 118-119; advises Taylor, 143; becomes Republican, 158; in campaign of 1856, 166; Seward's manager, 178-180; favors compromise, 1861, 185-186; and cabinet appointments, 186-187; in Johnson's convention, 1866, 207
Weeks, John W., 380, 382
Welch, Robert, H. W., Jr., 567
Welles, Gideon, 187, 207
Werdel, Thomas H., 535
West, Alanson, M., 296
Wheeler, Burton K., 415-416, 446, 466, 467, 477
Wheeler, William A., 239
Whig party, origins, 109-111; first elec-

Whig party (*cont.*)
tion, 111-113; first convention, 118-120; "log cabin" campaign, 120-123. *See also* Elections, Presidential, and important figures
Whigs (of the Revolution), 7-8
White, Byron ("Whizzer"), 555
White Citizens' Council, 607
White, George, 402, 471
White, Horace, 224, 228
White, Hugh L., 98, 112-113, 119
White, William Allen, 321, 365, 392, 447, 481
Whitney, W. C., 266, 268, 289, 291-292
Wilkins, William, 99, 105
Willard, Frances W., 271
Williams, G. Mennen, 530
Willis, Frank B., 419
Willkie, Wendell L., nominated for President, 461-465; in 1940 campaign, 468-476; internationalist views, 477, 480-481; defeated in primary, 481; death, 489
Wilmot Proviso, 136, 140, 141
Wilson, Henry, 140, 171, 212, 229
Wilson, Woodrow, governor, 366; in 1912 convention, 367-369; on campaign, 371-374; character and methods, 375-377; policies, 377-379; renominated, 383-384; reelected, 384-388; as war President, 388-390; and 1920 convention, 398
Wilson-Gorman Act, 301
Wirt, William, 75, 103, 105
Wise, Henry A., 99, 119, 158, 170
Wolcott, Oliver, 33, 38, 71
Wood, Leonard, 393-397
Woodin, W. H., 443
Work, Hubert, 425
Wright, Fielding L., 500
Wright, Silas, 128, 135
Wyatt, Wilson W., 518

Yancey, W. L., 138, 174, 175, 183
"Young Republicans," policies of, 73-74
Youth International party ("Yippies"), 597